COUTURE

D1205098

COUTURE

The Encyclopedia of
Native American
Biography

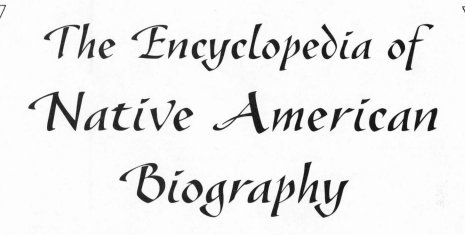

The Encyclopedia of Native American Biography

Six Hundred Life Stories of Important People,
from Powhatan to Wilma Mankiller

Bruce E. Johansen and Donald A. Grinde, Jr.

DA CAPO PRESS • NEW YORK

Library of Congress Cataloging-in-Publication Data

Johansen, Bruce E. (Bruce Elliott), 1950–
  The encyclopedia of Native American biography: six hundred life stories of
important people from Powhatan to Wilma Mankiller / Bruce E. Johansen
and Donald A. Grinde, Jr.—1st Da Capo Press ed.
    p.   cm.
  Originally published: New York: H. Holt, 1997.
  Includes bibliographical references and index.
  ISBN 0-306-80870-6 (pbk.: alk. paper).
  1. Indians of North America—Biography—Encyclopedias. I. Grinde, Donald
A., 1946– . II. Title.
E89.J69 1998
920′.009297—dc21
[B]   98-20903
                                                                                   CIP

First Da Capo Press edition 1998

This Da Capo Press paperback edition of *The Encyclopedia of Native
American Biography* is an unabridged republication of the edition first
published in New York in 1997. It is reprinted by arrangement with
Henry Holt and Company, Inc.

Copyright © 1997 by Bruce E. Johansen & Donald A. Grinde, Jr.

DESIGNED BY BETTY LEW

Published by Da Capo Press, Inc.
A Subsidiary of Plenum Publishing Corporation
233 Spring Street, New York, N.Y. 10013

All Rights Reserved

Manufactured in the United States of America

‹ ‹ ‹ Foreword › › ›

by Doug George-Kanentiio

People around the world have demonstrated an ongoing and deep interest in American Indians. From Germany to China they want to know about the rituals, history, and values that have shaped Native lives and given such a powerful definition to the Western Hemisphere.

Native culture has been idealized in the popular media, but altogether too much is excluded. Native people were more than guerrilla fighters, High Plains buffalo hunters, or grand orators. Theirs was and is a complex world composed of hundreds of different nations, with their own political, economic, linguistic, and cultural systems. They have little in the way of universal characteristics other than a common ethnic heritage and perhaps a deep appreciation for the environmental integrity of the land they call Turtle Island.

The journey toward a more complete understanding of Native people and their guests from the East has been a most difficult one. In the rush to dominate the terrain and exploit the resources of North America, the newcomers brushed aside Native people, perceiving them as little more than impediments to Christian manifest destiny.

They ignored the significant contributions Native scientists, political philosophers, architects, and engineers have made to humanity. Indian agriculturalists contributed vastly to the health of mankind by the introduction of foods such as corn, potatoes, and beans. Yet a few years ago we were all taught, Indian and non-Indian alike, that Native people were mere nomads, wandering across this great continent, leaving little more in their wake than pottery shards and arrowheads.

In addition, scholars—who should have known better—deliberately ignored Native accomplishments in astronomy, psychology, political science, music, economics, and athletics. It would be a far less colorful world without basketball, hockey, or lacrosse (all Native sports) or the rituals of gratitude as expressed on Thanksgiving Day.

Perhaps no other people have contributed so much to the betterment of humankind yet received so very little credit.

Only now are we acknowledging that Indian societies were far in advance of Europeans with regard to universal suffrage; the framers of the Iroquois Confederacy created a model democratic state that is reflected in the U.S. Constitution and in the egalitarian visions entertained by Karl Marx and Friedrich Engels.

But who are these people? What do we make of individuals most of us never heard of? How do we mark their achievements or share in the drama of their lives?

A reference guide such as the *Encyclopedia of Native American Biography* is an ideal place to start. By perusing the multitude of citations in this remarkable work we can learn, for example, of the spiritual genius of Black Elk, Lakota Nation, and the lesser known, although equally powerful, Tenskwatawa, the Shawnee brother of Tecumseh.

There are the famous military leaders such as Crazy Horse and Geronimo, but how many know of Little Turtle, the Miami/Mohican commander who masterminded the defeat in 1790 of a U.S. army five times the size of Custer's contingent at the Little Big Horn?

Such people make for fascinating reading. These are the ones who have given definition and substance to an entire race. They are our heroes and villains, our saints, saviors, and sinners.

Readers of this volume will surely be enlightened by the *Encyclopedia* and with this will come, one hopes, a proper appreciation for the indigenous peoples of this beautiful land we now share in common.

‹ ‹ ‹ *Introduction* › › ›

One may compare the writing of a book—or if one has a coauthor, part of a book—to a very long journey. At some turns, this journey is fascinating, full of revelations and discoveries and other surprises. Great stretches of any author's journey also are quite mundane, somewhat like driving long hours through the Texas Panhandle. During the trip, one must make certain decisions about which route to take and where to stop.

Before a trip, one may look for maps of the territory, in this case, earlier attempts to survey Native American biography. One quickly realizes that the creation of maps such as these is an extremely arbitrary exercise. Our first decision, among many, was deciding who would be used in the roughly 600 entries that take us from before the era of discovery (as Europeans defined it) to the present day. Of these entries, perhaps fifty would be included without question—the people whose names nearly every student of Native American history knows: GERONIMO, RED CLOUD, CRAZY HORSE, SITTING BULL, BLACK ELK, Joseph BRANT, SEATH'TL, TECUMSEH, and the like. It took us only a few weeks of biographical research to realize that a great deal has been written about the same few dozen people. Choosing the other 90 percent of the entries involved judgment calls and the diligent mining of many obscure sources. We chose to include non-Indians who have been important to Native Americans, one way or another.

Along the way, certain problems emerged. One of the most confounding was the fact that the records of Native American lives often do not leave written facts useful in a biographical encyclopedia. To cite one major example, we often did not know when a particular person was born, and available estimates varied widely. The reader will become very familiar with the phrases *circa*, abbreviated *c.*, Latin for "about"; and *fl.*, which is academic shorthand for "flourished"—

Red Cloud, about 1870.
[Nebraska State Historical Society]

denoting the period of time in which a particular person was known to history.

Problems befuddled our search for birthdates, particularly those before 1900, because many Native Americans were born into cultures that did not follow European systems of timekeeping. Most Native American cultures do not place the same value on precision in telling (and recording) of events on a linear time line. In some of the references we consulted, an emphasis on exactness with time exceeds the grasp of factual accuracy, as in one encyclopedia where we found the death date of the Oglala Lakota chief RED CLOUD listed as 1883. The date was very exact, with no *circa* or other approximation. The problem was that it was twenty-six years off. Red Cloud died in 1909. A Native oral history may include all the circumstances of a person's birth except a date that can be matched with the Roman calendar. In the case of CRASHING THUNDER, the Winnebago profiled by Paul Radin, our estimate of his birth year comes from Radin's observation that Crashing Thunder was about forty-five years of age when he was interviewed in 1910.

Names have also been an area of difficulty. In some cases, the same name would be used by different people in the same or different Native nations. The example of Standing Bear is instructive. The Northern Plains was home to a host of Standing Bears in the nineteenth and early twentieth centuries. Two of the best known were the Ponca chief who led his people back to their homeland along Nebraska's Niobrara River in the 1870s and the Lakota Sioux author Luther STANDING BEAR. There were many others, and as authors we had to sort them out. A father and a son might have had the same name, or several individuals might have used the same name in succession. There was one entry in another biographical effort that listed a man's name and then his birth and death dates, which were almost 140 years apart. The man in the photo used to illustrate the entry didn't look a day over forty. Actually, the birth and death dates referred to three individuals, a father, his son, and his grandson.

Many Native people also had different names at various stages of their lives and sometimes used one name in Native company and another in English, French, Dutch, or Spanish society. In our entry headings, we have listed the names that were used most frequently in the literature. On occasion, additional names appear within entries. We know some Native Americans by the English translations of the names their relatives gave them, such as Crazy Horse and Red Cloud. Other times, we know a Native American historical figure, such as CAPTAIN JACK, more familiarly by a name given him by non-Indians. Still others we know by their own untranslated names, such as MASSASOIT and OSCEOLA.

A Native person, particularly a man, might have as many as a half-dozen names during a lifetime. Some were given in respect to a grandparent; some were secret and not mentionable in public and were known only to the individual and his or her parents. Others had spiritual significance and were used only in connection with certain ceremonies. Usually public names venerated some outstanding moment in one's life or recognized a person's physical attributes. If one adds these Native-given names to those applied by various groups of settlers at different times in a person's life, the number of available names can rise to eight or ten for one person. Add to this variety the fact that many of the names were spelled phonetically (and spelling was not consistent) when they were written in English. CANASSATEGO, for example, may be spelled several ways in historical records.

Confusion may also arise in the matter of the names we have listed for tribal affiliations, because Native tribal and national names are a mixture of those given by European immigrants (in English, Spanish, French, etc.), those given Native people by other Native peoples (often unflattering labels for enemies), and those names given to Native peoples by themselves. For example, the Iroquois (French name) or Six Nations (English name) called themselves *Haudenosaunee,* or "People of the Longhouse." *Mohawk* is not a Mohawk name but an Algonquian one for their enemies. According to Edmund Wilson in *Apologies to the Iroquois,* it meant "eater of human flesh." The Mohawks knew themselves by a considerably more benign name meaning "People of the Flint."

The name *Sioux* may have been Chippewa for "Lesser Adders" or "Small Snakes," was adopted by the French to mean "enemy," and was then applied generally to a number of Native peoples in what is now the north-central United States. Since these peoples had no inclusive term for themselves, *Sioux* is used here as an umbrella term or in cases where a more precise identity is not possible. When more precise identification is available, we use linguistic groupings: Dakota (Santee), Nakota (Yankton), and Lakota (Teton). The Dakota can be delineated into four tribes: Mdewkanton, Wahpeton, Wahpekute, and Sisseton. The Nakota comprise one subdivision (Yankton), and the Lakota have seven (often called the "seven fires"): Oglala, Sicangu (Brulé), Miniconjou, Hunkpapa, Sihasapa (Blackfoot), Tazipcho (Sans Arcs), and the Oohenonpa (Two Kettles).

Linguistic brambles aside, this journey produced some wonderful surprises. We invite the reader to discover the Omaha Susan LAFLESCHE, who became one of America's first women physicians and then nearly worked herself to death trying to save her people from rampant epidemics.

We met the first person to run a mile in under four minutes (see Big Hawk Chief) and the first fatality in the American Revolution, who was also part African American (see Crispus Attucks). Along the way, certain scenes stand out. One is that of Tecumseh seated on a bench with William Henry Harrison, who would later become president of the United States. Tecumseh edged Harrison off the bench inch by inch and finally dumped him on the ground. The irritated Harrison then asked Tecumseh why he had done this. "This is what you're doing to my people," Tecumseh replied. Another scene involves Black Hawk, the Fox and Sauk leader who decided to fight for his homeland, and Keokuk, a Fox and Sauk who decided to accommodate the invading European Americans and moved his people from present-day Illinois into Iowa. At the end of the Black Hawk War, the U.S. Army tried to shame Black Hawk by forcing him to attend a ceremony in which Keokuk was recognized as chief of the Fox and Sauk. After taking several hours of this humiliation, Black Hawk removed his breechclout and slapped Keokuk across the face.

While looking for artwork, one finds that there exist a lot of people for whom we have faces and precious little other material. This may be because photography was more salable (especially on regional postcards) than written history was in the late nineteenth century. There were many more photographers flitting around the frontier in 1880 than historians. For every Native figure for whom we have reams of material (a Black Elk, a Chief Joseph, et al.), dozens have been left with next to no record at all. Looking at photos in archives tantalized us because it indicated how much we didn't know.

While gathering artwork for this volume, I visited the Nebraska State Historical Society several times. On one of those occasions, a Saturday, the main archive (where one may view artwork) was closed, so I was ordering from indexes. I requested a print of a piece called "Shooting Star" thinking I might get a line drawing of Tecumseh, since that was one of his names.

Instead, I got a stunning photo of what looked to me like a Sioux woman in the late nineteenth century. I could find no information on her, even after passing a copy of the photo to several people who are experts in the history of the Plains Indians. I

Shooting Star, a woman about whom a name—and nothing else—is known. [Nebraska State Historical Society]

learned something about her clothes—quill-work moccasins, trade blanket, dentalium shell choker and earrings, cotton calico dress—and that she was a Lakota woman of the 1890s. Still, there was nothing else to be found about her as a human being. All I knew was that her wonderful visage had passed in front of another human being with a camera.

While writing the entries for this volume, we read just about every available reference on and tangential to Native Americans. Along the way, we developed a critique of orthodox encyclopedia style. Sometimes we evade that style consciously. For example, one might find fault with us for including extended quotations from some of the more important leaders. Our purpose here is to convey feelings as well as facts, to transport the reader into the mind of another human being. Since this is an encyclopedia of biography, we believe that conveying this quality of humanity is very important. These biographies celebrate the vibrancy and endurance of Native American cultures. We hope that you will find the journey instructive.

As all authors do, we encountered people who gave us their time and energy as well as information. Among these are: Don Hannula, editorial writer, *Seattle Times*; Barbara Clements-Syring, Seattle; Shelly Price-Jones, Kingston, Ontario; Inga Ronke, Communication Department secretary at the University of Nebraska at Omaha; Vyrtis Thomas, Cathy Crook, Neil Hauck, and James L. Harwood, archivists at the National Anthropological Archives; John Carter (curator), Martha Vestecka-Miller, and Katherine F. Wyatt, Photographic Collections, Nebraska State Historical Society; and John Kahionhes Fadden, Six Nations Indian Museum, Onchiota, New York. Many thanks are also due our editors at Henry Holt: Mary Kay Linge, Kevin Ohe, and Ken Wright.

Bruce E. Johansen
Omaha, Nebraska
September 1996

The Encyclopedia of
Native American
Biography

ABOMAZINE (BOMBAZINE)
Abenaki or Kennebec
c. 1675–1724

Abomazine, a principal chief, resisted colonial expansion in New England during King William's War (1689–1697). He signed a peace treaty with the Massachusetts Bay Colony in 1693 but renewed hostilities in 1694 after he was arrested and imprisoned while carrying a flag of truce to a fort at Pemaquid, Maine. Attacks continued through Queen Anne's War (1702–1713). Abomazine was one of the Native signers of the peace treaty ending that war. Hostilities continued, however, evidenced by the fact that Abomazine was killed in 1724 as his family was being attacked by English soldiers at Norridgewock, Maine.

ABOUREZK, JAMES
Mixed Sioux
1931–

James Abourezk, son of American Indian and Lebanese parents, was elected to the U.S. Senate from South Dakota in 1972, as Native American

activists converged on Washington, D.C., on the Trail of Broken Treaties to protest mistreatment.

Abourezk was born and grew up on the Rosebud Reservation in South Dakota, where his father did business at a trading post. He was elected to the U.S. House of Representatives in 1970 and then to the Senate. Abourezk quickly became a spokesperson for Native American interests in the Senate during protests, including the occupation of Wounded Knee in 1973. He also played a key role in negotiations between the American Indian Movement (AIM) and the federal government during the occupation.

In early March 1973, Senators George McGovern and Abourezk, both from South Dakota, met with AIM leaders and federal authorities to calm tempers at Wounded Knee. On March 11, 1973, AIM members declared their independence as the Oglala Sioux nation, defining its boundaries according to the 1868 Treaty of Fort Laramie. At one point, federal officials considered an armed attack on the camp at Wounded Knee, but the plan was ultimately discarded. The occupation by AIM lasted seventy-two days. AIM leaders Dennis BANKS and Russell MEANS told Abourezk and McGovern that they would hold out until the Senate Foreign Relations Committee had reviewed all broken treaties, and the corruption of the Bureau of Indian Affairs had been exposed to the world. After much gunfire and negotiation, AIM's occupation of Wounded Knee ended on May 7, 1973.

In the U.S. Senate, Abourezk was a major advocate of legislation, passed in 1978, to protect Native American religious freedom. He also chaired the American Indian Policy Review Commission, created in the middle 1970s to assess governmental policies under the Self-Determination Act of 1974. Abourezk resigned from the Senate in 1979.

FOR MORE INFORMATION:

Churchill, Ward, and Jim Vander Wall. *The Cointelpro Papers: Documents from the FBI's Secret Wars Against Dissent in the United States.* Boston: South End Press, 1990.

Deloria, Vine, Jr. *Behind the Trail of Broken Treaties.* New York: Delacorte Press, 1974.

ABRAHAM
Mohawk
fl. 1750–1780

Abraham was a prominent figure at several treaty councils among the Iroquois, their allies, and colonial representatives during the middle and late eighteenth century, at a time when the United States was taking shape. He figured in the transference of Iroquois political ideas to colonial representatives who would be influential in the elemental statecraft of the United States.

A dramatic example of the influence of Iroquois political theories on Americans occurred at German Flats, New York, in August 1775, when treaty commissioners from the Continental Congress met with the sachems and

warriors of the Six Nations. This conference was so important that a delegate from the Continental Congress, Philip Schuyler, attended.

The sachems and treaty commissioners met on August 24, 1775, at Cartwright's Tavern near Albany, New York. According to protocol, the commissioners asked the sachems to appoint a speaker. The sachems deferred to the commissioners, so the Americans picked Abraham, a Mohawk, the adopted brother and successor to HENDRICK. On the next day, the treaty commissioners (who had specific instructions from John HANCOCK and the Second Continental Congress) told the sachems that they were heeding the advice Iroquois forefathers had given to the colonial Americans at Lancaster, Pennsylvania, in 1744. At this point, the commissioners quoted the words that CANASSATEGO had spoken at the Lancaster Treaty Council of 1744.

After quoting Canassatego on the power of political union, the Americans said their forefathers had rejoiced to hear his words, which had sunk

> deep into their Hearts, the Advice was good, it was Kind. They said to one another, the Six Nations are a wise people, let us hearken to their Council and teach our children to follow it. Our old Men have done so. They have frequently taken a single Arrow and said, Children, see how easy it is broken, then they have tied twelve together with strong Cords—And our strongest Men could not break them—See said they—this is what the Six Nations mean. Divided a single Man may destroy you—United, you are a match for the whole World. [Grinde and Johansen]

FOR MORE INFORMATION:

Grinde, Donald A., Jr., and Bruce E. Johansen. *Exemplar of Liberty: Native America and the*

Evolution of Democracy. Berkeley and Los Angeles: University of California Press, 1991.

ADAIR, JAMES
c. 1709–1783

As an Irish trader based in South Carolina who lived among the Chickasaws for nearly forty years in the mid-1700s, James Adair amassed a wealth of knowledge about American Indian manners and customs in the Southeast. He had several Indian wives and numerous children by them. Adair's *The History of the American Indians,* first published in 1775 when he returned to England, remains a classic early work on Southeastern Indian nations. His analysis, for its time and place, provided much in the way of ethnographic data for the Chickasaws, Cherokees, Creeks, and Catawbas and included helpful recommendations relating to Indian policy. However, the work is marred by his specious argument that American Indians are descended from the Ten Lost Tribes of Israel.

ADAMS, ALFRED
Haida
1867–1945

Born in Masset, British Columbia, Adams was the offspring of a long line of Haida nobles. He founded the Native Brotherhood of British Columbia in 1930 and served as its president until his death in 1945.

Adams was noted in his community for organizing a Native cooperative to compete with unfair traders; he also organized a thirty-piece band that lasted three decades. Across Canada, he was known as a tireless advocate of Native interests with the federal government.

ADAMS, HANK
Assiniboine-Dakota
1944–

Hank Adams was involved in many of the early "fish-ins" in the Puget Sound area of Washing-

ton State during the 1960s. These widespread acts of civil disobedience based on treaties signed in the 1850s presaged the landmark decision by Federal Judge George BOLDT in 1974 that entitled Native American treaty signatories to up to half the wild salmon catch. Although he was not a lawyer, Adams later represented several Native nations in treaty rights cases. Adams also played a major role in nationwide Native activism in the 1970s, including the 1972 Trail of Broken Treaties (organized by Dennis BANKS and Russell MEANS).

Adams was born in Poplar, Montana, and then attended the University of Washington (1961–1963). Between 1963 and 1967, he worked with the National Indian Youth Council and became involved in civil disobedience related to fishing rights in the Pacific Northwest. At one point, Adams led a Native American contingent in the 1963 march on Washington organized by Martin Luther King, Jr. During fishing rights protests, Adams was arrested several times. He also was shot by an unknown assailant and seriously injured once. Between 1965 and 1967, Adams worked with consumer advocate Ralph Nader and Senator Robert Kennedy on Native-related issues. During the late 1960s and early 1970s, Adams was a leader in the Survival of American Indians Association.

At the conclusion of the Trail of Broken Treaties, American Indian Movement (AIM) protesters occupied the Bureau of Indian Affairs headquarters building in Washington, D.C. As they vacated the building, protesters carried with them boxes of documents that later were released to the press. On January 31, 1973, Adams was arrested with Les Whitten, an associate of columnist Jack Anderson, after Anderson published some of the documents. Following their arrests by the FBI, a federal grand jury refused to return indictments against Adams and Whitten.

FOR MORE INFORMATION:

Adams, Hank. "A Citizen's Letter to His Governor," Tacoma, Washington, October 17–21, 1968. In *Now That the Buffalo's Gone: A Study of Today's American Indians*, edited by Alvin M. Josephy. New York: Knopf, 1982.

Deloria, Vine, Jr. *The Trail of Broken Treaties*. New York: Delacorte, 1974.

ADAMS, JOHN
1735–1826

John Adams, the colonial American lawyer, diplomat, and later President of the United States, occasionally weaved examples of Native American governance into his examinations of statecraft around the world during debates over the U.S. Constitution in 1787. His *Defence of the Constitutions*, a wide-ranging examination of confederate precedents that was used as a reference at the Constitutional Convention, examined the governmental systems of the Iroquois and Incas, along with old-world models. Although Adams had been selected as a Massachusetts delegate to the Constitutional Convention, he chose not to attend and published his lengthy essay instead.

In his preface, Adams mentioned the Inca, Manco Capac, and the political structure "of the Peruvians." He also noted that tribes in "North America have certain families from which their leaders are always chosen." Adams believed that American Indian governments collected their authority in one center (a simple or unicameral model). He also observed that in American Indian governments, "the people" believed that "all depended on them." Later in the preface, Adams observed that Benjamin FRANKLIN, the French Philosophes, and other "great philosophers and politicians" of the age were "attempting to . . . set up governments of . . . modern Indians." According to Adams, the French philosopher Turgot believed that the

new American constitutions that Franklin showed him were "an unreasonable imitation of the usages of England."

Adams, an ardent believer in the fundamentals of the British constitution, opposed Franklin's intimation that the new U.S. government should resemble the Native confederacies, but he did believe it would be productive to have "a more accurate investigation of the form of governments of the . . . Indians." In addition, Adams argued that it would be "well worth the pains . . . to collect . . . the legislation of the Indians" for study while creating a new constitution. Adams believed that in studying American Indian governments such as the League of the Iroquois, Americans could observe the best examples of governmental separation of powers. In fact, Adams stated that separation of powers in American Indian governments "is marked with a precision that excludes all controversy."

Indeed, Adams pointed out that American Indian governments were so democratic that the "real sovereignty resided in the body of the people." Personal liberty was so important to American Indians, according to Adams, that Mohawks might be characterized as having "complete individual independence."

While discussing the Mohawks, Adams referred to "fifty families governed by all authority in one centre." This statement reflects the extent of Adams's knowledge of the structure of the Iroquois Confederacy. In fact, Adams notes rather casually the number of Iroquois sachemships that would be delineated by Lewis Henry MORGAN, pioneer ethnographer of the league, more than sixty years later.

Adams's knowledge of Iroquois and other American Indian confederacies can be seen in his reference to the sachemship system in American Indian governments, which also presaged Morgan's work. Adams wrote that a sachem is elected for life and lesser "sachems are his ordinary council." In this ordinary council, all "national affairs are deliberated and resolved" except declaring war when the "sachems call a national assembly round a great council fire." At this council, the sachems "communicate to the people their resolution, and sacrifice an animal." No doubt the animal sacrifice is a reference to the White Dog Ceremony of the Iroquois, also described by Morgan more than six decades after Adams. Adams further describes Iroquois custom when he states that "the people who approve the war . . . throw the hatchet into a tree" and then "join in the subsequent war songs and dances." Adams also exhibits an understanding of the voluntary nature of Iroquois warfare when he asserts that those who do disapprove of the decision to go to war "take no part in the sacrifice, but retire."

FOR MORE INFORMATION:

Adams, Charles F., ed. *Correspondence Between John Adams and Mercy Warren.* 1878. Reprint, New York: Arno Press, 1972.

Adams, Charles F. *Works of John Adams.* Boston: Little, Brown, 1851.

Adams, John. *Defence of the Constitutions.* Philadelphia: Hall & Sellers, 1787.

Butterfield, Lyman H., ed. *The Diary and Autobiography of John Adams.* Cambridge, Mass.: Harvard University Press, 1961.

Grinde, Donald A., Jr., and Bruce E. Johansen. *Exemplar of Liberty: Native America and the Evolution of Democracy.* Berkeley and Los Angeles: University of California Press, 1991.

ADARIO (KONDIARONK)
Huron
c. 1650–1700

Adario, half-real and half-imagined, became a literary figure in France during the Enlightenment. Like other prominent Native Americans such as the Iroquois CANASSATEGO and HEN-DRICK, the European image of Adario was used as a counterpoint to European customs and assumptions.

The actual Adario sabotaged a peace agreement between the French and the Iroquois Confederacy, which caused the Iroquois to attack settlements in New France. At the time, the Iroquois were also destroying the Huron Confederacy. In 1688, Adario made an alliance with the French. Adario took this to be an alliance against the Iroquois as well, but on a visit to Cataracouy (present-day Kingston, Ontario), Adario was told to cease hostilities. The French commandant told him that an Iroquois delegation was due in Montreal to negotiate peace. Afraid that such negotiation would cause the French to abandon him to Iroquois aggression, Adario ambushed the Iroquois delegation and spread word that he did so under French urging. Adario released his Iroquois prisoners, except for one man who was later put to death by Frenchmen who had not heard that the Iroquois were about to negotiate peace. Adario then sent word to the Iroquois Grand Council that the French had murdered their kinsman. The Iroquois believed Adario's lie, and as a result about thirteen hundred Iroquois attacked Montreal on August 25, 1689, killing hundreds of settlers and burning large parts of the town.

Later in his life, Adario became a steadfast ally of the French. He was converted to Christianity by the Jesuits, who incorporated accounts of him into their *Jesuit Relations.* From these firsthand accounts, the fictional Adario made his way into French letters.

On several occasions, this imagined Adario, the cosmopolitan Indian, advised Europeans to "take my advice and turn Huron." The fictional Adario pointed out (inaccurately) that in French society "The Great Lords . . . are slaves to their . . . King," who is the only Frenchman who is happy with respect "to that adorable Liberty

Adario. [Courtesy of John Kahionhes Fadden]

which he alone enjoys." In a similar manner, the Jesuits related to the French stories of noble savages who were nonmaterialistic and possessed dignity and rights distinct from the powers of the state. In an era of divine right monarchies, this was a radical concept for Europeans.

AHATSISTARI
Huron
fl. 1640s
During the early and middle seventeenth century, Ahatsistari led Huron war parties on several raids against the Iroquois, their enemies at the time. On one occasion, Hurons under the direction of Ahatsistari routed a large force of Iroquois in war canoes on Lake Ontario; in 1641, Ahatsistari and fifty other Hurons defeated three hundred or more Iroquois.

As he lived, Ahatsistari died; in summer 1642, he was leading a group of Hurons and their French allies on Lake St. Peter when the party was ambushed by Mohawks, who later put him to death.

ALCHESAY (ALCHISE)
Chiricahua Apache
fl. 1870s–1880s
During General George Crook's 1872–1873 Arizona campaign against the Apaches and Yavapais, Alchesay served in the Indian scouts with the rank of sergeant. For his service in that conflict, he was awarded the Congressional Medal of Honor in 1875. In 1886, aided by other scouts including KAYATENNAE, Mickey FREE, and CHATO, he tracked GERONIMO. Although he reasoned that military resistance was futile and therefore collaborated with the U.S. military, Alchesay lobbied to better the lot of his people. He was a part of the Apache delegation that went to Washington, D.C., with LOCO and Chato in 1886 to meet with President Grover Cleveland. As an older man, he adapted well to reservation life and became a prominent cattleman.

ALEXANDER (WAMSUTTA)
Wampanoag
fl. 1660s
MASSASOIT fathered three boys and two girls. The two younger men, who would become chiefs of the Wampanoags after Massasoit's death, were named Wamsutta and METACOM by their father, Alexander and Philip by the English. Alexander succeeded Massasoit as principal chief of the Wampanoags after his father's death; and Philip, later called King Philip by the English, assumed the office among a people increasingly angry over English treatment after Alexander's death in 1662.

After Alexander had been chief less than a year, the English authorities at Plymouth summoned him to their colony to take a dressing-down in regards to his asserted lack of loyalty. Initially Alexander refused to go, but a detail of colonial troops arrived at his village to take him, and he went in humiliation. Alexander traveled with eighty of his people, including his wife, WEETAMOO, who also was a sachem of the Wampanoags. During his summons to Plymouth, Alexander became ill with a raging fever and asked to go home. The English let him go only after he left two of his own sons as hostages. His people carried Alexander away on a litter, but he became even sicker and died on the way home. Many Wampanoags believed that Alexander had been killed by the English, either by bitterness over his humiliation or by poisoning. Actually, he probably died of windborne viruses in the colony.

In this seething atmosphere, Metacom assumed the chieftainship of the Wampanoags; his life would culminate in King Philip's War a decade and a half later.

FOR MORE INFORMATION:

Josephy, Alvin M., Jr. "The Betrayal of King Philip." In *The Patriot Chiefs.* New York: Viking, 1961.

Waters, Frank. *Brave Are My People: Indian Heroes Not Forgotten.* Santa Fe, N. Mex.: Clear Light, 1993.

ALFORD, THOMAS WILDCAT (GAYNWAW-PIAHSIKA, GAYNWAH)
Shawnee
1860–1938

Thomas Wildcat Alford, a major Native American educator, lobbyist, and Bureau of Indian Affairs official, was born in the Canadian River region near Sasakwa, Oklahoma, in what was then Indian Territory. (Later in life he would be called Gaynwawpiahsika or Gaynwah, "the Leader.") Alford's mother was the great-granddaughter of TECUMSEH, and his father was called Gaytahkipiahsikah, or "Wildcat." His parents were absentee Shawnees passing on to their son their tribal heritage. At the age of twelve, he went to a mission school. Subsequently, he obtained a scholarship to attend the Hampton Institute

in Virginia. He became a convert to Christianity while a student.

When he went back to Indian Territory as an assimilated Indian and a Christian, he clashed with traditionalists who had warned him against losing his identity as a Shawnee. As a result, he left to teach elsewhere. A year later, he became principal of the new federal school for Shawnee children, settling in the Indian Territory for the rest of his life. For five years, he was principal of the school and also worked with Shawnee adults who were adjusting to life with the whites.

By the 1890s, the Shawnees were being pressured to register for allotments; many were very wary of the white man's ideas about land title papers. In 1893, Alford became chairman of a Shawnee business committee, the government that superseded the old Shawnee government. In this capacity, he lobbied in Washington for his nation. During this time, he tried to stop the speculative activities of unscrupulous whites trying to benefit from the Indians' unfamiliarity with the individualistic legal title inherent in the allotment system.

In arguing the virtues of the traditional Indian way of life, he would tap his knowledge of tribal customs and often recited the codes by which traditional Shawnees lived, stating that they were not that different from Christian ideals. In the 1890s, he also became an employee of the Bureau of Indian Affairs, thinking that this would give him more influence on the problems in Indian Territory. Married to the former Mary Grinnell, he had five children. He passed away at Shawnee, Oklahoma, on August 3, 1938; he was buried in the family plot.

ALLIGATOR (HALPATTER TUSTENUGGEE)
Seminole
c. 1795–c. 1850

Alligator, a principal chief during the Second Seminole War (1835–1842), probably as a young boy emigrated to central Florida from Creek country in Georgia and Alabama. On December 28, 1835, along with JUMPER (Ote Emathla) and MICANOPY, he commanded a force of three hundred men that attacked Major Francis L. Dade's detachment of 108 soldiers en route to reinforce Fort King in central Florida. Only three Americans survived that battle, while the Seminoles suffered fewer losses. On the same day, OSCEOLA attacked the party of Indian agent Wiley Thompson, slaying him.

On New Year's Eve, just three days later, Osceola and Alligator combined their forces to defeat General Duncan L. Clinch's contingent of five hundred Florida militiamen and three hundred army regulars on the banks of the Withlacoochee River. In December 1837 at Lake Okeechobee, Alligator's Seminole force, ARPEIKA's Miccosukee warriors, and WILD CAT's detachment of African Americans and Seminoles fought Colonel Zachary Taylor's contingent to a stalemate. As a result of brutal scorched earth policies in the swamps, Alligator was forced to lay down his arms in March 1838. After an attempted escape later in 1838, he was relocated to Indian Territory.

In 1843, he was a member of a Seminole delegation to Washington, D.C., that requested the settlement of land disputes between Seminoles and Creeks in the Indian Territory. The group also argued for better conditions for the Indians that had been removed there.

ALLIGATOR-STANDS-UP
Crow
fl. 1870s

Alligator-Stands-Up commanded a force of between one hundred and two hundred Crow scouts who served under General George Crook in the final phases of the Plains wars against Sioux, Cheyennes, and others the U.S. Army had defined as hostile.

Alligator-Stands-Up supplied scouts to General George Armstrong CUSTER at the Battle of the Little Bighorn in 1876. He mourned the demise of Custer and his men, despite the fact that Custer had disregarded the Crows' reports describing the size of the encampment they were about to attack. Alligator-Stands-Up followed the vision of Crow chief PLENTY COUPS, who believed that the invading Euro-Americans must be accommodated if the Crows were to survive in the midst of their traditional Native American enemies, notably the Sioux and Cheyennes.

FOR MORE INFORMATION:

Rosenberg, Bruce A. *Custer and the Epic of Defeat.* University Park: Pennsylvania State University Press, 1974.

Whittaker, Frederick. *A Complete Life of General George Armstrong Custer.* 1876. Reprint, Lincoln: University of Nebraska Press, 1993.

ALOKUT (OLLIKUT)
Nez Perce
fl. 1870s

An older brother of Chief JOSEPH, YOUNGER, Alokut (meaning "Frog") was one of the major war chiefs of the Nez Perce during their Long March through the Rocky Mountains in 1877. He tended to handle war strategy, while Young Joseph dealt with political matters. Alokut was killed September 30, 1877, in the Nez Perces' last battle with the U.S. Army in Montana's Bear Paw Mountains.

FOR MORE INFORMATION:

Josephy, Alvin M., Jr. *The Nez Perce Indians and the Opening of the Northwest.* New Haven, Conn.: Yale University Press, 1965.

———. *The Patriot Chiefs.* New York: Viking, 1961.

AMERICAN HORSE, ELDER (WASHICUN TASHANKA, IRON SHIELD)
Oglala Lakota
c. 1800–1876

American Horse was one of the Lakotas' principal chiefs, along with CRAZY HORSE, SITTING BULL, and others, during the Plains Indian wars of the last half of the nineteenth century. He was a principal military leader at the Battle of the Little Bighorn in 1876.

Following the Native victory over General George Armstrong CUSTER at the Little Bighorn in June 1876, the Sioux split up. Crazy Horse's band headed for the Little Bighorn Mountains, while Sitting Bull and his people headed for Canada. A third group of forty lodges, headed by American Horse, decided to go to an agency assigned by the United States. As they traveled to the agency, American Horse's band crossed paths with troops commanded by General George Crook at Slim Buttes. Crook attacked despite the fact that the Sioux were proceeding peacefully on land that was guaranteed to them by treaty.

A few escaped to join Sitting Bull's camp, but many in American Horse's camp were killed. Near the end of the fight, American Horse, four warriors, and fifteen women were backed into a cave. General Crook persuaded the women and children to leave the cave, but the five remaining warriors refused to surrender. During the shooting, American Horse was mortally wounded by a shot through his bowels. He died in excruciating pain as army surgeons struggled to save his life.

After the battle, Sitting Bull visited the site and was sickened by the sight of the women and children who had been killed. One woman was killed suckling her baby; another (who somehow survived) dropped her newborn child in the terror.

American Horse, Elder.
[Nebraska State Historical Society]

FOR MORE INFORMATION:

Sandoz, Mari. *Crazy Horse: Strange Man of the Oglalas.* New York: Alfred A. Knopf, 1942.

Schmitt, Martin F., and Dee Brown. *Fighting Indians of the West.* New York: Scribner's Sons, 1948.

Utley, Robert M. *The Lance and the Shield: The Life and Times of Sitting Bull.* New York: Henry Holt, 1993.

AMERICAN HORSE, YOUNGER (WASECHUN-TASHUNKA)
Oglala Lakota
c. 1840–1908

The nephew of American Horse (elder), American Horse (younger) was instrumental in signing a treaty that divested the Oglala Lakota of almost half their reservation lands in 1887.

American Horse (younger) was born in the Black Hills country of South Dakota, a son of Sitting Bear. American Horse supported accommodation with invading whites as the fervor for WOVOKA's Ghost Dance built on many Sioux reservations in the years before the 1890 massacre of BIG FOOT's band at Wounded Knee. Contemporary records indicate that he was involved in debates with traditional Sioux over whether to adapt to reservation life. He maintained that there was no future in resisting the white invasion, while traditional Sioux told him that he was one of those responsible for surrendering their former way of life. The people whom American Horse led were camped at Pine Ridge Agency during the Wounded Knee massacre but missed the bloodshed. A year later, American Horse was among delegates to Washington, D.C., who tried to secure fairness for Native people there with mixed results.

American Horse (younger) died at Pine Ridge on December 16, 1908.

FOR MORE INFORMATION:

Sandoz, Mari. *Crazy Horse: Strange Man of the Oglalas.* New York: Alfred A. Knopf, 1942.

Schmitt, Martin F., and Dee Brown. *Fighting Indians of the West.* New York: Scribner's Sons, 1948.

AMHERST, JEFFREY
1717–1797

In 1752, General Jeffrey Amherst, commander-in-chief of the British army in North America, was reported to have advocated the use of smallpox as a military tactic against the Ottawas, Ojibways, and other Indian tribes in the Great Lakes area. "You will be well advised," Amherst told his subordinates, "to infect the Indians with sheets upon which small pox patients have been lying or by any other means which may serve to exterminate this accursed race." [Josephy]

Amherst also recommended hunting Indians with dogs.

An oral history of the Ottawas related by Andrew J. Blackbird, a nineteenth-century Ottawa historian, indicates that smallpox came to them in a box from a white man. They opened the box only to find another one. Inside the second box was a third. Inside the last box the Ottawas found "mouldy particles," the smallpox "patients." (Blackbird's account has been questioned by historian William W. Warren, who says that smallpox reached the Ojibways and Ottawas after they took scalps from infected Gros Ventres, not from Gen. Amherst's troops.)

Amherst's policies regarding the conduct of Indian relations differed sharply from those of Sir William JOHNSON, the long-time British Indian agent for the Northeast. Amherst thought that Indians should be concerned with bringing in skins or they might become mischievous. Moreover, he directed his officers to hand out powder, arms, and clothing sparingly—for hunting purposes only—and to exercise caution in doing so. He also established a trading schedule at Fort Pitt and other posts, increasing the exchange rates for beaver pelts.

Amherst's policy of frugality bore bitter fruit. In May 1762 at Fort Pitt, Deputy Agent George Croghanbegan sent to his superiors reports of dissatisfaction among the neighboring tribes. Apparently they missed the more liberal trade policies of the French and those English officers before Amherst. As a result, war rumors began to circulate, and abuses by whites inevitably brought retaliations from the Indians.

FOR MORE INFORMATION:

Hamilton, Charles. *Cry of the Thunderbird.* Norman: University of Oklahoma Press, 1972.

Josephy, Alvin M., Jr. *The Patriot Chiefs.* New York: Viking, 1961.

ANDERSON, WALLACE "MAD BEAR"
Tuscarora
1927–

Wallace "Mad Bear" Anderson (given his Native name by his grandmother in relation to his hot-headedness) was one of the most noted Native rights activists in the 1950s before a general upsurge in Native self-determination efforts in the 1960s. Anderson later evolved into a noted spokesman for Native sovereignty in international forums.

Anderson was born in Buffalo, New York, and was raised on the Tuscarora Reservation near Niagara Falls. Serving in the U.S. Navy during World War II, he saw action at Okinawa and later served in Korea as well. Anderson became an activist after his request for a GI Bill loan to build a house on the Tuscarora Reservation was rejected.

Anderson led protests against Iroquois payment of New York State income taxes in 1957. At the height of the protest, several hundred Akwesasne (St. Regis) Mohawks marched to the Massena, New York, state courthouse, where they burned summonses issued for unpaid taxes. In 1958, Anderson played a leading role protesting a 1,383-acre seizure of Tuscarora land by the New York Power Authority for construction of a dam and reservoir. Anderson and other Iroquois deflated workers' tires and blocked surveyors' transits. When the Tuscaroras refused to sell the land, a force of about one hundred state troopers and police invaded their reservation. Anderson met the troopers and police with 150 nonviolent demonstrators who blocked their trucks by lying in the road. During the late 1950s, Anderson was profiled by Edmund Wilson in *The New Yorker* as Wilson was researching his book *Apologies to the Iroquois*.

In March 1959, Anderson was involved in a declaration of sovereignty at the Iroquois Six Nations Reserve in Brantford, Ontario, the settlement established by Joseph BRANT and his followers after the American Revolution. The declaration prompted an occupation of the reserve's council house by Royal Canadian Mounted Police. Also during the same month, Mad Bear attempted a citizens' arrest of Indian commissioner Glen L. Emmons in Washington, D.C., on allegations of misconduct in office. Emmons avoided the intended arrest but later resigned.

In July 1959, Anderson traveled to Cuba with a delegation of Iroquois and other Native Americans to exchange recognitions of sovereignty with Fidel Castro, whose revolutionary army had seized power only months earlier.

In 1967, Anderson formed the North American Indian Unity Caravan, which traveled the United States for six years as the types of activism that he had pioneered spread nationwide. He also gathered opposition to termination legislation from 133 Native tribes and nations and carried it to Washington, D.C., effectively killing the last attempt to buy out reservations in the United States. In 1969, he helped initiate the takeover of Alcatraz Island.

FOR MORE INFORMATION:

Anderson, Wallace (Mad Bear). "The Lost Brother: An Iroquois Prophecy of Serpents." In *The Way: An Anthology of American Indian Literature*, edited by Shirley Hill Witt and Stan Steiner. New York: Vintage, 1972.

Wilson, Edmund. *Apologies to the Iroquois*. New York: Farrar, Straus & Cudahy, 1960.

ANNAWAN ("COMMANDER")
Wampanoag
fl. 1670s

Annawan was METACOM's chief military strategist during King Philip's War. Making war as an ally of Metacom, Annawan was cornered in a swamp near Taunton, Massachusetts, by troops under Puritan military commander Benjamin Church. Annawan and a small group of warriors managed to elude Church's troops for several days. A number of Annawan's warriors were captured, however, and one prisoner led Church and his troops to Annawan's hiding place.

Church himself crept to the side of a sleeping Annawan and raised a tomahawk over the chief's head. Annawan woke suddenly then surrendered. As he was being transported to Boston for trial, Annawan developed a friendship with Church, who tried to keep Annawan from being executed. Church was unable to convince an angry mob, whose members seized Annawan and beheaded him.

FOR MORE INFORMATION:

Howe, George. "The Tragedy of King Philip." *American Heritage* (December 1958).

Leach, Douglas Edward. *Flintlock and Tomahawk*. New York: Macmillan, 1959.

ANTONIO, JUAN (COOSWOOTNA)
Cahuilla
c. 1783–1863

As a chief of the Kostakiklim lineage of the Cahuillas, Juan Antonio (as he was called by the Spanish) was probably born in the vicinity of Mount San Jacinto around 1783. He also was known as Yampoochee, meaning "Gets Mad Quickly." Juan Antonio was a principal chief during the California gold rush that began in 1849.

On July 4, 1842, Juan Antonio enters the historical record through a meeting with Daniel Sexton, an early Anglo pioneer who had come to California via the Santa Fe Trail. He let Sexton celebrate the holiday by erecting a flagpole. By 1845, Juan Antonio was listed as a leader of the Cahuilla mountain clan groups. At about the same time, Antonio, as leader of the Cahuillas around the San Jacinto Mountains, aided a U.S. Army detachment under Lieutenant Edward F. Beale, shielding the expedition against Ute assaults led by Walkara. On several occasions, Juan Antonio forced Walkara to abandon his attacks against Beale. Grateful for the efforts on his behalf, Beale gave the tribal leader some military epaulets that Antonio placed on his ceremonial garb.

In 1851, the white outlaw John Irving and his band of eleven men began to steal cattle and kill people in the Mount San Jacinto area. A group of Cahuillas under Juan Antonio tracked down and killed all but one of the renegades. Grateful for eliminating the outlaws, but fearful of the Indians' now obvious ability to kill white men, the whites attempted to depose Juan Antonio; but the Cahuillas ignored the white manifesto and continued to look to him as their chief. By 1852, he had become the titular leader of the Cahuillas by virtue of his leadership abilities, although he never became hereditary chief. In the chaotic 1850s, Antonio's Cahuillas vied with criminals, Cupeno Indians, miners, and Mormons for control over the area of present-day San Bernardino and Riverside Counties in southern California. Through the intercessions of his friend Paulino WEAVER (a mountain man of Cherokee descent living in the area) and some white ranchers, Antonio initially remained neutral and then decided to aid in the quelling of the 1851–1852 Cupeno uprising led by his Indian rival Antonio GARRA. Although his aid was crucial in suppressing the revolt, the California and U.S. Senates lobbied against the ratification of an 1852 treaty granting the Cahuillas dominion over their homelands. Frustrated by such duplicity, Antonio began raids on southern California settlers in 1854 and 1855. However, he was forced to stop when an expected alliance with the Mohaves and Quechans stalled. By 1856, predatory whites had cut off all water supplies to Juan Antonio's band, forcing them to move off their lands and become paupers in their own country.

In 1863, Juan Antonio succumbed to smallpox. Over ninety years later, in 1956, an archaeological dig disturbed an Indian grave near El Casco Schoolhouse in San Timoteo. Military epaulets on the shoulders of the interred man attested conclusively that it was Juan Antonio's body. Subsequently, the acclaimed leader of the Cahuillas was reburied with full tribal honors.

APEES, WILLIAM
Pequot
1798–c. 1836

William Apees, a lineal descendant of the Wampanoag war chief METACOM, was an ordained Methodist preacher who shared with Metacom a seething hatred for the Euro-Americans' treatment of his people. In 1836, 160 years after Metacom was killed then drawn and quartered, Apees delivered a passionate eulogy for him in Boston at the Odeon on Federal Street. His speech ended with a paraphrased quote from Dr. Increase Mather bidding God to come to the Puritans' aid in their pursuit of Metacom:

Nor could they, the Pilgrims, cease crying to the Lord against [King] Philip, until they had prayed the bullet through his heart. If this is the way they pray, that is bullets through people's hearts, I hope they will not pray for me; I should rather be excused. [Apees, *Eulogy*]

Shortly after this speech, at the age of thirty-eight, Apees disappeared from public view and was never heard from again. Many have specu-

lated that he was murdered, but the actual circumstances of Apees's death have been lost to history.

FOR MORE INFORMATION:

Apees, William. *Eulogy on King Philip.* Boston, 1836.

———. *Increase of the Kingdom of Christ.* New York, 1831.

———. *On Our Own Ground: The Complete Writings of William Apees, a Pequot.* Edited by Barry O'Connell. Amherst: University of Massachusetts Press, 1992.

———. *A Son of the Forest.* 2d ed. New York, 1831.

Hamilton, Charles. *Cry of the Thunderbird.* Norman: University of Oklahoma Press, 1972.

APODACA, PAUL
Navajo
1951–

Born in Los Angeles, Apodaca is of Spanish, Mexican, and Navajo descent. Since the early 1970s, Apodaca has been affiliated with the Bowers Museum (a museum of the cultural arts of the Pacific Rim, the Americas, African Art and California history) in Orange County, California, as curator of American Indian Art, artist-in-residence, head of the California History and Folk Art Collections, and exhibiting artist.

Throughout his career, Apodaca has worked with funding agencies like the Arizona Commission on the Arts, the Corporation for Public Broadcasting, the California Arts Council, and the Los Angeles Cultural Affairs Department. Apodaca was a consultant to Knott's Berry Farm and the Los Angeles Festival in the early 1990s. He is currently a consultant to the Smithsonian Institution's National Museum of the American Indian.

In addition, he has held academic appointments at Chapman University, California State University, Fullerton, and the University of California, Irvine. His numerous awards include: the Orange County Human Rights Award, the Smithsonian Institution Museum Professional Award, and the Academy of Motion Pictures Arts and Sciences Award for *Broken Rainbow* (1986), a documentary film that helped to stop the relocation of twelve thousand Navajos in northern Arizona. Apodaca wrote and played the musical score for the film and did much of the research. He is also responsible along with Henry Koerper of Cypress College and Jon Erikson of the University of California, Irvine, for California state legislation that made an eight-thousand-year-old carving of a bear in San Diego County the State Prehistoric Artifact. Apodaca continues to be an important figure in Hispanic, Native American, and arts communities at the national and state levels.

FOR MORE INFORMATION:

Champagne, Duane, ed. *Native America: Portrait of a People.* Detroit: Gale Research, 1994.

AQUASH, ANNA MAE
Micmac
1945–1976

Anna Mae Aquash, who was originally from Nova Scotia, Canada, became involved in the American Indian Movement (AIM) during its peak of activity shortly after 1970. She was a close friend of Leonard PELTIER, Dennis BANKS, Russell MEANS, and others who were arrested and charged in connection with the Wounded Knee occupation in 1973 and other events. At the height of violence at the Pine Ridge Reservation in 1976, she was found murdered near a Pine Ridge highway.

Following the shooting deaths of FBI agents Ronald Coler and Jack Williams at the Jumping Bull Compound on the Pine Ridge Indian Reservation in June 1975, Aquash was pursued and arrested by the FBI as a possible material witness to the crime (of which Peltier was eventually accused).

On February 24, 1976, Roger Amiott, a rancher, found Aquash's body near Wanblee, in the northeastern section of the Pine Ridge Indian Reservation. Dr. W. O. Brown, a pathologist who performed autopsies under contract with the Bureau of Indian Affairs, arrived the following day. After examining the body, Dr. Brown announced that the woman, who still had not been officially identified, had died of exposure to the brutal South Dakota winter.

The FBI decided that the only way to identify the woman was to sever her hands and send them to the FBI's crime laboratories in the Washington, D.C., area. Agents on the scene reasoned that the body was too badly decomposed to take fingerprints at Pine Ridge. Ken Sayres, BIA police chief at Pine Ridge, would say later that no one had been called to the morgue to attempt identification of the body before the hands were severed.

A week after the body was found, Aquash—now missing her hands as well as her identity—was buried at Holy Rosary Catholic Cemetery, Pine Ridge. On March 3, the FBI announced Aquash's identity.

Aquash's family was notified of her death on March 5. They did not believe that she had died of natural causes. At thirty-two, Aquash had been in good health and was trained to survive in cold weather. She did not drink alcohol or smoke tobacco. Her friends remembered that she had smuggled food past federal government roadblocks into Wounded Knee during another brutal South Dakota winter, almost three years to the day before her body had been found. A new autopsy was demanded.

In the midst of the controversy, Aquash's body was exhumed. Her family retained an independent pathologist, Dr. Gary Peterson of St. Paul, Minnesota. Dr. Peterson reopened the skull and found a .32-caliber bullet, which he said had been fired from a gun placed at the base of Aquash's neck. The bullet was not difficult to find; "It should have been discovered the first time," Peterson said. Asked about the bullet he had not found, Dr. W. O. Brown, the BIA coroner, replied, "A little bullet isn't hard to overlook." [Johansen]

Following identification of Aquash's decomposed body, the Canadian government and the U.S. Commission on Civil Rights demanded an investigation into her death. The U.S. Justice Department announced that it would look into the case, but the murder was never solved; the investigation languished in bureaucratic limbo. Aquash's friends refused to let her spirit pass away. On March 14, Anna Mae's body was wrapped in a traditional star quilt as the women of Oglala Village mourned her for two days and two nights.

FOR MORE INFORMATION:

Brand, Johanna. *The Life and Death of Anna Mae Aquash.* Toronto: Lorimer, 1978.

Johansen, Bruce E., and Roberto F. Maestas. *Wasi'chu: The Continuing Indian Wars.* New York: Monthly Review Press, 1979.

Weir, David, and Lowell Bergman. "The Killing of Anna Mae Aquash." *Rolling Stone* (April 7, 1977): 52–55.

ARAPOOSH
Crow
c. 1790–1834

Arapoosh, one of the principal chiefs of the Crow during their early-eighteenth-century assertions against the Cheyenne and Blackfoot, was probably born in the mountains that were later named for him. He was said to have had a surly disposition (thus his name, meaning "Sour Belly" or "Rotten Belly"). Arapoosh

was also known for his unyielding bravery in battle.

Arapoosh was thought of as a spiritual leader and something of a mystic. He painted a symbol from a vision, the "man in the moon," on his war shield and used it to help him make decisions. Crow leaders rolled the shield, and if the moon symbol came to rest upright, success was expected.

Arapoosh distrusted the whites who, in his time, were beginning to filter into the Crow country between the Black Hills and Rocky Mountains in what is today eastern Montana. He refused to sign treaties with them, although other Crows signed a treaty of friendship in 1825. Arapoosh did not like the idea of living on a reservation. He never had to make the choice between a free life and a reservation life because he died before the Anglo-American invasion reached its peak.

ARMIJO
Navajo
fl. mid-1800s

Armijo, a headman in the Navajo War of 1863–1864 and a farmer, took the name of the governor of New Mexico, Manuel Armijo, sometime before 1846, when the territory was still a part of Mexico. Residing in northwestern New Mexico in the foothills of the Chuska Mountains, Armijo was a prominent agriculturalist among the Navajo. Throughout the 1850s, Armijo was an advocate of peaceful relations between Indians and whites. However, when violence erupted in the early 1860s, he became an ardent supporter of Navajo chief MANUELITO. In April 1864, after a protracted struggle against the American forces, he went to Fort Canby, Arizona, and surrendered. Subsequently, he was relocated with his followers and other Navajos to Fort Sumner (Bosque Redondo) in New Mexico. Armijo was a signatory of the 1868 Navajo treaty that set up the original confines of the Navajo Reservation in his homeland, the Chuska Mountains of Arizona and New Mexico (surrounding present-day Fort Defiance, Arizona).

ARPEIKA (ARIPEKA, APAYAKA HADJO; SAM JONES)
Seminole-Miccosukee
c. 1765–1860

Arpeika was a spiritual leader and a chief in the Second Seminole War (1835–1842). It is generally thought that he was born in Georgia and emigrated south to Florida with other Miccosukees as a young man. In Florida, the modern town of Arpeika stands on the site of his principal village on the Weekwachee River just north of Tampa.

In 1841, he was residing in a village a few miles north of Lake Okeechobee. At the conclusion of the Third Seminole War of 1855–1858, he moved farther south into the Big Cypress Swamp.

Arpeika was reputed to be the most militant of the Seminole chiefs in resisting removal from Florida to Indian Territory. In 1835, he advised OSCEOLA to seek vengeance against Indian agent Wiley Thompson. During the Second Seminole War, Arpeika warned of white duplicity and the violation of truce flags. He participated in the Battle of Lake Okeechobee in December 1837 with WILD CAT and ALLIGATOR. They imposed heavy casualties on the Americans, but the Seminoles had to retreat from the battlefield.

Although most Seminoles had left southern Florida by 1860, Arpeika and his followers remained in their homeland. He and Billy BOWLEGS successfully thwarted attempts to relocate their bands during the Third Seminole War of 1855–1858. When Bowlegs decided to go to Indian Territory, Arpeika continued to live in the Florida Everglades. He died in 1860 at home in the swamps. Some Miccosukees said he was over a hundred years old at his demise.

ASAH, SPENCER (LALLO)
Kiowa
c. 1908–1954

As one of the leading Kiowa artists of the first half of the twentieth century, Spencer Asah (whose Kiowa name means "Little Boy") pioneered in portraying the esthetics of the Southern Plains Indians. Born the son of a buffalo medicine man, he was imbued with the rituals and traditions of his people at an early age. Educated at local government schools as a child, he graduated from St. Patrick's Mission School at Anadarko, Oklahoma.

He became affiliated with a fine arts club organized by Mrs. Susie Peters, an Indian service employee. Several of the artists in the club attended special classes at the University of Oklahoma in 1926–1927. Excited by what he observed, the head of the university art department, Professor Oscar B. Jacobson, obtained funds to enable five Kiowa artists to devote most of their time to their work. By the late 1920s, their watercolor works, including Asah's, were being shown in Europe and the United States to critical acclaim. Asah used no models, usually painting from memory. He also painted murals for several Indian schools and institutions.

Asah married a Comanche woman, Ida, and had three children before his death in 1954.

ASPENQUID
Abenaki
fl. mid-1600s to late 1600s

Aspenquid was one of the first Native Americans converted to Christianity by French

Jesuits. Born late in the sixteenth century (the precise date is unknown), Aspenquid became known in New England and eastern Canada for his skill as a preacher and orator as he spread the gospel. For many years after his death (which may have occurred as late as 1682), an Aspenquid Day was celebrated among many people in Halifax, Nova Scotia.

ASPINET
Wampanoag
fl. 1620s
A principal chief of the Nausets, who lived near the present-day town of Eastham on Cape Cod, Aspinet helped European colonists become established there despite the fact that he had ambushed an initial scouting party from the *Mayflower*. In 1621, he returned a lost English boy to the colonial settlement, and in 1622 he contributed beans and corn to the colonists, whose own harvest had all but failed.

Despite his overtures of friendship to the colonists, word leaked out to MASSASOIT in 1623 that Aspinet was among several Wampanoag subchiefs who were planning to drive the Plymouth colony into the sea. He died in hiding from colonists' reprisals.

ASSACUMBUIT
Abenaki
fl. 1700–1720
Assacumbuit provided continuing support to the French in their American wars with the English during the late seventeenth and early eighteenth centuries. He also traveled throughout France during 1706 and 1707, where he was knighted by Louis XIV and given a magnificent saber for having had a personal hand in the deaths of 150 "enemies of France."

Assacumbuit assisted the French in the battle of Fort St. Johns, Newfoundland, in 1696, and later allied with the French to attack several New England settlements in Queen Anne's War (1702–1713).

ATSIDI SANI (OLD SMITH)
Navajo
c. 1830–c. 1870
Atsidi Sani was an artist and medicine man generally given credit for the introduction of silversmithing among the Navajos. His Navajo name is from *atsidi*, or "smith." He also was sometimes called Herrero Delgado, "Small Ironworker," or Beshiltheeni, meaning "Metal Worker" or "Knife Maker." Although he was born about 1830 near present-day Wheatfields, Arizona, little is known of his parentage other than that he was of the Dibelizhini (Black Sheep people) clan. By the 1850s, he became friendly with Nakai Tsosi or the "Thin Mexican," who taught him the basic techniques of the silversmithing craft. In 1853, Captain Henry Linn Dodge (Indian agent to the Navajos) also brought a blacksmith, George Carter, to Fort Defiance, Arizona, to teach ironwork to the Navajo. Dodge's interpreter, Juan Anaya, was a skilled silversmith, also.

Although the exact date for the first Navajo silver pieces is debatable, there is general agreement that Atsidi Sani fashioned his first silver pieces (conchas, bracelets, and various other jewelry items) in 1853. Hence, the Navajos took some knowledge of silversmithing with them when they were taken to Fort Sumner. At Bosque Redondo, Atsidi Sani enhanced his knowledge through contacts with Mexican ironworkers. At first, he made bridle ornaments and other decorative items, but he also began to use silver coins in his work, improvising with whatever tools he could find. Other Navajos became interested in his craft, and he taught them what he knew. He apprenticed four of his sons to ironworking. One of them, Red Smith, became a prominent silversmith in the late nineteenth century. From this humble beginning, Navajo silversmithing developed a legacy of simple but fine designs that remain prevalent today.

Atsidi Sani was a minor headman who became a prominent chief at Fort Defiance by 1858. After 1858, he was a major force in Navajo affairs as a political leader and silversmith. He was the sixth chief to sign the 1868 treaty that returned the Navajos to their ancestral lands. He was also a ceremonial singer who performed the various chants he knew with fidelity and great detail. It is said he had an excellent memory and was widely sought after for curing chants. His silversmithing was a matter of great concern to him, and he maintained high standards for his workmanship. He died near Chinle, Arizona, in 1870, a respected elder honored by his people.

ATTAKULLAKULLA
Cherokee
c. 1700–c. 1778

Attakullakulla, meaning "Leaning Wood" is from Attacullaculla (more correctly Atagulkalu), which stems from the Cherokee *ata*, "wood," and *galkalu*, "something or someone leaning." He also was called Little Carpenter, which referred to his small size. His real name was White Owl or Onacona, Oukounaka, or Ukwaneequa in Cherokee. He was an ally of the English colonists, a peace chief, an uncle of Nancy WARD, and the father of DRAGGING CANOE.

The first historical mention of Attakullakulla appears in 1730, when he traveled with a group of Cherokee and Creek chiefs to the royal court in London. This delegation of prominent American Indian leaders was taken there by Sir Alexander Cumming. By 1738, he was listed as

a peace chief of the Cherokees, with OCONOSTOTA being the principal war chief. Throughout their long lives, Attakullakulla and Oconostota worked quite effectively in tandem. In fact, Attakullakulla was married to Oconostota's daughter.

By 1750, Attakullakulla was renowned as a gifted orator and was the speaker for Old Hop (Kanagatoga), a chief of the Cherokees. At a peace council with Governor John Glen of South Carolina in 1750, he was the principal speaker even though he was not the most powerful Cherokee chief at the time. Friendly to whites, he saved treaty commissioner William Byrd's life when he was the object of a proposed assassination by disgruntled Cherokee warriors. In 1755, as a result of his efforts, Fort Dobbs was built in Cherokee Territory on ceded land, and the Little Carpenter was granted a commission in the British colonial army.

At the Treaty of Broad River in 1756, Attakullakulla favored expanding the influence of the South Carolinians. In 1759, he obtained the release of Oconostota, who was being held by South Carolina authorities. During the Cherokee War of 1760–1761, he saved the life of Colonel John Stuart after his capture at Fort Loudon (eastern Tennessee) by Oconostota's Cherokee warriors. Subsequently, Attakullakulla escorted Stuart to safety in Virginia. After the war, Stuart became the English superintendent for the Southern Department. To nurture peace in the Southeast, Stuart held a conference at Augusta, Georgia, in 1763, attended by Attakullakulla and his people as well as Choctaws, Chickasaws, and Creeks. Numerous gifts and provisions were distributed to promote goodwill.

Despite his pro-British inclinations, Attakullakulla sided with the Americans at the outbreak of the American Revolution and raised a force of about five hundred Cherokee warriors on their behalf. He was probably angered by continued pressure from the British for land cessions. He continued as a significant leader in Indian-white relations in the Southeast until his death in Tennessee in 1777 or 1778.

FOR MORE INFORMATION:

Dockstader, Frederick. *Great North American Indians.* New York: Van Nostrand Reinhold, 1977.

ATTUCKS, CRISPUS (SMALL DEER)
Massachuset
c. 1725–1770

Son of an African American father and a Massachuset Indian mother, Crispus Attucks was the first casualty of the Boston Massacre of March 5, 1770—and the first death in the American Revolution. Attucks' father was a slave in a Framingham, Massachusetts, household until about 1750, when he escaped and became a sailor. His mother lived in an Indian mission at Natick.

During the Boston Massacre, which occurred five years before the first sustained combat of the American Revolution at Lexington and Concord, Boston residents upset with the Townsend Acts (which directed them to pay unwanted taxes) attacked a detachment of British troops in front of the city's customs house. The troops fired into the rioters (some accounts say that Attucks was their leader), killing Attucks first. Two others died on the spot of gunshot wounds, and two more died of their injuries later.

In 1888, a monument to Attucks was erected at the Boston Common.

$\mathcal{B}$

BAD HEART BULL, AMOS
Oglala Lakota
d. 1913

Amos Bad Heart Bull traced the late–nineteenth-century history of the Oglala Lakota in more than four hundred pictures, which, with captions that he composed, constitute a unique account. Bad Heart Bull's history provides an Oglala point of view on the CUSTER battle at the Little Bighorn, the Wild West shows of Buffalo Bill CODY and others, the massacre of BIG FOOT's band at Wounded Knee, and other events.

Bad Heart Bull inherited the role of tribal historian from his father. His artistic technique was self-taught but extremely detailed and allows glimpses into Lakota everyday life, as well as a chronicling of remarkable events.

On Bad Heart Bull's death in 1913, his records passed to his sister Dolly Pretty Cloud. The record was used by Helen Blish, a University of Nebraska graduate student in the 1920s, as the basis for a book, *A Pictographic History of the Oglala Sioux* (1967).

FOR MORE INFORMATION:

Blish, Helen. *A Pictographic History of the Oglala Sioux.* Lincoln: University of Nebraska Press, 1967.

BAD HEART BULL, WESLEY
Oglala Lakota
c. 1915–1973

Wesley Bad Heart Bull was knifed to death by a young white man near Custer, South Dakota, in 1973. Weeks later, the assailant was charged with second-degree manslaughter.

The manslaughter charge had become a political red flag for the American Indian Movement (AIM); the murder of Raymond YELLOW THUNDER had been handled the same way in Gordon, Nebraska. To many Indians, that charge—a common one in cases of a non-Indian killing an Indian—was worse than no charge at all; it implied that they were subhuman. Local Lakota residents asked AIM to arrange a discussion with magistrates in Custer in an attempt to have the charge changed to first-degree murder. On February 6, the Indians arrived at the

Custer County Courthouse to find a large group of police standing around it in riot gear. The meeting began, anyway. Bad Heart Bull's mother, Sarah, arrived late and requested entry to the courthouse. Police refused. A riot policeman grabbed Sarah and threw her to the ground. A melee followed, and the courthouse was set on fire. Sarah was charged with assaulting an officer, convicted, and sentenced to three to five years in prison. The man who had killed her son was later sentenced to two months' probation.

FOR MORE INFORMATION:

Bates, Tom. "The Government's Secret War on the Indian," *Oregon Times*, February–March 1976, pp. 14–17.

BANKS, DENNIS
Chippewa
1932–

Dennis Banks, born on the Leech Lake Reservation in northern Minnesota, was one of the founders of the American Indian Movement (AIM) in 1968. The group was first formed in Minneapolis to combat police brutality against Native Americans and the selective law enforcement policies of the Minneapolis police. Initially, an Indian patrol was established to follow the police as they traveled through Native American neighborhoods. Arrest rates of Native Americans fell to the city's general average nine months after the AIM patrols were introduced.

During the summer of 1972, Hank ADAMS (a leader of "fish-ins" in Washington), Banks, and about fifty other Native activists met in Denver to plan a Trail of Broken Treaties caravan. Their hope was to marshal thousands of protesters across the nation to march on Washington, D.C., to dramatize the issue of American Indian self-determination.

Upon arriving in Washington on November 3, 1972, the fifty to one hundred protesters found that there was not enough lodging available, so they elected to stay in the Bureau of Indian Affairs (BIA) building for several hours until security guards sought to forcibly remove them. At that point, events turned violent. The protesters seized the building for six days as they asserted their demands that tribal sovereignty be restored and immunity be granted to all protesters. Files were seized and damage was done to the BIA building (AIM leaders claimed that federal agents had infiltrated the movement and had done most of the damage). On November 8, 1972, federal officials offered immunity and transportation home to the protesters. The offer was accepted and the crisis was resolved for the moment.

Banks was a principal leader of AIM in 1973 during the occupation of the hamlet of Wounded Knee on the Pine Ridge Sioux Reservation. The two-month occupation of Wounded Knee, which began on February 28, 1973, demonstrated AIM's contempt for the BIA. The occupation also provided a platform from which to portray AIM's goals of tribal sovereignty and self-determination. At the same time, the occupation of Wounded Knee by Native American activists had a profound impact on non-Indians as news of the conflict was spread worldwide through the media.

Following the occupation of Wounded Knee, Banks and fellow AIM leader Russell MEANS were charged with three counts of assault on federal officers, one charge each of conspiracy, and one each of larceny, all arising from their activities during the occupation. Banks and Means, facing five charges each, could have been sentenced to as many as eighty-five years in prison. For several months in 1974, a year after Wounded Knee, the defense and prosecution presented their cases in a St. Paul, Minnesota, federal court. On September 16, Judge Fred J. Nichol dismissed all the charges. The judge said that the FBI's agents had lied repeatedly during the trial while under oath and had often furnished defense attorneys with altered documents. Judge Nichol said that R. D. Hurd, the federal prosecutor, had deliberately deceived the court. "The FBI," said Judge Nichol, "has stooped to a new low." To the chagrin of the judge and jurors, the Justice Department responded by presenting Hurd with an award for "superior performance" during the trial. [Bates]

Banks eluded capture during the FBI dragnet following the deaths of two agents at Pine Ridge (for which Leonard PELTIER was later convicted) in June 1975. He went underground before receiving amnesty from Jerry Brown, governor of California. Banks earned an associate of arts degree at the University of California (Davis campus) and during the late 1970s helped found and direct Deganawidah-Quetzalcoatl University, a Native-controlled college.

After Brown's term as governor ended, Banks, in 1984, was sheltered by the Onondagas on their reservation near Nedrow, New York. While there, Banks organized the Jim THORPE Run. In 1984, Banks surrendered to face charges stemming from his 1970s' activities in South Dakota. He later served eighteen months in prison, after which he worked as a drug and alcohol counselor on the Pine Ridge Reservation.

During the late 1980s, Banks's energies were concentrated on measures to protect Native graves and human remains. He organized a campaign in Kentucky, where he lived as a single parent, that resulted in statewide legal protections after robbers desecrated Native graves in Uniontown. Banks also organized several more ceremonial runs in the United States and Japan. His autobiography, *Sacred Soul*, was published in Japan in 1988.

Banks remained active in Native American politics throughout the 1990s, although he was not as often in the national spotlight. He had acting roles in several films, including *War Party*, *The Last of the Mohicans*, and *Thunderheart*. During the first half of 1994, Banks helped organize a five-month Walk for Justice across the United States on behalf of imprisoned Native activist Leonard Peltier. About four hundred people took part in the march, and twenty-eight walked the entire three-thousand-mile distance. The Walk for Justice ended in Washington, D.C., on July 15, at a rally calling on President Bill Clinton to free Peltier.

FOR MORE INFORMATION:

Bates, Tom. "The Government's Secret War on the Indian," *Oregon Times*, February–March 1976, p. 14.

Churchill, Ward, and Jim Vander Wall. *The Cointelpro Papers*. Boston: South End Press, 1990.

BANYACYA, THOMAS, SR.
Hopi
c. 1910–

Born in New Oraibi on the Hopi Reservation about 1910, Banyacya gained prominence in 1948 when the Hopi elders chose him as one of the four men to be their "tongue and ears." Banyacya and the three other men were directed to warn the white world of certain foreboding messages contained in the ancient Hopi prophecies. The Hopi prophecy predicted the gigantic "gourdful of ashes" (the advent of nuclear weapons in 1945) and warned the world of nuclear holocaust if the world's peoples refused to change their harmful ways. As the last surviving member of this group of men, Banyacya has become a major voice espousing the traditionalist point of view on a number of contentious issues in the American Southwest.

Banyacya gained national prominence in the 1970s when he opposed strip mining adjacent to Hopi lands. In 1972, the U.S. Congress passed Public Law 93-531 which forced the removal of more than ten thousand Navajos from Black Mesa in northeastern Arizona. Ostensibly, the U.S. government claimed that they were returning the land (the so-called Navajo-Hopi Joint Use Area) to the Hopi nation. This governmental action precipitated the Navajo-Hopi Land Dispute. Accordingly, a barbed wire fence 285 miles long was built to stop Navajos from using the area. By the early 1970s, Thomas Banyacya and his son, Thomas, Jr., had joined other Hopi traditionalists and Navajos to protest the government's actions. Banyacya and others asserted that the U.S. government was chiefly concerned with vacating the land so that tribal governments and mining companies could gain unfettered access to the area's vast amounts of oil shale, coal, and uranium. Banyacya opposes the proposed strip mining of the area and claims that the self-destructive tendencies of the U.S. government were revealed a long time ago in the Hopi prophecies. He continues these activities from his home on the Hopi reservation to this day.

FOR MORE INFORMATION:

Champagne, Duane, ed. *Native North American Almanac.* Detroit: Gale Research, 1994.

BARBONCITO (BARBON)
Navajo
c. 1820–1871

Growing up in the heart of Navajo country at Canyon de Chelly, Arizona, Barboncito became a prominent Navajo headman and spiritual singer. At different times in his life, Barboncito also was known as Hastin Dagha, Hastin Daagi ("Full-bearded Man"), Bislahalani ("the Orator"), and Hozhooji Naata ("Beautyway Chanter").

A brother of DELGADITO, Barboncito was born into the Ma'iideeshgiizhnii (Coyote Pass) clan about 1820. At the start of the Mexican War in 1846, he endorsed a treaty with U.S. Army Colonel Alexander W. Doniphan that established friendly relations with the newly arrived Anglos in the Southwest. Disliking Mexican and Pueblo Indian slave-raiding of their children, it seemed like a natural alliance for the Navajos. However, the U.S. government was not able to stop the long-standing warfare between the Navajos and the Mexicans.

By the 1850s, Barboncito was taking little part in these skirmishes, preferring to remain at Canyon de Chelly. On the eve of the U.S. Civil War, he counseled both sides to avoid violence and seek peace. In 1861, he signed the treaty at Fort Fauntleroy, New Mexico, which sought peaceful solutions to these dilemmas.

With the start of the Civil War, many western garrisons were abandoned or undermanned; the Navajos decided to take advantage of this power vacuum. Consequently, Colonel Kit CARSON was brought in to subjugate the Navajos and relocate them to Fort Sumner (Bosque Redondo). Although MANUELITO and other leaders resisted Carson's scorched earth policies, a lack of supplies and food eventually forced Barboncito to surrender in September 1864. Taken 350 miles to Fort Sumner, Barboncito found worse conditions there than he could have imagined. In June 1865, he escaped with about five hundred followers and rejoined Manuelito in the Navajo homeland. He surrendered a second time with twenty-one followers at Fort Wingate in November 1866.

The deplorable living conditions at Fort Sumner (the over eight thousand Navajos forced to stay there lived in foxholes with canvas coverings) were so scandalous that the U.S. government set up a meeting with General William T. Sherman and Barboncito and other chiefs. As a result of these talks, there emerged a proposal to relocate the Navajos to Indian Territory (Oklahoma). Horrified at this offer, Barboncito objected vociferously, stating, "I hope to God you will not ask us to go to another country except our own. It might turn out to be another Bosque Redondo. They told us this was a good place when we came here, but it is not." As a result of these protests, the U.S. government, in 1868, drew up a new treaty that returned the Navajos to the area within their four sacred mountains. Although the area was only about 20 percent of their former territory, the Navajos gladly returned and expanded their reservation through purchases derived from oil monies until the 1930s.

Barboncito never became a Navajo head chief, but he was renowned for his eloquence and persuasiveness in tribal councils. His voice was always strong and influential during crucial deliberations. On March 16, 1871, he died at Canyon de Chelly, respected and much loved by his people and by his Anglo adversaries.

BARNARD, TIMPOOCHEE
Yuchi and Caucasian
fl. early 1800s

The son of Scotsman Timothy Barnard and his Yuchi spouse, Timpoochee Barnard was the leader of a small band of pro-American Yuchis during the War of 1812. His father was employed by Benjamin Hawkins, an Indian agent in the Southeast.

At the start of the Creek War, Timpoochee Barnard led one hundred Yuchi warriors under the general command of Andrew Jackson, even though the majority of the Yuchi supported the Creek Red Sticks led by Red Eagle (William WEATHERFORD). At the Battle of Callabee Creek on January 2, 1814, Barnard's fearless attack allowed the beleaguered and outnumbered

forces commanded by Captain John Broadnix to withdraw from the battlefield with minimal losses. Barnard was a signatory of the disastrous and unjust Treaty of Fort Jackson, Alabama, in August 1814. After the War of 1812, he resided with his Creek spouse on the Flint River in Georgia.

BARREIRO, JOSE
Cuban/Taino
1948–

Jose Barreiro edited the Northeast Indian Quarterly (renamed Akwe:kon Journal in 1992 and Native Americas in 1995) at the American Indian Program, Cornell University, from its first issue in 1984. The journal and the Cornell AIP generally influenced a generation of scholars from the bachelor's to the doctoral level. Barreiro also contributed to Cornell AIP as it combined with other disciplines at Cornell to provide many early and critical studies of environmental pollution on Indian reservations, especially Akwesasne (St. Regis) in New York State.

Akwe:kon Journal and Cornell AIP also sponsored and published proceedings of a number of precedent-setting conferences, including "Cultural Encounter: The Iroquois Great Law of Peace and the United States Constitution" (1987), "Indian Corn of the Americas: A Gift to the World" (1989), and "Indigenous Economics: Toward a Natural World Order" (1992). Akwe:kon (which means "all of us" in Mohawk) combines missions of community service and scholarship. In 1993, Barreiro published a novelistic treatment of the first Spanish landfalls in the Americas through Native American eyes, The Indian Chronicles.

FOR FURTHER INFORMATION:
Barreiro, Jose. The Indian Chronicles. Houston: Arte Publico Press, 1993.

Jose Barreiro. [Tim Johnson]

BEAR HUNTER
Shoshone
fl. 1860s

Unlike WASHAKIE and TENDOY, the Shoshone Bear Hunter resisted white colonization in the Great Basin during the middle of the nineteenth century. With most federal troops occupied in the U.S. Civil War, Bear Hunter's war parties declared open season on Mormon settlers, telegraph workers, and wagon trains bound for the West Coast.

In 1862, a California vigilante infantry under the command of Patrick Conner established a fort in the Wasatch Range overlooking Salt Lake City to patrol the westward route through the Great Basin. During January 1863, soldiers marched out of the fort toward Bear Hunter's village. In less than a day of fighting on January 27, the infantry killed 224 Shoshones, including Bear Hunter, and took 164 women and children prisoner. The Indians killed twenty-one white infantry and injured forty-six others. Shortly thereafter, the Shoshones were forced to cede most of the Great Basin by treaty.

BENDER, CHARLES ALBERT
Chippewa/Ojibway
1883–1954

A pitcher with a fastball that was said to rival that of Walter Johnson, Charles Albert Bender was elected to the Baseball Hall of Fame at Cooperstown, New York, in 1953.

Born of mixed parentage near Brainerd, Minnesota, in the Bad River band of Chippewas, Bender attended Carlisle Indian School and earned a college degree at Dickinson College. His major league baseball career began in 1903 with the Philadelphia Athletics. During a dozen years under manager Connie Mack, Athletics teams on which Bender played won the American League pennant five times and the World Series three times. He was the best pitcher on the team, and he led the league in strikeouts in 1910, 1911, and 1914. Some Philadelphia sports writers called Bender "Connie Mack's meal ticket."

After 1914, Bender played a year for Baltimore in the short-lived Federal League and two more for the Philadelphia Nationals. During his career, Bender won 200 games and lost 111. Occasionally, fans for other teams would deride his ancestry; Bender would call them "foreigners" in return. When one fan remarked that she thought all Indians wore feathers, Bender quipped, "We do, madam, but this happens to be molting season." [Masin]

Later in his life, Bender worked as a baseball coach at the U.S. Naval Academy and for the Chicago White Sox and his old team, the Athletics. A year after he was elected to the Baseball Hall of Fame, Bender died of cancer.

FOR MORE INFORMATION:
Masin, Merman L. *Curve Ball Laughs.* New York: Pyramid Books, 1958.

BENNETT, ROBERT L.
Oneida
1912–

Robert L. Bennett, commissioner of the U.S. Bureau of Indian Affairs under President Lyndon Johnson, was born in Oneida, Wisconsin, and educated at the Haskell Institute. He later attended Southeastern University, earning an LL.B. degree in 1941. From 1943 to 1945, Bennett served in the Marine Corps during World War II. Following the war, Bennett held a number of posts in the BIA before becoming commissioner (1966–1969) by appointment of President Johnson.

As BIA director at the beginning of the self-determination era, Bennett tried to fashion programs that would hasten economic development on reservations. Bennett's administration also tried to extend the social welfare policies of Johnson's Great Society to reservation Indians, with various degrees of success. In addition, Bennett fought off the last attempts to further termination—the buying out of Native titles to reservations—in Congress.

After his retirement from the BIA, Bennett directed the American Indian Law Center at the University of New Mexico Law School. He served on a number of boards of directors and garnered many awards working with Native groups across the United States. His autobiography was published by Dillon Press, Minneapolis.

BIG BEAR
Cree
c. 1825–1888

Big Bear was a principal chief among the Cree during the Second Riel Rebellion, the most serious Native uprising on the Canadian frontier. Born in Fort Carlton in what would later become the Canadian province of Saskatchewan, Big Bear was noticed by Canadian authorities in 1876 when, as a chief of the Plains Cree, he refused to sign Treaty Number Six. Meeting with about two thousand other Native people at POUNDMAKER's reserve in Cut Knife, Big Bear, in 1876, denounced white dishonesty in treaty dealings.

Big Bear called on other Native nations to join his Cree in resisting Canadian colonization, but few responded. The Métis (French–Native Canadian mixed-bloods) allied with him and joined forces in the Second Riel Rebellion (1885), in which Big Bear was a prominent leader. Big Bear and Poundmaker joined the Riel Rebellion after Métis forces met Canadian troops at Duck Lake on March 26, 1885. A week later, a Cree war party led by Big Bear invaded a Battleford Catholic church during mass and took thirteen whites hostage. One of them, an Indian agent named Thomas Quinn, decided to fight back and was shot to death. Eight other whites died in the melee. One man escaped and reported the incident to the Royal Canadian Mounted Police at nearby Fort Pitt. The Mounties surveyed the battlefield logistics and noted that the Crees had several hundred more men under arms than they did. The post was soon abandoned, after which Big Bear's warriors ransacked and burned it.

The Canadian government brought in reinforcements and forced Poundmaker's surrender, but Big Bear and several of his warriors escaped. On June 3, a troop of RCMP caught the Crees at Loon Lake. They escaped again, but the constant pursuit was wearing down Big Bear's people. By June 18, he had released several white hostages along with a note pleading for mercy. Over the next few weeks, Big Bear and most of his warriors surrendered, a few at a time. Eight of the rebels were hanged after a

Big Bear's camp in the fall of 1888.
[Nebraska State Historical Society]

summary trial. Poundmaker and Big Bear were sentenced to three years in jail but were released early when it became obvious that illness and hopelessness would kill both of them much sooner. Both died within six months.

FOR MORE INFORMATION:

Dempsey, Hugh A. *Big Bear: The End of Freedom.* Vancouver: Douglas & McIntyre, 1984.

BIG BOW (ZIPKIYAH, ZIPKOHETA, ZEPKO-EETE)
Kiowa
c. 1830–c. 1900

In the latter half of the nineteenth century, Big Bow was known as one of the most outspoken anti-Anglo war chiefs of the Kiowas. Although little is known of his lineage and childhood, he earned a reputation as an astute warrior on the Central Plains in forays against the Navajos and the Utes. Along with BIG TREE, SATANK, SATANTA, and LONE WOLF, Big Bow made the early settlers of Kansas, Oklahoma, and Texas pay dearly for their incursions into the Kiowa homeland. A knowledgeable missionary, Thomas Battey, estimated that Big Bow scalped and killed more white people than any other Kiowa in the last half of the nineteenth century. In 1867, when the leaders of the Plains tribes negotiated the Medicine Lodge

Treaty, Big Bow refused to sign. He did not want to give up the traditional Kiowa life of roaming the Plains. Accordingly, he kept his people sequestered in the backcountry, emerging only for special visits and raids.

In 1871, the U.S. Army mounted a spirited campaign to subdue the Kiowas and keep them on their lands near Anadarko, Oklahoma. By 1874, Big Bow was the only major Kiowa chief that had not been forced onto the reservation. Pressured by the government, KICKING BIRD located Big Bow and told him that his cause was hopeless and that the best strategy for survival was surrender. Big Bow took Kicking Bird's message back to his people, and after much discussion, they agreed to settle on the reservation.

The U.S. government granted Big Bow and his band amnesty. Subsequently, he served commendably as a sergeant in the Indian Scouts for a few years. He lived peacefully on the reservation for twenty-five years until his death in 1900.

BIG EAGLE
Mdewakanton Sioux
c. 1827–1906

In 1857, Big Eagle, who would become a leader in the 1862 Great Sioux Uprising in Minnesota, succeeded his father, Mazarota (Gray Iron), as leader of a Mdewakanton Sioux band of about two hundred people at Crow Creek in Macleod County, Minnesota. In 1858, he traveled to Washington, D.C., to negotiate grievances with federal officials. Unhappy with the results, Big Eagle and his people joined LITTLE CROW and others in the general Sioux uprising in Minnesota during 1862 and 1863. Big Eagle fought with Mankato and probably witnessed his death at the hands of soldiers under the command of Henry Hastings Sibley at Wood Lake in September 1862. Big Eagle's band surrendered on September 26, 1862, after which he was imprisoned. Later in life, Big Eagle lived at

Granite Falls, Minnesota; his memoirs appeared in a book, *Big Eagle's Story of the Sioux Outbreak of 1862*, published in 1894.
FOR MORE INFORMATION:
Big Eagle. *Big Eagle's Story of the Sioux Outbreak of 1862*. N.p., 1894.

BIG ELK (ONGPATONGA)
Omaha
c. 1765–1846

Big Elk became principal chief of the Omahas on the death of Washinggusaba (Black Bird) in 1800; in 1821 and 1837, he traveled to Washington, D.C., to negotiate treaties and became known among whites as a spellbinding orator. He was the principal Omaha chief during the first sizable Euro-American migration through Omaha Territory by Mormons, who were traveling from Illinois to their eventual destination on the shores of the Great Salt Lake.

Big Elk was probably born in the principal village of the U'maha (which has been anglicized as "Omaha"), midway between contem-

Big Elk. [National Anthropological Archives]

porary Omaha, Nebraska, and Sioux City, Iowa. As a young man, he earned a reputation for courage in war, primarily against the Pawnees. Big Elk became very popular and was known for his fairness in making decisions—unlike his predecessor Black Bird, a tyrant who was said to have poisoned some warriors who disagreed with him.

Charles Bird King painted Big Elk's portrait in Washington, D.C., during his first visit in 1821; George Catlin painted his portrait in 1833.

Big Elk was head chief of the Omahas until 1843, when he went hunting alone one winter day and killed a deer with a tomahawk (which was unusual, since most Omahas used guns by this time). On his return from the hunt, Big Elk caught a fever and died three days later. He was buried in Bellevue, Nebraska, at a site that the whites called Elk Hill. The Omahas call it Onpontonga Xiathon, meaning, "the Place Where Big Elk [Onpontonga] Is Buried." He was succeeded by his son Big Elk, younger, who was followed by Joseph LaFLESCHE as the Omahas' principal chief.
FOR MORE INFORMATION:
Wilson, Dorothy Clarke. *Bright Eyes: The Story of Suzette LaFlesche, an Omaha Indian*. New York: McGraw-Hill, 1974.

BIG FOOT (SPOTTED ELK)
Miniconjou Sioux
c. 1820–1890

Big Foot was leader of the band of Sioux (some accounts say Cheyenne as well) who took the brunt of the casualties at the Wounded Knee massacre in December 1890.

Earlier in his life, Big Foot had been known as a master of diplomacy who tried to avoid war at all costs. Before he used the name Big Foot, he was generally known among the Sioux as Spotted Elk. Big Foot resisted efforts of whites to civilize him without being overtly hostile. Big

Foot also figured in the settlement of several intratribal conflicts between Sioux bands. He had advised his people to retain Lakota traditions but to adapt white ways, especially agriculture, after they surrendered in 1877 and took up residence on the Cheyenne River Reservation, South Dakota. Big Foot was among the first on the reservation to successfully harvest corn, and he also had a hand in building schools. In October 1888, Big Foot represented his people in Washington, D.C.

By 1890, the remaining Lakota were detained in concentration camp–like conditions on the Plains. The Ghost Dance religion arrived at their lowest ebb. Spawned by the prophet WOVOKA, a Paiute, the Ghost Dance spread among the destitute Native peoples of the West, from Oregon to Nebraska, into the Dakotas, where SITTING BULL endorsed its vision of Native restoration.

By late 1890, an estimated thirty-five hundred Indians were gathered against their wills in the hills near Wounded Knee Creek, which bisects the Pine Ridge Reservation. Many of them demanded the right to practice the Ghost Dance religion, which held that God would create a new world for them in which the buffalo would return and white people would vanish. The rules of the reservation laid down by the Indian Bureau forbade practice of the religion. Anglo settlers demanded protection from what they regarded as a revolutionary insurgency. In anticipation of renewed conflict, several thousand troops converged on the reservation from surrounding forts. Troops with itchy trigger fingers were spurred by settlers eager to extinguish the Indian threat.

Three days after Christmas 1890, soldiers of the Seventh Cavalry met Big Foot's band, 120 men and 180 women and children, who had come in from open country to surrender at Chankpe Opi Wakpala, Wounded Knee Creek. Big Foot had renounced the Ghost Dance and

Big Foot. [Nebraska State Historical Society]

called for peace. The soldiers herded the three hundred Hunkpapa Sioux into a circle and demanded their guns. The Indians were surrounded by five hundred cavalry. When Big Foot said they had no firearms, a search was ordered. Soldiers then tried to frisk some members of the party as shooting began. Most of the Indians surrendered their firearms, but one deaf man, Black Coyote, refused to relinquish his gun, which reportedly discharged. The troops then opened fire from four Hotchkiss guns—breech-loading cannons that hurled 3.2-inch explosive shells—and small arms as well. More than two hundred people were killed, including Big Foot, who died with a bullet in his head. Thirty-one soldiers were killed and twenty-nine less seriously injured. Several soldiers probably were killed by friendly fire.

The Hotchkiss guns' explosive shells were lobbed into the Indian camp at fifty a second, ripping people, tents, and other possessions to pieces. Photographs taken just after the massacre show seared tepee poles denuded of their coverings hovering ghostlike above a field strewn with broken bodies.

Soldiers pursued several dozen Indians, most of them women and children, as far as two miles from the scene of the massacre, killing another one hundred people in a maddened frenzy. Twenty-eight soldiers were awarded the Medal of Honor for their actions at Wounded Knee shortly after the bodies of 146 Native Americans were buried in an anonymous mass grave.

During the latter part of the twentieth century, descendants of the victims at Wounded Knee have joined with other Native Americans and supportive non-Indians in a remembrance

Big Foot's body, frozen where he fell in the slaughter. [Nebraska State Historical Society]

of the massacre. Usually traveling by horseback, often in subzero cold, the memorial riders start at Sitting Bull's former home on the Grand River near the North Dakota border, then ride through the Badlands, southward close to the Nebraska border, where Red Cloud's Oglala

A contemporary artist's rendering of the Sioux camp at Wounded Knee as it appeared just before the 1890 massacre. [Nebraska State Historical Society]

Victims of the Wounded Knee massacre are interred in a mass grave two days after their deaths.
[Nebraska State Historical Society]

Lakotas huddled against the winter of 1890. In 1990, the riders marked the hundredth year since the massacre.

FOR MORE INFORMATION:

Brown, Dee. *Bury My Heart at Wounded Knee.* New York: Holt, Rinehart & Winston, 1970.

BIG HAWK CHIEF (KOOTAHWECOOT-SOOLELEHOOLASHAR)
Pawnee
c. 1850–

Big Hawk Chief joined the U.S. Army scout corps under Captain Luther North in 1876; he fought the Sioux and their allies in the final years of the Plains Indian wars. As he was waiting for orders to muster out of the army, Big Hawk Chief twice ran a mile in under four minutes at Fort Sidney, Nebraska.

Captain North set up a mile-long course and put two stopwatches on Big Hawk Chief, who was reputed to be the fastest of a number of outstanding Pawnee runners. Big Hawk Chief was reported to have run the first half of the course in 2:00 and the second half in 1:58, at a time when the fastest recorded mile run by any other human being was 4:49. Captain North remeasured the course, and Big Hawk Chief again ran it in 3:58 to the astonishment of nearly everyone at the fort. The next sub-four-minute-mile would be run by Englishman Roger Bannister in 1954, three-quarters of a century later.

FOR MORE INFORMATION:

Waldman, Carl. *Who Was Who in Native American History.* New York: Facts on File, 1990.

BIG JIM (WAPAMEEPTO, DICK JIM)
Shawnee
1834–1900

Born in East Texas on the Sabine Reservation, Big Jim in 1872 became chief of the Absentee Shawnees (Kispicotha band). This group of traditionalist Shawnees had separated from the Shawnee bands in Indian Territory, who had a more assimilationist stance. As a leader, he tried to foster his people's traditions. Hence, he opposed agriculture, reasoning that plowing the ground did violence to Mother Earth. Also, he resisted the General Allotment or Dawes Severalty Act of 1887, which sought to break up tribal lands held in common into individual farms. Big Jim and other Shawnees relocated to Mexico to avoid these federal land policies for Indians. While in Mexico, he succumbed to smallpox during an epidemic there.

BIG MOUTH
Brulé Sioux
fl. 1860s–1870s

In 1866, Big Mouth was one of a few Sioux leaders who favored allowing the United States to build a road (which became known as the Bozeman Trail) through Sioux hunting grounds along the Powder River. Later, he changed his mind and opposed the construction of a railroad. After surrendering to reservation life, Big Mouth became principal chief of the Brulés at the Whetstone Agency on the upper Missouri River. When he stated his opposition to a Union Pacific railway extension along the Powder River in 1873, he was assassinated by SPOTTED TAIL, who favored the railroad.

BIG SNAKE
Ponca
fl. 1870s

Shortly after Omaha federal judge Elmer S. DUNDY denied the U.S. Army's presumed power to forcibly relocate Indians in the case of STANDING BEAR (Ponca), his brother Big Snake tested the law by moving roughly one hundred miles within Indian Territory from the Poncas' assigned reservation to one occupied by Cheyennes. Big Snake was arrested by troops and returned to the Ponca Reservation. On October 31, 1879, Ponca Indian agent William H. Whiteman called Big Snake a troublemaker and ordered a U.S. Army detail to imprison him. When Big Snake contended that he had committed no crime, for he did not know that Judge Dundy had restricted the ruling to Standing Bear's party, and refused to surrender, he was shot to death.

In a statement to Congress, the Ponca Hairy Bear said that Big Snake asked the agents who came to arrest him what he had done wrong. "He said he had killed no one, stolen no horses, and that he had done no wrong," Hairy Bear testified. Big Snake said he carried no knife "and threw off his blanket and turned around to show that he had no weapon." But Big Snake refused to go when an officer tried to arrest him forcibly. Big Snake fought off several such attempts from a sitting position. After that, six soldiers came at Big Snake and beat him with their rifle butts. Hairy Bear recalled, "It knocked him back to the wall. He straightened up again. The blood was running down his face. I saw the gun pointed at him, and was scared, and did not want to see him killed. So I turned away. Then the gun was fired and Big Snake fell down dead on the floor." [Moquin]

FOR MORE INFORMATION:

Moquin, Wayne. *Great Documents in American Indian History.* New York: Praeger, 1973.

BIG TREE (ADOEETTE)
Kiowa
c. 1847–1929

Big Tree (from the Kiowa Adoeette *ado,* meaning "tree," and *e-et,* meaning "large") was a major Kiowa war chief late in the nineteenth century.

Throughout the 1850s and 1860s, when Big Tree was young, the Kiowas raided the Texas Plains until their chief, Dohosan, died in 1866. Dohosan was succeeded by a new chief, LONE WOLF, who also resisted white settlement on their lands. Reared in this pattern of resistance, it is not surprising that in May 1871, Big Tree, SATANTA, and SATANK, along with a force of over three hundred, struck a wagon train in Young County, Texas, taking its mules and leaving seven men dead. Returning to their reservation at Fort Sill in Indian Territory, they openly boasted of the raid at the trading post. Shortly thereafter, Big Tree, Satanta, and Satank were arrested and jailed. The three were sent to Texas to stand trial for their depredations. On the way to Texas, Satank attempted to flee his captors and was killed. Big Tree and Satanta were tried and sentenced to death, but the protests of sympathetic whites over the harsh sentences deterred their execution; their sentences were commuted to life imprisonment at Huntsville, Texas. The Bureau of Indian Affairs argued that the two men should not be released since their raid was an act of war. Two years later in 1873, Big Tree and Satanta were paroled on assurances of good behavior and confined to Indian Territory.

In 1874–1875, violence erupted once again when the army confiscated some Kiowa horses.

Consequently, the government became alarmed when Quanah PARKER, Big Tree, and Satanta left Indian Territory while on a hunting expedition to Kansas. An army contingent of three thousand men pursued them until they surrendered at the Cheyenne Agency. Big Tree was briefly incarcerated at Fort Sill for violating parole, while Satanta was jailed at Huntsville, where he committed suicide.

Big Tree, when he was released in 1875, settled down to a peaceful life on the Kiowa Reservation, operating a supply train from Anadarko to Wichita. Wedding a Kiowa woman, Omboke, he became a Christian and attended the Rainy Mountain Baptist Church, where he taught Sunday school and was a deacon for over thirty years. Farming his allotment near Mountain View, Kiowa County, Oklahoma, he became a model and peaceful citizen in his later years. He died on November 13, 1929, at Fort Sill.

BIG TREE, JOHN, "CHIEF"
Seneca
fl. 1920s–1950s

Silent movies became popular within a generation after the final closing of the frontier at Wounded Knee. Until the 1920s, when sound replaced silent movies and non-Indians such as Clint Eastwood were hired to act as Indians, Native actors sometimes achieved stardom. One such star was the Seneca "Chief" John Big Tree, who played major roles in sixteen movies staged as early as 1922 and as late as 1950. Most of these movies, such as *Winners of the Wilderness* (1927) and *The Frontiersman* (1927), had western history themes.

BIG WARRIOR (TUSTENNUGEE THLOCCO)
Creek
fl. early 1800s

Although often thought to be a Creek Indian by birth, Big Warrior probably was of Miami or

Shawnee descent. As a chief of the Upper Creek village at Tuckabathee with a large traditionalist Red Stick constituency, Big Warrior nevertheless became a principal chief of the White Stick Lower Creeks, who were sympathetic to the American side in the Creek War of 1813–1814.

When Big Warrior and his men seized and killed Red Stick leader Little Warrior, he inflamed tensions within the Creek Confederacy and aided in the launching of the Creek War. During the War of 1812, Little Warrior had commanded a pro-English unit in the massacre at Raisin River. Big Warrior and his followers had also struck several settlements along the Ohio River.

As an ally of the Progressive Creek faction led by William MCINTOSH and General Andrew Jackson, Big Warrior made war against the traditionalist Red Sticks led by MENEWA and Red Eagle (William WEATHERFORD). When the Red Sticks laid siege to his village, the White Sticks came to his rescue. As a result, McIntosh's house at Coweta became Big Warrior's headquarters for the rest of the war.

When the Creek War ended, Selocta and Big Warrior were the chief spokesmen for the White Stick faction during treaty discussions with Jackson. As signers of the August 14, 1814, Treaty of Fort Jackson, the pro-American White Sticks felt betrayed when they were told by their ally, Jackson, that they had to compensate the U.S. government through land cessions for the cost of the Creek War. As a consequence of Jackson's duplicity, Big Warrior embraced the Red Sticks' political views with regard to the land-hungry Americans.

BISSONETTE, PEDRO
Oglala Lakota
fl. 1970s

Pedro Bissonette was a leader of the Oglala Sioux Civil Rights Organization (OSCRO) dur-ing the early 1970s, when Pine Ridge residents invited the American Indian Movement (AIM) onto the reservation to help them deal with what they described as a reign of terror imposed by tribal chairman Richard Wilson. This invitation and other incidents led to the 1973 siege at Wounded Knee. Shortly after the occupation, on October 17, 1973, Bissonette was shot to death at a Bureau of Indian Affairs roadblock on the reservation.

Bissonette, a scrappy man with a background as a boxer, was killed by sympathizers of tribal chairman Dick Wilson, whose "goons" inflicted more than sixty deaths on American Indian Movement activists during the early 1970s, a time during which the Pine Ridge Reservation had a higher murder rate than any city in the United States. A statement released by the OSCRO the day after Bissonette was shot to death said, "All day yesterday, October 17, there was an extensive manhunt for Pedro. The search involved about 20 police cars and several airplanes. They hunted Pedro down like an animal and murdered him in cold blood." [Johansen]

FOR MORE INFORMATION:

Johansen, Bruce E., and Roberto F. Maestas. *Wasi'chu: The Continuing Indian Wars.* New York: Monthly Review Press, 1979.

BLACK BEAVER (SEKETTU MAQUAH)
Delaware
1806–1880

He was born in Bellville, Illinois, but very little is known of Black Beaver's youthful days. It is known, however, that he left for an extended journey in the Rocky Mountains as a young man, thus gaining a thorough knowledge of that region. Eventually, he became one of the foremost mountain men of his time.

Black Beaver (who also was called Sucktum Mahway and Settu Maquah) and Jesse CHISHOLM were interpreters for General Henry Leavenworth and Colonel Henry Dodge during their 1834 expedition to the Comanches, Kiowas, and Wichitas in the upper Red River area. From that time onward, he was employed sporadically by the U.S. government in a variety of capacities. In 1846, during the Mexican War, he commanded a company of Indian scouts under General William S. HARNEY. Thereafter, he was known as Captain Black Beaver.

At the start of the California gold rush in 1849, Black Beaver led a large contingent of white miners from Fort Smith, Arkansas, to California via Albuquerque, New Mexico. Not content to retrace his steps from California, he blazed a new trail from northwest Texas to Fort Smith, Arkansas. Throughout the 1850s, he was on numerous trading expeditions to the Southern Plains, enhancing his knowledge of the area and its peoples. He also developed a trading business at this time.

Black Beaver.
[National Anthropological Archives]

When the Civil War began, Black Beaver led the U.S. garrisons at Fort Smith, Arbuckle, Cobb, and Washita out of Indian Territory to safety at Fort Leavenworth. Black Beaver and Jesse Chisholm served as interpreters once again to the Southern Plains tribes during the Little Arkansas Council of 1865.

After the Civil War, Black Beaver became a respected mediator for the Delaware tribe, which had moved to Indian Territory. He became a legend in his own time for his knowledge of the Far West and Indian languages, and his amiable ways, skillful diplomacy, and tenacity. He passed away on May 8, 1880, near present-day Anadarko, Oklahoma, at the age of seventy-four.

BLACKBIRD, WILLIAM
Ottawa
fl. 1830s

William Blackbird was a brother of Chief Andrew J. Blackbird, a historian of the Ottawa. Known as a powerful orator, William was summoned to seminary in Rome in 1832 as the first American Indian candidate for the Roman Catholic priesthood. He studied two years but died suddenly on the eve of his ordination as a priest in 1834. In 1885, Chief Andrew Blackbird speculated that his brother had been murdered to prevent an Indian from becoming a priest.

FOR MORE INFORMATION:

Blackbird, Chief Andrew J. *Education of Indian Youth.* Philadelphia, 1856.

———. *History of the Ottawa and Chippewa Indians of Michigan.* Ypsilanti, Mich., 1887.

BLACK ELK (HCHAKA SAPA)
Oglala Lakota
1863–1950

Black Elk, a Lakota Sioux spiritual leader, came of age during the late nineteenth century as European settlement reached his homeland. His views of Native American life at that time reached large audiences in the twentieth century through the books of John Neihardt, the best known of which is *Black Elk Speaks.*

Black Elk was eleven years old during the summer of 1874 when, by his account, an expedition under General George Armstrong Custer invaded the Paha Sapa ("Hills That Are Black"), the holy land of the Lakota. In *Black Elk Speaks,* the Lakota holy man told Neihardt that he had been a young warrior at the Battle of the Little Bighorn and that he had witnessed the battle. Young Black Elk tried to take the first scalp at that battle. The soldier under Black Elk's hatchet proved to have an unusually tough scalp, so Black Elk shot him. The battle provoked momentary joy among the Sioux and Cheyennes, who for decades had watched their hunting ranges curtailed by what Black Elk called "the gnawing flood of the wasi'chu."

After the Battle of the Little Bighorn, June 25, 1876, U.S. Army troops flooded the Northern Plains, crippled the last of the Indians' resistance, and ordered many Sioux, including Black Elk's people, onto reservations. Black Elk's memoirs describe the subjugation of his family, as well as the brief euphoria over WOVOKA's Ghost Dance before the Wounded Knee massacre (see BIG FOOT) in late December 1890. After the Wounded Knee massacre, Black Elk watched his people, once the mounted lords of the Plains, become hungry, impoverished prisoners, penned up on thirteen government reservations. "It was a beautiful dream. . . . The nation's hoop is broken and scattered. There is no center anymore, and the sacred tree is dead," said Black Elk. In 1886, when he was twenty-three, Black Elk joined Buffalo Bill CODY's Wild West Show. After a tour of large cities on the eastern seaboard, the troupe traveled to England.

Black Elk is one of the most studied and most written-about Native Americans. His long life

Black Elk (left), on tour in London.
[National Anthropological Archives]

has been subjected to several interpretations by different authors. The first three decades of Black Elk's life, to the 1890s, are chronicled in Neihardt's book-length poem *Black Elk Speaks,* first published in 1932; much of the same ground is covered in Joseph Epes Brown's *The Sacred Pipe: Black Elk's Account of the Seven Rites of the Oglala Sioux.* Both books tend to describe Black Elk as an Indian mystic and patriot. Another book, Michael Steltenkamp's *Black Elk: Holy Man of the Oglala,* describes a different Black Elk, who after 1900 became a Roman Catholic missionary. Steltenkamp, a Jesuit himself (as well as an anthropologist), said he learned of Black Elk's conversion from Lucy Looks Twice, Black Elk's only surviving child, who died in 1978.

Lucy Looks Twice recalled:

The Jesuits took my father to other different tribes—even though he couldn't understand their languages. He instructed Arapahoes, Winnebagos, Omahas, and others—teaching them the Catholic faith with the help of an interpreter. At that time, these tribes were going for peyote. . . . He converted a lot of these people. [Steltenkamp]

The church also sent Black Elk on fundraising trips to cities such as New York, Boston, Chicago, Washington, D.C., and Omaha. In 1934, shortly after publication of *Black Elk Speaks*, he complained that Neihardt hadn't said enough about his life as a Catholic. Black Elk added:

My family is all baptized. All my children and grandchildren belong to the Black-gown church and I am glad of that and I wish that all should stay in that holy way. . . . I will never fall back from the true faith in Christ. [Steltenkamp]

In his later years, Black Elk combined Catholic missionary work with occasional showmanship at South Dakota tourist attractions that capitalized on his reputation as a Lakota holy man. Steltenkamp says that Black Elk sensed no contradictions in mixing the two interpretations of the "great mystery." Black Elk died in 1950. He is said to have believed that lights in the sky would accompany his death. The night Black Elk died, the Pine Ridge area experienced an intense and unusually bright meteor shower.

FOR MORE INFORMATION:

Black Elk. *The Sacred Pipe*. Edited by Joseph Epes Brown. New York: Penguin, 1973, pp. 13–14.

Brown, Dee. *Bury My Heart at Wounded Knee*. New York: Holt, Rinehart & Winston, 1970.

Gibson, Arrell Morgan. *The American Indian, Prehistory to Present*. Lexington, Mass.: D. C. Heath, 1980.

Nabokov, Peter. *Native American Testimony*. New York: Viking, 1991.

Neihardt, Hilda. *Black Elk & Flaming Rainbow: Personal Memories of the Lakota Holy Man*. Lincoln: University of Nebraska Press, 1995.

Rice, Julian. *Black Elk's Story*. Albuquerque: New Mexico University Press, 1991.

Steltenkamp, Michael. *Black Elk: Holy Man of the Oglala*. Norman: University of Oklahoma Press, 1993.

Black Elk in 1947, in his eighties.
[National Anthropological Archives]

BLACKFOOT
Crow
c. 1795–1877

Blackfoot assumed a leadership role among the
Crows in the 1850s and represented them at the
negotiation of the important Treaty of Fort
Laramie in 1868. Noted as an outstanding orator, Blackfoot was generally an ally of the
United States against the Sioux, traditional
enemies of the Crows. Blackfoot's statements
at several treaty councils indicate his concern
that the immigrating whites might crowd his
people from their land and that hot-blooded
young warriors might retaliate.

BLACK HAWK (MAKATAIMESHIEKIAKIAK)
Sauk
c. 1770–1838

A member of the Thunder clan of the Sauk
nation, Black Hawk won renown as a warrior
from the time he carried home his first scalp at
fifteen to his leadership in the early 1830s of a
Native rebellion that bears his name.

Black Hawk was capable of both murderous
hatred and intense personal compassion. In one
battle with the Osages, he personally killed
nine people; but on another raid against the
Cherokees, he found only four people—three
men and a woman. He took the woman captive
and then freed the three men, figuring it was
dishonorable to kill so few. During the siege of
an American fort during the War of 1812—during which he was allied with the British—Black
Hawk found two white boys hiding in a bush. "I
thought of my own children," he said later,
"and passed on without noticing them." During the same war, Black Hawk learned that
some of his Indian allies, who were aiding the
British, were torturing white American prisoners. He halted the practice and poured his scorn
on Colonel Henry Procter, the British commander, for permitting it. "Go and put on petti-

Blackfoot. [National Anthropological Archives]

coats," Black Hawk stormed. "I conquer to
save, and you to murder!"

About 1820, the Fox and Sauk divided over
whether to resist Euro-American expansion
into their country in what is now southern
Illinois. KEOKUK and a number of his supporters decided to accommodate the expansion,
and they moved into Iowa. Black Hawk and
his supporters remained at their principal village, Saukenuk, at the confluence of the Rock
and Mississippi Rivers, the site of present-day
Rock Island, Illinois. The land provided abundant crops and the river was a rich source of
fish. Black Hawk consulted with the spiritual
leaders WHITE CLOUD and NEAPOPE, who
advised him to seek allies in defense of
the land.

In the meantime, George Davenport, Indian
agent in the area, had purchased the site on

which Saukenuk was built, including Black Hawk's own lodge and his people's graveyard. Settlers began to take land around the village. Illinois governor John Reynolds ordered the state militia to march on Saukenuk. Black Hawk and his band moved west across the Mississippi but pledged to return.

Black Hawk recalled:

> Upon our return to Saukenuk from our winter hunting grounds last spring, we found the palefaces in our lodges, and that they had torn down our fences and were plowing our corn lands and getting ready to plant their corn upon the lands which the Sauks have . . . cultivated for so many winters that our memory cannot go back to them. . . . They are now running their plows through our graveyards, turning up the bones and ashes of our sacred dead,

Black Hawk. [National Anthropological Archives]

whose spirits are calling on us from the land of dreams for vengeance on the despoilers. [Vanderwerth]

In 1832, Black Hawk's band recrossed the Mississippi into Wisconsin and sought Winnebago support. Contrary to the promises of Neapope and White Cloud, only a few Winnebagos joined. Black Hawk, his warriors, and their homeless families attacked frontier settlements in the area. In response, Governor Reynolds called out the militia again, assembling freshly recruited companies in the area. One of the new recruits was Abraham Lincoln, a young man at the time. (Lincoln's unit was disbanded after its members took a vote over whether to fight Black Hawk. The vote was a tie. Lincoln later reenlisted, but saw no fighting.)

Regular U.S. Army troops were brought in to pursue Black Hawk's band, whose members had been forced to subsist on roots in the swamplands near the Mississippi. Several army and militia units caught Black Hawk and his people, their backs to the river, where the Indians hoisted a flag of truce. General Winfield Scott and other officers ignored the appeal for a truce and engaged in a one-sided slaughter that became known as the Battle of Black Ax. General Scott later apologized for the large number of women and children killed by his men. He complained that they could not be distinguished from warriors in the heat of battle.

Black Hawk, Neapope, and other survivors of the battle fled north to a Winnebago village, where they were betrayed for a bribe of twenty horses and $100. Black Hawk was defiant in surrender:

> You know the cause of our making war. It is known to all white men. The white men

despise the Indians, and drive them from their homes. They smile in the face of the poor Indian, to cheat him; they shake him by the hand, to gain his confidence; they make him drunk, to deceive him.

[Black Hawk] has done nothing for which an Indian ought to be ashamed. He has fought for his countrymen . . . against white men who came, year after year, to cheat them and take away their lands. You know the cause of our making war. It is known to all white men. They ought to be ashamed of it. [Moquin]

Black Hawk was led away in chains by Jefferson Davis, who would later become president of the Confederate States of America. After several months' imprisonment, Black Hawk was taken on a tour of several eastern cities, during which he met with President Andrew Jackson at the White House. Jackson gave Black Hawk a military uniform and a sword, but the aging chief was not mollified. He told Jackson that he had made war to avenge injustice against his people. Behind Black Hawk's back, Jackson recognized Keokuk as principal chief of the Sauks and Foxes. The news came to Black Hawk and Keokuk as they stood together with army officers. Angry and frustrated, Black Hawk removed his breechclout and slapped Keokuk across the face with it.

Black Hawk's body was still lean and firm at the age of sixty. Author Frank Waters described his "hawk-like face with its long nose, luminous dark eyes, and firm mouth. . . . All the hair above his high forehead had been shaved off except for a scalp lock, and by this one knew he was a warrior."

Eventually, Black Hawk settled on land governed by Keokuk near Iowaville on the Des Moines River. Shortly before his death in 1838, Black Hawk acknowledged his defeat without lingering bitterness, telling a Fourth of July gathering near Fort Madison:

A few winters ago, I was fighting against you. I did wrong, perhaps, but that is past; it is buried; let it be forgotten. Rock River is a beautiful country. I liked my towns, my cornfields, and the home of my people. I fought for it. It is now yours. Keep it as we did; it will produce you good crops.

FOR MORE INFORMATION:

Armstrong, Virginia Irving, ed. *I Have Spoken: American History Through the Voices of the Indians.* Chicago: Swallow Press, 1971.

Beckhard, Arthur J. *Black Hawk.* New York: Julian Messner, 1957.

Black Hawk. *Life of Ma-ka-tai-me-she-kia-kiak, or Black Hawk, Dictated by Himself.* Boston, 1834.

Carter, Harvey Lewis. *The Life and Times of Little Turtle.* Urbana: University of Illinois Press, 1987.

Drake, Benjamin F. *The Life and Adventures of Black Hawk.* Cincinnati, 1838.

Hagan, William T. *The Sac and Fox Indians.* Norman: University of Oklahoma Press, 1958.

Hamilton, Charles. *Cry of the Thunderbird.* Norman: University of Oklahoma Press, 1972.

Jackson, Donald, ed. *Black Hawk: An Autobiography.* Urbana: University of Illinois Press, 1964.

Jones, Louis Thomas. *Aboriginal American Oratory.* Los Angeles: Southwest Museum, 1965.

Moquin, Wayne, ed. *Great Documents in American Indian History.* New York: Praeger, 1973.

Stevens, Frank E. *The Black Hawk War.* Chicago, 1903.

Thwaites, Reuben Gold. *The Story of the Black Hawk War.* Madison, Wis., 1892.

Vanderwerth, W. C. *Indian Oratory.* Norman: University of Oklahoma Press, 1971.

Waters, Frank. *Brave Are My People.* Santa Fe, N. Mex.: Clear Light, 1993.

BLACK KETTLE (MOKETAVATO)
Southern Cheyenne
c. 1800–1868

Born in the Black Hills, Black Kettle became a leading chief of the Southern Cheyennes before his people were massacred at Sand Creek in 1864. Four years later, he was killed in the Washita massacre by George Armstrong CUSTER's Seventh Cavalry.

The Southern Cheyennes and white settlers in the Denver area got along rather peacefully during their early years of contact. A village of Arapahoes camped in the heart of Denver around 1860. In 1861, Arapaho and Southern Cheyenne treaty chiefs were pressured into signing an agreement with the federal government without consulting their nations as a whole. Resentment rose among the Indians as more settlers and gold seekers moved in, further encroaching on hunting lands.

During spring 1864, Reverend J. M. Chivington, an officer of the Colorado volunteer militia, reported that Cheyennes had stolen a number of cattle. The report may have been faked as an excuse to retaliate—which he did, attacking Cheyenne camps and indiscriminately killing women and children as well as warriors. The governor of Colorado then persuaded the Cheyennes to settle at Sand Creek. On November 29, 1864, again acting on his own volition, Chivington raised between six hundred and one thousand men, mostly volunteers seething to drive the Indians out, and mounted a surprise attack on the village. Chivington shouted, "Kill and scalp all the big and little; nits make for lice."

As Black Kettle, the ranking chief in the village, hoisted a white flag and a U.S. flag, Chiv-

ington's men tore the Indians apart with sadistic enthusiasm. Black Kettle's wife was shot nine times but somehow survived, while he escaped. Another leader of the village, White Antelope, stood in front of his lodge and sang his death song, which included the often-quoted passage "Nothing lives long, except the earth and the mountains." The elderly White Antelope was unceremoniously shot down, along with at least three hundred other native men, women, and children. Chivington's detachment never accurately counted the casualties. The volunteers severed several Indians' limbs and heads, took them to Denver, and charged people admission to a theater for a glimpse of the bloody body parts.

The behavior of Chivington and his volunteers was so reprehensible to famed scout Kit CARSON that he called Chivington's men cowardly dogs. The Cheyennes retaliated with fire and fury, killing several hundred settlers during the next three years and capturing dozens more. Four years after Chivington's attack, a federal commission concluded that he and his men had acted with a degree of barbarism that even the most brutal of Indians could not match. The Sand Creek massacre sparked a war on the plains which cost the government $30 million.

Black Kettle tried to restore the peace again, figuring that his people would not survive any other way. In summer 1868, he and the survivors of the Sand Creek massacre moved west to the Washita Valley. On November 27, 1868, they were attacked again by Seventh Cavalry troops with orders to raze the village, hang all the men, and take women and children captive. These troops were under the command of General George Armstrong Custer, in his first campaign of the Indian wars. Between 40 and 110 Indians were killed, some in a very gruesome fashion. Though Arapahoes, Comanches, and

Kiowas came to the rescue of the Cheyennes, forcing Custer and his troops to withdraw before they had fully carried out the assigned extermination, it was too late for Black Kettle, who was found among the dead.

FOR MORE INFORMATION:
Hoig, Stan. *The Sand Creek Massacre.* Norman: University of Oklahoma Press, 1961.

BLACK PARTRIDGE
Potawatomi
fl. early 1800s

Black Partridge sought to support the Americans in the War of 1812 but was unable to restrain a larger body of Potawatomis under Metea, who had decided to raid in support of the British. Their target was Fort Dearborn on the contemporary site of Chicago.

On the eve of the Fort Dearborn massacre, August 15, 1812, Black Partridge warned Captain Nathan Heald to stay inside the fort, as he returned a peace medal given him at an earlier treaty conference.

I come to deliver up to you the medal I wear. It was given me by the Americans, and I have long worn it, in token of our mutual friendship. But our young men are resolved to imbue their hands in the blood of the Whites. I cannot restrain them and I will not wear a token of peace while I am compelled to act as an enemy. [Armstrong]

Heald led fifty regulars out of the fort, escorting a number of women and children to Detroit. The Potawatomis under Metea killed nearly all of them, as Black Partridge urged Metea's men to exercise mercy. Black Partridge personally saved at least one white woman in the battle. Despite his defense of the settlers, Black Partridge's village was later destroyed on orders of Illinois governor Ninian Evans.

FOR MORE INFORMATION:
Armstrong, Virginia Irving, ed. *I Have Spoken: American History Through the Voices of the Indians.* Chicago: Swallow Press, 1971.

BLACKSNAKE
Seneca
c. 1760–1859

Blacksnake was a nephew of both CORNPLANTER and HANDSOME LAKE. He also was a disciple of Handsome Lake, prophet of the Iroquois Longhouse religion. Blacksnake played a key role in the publication of *The Code of Handsome Lake* in 1850, thirty-five years after the prophet's death. The code combines elements of traditional Iroquois religion with Quakerism, which Handsome Lake had studied.

Born at Cattaraugus, a Seneca settlement in western New York, Blacksnake aided the British in the American Revolution, fighting with such notable Iroquois leaders as Cornplanter and Joseph BRANT. He participated in the Battle of Oriskany (1777), the raids in the Wyoming and Cherry Valleys (1778), and the Battle of Newtown (1779).

After Handsome Lake pronounced his vision for reforming Iroquois society in 1799, Blacksnake became one of his most dedicated disciples. He fought with the Americans against the British in the War of 1812 and later became the Senecas' principal chief. He often was called "Governor Blacksnake," and was known for his desire to combine Euro-American educational practices with retention of Native traditions. Late in his life, Blacksnake related memoirs that provide insight into the Iroquois role in the American Revolution, as well as the life and thoughts of Handsome Lake.

Blacksnake died at Cold Spring, New York, in 1859 at the age of ninety-nine.

FOR MORE INFORMATION:

Wallace, Anthony F. C. *The Death and Rebirth of the Seneca.* New York: Knopf, 1970.

Wright, Ronald. *Stolen Continents.* Boston: Houghton Mifflin, 1992.

BLOODY FELLOW (ISKAGUA, CLEAR SKY)
Cherokee
fl. late 1700s

In the 1770s and 1780s, during and after the American Revolution, the Chickamauga Cherokees of eastern Tennessee ravaged the Southeast with impunity partly because they were armed and supplied by the English in Pensacola, Florida. Bloody Fellow and DRAGGING CANOE spearheaded these attacks along the southern frontier.

As a diplomatic gesture, Bloody Fellow agreed to journey to the nation's capital, Philadelphia, in 1791 to seek peace through discussions with President George Washington and Secretary of War Henry Knox, but the talks were not fruitful. When he returned to his homeland, Bloody Fellow continued his policy of pitting the Americans and Spanish against each other. At the Treaty of Tellico Blockhouse in 1794, Bloody Fellow and his Chickamaugas finally agreed to end hostilities against the southern settlers.

BLOODY KNIFE
Arikara-Sioux
c. 1840–1876

Born in what would later be known as North Dakota of a Hunkpapa Sioux father and an Arikara mother, Bloody Knife turned a childhood of Hunkpapa insults over his mixed heritage into such a hatred for them that he joined the U.S. Army as a scout. Bloody Knife was a bitter lifelong enemy of the Hunkpapa Sioux chief GALL. Early in Bloody Knife's life, Gall headed a war party that killed two of Bloody Knife's brothers.

Later, after Bloody Knife had worked as a mail carrier between several army posts on the upper Missouri River, he took part in an attack on Gall. Having sliced him badly with bayonets, Bloody Knife offered to kill Gall with a bullet to the head, but the officer in charge elected to leave Gall for dead. The burly Hunkpapa somehow survived to become a leading war chief with SITTING BULL.

George Armstrong CUSTER admired Bloody Knife's scouting skills and obtained a transfer for him from Fort Abraham Lincoln in North Dakota to the Seventh Cavalry. Bloody Knife scouted for Custer during the invasion of the Black Hills (1874). He died with Custer in 1876 at the Battle of the Little Bighorn, during which Bloody Knife was killed in a charge led by Gall. As much as Custer admired Bloody Knife's scouting skills, he ignored his reports that the Sioux and Cheyenne camp at the Little Bighorn was much larger than Custer had expected.

FOR MORE INFORMATION:

Custer, George Armstrong. *My Life on the Plains.* 1891. Reprint, Lincoln: University of Nebraska Press, 1966.

Hyde, George E. *A Sioux Chronicle.* Norman: University of Oklahoma Press, 1956.

BLUE JACKET (WEYAPIERSENWAH)
Shawnee
fl. 1790s

As an ally of the Miami LITTLE TURTLE, Blue Jacket (who was sometimes called Jim Blue Jacket) resisted European American expansion west of the Appalachian Mountains late in the eighteenth century.

In April 1790, Blue Jacket refused to attend treaty councils that he feared would cost his people their lands; Blue Jacket then fought alongside Little Turtle for four years. Blue Jacket and Little Turtle shared in several victories over U.S. troops. In 1794, Little Turtle advised suing for peace from a position of strength, but Blue Jacket continued to advocate war. Blue Jacket then assumed command from Little Turtle; his forces were defeated by General Anthony ("Mad Anthony") Wayne at the Battle of Fallen Timbers. Afterward, Blue Jacket signed the Treaty of Greenville (1795) and the Treaty of Fort Industry (1805), ceding millions of acres of Native land.

FOR MORE INFORMATION:

Winger, Otho. *Last of the Miamis: Little Turtle.* N.p.: Lawrence W. Shultz, 1935.

BOGUS CHARLEY
Modoc
c. 1850–1880

As the most Americanized Modoc involved in the Modoc uprising in California, Bogus Charley was an accomplished interpreter who could speak excellent English and Modoc. He was also a noted chief and warrior.

Bogus Charley took his name from Bogus Creek, the place of his residence. As a young man, he had extensive interaction with whites. Because of his excellent English, he regularly acted as interpreter in negotiations. During the fateful April 11, 1873, negotiations when CAP- TAIN JACK shot and killed General Edward S. Canby, Bogus Charley and another English- speaking Modoc, Boston Charley, acted as interpreters. For a while, Bogus Charley fought in the Lava Beds of northern California against the U.S. Army. Despairing of any chance to win, he laid down his arms with HOOKER JIM. Bogus Charley then worked as a tracker for the U.S. Army while Captain Jack was being sought.

After all of the Modoc leaders had surrendered, Bogus Charley testified for the prosecu- tion against Captain Jack during the government trial. His testimony resulted in the hanging of Captain Jack and others on October 3, 1873. Subsequently, he was one of the 155 Modocs removed to Indian Territory. After SCARFACED CHARLEY (the principal chief of the Modocs in Indian Territory) refused to take government orders, Bogus Charley became principal chief of the Modocs in the latter part of the 1870s. He died while traveling to visit his sister in Walla Walla, Washington, on October 25, 1880.

BOLDT, GEORGE HUGO
1903–

On February 12, 1974, U.S. District Court judge George Boldt ruled that Indians were entitled to an opportunity to catch as many as half the fish returning to off-reservation sites, which had been the "usual and accustomed places" when treaties were signed with Puget Sound Indian tribes in the 1850s. The case became an object of major controversy between Indians and commercial and sports fishermen.

Boldt put three years into the case; he took two hundred pages to interpret one sentence of the treaty in an opinion that some legal scholars say is the most carefully researched, thoroughly analyzed decision ever handed down in an Indian fishing rights case. The nucleus of Boldt's ruling had to do with nineteenth-century dictionaries' definitions of "in common with." Boldt said the word meant "to be shared equally." During the next three years, the Ninth Circuit Court of Appeals upheld Boldt's ruling, and the U.S. Supreme Court twice let it stand by refusing to hear an appeal.

Judge Boldt's ruling had a profound effect not only on who would be allowed to catch salmon in Puget Sound, but on white-Indian relations generally.

The relative powerlessness of the Indian communities left non-Indians unprepared for the sudden turn of events brought about by the Boldt decision, and the shocked white community reacted immediately. Non-Indians, who had long come to regard the salmon harvest as virtually their own, were suddenly faced with the possible prospect of being forced out of the fishing industry or at least of experiencing large reductions in their catch. Hostility became so serious that Indians armed their fishing camps after enduring attacks on themselves and their equipment. Many whites displayed their reaction to the decision with bumper stickers proclaiming "Can Judge Boldt" on their cars. A widely held view was that the Boldt decision gave an unfair advantage to Indians in the fisheries.

State officials and the fishermen whose interests they represented were furious at Boldt. Rumors circulated about the sanity of the seventy-five-year-old judge. It was said that he had taken bribes of free fish and had an Indian mistress, neither of which was true. Judge Boldt was hung in effigy by angry non-Indian fishermen, who on other occasions formed convoys with their boats and rammed Coast Guard vessels dispatched to enforce the court's orders. At least one Coastguardsman was shot.

Lost in the fray were a number of small, landless western Washington tribes that were not recognized by the federal government and therefore not entitled to participate in the federally mandated solution. A few such tribes, such as the Upper Skagit and Sauk-Suiattle, were recognized after the Boldt decision. A number of others remained in legal limbo as nonpersons with no fishing rights under federal law. While the commercial interests raged, the Indians were catching nothing close to the 50 percent allowed by the Boldt ruling. In 1974,

they caught between 7 and 8 percent; in 1975, between 11 and 12 percent; in 1976, between 13 and 25 percent; and in 1977, 17 percent.

Among state officials during the middle and late 1970s, a backlash to Indian rights formed that would become the nucleus for a nationwide non-Indian campaign to abrogate the treaties. Washington State attorney general (later U.S. senator) Slade Gorton called Indians "supercitizens" with "special rights" and proposed that constitutional equilibrium be reestablished not by open state violation of the treaties (Boldt had outlawed that), but by purchasing the Indians' fishing rights. The tribes, which had been listening to offers of money for Indian resources for a century, flatly refused Gorton's offer. To them the selling of fishing rights would have been tantamount to termination.

FOR MORE INFORMATION:

American Friends Service Committee. *Uncommon Controversy: Fishing Rights of the Muckleshoot, Puyallup, and Nisqually Indians.* Seattle: University of Washington Press, 1970.

Barsh, Russell L. *The Washington Fishing Rights Controversy: An Economic Critique.* Seattle: University of Washington School of Business Administration, 1977.

Brack, Fred. "Fishing Rights: Who Is Entitled to Northwest Salmon?" *Seattle Post-Intelligencer Northwest Magazine* supplement (January 16, 1977).

Brown, Bruce. *Mountain in the Clouds.* New York: Simon & Schuster, 1982.

Miller, Bruce J. "The Press, the Boldt Decision, and Indian-White Relations." *American Indian Culture & Research Journal* 17:2 (1993).

Roderick, Janna. "Indian-White Relations in the Washington Territory: The Question of

Treaties and Indian Fishing Rights." *Journal of the West* 16:3 (July 1977).

United States v. *Washington*, 384 F. Supp 312 (1974).

BOLEK (BOLECK, BOWLEGS)
Mixed Seminole
fl. early 1800s

Bolek was a Seminole chief who opposed the United States in 1812 during the wars along the Georgia/Florida frontier. His village was on the Suwanee River in western Florida. He joined his brother, King Payne, in 1812 to try to stop the Georgians from pursuing runaway slaves into Florida. Already some of these African Americans were marrying into the Seminole bands. Bolek and his brother engaged in numerous skirmishes on the Georgia/Florida frontier. King Payne was killed and Bolek wounded in one of these altercations with the Georgians under the command of Daniel Newman. These border tensions continued unresolved after the end of the War of 1812.

During the First Seminole War (1817–1818), General Andrew Jackson's American forces invaded northern Florida (nominally under Spanish colonial rule but controlled by the British), taking KINACHE's village of Miccosukee as well as the British town of St. Marks and then heading for Chief Bolek's village. The Seminoles under Bolek had abandoned their village, but Jackson's men apprehended two Englishmen, Robert Ambrister and Peter Cook. These two British subjects were marched to St. Marks, sentenced to death by Jackson for aiding the Indians, and then executed. Jackson's caprice created an international incident, and he narrowly avoided ruining his future political career. After the executions, Jackson retook Pensacola. In 1819, a treaty between Spain and the United States granted the sale of Florida to the United States.

Bolek became principal chief of the Seminoles when King Payne died, but he passed away shortly after the end of the First Seminole War. King Payne's grandson, MICANOPY, succeeded Bolek.

BONNIN, GERTRUDE (ZITKALA-SA)
Yankton Dakota
1876–1938

Along with Charles EASTMAN and Luther STANDING BEAR, Gertrude Bonnin provided a written window on Sioux life at the juncture of two worlds. Born the year of the Battle of Little Bighorn, she died on the eve of World War II.

Bonnin distrusted most non-Indians but early sought a formal education against her mother's wishes, eventually attending the Boston Conservatory of Music. Her articles and poetry were published in large-circulation magazines. One of Bonnin's books, *American Indian Stories* (1921), was autobiographical. It described her changing perceptions of the Euro-American world and her gradual acceptance of Christianity. She also wrote *Old Indian Legends* (1901).

With Eastman, Bonnin was a founder of the Society of American Indians, an early pan-Indian advocacy organization in the 1920s. She taught for a time at Carlisle Indian School and was known for her talent on the violin. Bonnin, under the pen name Zitkala-sa, investigated the swindling of Indians in Oklahoma by settlers who swarmed the area after the discovery of oil. She also advised the government's Meriam Commission in the late 1920s. Bonnin remained active in Indian affairs until her death in 1938.

FOR MORE INFORMATION:

Bonnin, Gertrude. *American Indian Stories.* 1921. Reprint, Lincoln: University of Nebraska Press, 1985.

———. *Old Indian Legends.* 1901. Reprint, Lincoln: University of Nebraska Press, 1985.

BOSOMWORTH, MARY (MARY MUS-GROVE OR MATTHEWS; COOSAPONSKEESA)

Mixed Creek

c. 1700–c. 1763

Born on the Chattahoochee River in what would become Alabama, young Mary was the daughter of a Creek woman and her white trader husband. She was taken to South Carolina by her father at the age of seven, where she attended school and became a member of the Church of England. When she was sixteen, she returned to her mother's people. Bosomworth would become an important interpreter, trader, and leader in the Creek nation.

After marrying a trader named John Musgrove, she and her husband established a trading post at Yamacraw Bluff (present-day Savannah, Georgia) on the Savannah River in 1732. In 1733, Sir James Oglethorpe, the founder of Georgia, made Mary his interpreter to the Creeks and paid her about $500 per year. A second trading post on the Altamaha River at Mount Venture was soon set up by the Musgroves. Mary Musgrove's power and influence among the Creeks burgeoned. Since she was pro-English, she encouraged the Creeks to support the British against the Spanish in the colonial struggle for the Southeast.

In 1739, Mary was widowed, but she soon married Jacob Matthews, a British army captain. While they were residing in Savannah, she was widowed once more in 1742. In 1749, Mary took a third spouse, the Reverend Thomas Bosomworth, thus taking the surname by which she is widely known. Thomas Bosomworth became the South Carolina agent to the Creeks soon after their marriage. At about this time, Mary Bosomworth claimed that she owned Sapelo, Ossabaw, and St. Catherine's Islands (some of the coastal islands of Georgia) as well as significant parcels on the Georgia mainland. To assert their land claims and the failure of the colonial government to properly pay for their services, Mary and Reverend Bosomworth marshaled a force of Creek warriors at Savannah, Georgia, in 1749. British authorities, discounting their declarations, arrested the pair and bribed her Creek supporters with gifts so that they would go home.

Shortly after they were released from custody unharmed, the Bosomworths went to England to continue their legal battle with the British Crown. Receiving a small compensation for their claims and services in 1759, the Bosomworths received permission to sell Sapelo and Ossabaw Islands. Four years later on St. Catherine's Island, Mary Bosomworth, the self-styled "Empress" of the Creeks, passed away.

BOUCHARD, JAMES (WATOMIKA)

Delaware

1823–1889

Born of a French mother called Monotowa who had been reared by the Comanches and a Delaware father named Kistalwa who was a chief, James Bouchard (whose Native name means "Swift Foot") became a Presbyterian when his father was slain by the Sioux in 1834. Subsequently, he studied in Ohio at a mission school. Converting to Roman Catholicism in 1846, he studied to be a Jesuit in Missouri. Bouchard became a Catholic priest in 1855; he traveled widely and spoke to audiences about his life as a Christian Indian. In 1861, he became a missionary to miners in the San Francisco area.

BOUDINOT, ELIAS (GALEGINA)

Mixed Cherokee

c. 1803–1839

An outspoken editor of the *Cherokee Phoenix* and early opponent of the removal policy that led to the Trail of Tears, Elias Boudinot was born near Rome, Georgia, as Buck Watie. In 1818, he took the name of his benefactor, philanthropist Elias Boudinot. He was also known as Galegina (meaning "Mule Deer") and Stag Watie.

Boudinot was a son of David Uwati and a mixed-blood Cherokee woman named Susannah Reese. As a young boy, he studied at the Moravian school in Salem, North Carolina. From 1818 to 1822, he attended the Cornwall Foreign Mission School in Cornwall, Connecticut, through a scholarship provided by Elias Boudinot of New Jersey. Boudinot met a local white girl, Harriet Ruggles Gold, while at the Cornwall school; he married her in 1826. The marriage was violently opposed by most of the town, and Harriet's brother, in protest, burned the two in effigy. However, Harriet remained firm in her decision to marry her love.

In December 1822, Boudinot journeyed back to his homeland and served as clerk of the Cherokee National Council. In 1827, the Cherokee Council authorized a national newspaper; and on February 21, 1828, Boudinot's name appeared as the first editor of the weekly *Cherokee Phoenix*, a bilingual tribal newspaper published in SEQUOYAH's newly fashioned syllabary and in English. The associate editor was Stephen Foreman. As editor, Boudinot took a strong position against removal. In 1831, Boudinot traveled in the North to raise funds to continue publishing the *Phoenix*. At this time, he wrote the first novel published in Cherokee, *Poor Sarah, or the Indian Woman* (1831). Boudinot also collaborated on a translation of the Bible into Cherokee with Foreman and Samuel Worcester. In September 1833, he resigned as editor.

Late in 1832, Boudinot reversed his earlier opposition to removal, fearing annihilation of the Cherokees if they stayed. His brother Stand WATIE, Major RIDGE, John RIDGE, and Boudinot all became prominent members of the Treaty Party. Georgia had begun to survey Cherokee lands in 1832; the Treaty Party felt that removal was unavoidable and counseled that the best possible terms for removal should therefore be secured. John ROSS and his faction decided to oppose removal through the courts. Boudinot, John Ridge, and several others journeyed to Washington, D.C., in 1835 to negotiate removal, but their efforts were not sanctioned by the Cherokee government. On December 29, 1835, Boudinot and nineteen other Cherokees signed the Treaty of New Echota, ceding Cherokee lands to the United States in exchange for lands in Oklahoma. Removal was to be accomplished in two years. On May 23, 1836, this controversial treaty was ratified by a one-vote margin in the U.S. Senate. This removal treaty led to the Trail of Tears, the 1,000-mile march that caused over 20 percent of the tribe—4,000 people—to die on the way to present-day Arkansas.

Upon the Cherokees' arrival in Indian Territory in late 1837, Boudinot settled at Park Hill. On June 22, 1839, Boudinot was killed by several Cherokee traditionalists who invoked the Law of Blood for his unsanctioned sale of Cherokee lands.

Boudinot's first wife, Harriet, died in 1830, leaving him with six children; Boudinot's second wife, Delight Sargent Boudinot, took these children to the East for education. Boudinot's most famous son, Elias Cornelius Boudinot, went to school in Vermont, studied civil engineering, and later became a leader among the Western Cherokees. He sided with the Confederacy during the Civil War along with his uncle, Stand Watie. Elias Cornelius Boudinot was also a member of the Confederate Congress (he attended as a delegate from the Cherokee nation) in Richmond, Virginia.

BOWL (DIWALI)
Mixed Cherokee
1756–1839

Bowl, a major chief of the Western Cherokees, was born in North Carolina and grew up in the Cherokee village of Chickamauga in Tennessee. He was the son of a Scots-Irish trader named Bowles and a Cherokee mother. His name is a translation of the Cherokee word *diwali*, meaning "the Bowl Used for Black Drink." He was also called Colonel Bowles by Texans.

Little is known about Bowl's childhood. He emerged as a leader of a large group of pro-British Cherokee militants during the American Revolution when he fought with DRAGGING CANOE. After the Revolution, he avoided contact with the new American nation and continued his alliance with the English. By 1791, he was chief of the Cherokee village at Running Water, Georgia.

In June 1794, he and a band of warriors struck a white settlement at Muscle Shoals, Alabama, on the Tennessee River, slaying several white settlers. The Cherokees under Bowl asserted that the settlers had defrauded them in trade. Subsequently, the Cherokee Tribal Council condemned the attack and even offered to aid U.S. authorities in Bowl's arrest. Bowl took his band across the Mississippi River into present-day Arkansas to escape prosecution. But after the Louisiana Purchase of 1803, Bowl found himself once again under U.S. jurisdiction.

In 1820, because of government surveyors and white settlers, the Cherokees led by Bowl left Arkansas and crossed the Sabine River into Texas, taking lands surrounded by the Angelina, Neches, and Sabine Rivers along with other tribes like the Delaware, Shawnee, and Kickapoo. These groups were persuaded by Mexican officials, who hoped to keep Texas

from succumbing to U.S. expansion or Kiowa and Comanche attacks, to settle there. In 1827, Bowl was commissioned a lieutenant colonel in the Mexican army for his efforts in quelling an insurrection against the Mexican government.

When the Texans gained independence from Mexico in 1835, Bowl's Cherokees had to negotiate a new treaty for their lands. This treaty with the provisional government of Texas, initiated by Sam Houston, was finalized in February 1836 and granted the Cherokees the right to stay in Texas. However, the treaty was never ratified by the Texas Senate, since most Texans wanted the removal of all Indian nations. The Texans feared that the tribes would conspire against them with the Mexicans. In 1839, Texas governor Mirabeau B. Lamar, successor to Houston, tried to negotiate a removal treaty with Bowl. When the Cherokees refused to leave their homes, troops from Texas were dispatched; in July 1839, the Cherokees were massacred in two engagements along the Angelina River. War chief Hard-Mush and Bowl were slain in the bloody melee; their followers were driven northward. The dead Bowl was discovered gripping a metal box with the 1836 treaty inside.

BOWLEGS, BILLY (HOLATA MICO)
Seminole
c. 1810–1864

Billy Bowlegs, a hereditary war chief (also known as Holata Mico, Halpatter-Micco, and Halpuda Mikko, all meaning "Alligator Chief"), headed one of the last bands of Seminoles to stay in Florida and fight U.S. authorities. He was born on the Alchua Savannah (present-day Cuscowilla, Florida) of full-blooded Seminole parents; his father was called Secoffee. It is said that his nickname stemmed from Bolek or Bowleck, the surname of a prominent trader.

Billy Bowlegs. [Nebraska State Historical Society]

The common assumption that he was bow-legged from horseback riding cannot be substantiated. It is thought that Chief MICANOPY was his uncle.

Although he signed the Treaty of Payne's Landing in 1832, Bowlegs subsequently avoided the removal of his band to Indian Territory for over twenty years. He was known as a skilled warrior; to be sure, he eluded the U.S. Army long after WILD CAT's, OSCEOLA's, and other Seminole bands had been apprehended. Through an excellent knowledge of the Everglades, Bowlegs and his band maintained an independent existence unhindered by U.S. authorities until the eve of the Civil War.

From 1835 to 1842, Billy Bowlegs was a significant leader in the Second Seminole War along with ARPEIKA, Osceola, Micanopy, JUMPER, Wild Cat, and ALLIGATOR. Even after the death of

Osceola and the surrender of Micanopy, head chief of the Seminoles, in 1837, Bowlegs and his two hundred warriors continued to resist removal to Indian Territory. On July 22, 1839, his name is mentioned in government reports relating to an attack on a Camp Harney. This raid was one of a series of successful forays against the army and settlers by Bowlegs, the new chief of the Florida Seminoles. His guerrilla tactics enabled him to secure, on August 14, 1842, a peace treaty that ended over seven years of hostilities. This eight-year war cost the U.S. government $30 million and fifteen hundred dead. To secure an enduring peace and impress Bowlegs and other Seminole chiefs with American might, a group of Seminole chiefs were brought to Washington, D.C., to see the power of the U.S. capital.

As a result, from 1842 to 1855 a period of relative peace prevailed in Florida. However, a small group of army engineers and surveyors in 1855 invaded Bowlegs's homeland in the Great Cypress Swamp, stealing crops, cutting down banana trees, and destroying property only two miles from Bowlegs's main village just to see how he would react. This created what some have called the Third Seminole War. When the engineers and surveyors were confronted about their depredations, they proffered the Seminoles neither restitution nor remorse. Consequently, the Seminoles in southern Florida under Bowlegs launched two years of sporadic raids against Anglo trappers, settlers, and traders in the area. Settlers demanded that the U.S. Army mount a campaign to remove all remaining Seminoles.

Containing the ravages of the Seminole militants once again proved difficult for the U.S. military. In 1858, a group of Western Seminoles that were under the leadership of Wild Cat and that had been removed to Indian Territory were brought back to convince Bowlegs and his followers of the wisdom of moving west. Bowlegs, upon hearing that Wild Cat was coming, stated, "Tell him not to come out to our country until I send for him." Bowlegs was offered $10,000 and each of his followers $1,000 if they agreed to go to Indian Territory, but they initially refused, fearing harsh treatment in the West. Under enormous pressure, Bowlegs and 123 of his followers, plus 41 captives, finally agreed to removal in 1858.

After his arrival in the West, Bowlegs became an important Seminole village chief in Indian Territory. At the start of the Civil War, he became a leader of the pro-Union Seminole forces (the Loyal Seminoles); his unit fought on the Union side in Kansas. As captain of the First Regiment, Indian Home Guard, Bowlegs served with distinction until he succumbed to smallpox in 1864.

BRANDO, MARLON
1924–

Actor Marlon Brando has participated in Native American rights struggles beginning with the 1960s "fish-ins" near Puget Sound. On March 2, 1964, Brando was arrested for illegal net fishing, but he was released on a technicality and was not tried. A day later, Brando helped lead a march on the state capital in Olympia, Washington, joined by about one thousand Native fishing people and their non-Indian allies.

Brando refused to accept an Academy Award for his performance in *The Godfather* (1972), which was presented during the siege of Wounded Knee, South Dakota, as protest of Indians' treatment there. Instead he sent a woman named Shasheen Littlefeather to deliver a prepared statement criticizing Hollywood for its degrading portrayals of Indians. (She was not permitted to read the statement, which was released to the press after the ceremony.)

BRANT, JOSEPH (THAYENDANEGEA)
Mohawk
1742–1807

Brant was the son of Aroghyiadecker (Nicklaus Brant), who was prominent on the New York frontier during the mid-1700s as an Iroquois leader and an ally of the British in the American Revolution. His grandfather, SA GA YEAN QUA PRAH TON, was one of the four "American kings" invited to London to visit Queen Anne's court in 1710.

Brant joined the British Indian agent William JOHNSON at the age of thirteen, and with other Mohawk allies, was present at the Battle of Lake George when the elderly HENDRICK was killed.

In 1758, Brant was one of the guides who led the Bradstreet expedition to the French Fort Frontenac on the north shore of Lake Ontario. Two hundred and fifty Redcoats marched with the Mohawks, and another twenty-seven hundred colonial volunteers tagged along. Fort

Joseph Brant. [National Anthropological Archives]

Frontenac fell, and Brant began to appear more often at Johnson Hall.

After the war with the French ended in 1763, Brant, who was still a young man, was tutored by Eleazer Wheelock at the Indian Charity School in Connecticut, which would later move to New Hampshire and become known as Dartmouth College. He was an able student but dropped out after a year. Brant was married for a time to Margaret, a daughter of the Oneida sachem SKENANDOAH. After Margaret's death, Brant married Catherine Croghan, the Mohawk daughter of George Croghan, a British Indian agent who was a close friend of William Johnson.

By 1765, Joseph Brant was married and settled in the Mohawk Valley. He had accepted a job as a secretary to Johnson and had acquired farmland, cattle, and an interest in a gristmill. As personal secretary to Johnson, Brant became known as the most able interpreter available to the British in northeastern North America. As a Mohawk leader, Brant attended meetings of the Iroquois Grand Council at Onondaga and provided firsthand intelligence to the British military.

After William Johnson died in 1774, Brant became secretary to his nephew Guy JOHNSON, who had taken over the Indian superintendency for the Crown. In November 1775, Brant sailed for England with Johnson. "As a Pine Tree Chief of the Iroquois, he wore knee-high moccasins and a blanket draped over one shoulder. And as Col. Guy Johnson's secretary, he was equally at home in starched linen and broadcloth," wrote historian Frank Waters.

Brant played a major role in rallying some of the Iroquois to the British cause during the American Revolution. Brant was told that some Mohawk lands would be returned to them if they allied with the British. An artistic likeness of him appeared in the July 1776 edition of *Lon-*

don Magazine just as (unknown to Londoners until mid-August) American revolutionaries were posting their Declaration of Independence in Philadelphia. On another visit to London in 1785, Brant was sought after by Boswell and sat for a portrait by Romney; he also dined with the Prince of Wales. Brant made a favorable impression upon society in London. He fascinated the English, since he spoke good English and had a European education. He was a Mason, a staunch churchman, and a translator of the Gospel of St. Mark into his native tongue. The British government provided him with personal guides to the sights of London.

On his return to America, Brant recruited most of the Mohawks, Senecas, Cayugas, and Onondagas to support the British. Most of the Oneidas and Tuscaroras supported the revolutionaries. The league was split for the first time in several hundred years. Brant's ferocity as a warrior was legendary; many settlers who supported the Americans called him "Monster Brant." The revolutionaries were no less fierce; revolutionary forces often adopted a scorched earth policy against Iroquois who supported the British. George Washington's forces ended the battle for the Mohawk Valley by defeating the British and their Iroquois allies at the Battle of Johnstown.

The Grand Council met in late 1774 for nearly a month to deliberate important matters relating to alliances in the coming American Revolution. Brant, a brother of Mary BRANT, was sent by Guy Johnson to take notes and report back to him. Thayendanega would become a key figure in the military operations of the Iroquois Confederacy as the war for American independence dragged on.

By 1780, after Brant and Guy Johnson had crossed the Atlantic together several times and worked closely for a half-dozen years, they had a falling out. Evidence mounted that Guy Johnson was padding reports to the Crown to swindle large amounts of money in league with several traders at Niagara. For example, Johnson debited the king for 1,156 kettles when the actual number was 156.

The war had ended along the American frontier, but the efforts of the Iroquois went unrewarded by both sides. The British discarded their Mohawk, Onondaga, Cayuga, and Seneca allies at their earliest convenience. The Americans did the same to their own allies, the Tuscaroras and Oneidas. At the conclusion of the Revolutionary War, the border between the new United States and Canada (still under British dominion) was drawn straight through the middle of Iroquois country without consultation.

Brant emigrated to British Canada with a number of Mohawks and other Iroquois, along with many other Tories, non-Indian British sympathizers. He was commissioned as an officer in the British army, which maintained his rank at half pay and granted him land along the Grand River in Ontario after he retired. Today this is the site of the Grand River Iroquois Council. He visited England again in 1786 at the Court of St. James. Brant devoted many of his later years to translating the rest of the Bible and other religious works into Mohawk and to raising seven children by three wives. He died November 24, 1807.

FOR MORE INFORMATION:

Edmunds, R. David. *American Indian Leaders: Studies in Diversity.* Lincoln: University of Nebraska Press, 1980.

Graymont, Barbara. *The Iroquois in the American Revolution.* Syracuse, N.Y.: Syracuse University Press, 1972.

Grinde, Donald A., Jr. *The Iroquois and the Founding of the American Nation.* San Francisco: Indian Historian Press, 1977.

Kelsay, Isabel Thompson. *Joseph Brant.* Syracuse, N.Y.: Syracuse University Press, 1984.

Stone, William L. *The Life of Joseph Brant.* 1838. Reprint, New York: Kraus, 1969.

Waters, Frank. *Brave Are My People: Indian Heroes Not Forgotten.* Santa Fe, N. Mex.: Clear Light, 1993.

BRANT, MARY (MOLLY, DEGONWADONTI)
Mohawk
c. 1735–c. 1795

Mary Brant, sister of Joseph BRANT, married Sir William JOHNSON and wielded considerable influence on both sides of the frontier in bringing many Iroquois to the British side in the American Revolution. Born at Canajoharie, New York, of Nicklaus Brant, a Mohawk, and a mixed-blood Mohawk woman, Mary grew up with her brother Joseph at the family home in the Mohawk Valley. She met Johnson in 1753, when she was about eighteen. Between that year and Johnson's death in 1774, she bore him nine children.

Mary Brant suffered at the hands of patriots during the American Revolution. The 1777 plundering of her home by fellow Iroquois allied with the patriots provides a study in microcosm of the divisions that bedeviled the Iroquois Confederacy during the American Revolution. During the raid, the chairman of the Tryon County Committee of Safety enriched himself by carrying off wagonloads of goods. The patriots also urged the Oneidas of Oriska to make up their losses at the hands of the raiding Mohawks. Peter Deygart of the Committee of Safety urged the Oneidas to take two cows, horses, sheep, and hogs for every one that the Mohawks had earlier taken from them. Many of the Mohawks had lived in greater comfort than the struggling white settlers; thus, the settlers were only too pleased to loot Indian homes. A cursory glance at some of the articles taken in these raids reflects the wealth of these Indian communities. Agricultural products such as Indian corn, turnips, and potatoes were taken, as well as livestock, wagons, farm implements, and sleighs. Many Mohawk houses were sturdily built and had window glass, a rare item on the frontier. The result of this devastation was to persuade the Mohawk nation that their only ally would be the British government. Among the things they took were "Sixty half Johannesses, two quarts full of silver, several Gold Rings, Eight pair silver Buckels; a large quantity of Silver Brooches, Together with several silk Gowns." [Grinde]

Due to her position, Mary was actually more influential within the confederacy than her younger brother, Joseph. As a clan mother and consort of Sir William Johnson, she was a powerful figure within the traditional framework. She also knew the ways of the white man. An unnamed observer commented that "one word from her goes farther with them than a thousand from any white Man." [Grinde]

By fall 1777, Major John Butler had returned to Fort Niagara and invited Mary Brant to come to the frontier to live. The Iroquois clan mother hesitated, not wanting to alienate her friends and relatives at Cayuga. Later, however, she did move to Niagara. While there, she maintained an open house for all the leading men and women of the confederacy. Niagara was a busy place, as the Iroquois were constantly visiting the post to trade. She freely gave her advice on affairs of state and encouraged her people to remain loyal to the English cause, listening sympathetically to the grievances of the influential chiefs and providing counsel to those in doubt.

Mary Brant moved to Canada with the rest of Joseph Brant's band after the American Revolution, and the details of her life became sketchy at this point. It is probable that she died about 1795 in or near Brantford, Ontario.

FOR MORE INFORMATION:

Anonymous. "Molly Brant—Loyalist." *Ontario History* XLV, 3 (Summer 1953).

"Anecdotes of Brant," Claus Papers, Buffalo Publications, IV.

Graymont, Barbara. *The Iroquois in the American Revolution.* Syracuse, N.Y.: Syracuse University Press, 1972.

Grinde, Donald A., Jr. *The Iroquois and the Founding of the American Nation.* San Francisco: Indian Historian Press, 1977.

BRIDGES, AL
Nisqually
1922–1982

During the 1960s and early 1970s, Al Bridges was a leader among Native Americans in the Puget Sound area of Washington State. He went to virtual war with state fisheries police to enforce Indian rights to fish in accord with treaties signed in the 1850s. This method of defending fishing rights ended in 1974 with a decision by Federal Judge George BOLDT that Indians were entitled to up to half the catch.

Born in Gig Harbor, Washington (near Tacoma), Bridges was one of the earliest leaders of the "fish-ins," which helped spur Native American defenses of treaty rights nationwide during the 1960s. For a decade and a half, Native Americans around Puget Sound had fished as they said the treaties allowed. State game officials tried to stop them by disabling their boats, cutting their nets, and making arrests once Indians returned to shore with their catch. Judge Boldt's ruling followed several setbacks for Bridges and other Native people in state courts. Bridges was among a nucleus of fishing rights activists from Franks Landing—only a few miles from the site at which the Medicine Creek Treaty had been signed in 1855—who continued to fish on the basis of the treaty, which gave them the right to fish there as long as the rivers should run. Day by day, the state fishery police descended on the fishing Indians as the legal battle continued in the courts. Vigilante sports fishermen joined state fisheries police in harassing the Indians, stealing their boats, slashing their nets, and sometimes shooting at them. The elders and women stood with the younger men. Al Bridges and his wife, Maisel, fished beside their daughters, Suzette Mills and Valerie and Allison Bridges. All stood alongside the young men, Hank Adams, Sid Mills, and others.

Supporters from Seattle joined the Indians in their confrontation with the police, the vigilantes, and the cold rain. Chicanos from Seattle's El Centro de la Raza took an active part in these early battles, as did the National Indian Youth Council of Albuquerque, New Mexico. Actors Marlon Brando, Dick Gregory, and Jane Fonda stopped by to hoist nets and to spread the aura of national celebrity, making the Northwest conflict over fish the first widely publicized treaty rights defense of the late twentieth century. Many other treaty struggles were surfacing at this time, particularly in the North and West, where the subjugation was little more than a century in the past.

FOR MORE INFORMATION:

American Friends Service Committee. *Uncommon Controversy: Fishing Rights of the Muckleshoot, Puyallup, and Nisqually Indians.* Seattle: University of Washington Press, 1970.

BRUCE, LOUIS R.
Dakota and Mohawk
1906–1989

Bruce, who was raised among the Onondagas of the Iroquois Confederacy, served as commissioner of the Bureau of Indian Affairs (BIA) during President Richard M. Nixon's first term. His tenure coincided with activist movements during the late 1960s and 1970s. Nixon fired Bruce after Indian activists seized the BIA headquarters in Washington, D.C., less than a week before the 1972 election.

Bruce's father, Louis Bruce, a Mohawk, worked as a dentist, a major league baseball player, and a Methodist missionary. His mother, Nellie Rooks, was Dakota (Sioux). Bruce attended Cazenovia Seminary, then worked his way through Syracuse University and became known as a star pole vaulter. After his graduation from college, Bruce worked as a clothing store manager, as an official in the Works Progress Administration, and as a dairy farmer. He married Anna Wikoff, a former classmate at the Cazenovia Seminary, in 1930.

In 1957, Bruce played a major role in organizing the first Native American Youth Conference. He was a founder and executive secretary of the National Congress of American Indians. After Bruce was named BIA commissioner by President Nixon in 1969, he set out to "Indianize" the bureau by appointing a number of Native Americans to influential positions. His policies ran up against considerable opposition from interests that had benefited by keeping Indians in a subordinate position. In this respect, his ouster recalled that of the first BIA commissioner of Native American descent, Ely PARKER, who had been drummed out of the office almost exactly a century earlier.

FOR FURTHER INFORMATION:

Ballantine, Betty, and Ian Ballantine. *The Native Americans Today.* Atlanta: Turner Publishing, 1993.

BUCKONGAHELAS
Delaware
fl. 1800

Born in the mid–eighteenth century in western Ohio, Buckongahelas resisted white expansion into the Ohio country, but did so with a human demeanor that sometimes won the admiration even of his enemies. As chief of the Delawares along the Miami and White Rivers, Buckongahelas tried to remove his people from the tide of Euro-American immigration, moving to the upper Miami River in 1781.

Later in the century, Buckongahelas was among the Native leaders of a major revolt led by the Miami LITTLE TURTLE. Buckongahelas took part in the defeat of General Arthur Saint Clair in 1791 and the defeat of the Native alliance at the Battle of Fallen Timbers in 1794. He signed the Treaty of Greenville a year later.

Buckongahelas died in 1804 or 1805, probably on the White River near the present-day site of Muncie, Indiana.

FOR MORE INFORMATION:

Winger, Otho. *Last of the Miamis: Little Turtle.* N.p.: Lawrence W. Shultz, 1935.

BUFFALO HORN
Bannock
fl. 1870s

Like many other native peoples in the Pacific Northwest, Buffalo Horn and the Bannocks initially were friendly to white immigrants, who arrived at first in small numbers. Early in the 1870s, Buffalo Horn worked as a scout for several U.S. Army officers, including Nelson A. Miles, Oliver O. Howard, and George Crook.

The Bannocks' anger rose as white immigration increased and especially as hogs began to root in areas used by the Indians to harvest their prized camas root in southern Idaho. In May 1878, a Bannock wounded two whites. As the settlers mobilized for war, Buffalo Horn agreed, after considerable pressure by young warriors, to lead about two hundred Bannocks and Northern Paiutes into battle with a volunteer regiment from Silver City. Buffalo Horn was killed in that brief battle in 1878, but the

Bannock War dragged on in occasional incidents until the early fall.

FOR MORE INFORMATION:

Howard, O. O. *Famous Indian Chiefs I Have Known.* 1908. Reprint, Lincoln: University of Nebraska Press, 1989.

BUFFALO HUMP (BULL HUMP, POCHANAW-QUOIP)
Comanche
fl. mid-1800s

As a young Comanche war chief, Buffalo Hump's raids, involving over one thousand warriors, ranged into Chihuahua, Mexico, on foraging expeditions for horses and slaves. By the 1830s, he was also a part of war parties directed against the Arapahos and Cheyenne. At the conclusion of these raids, a firm peace was set up in 1840 among the Kiowa, Cheyenne, Arapaho, and Comanches. Later, Buffalo Hump became the principal chief of the Comanches and led their resistance to subjugation by the Texas Rangers.

In the Council House Affair of 1838, the Texas Rangers attempted to emancipate hostages by seizing Comanche chiefs under a flag of truce at a peace conference near San Antonio, Texas. Violence erupted and several Comanches were slain in the melee. Angered by this treachery, Buffalo Hump marshaled warriors for revenge from the Comanche homeland north of the Red River along the Guadalupe Valley. They rode toward the Gulf of Mexico, raiding and pillaging the settlements of Linnville and Victoria. The Texas Rangers intercepted and attacked the Comanches near Lockhart. They suffered some casualties, but Buffalo Hump and his men successfully eluded the Rangers.

After the cholera epidemic of 1849, Buffalo Hump became the principal chief of the Comanches. In the late 1850s, the U.S. Army and the Texas Rangers mounted a cooperative military operation against the Comanches. In May 1858, the Texas Rangers struck Chief Iron Jacket's village north of the Red River at Antelope Hills, in present-day Oklahoma. In the ensuing battle, two women died. The escaping Comanches, including Buffalo Hump, had to abandon three hundred ponies. The Rangers also burned their possessions and tepees. The next year, fifty-four Comanches were killed by the U.S. Army at Crooked Creek in Kansas.

After the U.S. Civil War, in October 1865, Buffalo Hump was a member of a meeting on the Little Arkansas River with other chiefs from Southern Plains tribes. As a result of this parlay, the Southern Cheyenne, Kiowa-Apaches, Kiowas, Comanches, and Southern Arapahoes reluctantly renounced their rights to the lands north of the Arkansas River. But this agreement did not end the strife on the Southern Plains; Buffalo Hump's son, taking his father's name, would carry on armed resistance with Quanah PARKER.

BULLHEAD
Sioux
fl. 1880s–1890s

Bullhead, who assassinated SITTING BULL, was at the head of a column of forty-three Indian police sent to arrest Sitting Bull at the Standing Rock Agency on December 15, 1890, only a few days before the massacre of BIG FOOT's band at Wounded Knee. Bullhead, RED TOMAHAWK, and the other Indian police faced off with a large number of Sitting Bull's supporters, who were armed and ready for a fight. Sitting Bull refused to surrender, and shooting broke out. Bullhead shot Sitting Bull in the back as he was falling from a bullet wound. Red Tomahawk also shot into Sitting Bull's body as the aging chief fell from Bullhead's wound.

The death of Sitting Bull was the culmination of his rivalry with Indian agent William ("White Hair") McLaughlin, who had used the Indian police to harass Sitting Bull and who had appointed four recognized chiefs to undermine his authority among the Sioux.

FOR MORE INFORMATION:
Utley, Robert M. *The Lance and the Shield: The Life and Times of Sitting Bull.* New York: Henry Holt, 1993.
Vestal, Stanley. *Sitting Bull: Champion of the Sioux.* 1932. Reprint, Norman: University of Oklahoma Press, 1957.

BURNETTE, ROBERT
Sioux
1926–

Robert Burnette served as executive director of the National Congress of American Indians between 1962 and 1964 after eight years (1954–1962) as tribal chairman of the Rosebud Sioux. He authored *The Tortured Americans* (1971), a dissection of twentieth-century Sioux politics and exploitation of Native political divisions by state and federal bureaucracies. With coauthor John Koster, Burnette wrote *The Road to Wounded Knee* (1974).

FOR MORE INFORMATION:
Burnette, Robert. *The Tortured Americans.* Englewood Cliffs, N.J.: Prentice Hall, 1971.
———, and John Koster. *The Road to Wounded Knee.* New York: Bantam, 1974.

BUSHYHEAD, DENNIS WOLF (UNADUTI)
Mixed Cherokee
1826–1898

Born on Mouse Creek near Cleveland, Tennessee, on March 18, 1826, Dennis Wolf Bushyhead was the son of the Reverend Jesse Bushyhead, a Cherokee Presbyterian minister. Young Dennis, who would become a principal chief of the Western Cherokees, attended mission schools in the East until his father led a contingent of twelve hundred Cherokees on the Trail of Tears (see John ROSS) to Indian Territory in 1838–1839. In 1841, he was a member of a Cherokee delegation to Washington, D.C. In 1844, he began college at Princeton University but failed to finish, dropping out of school to take over his father's business interests in Oklahoma at Fort Gibson.

By 1848, Bushyhead assumed the clerkship of the Cherokee National Committee. The next year, however, he headed to California hoping to make his fortune in the gold rush. Although he did not strike it rich, he was more successful than most of the forty-niners. He did not return to Indian Territory until after the Civil War, settling at Tahlequah in 1868. In 1871, he became the treasurer of the Cherokee nation. In 1879, as head of the National Party, he was made principal chief, serving two terms (1879–1887).

As a Progressive mixed-blood, Bushyhead was a staunch supporter of the General Allotment Act of 1887, while many traditionalist Cherokees represented by the Keetowah Society (see Redbird SMITH) opposed individual allotments that fragmented communal lands. He later became a tribal delegate to Washington, D.C., in 1889 and 1890 seeking Cherokee allotment, but the traditionalist Cherokees thwarted his efforts. Although often thought of as being in the vanguard of Cherokee Progressive politics, Bushyhead always thought of himself as a compromiser between the Progressive and traditionalist factions of his people. He sought education for all Cherokees and economic development through railroad, mineral, timber, and cattle-grazing leases on Cherokee lands. Bushyhead died at Tahlequah in Indian Territory in 1898, just a few years before the creation of the state of Oklahoma.

C

CAMEAHWAIT
Shoshoni
fl. early 1800s

Cameahwait made his first acquaintance with Anglo-American history as the brother of SACA-JAWEA, guide to Lewis and Clark and thus a friend of the expedition. A leading chief among the Shoshonis, Cameahwait was present when WASHAKIE, who later succeeded him as principal chief, was born as Lewis and Clark swaddled him in an American flag. Cameahwait established a tradition of friendliness to immigrating Americans that continued with Washakie.

CAMPBELL, BEN NIGHTHORSE
Northern Cheyenne
1933–

Ben Nighthorse Campbell was elected to the U.S. House of Representatives from Colorado in 1986 and in 1992 became the first Native American to serve in the U.S. Senate. At the same time, Campbell was a member of the traditional Council of Forty-four in his Northern Cheyenne homeland in Montana. In March 1995, Campbell resigned from the Democratic Party and joined the Republicans.

Campbell's long career, following his birth in Auburn, California, included U.S. Air Force service in the Korean War. As a student at San Jose State College, Campbell became a championship competitor in judo in 1957. He won the U.S. collegiate championship in his weight class three times and took a gold medal at the 1963 Pan-American Games. Campbell represented the United States in judo at the 1964 Olympic Games and later wrote a judo training manual.

In 1983, Campbell became the second Native American to be elected to Colorado's legislature, where he served until his 1986 election to the U.S. House of Representatives. Campbell, who is married and the father of two, also maintains a jewelry design business.

FOR MORE INFORMATION:

Viola, Herman J. *An American Warrior: Ben Nighthorse Campbell.* New York: Orion Books, 1993.

CANASSATEGO
Onondaga
c. 1690–1750

Canassatego was *tadadaho* (speaker) of the Iroquois Confederacy in the middle of the eighteenth century and a major figure in diplomacy with the French and English colonists. His advice that the colonies should form a union on the Iroquois model influenced the plans of Benjamin FRANKLIN for colonial union as early as 1754. Later in the century, a fictional Canassatego became a figure in English social satire and other literature.

Canassatego. [Courtesy of John Kahionhes Fadden]

In 1744, Pennsylvania officials met with Iroquois sachems in council at Lancaster, Pennsylvania. This meeting was one of a number of significant diplomatic parlays between British colonists, the Iroquois, and their allies. It preceded and helped shape the outcome of the French and Indian War. At the meeting, Canassatego and other Iroquois complained that the colonies, with no central authority, had been unable to restrain invasion of Native lands by settlers. In that context, Canassatego advised the colonists to form a union emulating that of the Iroquois:

> Our wise forefathers established Union and Amity between the Five Nations. This has made us formidable; this has given us great Weight and Authority with our neighboring Nations. We are a powerful Confederacy; and by your observing the same methods our wise forefathers have taken, you will acquire such Strength and power. Therefore whatever befalls you, never fall out with one another. [Grinde and Johansen]

Richard Peters, delegate from Pennsylvania, described Canassatego at Lancaster as "a tall, well-made man," with "a very full chest and brawny limbs, a manly countenance, with a good-natired [sic] smile. He was about 60 years of age, very active, strong, and had a surprising liveliness in his speech." [Grinde and Johansen]

At the time of the Lancaster Treaty Council, Franklin, a Philadelphia printer, was publishing the transcripts of Indian treaty councils as small booklets, which enjoyed a lively sale in the colonies and in England. The Lancaster Treaty was one of several dozen treaty accounts that he published between 1736 and 1762. Franklin read Canassatego's words as they issued from his press; he became an advocate of colonial union by the early 1750s, when he began his diplomatic career as a Pennsylvania delegate to the Iroquois and their allies. In a letter to his printing partner, James Parker, in 1751, Franklin urged the British colonies to unite in emulation of the Iroquois Confederacy, and he drew up his Albany Plan of Union in 1754.

After he advised colonial leaders to form a federal union at the Lancaster Treaty Council of 1744, Canassatego also became a British literary figure, the hero of John Shebbeare's *Lydia, or, Filial Piety*, published in 1755. The real Canassatego had died in 1750. With the flowery eloquence prized by romantic novelists of his time, Shebbeare portrayed Canassatego as something more than human—something more, even, than the "Noble Savage" that was so popular in Enlightenment Europe. Having saved the life of a helpless English maiden from the designs of a predatory English ship captain en route, Canassatego, once in England, becomes judge and jury for all that is contradictory and corrupt in mid–eighteenth-century England.

Canassatego's words echoed to the eve of the American Revolution, amplified by Franklin's talents as author and publisher. In 1775, Canassatego's thirty-one-year-old advice was recalled at a treaty between colonial representatives and Iroquois leaders near Albany. The treaty commissioners told the sachems that they were heeding the advice Iroquois forefathers had given to the colonial Americans at Lancaster, Pennsylvania, in 1744. At this point, the commissioners quoted Canassatego's words:

> Brethren, We the Six Nations heartily recommend Union and a good agreement between you our Brethren, never disagree but preserve a strict Friendship for one another and thereby you as well as we will become stronger. Our Wise Forefathers established Union and Amity between the Five Nations. . . . We are a powerful Confederacy, and if you observe the same methods . . . you will acquire fresh strength and power. [Grinde and Johansen]

FOR MORE INFORMATION:

Boyd, Julian. "Dr. Franklin, Friend of the Indian." In *Meet Dr. Franklin*, edited by Ray Lokken, Jr. Philadelphia: Franklin Institute, 1981.

Grinde, Donald A., Jr., and Bruce E. Johansen. *Exemplar of Liberty: Native America and the Evolution of Democracy.* Berkeley and Los Angeles: University of California Press, 1991.

Van Doren, Carl, and Julian P. Boyd, eds. *Indian Treaties Printed by Benjamin Franklin 1736–1762.* Philadelphia: Historical Society of Pennsylvania, 1938.

Wallace, Paul A. W. *Indians in Pennsylvania.* Harrisburg: Pennsylvania Historical and Museum Commission, 1961.

CANONCHET
Narraganset
c. 1630–1676

Son of MIANTINOMO, Canonchet was a leader in and casualty of King Philip's War. Canonchet was pressured by the Puritans to surrender refugee Wampanoags, and he even signed a treaty indicating he would, though he told his followers he would not. The Narragansets were reluctant to join Metacom but took an active part in King Philip's War after December 19, 1675, when a force of about one thousand colonial soldiers attacked Canonchet's village, killing as many as six hundred Native people. Warriors fought hand-to-hand with soldiers as fire swept through the village. According to the Puritan minister Cotton Mather, most of the Native people were "terribly Barbikew'd." Canonchet and some of his warriors escaped the carnage.

Later in King Philip's War, Canonchet offered refuge to Metacom, who hid in a swamp until he was captured then drawn and quartered. While sheltering Metacom and his warriors,

Canonchet's warriors obliterated a small invading force of colonial soldiers on March 26, 1676. In retaliation for this act of friendship to Metacom, Puritan forces under Captain Benjamin Church again burned Canonchet's village, killing all the women and children in it. Most of the men were taken prisoner. Canonchet himself was turned over to colonists in Stonington, Connecticut, who offered him freedom if he would order his warriors to lay down their arms. Canonchet refused, saying, "I shall die before my heart is soft, or I have done anything unworthy of myself." [Peirce] After his refusal to surrender, Canonchet was turned over to Mo-hawks and Pequots—his traditional enemies—who beheaded him then presented his dismem-bered head to the governor of Connecticut at Hartford.

FOR MORE INFORMATION:

Peirce, Ebenezer Weaver. *Indian History, Biography, and Genealogy Pertaining to the Good Sachem Massasoit.* Freeport, N.Y.: Books for Libraries, 1972.

CANONICUS
Narraganset
c. 1560–1647

Canonicus was one of the earliest major Native American leaders to observe the settlements of the English Puritans in New England. He also was a major source of support for the dissident Roger WILLIAMS in his struggle to establish an independent egalitarian colony in Providence Plantations, later renamed Rhode Island.

When the Pilgrims arrived in New England, Canonicus nearly declared war on them. He sent to Plymouth a traditional declaration of war, a bundle of arrows in a rattlesnake skin. Governor William Bradford of the Plymouth colony answered this ultimatum with one of his own; he filled the rattlesnake skin with powder and shot and sent it back to Canonicus,

who refused to accept it to avert a possibly bloody war.

Williams became close to Canonicus, elderly leader of the Narragansets, as well as his Wampanoag counterpart MASSASOIT. With both men, Williams traveled the forest for days at a time, learning what he could of their languages, societies, and opinions. Canonicus regarded Williams nearly as a son. At their height, the Narragansets, with Canonicus as their most influential leader, held sway over the area from Narraganset Bay on the east to the Pawcatuck River on the west. The Narragansets were rarely warlike, but their large numbers (about four thousand men of warrior age in the early seventeenth century) usually prevented other Native nations from attacking them.

William Wood, in *New England's Prospect*, characterized the Narragansets as "the most numerous people in those parts, and the most rich also, and the most industrious, being a storehouse of all kinds . . . of merchandise." The Narragansets fashioned wampum in bracelets and pendants for many other Indian nations. They also made smoking pipes "much desired by our English tobacconists for their rarity, strength, handsomeness, and coolness." According to Wood's account, the Narragansets had never desired "to take part in any martial enterprise. But being incapable of a jeer, they rest secure under the conceit of their popularity, and seek rather to grow rich by industry than famous by deeds of chivalry." In this fashion, the Narragansets built a confederacy in which they supervised the affairs of Indian peoples throughout most of present-day Rhode Island and eastern Long Island, about thirty thousand Native people in the early seventeenth century.

When word reached Boston that the Pequots were urging other Indians, including Canonicus's Narragansets, to drive the Massachusetts

Bay settlements into the sea, the Massachusetts Council sent urgent pleas to Williams to use his "utmost and speediest Endeavors" to keep the Narragansets out of it. Within hours after the appeal arrived in the hands of an Indian runner, "scarce acquainting my wife," Williams boarded "a poor Canow & . . . cut through a stormie Wind and with great seas, euery [sic] minute in hazard of life to the Sachim's [Canonicus's] howse." After traveling thirty miles in the storm, Williams put into port in a Narraganset town larger than most of the English settlements of his day, knowing that the success or failure of the Pequot initiative might rest on whether he could dissuade his friends from joining them in the uprising.

Canonicus listened to Williams with Miantinomo at his side. The younger sachem was assuming the duties of leadership piecemeal as his father aged. The three men decided to seal an alliance, and within a few days, officials from Boston were double-timing through the forest to complete the necessary paperwork. Later, Williams also won alliances with the Mohegan and Massachusetts nations, swinging the balance of power against the Pequots and their allies. The Indians welcomed the Puritan deputies with a feast of white chestnuts and cornmeal with blackberries (hasty pudding, later a New England tradition) as Williams translated for both sides, sealing the alliance.

The Puritan deputies were awed at the size of the Narraganset town, as well as the size of the hall in which they negotiated the alliance. The structure, about fifty feet wide, was likened to a statehouse by the men from Boston. Canonicus, so old that he had to lie on his side during the proceedings, surprised the Puritans with his direct questions and shrewd answers. The treaty was finally sealed much to the relief of the Puritans, who thought the Narragansets

capable of fielding thirty thousand fighting men. Although they had only a sixth that number, the Narragansets still were capable of swinging the balance of power for or against the immigrants, who had been in America only sixteen years at the time.

FOR MORE INFORMATION:

Chapin, Howard H. *Sachems of the Narragansetts*. Providence: Rhode Island Historical Society, 1931.

Covey, Cyclone. *The Gentle Radical: A Biography of Roger Williams*. New York: Macmillan, 1966.

Guild, Reuben Aldridge. *Footprints of Roger Williams*. Providence, R.I.: Tibbetts & Preston, 1886.

Josephy, Alvin M., Jr. *The Patriot Chiefs*. New York: Viking, 1961.

Wood, William. *New England's Prospect*. Amherst: University of Massachusetts Press, 1977.

CAPTAIN JACK (KINTPUASH)
Modoc
c. 1837–1873

Kintpuash, called Captain Jack by Anglo colonists of California because he wore a uniform coat with brass buttons that was given to him by the army, played a major role as a leader in the Modoc War of 1872–1873. He was born at the Wa'chamshwash Village on the Lower Lost River near the California-Oregon border. Kintpuash's father was ambushed and slain by treacherous whites in the Ben Wright massacre of 1846. There is little knowledge of Kintpuash's life until he was twenty-five. We do know that his Modoc name, Kintpuash, meant "He Has Water Brash [pyrosis]."

The Modocs had little to do with Anglos until the advent of the California gold rush. Although the Modocs opposed white expansion into their lands, Captain Jack counseled peace and encouraged trade with the settlers living near Eureka, California, in the 1840s.

However, the gold rush accelerated tensions and hostilities in the 1850s until SCHONCHIN JIM, a Modoc chief, signed a treaty removing his band to a reservation in Oregon in 1864. Unfortunately, the area was also the traditional homeland of the Klamaths, who did not relish Modoc resettlement in Oregon. Realizing that the land in Oregon was insufficient, Captain Jack and his followers went back to California and requested a reservation there. Federal and state authorities denied their request. Subsequently, Anglo settlers began to insist on the removal of the Modocs in California. On November 28, 1872, federal forces invaded Captain Jack's camp and coerced him into consenting to removal. As tensions mounted at the meeting, violence broke out. SCARFACED CHARLEY, a Modoc leader angered by the army's behavior, refused to give up his gun, and shots were fired in the ensuing struggle. When the fighting stopped, eight soldiers and fifteen Modocs were dead.

Fearing reprisals, the Modocs under Captain Jack fled to the nearby Lava Beds of northern California, thinking they would be safe there. However, this was not to be the case. HOOKER JIM, another Modoc leader, and his people, encamped on the Oregon side of the Lost River, were under attack by white settlers at the same time. In their own retreat to the Lava Beds, they killed twelve whites in revenge. In this hostile environment, Modoc leaders Captain Jack, SCHONCHIN JOHN, and Hooker Jim prepared to defend themselves against an attack in the vast and inaccessible volcanic area. Captain Jack still counseled peace and negotiation, arguing that the government would ultimately win. However, more militant factions under Hooker Jim and Schonchin John outvoted him.

On January 13, 1873, U.S. Army troops moved into the Lava Beds to quell the Modoc uprising. On February 28, 1873, Captain Jack's cousin WINEMA—a Modoc woman married to a white man, Frank Riddle—and a peace delegation began talks with the rebellious Modocs. Hooker Jim and Schonchin John believed Captain Jack to be a coward for consenting to the talks, so they insisted that Captain Jack kill General Edward S. Canby, the head of the delegation, believing that American resolve would be damaged by Canby's death. Reluctantly, Captain Jack agreed to their terms, but only if the Modocs were refused amnesty and a return to their California homeland in the talks. At an April 11 meeting, Captain Jack at last shot Canby. In the ensuing melee, Reverend Eleazar Thomas was killed, and Albert Meachum, the Indian superintendent, was also severely wounded. Winema and her husband managed to escape with the remaining members of the peace party.

The government quickly fielded more troops and heavier weapons. The rugged lava rock terrain worked to the Modocs' advantage at first, but dissension among the Modoc leaders and harsh conditions weakened their position. Finally, when the Modocs quarreled among themselves and left the Lava Beds, the government secured their capture. Captain Jack surrendered in late May 1873. After a military trial in which Hooker Jim testified for the prosecution, Captain Jack, Schonchin John, and two other Modoc warriors were hanged on October 3, 1873.

Since the administration of President Ulysses S. Grant had instituted a peace policy toward Indians, the American people were stunned by the uprising and the consequent inhumanity and insensitivity. In the final analysis, white prejudice, Indian betrayal, greed, and an opportunistic press made a deplorable situation far worse. Employing over one thousand soldiers to fight a Modoc force that never numbered over fifty-three, the army incurred losses that totaled the dead at seven officers, thirty-nine soldiers, two scouts, and sixteen civilians. The Modoc dead numbered eleven women and seven men. The enormous human and fiscal cost in capturing and removing 155 Modocs to Indian Territory seemed ridiculous. This bloody affair produced no glory for the army or the Modocs. A few did manage to profit from the war: a staged melodrama entitled *Captain Jack* ran for a brief time in 1873. In a more grisly venture, grave robbers dug up Captain Jack's body one day after his execution, embalmed it, and put it on display in a carnival sideshow that toured profitably in many eastern cities.

In 1909, fifty-one of the Oklahoma Modocs were permitted to return to their reservation in Oregon.

CARR, PADDY
Mixed Creek
1808–c. 1840

As the name aptly indicates, Paddy Carr was the son of an Irishman married to a Creek woman. Born near Fort Mitchell, Alabama, he was reared by Colonel John Crowell, the Creek Indian agent. It was in the Crowell household that he acquired his knowledge of English. An intelligent boy, young Paddy retained his knowledge of Creek as well.

In 1826, he accompanied a Creek delegation led by OPOTHLEYAHOLO to Washington, D.C., for a meeting with President John Quincy Adams on the question of Creek removal; this parlay resulted in the Treaty of Washington. Shortly thereafter, Carr wed the daughter of a wealthy Creek mixed-blood, thus procuring a considerable dowry to launch a career as a trader and

planter. By 1837, he possessed some eighty slaves, a large-landed estate, and a sizable amount of livestock and horses. He was fond of horse racing, and it is said that he often rode his own horses during races. Eventually, he took two more wives (one of them the daughter of Creek leader William McINTOSH). His wives and large family lived on a plantation on the Chattahoochee River.

When Creek hostilities flared in 1836, Carr was drawn out of his agricultural pursuits to serve as an interpreter and guide for the U.S. Army under General Thomas Jesup. During the Second Seminole War in 1836, Carr marched to Florida and was second in command of about five hundred Creek volunteers in an expedition against the Seminoles and their Creek traditionalist supporters. Although Carr rendered invaluable service to the American cause, relocation to Oklahoma was, nevertheless, forced upon him in 1837.

CARSON, CHRISTOPHER "KIT"
("ROPE THROWER")
1809–1868

Soon after his birth in Kentucky on December 24, 1809, Christopher "Kit" Carson, who would become famous as an army officer, trader, guide, scout, and Indian agent, moved with his family to the Missouri frontier. At sixteen, he abandoned his training as an apprentice saddler and went west on a caravan bound for Santa Fe, New Mexico. Roaming the Rocky Mountains from 1827 to 1842, he became a prominent fur trapper and trader in the Southwest.

During this time, Carson acquired a great deal of firsthand knowledge about the American Indians in the Far West, since he lived for lengthy periods with them. They called him "Rope Thrower"; WASHAKIE, the well-known Shoshone chief, was a good friend. Because he was so knowledgeable about the Indian nations and the geography of the West, he was recruited in 1842 as a guide for John C. Frémont's explorations in California and Oregon.

Carson took an Arapaho wife, who died in childbirth though their daughter survived. His second wife was a Cheyenne woman, who divorced him a few years later. In 1843, he took a third wife, Maria Josefa Jaramillo, scion of an affluent trading family in Taos, New Mexico.

In 1849, Carson returned to northern New Mexico and engaged in sheepherding. He also scouted for the U.S. Army in 1849, pursuing Ute and Jicarilla Apache warriors raiding up and down the Santa Fe Trail. From 1853 to 1861, he was Indian agent to the Mouache Utes and Jicarilla Apaches in spite of the fact that he could neither read nor write. During the 1850s, Carson participated in several campaigns against the Navajos, Apaches, and Kiowas.

At the start of the Civil War, he quit his job as Indian agent to become colonel of the New Mexico volunteers. William Arny succeeded him as agent to the Utes and Jicarillas. In 1861–1862, he engaged in military operations that sought to pacify the Navajos and Mescalero Apaches. By the end of 1862, Carson had obtained the surrender of the remaining rebellious Mescaleros; he then resettled them to Bosque Redondo (Fort Sumner, New Mexico). By early 1864, Carson was leading forces against Navajos reluctant to relocate to Fort Sumner. At the Navajo bulwark in Canyon de Chelly, Carson attacked the Navajos led by MANUELITO. After decimating the Navajo stronghold, Carson ravaged Navajo livestock and crops, thus coercing the surrender of thousands of Navajos. Carson then relocated the Navajos to Fort Sumner, where they remained until 1868.

Carson also distinguished himself in repelling a Confederate invasion of New Mexico. In

November 1864, Carson commanded an assault on Kiowa and Comanche forces at the Battle of Adobe Walls. When Carson's detachment of New Mexico volunteers and Ute and Jicarilla Apaches destroyed the Indian village, he discovered that he was outmanned during an ensuing counterattack. Two small howitzers saved the day for Carson's forces when they fired grapeshot at their adversaries, enabling an orderly retreat with limited Union losses.

Just after the Civil War's conclusion, Carson became a brigadier general (brevetted) in the U.S. Army for his valor. After having a brief command of U.S. forces at Fort Garland, Colorado, Carson retired in 1867. The next year, he passed away at Fort Lyon, Colorado, already a legendary figure.

CATAHECASSA
Shawnee
c. 1740–1831

The Shawnee orator, principal chief, and war chief Catahecassa (meaning "Black Hoof") was probably born in Florida and then forced to emigrate northward in the face of white expansion. He sided with the French in the French and Indian War. Catahecassa's forces contributed to the defeat of General Edward Braddock's troops in 1755 in western Pennsylvania. Later, he also allied with PONTIAC in 1763 during his rebellion. His youthful successes in war made him the principal chief of the Shawnee in later years.

During Lord Dunmore's War in 1774, his warriors aided in the defeat of colonial forces at Point Pleasant. During the American Revolution, Catahecassa sided with the English. In LITTLE TURTLE's War of 1790–1794, Catahecassa fought American troops with another Shawnee leader, BLUE JACKET.

After the American victory at the Battle of Fallen Timbers, he became an advocate of peace and reconciliation with the Americans. He was one of the signatories of the Fort Greenville Treaty of 1795, which ceded land in the Old Northwest. Like Wyandot leader TARHE, he did not back TECUMSEH and his Indian barrier state strategies in 1809–1811. Known as a renowned and talented speaker, Catahecassa died of old age near Wapakoneta, Ohio.

FOR MORE INFORMATION:

Carter, Harvey Lewis. *The Life and Times of Little Turtle.* Urbana: University of Illinois Press, 1987.

CATLIN, GEORGE
1796–1872

An artist whose paintings of the frontier world serve as historical resources a century later, George Catlin was born in 1796 at Wilkes-Barre, Pennsylvania. As a youth, Catlin studied to become a lawyer, and he passed the Pennsylvania bar examination in 1818. By 1820, however, he had set up an artist's studio and was beginning his career as a painter. A visit by several Native American leaders to Philadelphia in 1824 stirred Catlin's interest in painting Indian portraits. The first notable Native leader that he painted may have been RED JACKET, in 1826.

Catlin traveled to St. Louis in 1830 and became friends with explorer William Clark, who was an Indian agent there. For several years thereafter, Catlin traveled the Midwest painting Native portraits. During the late 1830s, while painting portraits in Minnesota, Catlin was the first non-Indian to observe the mining of a previously unknown (to whites) variety of pipestone, which was later named "catlinite" after him. By the late 1830s, Catlin had assembled about six hundred paintings for exhibition. Catlin had hoped to sell the paintings to the U.S. government to begin a national Indian museum, but this possibility was foreclosed by his criticism of government policies toward Indians. In 1839, Catlin exhibited his collection in Europe to considerable critical praise.

In 1852, Catlin went bankrupt and lost many of his paintings, as well as a collection of artifacts, to creditors. By the end of the decade, Catlin had improved his financial condition to the point where he was able to take up traveling and painting again, this time in Central and South America, the far Northwest, and Alaska. Catlin returned to the United States in 1870 and died in Jersey City, New Jersey.

Catlin was a trenchant social commentator as well as an artist. He said, recapitulating words spoken in an earlier century by Benjamin FRANKLIN and Thomas PAINE, and later in the nineteenth century by Friedrich Engels:

> I love a people who have always made me welcome to the best they had . . . who are honest . . . who have no jails and no poorhouses . . . who never take the name of God in vain . . . who worship God without a Bible, and I believe that God loves them also . . . who are free from religious animosities . . . who have never raised a hand against me, or stolen my property, where there was no law to punish either . . . who never fought a battle with white men except on their own ground. . . . and, oh, how I love a people who don't live for the love of money. [Catlin]

Catlin watched the devastation of Native peoples by disease. Epidemics swept many villages as he visited: "merely to sympathize with them (and but partially to do that) when they are dying at our hands . . . would be to subvert the simplist law of nature, and turn civilized man, with all his boasted virtues, back to worse than savage barbarism." [Catlin]

FOR MORE INFORMATION:

Armstrong, Virginia Irving, ed. *I Have Spoken: American History Through the Voices of the Indians.* Chicago: Swallow Press, 1971.

Catlin, George. *North American Indians, Being Letters and Notes on Their Manners, Customs, Written During Eight Years' Travel.* Edinburgh: John Grant, 1933.

Haberly, Lloyd. *Pursuit of the Horizon: A Life of George Catlin.* New York: Macmillan, 1944.

McCracken, Harold. *George Catlin and the Old Frontier.* New York: Dial Press, 1959.

Moquin, Wayne, ed. *Great Documents in American Indian History.* New York: Praeger, 1973.

CHAMPAGNE, DUANE
Turtle Mountain Chippewa
1951–

As an author, professor of sociology, editor of the *American Indian Culture & Research Journal,* and director of the American Indian Studies Center at the University of California at Los Angeles, Duane Champagne has helped shape many influential publications about Native America. Champagne is author of two books, *American Indian Societies: Strategies and Conditions for Political and Cultural Survival* (1989) and *Social Order and Political Change: Constitutional Governments Among the Cherokee, the Choctaw, the Chickasaw, and the Creek* (1992). He completed a master's degree in sociology at North Dakota State University in 1975 and a Ph.D. in the same field at Harvard University in 1982.

Champagne began his full-time college teaching career in 1983 at the University of Wisconsin (Milwaukee), after spending a year on a Rockefeller Foundation award among the Tlinget. Champagne began teaching at UCLA in 1984, and in 1986 he became editor of UCLA's *American Indian Culture & Research Journal.* In 1991, he was appointed as director of UCLA's American Indian Studies Center, which publishes the journal as well as books. Champagne was also general editor of *The Native North American Almanac,* published in 1994 by Gale Research of Detroit.

CHARBONNEAU, JEAN BAPTISTE ("POMP")
Shoshoni
1805–1866

Jean Baptiste Charbonneau was born February 11, 1805, son of French Canadian Toussaint CHARBONNEAU and SACAJAWEA, his Shoshoni wife, while both served as guides for the Lewis and Clark expedition as it passed among the Mandans. The infant boy was nicknamed "Pomp." Sacajawea carried him on her back for the rest of the expedition.

After 1806, Charbonneau was taken under the care of William Clark, who had become an Indian agent in St. Louis after the expedition. The young man attended Catholic schools; in 1823, he traveled to Europe with Prince Paul Wilhelm of Germany and spent six years traveling the Continent and studying languages. Charbonneau returned to the United States in 1829 with Prince Wilhelm. Together, they explored the upper Missouri River watershed. Charbonneau later was employed as a trapper in the Rocky Mountains by the American Fur Company. He became friends with several well-known mountain men of the time, including Jim Bridger, and attended a famous mountaineers' rendezvous on the Green River of Wyoming in 1833.

As the fur trade exhausted animal stocks, Charbonneau became a guide for government officials and some European dignitaries. He died on the Owyhee River, near the spot where the borders of Oregon, Idaho, and Nevada would later meet.

FOR MORE INFORMATION:

Hebard, Grace Raymond. *Sacajawea. With an Account of the Travels of Toussaint Charbonneau.* Glendale, Calif.: Arthur H. Clark, 1933.

CHARBONNEAU, TOUSSAINT
c. 1760–c. 1840

Toussaint Charbonneau, a French-Canadian trader, joined the Lewis and Clark expedition with his wife, the Shoshoni SACAJAWEA, and provided invaluable guidance for nineteen months as the expedition crossed the Rocky Mountains and reached the Pacific Coast near Astoria, Oregon. Charbonneau's particular talent was interpretation—he provided communication with many Native American peoples whom Lewis and Clark encountered on the expedition. For nineteen months of work, Charbonneau and Sacajawea were paid $500.33.

After the expedition, Charbonneau was instrumental in convincing many Native tribes in the Missouri Valley to back the United States in the War of 1812. He was a well-known guide for several government parties and visiting dignitaries until late in a life that included marriages to many Native American wives, the most famous of whom was Sacajawea.

FOR MORE INFORMATION:

Hebard, Grace Raymond. *Sacajawea. With an Account of the Travels of Toussaint Charbonneau.* Glendale, Calif.: Arthur H. Clark, 1933.

CHARLOT, ELDER
Flathead/Salish
fl. mid-1800s

Old Charlot was among the Flathead/Salish people in the Bitterroot Mountains of Montana who took up farming on U.S. government instructions. Their land was fertile, and the farms became productive. Non-Indians, noting the success of the Indians, later moved to take over their farms during the early 1890s. Martin CHARLOT (son of the chief Old Charlot) was among Flathead/Salish who were forced to move to less fertile land on the Pend d'Oreille Reservation.

Old Charlot said that the tribe's land was guaranteed to them by a treaty signed in 1855. "A general who was with Garfield spoke up and told my father that he would send an army in there and kill us if we didn't move." [Armstrong]

In 1870, an embittered Old Charlot spoke of the whites he knew whose presence had been growing in the Bitterroot Valley for seventy years:

We were happy when he first came, . . . [but now] to take and to lie should be burned on his forehead, as he burns the sides of my stolen horses with his own name. . . . He has filled graves with our bones. . . . The white man fathers this doom—yes, this curse on us and on the few that may see a few days more. . . . He says one of his virgins had a son nailed to death on two cross sticks to save him. Were all of them dead when that young man died, we would all be safe now, and our country our own. [Armstrong]

FOR MORE INFORMATION:

Armstrong, Virginia Irving, ed. *I Have Spoken: American History Through the Voices of the Indians.* Chicago: Swallow Press, 1971.

CHARLOT, MARTIN, YOUNGER
Flathead/Salish
1831–1900

Martin Charlot was among Flathead/Salish people in the Bitterroot Mountains of Montana who created fertile farms only to have them seized by immigrants. In the early 1890s, Charlot (son of the chief Old CHARLOT) was among Flathead/Salish who were told to move to less fertile land on the Pend d'Oreille Reservation. The dissident band of Flathead/Salish people led by Charlot delayed relocation for several years. Charlot even traveled to Washington, D.C., in 1884 with Indian agent Peter Ronan to discuss the issue. Charlot still refused to cooperate in removal to a reservation. As whites enveloped their homeland, many of Charlot's followers moved in the 1880s; but he and a few followers held out until 1900, when they were removed by force during the same year that Charlot died.

Martin Charlot.
[National Anthropological Archives]

Charlot recalled: "Everything was going fine. We were making a good living and learning the White Man's way. . . . Garfield [an Indian agent] told my father that he would have to move out of the Bitterroot. 'I am doing some farming,' my father said. 'I am getting good crops and my people and I are living here as agents and priests have taught us to do. I am not going to move.' " [Nabokov]

FOR MORE INFORMATION:

Nabokov, Peter. *Native American Testimony.* New York: Viking Penguin, 1991.

CHATO (ALFRED CHATO, CHATTO)
Chiricahua Apache
c. 1860–1934

Chato, a leader in the Apache Wars of 1881–1886, accompanied GERONIMO when both left the San Carlos Reservation in 1881, disgruntled with U.S. policies. They headed for the Sierra Madre region in Mexico. By 1882, Chato returned periodically to the United States with Geronimo to engage in several raids. When Geronimo and his followers went south to Sonora, Mexico, looking for cattle and other foodstuffs in March 1883, Chato and another leader, Benito, went north into present-day Arizona seeking ammunition and other supplies with about two dozen men. Chato and his men, before they went back to Mexico, killed about a dozen Anglos while on this expedition. General George Crook responded to these raids by attacking Chato's stronghold in Mexico in May 1883. These tactics did not deter Chato's forays throughout 1883; but by the next year, in February 1884, Chato and about sixty Apaches were forced to surrender. By the next month, Geronimo and a force of eighty men capitulated as well.

In 1885, Geronimo, disliking policies toward his band of Chiricahuas, left the reservation again. Chato balked at following him this time and instead attempted to persuade Geronimo to stay. By 1886, Chato was helping Crook pursue Geronimo in Mexico with the aid of other scouts such as Mickey FREE, KAYATENNAE, and ALCHESAY. As a leader of the Apache delegation to Washington, D.C., in 1886, Chato begged for the captured Apaches' right to stay in their native land.

In spite of his aid in capturing Geronimo, Chato was forced to go to Florida with some of the Apache prisoners that he had pursued. As a result, he relinquished his livestock and land at the San Carlos Reservation. Tragically, his children were all forced to go to the Carlisle Indian School by the U.S. government, where they died. Eventually, Chato came back to New Mexico, where he resided on the Mescalero Apache Reservation. In 1934, an automobile accident took his life.

CHICAGO (CHIKAGOU)
Illinois
fl. early 1800s

The man for whom Chicago, Illinois, is named made his reputation by visiting France in 1725 at the behest of Jesuits who had converted him to Catholicism and wanted him to raise money for their missionary efforts. Chicago remained a firm ally of the French throughout his life, even though many other Native people refused to believe his enthusiastic portrayals of the wonders of life in Paris.

CHICKHONSIC (LITTLE BUFFALO)
Winnebago
fl. 1820s

Following a surge in illegal immigration of lead miners onto Winnebago land in southwestern Wisconsin, Chickhonsic, along with WEKAU and RED BIRD, led a brief insurgency in 1827. Chickhonsic was convicted of murder but pardoned as a peace gesture by President John Quincy Adams in 1828.

The Winnebagos had supported TECUMSEH and the British in the War of 1812, as their mixed-blood chief DECORA (also known as Konoka) led Winnebago warriors in British campaigns at Sandusky River and the Battle of the Thames. Following the war, most Winnebagos remained under British influence. They were generally unfriendly to the Americans who began to flood their territory.

The Winnebagos' anger rose when U.S. officials forbade their sale of lead to traders—the same trade that whites were carrying out illegally on their land. This, and widespread abuse of Winnebago women by white frontiersmen, led the Winnebagos' headmen to seek vengeance. Red Bird was selected to seek revenge for the offenses. Red Bird, Wekau, and Chickhonsic entered the trading town of Prairie du Chien on June 26, 1827. In an unplanned incident, Red Bird shot trader Registre Gagnier in his cabin. Chickhonsic also killed Solomon Lipcap, another trader, during the fray. Wekau had his rifle taken from him by Gagnier's wife. Enraged, he scalped her eleven-month-old infant, who somehow survived the incident. On June 30, a party of Winnebagos, drunk on whiskey, ambushed the keelboat *O. H. Perry* near the mouth of the Bad Axe River, killing two whites. The whites on the keelboat said they killed a dozen Winnebagos in retaliation.

The Winnebago chiefs urged a number of neighboring Native peoples to rise up with them, but few responded. The area was flooded with U.S. Army troops as well as militia composed of white miners. On February 16, 1828, Red Bird died in prison of dysentery and a general lack of will to live. In September 1828, the other two leaders were found guilty of being accomplices to Red Bird in the murder of Gagnier; Wekau was convicted of assault and battery with intent to kill the Gagnier infant. Chickhonsic was convicted of murdering Lipcap. They were sentenced to hang but were later pardoned by President John Quincy Adams, who was seeking peace with a delegation of Winnebagos in Washington, D.C., at the time.

CHILD, LYDIA MARIA FRANCIS
1802–1880

Pressure to broaden civil rights for women grew early in the nineteenth century at roughly the same time as the abolitionist movement against slavery. Although the landmark Seneca Falls conference, usually credited with beginning the modern feminist movement in the United States, was not held until 1848, the ideological basis for the movement was set down by Lydia Maria Child in her *History of the Condition of Women, in Various Ages and Nations,* published in 1835. Child's book used the Iroquois and Huron cultures to counterpose notions of European patriarchy, illustrating the importance of Native American women in political decision making.

According to Professor Gail Landsman of the State University of New York at Albany, "Child's work was mined extensively by later suffragists, including Matilda Joslyn GAGE, who furthered Child's concept of Indian culture as a matriarchal alternative to American white patriarchy through her contact with the Iroquois." With Elizabeth Cady STANTON and Susan B. Anthony, Gage coauthored the landmark *History of Woman Suffrage.*

FOR MORE INFORMATION:

Child, Lydia Maria. *Hobomok and Other Writings on Indians.* Edited by Carolyn L. Karcher. New Brunswick, N.J.: Rutgers University Press, 1986.

––––––. *Selected Letters, 1817–1880.* Edited by Milton Meltzer and Patricia G. Holland. Amherst: University of Massachusetts Press, 1982.

CHISHOLM, JESSE
Mixed Cherokee
c. 1805–1868

Born in Tennessee of a Scottish trader father and a Cherokee mother, Chisholm emigrated to Arkansas about 1816, settling near Fort Smith, Arkansas, with a band of Cherokees. As a young man, Chisholm became involved in the fur trade with the Osages, Comanches, Kiowas, and Wichitas as well as other tribes in the region that would soon be constituted into Indian Territory. He soon became known as a trader and interpreter; his name remains on the Chisholm Trail.

Because of his trade contacts, his familiarity with the terrain, and his linguistic abilities (it is reputed that he spoke fourteen Indian languages), Chisholm became a guide and interpreter for many expeditions of the U.S. military. Chisholm and the Delaware BLACK BEAVER were in the employ of General Henry Leavenworth and Colonel Henry Dodge's 1834 western expedition. They were interpreters at councils with Kiowas, Wichitas, and Comanches. During negotiations at Fort Concho, Texas, in 1846, Chisholm served as a government interpreter to the Southern Plains tribes.

Chisholm ran three trading posts in Indian Territory (Oklahoma City, Lexington, and Camp Holmes). At the outbreak of the Civil War, he worked for the Confederacy and then accompanied OPOTHLEYAHOLO's band to Wichita, Kansas, to maintain his neutrality. He was married to the daughter of James Edward, an Anglo trader, and had thirteen children.

At the end of the Civil War in 1865, Chisholm drove a load of trade goods from Kansas through Indian Territory to the Red River country in Texas to trade with tribes in the vicinity. Returning with a wagon of buffalo hides, cutting ruts in the prairie, he instituted the famous Chisholm Trail, along which Texas longhorns by the thousands were herded from central Texas to marketplaces and railheads like Abilene, Kansas, through the 1880s.

Chisholm continued his work at Indian treaties; the signing of treaties at both Little

Arkansas in 1865 and Medicine Lodge in 1867 were facilitated by him. In 1868, he died at Left Hand Spring near present-day Oklahoma City.

CHITTO HARJO
Creek
1846–1912

Chitto Harjo, whose name comes from the Creek *chitto*, meaning "recklessly brave or foolhardy," and *harjo*, meaning "snake," became a leader in the 1901 Snake uprising in Indian Territory, later called Oklahoma. Born in Indian Territory near what would become Boley, Oklahoma, Chitto Harjo was a noted traditionalist and advocate of tribal restoration and sovereignty. He resisted the tribal enrollment of Creeks by the federal government as well as the General Allotment Act of 1887, which called for the fragmentation of tribal lands into fee simple deeds for individuals and paved the way for Oklahoma statehood.

Harjo and others believed that these policies undermined the old land tenure system of the Creeks, in which all tribal lands were held in common, as well as their political structure. With other traditionalist Creeks (calling themselves Snakes), Harjo established his own Snake government in 1897 to deter such assimilationist policies. Their capital was at Hickory Ground, Oklahoma, where they created a legislative and judicial branch and other legal mechanisms that bolstered their independence.

In January 1901, some of Harjo's followers attacked Indians who had accepted allotments and began to intimidate white settlers in the region. Federal authorities mounted an offensive against the Snakes and arrested Chitto Harjo. Although in February 1901 Harjo was tried and found guilty for his actions, he was allowed to return home.

Chitto Harjo and his traditionalist Creeks then shifted their resistance to legal actions;

they hired Anglo attorneys and lobbied the U.S. Congress. In 1906, he testified before the Senate Committee on Land Treaties protesting allotment policies. In spite of his continued efforts, Oklahoma became a state and the allotment policy remained in force.

Soon after statehood, the Snakes revolted again in an action called the Smoked Meat Rebellion. Anglo police, in their search for the alleged thief of a thousand pounds of smoked bacon, interrupted a council of Creek fullbloods at Hickory Hills. Tempers flared and violence erupted, wounding a white man, killing a Creek, and resulting in the arrest of forty Snakes. With whites becoming hysterical, the police returned to arrest even more Snakes. Shots were fired, and Harjo, with a small band of followers, escaped into the backcountry. For two years, he lived in the hills as a fugitive, only coming to small towns occasionally. In one attempt to arrest him, he was wounded but again escaped into the hills. He died April 11, 1912, near Smithville, Oklahoma, at a friend's house where he had taken refuge.

As a militant advocate of traditional ways, Harjo used his remarkable oratorical skills to galvanize resistance against Anglo encroachment in Indian Territory. Although he appeared to be a renegade in the eyes of white authorities, he was a man of courage and conviction in his pursuit of justice and self-determination for his people.

CHRYSTOS
Menominee
1946–

As a poet, and as a gay and Native American activist, Chrystos enraged Senator Jesse Helms after she published poems describing lesbian love in a book that acknowledges support from the National Endowment of the Arts. Chrystos, who read her poetry on nationwide tours in the 1990s, was born in San Francisco of a Menominee father and a Lithuanian and Alsace-Lorrainian mother. By the mid-1990s, she had published several volumes of poetry, including *Not Vanishing* and *Dream On.* She has also been active in several Native American political issues, notably the campaign to free Leonard PELTIER.

CLERMONT
Osage
fl. early 1800s

In 1802, Clermont, a principal chief of the Arkansas River Osage, led a group of Osages from western Missouri and resettled them farther west along the Arkansas River in present-day northeastern Oklahoma and southeastern Kansas. During his life, Clermont was known by many names including Clermore, Claremore, Clermos, Tawagahe or Tawhangage ("Town Builder"), Gra-Mo'n ("Arrow Going Home"), and Manka-Chonka ("Black Dog").

WHITE HAIR carried on as the chief of the remaining band in Missouri. Because of increased pressures from growing numbers of Anglo settlers and traders in their ancestral lands, the traditional ways of the Osages were threatened by increasing white influence. In this environment, Clermont deplored alcohol abuse and dependence on white trade goods by the Osages. His efforts to restrict the sale of liquor and continue traditional practices fostered peace and prosperity for his band of Osages. As a result, the name Clermont was also used by subsequent Osage chiefs.

CLOUD, HENRY ROE (WONAH'ILAY-HUNKA)
Winnebago
1884–1950

Henry Roe Cloud's Winnebago name was Wonah'ilayhunka, meaning "War Chief." Con-trary to that name, Roe fused Native and Euro-American cultures in a peaceful way as an educator and as a reformer of U.S. government policies toward Native Americans.

Born in Thurston County, Nebraska, to full-blooded Winnebago parents, Roe knew almost nothing of non-Indian life until his teenage years. Cloud's English name was borrowed from Reverend and Mrs. Walter C. Roe, who shaped his desire for education. In 1910, he was the first Native American student to earn a degree from Yale University; in 1914, he also earned a master's degree there.

In 1915, Roe established the American Indian Institute in Wichita, Kansas, where he educated Native young men for thirteen years. This school was notable because it prepared Native Americans for college at a time when all other schools offered them only vocational (often called industrial) training. Roe married Elizabeth G. Bender, sister of baseball pitcher Charles Albert BENDER. Mrs. Bender Roe Cloud had attended Hampton Institute, the University of Wichita, and the University of Kansas. She worked with her husband for many years with the National Congress of American Indians and the Society of American Indians.

Roe became the only Native American member of the Institute for Government Research (later called the Brookings Institution); there, in 1926, he helped to initiate the Meriam Report, which documented miserable conditions on many Indian reservations. In 1933, he became the first Native American to preside over the Haskell Institute. Roe also held several posts in the Bureau of Indian Affairs and advised several government committees on Indian affairs. He died while serving as superintendent of the Umatilla Reservation Agency in Oregon.

FOR MORE INFORMATION:

Gridley, Marion. *Indians of Today.* Chicago: Millar Publishing, 1947.

COCHISE (HARDWOOD)
Chiricahua Apache
c. 1823–1874

Cochise, a major leader in the Apache wars of the 1870s, was the son of an Apache chief. After his father's death, Cochise became the leader of his father's band.

In the early 1800s, the Apaches had been victimized by unscrupulous Mexican and Spanish scalp hunters and slavers in what would become Arizona and New Mexico and were driven from some of their lands. By the 1850s, the Chiricahua Apaches had granted safe passage to Americans going to California, and some of Cochise's people worked for a stagecoach at Apache Pass.

But these peaceful relations were ended by the pointless actions of the U.S. military. During the 1860s, Cochise waged a formidable military campaign to retain the traditional homelands of the Apaches. In 1861, Cochise was summoned to see Lieutenant George N. Bascom at Apache Pass; a rancher had accused Cochise of stealing cattle and kidnapping an Anglo settler's child named Mickey FREE. Along with members of his family, including his son NAICHE, Cochise came to meet with Bascom under a flag of truce. Bascom accused Cochise of the earlier raid. Although Cochise denied any wrongdoing, Bascom attempted to arrest him. A fight resulted and Cochise was badly wounded. However, he slashed his way through the tent with a knife and managed to escape. One Apache was killed, and Bascom took the others hostage. In the next few days, Cochise took a number of whites as prisoners, offering them in exchange for the Apache captives. When Cochise's negotiations broke down with Bascom, both sides killed their hostages.

The Bascom fiasco began the Apache wars. Under Cochise's father-in-law, MANGAS COL-ORADAS, the Mimbreno Apaches joined the Chiricahuas and the White Mountain (Coyotero) Apaches. During the early Civil War years, Apache depredations sought to drive both Mexican and Anglo-Americans from Arizona. In July 1862, three thousand California volunteers under Colonel James H. Carleton were sent to remedy the situation. Meanwhile, Mangas Coloradas and Cochise set a trap for the newly arrived troops. At Apache Pass, with about five hundred men behind fortifications, the Apaches held off the California forces until Carleton utilized howitzers against them. The Apaches then retreated to Mexico with a wounded Mangas Coloradas; Cochise got a Mexican surgeon to heal his father-in-law's wounds. The following year, Mangas Coloradas was captured and slain under a flag of truce by the Americans (his brain was shipped to the Smithsonian Institution). With the death of his father-in-law, Cochise became the leader of the rebellious Apaches.

For over a decade, Cochise and some two hundred warriors raided white settlements along the Butterfield Trail and adjacent areas from his stronghold in the Dragoon Mountains of southern Arizona. He resisted all efforts to exterminate him and his men.

In 1871, Colonel George Crook took command of the army's Department of Arizona. Realizing the futility of annihilatory warfare, Crook developed a group of highly effective Indian scouts who pursued Cochise in the rugged terrain of southern Arizona. When Cochise heard news that his band was to go to a reservation near Fort Tularosa, New Mexico, he refused to do so. As a result, General Oliver O. Howard, dispatched by President U. S. Grant, arranged a meeting with Cochise in fall 1872. After eleven days of deliberations, Howard gave in to Cochise's wishes to have a reservation along Apache Pass. Shortly after this meeting,

Cochise's two hundred men surrendered, and Cochise promised Howard to keep order along the pass. He remained peaceful until his death in 1874. TAZA, his oldest son, who became chief after Cochise's death, attempted to continue the peace agreement. But when Taza died, Naiche joined forces with Geronimo. In 1876, owing to these hostilities, the Chiricahua Reservation was dissolved.

All those who dealt with Cochise accorded him great respect. He was a powerfully built man who carried himself with dignity. In peaceful situations, he was mild mannered, but during war, he was capable of ferocity, great courage, and cruelty. Ultimately, he understood that a lasting peace was the only way to ensure the survival of his people in the Southwest.

CODY, WILLIAM FREDERICK ("BUFFALO BILL")
1846–1917

William Cody, the creator of Buffalo Bill's Wild West Show, was born near Davenport, Iowa, but moved at the age of eight to Kansas, where his father became embroiled in antislavery politics. When Cody was eleven, his father died of an attack motivated by his politics. The younger Cody then moved to Colorado, where he tried panning for gold and spent some time as a rider on the Pony Express. During the early 1860s, Cody began serving as a scout for the U.S. Army. The name "Buffalo Bill" was given to him by Union Pacific railway workers whom he supplied with buffalo meat under contract about 1866.

By 1868, Cody was working as an army scout again; he may have killed the Cheyenne leader TALL BULL. In the meantime, Edward Zane Carroll Judson was beginning to glorify Buffalo Bill's real and imagined exploits in the earliest of seventeen hundred dime novels. By 1872, Cody had taken advantage of the publicity to

become an entertainer. He engaged in Wild West shows staged by a number of army scouts who toured the urban areas of the eastern United States. Between show tours, Cody returned to work as an army scout. On July 17, 1876, Cody reportedly killed the Cheyenne chief YELLOW HAIR and scalped him.

By the early 1880s, the Indian wars were winding down, and Cody became a full-time showman with his own Wild West show. He was known as a benevolent employer as he became friends with some of the same Native leaders he had once pursued as a scout, particularly SITTING BULL.

William "Buffalo Bill" Cody poses with Sitting Bull. [Nebraska State Historical Society]

As tensions mounted in South Dakota in late 1890, Cody was asked by General Nelson Miles—an adversary of Standing Rock Indian agent James McLaughlin—to help mediate the conflict. But on his arrival in Nebraska on November 20, Cody was detained by associates of McLaughlin. McLaughlin had Cody's authority rescinded as he hurried along his own plans to arrest Sitting Bull, who was shot to death by Indian agency police on December 15.

FOR MORE INFORMATION:

Russell, Don. *The Lives and Legends of Buffalo Bill*. Norman: University of Oklahoma Press, 1960.

Sell, Henry B., and Victor Weybright. *Buffalo Bill and the Wild West*. New York: Oxford University Press, 1955.

COHEN, FELIX
1907–1953

Felix Cohen was the author of the *Handbook of Indian Law* (1942), a basic reference book of this field for decades. He was also a student of Native American societies and a social critic. On one occasion, Cohen compared Native American influence on immigrants from Europe to the ways in which the Greeks shaped Roman culture: "When the Roman legions conquered Greece, Roman historians wrote with as little imagination as did the European historians who have written of the white man's conquest of America. What the Roman historians did not see was that captive Greece would take captive conquering Rome [with] Greek science [and] Greek philosophy." [Cohen, "Americanizing"]

Cohen wrote that American historians had too often paid attention to military victories and changing land boundaries while failing to see that "in agriculture, in government, in sport, in education, and in our views of nature and our fellow men, it is the first Americans who have taken captive their battlefield conquerers." American historians "have seen America only as an imitation of Europe," Cohen asserted. In his view, "The real epic of

America is the yet unfinished story of the Americanization of the white man." [Cohen, "Americanizing"]

In 1952, Cohen argued:

It is out of a rich Indian democratic tradition that the distinctive political ideals of American life emerged. Universal suffrage for women as for men, the pattern of states that we call federalism, the habit of treating chiefs as servants of the people instead of their masters, the insistence that the community must respect the diversity of men and the diversity of their dreams—all these things were part of the American way of life before Columbus landed. [Cohen, "Americanizing"]

Cohen was a law professor at the City University of New York and Yale University. He also worked for the U.S. Department of the Interior as associate solicitor.

FOR MORE INFORMATION:

Cohen, Felix. "Americanizing the White Man." *The American Scholar* 21:2 (1952).

———. *Legal Conscience: Selected Papers of Felix S. Cohen*. Edited by Lucy Kramer Cohen. New Haven, Conn.: Yale University Press, 1960.

COLBERT, GEORGE
Mixed Chickasaw
1764–1839

Like his brother William COLBERT, George Colbert sided and fought with the Americans during the War of 1812. He had a large plantation and ferry near what would become Tupelo, Mississippi, with over 150 slaves. He was opposed to removal of the Chickasaws and protested the treaty of 1832 that called for it. When the Chickasaws were finally moved to Indian Territory, Colbert helped with the expenses to relocate over three hundred Chickasaws in addition to bearing the costs of moving his own family and slaves. He died a few years after he was removed to present-day Oklahoma.

COLBERT, LEVI
Mixed Chickasaw
fl. 1820s–1830s
Levi Colbert invited Presbyterian missionaries to proselytize and establish churches among the Chickasaws in the 1820s. He encouraged the building of the Charity Hall mission school outside of Cotton Gin Port, Mississippi; he reasoned that education was a good way for Chickasaws to accommodate to white expansion into Indian lands. He lived in a grand manner and was renowned for his graciousness and lavishness. Late in life, a few years before Chickasaw removal to Indian Territory, he became the unofficial chairman of the Chickasaw nation. He opposed Chickasaw removal and died en route to Washington in 1834 to discuss the problems pursuant to their removal to Indian Territory.

COLBERT, PITTMAN
Mixed Chickasaw
fl. 1830s–1840s
With accounting and surveying skills, Pittman Colbert, like his brothers George COLBERT, Levi COLBERT, and William COLBERT, became a respected planter and businessman as well as an influential Chickasaw leader. When the Choctaws were removed to Indian Territory, he paid the removal costs of many needy families. Upon his own removal to Oklahoma, he set up a prosperous cotton plantation. He also negotiated the surveying and separation of Chickasaw and Choctaw lands. He was instrumental in setting up the Chickasaw government in Indian Territory during the 1840s.

COLBERT, WILLIAM ("GENERAL" COLBERT)
Mixed Chickasaw
fl. 1790s–1810s
William Colbert was the oldest son of James Logan Colbert, a Scottish trader, and a Chickasaw woman from what would become Mississippi. James Logan Colbert had two other Chickasaw wives. With the three of them, he fathered six sons, William, George, Levi, Samuel, Joseph, and Pittman. By the early nineteenth century, the Colberts had become the most influential leaders among the Chickasaws. William Colbert sided with the patriots during the American Revolution, leading a contingent of Chickasaws into battle on the colonists' behalf.

Colbert continued his alliance with the Americans during LITTLE TURTLE's War of 1790–1794, supporting General Arthur St. Clair's forces. He also counseled the Chickasaws against joining TECUMSEH's Rebellion from 1809 to 1811. He further demonstrated his pro-American views when he fought in the U.S. infantry for nine months during the War of 1812. He then led a Chickasaw unit in support of General Andrew Jackson in the 1813–1814 Creek War. Colbert's men successfully battled William WEATHERFORD's Red Sticks, once taking eighty-five prisoners to Montgomery, Alabama. After the War of 1812, Colbert was the head of a Chickasaw delegation to Washington, D.C., that signed a series of treaties ceding Chickasaw lands in 1816. The Anglos called him "General" Colbert.

COLDEN, CADWALLADER
1688–1776
Cadwallader Colden was, in the words of historian Robert Waite, "the best-informed man in the New World on the affairs of the British-

American colonies." He provided the first systematic English-language study of the Six Nations or Iroquois Confederacy in 1727 and augmented it in 1747. In his *History of the Five Nations Depending on the Province of New York in America,* Colden, an adopted Mohawk, compared the Iroquois to the Romans because of their skills at oratory, warfare, and diplomacy, as well as the republican nature of their government. "When Life and Liberty came in competition, indeed, I think our Indians have outdone the Romans in this particular. . . . The Five Nations consisted of men whose courage could not be shaken," Colden wrote.

Describing the Iroquois's form of government extensively, Colden wrote that it "has continued so long that the Christians know nothing of the original of it." According to his account, "Each Nation is an Absolute Republick by its self, governed in all Publick affairs of War and Peace by the Sachems of Old Men, whose Authority and Power is gained by and consists wholly in the opinions of the rest of the Nation in their Wisdom and Integrity. . . . They never execute their Resolutions by Compulsion or Force Upon any of their People." Colden also held that "the Five Nations have such absolute Notions of Liberty that they allow no Kind of Superiority of one over another, and banish all Servitude from their Territories."

Colden's *History of the Five Nations* was read by Benjamin FRANKLIN before he began his diplomatic career by representing Pennsylvania with the Iroquois and their allies. In a letter to Colden of October 25, 1753, Franklin noted that he had seen extracts of Colden's book "in all the magazines." Upon his return to Philadelphia, Franklin wrote to Colden that he had journeyed "to meet and hold a treaty with the Ohio Indians." Franklin promised Colden a copy of the treaty and stated that he had left his

copy of Colden's book with a friend in Boston. Shortly after attending the Albany Congress in 1754, Franklin made his first stop at Colden's estate to thank him for the notes that Colden had sent to him while at Albany.

Colden held several colonial offices including the lieutenant governorship of New York. He also carried on extensive research in various natural sciences. Colden's belief that the Indians, particularly the Iroquois, provided the new Americans with a window on their own antiquity was not unique to him. It was shared as well by Franklin, Jefferson, and Paine, and, a century later, by the founders of modern feminism, as well as Marx and Engels. Such a belief provided a crucial link between Indian societies and their own, as well as a counterpoint by which to judge society's contemporary ills for two centuries of revolutionaries and reformers. "We are fond of searching into remote Antiquity to know the manners of our earliest progenitors; if I be not mistaken, the Indians are living images of them," Colden wrote.

FOR MORE INFORMATION:

Colden, Cadwallader. *History of the Five Indian Nations Depending on the Province of New York in America.* 1727 and 1747. Reprint, Ithaca, N.Y.: Great Seal Books, 1958.

COMCOMLY
Chinook
c. 1766–1830

A leader among Chinooks who lived near the mouth of the Columbia River, Comcomly warmly greeted explorers Lewis and Clark in late 1805. Shortly afterward, Comcomly's daughter married the leader of the Astor expedition, Duncan M'Dougal. This expedition founded Astoria, Oregon, in 1811 and claimed the Oregon Territory for the United States in the face of British counterclaims. In 1813, when the British challenged the American claims, Comcomly sent several hundred warriors to the Americans' aid. He met with the British and accepted their gifts, however.

Comcomly was reared in a hierarchical society; unlike many Native peoples, who governed themselves democratically, the peoples of the Northwest Coast observed very strict social and class structures. When Comcomly traveled, he moved with up to three hundred slaves, some of whom laid a path of otter and beaver skins under his feet whenever he made landfall in another Native community.

Comcomly, although blind in one eye, became noted as the first maritime pilot of the Columbia River. He died in 1830 during a smallpox epidemic and was buried in a canoe according to Chinook custom. After the burial ceremony, an unknown person entered his grave and removed Comcomly's head, which was later offered for sale in Scotland.

CONQUERING BEAR
Brulé Sioux
c. 1800–1854

In 1854, a cow strayed away from a Mormon group traveling along the North Platte River in Wyoming. The cow wandered into a Brulé Sioux camp led by Conquering Bear. The Mormons reported that the Brulés had stolen their livestock. In the meantime, High Forehead, a Miniconjou Sioux visiting the camp, had slaughtered the wayward bovine.

Conquering Bear visited the U.S. Army garrison at Fort Laramie and attempted to make restitution for the cow. The commander of the garrison insisted that High Forehead be arrested. He gave the order to Lieutenant John GRATTAN, who had just graduated from the U.S. Army Academy at West Point. On August 19, 1854, Grattan set out for the Brulé camp with thirty men and two cannons. Conquering Bear tried to restrain his warriors, but shooting broke out, during which Conquering Bear was killed. Brulé braves, now led by Little Thunder, wiped out Grattan and his small force to the last man. A little more than a year later, Colonel William HARNEY was ordered into the area to take retribution on the Sioux for the Grattan fight, initiating the Battle of Blue Water Creek near Ash Hollow, Nebraska, the first major battle of the Plains Indian wars.

COON-COME, MATTHEW
Cree
1956–

As president of the Canadian Assembly of First Nations and as grand chief of the nine Cree councils, Matthew Coon-Come has become one of the late twentieth century's major Canadian Native leaders, especially in the campaign to halt exploitation of the James Bay region by Hydro-Quebec.

In the early 1990s, Coon-Come fought Hydro-Quebec's James Bay II proposal to dam eight major rivers that flow into James Bay in northern Quebec at a cost of up to $170 billion to provide electricity for urban Canada and for several states in the northeastern United States. The area is virtually unknown to most Euro-Americans but has been home for thousands of years to roughly ten thousand Cree, many of whom would be forced from their homelands by flooding and toxic contamination if the project were completed. After considerable opposition by the Crees, "James Bay II" was stopped by Hydro-Quebec in 1995.

Coon-Come's Crees had also opposed construction of James Bay I, completed in 1985, which dammed or diverted five large rivers and flooded four thousand square miles of forest. Rotting vegetation in the area had released about 184 million tons of carbon dioxide and methane gas into the atmosphere by 1990, possibly accelerating atmospheric warming around the world and meanwhile saddling Quebec electric ratepayers with a debt of $3,500 per person. Rotting vegetation also caused an acceleration in microbial activity converting elementary mercury in submerged glacial rock to toxic methyl mercury, which was rapidly diffusing through the food chain. Methyl mercury poisoning can cause loss of vision, numbness of limbs, uncontrollable shaking, and chronic neurological disease. By 1990, some Cree elders had twenty times the level of methyl mercury in their bodies that the World Health Organization considers safe. A 1984 survey of people residing in Chisasibi, a village in Quebec, showed that 64 percent of its people had elevated levels of this toxin in their bodies. The Quebec government responded to these findings by telling the Cree not to eat fish, one of their main sources of protein.

The human problems brought on by James Bay I are not limited to the flooding of forestland and increasing discharge of toxins. The large-scale construction in the area (including road building) brought in large numbers of non-Indians and is linked by Coon-Come and other Cree leaders to rising levels of alcoholism (as well as abuse of other drugs), violence, and suicide in their communities. Traditional family patterns and ways of making a living have been breaking down; one-quarter of the Crees' caribou herds, about twelve thousand animals, drowned in the first phase of the project.

The Cree believe that the demise of their environment will kill them. The entire culture and cosmology of the Cree revolves around seasonal activities associated with the land and its waters. Coon-Come told a 1991 gathering in Seattle:

My people live in and use every inch of that land. We have lived here for so long that everything has a name: every stream, every hill, almost every rock. The Cree people have an intimate relationship with the land. It is very difficult to describe, but I think "intimate" is very close to describ[ing] how close we are to the land; how we care for it and how we know it. [Coon-Come]

Coon-Come and the Crees enlisted international support as they fought the first phase of the James Bay project through the Canadian courts, but they lost. In their efforts to stop the second phase, the Crees forged alliances with environmental groups around the world, with special emphasis on the northeastern United States, where a large proportion of the power generated by the project would be sold. By 1993, New York State had withdrawn from agreements to purchase power from Hydro-Quebec.

The James Bay projects are not single dams across single rivers that flood valleys between mountains. They are massive earth-moving projects across an area as large as the state of Oregon. According to Coon-Come,

A project of this kind involves the destruction and rearrangement of a vast landscape, literally reshaping the geography of the land. This is what I want you to understand: it is not a dam. *It is a terrible and vast reduction of our entire world* [emphasis added]. It is the assignment of vast territories to a permanent and final flood. The burial of trees, valleys, animals, and even the graves [of the Cree] beneath tons of contaminated soil. All of this serves only one purpose: the generation of more electricity to get more revenue and more temporary jobs and to gain political power. [Coon-Come]

In 1994, Coon-Come was awarded the Gold-man Environmental Prize for his activism against the James Bay projects. It carries a $60,000 stipend. In November 1994, Hydro-Quebec announced that it was shelving the second phase of the James Bay project indefinitely, a major victory for the Crees.

FOR MORE INFORMATION:

Coon-Come, Matthew. "A Vast Reduction." In *Our People, Our Land: Perspectives on Common Ground*, edited by Kurt Russo. Bellingham, Wash.: Lummi Tribe and Kluckhohn Center, 1992.

Fadden, Mary. "The James Bay Hydro-electric Project." *Northeast Indian Quarterly* 8, no. 2 (Summer 1991).

Gorrie, P. "The James Bay Power Project—The Environmental Cost of Reshaping the Geography of Northern Quebec." *Canadian Geographic* (February–March 1990): 20–31.

Rosenthal, J., and J. Beyea. "The Long-term Threats to Canada's James Bay from Human Development." National Audubon Society Environmental Policy Analysis Report No. 29 (1989).

COPWAY, GEORGE (KAHGEGWAGEBOW)
Chippewa/Ojibway
1818–c. 1863

Historian Charles Hamilton suggests that Copway may have been the model for Longfellow's Hiawatha. Copway (whose Native name, Kahgegwagebow, means "Stands Fast") was a close friend of Longfellow and was noted among the Ojibways for his physical strength and skill at hunting. Copway was also one of the first Native Americans to write books that were widely read by non-Indians.

Copway was born near the mouth of the Trent River, Ontario, in 1818. He was raised as a traditional Ojibway—his father was a noted leader and medicine man—but the family often went hungry during Copway's youth. His traditional training included stress on physical strength; Copway once carried two hundred pounds of flour and other supplies on his back for a quarter mile without rest. In spring 1841, he is said to have run across much of Wisconsin to warn the Ojibways of a Sioux raiding party, traveling 240 miles in four days.

George Copway.
[State Historical Society of Wisconsin]

Copway was converted to Methodism in 1830 and attended Ebenezer Academy in Jacksonville, Illinois, for two years. Copway became a Methodist minister in 1834, after which he translated several religious texts from English into Algonquian and worked with several religious publishers. In 1851, in New York City, Copway started a newspaper about American Indian affairs, *Copway's American Indian.*

Only one issue is known to have been published, on July 10, 1851.

Copway wrote *The Life, History and Travels of Kah-Ge-Ga-Gah-Bowh* (1847), which was revised in 1850 as *The Traditional History and Traditional Sketches of the Ojibway Nation.* The same book was reissued again in 1858 as *Indian Life and Indian History.* He also wrote *The Ojibway Conquest* (1850); *The Organization of a New Indian Territory East of the Missouri River* (1850); and *Running Sketches of Men and Places in England, Germany, Belgium, and Scotland* (1851). Copway also made a lecture tour of Europe; in England he denounced European and American deals for Ojibway ancestral lands as frauds and robberies.

Copway died near Pontiac, Michigan, at forty-five.

FOR MORE INFORMATION:

Copway, George (Kah-ge-ga-gah-bowh). *The Life, Letters, and Speeches.* New York, 1850.

Hamilton, Charles. *Cry of the Thunderbird.* Norman: University of Oklahoma Press, 1972.

CORBITANT
Wampanoag
fl. early 1600s

Corbitant, a subchief under MASSASOIT in the Wampanoag Confederacy, counseled resistance to European invasion, contrary to Massasoit's policies. In 1621, Corbitant was one of the primary authors of plans for a rebellion with the Narragansets and other tribes aiming to drive the colonists into the sea. As part of the plan, Corbitant's warriors waited until Miles Standish and most of the colony's other fighting men were absent from Plymouth; then they seized their Native allies, including SQUANTO and HOBOMOK. Hobomok escaped and led Standish and his men to the scene of the insurrection. Corbitant and the hostile Narraganset leaders then made peace.

FOR MORE INFORMATION:

Peirce, Ebenezer Weaver. *Indian History, Biography, and Genealogy Pertaining to the Good Sachem Massasoit.* Freeport, N.Y.: Books for Libraries, 1972.

CORNPLANTER (JOHN O'BAIL)
Seneca
c. 1735–1836

Cornplanter was a major Iroquois leader of the late eighteenth century. He figured importantly in the shifting alliances that accompanied the American Revolution and became a personal friend of George Washington through the Tammany Society, a group that observed the fusion of European and Native American cultures in America.

Cornplanter's father was a white trader, John O'Bail (sometimes Abeel). Some sources contend he was Irish; others say he was Dutch. All

Cornplanter.
[National Anthropological Archives]

agree, however, that he was one of the biggest sellers of liquor to the Senecas. O'Bail had been heard to boast that his trade had a profit margin of 1,000 percent. While more proper Englishmen detested O'Bail, they relied on his intelligence about the French, gathered from Indians with whom he did business.

Cornplanter was raised by his Seneca mother. He knew his father only slightly, having met him a few times as a child. In 1780, Cornplanter led a raiding party in the Schoharie Valley, taking a number of prisoners including his father. Cornplanter released his father, who still made his living by bartering guns, rum, and other things for furs, and invited him to join his Seneca family in his old age. The elder O'Bail chose to return to his Euro-American family at Fort Plain, New York.

As French allies in the French and Indian War (1754–1763), Cornplanter's warriors raided several British settlements. He may have been part of the French force that defeated British general Edward Braddock and his aide George Washington at Fort Duquesne (now Pittsburgh).

Cornplanter generally favored neutrality in the American Revolution. The Iroquois Grand Council could not reach consensus on alliance in that war. Joseph BRANT spoke eloquently about the necessity of taking up the hatchet, stating the neutrality would lead to disaster and that the Americans or the British might turn on the confederacy with a vengeance. RED JACKET and Cornplanter argued against Brant. They insisted that this quarrel was among the whites; interfering in something they did not fully understand was a mistake. As the meeting broke up in a furor, Brant called Cornplanter a coward. The Senecas divided into two camps and discussed the issue of going to war. In general, the Senecas were disposed to neutrality. HANDSOME LAKE also advocated neutrality. However, the words of Brant stung the ears of the Senecas. They could not bear to be called cowards. Finally, after lengthy discussion, the Senecas were swayed along with other wavering groups to take up the King's cause. Of great importance was the consent of the clan mothers. The Senecas took this defeat gracefully and exhorted the warriors to unite in the fight against the Americans. With this meeting, the resolution was made unanimous. The majority of the Six Nations broke its neutrality and took up the British cause.

After the Revolution, Cornplanter secured for his people a tract of land on both sides of the Allegheny River. He brought in Quaker teachers and helped sustain a prosperous agricultural community that included large herds of cattle. Cornplanter signed several treaties on behalf of the Senecas, including those concluded at Fort Stanwix in 1784 and others at various locations in 1789, 1797, and 1802. Through his many associations with Euro-Americans (including a trip to England), Cornplanter picked up English clothes and mannerisms. On one occasion, fellow Senecas tore off Cornplanter's English clothes and dressed him in traditional attire, greasing his body.

In April 1786, the Tammany Society welcomed Cornplanter and five other Senecas to Philadelphia. In a remarkable ceremony, the Tammany sachems escorted the Senecas from their Indian Queen Tavern lodgings to Tammany's wigwam on the Schuylkill River for a conference. Within a few days, Cornplanter and the Senecas proceeded to New York City to address the U.S. Congress.

In Philadelphia, on May 1, 1786, St. Tammany's Day was marked with celebrations and feasts, after which a portrait of Cornplanter was given to the Tammany Society. More than a dozen toasts were made, including: "The Great Council Fire of the United States—May the thirteen fires glow in one blended blaze and illumine the Eagle in his flight to the stars," "Our great grand sachem George Washington, Esq.," "Our Brother Iontonkque or the Corn Plant—May we ever remember that he visited our wigwam and spoke a good talk from our great-grand-fathers," and "The Friendly Indian Nations—our warriors and young men who fought, bled and gave good council for our nation."

Later in life, Cornplanter lost some of his prestige among the Senecas because of his ready agreement to land cessions. He retained enough influence to bring the Senecas to the American side in the War of 1812, however. Shortly before he died in 1836, Cornplanter had a dream that indicated his friendship with all Euro-Americans had been mistaken. After the dream, he destroyed all the presents that had been given to him by non-Indians.

Cornplanter's people occupied the thirteen-hundred-acre piece of land along the Allegheny River that had been given to them by George Washington until the mid–twentieth century. At that time the Army Corps of Engineers decided that the land better suited the public convenience and necessity under water. The scope of the army's engineering projects had grown grandiosely since Washington himself helped survey the mountains that now make up West Virginia, long before the pursuit of electricity became a legally valid reason for the state to seize land. In 1964, the bones of Cornplanter's people were moved from their land to make way for rising waters behind the Kinzua Dam. In the valleys at the Western Door, Senecas still ask sardonically if George Washington had ever asked Cornplanter if he knew how to swim.

FOR MORE INFORMATION:

Grinde, Donald A., Jr. *The Iroquois and the Founding of the American Nation.* San Francisco: Indian Historian Press, 1977.

CORNSTALK (WYNEPUEHSIKA)
Shawnee
c. 1720–1777

Cornstalk, a principal chief of the Ohio Shawnees, was born in western Pennsylvania but in 1730 moved to Scioto, in the Ohio country, with his parents. As an adult, Cornstalk became an ally of the French in the French and Indian War. Cornstalk, who was well known as an orator and military strategist, joined forces with Pontiac after the war with the French in an attempt to forestall Euro-American expansion on the western side of the Appalachian Mountains.

As an ally of Pontiac, Cornstalk led early Shawnee resistance to Euro-American expansion into the Ohio Valley during the 1770s. He headed a coalition of Ohio country Native peoples who tried to prevent whites from planting corn north of the Ohio River. After raiding settlers' villages in West Virginia and suffering reprisals, including the shooting of his brother Silver Heels, Cornstalk requested a peace treaty but was ignored. Instead, Lord Dunmore, governor of Virginia, ordered one thousand troops into the area. During an intense day-long battle at Point Pleasant (on the present-day Ohio–West Virginia border), both sides suffered heavy losses. Cornstalk said: "What shall we do now? The big knife is coming on us, and we shall all be killed. Now we must fight, or we are done. Then let us kill our women and children and go fight until we die? I shall go and make peace!" [Armstrong]

A moderate while he lived, Cornstalk was twice taken hostage by settlers. His life ended violently while he was at Point Pleasant to discuss peace with settlers. During that time, Shawnees killed a settler, and a vengeful white militia stormed the stockade where Cornstalk was being held. The militia lynched Cornstalk and killed his son Elinipsico and another Shawnee, Red Hawk.

Cornstalk's people remained at war with the United States until they signed the Treaty of Greenville in August 1795. The smoldering resentment at the murder of Cornstalk re-emerged under the leadership of TECUMSEH, who had fought beside Cornstalk when he was young and idolized him.

FOR MORE INFORMATION:

Armstrong, Virginia Irving, ed. *I Have Spoken: American History Through the Voices of the Indians.* Chicago: Swallow Press, 1971.

COSTO, RUPERT
Cahuilla
1906–1989

As a football player in the 1920s at Haskell Institute and Whittier College (where he played with future President Richard M. Nixon), Rupert Costo, early in life, demonstrated his athletic and intellectual aptitudes to the Indian and non-Indian world. From the 1930s to the 1950s, he was active in national and tribal politics, serving both as a vocal critic of the Indian New Deal in the 1930s and as tribal chairman of the Cahuillas in the 1950s. For most of his working life, he was employed as an engineer in California's highway department.

Upon his retirement in 1964, Costo and his wife, Jeannette Henry Costo (an Eastern Cherokee), founded the San Francisco–based American Indian Historical Society. The organization was often in the forefront of American Indian issues such as the protection of American Indian cemeteries and American Indian human remains and the correction of American Indian textbooks. The group began to develop publications that accurately reflected the historical role of American Indians in American society.

Initially, the American Indian Historical Society published three journals: *Wassaja*, a national Indian newspaper; *The Indian Historian*, a respected academic journal; and *Weewish Tree*, a

national magazine for Indian young people. Rupert Costo coedited all three publications with his wife. Through *Wassaja*, Costo advocated increased sovereignty for Native American nations in order to enhance land and water rights. He also worked tirelessly for the protection of American Indian civil, social, and religious rights. In 1970, the society founded another publication arm, the Indian Historian Press, an American Indian–controlled publishing house that published fifty-two titles.

At the end of his life, Costo endowed the Rupert Costo Chair in American Indian History at the University of California, Riverside. He and his wife also established the Costo Library of the American Indian at the University of California, Riverside, one of the most comprehensive collections of American Indian books in the United States. In 1994, the University of California, Riverside, renamed its Student Services Building as Costo Hall in honor of the outstanding contributions of Rupert Costo and Jeannette Henry Costo to the university.

COTA, MANUELITO
Mixed Luiseno
fl. mid-1800s

Manuelito Cota, a principal chief of the Luisenos during the 1850s, resided on the San Luis Rey River near San Diego, California, in the Mission Indian village of Pauma. He was of both Spanish and Luiseno descent. He often clashed with Cahuilla leader Juan ANTONIO as well as Antonio GARRA, the Cupeno leader, about Mission Indian policies toward the Americans. In 1847, Cota broke with the more militant Antonio in regard to the treatment of Anglos in southern California. As a result of his peaceful views, he rejected Garra's overtures for support in the Garra uprising of 1851 against the Anglos. Because of his conciliatory nature toward the Americans, Cota remained the Luisenos' chief until 1855.

CRASHING THUNDER (JASPER BLOWSNAKE)
Winnebago
fl. early 1900s

Profiled by ethnologist Paul Radin, Crashing Thunder and his Winnebago relatives became known to generations of students. MOUNTAIN WOLF WOMAN, Crashing Thunder's sister, was similarly profiled by anthropologist Nancy Lurie.

Like Mountain Wolf Woman, Crashing Thunder, born about 1865, was not a remarkable figure in the context of his place and time. His life reveals the daily texture and fundamental beliefs of the Winnebago. Crashing Thunder's experiments with peyote and his erotic yearnings as a young man were similar to incidents in the lives of many Winnebago. At one point, he joined a rodeo, passing himself off as a cowboy; at another, he was placed on trial (and acquitted) for killing a sheep. Crashing Thunder's life is described in Radin's *Crashing Thunder: The Autobiography of an American Indian* (New York, 1926).

FOR MORE INFORMATION:

Radin, Paul. *The Winnebago Tribe.* Bureau of American Ethnology, 37th Annual Report. Washington, D.C., 1923.

CRAZY HORSE (TASHUNKA WITCO)
Oglala Lakota
c. 1842–1877

Crazy Horse, a daring military strategist, was a major Lakota leader during the last half of the nineteenth century, during the final phases of the Plains Indian wars. Alone among the leaders of the Plains wars, he never signed a treaty with the United States, and he repudiated the idea of reservation life until his violent death at

the young age of about thirty-five. Crazy Horse never wore European-style clothing, and his photograph was never taken. To Oglala Lakota and to many other Native people generally, his memory has become the essence of resistance to European colonization.

"Crazy Horse" is an old name among the Oglalas and has been handed down from generation to generation. For several centuries, Crazy Horse's ancestors kept Oglala historical records on buckskin, a method of historical record keeping related to the "winter counts" of other Sioux tribes. Crazy Horse married a Cheyenne and thus cemented the alliance that functioned during the final phases of the Plains Indian wars. He was a son-in-law of RED CLOUD.

Crazy Horse was born about 1842 on what would later become the site of Rapid City, South Dakota. His father was a Lakota holy man, and his mother was Brulé Sioux. As a youth, Crazy Horse was called "the Light-haired One" or "Curly." He got the name "Crazy Horse" from his father after a battle with the Arapahos in 1858, at about sixteen. From an early age, Crazy Horse was a master of the psychological aspects of Plains warfare. According to historian Frank Waters, Crazy Horse often rode into war naked except for a breechclout around his loins, "his body painted with white hail spots, and a red lightning streak down one cheek. . . . His battle cry was 'It's a good day to die!'" Crazy Horse was never seriously injured in battle, and he made a point of never scalping anyone he killed. Crazy Horse is recalled as having been of average height, with a complexion that was lighter than most other Lakota. He was known to wander away from his village after a battle with the detachment of a poet. After attaining "shirt wearer" rank—a position of political and spiritual prestige among the Oglalas—in 1865, he attended leadership meetings but rarely spoke. Introverted and eccentric, Crazy Horse was shot in the face and relieved of the shirt of rank in 1870 following an attempt to seduce another man's wife.

In 1874, Crazy Horse and other Lakota learned that George Armstrong CUSTER had led an expedition into their sacred Black Hills and found gold at French Creek. Hordes of prospectors followed, ignoring the fact that the Black Hills had been guaranteed to the Lakota by the Fort Laramie Treaty of 1868. Crazy Horse and others ignored government edicts that sought to keep them on the Great Sioux Reservation, arguing that all the land guaranteed to them under the 1868 treaty was theirs to use.

Several allied Native peoples, including several bands of Lakota and Cheyenne, began to converge at the ridge called the Little Bighorn in southeastern Montana in spring 1876. On June 17, Crazy Horse and an estimated fifteen hundred warriors engaged a force under General George Crook in the Valley of the Rosebud in Montana. The fight was a standoff, but it did prevent Crook from making a planned rendezvous at the Little Bighorn with two other armies.

The Indian camp at the Little Bighorn River, perhaps as many as five thousand people, including two thousand warriors, followed the river for about three miles. The elite Seventh Cavalry under George Armstrong Custer had expected only a thousand. Even after he discovered that the camp was much larger than he expected, Custer decided to attack the Indians on their home ground. That decision resulted in the deaths of Custer and his entire force of about 225 men. A furious assault led by Crazy Horse and GALL dismembered Custer's force.

After the Battle of the Little Bighorn, Indians who remained free of reservations were hounded relentlessly by reinforced U.S. Army troops. The Lakota who had defeated Custer were pushed onto the Great Sioux Reservation, band by band. As he watched his people suffer

owing to the destruction of their buffalo-based economy, Crazy Horse's defiant will began to soften. Crazy Horse and his contingent of eight hundred Oglalas, in 145 lodges with seventeen hundred ponies, were among the last to surrender. On May 5, 1877, the Oglalas formed a parade two miles long as they marched into Red Cloud Agency. They gave up their horses and guns. Red Cloud met the Oglalas en route and guided them to Fort Robinson, near the agency.

Shortly after the surrender, Crazy Horse's wife, Black Shawl, became sick with tuberculosis. He asked permission to take her to SPOTTED TAIL's people at the Brulé Agency, forty miles away, but was denied. He left Fort Robinson anyway. Several dozen soldiers chased Crazy Horse to the Brulé Agency but failed to catch him. Instead, the Brulé Indian agent and Spotted Tail himself convinced Crazy Horse to return to Fort Robinson.

Crazy Horse began to return, but fifteen miles from the Brulé Agency, he was surrounded by forty government scouts. Crazy Horse was taken prisoner and escorted back to Fort Robinson. Rumor had it that Crazy Horse would be killed or taken in chains to Fort Augustine, Florida, to be imprisoned for life. At Fort Robinson on September 5, 1877, Crazy Horse was led toward a stockade. He rebelled at the sight of the prison and tried to escape. LITTLE BIG MAN and several other Indian scouts grabbed Crazy Horse as U.S. Army private William Gentles ran his bayonet through Crazy Horse's body.

On his deathbed, Crazy Horse recalled why he had fought:

> I was not hostile to the white man. . . . We had buffalo for food, and their hides for clothing and our tipis. We preferred hunting to a life of idleness on the reservations, where we were driven against our will. At

times, we did not get enough to eat, and we were not allowed to leave the reservation to hunt.

We preferred our own way of living. We were no expense to the government then. All we wanted was peace, to be left alone. . . . They tried to confine me, I tried to escape, and a soldier ran his bayonet through me.

I have spoken. [Clark]

After Crazy Horse's assassination, about 240 Lakota lodges occupied by people who had supported him migrated to Canada, where they joined SITTING BULL's people. With the Crazy Horse band, Sitting Bull's camp grew to about eight hundred lodges.

A statue of Crazy Horse is being sculpted in the Black Hills of South Dakota, near the town of Custer. The statue will rival the monument of Mount Rushmore in size. Sculptor Korczak Ziolkowski will have worked on the 883-foot-high rock statue nearly a half century by the time it is finished, having moved six million tons of rock.

FOR MORE INFORMATION:

Ambrose, Stephen E. *Crazy Horse and Custer.* New York: New American Library, 1986.

Brininstool, E. A. *Crazy Horse.* Los Angeles, 1949.

Clark, Robert A. *The Killing of Crazy Horse.* Lincoln: University of Nebraska Press, 1976.

Josephy, Alvin M., Jr. *The Patriot Chiefs.* New York: Viking, 1961.

Kadlecek, Edward, and Mabell Kadlecek. *To Kill an Eagle.* Boulder, Colo.: Johnson Publishing, 1981.

Nabokov, Peter. *Native American Testimony.* New York: Viking, 1991.

Parkman, Francis. *The Oregon Trail.* 6th ed. New York, 1847. Boston: Little, Brown, 1878. Reprint, n.p.: 1918.

Sandoz, Mari. *Crazy Horse: Strange Man of the Oglalas.* New York: Alfred A. Knopf, 1942.

Schmitt, Martin F., and Dee Brown. *Fighting Indians of the West.* New York: Scribners, 1948.

Utley, Robert M. *The Lance and the Shield: The Life and Times of Sitting Bull.* New York: Henry Holt, 1993.

Waters, Frank. *Brave Are My People: Indian Heroes Not Forgotten.* Santa Fe, N. Mex.: Clear Light, 1993.

CROW DOG (KANGI SUNKA)
Brulé Sioux
c. 1833–1910

Crow Dog was present when CRAZY HORSE was killed at Fort Robinson, Nebraska, in 1877; he helped prevent a retaliatory attack on U.S. Army soldiers at the fort. He was police chief at the Rosebud Reservation in 1879–1880, during which time he assassinated SPOTTED TAIL.

Crow Dog. [Nebraska State Historical Society]

Crow Dog was born at Horse Stealing Creek, Montana Territory, into a family of esteemed warriors. Before submitting to reservation life, he made his reputation in battle. As the Sioux were confined on reservations following the CUSTER battle at the Little Bighorn, dissension arose among some of their leaders. On one occasion, Spotted Tail was accused by RED CLOUD of pocketing the proceeds from a sale of tribal land. Crow Dog heard rumors that Spotted Tail was selling Lakota land to the railroads, building himself an enormous white-styled mansion with the proceeds. In mid-July 1880, Spotted Tail was called before the general council by Crow Dog's White Horse Group, where he denied the charges. The council voted to retain him as head chief, but Crow Dog continued to assert the chief's complicity in various crimes against the people. Crow Dog carried

out his own death sentence on Spotted Tail on August 5, 1881. Blood money was paid in traditional Brulé fashion for the crime. Crow Dog was also convicted of murder in a Dakota Territory court; he was later freed on order of the U.S. Supreme Court, which ruled that the territorial government had no jurisdiction over the crime.

Later, Crow Dog was one of the leaders in popularizing WOVOKA's Ghost Dance among the Lakota. Crow Dog adopted the religion from SHORT BULL. Crow Dog vociferously opposed U.S. Army occupation of South Dakota Indian reservations and was one of the last holdouts after the massacre of BIG FOOT's people at Wounded Knee during December 1890. Crow Dog spent the last years of his life in relative peace on the Rosebud Sioux Reservation in South Dakota.

Crow Dog's camp, 1890. [Nebraska State Historical Society]

CROW FOOT (ISAPO-MUXILA)
Blood/Blackfoot
c. 1825–1890

Born a Blood near contemporary Calgary, Alberta, Crow Foot was raised as a member of the Siksika Blackfoot. He became a leading chief in the Blackfoot Confederacy, an ally of immigrating whites and an advocate of peace with them.

Crow Foot. [J. A. Ross/National Archives of Canada/Neg. no. PA134918]

Among his people's traditional Native enemies, especially the Cree, Crow Foot was known as a fierce warrior who took part in his first battle at thirteen. In 1866, Crow Foot became known to settlers after he rescued Albert Lacombe, a Catholic priest. Crow Foot also refused to ally with SITTING BULL's Oglala Lakota after they escaped to Canada following the Battle of Little Bighorn (1876).

In 1877, Crow Foot was a principal spokesman for the Blackfoot Confederacy as several chiefs signed Canadian Treaty No. 7, which ceded most of the land in what would become southern Alberta to Canada. In 1883, Crow Foot sought peace between Native peoples and the Canadian Pacific Railway, which was building track across the Canadian prairies. The railroad all but obliterated the Blackfoots' hunting economy, but Crow Foot himself was rewarded by the railroad with a pension.

In 1885, Crow Foot's adopted son POUND-MAKER sought his alliance in the Second Riel Rebellion. By adopting Poundmaker, a dissident Cree, Crow Foot had subverted the Blackfoots' traditional enemies. By declining participation in the Second Riel Rebellion, Crow Foot again refused to fight the encroaching whites. Crow Foot spent his later years traveling as a peacemaker between various tribes after his personal life had been marked by the tragedy of losing nearly all his children to smallpox and other diseases imported from Europe.

FOR MORE INFORMATION:

Dempsey, Hugh A. *Crowfoot: Chief of the Blackfeet.* Norman: University of Oklahoma Press, 1989.

CROW FOOT
Oglala Lakota
c. 1878–1890

When a detail of forty-three Indian agency police sent by Agent James McLaughlin killed SITTING BULL in an attempt to arrest him on December 15, 1890, they also killed his young son Crow Foot. During the riot that followed Sitting Bull's assassination, the police noticed movement under a pile of blankets. Lone Man, one of the police, uncovered Crow Foot and asked his commander, BULLHEAD, what to do as

Crow Foot cried out, "My uncles. . . . Do not kill me. I do not wish to die." Bullhead, who had been seriously injured by four bullet wounds, told Lone Man to "do what you like with him." Lone Man hit Crow Foot with the butt of a rifle, sending him reeling. Lone Man and two other Indian police then pumped bullets into young Crow Foot as tears ran down their cheeks.

CROW KING
Hunkpapa Sioux
fl. 1870s–1880s

Along with SITTING BULL and GALL, Crow King was a leading war chief of the Hunkpapas during the defeat of General George Armstrong CUSTER at the Little Bighorn (1876). He escaped to Canada with other Hunkpapas but returned to the United States several months before most of Sitting Bull's band.

Crow Foot, son of Sitting Bull.
[Nebraska State Historical Society]

Crow King.
[National Anthropological Archives]

FOR MORE INFORMATION:
Utley, Robert. *The Lance and the Shield: The Life and Times of Sitting Bull.* New York: Henry Holt, 1993.

FOR MORE INFORMATION:
Utley, Robert. *The Lance and the Shield: The Life and Times of Sitting Bull.* New York: Henry Holt, 1993.

CRUZ, JOSEPH DE LA
Quinault
1937–

A veteran of twenty-five years as president of the Quinault nation, Joseph de la Cruz gained a national reputation by serving as president of the National Tribal Chairmen's Association (1977–1981) and as head of the National Congress of American Indians (1981–1985). De la Cruz stepped down from the Quinaults' leadership in 1994 to make way for Pearl Capoeman Baller, the tribe's first woman chief in modern times.

At home in the Quinault nation along the Pacific coast of Washington State, de la Cruz played an active role in founding many tribal enterprises, including forestry management, land restoration, housing construction, and seafood processing. Between 1985 and 1988, de la Cruz also became influential in fisheries management on an international level as a mediator between the United States, Canada, and Native nations in the Pacific Salmon Fisheries Treaty.

FOR MORE INFORMATION:

Johansen, Bruce E. "Sovereignty Summit." *Akwesasne Notes*, n.s., 1:3 & 4 (Fall 1995): 78–81.

CUERNO VERDE ("GREEN HORN")
Comanche
fl. 1770s

During the 1770s, Cuerno Verde led many raids on Spanish settlements along the Rio Grande in New Mexico for food, horses, and slaves. In order to pacify the frontier, the governor of New Mexico, Juan de Anza, led a force of 85 soldiers and 259 Indians against the Comanches in 1779, engaging Cuerno Verde in what is now Colorado. Cuerno Verde, his son, four band chiefs, his medicine man, and thirty-two other warriors died in a bitter battle against Spanish guns.

CUFFE, PAUL, JR.
Mixed Pequot
fl. early 1800s

Paul Cuffe was born into a Pequot family that had intermarried with freed or escaped slaves in New England. (His father, Paul Cuffe, Sr., became known for his attempt to begin an African American colony in Sierra Leone.) Paul Cuffe, Jr., made his living as a whaling harpooner and probably came to know Herman Melville, the author of *Moby Dick* and other works. It is probable that Melville modeled his character Queequeg, the aboriginal harpooner, after the younger Cuffe.

CURLY (SHISHI'ESH)
Crow
c. 1860–1923

Curly (whose Crow name means "the Crow"), a well-known scout for the U.S. Army, was born along the Rosebud River, Montana, and married Takes a Shield, a Crow woman, before he became a scout for General George Armstrong Custer at the time of the Battle of the Little Bighorn (1876). After taking a look at the odds (expressed in men under arms on each side), Curly is alleged to have escaped the battlefield. Accounts say that he disguised himself as a Sioux by braiding his hair and hiding his Crow clothing before he slipped away.

Two days later, at the junction of the Yellowstone and Missouri Rivers, Curly met the crew of Custer's supply boat and told them Custer's army had been killed to the last man. Curly, who did not speak English, described the battle with hand signals and drawings and provided the outside world with the first account of the battle.

Curly became controversial after he allegedly refused to render aid to U.S. forces; he also refrained from reporting the battle to General Alfred Terry, who could have provided reinforcements to Custer's cause. Curly later told reporters (according to the *Helena Herald,* July 15, 1876) that his army commanders had told him to "go home" after locating the Sioux-Cheyenne camp at the Little Bighorn.

Curly in 1913.
[Nebraska State Historical Society]

Curly continued to provide accounts of the Custer battle to the press well into the twentieth century. He also carried on a long battle with the army over his right to retirement pay. His pension was granted for life in April 1923. Curly died a month later at the approximate age of seventy. He was buried at the Little Bighorn National Monument in eastern Montana.

FOR MORE INFORMATION:

Camp, Walter M. *Custer in '76: Walter Camp's Notes on the Custer Fight.* Edited by Kenneth

Hammer. Provo, Utah: Brigham Young University Press, 1976.

Rosenburg, Bruce A. *Custer and the Epic of Defeat.* University Park: Pennsylvania State University Press, 1974.

Sandoz, Mari. *The Battle of the Little Bighorn.* New York: J. B. Lippincott, 1966.

Stewart, Edgar Irving. *Custer's Luck.* Norman: University of Oklahoma Press, 1955.

CURLY CHIEF
Pawnee
fl. 1840s

Curly Chief was one of the principal leaders of the four-tribe Pawnee Confederation, which lived along the Platte River in Nebraska. He witnessed the arrival of wagon trains bearing settlers bound for the gold fields of California. He was chief in 1849, at the height of the California gold rush, when the Pawnees lost a quarter of their people to smallpox and cholera.

CURTIS, CHARLES
Kansa (Kaw) and Osage
1860–1936

As a Republican politician, Charles Curtis served as a member of the U.S. House of Representatives, a U.S. senator, and as vice president of the United States.

Born on Indian land later incorporated into North Topeka, Kansas, Charles Curtis was the son of Oren A. Curtis (an abolitionist and Civil War Union cavalry officer) and Helen Pappan (Kaw/Osage). His mother died when he was three, and he was raised under the care of his maternal grandmother on the Kaw Reservation and in Topeka. Following an attack on Kaw Indians at Council Grove by Cheyenne militants, Curtis (one-eighth Indian) left the Indian mission school on the Kaw Reservation in 1868 and returned to Topeka, where he attended Topeka High School. For several years as a young man, he was a jockey and worked odd jobs until he met A. H. Case, a Topeka lawyer. Studying law and working as a law clerk, Curtis was admitted to the Kansas bar in 1881.

Entering politics as a Republican, Curtis was elected county prosecuting attorney in 1884 and 1886. From 1892 to 1906, he served eight terms in the U.S. House of Representatives. He authored the Curtis Act of 1898, which dissolved tribal governments and permitted the institution of civil government within the Indian Territory. The Curtis Act tried to force assimilation on American Indian peoples. It brought the allotment policy to the Five Civilized Tribes of Oklahoma, who had been exempt from the Dawes Severalty Act of 1887. That law had empowered the DAWES Commission, created in 1893, to extinguish tribal title to lands in Indian Territory. Once tribal title was eliminated, the commission proceeded with allotment of reservation lands to individuals. Curtis's endeavors to foster detribalization, allotment, and assimilation were opposed by many of the tribal leaders of Indian Territory. In essence, the Curtis Act paved the way for Oklahoma statehood in 1907 by destroying tribal land titles and governments.

Curtis served in the U.S. Senate from 1907 to 1913 (he was the first U.S. Senator of American Indian ancestry) and 1915 to 1929. During his tenure in the Senate, he was Republican party whip (1915–1924) and then majority leader (1924–1929). As chairman of the Senate Committee on Indian Affairs in 1924, Curtis sponsored the Indian Citizenship Act, which made American Indians U.S. citizens and yet still protected their tribal property rights. After an unsuccessful campaign for the presidential nomination, he ran as vice president with Herbert Hoover in 1928. He served as vice president from 1929 to 1933. He was a deft politician who used his Indian background for personal advan-

tage, even though his political adversaries called him "the Injun." Although a fiscal conservative, he supported veterans' benefits, farm relief, women's suffrage, and national prohibition.

The Hoover-Curtis ticket's bid for a second term in 1932 was defeated by Franklin Delano Roosevelt. Upon his retirement in 1933, Curtis had served longer in the nation's capital than any active politician. After leaving public office, he headed the short-lived National Republican League and practiced law in Washington, D.C. He was also president of a gold mining company in New Mexico. In 1936, Curtis died of heart disease.

CURTIS, EDWARD SHERIFF
1868–1952

Born in Whitewater, Wisconsin, Edward Curtis showed an interest in both the mechanics and art of photography at an early age. He learned to build his own cameras and, in 1887, moved with his family to Seattle, where he photographed many Native Americans in the area. In 1892, Curtis opened his first studio there.

In 1898, Curtis was photographing on the slopes of Mount Rainier when he found a party of lost climbers and helped them to safety. The group included C. Hart Merriam, chief of the United States Biological Survey, who a year later arranged for Curtis to be official photographer with the Harriman expedition to Alaska. Also among the lost climbers was George Bird Grinnell, the well-known photographer and naturalist who edited *Forest and Stream* magazine. Grinnell later invited Curtis to journey to Montana where they planned to make a definitive photographic record of Native Americans at the turn of the century.

With a $75,000 grant from banker J. P. Morgan, who gave the money at the behest of President Theodore Roosevelt, Curtis began to compile a twenty-volume set of photographs and text. Curtis spent more than thirty years on the project. He traveled throughout North America taking more than forty thousand photographs. About two thousand of these photographs were published in *The North American Indian*, a series of books issued by the Smithsonian Institution between 1907 and 1930.

Introducing the twenty-volume set, Curtis said that he undertook the task because "it represents the result of a personal study of a people who are rapidly losing the traces of their aboriginal character and who are destined to ultimately become assimilated with the 'superior race.' " Curtis thought the Indians' demise inevitable because of Euro-American immigrant behavior that "has been worse than criminal," by people who "lay claim to civilization and Christianity."

Curtis also made *In the Land of the War Canoes*, the first moving picture of Native Americans, filmed in 1914 with the help of George HUNT, a primary informant of pioneer anthropologist Franz Boas. Curtis continued his photography until late in his life; he died in Los Angeles.

FOR MORE INFORMATION:

Lawlor, Laurie. *Shadow Catcher: The Life and Work of Edward S. Curtis.* New York: Walker & Co., 1995.

CUSTER, GEORGE ARMSTRONG
1839–1876

Best known as the loser of one of the most spectacular battles of the Plains wars in the late nineteenth century, George Armstrong Custer had earned the enmity of Native Americans for his participation in earlier campaigns against them, as well as for leading a U.S. Army expedition into the Lakotas' sacred Paha Sapa (Black Hills) in 1874.

Following the massacre of Southern Cheyennes at Sand Creek by Colorado volunteers

George Armstrong Custer.
[Nebraska State Historical Society]

under the command of Colonel J. M. Chivington, BLACK KETTLE and other chiefs tried to restore the peace again, figuring that their people would not survive any other way. The survivors of this massacre camped near the Washita River in Oklahoma. During the winter of 1868, they were attacked again by troops with orders to raze the village, hang all the men, and take women and children captive. The leader of this attack was Custer, the brash "boy general," fresh from a decorated tour of duty in the Civil War. His desire for a big victory would cost him his scalp at the Little Bighorn a dozen years later.

Custer had won a number of battlefield promotions during the Civil War, and he was the U.S. Cavalry's youngest general, a rank that he held on a brevet (temporary) basis. The attack on Black Kettle's camp was his first participation in an Indian war. Between 40 and 110 Indians were killed, including Black Kettle himself. During the attack, Arapahoes, Comanches, and Kiowas came to the rescue of the Cheyennes, forcing Custer and his troops to withdraw before they had fully carried out the assigned extermination.

In 1874, Custer led an army expedition into the Black Hills, which were guaranteed to the Lakota under the 1868 Fort Laramie Treaty. The expedition was less a military invasion than a geological assay; Custer brought with him a sixteen-piece brass band as well as civilians to catalog the area's flora and fauna and to tell the world that the Black Hills were laden with gold, as he once put it, "from the grass roots down." This announcement by Custer caused a gold rush in the area.

According to Native American accounts (see CRAZY HORSE, CURLY, and RED HORSE), Custer ignored the advice of his own scouts regarding the size of the Indian encampment at the Little Bighorn. Custer found himself facing two thousand warriors—a force almost ten times his own—on their own home ground. The Battle of the Little Bighorn presented the Indians with the unexpected opportunity to avenge the invasion of the Black Hills as well as Custer's role in the massacres at Sand Creek and Washita. The June 25, 1876, "Custer Battle," as it soon became known, rather effectively spoiled the United States' centennial celebration nine days later. In an ironic twist, Custer's name was invoked by the U.S. Army as a martyr during the following decade as ever-larger numbers of army troops extinguished the last Indian resistance on the Plains. Custer himself became a hero in some quarters, despite his sloppy soldiering.

In 1991, the Custer Battlefield National Monument's name was changed to Little Bighorn (the geographical name of the area) by an act of Congress that had been initiated by Native groups. A monument to the Indians who fell in the battle was also planned to stand on equal footing with one honoring Custer and his men. Until 1991, white marble markers placed amidst the buffalo grass and purple wildflowers designated where each of Custer's men had died. There was no indication at the site that Indians had spilled any blood at all.

At about the same time, Barbara Booher, daughter of a Cherokee and a Northern Ute, became the first Native American superintendent of the battlefield. All of this stirred the ire of Custer buffs, who maintain an organization (the Little Bighorn Association) that polishes the general's mythic image. Dennis Farioli, a member of that group, said that General Custer had been a dashing hero in the Civil War before he lost his life at the Little Bighorn. "[He was] a General Schwartzkopf of his day," Farioli said. Another member of the Little Big Horn Association, Bill Wells, has said: "The simple fact is that [the Indians] were the enemy of the federal government. The battlefield was named and the monument placed there to honor the soldiers who died under the flag of the United States." [*Wall Street Journal*] The newsletter of the seven-hundred-member Order of the Indian Wars suggested sardonically that the government's next step might be to build a Japanese Shinto temple on the site where the USS *Arizona* sank during the attack on Pearl Harbor. Three organizations enrolling forty-six hundred members have dedicated themselves to upholding Custer's side of the story.

Following his defeat, Custer has been the subject of hundreds of books and articles and at least a dozen movies. Ronald Reagan played Custer in the 1940 release *Santa Fe Trail*. General Custer's legacy is all the more surprising because he is known to historians generally as the loser in one of the most one-sided defeats in U.S. Army history. In 1990, about 250,000 people visited the battlefield at the Little Bighorn.

FOR MORE INFORMATION:

Ambrose, Stephen E. *Crazy Horse and Custer.* New York: New American Library, 1986.

Custer, Elizabeth. *Boots and Saddles.* 1885. Reprint, Norman: University of Oklahoma Press, 1961.

Custer, George Armstrong. *My Life on the Plains.* 1891. Reprint, Lincoln: University of Nebraska Press, 1966.

Gibson, Arrell Morgan. *The American Indian: Prehistory to Present.* Lexington, Mass.: D. C. Heath, 1980.

Graham, W. A. *The Custer Myth.* Lincoln: University of Nebraska Press, 1953.

Hyde, George E. *A Sioux Chronicle.* Norman: University of Oklahoma Press, 1956.

Luce, Edward S., and Evelyn S. Luce. *Custer Battlefield.* Washington, D.C., 1952.

Monoghan, Jay. *Custer.* Lincoln: University of Nebraska Press, 1959.

Rosenberg, Bruce A. *Custer and the Epic of Defeat.* University Park: Pennsylvania State University Press, 1974.

Utley, Robert. *The Lance and the Shield: The Life and Times of Sitting Bull.* New York: Henry Holt, 1993.

The Wall Street Journal, October 15, 1990, p. A-1.

Whittaker, Frederick. *A Complete Life of General George Armstrong Custer.* 1876. Reprint, Lincoln: University of Nebraska Press, 1993.

DATSOLALEE (DATSOLAI)
Washo
c. 1835–1925

Born in Nevada in the Carson Valley near the California border, Datsolalee (who was also known as Louisa Keyser and Dabuda, meaning "Wide Hips") learned traditional Washo basketry skills at an early age. Washo basket making was a refined art with complex designs and as many as thirty-six stitches to an inch. Datsolalee, who became one of the Washos' best-known basket makers, was also one of the Washos who welcomed John C. Fremont's expedition to Nevada in 1844. Her first marriage was to a Washo man named Assu, and they had two children. Soon after the birth of the second child, she was widowed. Years later, in 1888, she married her second husband, a Washo man called Charley Keyser.

By the 1850s, the Paiutes, having defeated the Washos in battle, had suppressed the production of Washo baskets to enhance the price of Paiute baskets sold to the whites. This policy forced the Washos into extreme poverty. But in 1895, Datsolalee disregarded the Paiute restrictions and showed several glass bottles woven on the outside with willow reeds and fern fibers to Abram Cohn, the owner of a dry goods store in Carson City, Nevada. Cohn bought the baskets and stated that he would purchase any other baskets that she might make. By the time of Datsolalee's death, Cohn had bought 120 baskets from her. It is estimated that she made about three hundred baskets during her lifetime. Many of her larger works required more than a year to fashion and had names like "Myriad Stars Shine over the Graves of Our Ancestors."

Although she was almost blind and losing her strength in her later years, Datsolalee continued to weave baskets until her death. Her works were highly valued by collectors. Five years after her death, one basket was purchased for $10,000. Today, her works are still shown in museums and are valued in the hundreds of thousands of dollars.

DAWES, HENRY
1816–1903

Senator Henry Dawes of Massachusetts was the principal author of legislation designed to break down common landholdings among Indians and replace them with individual family farms. The idea, born of late-nineteenth-century non-Indian reform efforts (such as those of Helen Hunt JACKSON), was designed to transform Indians into self-sufficient farmers.

As the law was originally written, Indians could not sell their land for twenty-five years. This was meant to protect them from speculators, but land-hungry settlers found many ways to get around the limit. If Indians refused allotment (and many did), the law specified that it could be ordered for them. To thwart these efforts, Yakimas in eastern Washington pulled up surveyors' markers; in Wyoming, Arapaho horsemen destroyed surveyors' tapes. When WASHAKIE, an elderly Shoshoni, was told the virtues of vegetable gardening, he swore, "God damn a potato."

Once the legislation was implemented, its intent fell to the land speculators and Indian agents who made their livings off Native Americans. The law was written so that after each Native family had been allocated 160 acres, the remaining reservation lands would be opened for non-Indian homesteaders. The first Native tribe to be affected by allotment was the Iowas. After alloting each family 160 acres, 90 percent of the Iowas' reservation land was thrown open to non-Indian settlement. Cheyennes and Arapahoes who had been forcibly moved to Indian Territory (now Oklahoma) lost 80 percent of land that had been guaranteed to them forever just twenty years before.

Allotment-related frauds were especially common in Oklahoma after oil was discovered on some Indian lands (see Gertrude BONNIN). According to historian Peter Nabokov, "Fraud-ulent wills were drafted for dead Indians. Deeds were forged for tribespeople who never existed. White opportunists were appointed as guardians for Indian children soon to inherit land from their parents. Allottees were bribed or murdered to steal their property."

In the final analysis, allotment, which had been promoted for the Indians' own good, ended up as one of the largest transfers of land from Native Americans to non-Natives in U.S. history. In 1887, Indians owned about 138 million acres within the United States. By 1932, ninety million of those acres had passed into non-Indian ownership under allotment's provisions.

FOR MORE INFORMATION:

Josephy, Alvin M., Jr. *The Indian Heritage of America.* New York: Bantam, 1969.

Nabokov, Peter. *Native American Testimony.* New York: Viking Penguin, 1991.

DECORA (KONOKA)
Winnebago
1747–1836

Decora became the Winnebagos' principal chief in 1816 on the death of his father Spoon DECORA. He sided with the British in the War of 1812 but counseled peace with the whites afterward. He was held hostage by whites for a time during the Winnebago War (1827), although he did not take an active part in the hostilities.

DECORA, SPOON (DEKAURY, CHOUKEKA)
Winnebago
1730–c. 1816

Also called Choukeka, Spoon Decora was one of the first of several Winnebago leaders to carry the name "Decora." Spoon Decora was one of six sons and five daughters born to a French trader (Joseph des Caris) and the Winnebago Hopokaw, a daughter of NAWKAW. He took a leading role in the Winnebagos' conflicts with the Chippewas but generally refrained from becoming involved in Euro-American conflicts. Decora played a leading role in negotiating the St. Louis Treaty of 1816; he died shortly afterward.

DEER, ADA
Menominee
1935–

Ada Deer is Undersecretary at the Bureau of Indian Affairs (BIA); President Bill Clinton appointed her to the post in 1993.

Deer was born in Keshena, Wisconsin. She earned a bachelor's degree at the University of Wisconsin/Madison in 1957 and a masters of social work from Columbia University in 1961. Her principal avocation became social work, including lecturing in the fields of social work and Native American studies at the University of Wisconsin's Madison campus.

In addition, Deer chaired the Menominee Restoration Committee between 1973 and 1975; she also worked as a lobbyist for the Menominees in Washington, D.C. During the late 1970s, Deer was a member of the American Indian Policy Review Commission.

FOR MORE INFORMATION:

Katz, Jane B., ed. *I Am the Fire of Time.* New York: E. P. Dutton, 1977.

DEGANAWIDAH
Huron
fl. 1100–1150 (?)

The Iroquois Confederacy was founded by the Huron prophet Deganawidah, who is called "the Peacemaker" in oral discourse among many Iroquois. Deganawidah enlisted the aid of a speaker, Aionwantha (sometimes called HIAWATHA), to spread his vision of a united Haundenosaunee Confederacy. The date that Deganawidah united the Haudenosaunee ("People of the Longhouse") has long been debated by historians and anthropologists. Some of the Iroquois oral history indicates a founding date as early as A.D. 900 on the Christian calendar. Some anthropologists date the origin of the confederacy as late as A.D. 1550 to 1600, in reaction to European contact. Others use astronomical data or genealogical lines to pinpoint a founding date of A.D. 1145. Deganawidah himself was a historical personage whose life story has been embellished as myth. He has sometimes been compared to Jesus Christ in this regard.

Deganawidah needed a spokesman in the oral culture of the Iroquois because he stuttered so badly he could hardly speak, a manifestation that Iroquois oral history attributes to a double row of teeth. The confederacy was founded before first European contact in the area, possibly as early as A.D. 900 or perhaps as late as A.D. 1500. Deganawidah sought to replace blood feuds that had devastated the Iroquois with peaceful modes of decision making. The result was the Great Law of Peace (sometimes called the Great Binding Law) of the Iroquois, which endures to this day as one of the oldest forms of participatory democracy on earth. The confederacy originally included the Mohawks, Oneidas, Onondagas, Cayugas, and Senecas. The sixth nation, the Tuscaroras, migrated into Iroquois country in the early eighteenth century. They called themselves the Haudenosaunee ("Iroquois" was applied to them by the French).

Peace among the formerly antagonistic nations was procured and maintained through the Haudenosaunee's Great Law of Peace (Kaianerekowa), which was passed from generation to generation by use of wampum, a beaded form of written communication. The Great Law outlined a complex system of checks and balances between nations and sexes. A complete oral recitation of the Great Law can take several days; encapsulated versions of it have been translated into English for more than a hundred years.

According to Iroquois oral history, the visionary Hiawatha tried to call councils to eliminate the blood feuds, but they were always thwarted by the evil and twisted wizard TADADAHO, an Onondaga who used magic and spies to rule by fear and intimidation. Failing to defeat the wizard, Hiawatha traveled to Mohawk, Oneida, and Cayuga villages with his message of peace and brotherhood. Everywhere he went, his message was accepted—with the proviso that he persuade the formidable Tadadaho and the Onondagas to embrace the covenant of peace.

Just as Hiawatha was despairing, the prophet Deganawidah entered his life. Together, the two men developed a powerful message of peace. Deganawidah's vision gave Hiawatha's oratory substance. Through Deganawidah's vision, the constitution of the Iroquois was formulated. In his vision, Deganawidah saw a giant white pine reaching to the sky and gaining strength from three counterbalancing principles of life. The first axiom was that a stable mind and healthy body should be in balance so that peace between individuals and groups could occur. Second, Deganawidah stated that humane conduct, thought, and speech were a requirement for equity and justice among peoples. Finally, he foresaw a society in which physical strength and civil authority would reinforce the power of the clan system.

Deganawidah comes ashore in a stone canoe—an artist's rendering of a scene from the Iroquois Confederacy's founding story. [Courtesy of John Kahionhes Fadden]

With such a powerful vision, Deganawidah and Hiawatha were able to subdue the evil Tadadaho and transform his mind. Deganawidah removed evil feelings and thoughts from the head of Tadadaho and said, "Thou shalt strive . . . to make reason and the peaceful mind prevail." [Wallace] The evil wizard became reborn into a humane person charged with implementing the message of Deganawidah. After Tadadaho had submitted to the redemption, Onondaga became the central fire of the Haudenosaunee, and the Onondagas became the "firekeepers" of the new confederacy. To this day, the Great Council Fire of the confederacy is kept in the land of the Onondagas.

Deganawidah outlined a system that Benjamin FRANKLIN speculated had "subsisted ages" before he factored some of its attributes into his Albany Plan of Union (1754). The Great Law of Peace outlined a federal system of government not unlike that of the United States. Each of the five Iroquois nations in Deganawidah's confederacy maintained its own council, whose sachems were nominated by the clan mothers of families holding hereditary rights to office titles. The Grand Council at Onondaga was drawn from the individual national councils. The Grand Council could also nominate sachems outside the hereditary structure and based on merit alone. These sachems, called "pine tree chiefs," were said to have sprung from the body of the people as the symbolic Great White Pine springs from the earth.

Rights, duties, and qualifications of sachems were explicitly outlined, and the clan mothers could remove (or impeach) a sachem found guilty of any of a number of abuses of office, from missing meetings to murder. An erring chief was summoned to face charges by the war chiefs, who acted in peacetime as the peoples' eyes and ears in the council, somewhat as the role of the press was envisaged by Thomas Jefferson and other founders of the United States. A sachem was given three warnings then removed from the council if he did not mend his ways. A sachem guilty of murder not only lost his title but also deprived his entire family of its right to representation. The women relatives holding the rights to the office were "buried," and the title transferred to a sister family.

Deganawidah said that the sachems' skins must be seven spans thick to withstand the criticism of their constituents. The law pointed out that sachems should take pains not to become angry when people scrutinized their conduct in governmental affairs. A similar point of view pervades the writings of Jefferson and Franklin, although it was not fully codified into U.S. law until the Supreme Court's 1964 decision, in *New York Times* v. *Sullivan*, made it virtually impossible for public officials to sue successfully for libel. Sachems were not allowed to name their own successors. Nor could they carry their titles to the grave. The Great Law provided a ceremony to remove the antlers of authority from a dying chief. The Great Law also provided for the removal from office of sachems who could no longer adequately function in office, a measure remarkably similar to a constitutional amendment adopted in the United States during the late twentieth century providing for the removal of an incapacitated president.

Deganawidah's Great Law also included provisions guaranteeing freedom of religion and the right of redress before the Grand Council. It also forbade unauthorized entry of homes—all measures that sound familiar to U.S. citizens through the Bill of Rights.

As it was designed by Deganawidah, the procedure for debating policies of the confederacy begins with the Mohawks and Senecas (the Mohawks, Senecas, and Onondagas are called the elder brothers). After being debated by the Keepers of the Eastern Door (Mohawks) and the Keepers of the Western Door (Senecas), the question is then thrown across the fire to the Oneida and Cayuga statesmen (the younger brothers) for discussion in much the same manner. Once consensus is achieved among the Oneidas and the Cayugas, the discussion is then given back to the Senecas and Mohawks for confirmation. Next, the question is laid before the Onondagas for their decision.

At this stage, the Onondagas have a power similar to judicial review in the U.S. legislative system; they can raise objections to the proposed measure if it is believed to be inconsistent with the Great Law. Essentially, the legislature can rewrite the proposed law on the spot so that it can be in accord with the constitution of the Iroquois. When the Onondagas reach consensus, Tadadaho gives the decision to Honowireton (an Onondaga chief who presides over debates between the delegations) to confirm the decision if it is unanimously agreed upon by all of the Onondaga sachems. (When Deganawidah convinced the evil wizard Tadadaho to accept his vision of the Great Peace, his name became that of the office of speaker of the confederacy—evidence, according to Iroquois law, that good triumphs over evil.) Finally, Honowireton or Tadadaho gives the decision of the Onondagas to the Mohawks and the Senecas so that the policy may be announced to the Grand Council as its will. This process reflects the emphasis of the league on checks and balances, public debate, and consensus. The overall intent of such a parliamentary procedure is to encourage unity at each step.

Public opinion is of great importance within the League of the Iroquois. Iroquois people can have a direct say in government policy formulation even if the sachems choose to ignore the will of the people. The Great Law of Peace stipulates that the people can propose their own laws even when leaders fail to do so: "If the conditions . . . arise . . . to . . . change . . . this law, the case shall be . . . considered and if the new beam seems . . . beneficial, the . . . change . . . if adopted, shall be called, 'Added to the Rafters.' " [Wallace]

This provision resembles provisions for popular initiative in several states of the United States, as well as the mechanism by which the federal and many state constitutions may be amended.

FOR MORE INFORMATION:

Colden, Cadwallader. *The History of the Five Nations.* 1727 and 1747. Reprint, Ithaca, N.Y.: Great Seal Books, 1958.

Dennis, Matthew. *Cultivating a Landscape of Peace.* Ithaca, N.Y.: Cornell University Press, 1993.

Fenton, William N. *Roll Call of the Iroquois Chiefs.* Washington, D.C.: Smithsonian, 1950.

———. "Seth Newhouse's Traditional History and Constitution of the Iroquois Confederacy." *Proceedings of the American Philosophical Society* 93:2, 141–158.

Hale, Horatio. *The Iroquois Book of Rites.* 1883. Reprint, Toronto: University of Toronto Press, 1963.

Hamilton, Charles. *Cry of the Thunderbird.* Norman: University of Oklahoma Press, 1972.

Henry, Thomas R. *Wilderness Messiah.* New York: Sloane Associates, 1955.

Hewitt, J. N. B. *A Constitutional League of Peace in the Stone Age of America.* Washington, D.C.: Smithsonian, 1918.

———. *Iroquois Cosmology.* Washington, D.C.: Smithsonian, 1903.

———. *Legend of the Founding of the Iroquois League.* Washington, D.C.: Smithsonian, 1892.

Wallace, Paul A. W. *The White Roots of Peace.* Santa Fe, N. Mex.: Clear Light , 1994.

Wampum belt, made by Techanetorens. Onchiota, N.Y.: Six Nations Museum, n.d.

Waters, Frank. *Brave Are My People: Indian Heroes Not Forgotten.* Santa Fe, N. Mex.: Clear Light, 1993.

White Roots of Peace. *The Great Law of Peace of the Longhouse People.* Rooseveltown, N.Y.: White Roots of Peace, 1971.

Wilson, Edmund. *Apologies to the Iroquois.* New York: Farrar, Straus & Cudahy, 1960.

DEKANISORA
Onondaga
c. 1650–1730

Dekanisora was a principal Iroquois leader in their late-seventeenth-century war with the Hurons. He was also an outstanding orator and a member of the Iroquois Grand Council, possibly holding the office of speaker, or *Tadadaho.* In 1688, he was among Iroquois who were traveling to Montreal for a peace parlay when they were captured by Huron leader ADARIO, who was trying to instigate Iroquois-French conflict. Dekanisora and the other Iroquois were led to believe that the French were responsible for the death of one warrior whom Adario did not release, and as a result they made war on Montreal, killing several settlers.

Dekanisora's reputation as an orator reached historian Cadwallader COLDEN, who wrote that as a speaker, he could stand with the best in the world. Dekanisora was a frequent spokesman for the Iroquois at councils with both the English and the French, and he tried to maintain the Iroquois' distance from both. Dekanisora died at Albany in 1730 during a treaty council.

DELAWARE PROPHET (NEOLIN)
Delaware
c. 1725–c. 1775

The Delaware Prophet, who also was widely called Neolin, combined the political and reli-gious aspects of a revivalist movement in the 1760s to renounce whites' liquor, trade goods, and customs—themes that would later echo through the visions of HANDSOME LAKE about 1800 and WOVOKA about 1880. The Delaware Prophet's message that all Native Americans should unite against the white invaders had an effect on PONTIAC, who adapted its military and political aspects.

The Prophet lived on the banks of the Cuyahoga River near Lake Erie (the site of present-day Cleveland). He is said to have had visions in which the Creator spoke to him. While communicating with the Creator, this man received a code of detailed instructions to follow to avoid the perils of worldly misery and damnation confronting the Ohio and Iroquois Indians along the frontier. If the code were followed, it was said that the Indians would be able to drive the white men out of their country and return to the simplicity and happiness of their original state.

As he assumed the title of Neolin, "the Enlightened," he told the people that the Great Spirit had ordered them to make sacrifices and renounce the ways of the white man. They were to give up guns for the bow and arrow, dress in skins instead of cloth, and stop using trade goods. Indian people would then return to a former happier state. He talked of giving up alcohol. He said that fire should not be made by flint and steel but by rubbing two sticks together. People were to learn to live again without trade with the Europeans. The message was one that stressed the revival of ancient customs in order to give the people the strength and resolve to resist the encroachments of the white man. Neolin prophesied that, after a period of negotiations with the Europeans, there would be an Indian uprising in 1762.

The Delaware Prophet's message was a mixture of the old and the new. Some of his recommendations were not at all traditional. He asked that people give up medicine songs and war rituals. He utilized such European concepts as a high-god for both white and Indian, as well as written prayers and a Great Book. But his ideas were so effective that a Pittsburgh trader said that the Delaware "have quit hunting any more than to supply nature in that way." [Wallace]

Pontiac became a convert and used the message to fuel his rebellion. During Pontiac's Rebellion, Handsome Lake may have heard the Delaware Prophet's message, although the Delaware Prophet made few converts among the Senecas.

FOR MORE INFORMATION:

Wallace, Anthony. *Death and Rebirth of the Seneca.* New York: Knopf, 1970.

DELGADITO
Navajo
c. 1830–c. 1870

Delgadito, also known as Herrero Delgadito ("Slender Little Metalworker"), Beshiltheen ("Knife Maker"), and Atsidi Sani ("Old Smith"), is thought to have been the first Navajo to learn silversmithing. He was also a participant in the Navajo War of 1863–1866, as well as a Navajo spiritual leader and ceremonial singer.

Delgadito resisted U.S. Army efforts to relocate the Navajos to Bosque Redondo (Fort Sumner), New Mexico, during the Civil War. Beginning in 1863, Delgadito and his brother BARBONCITO led over five hundred followers in the Navajo War of 1863–1866. When Kit CARSON started his scorched earth offensive against the Navajos by destroying livestock and grain supplies in 1863, Delgadito and Barboncito sent a third brother, El Sordo, and another man to Fort Wingate, New Mexico, under a flag of truce to surrender. General James Carleton told Delgadito that he and his family could return to

their homeland if they could persuade the other Navajos to go to Fort Sumner.

By January 1864, Delgadito had persuaded 680 Navajos to surrender. Still other Navajos remained at Canyon de Chelly with Barboncito until a march by soldiers on that Navajo stronghold in 1864. Although he was among the first Navajos to be taken to Bosque Redondo in eastern New Mexico in early 1864, Delgadito, Barboncito, and MANUELITO later signed the treaty of June 1, 1868, allowing the Navajos to return to their ancestral lands as Carleton had promised.

In the 1850s, Delgadito learned silversmithing from a Mexican called Nakai Tsosi. The Indian agent at Fort Defiance, Captain Henry L. (Red Shirt) Dodge, brought in a blacksmith, George Carter, at about the same time to teach Navajos ironwork. It is believed that by 1853, Delgadito was crafting his first pieces of jewelry from silver coins. In teaching this new craft to other Navajos and his son Red Smith, he established jewelry making among the Navajos.

FOR MORE INFORMATION:

Frink, Maurice. *Fort Defiance and the Navajo.* Boulder, Colo.: Fred Parrett, 1968.

DELORIA, ELLA CARA (ANPETU WASTEWIN)
Standing Rock Sioux
1889–1971

As a Columbia University faculty member beginning in 1929, Ella Cara Deloria gained notice as an outstanding anthropologist and linguist. She wrote *Dakota Texts* (1932), which is bilingual in Dakota and English, and *Speaking of Indians* (1944), a description of Native life before the arrival of Europeans.

Deloria was born in Wakpala, South Dakota; her Dakota name, Anpetu Wastewin, means

"Good Woman of the Day." Her father was an Episcopalian minister who had earned a wide-ranging reputation in the Plains region. Deloria attended Oberlin College and Columbia University, from which she graduated in 1915 with a bachelor's degree. After working as a school-teacher and an employee of the YMCA (in Indian education), Deloria returned to Columbia as a professor of anthropology. There she worked with Franz Boas on two major studies of Dakota language. Deloria also authored a novel, *Waterlily*, during the 1940s. It was published in 1988, seventeen years after her death.

In her later years, Deloria continued to write, speak, and work with reservation mission schools as she completed her Dakota grammar, fearing that it might join other Native languages in historical oblivion before she could finish. Deloria died of pneumonia at the Tripp Nursing Home, Vermillion, South Dakota, on February 12, 1971. Thanks in part to her work, her language lives on.

FOR MORE INFORMATION:

Deloria, Ella. *Dakota Texts.* 1932. Reprint, New York: AMS Press, 1974.

———. *Waterlily.* Lincoln: University of Nebraska Press, 1988.

Rice, Julian. *Deer Women and Elk Men: The Lakota Narratives of Ella Deloria.* Albuquerque: University of New Mexico Press, 1992.

DELORIA, PHILIP
Yankton Sioux
1854–1931

One of the first American Indians to become an Episcopal priest, Philip Deloria is one of about ninety historical figures whose statues surround *Christ in Majesty* at the Washington, D.C., National Episcopal Cathedral. He was born in South Dakota and educated at colleges

in Nebraska. As longtime rector of St. Elizabeth Mission on the Standing Rock Reservation, Deloria was said to have converted thousands of Sioux to Christianity. He is the father of Ella DELORIA and the grandfather of Vine DELORIA, Jr.

DELORIA, VINE, JR.
Standing Rock Sioux
1933–

Vine Deloria, Jr., rose to prominence with the Native self-determination movements of the 1960s and 1970s, becoming a widely respected professor, author, and social critic. He is one of the founders of Native American studies as a field of scholarly inquiry. In the early 1990s, Deloria was teaching and writing at the University of Colorado Institute for the Study of Race and Ethnicity in the United States.

Deloria was born in Martin, South Dakota; he served in the Marine Corps between 1954 and 1956, before he earned a bachelor's degree at Iowa State University (1958) and a theology degree at the Lutheran School of Theology in 1963. After that, Deloria served as executive director of the National Congress of American Indians.

As early as the 1950s, Deloria was engaging in criticism of the Indian Claims Commission, arguing that it was a device by which to avoid, not solve, treaty issues. He pointed out that laws and regulations announced as help to Indians often, in practice, perpetuated colonialism. Historically, Deloria argued, the rights of Native Americans have trailed those of other social groups in the United States. For example, slavery of Alaskan natives was not outlawed until 1886, two decades after the Civil War. The U.S. Supreme Court ruled in *Elk* v. *Wilkins* (1884) that the Fourteenth Amendment had freed black slaves but not Indians in bondage, because many Native peoples were not citizens of the United States, a status generally accorded them in 1924. Deloria also notes that Los Angeles ran a thriving Indian slave market after the Civil War.

Deloria's writings compare the metaphysics of Native and European points of view, especially in religious matters. In *God Is Red* (1992), he contrasts Native American religion's melding of life with a concept of sacred place to the artifices of Christianity and other Near Eastern religions. Deloria compares the nature of sacredness in each perceptual realm. His discussion of sacredness leads to ecological themes in Native American religions. Deloria also compares the ways in which each culture perceives reality—Europeans see time as lineal and history as a progressive sequence of events; most Native cultures see neither of these. Christianity usually portrays God as a human-like being, often meddlesome and vengeful, whereas many Native religions place supreme authority in a great spirit or great mystery symbolizing the life forces of nature.

The great mystery becomes an ecological metaphor as Deloria explains ways in which Native religions weave a concept of cycles into life, reinforcing reverence for the land and the remains of ancestors buried in it, in contrast to Europeans' ability to move from place to place without regard for location, until the reality of the American land and its often unwritten history begins to absorb them. What follows is described by Deloria as a "surplus of shamans," lost European souls trying to put down ideological roots in American soil.

In the late twentieth century, Deloria continued to write a number of books and articles in scholarly journals that often took issue with ethnocentric interpretations of reality. His early books, such as *Custer Died for Your Sins* (1969), *We Talk, You Listen* (1970), and *Of Utmost Good Faith* (1971), continue to spread to new,

younger audiences. On January 6, 1994, Deloria's home in Boulder, Colorado, was ravaged by fire, destroying archives including his personal library of more than one thousand books. Deloria's computer, containing five chapters of a work in progress, was also destroyed in the fire.

FOR MORE INFORMATION:

Deloria, Vine, Jr. *American Indian Policy in the Twentieth Century.* Norman: University of Oklahoma Press, 1985.

———. *Behind the Trail of Broken Treaties.* New York: Delacorte, 1974.

———. *Custer Died for Your Sins: An Indian Manifesto.* 1960. Reprint, Norman: University of Oklahoma Press, 1988.

———. *God Is Red: A Native View of Religion.* Golden, Colo.: North American Press, 1992.

———. *The Indian Affair.* New York: Friendship Press, 1974.

———. *The Nations Within.* New York: Pantheon, 1984.

———, and Clifford Lytle. *American Indians: American Justice.* Austin: University of Texas Press, 1984.

DELSHAY
Tonto Apache
c. 1835–1874

As an Apache leader in the early 1870s facing the starvation of his people, Delshay fought General George Crook and the U.S. Army in Arizona Territory. He is remembered best for having lost two heads.

In 1868, Delshay and his Tonto band had agreed to settle near Camp McDowell on the Verde River in Arizona, reporting to an agent there. However, the military in Arizona was in utter confusion. Indian agents and military officers quarreled among themselves over political power, while unscrupulous government contractors reaped huge profits supplying shoddy goods to corrupt Indian agents. An influx of miners and settlers forced the Apaches onto less productive land. Game was vanishing. The Tonto Apaches were forced to either starve or steal.

After the 1871 massacre at Camp Grant of ESKIMINZIN's Aravaipa Apaches and the shooting of Delshay himself by an officer at Camp McDowell, he asked that his people be relocated to the Sunflower Valley, near their traditional homeland. Delshay did not even receive a reply to his request. By 1872, to calm the public outcry about increased Apache raids, General Crook began his Tonto Basin campaign. Although the army had some success in quelling unrest among other Apache groups, Delshay remained at large for some time, and his band remained one of the strongest. But by April 1873, Delshay and his band, surrounded by the army, surrendered and were placed on the White Mountain Apache Reservation near Fort Apache.

Unhappy in their confinement, the Tonto Apaches under Delshay fled in July 1873 to Camp Verde, where the Indian agent in charge agreed to let them stay if they stopped all raiding. For a short time, the Tontos lived peacefully until a group of Apaches that had killed Lieutenant Jacob Almy joined forces with them and their raiding resumed.

In early 1874, Crook ordered his men to take no prisoners and shoot all non-reservation Apaches on sight. A cruel winter forced the raiding Apaches to sue for peace. Refusing at first, Crook at last stated that he would allow the Apaches to surrender and return to the San Carlos Reservation if they would bring him the heads of their leaders, including Delshay. Two days after his offer, a group of Apaches brought Crook (at San Carlos) a grain sack containing seven heads, one of them allegedly Delshay's. Although the identity of the seven heads was never certain, Crook then gave the Tonto

Apaches the same offer of a reward for Delshay's head; they responded by bringing in his alleged head to Camp Verde. Faced with the problem of deciding which was the real head of Delshay, Crook stated, "When I visited the Verde Reservation they would convince me they had brought in his head; when I went to San Carlos they would convince me they had brought in his head. Being satisfied that both parties were earnest in their belief, and the bringing of the extra head was not amiss, I paid both parties." Paradoxically, Crook then displayed one head at Camp Verde and the other on the San Carlos Reservation. According to informed Apache scouts who knew Delshay well, the head at San Carlos was authentic.

DEMMERT, WILLIAM
Tlingit and Sioux
1934–

Born on March 9, 1934, William Demmert received a doctorate in education from Harvard University in 1973. His doctoral dissertation was on "Critical Issues in Indian Education." He also coauthored a book entitled *Characteristics of Successful Leaders* (1986).

Demmert has taught at Stanford University, the University of Alaska at Juneau, Harvard University, and the University of Washington. From 1975 to 1976, he was Deputy Commissioner of Education at the U.S. Office of Education. From 1976 to 1978, he was Director of Indian Education for the Bureau of Indian Affairs. In the 1980s, he was Commissioner of Education for the State of Alaska.

DESERSA, BYRON
Oglala Lakota
c. 1955–1976

Byron DeSersa's father was the editor of a monthly newspaper in Manderson on the Pine Ridge Reservation. The elder DeSersa had often editorialized against the regime of Pine Ridge tribal chairman Richard WILSON and his policies. On January 31, 1976, twenty-year-old Byron DeSersa was murdered by tribal police after an automobile chase. DeSersa's car, carrying five unarmed passengers, was chased by six cars driven by tribal police. After DeSersa's car was driven off the road, the police prevented him from receiving any medical attention, and DeSersa bled to death. DeSersa's murder was one of several that occurred at Pine Ridge after the 1973 occupation of Wounded Knee, during a violent conflict between Wilson and supporters of the American Indian Movement (AIM).

Following DeSersa's death, federal and tribal authorities showed reluctance to investigate and prosecute the case. Several witnesses did the investigating for them, collecting affidavits from people near the murder scene, which was close to Wanblee on the Pine Ridge Reservation. One man, Charles D. Winters, was charged in connection with the crime, although several men had surrounded DeSersa while he was bleeding to death. DeSersa's father demanded justice. In June 1976, he wrote on the front page of his newspaper:

> The DeSersas have waited for many months for the U.S. attorney and his puppet grand jury to bring Byron DeSersa's killers to justice. There is [sic] only 30 days left to bring justice for the DeSersa killing. After that, then justice will come to the guilty ones. The family will not allow one of its kins to be killed without the forfeit of another. Violence may well occur again. [Johansen and Maestas]

FOR MORE INFORMATION:
Johansen, Bruce E., and Roberto M. Maestas. *Wasi'chu: The Continuing Indian Wars.* New York: Monthly Review Press, 1979.

Wounded Knee Legal Defense-Offense Committee. "Chronology of Violence." Rapid City, S.D.: Wounded Knee Legal Defense-Offense Committee, 1976.

DESKAHEH (LEVI GENERAL)
Cayuga
1873–1925

Deskaheh was *Tadadaho* (speaker) of the Iroquois Grand Council at Grand River, Ontario, in the early 1920s, when Canadian authorities closed the traditional Longhouse, which had been asserting independence from Canadian jurisdiction. The Canadian authorities proposed to set up a governmental structure that would answer to its Indian affairs bureaucracy. With Canadian police about to arrest him, Deskaheh traveled to the headquarters of the League of Nations in Geneva, Switzerland, with an appeal for support from the international community.

Deskaheh. [Courtesy of John Kahionhes Fadden]

Several months of effort did not win him a hearing before the international body in large part because of diplomatic manipulation by Great Britain and Canada, governments that were being embarrassed by Deskaheh's mission. Lacking a forum at the League of Nations, Deskaheh and his supporters privately organized a meeting in Switzerland, which drew several thousand people who roared approval of Iroquois sovereignty.

In his last speech, March 10, 1925, Deskaheh had lost none of his distaste for forced acculturation. "Over in Ottawa, they call that policy 'Indian Advancement.' Over in Washington, they call it 'Assimilation.' We who would be the helpless victims say it is tyranny. . . . If this must go on to the bitter end, we would rather that you come with your guns and poison gas and get rid of us that way. Do it openly and above board." ["Deskaheh"]

As Deskaheh lay dying, his relatives who lived in the United States were refused entry into Canada to be at his bedside. Deskaheh died two and a half months after his last defiant speech. His notions of sovereignty have been maintained by many Iroquois into contemporary times. The Iroquois Grand Council at Onondaga issues its own passports, which are recognized by Switzerland and several other countries but not by the United States or Canada.

FOR MORE INFORMATION:

"Deskaheh: Iroquois Statesman and Patriot." Six Nations Indian Museum Series. Akwesasne, N.Y.: *Akwesasne Notes*, n.d.

Deskaheh (Levi General) and Six Nations Council. *The Redman's Appeal for Justice.* Brantford, Ontario: Wilson Moore, 1924.

Rostkowski, Joelle. "The Redman's Appeal for Justice: Deskaheh and the League of Nations." In *Indians and Europe*, edited by Christian F. Feest. Aachen, Germany: Edition Herodot, 1987.

DIETZ, ANGEL DECORA
Winnebago
c. 1871–1919

Born on the Nebraska Winnebago Reservation, Angel DeCora Dietz was also known as Hinookmahiwi-kilinaka ("Floating Fleecy Cloud") and "the Word Carrier." She became an influential artist and political activist on a national level in the early twentieth century.

Dietz worked with author Gertrude BONNIN, creating artwork for several of her books. Both women shared an interest in trying to improve reservation living conditions. At one point, Dietz visited President Theodore Roosevelt to brief him on reservation conditions. In 1908, she married William Dietz (Lone Star), a Sioux with whom she collaborated on several artistic projects. They divorced a decade later.

In 1919, Dietz was living in New York City when she died of influenza during an epidemic.

FOR MORE INFORMATION:

Bataille, Gretchen M. *Native American Women.* New York: Garland Publishing, 1993.

DOCKSTADER, FREDERICK J.
Oneida/Navajo
1919–

Although he was born in Los Angeles, Dockstader spent most of his early years on the Navajo and Hopi Reservations in Arizona. He became an outstanding anthropologist, author, and silversmith. Dockstader became the staff ethnologist at the Cranbrook Institute in 1950. Later he became curator of anthropology at Dartmouth College. In 1955, he became assistant director of the Museum of the American Indian (Heye Foundation), and in 1960, he was named director. Since his primary field of study was Indian art, he was also appointed commissioner of the Indian Arts and Crafts Board of the U.S. Department of the Interior in 1955. His books include *Indian Art in America* (1962),

Indian Art in Middle America (1964), *Indian Art in South America* (1967), and *Great American Indians* (1977).

DODGE, HENRY CHEE
Navajo
1860–1947

Henry Chee Dodge, who became the first tribal chairman of the Navajo nation, was born February 22, 1860, of Bisnayanchi (a Navajo/Jemez woman of the Coyote Pass clan) and Juan Anaya, the Mexican silversmith and interpreter for Captain Henry Linn Dodge, the Indian agent to the Navajos. Chee Dodge's father died in 1862 and his mother renamed him after Captain Dodge. As a young lad, he was called Kilchii or "Red Boy," which is the derivation for his Navajo name "Chee." Dodge was also known as Adits'aii, in Navajo meaning "the Hearing and Understanding Person," and Ashkihih Diitsi, "the Boy Interpreter."

When he was orphaned by his mother's death during the Navajo Wars of 1863–1866, he was taken to Fort Sumner (Bosque Redondo) by his adoptive Navajo parents. A few years later, he was adopted by an agency worker, Perry H. Williams, who taught him English. Consequently, he became a useful Navajo interpreter for the U.S. government and a friend of Kit CAR-SON. On April 19, 1884, Dodge became the successor to the great Navajo chief MANUELITO and was made tribal chief by Dennis M. Riordan, Superintendent of Indian Affairs. He traveled to Washington, D.C., to meet President Chester A. Arthur shortly after his appointment. Realizing the cultural and artistic importance of Navajo silversmithing, Dodge was a patron of DELGA-DITO, the first influential Navajo silversmith. About 1890, he invested in a sheep ranch and trading post. These enterprises were economic successes; he built his home, Tso Tsela, "Stars Laying Down," near Crystal, New Mexico, and

he became a prominent and wealthy man. Dodge resided in Crystal for the rest of his life. He married four wives. He divorced his first wife, Adzaan Tsinajinnie, to marry Nanabah and her younger sister. Upon Nanabah's death, he married K'eehabah. He was the father of five children (one daughter died young); the remaining offspring, Tom, Ben, Mary, and Annie, became prominent in Navajo affairs.

In 1922, he became one of three members of the Navajo Business Council that negotiated corporate agreements and investments with economic interests in the area. On July 27, 1923, the Navajo Tribal Council was created, and Chee Dodge was chosen its first chairman. In this position he helped to institute a more formal system of centralized government for the Navajo nation. Although he stepped down as chairman in 1928, he remained highly influential in tribal affairs. Working with Commissioner of Indian Affairs John Collier in 1933, Chee Dodge helped introduce a controversial program to reduce the amount of livestock grazing on the Navajo Reservation, even though it meant he would have to reduce his own herds by about half. Opposed by many Navajos as harsh and unresponsive, the program was a social and economic disaster. In the violence that ensued, many sheepherders were incarcerated by federal authorities. Ironically, the Navajos were being penalized for adapting to changing economic conditions and becoming successful herders as governmental policies dictated. The spiritual shock of the wasteful slaughter of livestock persists to this day; the Navajos believe that this government policy was sacrilegious.

In 1942, Chee Dodge was elected tribal chairman once again. Even though he was an old man by this time, he journeyed to Washington many times to plead the Navajo cause. Although he was reelected in 1946, he was not able to take office owing to ill health. He was admitted to

Sage Memorial Hospital in Ganado, Arizona, with pneumonia and died at the age of eighty-seven on January 7, 1947. Buried at Fort Defiance, he was admired and respected by Indian and non-Indian alike at the time of his demise.

FOR MORE INFORMATION:

Dockstader, Frederick. *Great North American Indians.* New York: Van Nostrand Reinhold, 1977.

DOHOSAN (LITTLE BLUFF)
Kiowa
c. 1805–1866

Noted for his courage and defiance in the face of threats from the U.S. government, Dohosan is considered by many to be the greatest of a hereditary line of chiefs of the Kiowas. In 1833, he became chief after the Osages decimated a band of Kiowas and took their Sun Dance gods. As a result, his predecessor, Dohate or "Bluff," was deposed.

Although he signed several treaties (notably the Fort Atkinson Treaty of July 27, 1853, and the Little Arkansas River Treaty of October 18, 1865), Dohosan had little regard for the white man and his agreements. He believed that Indians should fight to retain their lands and rights as free people. However, he identified with and respected the Mexicans, who thought and fought much as he did. When he died in 1866 at the hands of a Dakota man, his name was bestowed upon his son, also a distinguished warrior.

DOONKEEN, EULAMAE NARCOMEY (HAH GAY KEE HOODYH LEE)
Seminole
1931–

Also known as Hah Gay Kee Hoodyh Lee or "Crying Wind," she was vice chief of the Seminole nation of Oklahoma in the mid-1970s. As a political activist for social action programs, an active leader in the National Congress of American Indians, and a spearhead for Oklahomans for Indian Opportunity, she gained national prominence as an outspoken leader.

DONNACONNA
Huron
fl. 1530s

As chief of Stadacona, a village on the St. Lawrence River near present-day Quebec City, Donnaconna met French explorer Jacques Cartier about 1534. Donnaconna lent Cartier the services of two of his sons as guides. In 1536, Cartier returned to France with Donnaconna on board, the victim of a kidnapping. The chief died in France in 1539, one of the first Native North Americans to visit that country. The kidnapping of Donnaconna so outraged the Iroquois that in 1580, more than forty years later, it was a major reason why the Iroquois denied the French access to the St. Lawrence River.

DORRIS, MICHAEL A.
Modoc
1945–

Dorris studied English and the classics at Georgetown University, graduating with honors in 1967. He also studied anthropology at Yale University, receiving a master's degree in 1970. An American Indian anthropologist and novelist who has taught at Franconia College, University of Redlands, and Dartmouth College (where he was director of Native American Studies throughout most of the 1970s and 1980s), he is the author of numerous scholarly articles and books including *Native Americans: Five Hundred Years After* and *A Guide to Research on North American Indians* (with Arlene Hirschfelder and Mary Lou Byler). His novels include *A Yellow Raft in Blue Water* and *The Crown of Columbus* (with Louise ERDRICH, his wife). Dorris is a descendant of the noted Modoc leader Kintpuash, or CAPTAIN JACK.

DOUBLEHEAD
Cherokee
c. 1755–1807

Doublehead, as speaker for the Cherokee nation between 1796 and 1807, ceded large tracts of land to the U.S. government. Although in 1793 he led a force that killed two white men in retaliation for attacks on Cherokee villages, he became a spokesman for the Cherokees in talks with the federal government. While prominent in the 1798, 1804, and 1805 negotiations that led to the cession of vast tracts of Cherokee land, it is generally believed that he received bribes in all these transactions. Upon being promised two tracts of land especially for him in 1806, he illegally ceded still more lands to the U.S. government. In 1807, for his treachery to his people, he was killed by the Cherokees.

DOZIER, EDWARD P. (AWA TSIDE)
Santa Clara Pueblo
1916–1971

Born on the Santa Clara Pueblo in New Mexico, Edward P. Dozier (whose Native name means "Cattail Bird") was reared imbued with the cultures and traditions of his people, a fact that was appreciated by many scholars and students as he became a renowned anthropologist and Indian rights activist. Dozier attended reservation schools. While serving as an officer in the U.S. Army Air Force during World War II, Dozier became interested in anthropology. He was one of the earliest Native American scholars to make his way into this scholarly discipline.

After World War II, Dozier attended the University of New Mexico and received his B.A. (1947) and M.A. (1949) degrees, specializing in Pueblo linguistic studies. Subsequently, he pursued further graduate studies at the University of California, Los Angeles, and received his

Ph.D. in anthropology in 1952. His doctoral dissertation focused on a group of Tewa people that moved to the Hopi Pueblo in the late seventeenth century, where they developed a distinctive community. He held academic positions at the University of Oregon, University of Arizona, the University of the Philippines, and the University of Minnesota. Dozier authored over twenty scholarly articles and two books, *Hano: A Pueblo Community in Arizona* (1967) and *Pueblo Indians in the Southwest* (1970). His career was cut short by a fatal heart attack in 1971.

DRAGGING CANOE (TSIYU-GUNSINI, TSUNGUNSINI, CHEUCUNSENE, KUNMESEE)
Cherokee
c. 1730–1792

Dragging Canoe, also known as Tsiyu-Gunsini (from *tsiyi*, "canoe," and *gunsini*, "he is dragging it"), was a principal chief of the Chickamauga band of Cherokees who allied with the British in the American Revolution. He was a son of ATTAKULLAKULLA and a cousin of Nancy WARD.

Dragging Canoe was born along the Tennessee River at Running Water Village or Natchez Town in present-day eastern Tennessee. As a leader, he violently opposed the white man's expansion into his people's lands. In 1775, at the Treaty of Sycamore Shoals, Cherokee leaders sold much of what would become Kentucky and northern Tennessee for ten thousand pounds of trade goods. Furious, Dragging Canoe refused to sign the agreement, and he declared that "finally, the whole country we . . . have for so long occupied, will be demanded; and the [Cherokee] . . . will be obliged to seek further refuge in some distant wilderness . . . until they again behold the advancing banners of the same greedy host." He concluded his speech by predicting that "you will find the settlement of this land dark and bloody."

As a result of the treaty, Dragging Canoe accepted arms from the British during the American Revolution. In July 1776, Dragging Canoe's warriors struck the trans-Appalachian settlements at Watauga. His cousin Nancy WARD, council member of the Cherokees, warned the white settlers before the attack and many lives were saved. When James Robertson and John Sevier counterattacked, Dragging Canoe retreated to Chickamauga Creek near what is now Chattanooga, Tennessee. In response, militia units destroyed Cherokee villages and crops.

In 1777, Cherokee leaders ceded vast areas of the Cherokee homeland. But Dragging Canoe, another Cherokee chief named BLOODY FELLOW, and the Creek chief Alexander McGILLIVRAY fought on. In 1778, British agents out of Pensacola, Florida, resupplied Dragging Canoe, Bloody Fellow, and McGillivray, and they began another wave of attacks on the white frontier. Frontier militias responded by devastating many Native settlements. The cycle of war and destruction in the Southeast carried on until all Chickamauga villages were decimated by the end of the American Revolution.

In 1782, as a result of these depredations, Dragging Canoe led his people downriver to present-day Chickamauga, Tennessee, and built the Chickamauga Lower Towns including Mialaquo, his new home. In 1784, when these towns were ravaged, he agreed to sue for peace.

In 1785, the Treaty of Hopewell established formal boundaries for the Cherokee nation and abandoned all lands outside those boundaries. By treaty, no white people could squat on Cherokee lands, but the American government would not enforce the treaty. Dragging Canoe responded by raiding settlements, burning cab-

ins, and deterring land speculators. As a result of this friction, the Treaty of Halston was signed in 1791. This treaty reaffirmed the land rights of the Cherokees, provided for an annual stipend, and accelerated the development of an agricultural economy among the Cherokees. However, the land grabbers and squatters continued unabated.

Dragging Canoe died at Running Water, Tennessee, on March 1, 1791, still resisting the invasion of his homeland. The relentless pattern persisted after his death, finally resulting in the tragic removal of the Cherokees to Arkansas and Oklahoma in the 1830s; this ill-fated removal process was called the Trail of Tears because thousands of Cherokees died along the way.

FOR MORE INFORMATION:

Dockstader, Frederick. *Great North American Indians.* New York: Van Nostrand Reinhold, 1977.

DROUILLARD, GEORGE (DREWYER)
Mixed Pawnee
fl. 1807–1810

Born of a French father and Pawnee mother, George Drouillard served with British forces that opposed the Americans led by George Rogers Clark during the American Revolution. Clark recommended Drouillard for his brother William's Lewis and Clark expedition in 1803. On December 3, 1803, Drouillard became a part of the Lewis and Clark expedition at Fort Massac in the vicinity of Paducah, Kentucky. An excellent shot, he bagged many of the expedition's 131 elk and 20 deer that were killed for food. William Clark relied heavily on Drouillard's cartographic knowledge of the West when he drafted his map of the West. Adept at sign language, Drouillard was able to communicate with many of the Indian nations while the expedition was en route to the Pacific Coast.

After the expedition's end, Drouillard and Manuel Lisa, along with Antoine Pierre Menard and William Morrison, established the first U.S. trading operation up the Missouri. Edward ROSE and John Colter were a part of this venture; they instituted the first trading post in what would become Montana and also initiated trade with the Crow nation. Upon returning to St. Louis, Drouillard was tried for the murder of Antoine Bissonette but was acquitted; Bissonette had stolen from the trading party and then deserted it.

On another venture up the Missouri, Lisa established Fort Mandan, while Drouillard, Menard, Colter, and Andrew Henry proceeded up the Missouri River to Three Forks in Blackfoot country. There they established a stockade. Renowned as an explorer, pioneer trader, and marksman throughout the upper Mississippi River valley in his later years, Drouillard died in 1810.

FOR MORE INFORMATION:

Skarstan, M. O. *George Drouillard: Hunter and Interpreter for Lewis and Clark . . . 1807–1810*. Glendale, Calif.: A. H. Clark Co., 1964.

DUKES, JOSEPH
Mixed Choctaw
1811–1861

As a young Choctaw Indian born in Mississippi, Joseph Dukes went to religious schools and then became an interpreter for several missionaries to his nation. He was instrumental in the creation of a Choctaw grammar book and dictionary. Although Dukes stayed in Mississippi after Choctaw removal, he later relocated to Indian Territory. In 1851, Dukes started to collaborate on the translation of the Christian Bible into the Choctaw language. It was completed in 1852.

DULL KNIFE (MORNING STAR)
Cheyenne
c. 1810–1883

Dull Knife—called Dull Knife by the Lakota and Morning Star by the Cheyenne—was one of two principal Cheyenne leaders (with LITTLE WOLF) who led the trek back to their homeland in eastern Montana after the exile to Indian country (later Oklahoma) late in the 1870s and 1880s. The harrowing march back to the Cheyenne homeland is described in Mari Sandoz's *Cheyenne Autumn* (1953).

Dull Knife, Little Wolf, and other Cheyennes may have enjoyed a brief euphoria after they allied with the Lakota and other tribes to defeat George Armstrong CUSTER at the Little Bighorn in 1876. Within a year, however, reinforced army columns were chasing bands of Lakota and Cheyenne across the Plains. Dull Knife was weary and depressed as he led his people into the Bighorn Mountains near the head of the Powder River. General Ranald S. MacKenzie moved out of Fort Fetterman in November 1876 and encountered Dull Knife's band in the course of a search for CRAZY HORSE's Oglalas. Nearly half of MacKenzie's force was made up of reservation-bound Cheyennes and Pawnees, recruited from near-starving conditions. Dull Knife's band had four hundred warriors. MacKenzie's force devastated them. A band of survivors hobbled to Crazy Horse's camp at Beaver Creek. Eleven children froze to death during the march, and the Cheyennes were forced to eat nearly all of their horses.

Crazy Horse shared his band's scanty food supplies and blankets but refused to rise to the invocations of some of the more hotheaded Cheyennes to stage a last-ditch fight against the army. "The Wasi'chus [white men] outnumber the blades of grass on the prairie," said Crazy Horse. "It is time to take the white man's road. . . . or we shall all be killed." Dull Knife agreed. "We Cheyennes are trying to fight the whirlwind." [Sandoz]

In spring 1877, the Cheyennes who had lodged with Crazy Horse during the winter surrendered to General Nelson Miles at Fort Keough. About thirty young warriors—those who had felt betrayed by Crazy Horse's refusal to aid them in a last-ditch battle—enlisted as scouts for Miles against Crazy Horse's band, which was still free. The rest were sent to Darlington Reservation in Indian Territory. Dull Knife realized with growing bitterness that promises of abundant game in Oklahoma were a lie. The buffalo were gone, and smaller game had been hunted to near extinction by the Indians who had been sent there earlier. Cheyennes began to die of a fever, probably malaria; others starved. Promised government rations did not arrive on time.

In the middle of August 1878, Dull Knife and Little Wolf pleaded with Indian agent John Miles to let the Cheyennes return home. Half the band had died in their year in Oklahoma. Dull Knife himself was shaking with fever as they talked. Miles asked for a year to work on the problem, and Little Wolf told him the Cheyennes would be dead in a year. Miles refused to relent.

The next morning at sunrise, the three hundred surviving Cheyennes broke for the open country, heading for their home on the Powder River, a thousand miles away. The next afternoon, two companies of cavalry caught up with them on the Little Medicine Lodge River. The Cheyennes refused promises of good treatment and drove off an attack, continuing northwestward. The Cheyennes repelled several more attacks over the next few weeks, capturing some non-Indian traders' small arms and buffalo meat along the way. They crossed the

Dull Knife. [National Anthropological Archives]

Arkansas and the South Platte Rivers, skirmishing again with soldiers. At White Clay Creek, Nebraska, the Cheyennes split into two groups. Dull Knife and 150 others went into Red Cloud Agency to surrender. Little Wolf and a roughly equal number headed into the Nebraska Sand Hills, where they spent the winter in hiding.

Back in Nebraska, Dull Knife's band had found Red Cloud Agency abandoned, so they moved on to Fort Robinson. For two months, Dull Knife's Cheyennes lived at the fort while the commanding officer awaited orders. When they finally came, the orders were to send the

Indians back to Indian Territory. Dull Knife refused to go. "No! I am here on my own ground, and I will never go back. You may kill me here, but you cannot make me go back!" [Sandoz] Captain Wessells, the commanding officer, sought to make the Cheyennes change their minds by locking them in a freezing barracks with no food or water. For three days, the Cheyennes remained in the barracks in below-freezing weather. Wessells gave them a last chance to surrender, and the Cheyennes again refused.

Just after sunset on January 9, 1879, Little Shield, a Dog Soldier Society leader, led the Cheyennes in a desperate breakout. The Dog Soldiers led people out of the barracks' windows. Shooting wildly, soldiers chased them out of the fort. Fifty Cheyennes died in the snow that evening. Twenty more died of wounds and exposure; most of the remaining Cheyennes, fewer than a hundred now, were herded back to Fort Robinson.

Dull Knife, his wife, and their son were among the few who escaped. They walked eighteen nights, resting by day, to Pine Ridge. They ate bark and their own moccasins to survive. At the Pine Ridge Agency, Bill Rowland, an interpreter, took the family in.

Thirty-one other warriors had escaped the soldiers from Fort Robinson but found themselves pinned down at Hat Creek Bluffs. The soldiers pummeled the area with gunshot and then called on the warriors to surrender. Their answer was three shots—the last three bullets the warriors had. More shooting followed, killing twenty-eight of the men. The surviving three stood up, took up their empty rifles as clubs, and charged the three hundred soldiers, who cut them to pieces.

The bones of the dead Cheyennes later were turned over to the Army Medical Museum for scientific study. On October 8, 1993, the remains were returned to a delegation of sixteen Cheyennes in Washington, D.C., for reburial under the Native American Graves Protection and Repatriation Act of 1990.

Dull Knife lived out his days on a reservation assigned to the surviving Cheyennes in the Rosebud Valley. He died in 1883 and was buried on high ground near his home.

FOR MORE INFORMATION:

Little Eagle, Avis. "Remains of Dull Knife's Band Make Final Journey Home." *Indian Country Today* (October 14, 1993).

Sandoz, Mari. *Cheyenne Autumn*. New York: Hastings House, 1953.

Wiltsey, Norman B. *Brave Warriors*. Caldwell, Idaho: Caxton, 1963.

DUNDY, ELMER S.
1830–1896

Elmer S. Dundy was the federal judge in Omaha who ruled during 1879, in the case of the Ponca STANDING BEAR, that Indians must be treated as people under U.S. law. The ruling implicitly denied the U.S. Army's presumed right to relocate individual Native Americans against their will, but it was restricted to Standing Bear's group.

Hearing of the travail of Standing Bear and his people as they camped near Omaha, local citizens obtained a writ of habeas corpus and brought the army into the federal court of Judge Dundy, who ruled: "An Indian is a person within the meaning of the law, and there is no law giving the Army authority to forcibly remove Indians from their lands." [Massey] Ironically, the case was prepared with the help of the old Indian fighter George Crook, who was swayed by the manifest injustice of the case. The harsh treatment of the

Ponca also received publicity in Omaha newspapers, was wired to larger newspapers on the East Coast, and caused a storm of protest letters to Congress.

Shortly after the ruling, Standing Bear's brother BIG SNAKE tested it by moving roughly one hundred miles within Indian Territory, from the Poncas' assigned reservation to one occupied by Cheyennes. Big Snake did not understand that the ruling had been limited to Standing Bear's party. He was arrested by troops and returned to the Ponca reservation. On October 31, 1879, Ponca Indian agent William H. Whiteman called Big Snake a troublemaker and ordered a detail to imprison him. When Big Snake refused to surrender, contending he had committed no crime, he was shot to death. Later, the U.S. Senate called for an investigation of the shooting and other aspects of the Poncas' tragedy.

FOR MORE INFORMATION:

Massey, Rosemary, et al. *Footprints in Blood: Standing Bear's Struggle for Freedom and Human Dignity.* Omaha: American Indian Center of Omaha, 1979.

Tibbles, Thomas Henry. *The Ponca Chiefs: An Account of the Trial of Standing Bear.* Lincoln: University of Nebraska Press, 1972.

DURANT, WILLIAM A.
Choctaw
c. 1866–1948

Born in Oklahoma Territory, Durant was the sergeant-at-arms at the Oklahoma Constitutional Convention (in 1907), which established the government for the state of Oklahoma. He served as a member of the Oklahoma House of Representatives from 1907 to 1912. He was Speaker of the House during his last term of office. In 1934, he was chosen as principal chief of the Choctaw nation when the tribal government was reorganized.

DUSTIN, HANNAH
fl. 1690s

Hannah Dustin became a heroine among residents of Haverhill, Massachusetts, after an Indian attack on the town in 1697. She, her week-old infant, and a nursemaid were kidnapped by Indians (the historical record is not clear on the tribe to which they may have belonged). After the raiders killed the baby for crying, Dustin waited for the right instant to seize the initiative and killed all but two of her captors with an axe or tomahawk. Returning to the town with scalps in hand, Dustin found herself a heroine and recipient of a £25 sterling reward.

E

EASTMAN, CHARLES (OHIYESA)
Santee or Mdewakanton Sioux
1858–1939

Along with his contemporaries Luther STAND-ING BEAR and Gertrude BONNIN, Charles Eastman provided a historical voice for the Sioux during the generations after subjugation by the United States. Eastman was also educated as a medical doctor and was a founder of the Society of American Indians.

Eastman was born near Redwood Falls, Minnesota; he was four years old when his family was caught up in the 1862 Great Sioux Uprising in Minnesota. The family fled to Canada with other Santee Sioux, but Eastman's father was later turned over to U.S. authorities. His father was one of the Sioux sentenced to hang after the uprising but was also among those pardoned by President Abraham Lincoln. His death sentence was commuted to a prison term.

Eastman was raised by relatives near Fort Ellis in southern Manitoba. Known in adulthood by the Sioux name Ohiyesa ("the Winner"), Eastman attended Dartmouth College, entering the freshman class of 1883 and graduating in 1887. Eastman earned a medical degree from Boston University in 1890; in his capacity as a medical doctor, he observed (and later published his recollections of) the aftermath of the Wounded Knee massacre. Later, he had a harrowing experience as a government physician at Pine Ridge during a time when epidemics were still sweeping reservation-bound Indians. Eastman later turned to private practice and, still later, with encouragement from his wife, Elaine Goodale, to writing and lecturing.

Eastman was an unusually brilliant student as a young man. He was involved with the organization of the Boy Scouts of America and the Campfire Girls from their inception and is credited as being the person most responsible for the incorporation of Indian lore into these groups. Eastman wrote nine books, some of which were translated into several languages other than English. Two of his books were autobiographical: *Indian Boyhood* (1902) and *From the Deep Woods to Civilization* (1916).

Eastman was one of a number of Sioux who watched their culture crushed in the late nineteenth century. His books enjoyed wide popularity early in the 1900s. In his autobiographical *Indian Boyhood,* Eastman recalled how his uncle had first portrayed Euro-Americans:

I had heard marvelous things about this people. In some things, we despised them; in others we regarded them as wakan (mysterious), a race whose power bordered on the supernatural. . . . I asked my uncle why the Great Mystery gave such power to the Wasi'chu . . . and not to us Dakotas.

"Certainly they are a heartless nation;" [the uncle said] "they have made some of their people servants—yes, slaves! We have never believed in keeping slaves. . . . The greatest object of their lives seems to be to gather possessions—to be rich. They desire to possess the entire world."

Eastman died on January 8, 1939, at his home in Detroit, Michigan. He was eighty years old.

FOR MORE INFORMATION:

Eastman, Charles (Ohiyesa). *From the Deep Woods to Civilization.* Boston, 1916. Reprint, Lincoln: University of Nebraska Press, 1977.

———. *Indian Boyhood.* New York: McClure, Phillips, & Co., 1902.

———. *Indian Heroes and Great Chieftains.* Boston, 1923. Reprint, Lincoln: University of Nebraska Press, 1991.

———. *Indian Scout Talks.* Boston, 1914.

———. *The Indian Today.* New York, 1915.

———. *Red Hunters and the Animal People.* New York, 1904.

———. *The Soul of the Indian: An Interpretation.* Boston and New York: Houghton-Mifflin, 1911.

———, and Elaine Goodale Eastman. *Wigwam Evenings: Sioux Tales Retold.* Boston, 1909. Reprint, Lincoln: University of Nebraska Press, 1990.

Nabokov, Peter. *Native American Testimony.* New York: Viking Penguin, 1991.

ECHOHAWK, JOHN
Pawnee
1945–

As an attorney and as executive director of the Native American Rights Fund since the middle 1970s, John Echohawk has made the organization a national force in Native legal affairs. From land rights to water rights to the reburial of Native bones and burial artifacts, the Native American Rights Fund has helped shape law and public opinion in late-twentieth-century America.

Echohawk was born in Albuquerque, New Mexico, and earned a bachelor's degree from the University of New Mexico in 1967. He earned a law degree from the same university in 1970, the same year he began his career at the Native American Rights Fund (NARF) as a staff attorney. Serving as senior staff attorney at the NARF is Walter Echohawk (b. 1948), John Echohawk's brother, who played a lead role in negotiations with the Smithsonian Institution in 1989 for the return of Native artifacts and human remains to tribes. He was a national leader in efforts to pass federal laws protecting Native graves.

ECHOHAWK, LARRY
Pawnee
1948–

After serving as attorney general of Idaho, Larry Echohawk ran for governor of Idaho as a Democrat in 1994. He lost to Republican Phil Batt in a nationwide Republican landslide, scuttling Echohawk's hopes to become the United

States' first Native American state governor. Echohawk advocated environmental issues, consumer protection, and crime victims' rights in his campaign.

Echohawk was born at Cody, Wyoming, and grew up in Farmington, New Mexico, one of six children of a full-blooded Pawnee father and a German mother. Echohawk's father was a land surveyor and worked in the oil supply business. His father was a severe alcoholic until he was converted to Mormonism.

Larry Echohawk won a football scholarship to Brigham Young University, where he played quarterback and earned an undergraduate degree in 1970. He also earned a juris doctor in 1973 at the University of Utah. Echohawk's legal career began with California Indian Legal

Larry Echohawk.
[Echohawk for Governor campaign]

Services. After that, Echohawk practiced law privately in Salt Lake City.

Echohawk served as general counsel for the Shoshoni-Bannock tribes at Fort Hall between 1980 and 1986, before he served a term as Bannock County prosecutor. He also served in the Idaho House of Representatives after election in 1982 and reelection in 1984. In 1991, Echohawk became the United States' first Native American to be elected to an attorney general's position. Echohawk spoke to the 1992 Democratic National Convention and was the first Native American to head a state delegation to that convention.

Echohawk is a holder of the George Washington University Martin Luther King Award for contributions to human rights.

FOR MORE INFORMATION:

Echohawk, John. "Our People—Native Americans, Then and Now." *Earth Journal* (January 1994): 38–43.

ECOFFEY, ROBERT D.
Oglala Lakota
c. 1955–

Early in 1994, Robert Ecoffey became the first Native American to hold the office of United States Marshal in the Justice Department. Ecoffey was appointed marshal for South Dakota, one of ninety-four in the United States. Ecoffey was sworn in with the traditional marshal's oath at Pine Ridge High School on March 16. Native acquaintances presented him with an eagle feather, symbolic of accomplishment in battle. More than eight hundred people attended the swearing-in for Ecoffey at the high school from which he had graduated twenty-one years earlier.

FOR MORE INFORMATION:

McElwain, Judy. "Ecoffey Sworn in as Federal Marshal." *Indian Country Today* (March 23, 1994): B-1.

EDENSHAW
Haida
fl. 1880s

As leader of the Stustas on Graham Island in the Queen Charlotte Islands, Edenshaw was one of the wealthiest of Haida chiefs. He is recalled as a friend of white explorers and missionaries. He requested a missionary for his village and at one time saved several U.S. sailors when their ship was besieged by other Native peoples. He died in 1885.

EDENSHAW, CHARLES
Tlinget
1839–1924

Nephew of EDENSHAW (the name probably means "Glacier" in Tlinget), Charles became a noted carver and silversmith, as well as chief of Yatza village on Graham Island in the Queen Charlottes. Charles Edenshaw's carvings and silver work have been exhibited by museums and galleries worldwide as evidence of the sophistication of Northwest Coast Native art.

FOR MORE INFORMATION:

Blackmore, Margaret. *During My Time: Florence Edenshaw, A Haida Woman.* Seattle: University of Washington Press, 1982.

EDWARDS, J. R. ("JUNIOR")
Mohawk
1958–1990

Junior Edwards was killed during the early hours of May 1, 1990, during the culmination of firefights over commercial gaming that wracked the Akwesasne Mohawk (St. Regis) Reservation. Mathew PYKE was also killed that night before police agencies from the United States and Canada occupied the area the next day. The body of Edwards, thirty-two, was found roughly six hundred yards from where Pyke had been killed along the River Road in an area of Akwesasne called Snye. Edwards had been killed by a blast to the stomach.

Harold Edwards, Sr., father of Junior Edwards, said that the young man had been an innocent victim most of his life. The younger Edwards lived alone in a house owned by his father near Snye, drew welfare, and "at times drank too much." While the younger Edwards did not overtly support gambling interests (the senior Edwards said his four other sons were gambling supporters), he was impressionable and sometimes hung out with gaming sympathizers. Edwards said that the blame for his son's death lay with the people who had brought the guns to Akwesasne.

> Whoever killed my son, I don't blame them as much as the people bringing in the weapons in the first place," he said. "It's some other people who are bringing them in, and giving them to the Warriors, and then they go crazy. I want the police to get the people who are bringing in the guns and the dope, even if they have to search every house to do it.

Edwards's murder was not solved; Doug GEORGE, Akwesasne newspaper editor and antigaming activist, was charged with the murder by Quebec authorities but was exonerated before trial by a judge who said the charge was baseless.

FOR MORE INFORMATION:

Johansen, Bruce E. *Life and Death in Mohawk Country.* Golden, Colo.: North American Press, 1993.

EL MOCHO
Tonkawa-Apache
c. 1730–1784

It is believed that El Mocho was born an Apache and then captured as a youth by the Tonkawas and taken to central Texas. Displaying valor and persuasiveness to his abductors, he quickly gained release from his captivity. He acquired his Spanish name (which means "the Cropped One") as a result of losing his right ear in a battle with some Osages. During an epidemic in 1777–1778, the Tonkawa chief died and El Mocho became the new chief. In 1782, he sought to fashion an alliance between the Tonkawas and Apaches to fight the Spanish. But at a council attended by more than four thousand people, El Mocho failed to cement a Tonkawa/Apache alliance. In 1784, the Spanish killed him because they feared his diplomatic and military skills.

ELOW-OH-KAOM
Mohawk
fl. early 1700s

Elow-Oh-Kaom was one of four Mohawks who visited England as a guest of Queen Anne in 1710, part of English diplomatic activity to bring the Mohawks and other Iroquois to the side of Britain in the conflict with France. One of the four, HENDRICK, later became well known as a British ally and participant in the Albany Congress of 1754. Elow-Oh-Kaom was christianized as Nicholas; he was called "King of the River Nation" during the visit. He may have been born a Schacook or Mohican, whom the English sometimes called the "River Indians," and adopted as a Mohawk. He was in the Turtle Clan.

FOR MORE INFORMATION:

Bond, Richmond P. *Queen Anne's American Kings.* Oxford: Clarendon Press, 1952.

EMATHLA, CHARLEY (CHARLES EMARTHLA, AMATHLA)
Seminole
c. 1790–1835

Born a Creek Indian in Georgia, Charley Emathla moved to Florida in the late 1820s and became a Seminole and an opponent of OSCE-OLA. Many of the Georgia Creeks were forcibly relocated west of the Mississippi at the time. Emathla settled on a small farm near Fort King (in the region of present-day Tampa, Florida) with a herd of cattle. He subsequently assumed a leadership role among the Seminoles. As a signatory of the Treaty of Payne's Landing in 1832, he agreed to relocate to Indian Territory (Oklahoma). While accompanying a Seminole delegation to inspect the new lands promised in Indian Territory, he signed the 1833 Treaty of Fort Gibson. In 1835, Emathla was ambushed and killed by Osceola and other warriors after he had readied himself for removal through the sale of his cattle. It is said that Osceola threw the cattle money gained from whites over Emathla's dead body as it awaited burial.

EMISTESIGO (GURISTERSIGO)
Creek
c. 1752–1782

Near the end of the American Revolution in June 1782, a British force marched out of Savannah, Georgia, to join forces with a group of Creek warriors led by Emistesigo. General "Mad Anthony" Wayne, leading a contingent of American patriots, intercepted and defeated the British. However, Emistesigo's warriors boldly attacked Wayne's men and captured two of his cannons. Emistesigo sustained a mortal wound from a bayonet. The close fighting with the Americans caused seventeen Creeks to lose their lives, and the remaining warriors beat a retreat.

ENSENORE
Secotan
fl. 1580s

When Sir Walter Raleigh's Roanoke colony under Richard Grenville was established in North Carolina in 1585, Ensenore was the aged

principal chief of the Secotan Indians. The Sec-
otans, an Algonquian-speaking group, lived
between Pamlico and Albemarle Sounds in
northeastern North Carolina. The artist John
White was a member of the first expedition and
led the second Roanoke colony in 1587, which
mysteriously disappeared. Ensenore and his
son, Granganameo, a lesser chief, aided the
colonists and were friendly to Grenville, regularly supplying the Roanoke colonists with
fish, meat, fruit, and vegetables. Granganameo
and Ensenore died in 1585. Consequently,
another son of Ensenore, Vingina, assumed
leadership and decided to forcibly eject the
colonists.

ERASMUS, GEORGES HENRY
Dene
1948–

Georges Erasmus achieved a national reputation
in Canadian Native affairs as president of the
Assembly of First Nations, which represents
about six hundred thousand Native people
across Canada. He was born at Fort Rae, Northwest Territories, and attended high school in
Yellowknife. Afterward, he became active in
Dene political affairs, serving as secretary of the
Yellowknife Band Council. Erasmus became
president of the Dene nation in 1976 and led a
successful campaign to stop the Mackenzie Valley pipeline, a natural gas transport line that
would have run from Alaska through Dene
lands in the Northwest Territories.

Erasmus also worked in several other posts as
a community advocate before becoming a
regional leader in the Assembly of First Nations
in 1983. He became national chief in 1985 and
was reelected in 1988, meanwhile becoming
known around the world through attendance at
various Native conferences. He also persuaded
the environmental activist organization Greenpeace to halt an anti–fur harvesting campaign

that was harming the economy of the Dene.
Erasmus served as cochair of the Canadian
Royal Commission on Aboriginal Peoples in
the early 1990s. The commission held hearings
and issued reports detailing the role of Native
peoples in debates over Canada's new constitution.

ERDRICH, LOUISE
Turtle Mountain Chippewa
1954–

An acclaimed writer in the late twentieth century, Louise Erdrich composed several best-
selling novels and volumes of poetry, many of
which described the evolution of Native American life among reservation Chippewas in
North Dakota early in the century.

Erdrich's novels include: *Love Medicine*
(1984), *The Beet Queen* (1986), *Tracks* (1988),
The Crown of Columbus (1991), and *The Bingo
Palace* (1993). All of Erdrich's novels except *The
Crown of Columbus* (which was written with
Erdrich's husband, Michael DORRIS) chronicle
the lives of an Indian family for four generations. Her poetry includes *Jacklight* (1984)
and *Baptism of Desire* (1989). Erdrich has also
contributed fiction and journalism to several
mass-circulation magazines and newspapers,
including the *New York Times Sunday Magazine and Book Review, Esquire, Harpers, Ms.,*
and *The Atlantic Monthly.*

ESKIMINZIN
Aravaipa-Pinal Apache
c. 1825–1890

Eskiminzin, also called Eskaminzin, Hack-
ibanzin (meaning "Angry Men Standing in Line
for Him"), and Big Mouth, was a principal chief
and proponent of peace whose band was massacred at Camp Grant in 1871.

Although a Pinal Apache, Eskiminzin married into the Aravaipas and became their head

chief. (The Aravaipas of the San Carlos group of Western Apaches inhabited south-central Arizona along Aravaipa Creek between the San Pedro Creek and Galiuro Mountains.) In 1871, with increasing tensions between Apaches and whites, Eskiminzin went to Lieutenant Royal Whitman near Tucson to express a desire to remain on their ancestral lands instead of relocating to the White Mountain Reservation. Whitman asserted that he would relay the request to his superiors while the Aravaipas encamped near Fort Grant as technical prisoners of war.

The band relocated their village, planting fields of corn and gathering agave outside of Tucson. At this time, some of the Aravaipas worked cutting hay to feed ranchers' horses. Eskiminzin's band was also joined by others, especially the Pinals, who desired a cessation of hostilities.

In March 1871, several Apache raids aroused indignation among the whites. On April 10, San Xavier, south of Tucson, was raided by an Apache band that took a great deal of livestock. Eskiminzin's band was blamed, and a vigilante force of 148 under William Ouray—consisting

A family of San Carlos Apaches, members of Eskiminzin's band. [Nebraska State Historical Society]

of Anglo-Americans, Mexican Americans, and Papago mercenaries—was constituted. In the early morning hours of April 30, the vigilantes killed about 150 (mostly women and children) of Eskiminzin's band. Eskiminzin lost eight family members. Twenty-nine children became slaves to Tucson whites or Papagos.

Horrified by the lawlessness, President Ulysses S. Grant directed that the vigilantes should be put on trial. As a result of this incident, Grant expanded his peace plan to include the Apaches. Predictably, the vigilantes were acquitted in December 1871, and hostile Apaches increased their raids on Arizona white settlements.

Although Eskiminzin's band peacefully rebuilt their village and continued to farm, they had to relocate to the San Carlos Reservation on the Gila River in 1873. When the San Carlos Apaches revolted again in 1874 and Lieutenant Jacob Almy was killed, Eskiminzin was mistakenly blamed by the local whites and ordered arrested by General George Crook (the Tonto Apache DELSHAY was subjected to the same treatment). Although exonerated, Eskiminzin was again imprisoned as a military precaution in 1874. Realizing Eskiminzin's innocence, John P. Clum, the new Indian agent, released Eskiminzin and he returned to his people.

In 1886, Eskiminzin and Clum went to Washington to negotiate an end to the hostilities. While traveling with Eskiminzin, the Chiricahua Apache TAZA, one of COCHISE's sons, caught pneumonia and died. NAICHE, Taza's brother, complained that Eskiminzin had not taken proper care of Taza. As tensions mounted, Eskiminzin left the San Carlos Reservation and decided to ranch along the San Pedro River. When unscrupulous whites destroyed his ranch, Eskiminzin went back to San Carlos. In 1888, he was incarcerated for fraternizing with the outlaw known as the Apache Kid (Chita, the Apache Kid's wife, was Eskiminzin's daughter). He was sent to Florida and later Alabama, with GERONIMO's Chiricahuas. While imprisoned, he became the head gardener. The next year, he was permitted to return to Arizona. He died soon after.

FOR MORE INFORMATION:

Dockstader, Frederick. *Great North American Indians.* New York: Van Nostrand Reinhold, 1977.

ESPANOW (APANNO)
Wampanoag
fl. early 1600s

Espanow was taken hostage in 1611 by Captain Edward Harlow as part of an early English attempt to colonize New England. Harlow had intended to use Espanow as a guide and translator for a colony, but Espanow had his own plan.

He convinced his masters that gold was to be found in Martha's Vineyard, his homeland. In 1614, Espanow and his gold-hungry captors sailed into Martha's Vineyard where, on a pre-arranged signal, warriors sprayed the ship with arrows as Espanow leaped to his freedom and swam safely to shore. Several of the prospective colonists were injured, and the colonizing expedition was abandoned.

In 1620, Espanow led an attack on another British ship that was attempting to land at Martha's Vineyard. Captain Thomas Dermer died of fourteen arrow wounds sustained during the battle, which killed most of his men. The survivors sailed to Virginia posthaste. A year later, Espanow made peace with the Pilgrims, who finally succeeded in establishing a colony at Plymouth.

FADDEN, JOHN KAHIONHES
Mohawk
1938–

John Kahionhes Fadden, his father, Ray FADDEN, and their families have played a major role in preserving and reviving Mohawk language and culture through artistic and educational endeav-

John Kahionhes Fadden.
[Courtesy of John Kahionhes Fadden]

ors spanning much of the last half of the twentieth century. Their efforts have reached people across the United States and in many other countries through correspondence and books. The Faddens' major impact in upstate New York, however, has been through the family's Six Nations Indian Museum at Onchiota.

Born in Massena, New York, John Kahionhes Fadden earned a bachelor's degree in fine art at the Rochester Institute of Technology (1961) and took graduate work at Saint Lawrence University and at the State University of New York at Plattsburgh. As his artistic talents developed, Fadden melded with them an intense political awareness of the changes taking place at Akwesasne, his homeland, where he often illustrated for the newspaper *Akwesasne Notes.* His art also portrays worldwide indigenous and ecological themes.

John Fadden's artwork had reached audiences around the world in fifty-two books by the early 1990s, including eighteen book covers, thirty exhibitions, eleven calendars, and other media. Fadden also has been a leader in efforts to provide Iroquois-produced materials for New York State schools. Until early 1994, he taught middle school art for thirty-two years in the Saranac Central School System.

John Fadden's wife, Eva, is an accomplished carver in wood and soapstone, and his son, David, is a graphic artist who by his early twenties had illustrated several books and magazines.

FOR MORE INFORMATION:

Whitaker, Robert. "Akwesasne Seek to Rebuild a Nation." *Plattsburgh [New York] Press-Republican*, 15 January 1989.

FADDEN, RAY TEHANETORENS
Mohawk
1910–

During most of the last half of the twentieth century, Ray Tehanetorens Fadden has been a principal figure in the preservation of Mohawk and other Iroquois language and culture. As founders of the Six Nations Indian Museum at Onchiota, New York, the Fadden family since the 1950s have been active in cultural affairs in New York State. Fadden's dedication to teaching began in the 1940s with the founding of the Akwesasne Mohawk Counsellor Organization, which taught Mohawk language and culture to several generations. Fadden has prepared twenty-six pamphlets and forty-two charts detailing Iroquois history as part of the Six Nations Museum Series.

Much of Ray Fadden's life and that of his wife and family have been dedicated to fighting environmental degradation in the Adirondack Mountains, their home. Fadden says that acid rain and other pollutants are destroying the abundance and variety of life in the forest. "If you kill the forest life, you kill your own grandchildren," Fadden says.

To many of his former students, Ray Fadden is a living legend. "He was father, grandfather,

Ray Fadden (left) with his wife, Christine. [Courtesy of John Kahionhes Fadden]

teacher [and] friend to three generations of Mohawks," said Ron LaFrance, a Mohawk and a former student of Fadden. [Clyne]

FOR MORE INFORMATION:

Clyne, Patricia Edwards. "Ray Fadden: Sachem of Onchiota." *Adirondack Life* (Summer 1975): 9–12.

Whitaker, Robert. "Akwesasne Seek to Rebuild a Nation." *Plattsburgh [New York] Press-Republican*, 15 January 1989.

FETTERMAN, WILLIAM JUDD
c. 1834–1866

In 1866, William Fetterman told other U.S. Army officers who were mired in an ineffective war against the Sioux and their allies that he could ride through territory under the control of RED CLOUD and his warriors with eighty men and survive. His party was lured into a deadly ambush, one of several defeats that set the military stage for the Fort Laramie Treaty of 1868, which forced the dismantling of part of the U.S. military's westward expansion.

In December 1866, Captain Fetterman set out with eighty-one men and high ambitions only to be decoyed by a band of ten warriors and led into an ambush by CRAZY HORSE, DULL

KNIFE, and others. Crazy Horse in particular goaded Fetterman with obscene gestures. Once Fetterman took the bait, all of his men were killed. About sixty-five Indians also died in the battle, which took place near Fort Phil Kearney in present-day Wyoming.

In 1868, with the wagon road still closed, the government signed a treaty at Fort Laramie that caused the forts to be dismantled. The Powder River country as well as the Black Hills were reserved for the Lakotas forever according to the treaty. In this case, forever lasted about a decade. By 1877, the army, having suffered George Armstrong CUSTER's defeat, pursued surviving Sioux and Cheyenne bands from newly erected forts, one of which was named in memory of Fetterman.

FIRE, JAKE
Mohawk
1846–1899

The shooting deaths of Mathew PYKE and Junior EDWARDS at Akwesasne on May 1, 1990, created an ironic coincidence. In 1985, the Canadian Mohawk Council of Akwesasne had declared May 1 a national Mohawk holiday in memory of Jake Fire. He was shot and killed at 4 A.M. on May 1, 1899, by a contingent of Canadian Dominion Police, as Fire was protesting the imposition by Canada of the band system (a sanctioned tribal government structure) mandated by the Indian Advancement Act of 1884.

In 1898, the Akwesasne clan mothers had written to Canada's governor general contending that the Mohawks' traditional political system suited them and that they did not wish to change it. Nonetheless, in March 1899, a contingent of Royal Canadian Mounted Police arrived on the Canadian side of Akwesasne to enforce the change of governments. A crowd of two hundred Mohawks caused them to retreat,

but the police returned two months later. On May 1, 1899, the police occupied the traditionals' council house and summoned the chiefs to a meeting. Seven who arrived were thrown to the ground and handcuffed. Jake Fire, who was head chief, heard of the arrests and demanded the chiefs' release. As he arrived at the council house, Fire was shot twice and killed. "This," observed Mike Mitchell, Canadian Mohawk Council of Akwesasne head chief in the 1990s, "[was] the way Canada introduced our people to the principles of their democracy."

Canadian records express some confusion over whether the man the Mounties killed was named Jake Fire or Jake Ice. According to Akwesasne historian Salli Benedict, Jake Fire was one of two brothers, Jacob and John Fire. John, who was often called Jake, had a Mohawk name that referred to ice, so he was sometimes called Jake Ice to distinguish him from his brother, Jacob Fire.

FOR MORE INFORMATION:

Wright, Ronald. *Stolen Continents.* Boston: Houghton Mifflin, 1992.

FISH CARRIER (OJAGEGHT)
Cayuga
fl. late 1700s

Fish Carrier was among the minority of Iroquois chiefs who supported the patriot cause in the American Revolution. He led forces that took part in the Wyoming Valley massacre in 1778 and the Battle of Newtown the following year. During the Revolutionary War, he worked to defuse tensions between the Senecas, who sided with the British, and the Oneidas, allies of the Americans. In 1790, Fish Carrier signed the Tioga Point Treaty in return for a tract of land and a peace medal from George Washington. In 1794, he was present at the signing of the Treaty of Canandaigua.

FLAT MOUTH
Chippewa/Ojibway
1774–c.1860

Flat Mouth (whom the French knew as Guelle Plat) was one of several war chiefs who led various Chippewa bands during an enduring rivalry with the Sioux in the upper Missouri watershed. Some accounts say that Flat Mouth was converted from the practice of poisoning his rivals by a visit from TENSKWATAWA, the Shawnee prophet. Flat Mouth's father, Wasonaunequa, had maintained his position using this practice. If Tenskwatawa influenced Flat Mouth religiously, he was unable to sway him politically toward his brother and ally TECUMSEH. Flat Mouth refused to attack American settlements during Tecumseh's Rebellion (1809–1811) and the War of 1812.

FOR MORE INFORMATION:

Eckert, Allan W. *A Sorrow in Our Heart: The Life of Tecumseh.* New York: Bantam, 1992.

Edmunds, R. David. *The Shawnee Prophet.* Lincoln: University of Nebraska Press, 1983.

FLETCHER, ALICE CUNNINGHAM
1838–1923

Born in Cuba as her parents visited from New England, Alice Fletcher, who would become known as one of the foremost ethnologists in nineteenth-century America, was steered toward anthropology by Frederic Ward Putnam of Harvard's Peabody Museum. In 1879, Fletcher met Francis LAFLESCHE and Susette LAFLESCHE, both Omahas, as they traveled on behalf of the Ponca STANDING BEAR. In 1883, Fletcher was hired by the United States to supervise the allotment of Omaha lands. Her work was cited with approval during debates over the General Allotment Act (1887). She later worked in similar positions during allotment of Winnebago and Nez Perce lands.

Aside from her government duties, Fletcher became a noted ethnologist among the Omahas. Speaking before the International Council of Women in 1888, Fletcher contrasted the treatment of women in nineteenth-century American society with that of many American Indian societies. She posed the case of a brother coming to the aid of a woman being beaten by her husband. Under Iroquois custom, the brother was honor-bound to defend her. Under U.S. law at that time, he could have been charged with a criminal act for doing so.

At the same conference, Fletcher said that an Indian woman with whom she had once lodged gave away a very fine horse. Fletcher, surprised that she had given the horse away without asking her husband's permission, asked whether he would be upset. According to Fletcher, the woman's eyes danced, and she laughed gently, hastening to tell the story to other women in her tent. The Indian women were more than a little amused at the hold a white man had on his wife's property, Fletcher said.

Alice Fletcher (left) *talks with two of her sources.*
[National Anthropological Archives]

FOR MORE INFORMATION:

Fletcher, Alice C. *A Study of Omaha Indian Music.* Cambridge, Mass.: Peabody Museum, 1893.

———, and Francis LaFlesche. *The Omaha Tribe.* Lincoln: University of Nebraska Press, 1972.

FLYING HAWK
Oglala Lakota
1852–1931

Born near present-day Rapid City, South Dakota, Flying Hawk became known among the Lakotas as a warrior at a young age. He allied with CRAZY HORSE at the Battle of the Little Bighorn in 1876. After the surrender of Crazy Horse's band, Flying Hawk settled at Pine Ridge Agency. He was known as a performer in Buffalo Bill's Wild West Show run by William CODY, as well as in several other touring attractions, including the Sells-Floto Circus.

FOR MORE INFORMATION:

Ambrose, Stephen E. *Crazy Horse and Custer.* New York: New American Library, 1986.

FOKE LUSTE HAJO
Seminole
fl. 1830s

Charley EMATHLA and Foke Luste Hajo were signers of the 1832 Treaty of Payne's Landing. Emathla and Hajo (who also was called Foke-Lustee Hadjo, Fuche Luste Hadjo, and Black Dirt) also signed the 1833 Treaty of Fort Gibson. In both treaties, they agreed to relocate Seminoles to Indian Territory, enraging anti-removal Seminoles who supported OSCEOLA.

Two years later in council, Osceola and other Seminoles decided to forcibly resist removal from Florida. As a result of this decision, they killed Emathla. Fearing for their lives, Foke Luste Hajo and other pro-removal Seminoles fled to Fort Brooke (present-day Tampa, Florida),

where they sought the protection of the U.S. military authorities. They were subsequently removed to Indian Territory.

FOLSOM, DAVID (COLONEL FOLSOM)
Choctaw
1791–1847

David Folsom resided near present-day Starkville, Mississippi. Along with Peter P. PITCHLYNN, he was a staunch advocate of education for the Choctaws and encouraged Presbyterian, Methodist, and Baptist missionaries to come among the Choctaws. He was also a negotiator of Choctaw removal.

In 1824, Folsom journeyed to Washington, D.C., for removal talks with the federal government. PUSHMATAHA, a respected tribal leader, died on this trip. By 1826, Folsom had become the first leader of the tribe's three districts. With the aid of Greenwood LE FLORE, he achieved the best possible removal deal for the Choctaws by opposing land cessions and then reluctantly signing the Treaty of Dancing Rabbit Creek in 1830. After removal to Indian Territory, he settled on a farm a few miles south of the town of Caddo.

FONSECA, HARRY
Maidu
1946–

Growing up in Sacramento, California, Harry Fonseca did not fully appreciate his Native American heritage until he was about twenty-five years old. At that time in his life, he became captivated by the images in ancient Maidu mythologies. Enthralled, he would listen for hours to the tales told by his Maidu uncles and cousins. He also began to do some academic research on Native American cultures but soon found these studies sterile and lacking the personal depth that his family's stories had. Much of Fonseca's art involves depictions of Coyote, who is the trickster of Maidu mythology. In his portrayals of Coyote, Fonseca satirizes modern society by rendering Coyote in modern garb and absurd contemporary situations.

Fonseca's work has been displayed at the Wheelwright Museum in Santa Fe, New Mexico, since the 1970s. He is currently residing in Santa Fe, where he is exploring new images and new forms in prints and paintings. He remains an important figure in American Indian art.

FOR MORE INFORMATION:

Champagne, Duane, ed. *Native North American Almanac.* Detroit: Gale Research, 1994.

FOOLS CROW, FRANK
Oglala Lakota
c. 1890–1990

Frank Fools Crow was a major political and spiritual leader of the Oglala Lakota early in the twentieth century. Fools Crow was born between 1890 and 1892, by his own account, in a log cabin on the Pine Ridge Reservation. His mother's father was Porcupine Tail, after whom the Porcupine District of Pine Ridge was named. His mother, Spoon Hunter, died four days after Fools Crow was born. His father was called both Eagle Bear and Fools Crow. The younger Fools Crow's father raised his son in traditional ways and kept him out of formal schooling in reservation missions. A reservation agent tried to force Fools Crow into school at the age of eighteen but discovered he was too old for compelled attendance.

In 1914, at the behest of elderly holy man Stirrup, Fools Crow set out on a vision quest, a trip of a hundred miles on horseback to Bear Butte, "the most awesome vision-questing place in the Black Hills." After this vision quest, Fools Crow became a major spiritual leader among the Lakotas.

Fools Crow also became a political leader in the Porcupine District; he participated in several Wild West shows early in the century as well. In 1975, at the invitation of South Dakota Senators James ABOUREZK and George McGovern, Fools Crow traveled with a Sioux delegation to Washington, D.C., where he became the first Native American to lead the U.S. Senate in an opening prayer. He also served as a spiritual advisor to American Indian Movement activists occupying Wounded Knee in 1973.

FOR MORE INFORMATION:

Mails, Thomas E. *Fool's Crow.* Garden City, N.Y.: Doubleday, 1979.

FORBES, JACK D.
Powhatan and Lenape
1934–

Born on January 7, 1934, in Long Beach, California, Jack Forbes grew up in Southern California. He received his B.A. in anthropology (1953), M.A. in anthropology (1955), and Ph.D. (1959) from the University of Southern California.

He became an American Indian activist during the 1960s when he became involved with the Native American Movement, the Coalition of Eastern Native Americans and the United Native Americans. He was also a co-founder and volunteer instructor at Deganawidah-Quetzalcoatl (D-Q) University in the 1960s. In 1969, he became a member of the faculty and department chairman of Native American Studies at the University of California at Davis.

He has published a variety of books on important American Indian subjects. His most prominent works are: *Warriors of the Colorado: The Yuma of Quechan Nation* (1955), *The Indian in America's Past* (1964), *Native Americans of California and Nevada* (1969), and *Native Americans and Nixon: Presidential Politics and Minority Self-Determination* (1981).

FOR MORE INFORMATION:

Champagne, Duane, ed. *Native North American Almanac.* Detroit: Gale Research, 1994.

FOREMAN, STEPHEN
Cherokee
1807–1881

Born in Rome, Georgia, Stephen Foreman was one of twelve children of a Scottish trader and a Cherokee woman. His father died shortly after moving the family to Cleveland, Tennessee, when Stephen was a young child. Foreman, who would become a noted Cherokee educator, missionary, editor, and translator, attended a small mission school close to home and then went for more advanced study under the Congregationalist missionary Samuel Worcester at New Echota, Georgia. He furthered his studies at the College of Richmond in Virginia and Princeton Theological Seminary in New Jersey. In 1835, he gained his license to preach through the Union Presbytery of Tennessee.

Foreman worked with both Worcester and Elias BOUDINOT on Cherokee translations of the Bible. As a result of his support of the anti-removal faction, led by Chief John ROSS, Foreman was jailed for his views in 1838. Subsequently, he became a leader of a group of Cherokees on the Trail of Tears.

Once removed to Indian Territory (present-day Oklahoma), Foreman remained both a political and a spiritual leader among the Cherokees. In 1841, he was instrumental in organizing a public school system for his people and was its first superintendent. He was elected to the Supreme Court of the Cherokee nation in 1844; from 1847 to 1855, he served as executive councilor.

Foreman did not support either side during the Civil War; he served as a missionary in Texas during that time. Upon returning to Indian Territory, he founded a church in the former home of Elias Boudinot. He had two marriages and fourteen children.

FOR MORE INFORMATION:

Dockstader, Frederick. *Great North American Indians.* New York: Van Nostrand Reinhold, 1977.

FOWLER, HERBERT BURWELL (OHIYESA)
Santee Sioux
1919–1977

Herbert Fowler combined the practices of western and Native medicine into a unique blend. He was trained as a traditional healer and as a medical doctor, having earned his M.D. degree from the University of Michigan in 1946.

Fowler served his internship at Detroit's Harper Hospital and his residency at the University of Utah College of Medicine. He also traveled to Europe under sponsorship of the National Institutes of Mental Health to survey psychiatric hospitals there. Fowler later practiced as a medical doctor and also developed an interest in police-Native relations in Alaska. He wrote a textbook, *Police and the Emotionally Disturbed* (1975), on the subject.

Fowler received both a National Institute of Mental Health Career Teacher Award (in 1960) in the United States and a Lenin Prize Laureate in Science worth $50,000 (in 1977) in the Soviet Union. Fowler died in 1977. His wife, Julia M. Hansen Fowler, survived him, as did his seven children. He was buried in Spokane, Washington.

FRANCIS, JOSIAH
Mixed Creek-Seminole
fl. 1810s

The tribal affiliation of Josiah Francis is murky. Although he had white ancestry and was originally thought to be of Alabama descent, some believe that he was descended from the Tawasa- or Tuskegee-related tribes. However, he did take part in the Red Stick Creek uprising. He went on to become a spiritual leader in the Creek and Seminole Wars, and the father of Milly Hayo FRANCIS. He was also known as Hillis Hayo or Hillis Hadjo—a Muskogean term for "Medicine Man."

As a friend and advocate of TECUMSEH's ideas, Francis traveled in 1811 throughout the Mississippi Valley, spreading the notion of a great Indian barrier state from present-day Ohio as far southwest as the Osages in what would become Oklahoma. From 1813 through 1814, along with William WEATHERFORD and the traditionalist Red Sticks, Francis fought against General Andrew Jackson. Jackson called Francis the great prophet of the Seminoles. In 1815, at the end of the War of 1812, he went to England asking for aid against the Americans.

In 1817, Francis's daughter, Milly, stopped the execution of a Georgia militiaman, Duncan McKrimmon. Milly insisted to her father she was willing to die with McKrimmon if the execution proceeded. Understandably, her father spared McKrimmon's life. The next year, 1818, Francis was captured by whites on the St. Marks River and killed.

FRANCIS, MILLY HAYO
Mixed Creek-Seminole
1802–1848

In the First Seminole War (1817), some Seminoles seized Duncan McKrimmon, an officer in the Georgia militia, and brought him to a Miccosukee settlement in west Florida known as Kinache's Village. Josiah FRANCIS, a spiritual leader, decided to execute McKrimmon by burning him at the stake. As the torch was being placed at his feet, Milly Hayo Francis pleaded with her father to spare McKrimmon's

life. Disregarding her requests for mercy, her father relented only when she demonstrated that she was also willing to be burned at the stake. McKrimmon was given a reprieve with the proviso that he shave his head and live among the Seminoles. Several months later, McKrimmon was sold to the Spanish as a slave.

A few months after this incident, Andrew Jackson captured and executed Josiah Francis. As the war wound down, Milly, her mother, and her sister, along with other Seminole civilians, went to an army post for food. McKrimmon, who had escaped captivity, now saved Milly's life. Folklore has it that McKrimmon asked Milly to marry him, and she refused. She believed that he offered marriage only out of kindness and obligation because she had saved his life, and so she decided to remain with her kin.

Subsequently, she was removed to the Indian Territory and settled near present-day Muscogee, Oklahoma. Because of her largesse during the First Seminole War, she was awarded, in 1844, a small pension by the United States. The annuity was delayed, and she died of tuberculosis four years later without having received any compensation.

FRANCISCO
Yuma
c. 1815–1857

In 1850, two young white girls were abducted by a group of Tonto Apaches who had attacked some settlers at Gila Bend, Arizona. Some two years later, the captive sisters were sold to the Mohaves. One child died soon after the transaction. A brother of the captive girls, left for dead during the raid, admonished the military command at Fort Yuma, California, to find his sisters. Although their efforts failed, Francisco, in

1856, professed knowledge of the whereabouts of the surviving girl.

To aid him in his mission, he obtained four blankets and some beads and went to purchase the girl. The Mohaves attempted to disguise her identity by staining her skin, but Francisco saw through the ruse and bought the girl anyway. Shortly after this incident (probably because of the notoriety he gained in rescuing the girl), Francisco became chief of his tribe, but he passed away the next year. He may have been assassinated as a result of his ineptness in war, since it was rumored that he lost seventy-five out of seventy-eight warriors in a battle with the Maricopas and Papagos shortly before his death.

FRANK, BILLY, JR.
Nisqually
1931–

Billy Frank, Jr., played a major role in Native American assertions of fishing rights in western Washington, which resulted, in 1974, in the landmark case popularly called the BOLDT decision. This decision reserved up to half the annual catch for Indians who had signed treaties, in the 1850s, that ceded large tracts of land but retained their rights to fish "in common with" citizens of Washington Territory at "usual and accustomed places." After that decision, Frank became influential in fisheries decision making in the Northwest and as an environmental advocate.

Despite the treaties, state agencies and courts regularly arrested Indians who attempted to fish in accordance with the old agreements. During the 1960s and early 1970s, Indians militantly protected their fishing rights in the face of raids by state fisheries authorities. A nucleus of fishing rights activists from Franks Landing, only a few miles from the site at which the Medicine Creek Treaty had been signed, continued to fish

on the basis of the treaty, which gave them the right to fish as long as the rivers run.

Frank recalled:

I went to jail when I was fourteen years old. That was the first time I ever went to jail for treaty rights. The State of Washington said I couldn't fish on the Nisqually River. So, at fourteen, I went to jail. Ninety times I went back to jail. . . . The State of Washington said "you can't go on that river and go fishing anymore." That's what they told us Indians. . . . "If you go on that river, you're going to jail." We went back fishing and we went to jail over and over until 1974. [Russo]

Resistance to the Boldt decision was soon organized among Washington State business leaders in the Washington Water Resource Committee. Frank and other fishing rights activists decided to boycott Seattle-First National Bank, a member of the Water Resource Committee; they discussed the idea with friends at El Centro de la Raza, a Seattle social service agency. All agreed they had a good idea, with one flaw. They did not have enough money in the bank to make a boycott hurt. Within a few weeks, however, they began to talk to other people. Frank later said, "We got the Colvilles to pull out sixteen million. . . . Then, the Washington State University kids started pulling their money out and the Teamsters Union, and other local people. . . . Then I flew up to Alaska to our native friends up there. . . . They passed a resolution and pulled out eighty million dollars." [Russo]

By this time, the boycott had drawn notice at the bank (commonly known as Sea-First).

At that time, Mike Barry was the president of Sea-First. He called me up and he said, "Bill, before I jump out of the seventeenth floor of the Sea-First bank, we got to have a meeting." So, I brought in all my tribal leaders again. . . . He asked, "What do you want us to do?" He said, "Fly back to Alaska and tell the Natives to put that money back in the bank because that was only the beginning. They had another hundred fifty million that they were going to pull out." [Russo]

"We know who the boss is in this country. It sure as hell isn't us," said Frank. Nevertheless, the boycott was pinching the bank, the region's largest at the time (before mismanaged oil investments caused its near-bankruptcy in the 1980s). The Indians refused to restore their deposits unless Sea-First and other businesses called off their attack on the Boldt decision.

The Washington State offensive was one part of a nationwide backlash that emerged against treaty rights during the middle and late 1970s. This movement was fueled, as expropriation of Indian resources always have been, by non-Native economic interests. During the 1980s, the battle over who would harvest how many fish continued in western Washington and spread to other states such as Wisconsin.

Frank became a nationally recognized leader in the cooperative effort to restore salmon runs of the eastern Pacific. Fisheries officials returned one of the boats they had seized from him during the "fish-ins," and Frank installed the old cedar dugout canoe in a spot of honor alongside the riverbank where his quest to fish in accordance with the treaties had begun. By the early 1990s, Frank had become chairman of the Northwest Indian Fish Commission and a leading spokesman for environmentalism in the Pacific Northwest. In 1992, he was awarded the Albert Schweitzer Prize for humanitarianism by Johns Hopkins University.

FOR MORE INFORMATION:

Russo, Kurt, ed. *Our People, Our Land: Reflections on Common Ground.* Bellingham, Wash.: Lummi Tribe and Kluckhohn Center, 1992.

FRANK, BILLY, SR.
Nisqually
1880–1980

Billy Frank, Sr., father of Billy FRANK, Jr., was the original owner of Frank's Landing, a tract of land along the Nisqually River near Olympia, Washington, that became a center of fishing rights protests during the 1960s and early 1970s.

The land was outside the bounds of the original Nisqually Reservation but was purchased for Frank and given trust status after his allotted land was taken as part of the Fort Lewis army base. The river bend at Frank's Landing proved to be a rich fishing ground, thus a focus of conflict between state fish and game police and Native Americans seeking to exercise their fishing rights under treaties signed in the 1850s. In 1974, Federal Judge George BOLDT ruled that Indians were entitled to up to half the catch returning to the Indians' "usual and accustomed" fishing grounds.

FOR MORE INFORMATION:

American Friends Service Committee. *Uncommon Controversy: Fishing Rights of the Muckleshoot, Puyallup, and Nisqually Indians.* Seattle: University of Washington Press, 1970.

FRANKLIN, BENJAMIN
1706–1790

Benjamin Franklin's life was frequently intertwined with the lives, societies, and affairs of Native Americans. As a printer, he published accounts of Indian treaties for more than two decades. Franklin began his diplomatic career by representing the colony of Pennsylvania at councils with the Iroquois and their allies. His designs for the Albany Plan of Union and later Articles of Confederation contain elements of the Native American systems of confederation that he had come to know as a diplomat. Franklin also speculated liberally in Native land.

Born in Boston, Franklin worked with his brother, James, as a printer until the age of seventeen. In 1723, he left Massachusetts for Philadelphia, where he became a successful printer and made his mark on history as an inventor, statesman, and philosopher.

Franklin's earliest contacts with Indians occurred in Philadelphia, where his printing company published the Indian treaties entered into by the colonial Pennsylvania Assembly. He was later a delegate to the 1753 treaty with the Ohio Indians at Carlisle, Pennsylvania. In 1744, at the Lancaster Treaty Council, CANAS-SATEGO, an Onondaga sachem, urged the colonies to unite in a manner similar to that of the Iroquois Confederacy. Franklin learned of Canassatego's words as he published the treaty proceedings. Franklin's press issued Indian treaties in small booklets that enjoyed a lively sale throughout the colonies. Beginning in 1736, Franklin published Indian treaty accounts on a regular basis until the early 1760s, when his defense of Indians under assault by frontier settlers cost him his seat in the Pennsylvania Assembly. Franklin subsequently served the colonial government in England.

At the Albany Congress in 1754, Franklin outlined a plan for colonial government and union that was the first blueprint for American government and intercolonial unity. Both Franklin and subsequent historians have acknowledged Franklin's debt to the basic tenets of the constitution of the Iroquois Con-

federacy. When the French and Indian War erupted in western Pennsylvania in 1754, Franklin aided General Edward Braddock's unsuccessful attempt to retake Fort Duquesne from the French. He also took part in a campaign that built defensive positions at Gnaddenhutten (where Christianized Delaware Indians were located).

Franklin believed in European settlement of the frontier. In "The Interest of Great Britain Is Considered" (1760), he asserted that the English colonization of the Ohio Valley would result in a large farming community with a lucrative demand for British manufactured goods. Before the American Revolution, Franklin believed that British control over the West was a result of God's will. Although he was critical of many Indian ways, he expected moral behavior of Europeans and Euro-Americans in Indian affairs.

In Franklin's "Narrative of the Late Massacres in Lancaster County" (1763), he condemned the massacre of Christianized Conestoga Indians by a mob from Paxton, Pennsylvania. He called these vigilantes "Christian white savages." He also argued that liquor and disease, brought on by increasing white contact, would cause the Indians' decline in North America. When the Paxton Boys marched on Philadelphia to exterminate the city's Indians in February 1764, Franklin led a delegation to the Indian camp and counseled peace.

While in the Pennsylvania Assembly, Franklin urged various forms of payments for obtaining Indian land rather than utilizing force. He advocated British regulation of Indian traders to diminish unscrupulous practices.

In 1776, Franklin ardently supported the idea of American independence, and his revised Albany Plan of Union became the basis for the new American nation's first instrument of government, the Articles of Confederation. It is known that he based some of his political concepts about governmental unity on the Iroquois League of Six Nations.

At the Treaty of Paris (1783), which ended the American war for independence, Franklin gained British recognition of the Great Lakes and the Mississippi as the northern and western boundaries of the newly created United States. This paved the way for the future displacement of the Ohio Valley tribes.

Franklin used his image of Indians and their societies as a critique of Europe: "The Care and Labour of providing for Artificial and fashionable Wants, the sight of so many Rich wallowing in superfluous plenty, while so many are kept poor and distress'd for want; the Insolence of Office . . . [and] restraints of Custom, all contrive to disgust them [Indians] with what we call civil Society." [Johansen]

Franklin described Indians' passion for liberty while making it a patriotic rallying cry; they admired Indians' notions of happiness while seeking a definition that would suit the new nation. Franklin wrote:

All the Indians of North America not under the dominion of the Spaniards are in that natural state, being restrained by no Laws, having no Courts, or Ministers of Justice, no Suits, no prisons, no governors vested with any Legal Authority. The persuasion of Men distinguished by Reputation of Wisdom is the only Means by which others are govern'd, or rather led—and the State of the Indians was probably the first State of all Nations. [Grinde and Johansen]

As U.S. Ambassador to France, Franklin often wrote about Indians. Indeed, among the French philosophes he was known as the "Philosopher as Savage." In his tract, "Remarks Concerning the Savages of North America" (1784), Franklin asserted that Indians should not be termed "savages." Although sometimes contradictory in his outlook, Franklin often compared the virtues and shortcomings of both Indian and white cultures, asserting that Indian ideas and customs had great wisdom and value.

Franklin died in 1790, shortly after the fashioning of the United States Constitution, which he had helped shape with his ideas of an amalgam between Native American and European cultures.

FOR MORE INFORMATION:

Aldridge, Alfred O. *Benjamin Franklin: Philosopher and Man.* Philadelphia: J. B. Lippincott, 1965.

———. "Franklin's Deistical Indians." *Proceedings of the American Philosophical Society* 44 (August 1950): 398–410.

Franklin, Benjamin. *The Autobiography of Benjamin Franklin.* Edited by John Bigelow. Philadelphia: J. B. Lippincott, 1868.

Grinde, Donald A., Jr., and Bruce E. Johansen. *Exemplar of Liberty: Native America and the Evolution of Democracy.* Berkeley and Los Angeles: University of California Press, 1991.

Johansen, Bruce E. *Forgotten Founders.* Ipswich, Mass.: Gambit, 1982.

Labaree, Leonard, and William B. Willcox [Whitfield J. Bell after 1962]. *The Papers of Benjamin Franklin.* New Haven, Conn.: Yale University Press, 1950– .

Van Doren, Carl, and Julian P. Boyd, eds. *Indian Treaties Printed by Benjamin Franklin, 1736–1762.* Philadelphia: Historical Society of Pennsylvania, 1938.

FREE, MICKEY (MIG-GA-N'-LA-AIE)
Pinalino Apache
1851–1913

Born in Mexico's Sonoita Hills along the upper Santa Cruz River to a father who was part Irish and a Mexican mother, Free was also of

Mickey Free with his youngest daughter.
[Nebraska State Historical Society]

Pinalino Apache descent. He may have taken his adult name on his own, referring to his gaining freedom from the Apaches who had captured him. At about fourteen, after having gained his own freedom, Free rescued his wife from the sexual advances of an army captain at Fort Bowie, Arizona, killing two Mexicans with a knife. At twenty, Free became an interpreter and scout under General George Stoneman, U.S. Army, Department of Arizona.

Free also helped Agent John P. Clum, General George Crook, and General Nelson A. Miles trail GERONIMO through Arizona, New Mexico, and northern Mexico in the 1870s and 1880s. During much of his career, Albert Sieber was Free's chief of scouts. He also worked with Lieutenant Britton Davis.

Free also acted as the Chiricahua Apaches' official interpreter on the San Carlos Reservation. In 1886, he visited Washington, D.C., as interpreter for an Apache delegation (including CHATO, LOCO, and ALCHESAY) trying to stop the incarceration of Apache prisoners in Florida. After his visit to Washington, Free trailed the escaped Apache, MASSAI, the outlaw known as the Apache Kid, and many other fugitives. Although he never apprehended Massai, Free asserted that he had located the remains of the Apache Kid in 1897 in New Mexico. In 1906, Free retired from the army.

G

GAGE, MATILDA JOSLYN
1826–1898

Matilda Joslyn Gage compared the status of women in Iroquois society with that of other women in nineteenth-century America in her groundbreaking *Woman, Church and State* (1893)—a book that was part of what Dr. Sally R. Wagner calls "the first wave of feminism." In the book, Gage acknowledges, according to Wagner's research, that "the modern world [is] indebted to the Iroquois for its first conception of inherent rights, natural equality of condition, and the establishment of a civilized government upon this basis."

Gage, with Elizabeth Cady STANTON and Susan B. Anthony, was one of the three most influential feminist architects of the nineteenth-century women's movement, according to Wagner, whose research was among the first to provide a scholarly basis for a resurgent feminist movement in the late twentieth century. Gage was later "read out" of the movement and its history because of her radical views, especially regarding women's oppression by organized religion.

Knowledge of the Iroquois' matrilineal system of society and government was widespread among early feminists, many of whom lived in upstate New York. The early feminists learned of the Iroquois not only through reading the anthropological works of Lewis Henry MORGAN, Schoolcraft, and others, but also through direct personal experience. With Stanton and Anthony, Gage coauthored the landmark *History of Woman Suffrage* (published in six volumes from 1881 to 1922). In *Woman, Church and State,* her last book, Gage opened with a chapter on the matriarchate, a form of society she believed existed in a number of early societies, specifically the Iroquois. Gage discussed several Iroquois traditions that created checks and balances between the sexes, including descent through the female line, the ability of women to nominate male leaders, the fact that women had a veto power over decisions to go to war, and the woman's supreme authority in the household. Gage also noted that

Iroquois women had rights to their property and children after divorce.

Gage herself was admitted to the Iroquois Council of Matrons and was adopted into the Wolf clan with the name Karonienhawi, "She Who Holds the Sky." Wagner asserts that "nineteenth-century radical feminist theoreticians, such as Elizabeth Cady Stanton and Matilda Joslyn Gage, looked to the Iroquois for their vision of a transformed world."

As contemporaries of Morgan, Engels, and Marx, Gage and the other founding mothers of modern feminism in the United States shared a chord of enthusiasm at finding functioning societies that incorporated notions of sexual equality. All seemed to believe that the Native model held promise for the future. Gage and Stanton looked to the Native model for a design of a "regenerated world." "Never was justice more perfect, never civilization higher than under the Matriarchate," Gage wrote. "Under [Iroquois] women the science of government reached the highest form known to the world."

FOR MORE INFORMATION:

Allen, Paula Gunn. *The Sacred Hoop: Recovering the Feminine in American Indian Traditions*. Boston: Beacon Press, 1986.

Anthony, Susan B., Elizabeth Cady Stanton, and Matilda Joslyn Gage. *History of Woman Suffrage*. Reprint, Salem, N.H.: Ayer Co., 1985.

Brown, Judith K. "Economic Organization and Position of Women Among the Iroquois." *Ethnohistory* 17: 3–4 (Summer–Fall 1970).

Carr, Lucien. *The Social and Political Position of Women Among the Huron-Iroquois Tribes*. Salem, Mass.: Salem Press, 1884.

Gage, Matilda Joslyn. *Woman, Church and State*. 1893. Reprint, Watertown, Mass.: Persephone Press, 1980.

Landsman, Gail. "Portrayals of the Iroquois in the Woman Suffrage Movement." Paper presented at the Annual Conference on Iroquois Research, Rensselaerville, N.Y., October 8, 1988.

Wagner, Sally Roesch. "The Iroquois Confederacy: A Native American Model for Nonsexist Men." *Changing Men* (Spring–Summer 1988).

———. "The Root of Oppression Is the Loss of Memory: The Iroquois and the Early Feminist Vision." *Akwesasne Notes* (Late Winter 1989).

GALL (PIZI)
Hunkpapa Sioux
c. 1840–1895

Gall was one of several Lakota and Cheyenne military leaders who dismembered George Armstrong CUSTER's elite Seventh Cavalry at the Little Bighorn in 1876. A large, mercurial man, Gall was an adopted younger brother and close confidant of SITTING BULL until the 1880s, when he was recognized as a chief of the reservation-bound Hunkpapas by the U.S. government, as Sitting Bull was ignored.

Gall fought beside Sitting Bull at the Little Bighorn; at the beginning of the troops' attack, as Major Marcus Reno's troops swooped down upon the Sioux-Cheyenne encampment, Gall's two wives and three children were killed. Gall then led the counterattack that drove off Reno's forces and set the scene for the obliteration of Custer's command.

Gall's feats as a warrior verged on the legendary. At one point, it was said that a detachment of soldiers surrounded his lodge and demanded that he surrender. Gall stuck his head out of the tepee door and took a shot then ripped a hole in the back of the tepee and stepped into a line of soldiers who knocked him to the ground with their rifles and bayonets. They slugged him, clubbed him, and shot him. After one soldier stepped on Gall's chest to

Gall. [Nebraska State Historical Society]

retrieve his bayonet, they left him for dead. Gall wasn't dead, however. Somehow he dragged his lacerated body through the snow to a friend's lodge about twenty miles away and recovered, nursing a hatred for the army as well as his wounds. These wounds were a factor in his death.

Indian agent Major James ("White Hair") McLaughlin set up Gall as a rival chief to Sitting Bull after the latter had surrendered in 1881. This was an attempt to break Sitting Bull's influence over the Sioux by denigrating him. Gall served McLaughlin's purposes as he ranged about the reservation attending official events in a business suit that fit tightly over his large frame.

FOR MORE INFORMATION:

Utley, Robert M. *The Lance and the Shield: The Life and Times of Sitting Bull.* New York: Henry Holt, 1993.

Vestal, Stanley. *Sitting Bull: Champion of the Sioux.* 1932. Reprint, Norman: University of Oklahoma Press, 1957.

GANADO MUCHO
Navajo
c. 1809–1893

Ganado Mucho was also called Ganodos Muchos or Mucho Ganado ("Many Cattle" in Spanish), and Aguas Grandes (meaning "Big Water"), as well as Hosteen Totsohnii. Born of a Navajo mother and a Hopi father, he was a Navajo headman, a proponent of peace with whites, and as his name indicated, a cattleman in the vicinity of present-day Klagetoh on the Navajo Reservation.

In the 1850s, Ganado was accused by non-Indians of cattle theft because of his large herds. He denied such allegations and, along with other Navajos, signed an agreement in 1858 to return any stolen livestock discovered among the Navajo people.

In the Navajo War of 1863–1866, under the tutelage of Manuelito, Ganado Mucho counseled peace. At first, he hid out with his followers from U.S. troops led by Kit Carson. In 1865, he led his group to Bosque Redondo (Fort Sumner, New Mexico) as ordered. At this time, his son and two daughters were lost to slave raids by Mexicans and Utes. He signed the Navajo Treaty of 1868, which allowed the Navajos' return to their homeland in the Four Corners area. Subsequently, Ganado rebuilt his herd and maintained his role as headman and peacemaker between the Navajos and the neighboring non-Indians.

GARAKONTIE, DANIEL
Onondaga
c. 1600–1676

Daniel Garakontie ("Moving Sun"), a lifelong ally of the French, was born at Onondaga. He spent some of his younger years in Montreal and made many friends as he became known around the community as a person who could redeem French captives from the Iroquois. In 1658, he also helped Jesuit missionaries avoid a planned massacre by Iroquois. By 1661, Garakontie had become one of the most influential leaders within the Iroquois Grand Council, and he may have served as Tadadaho (speaker) of the confederacy.

Also in 1661, Garakontie welcomed Jesuit Father Simon LeMoyne to his community; he converted his cabin into a missionary chapel for religious services. A year later, he foiled an attempt to assassinate LeMoyne. Garakontie was ridiculed at times for his passive acceptance of the whites and their religion, but he replied that they were too strong to effectively resist. He also urged Indians to reject alcohol and exhorted the benefits of schooling. All the while, Garakontie continued to arrange freedom for French captives. He also sought peace with the English. Garakontie was baptized in Quebec in 1669, when he was about seventy years of age, at which time he accepted the name Daniel. Garakontie died at Onondaga in 1676 and was buried with Christian services at his request.

GARRA, ANTONIO
Cupeno
c. 1805–1852

As chief of the Cupeno Indians living at the headwaters of the San Luis Rey River in southern California, Antonio Garra was a rival of the Cahuilla Juan ANTONIO to the east and the Luiseno Manuelito COTA to the west. In 1849, at the beginning of the California gold rush, numerous Americans entered southern California and vied for Indian lands and resources. Dismayed, Garra urged a coordinated general revolt among tribes from the San Diego to the Colorado Rivers, including the Luisenos, Mohaves, Cocopahs, Cahuillas, Kamias, Chemehuevis, and Quechans.

As a medicine man, Cota announced to his followers that he could turn the white man's bullets into water. Doubtful of Garra's powers, Manuelito Cota and his Luisenos maintained their neutrality, along with many other bands in the area. Paulino WEAVER, a noted mountain man and a friend of Juan Antonio, also advocated peace in the region.

In spite of his failure to generate a general uprising, Garra's followers raided many ranches and gained control of the Colorado River and desert country. Finally, Juan Antonio threw his support to the whites and aided in the capture of his rival, Garra, in December 1851. Garra was executed after a court martial by the state militia. Garra had a son with the same name, who fought with his father in the uprising.

GELELEMEND (KILLBUCK, WILLIAM HENRY)
Delaware
c. 1722–1811

Gelelemend was born in Pennsylvania about 1722. His father was Killbuck (the name Gelelemend, which means "Leader," was adopted in later years). In 1778, following the death of WHITE EYES, Gelelemend was made chief of the Delaware people owing to his wisdom and diplomatic ability. At this time, he also joined the Moravian Christian faith and was baptized William Henry.

While Gelelemend counseled peace with the American colonists, HOPOCAN, the leader of the Delaware war faction, opposed such a course as the American Revolution unfolded. Eventually, Hopocan's arguments for war prevailed, and Gelelemend and his followers, fearing reprisals from Hopocan, agreed to settle on an island in the Allegheny River (at the suggestion of an American military officer in western Pennsylvania). However, Gelelemend's band actually suffered several attacks from the Americans and none from Hopocan during the American Revolution. In 1782, white vigilantes massacred about one hundred Christianized Indians at Gnadenhutten; as the Indians returned to their homes along the Allegheny River, the vigilantes killed several of Gelelemend's people as well. Gelelemend and others escaped by swimming away from the attackers. During his watery flight, he lost treaty documents given to his tribe in 1682 by William Penn.

Gelelemend was dedicated to the maintenance of peaceful relations with the Americans; however, his Christianity and his many white friends made him suspect among his own people. He relocated to Pittsburgh, Pennsylvania, to avoid the wrath of fellow Delawares who blamed him for white attacks upon their settlements. He died there in 1811.

GEORGE, DAN
Suquamish
1899–1981

Born near Vancouver, British Columbia, Dan George spent nearly a quarter century as a logger and longshoreman before becoming an acclaimed actor and Native spokesman. Beginning about 1960, he acted in several television shows and movies, at first in Canada, then in the United States. He won the New York Film Critics' 1970 award for best supporting actor for his role as Old Lodge Skins in the feature film *Little Big Man*. The same role won him an Academy Award nomination.

On July 1, 1967, Chief Dan George spoke to thirty-two thousand people at Vancouver's Empire Stadium on the occasion of Canada's centenary. He reminded Canada of how difficult it was for Native people to celebrate Canada's centenary. His remarks were reported by the Associated Press:

> Oh, Canada, how can I celebrate with you this centenary. . . . Shall I thank you for the loss of pride and authority? . . . No! I must forget what is past and gone. . . . Give me back the courage of the olden chiefs. . . . Like a Thunderbird of old, I shall rise again out of the sea. . . . I shall see our young braves and our chiefs sitting in the houses of law and government. . . . Ruling and being ruled by the knowledge and freedom of our great land. So shall we shatter the barriers of our isolation. So shall the next 100 years be the greatest in the proud history of our tribes and nations.

GEORGE-KANENTIIO, DOUGLAS MITCHELL
Akwesasne Mohawk
b. 1955

Doug George-Kanentiio has been a key figure in Mohawk political and cultural life in the late twentieth century. He has participated in Mohawk land claims negotiations, was a member of the Mohawk Nation business committee, a founder of Radio CKON (the only exclusively Native licensed broadcasting facility in North America), and a founder of the Native American Journalists Association, from which he received, in 1994, its highest honor: the Wassaja Award for Journalism Excellence.

George was also the editor of the news journals, *Akwesasne Notes* and *Indian Time*, and a columnist for the Syracuse *Herald American* and *News from Indian Country*. He has served as a member of the Board of Trustees for the National Museum of the American Indian and the Haudenosaunee Standing Committee on Burial Rules and Regulations (the repatriation group of the Haudenosaunee Confederacy).

George-Kanentiio played a direct role in the Mohawk "civil war" at Akwesasne as a newspaper editor and ultimately as a participant in a four-day gun battle in 1990 that resulted in the death of two Mohawk men. George-Kanentiio attributed the violence at Akwesasne to illicit casino gaming, an activity that began in 1986 and quickly expanded until the Mohawk reservation became the fourth-largest gambling center in North America. His articles traced the rise of gaming to the displacement of the Mohawks from their ancestral lifestyles of fishing and farming that began after the Second World War and accelerated with the completion of the St. Lawrence Seaway and its subsequent contamination of the Akwesasne environment.

George-Kanentiio also wrote numerous essays and editorials about the political divisions at Akwesasne, which was governed by three Native councils yet subject to the jurisdiction of Canada and the United States. He was an advocate for the revitalization of the ancestral Mohawk government called the Mohawk Nation Council of Chiefs. He attempted, with others, to create an economy based on ancestral values with attendant regulations.

George-Kanentiio was also critical of the smuggling of narcotics, tobacco, firearms, and illegal aliens through the Akwesasne territory. As a result, his newspapers were banned in some businesses, his offices firebombed twice, and his personal residence raked with machine-gun fire. He persisted in his opposition and received many threats against his life, yet was given considerable encouragement by the Mohawk Nation Council and its supporters at Akwesasne.

In March 1990 the Akwesasne community split into two factions resulting in an escalation of violence and terror serious enough to warrant evacuation of the reservation on April 26. Thousands fled the community, yet there were a few isolated holdouts, one of whom was David George, Jr., the brother of George-Kanentiio. Rather than have his brother stand alone against the attacks of the pro-gaming "Mohawk Sovereignty Security Force" (or the "warrior society"), George-Kanentiio elected to pick up a firearm and support his brother. Along with eleven other Mohawk men, he then withstood four days of intense fighting (April 27–May 1) against greatly superior forces. They were finally relieved when the New York State Police, the Royal Canadian Mounted Police, and a contingent of the Canadian army arrived to occupy Akwesasne. On May 13, 1990, George-Kanentiio was arrested by the Surété du Québec and charged with the shooting death of Harold "J.R." Edwards, one of the two men killed. He was cleared during the preliminary hearing stage of the judicial proceedings for lack of evidence. George maintained that his arrest was a political action resulting from his severe public criticisms of the U.S. and Canadian police.

George-Kanentiio resigned as editor of *Akwesasne Notes* and *Indian Time* in 1992 and moved to the Oneida Territory in central New York State. He secured a position as a columnist with the *Syracuse Herald American* and, with his wife, Joanne SHENANDOAH, formed Round Dance Productions, a nonprofit corporation dedicated to the preservation of Iroquois culture through music, art, and film. He assisted Mohawk spiritual leader Tom PORTER in the relocation of Mohawks from Akwesasne to their ancient homes in the Mohawk Valley region.

George-Kanentiio has worked with the Haudenosaunee Confederacy on economic issues, played a key role in the repatriation of sacred items from the National Museum of the American Indian back to the Iroquois, and was retained as a consultant to the Mohawk Nation Council on many issues. He has lectured on Iroquois issues throughout North America and Europe.

FOR MORE INFORMATION:

Johansen, Bruce E. *Life and Death in Mohawk Country*. Golden, Colo.: North American Press, 1993.

GERONIMO (GOKHLAYEH, GOYATHLAY)
Chiricahua Apache
c. 1825–1909

The man the Spanish would come to call Geronimo was born along the upper Gila River, very likely on the Arizona side of the New Mexico–Arizona border. Taklishim, his father, was a Chiricahua as was his mother, Juana,

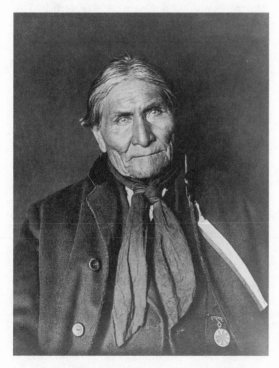

Geronimo. [Nebraska State Historical Society]

although she had been a captive among the Mexicans during childhood. (His Chiricahua name means "One Who Yawns.") In his youth, Geronimo served under the Chiricahua leader COCHISE and under MANGAS COLORADAS, a Mimbreno. While Geronimo was not a hereditary chief, his repute among the Apaches increased owing to his bravery and prowess in battle. In 1858, Mexicans killed his wife, mother, and three children, causing Geronimo to dislike Mexicans intensely and mount campaigns against them for revenge. Geronimo was also a respected medicine man.

After Cochise's death in 1874, the number of Chiricahua raids in Mexico increased despite the efforts of Indian agent Thomas J. Jeffords. Apache war parties would cross into Mexico then return to use the reservation at Apache Pass on the Butterfield Trail as a safe haven. After an altercation involving the killing of two stagecoach attendants, the reservation was dissolved by the U.S. government. Subsequently, John P. Clum, Indian agent to the Chiricahuas, moved them north to the San Carlos Reservation in Arizona where they joined four thousand other Apaches from other bands. Refusing to relocate, Geronimo fled into Mexico and took refuge in the Sierra Madre. He merged his group with JUH's Nednhi band and began carrying out raids on the American side of the river. In the wake of these raids, Clum left San Carlos to subdue Geronimo, who was finally seized in April 1877 and then transported to San Carlos Reservation. VICTORIO, a Mimbreno, was relocated along with his Warm Springs band at that time as well. During the late 1870s, Geronimo remained at San Carlos although he went raiding in Mexico once with Juh, withdrawing quickly to San Carlos after the buildup of Mexican troops.

These events ushered in the final stages of the Apache wars, which began in summer 1881

Geronimo at Fort Sill in 1909.
[Nebraska State Historical Society]

and ended in 1886 with Geronimo's surrender. The U.S. military decided on August 30, 1881, to arrest NAKAIDOKLINI, a White Mountain Apache prophet. He was accused of espousing a new vision that postulated the resurrection of dead warriors to overwhelm the whites. The U.S. Army killed Nakaidoklini at a battle near Cibecue Creek. Subsequently, some of Nakaidoklini's group attacked Fort Apache unsuccessfully. Military reinforcements were brought in against the rebellious Apaches to forestall further chaos.

In September 1881, after the battle at Cibecue Creek, Geronimo, Juh, NAICHE (the son of Cochise), the hereditary chief CHATO, and seventy-four followers left San Carlos for Mex-

ico. Returning in April 1882 to raid the reservation, Geronimo and others slew the chief of police and forced Loco and his band of Mimbrenos to follow them into Mexico, uniting them with NANA's more warlike Mimbrenos.

Consequently, by the end of 1882, General George Crook was ordered to the Southwest to subdue the Apaches. Believing in the virtues of mobility, Crook quickly instituted a number of mounted units with Apache scouts that could effectively track their fellow Apaches. Crook, in May 1883, led units into the Sierra Madre of Mexico (with Mexican permission). These detachments were led by Captain Emmet Crawford and Lieutenant Charles Gatewood. Because of the desert conditions, they used mules instead of horses. On May 25, 1883, the U.S. military struck Chato's camp. As a result, some Apache leaders agreed to return to the reservation, though it was a year before Nana, Naiche, Loco, and Chato slowly returned to San Carlos with their bands (Juh had died earlier in an accident). Geronimo himself, still one of the most revered war chiefs, returned to the reservation in March 1884.

When government authorities banned *tiswin*, an Apache alcoholic beverage, a year later, Geronimo, Nana, Naiche, and about 150 others headed for Mexico again. Crook's men trailed them until the fleeing Apaches agreed to talk at Canyon de los Embudos on March 25, 1886. Crook insisted that the Apaches submit to unconditional surrender and imprisonment in the East for two years. Geronimo acceded to the army's terms. While being escorted to Fort Bowie, Naiche, Geronimo, and twenty-four followers escaped. As a result, Crook was replaced with General Nelson A. Miles. To capture the twenty-four escaped Apaches, Miles placed five thousand soldiers in the field with Apache scouts. While leading a unit into Mexico, Captain Henry Ware Lawton skirmished with the Apaches on July 15, 1886. However, Geronimo was able to escape the grip of the army. After avoiding the army for over a month, Geronimo agreed to surrender, but only to Miles personally. At Skeleton Canyon, sixty-five miles south of Apache Pass, Geronimo and the remaining members of his group finally surrendered.

Geronimo and his band as well as hundreds of more peaceful Apaches were transported in chains to Forts Pickens and Marion in Florida via the railroad. In 1887, Geronimo and others were transferred west to Mount Vernon Barracks in Alabama. Tuberculosis, swamp fevers, and other diseases killed many of the Apaches there. Subsequently, ESKIMINZIN's Aravaipas were permitted to return to Arizona, but Geronimo's and Naiche's Chiricahuas were not allowed to return to their homeland. Eventually, Geronimo and his followers accepted the Comanches' and Kiowas' offer to share their reservation in the Indian Territory; in 1894, the remaining incarcerated Apaches were relocated to Fort Sill in western Oklahoma.

At Fort Sill, Geronimo played baseball, tried farming, and became a member of the Dutch Reformed Church. He also collaborated with S. M. Barrett on the publication of his memoirs, *Geronimo's Story of His People,* in 1906. He died of pneumonia on February 17, 1909, at Fort Sill, never having been allowed to return to his beloved homeland. SITTING BULL and Geronimo are widely considered to be the two most famous American Indians of the nineteenth century.

GIAGO, TIM (NANWICA KCIJI)
Oglala Lakota
1934–

As editor and publisher of *Indian Country Today,* Tim Giago became one of the best-known journalists of Native American descent in North America during the 1990s. In 1981, Giago became owner of the *Lakota Times,* a newspaper serving Native American South Dakota. In 1992, Giago added a national newspaper, *Indian Country Today,* with help from the Freedom Forum. (The Freedom Forum is the charitable arm of the Gannett Corporation, which publishes *USA Today,* after which Giago modeled some of his news format.) Giago was born at Pine Ridge. His Lakota name, Nanwica Kciji, means "Defender."

Giago's work is part of a growing Native American press in North America. The number of reservation newspapers increased from 18 in 1963 to more than 220 in 1978. By the mid-1990s, Giago's newspaper was reaching fifty thousand readers a week on a circulation of fourteen thousand copies. Giago, who attended San Jose (California) State College and the University of Nevada at Reno, began his journalistic career in the 1970s as a reporter and columnist at the *Rapid City Journal.* He also became the first Native American to receive a Nieman Fellowship at Harvard University. He has won a number of prizes for distinguished journalism and human rights activism. Giago has also authored three books, including *The Aboriginal Sin* (1978), *Notes from Indian Country* (1984), and *The American Indian and the Media* (1991). He also writes a column that is syndicated by the Knight-Ridder newspaper chain.

Giago has been outspoken in defense of Native American interests generally and Lakota concerns specifically. During South Dakota's centennial celebration in 1990, the fact that several army officers were awarded Medals of Honor after the 1890 massacre at Wounded Knee became an issue. "Should the American soldiers involved in My Lai in Vietnam have been awarded Medals of Honor for their actions?" asked Giago.

For four years in a row, *Indian Country Today* so dominated the South Dakota press association's awards for weekly newspapers that the group decided to classify it as a daily newspaper for purposes of its contests; Giago then withdrew from the association. In 1985, Giago was given the H. L. Mencken Award for column writing. He returned the award in 1989 after the disclosure of several bigoted statements in Mencken's papers.

FOR MORE INFORMATION:

Giago, Tim. "I Hope the Redskins Lose." *Newsweek* (January 27, 1992).

———. *Notes from Indian Country.* Rapid City, S.D.: Cochran Publishing, 1985.

GODFROY, FRANCIS
Miami
1788–1840

Francis Godfroy was born of a French father (Jacques Godfroy) and a Miami mother near the present-day site of Fort Wayne, Indiana. He won renown as a war chief and an ally of TECUMSEH in his attempt between 1809 and 1811 to stop white immigration into the Old Northwest. He was a large, stout man. Late in his life, Godfroy weighed more than four hundred pounds.

Godfroy allied with the British during the War of 1812 and at one point commanded a Miami force of three hundred men that routed troops sent against Miamis under the command of William Henry Harrison. With the defeat of the British, Godfroy accommodated the American advance as he moved to his father's former trading post site on the Wabash River and became a prosperous trader. He also benefited from cash and land grants as he signed away much of the Miamis' homelands to the United States until his death in 1840.

GOOD THUNDER (WAKUNTCHAPINKA)
Winnebago
c. 1790–1863

As an influential band chief among the Winnebagos, Good Thunder was one of a substantial number who refused to support BLACK HAWK's appeal for aid in an alliance to forestall white immigration. Despite his support for the United States, Good Thunder's band was uprooted from its ancestral lands and relocated to northeastern Iowa, then to Blue Earth County, Minnesota. During the Great Sioux Uprising of 1862–1863, Good Thunder supported the colonists. After the suppression of the uprising, Good Thunder's band was relocated to South Dakota and abandoned there without promised supplies. Nearly starving, members of the band found a home among the Omahas, where Good Thunder died.

FOR MORE INFORMATION:

Tebbel, John. *The Compact History of the Indian Wars.* New York: Hawthorn Books, 1966.

GOOD THUNDER (STOSA YANKA)
Sioux
fl. 1890s

Good Thunder was a Rosebud Sioux spiritual leader who advocated the Ghost Dance prior to the Wounded Knee massacre of 1890. Good Thunder was born of a Brulé father and a Miniconjou mother and called Stosa Yanka, or "Sits Up Straight." He minimized his own role in the massacre of BIG FOOT's band at Wounded Knee, but subsequent historiography indicates that he was the Ghost Dancer who threw dust at soldiers during the tense moments that preceded the shooting. He was wounded in the subsequent shooting but did not die. Many of the soldiers apparently thought that the throwing of dust was a signal for the Indians to attack—or so they argued after the massacre. The throwing of dust was in fact part of the Ghost Dance ritual.

In fall 1889, Good Thunder, Brave Bear, and as many as four others slipped away from the Pine Ridge Agency without the agent's permission to investigate WOVOKA's claims to have seen the messiah in the Ghost Dance. They returned to Pine Ridge convinced that the Ghost Dance could restore their old lives as they were before the coming of the European Americans. In spring 1890, a larger delegation of Indians from the Pine Ridge, Cheyenne River, and Rosebud Agencies visited Wovoka in Nevada with sanction from some of the leading chiefs on the Northern Plains. This delegation included Good Thunder, SHORT BULL, and KICK-ING BEAR, all of whom became leading advocates of the Ghost Dance during the months leading up to the massacre at Wounded Knee in late December 1890.

Shortly after the turn of the century, Good Thunder is reported to have worked as an Episcopalian minister.

FOR MORE INFORMATION:

Brown, Dee. *Bury My Heart at Wounded Knee.* New York: Holt, Rinehart & Winston, 1970.

GORMAN, CARL NELSON
(KIN-YA-ONNYBEYEH)
Navajo
1907–

Born on October 5, 1907, at Chinle, Arizona, on the Navajo Reservation, Gorman is a member of the Black Sheep clan. His mother and father founded the first Presbyterian mission at Chinle. Gorman's father was also a trader and rancher; his mother pursued artistic interests through Navajo weaving.

With the outbreak of World War II, Gorman joined the U.S. Marines and became a Navajo Code Talker (their coded radio messages in Navajo were never broken by the Japanese in the Pacific theater of the war). At the conclusion of World War II, Gorman went to study art on the GI Bill at the Otis Art Institute in Los Angeles. After completing his training, he became a technical illustrator for Douglass Aircraft, set up his own silk-screen company, and became an instructor in Native American Art at the University of California at Davis. Gorman's work is displayed in national and international galleries; he is known as an innovator in a variety of styles and media.

FOR MORE INFORMATION:

Klein, Barry T., ed. *Reference Encyclopedia of the American Indian.* West Nyack, N.Y.: Todd Publications, 1993.

GORMAN, R. C.
Navajo
1932–

Born on July 26, 1932, in Chinle, Arizona, on the Navajo Reservation, R. C. Gorman is the son of Carl Nelson GORMAN. R. C. Gorman was encouraged as a young man to become an artist like his father. As a boy, he herded sheep with his grandmother in Canyon de Chelly. After graduating from high school, he studied art at Northern Arizona University and San Francisco State University. Subsequently, he was awarded a grant by the Navajo Tribal Council to study art at Mexico City College where he was deeply influenced by the work of Diego Rivera. Gorman is the most renowned of all contemporary Native American artists. In 1973, he was honored as the only living artist to be in the "Masterworks of the American Indian" exhibit at the Metropolitan Museum in New York City. In 1975, he became the first artist to be selected for a series on contemporary American Indian art at the Museum of the

American Indian in New York. Gorman has also published several essays on Mexican artists, petroglyphs, and cave paintings.

FOR MORE INFORMATION:

Klein, Barry T., ed. *Reference Encyclopedia of the American Indian.* West Nyack, N.Y.: Todd Publications, 1993.

GRANGULA (HAASKOUAN, BIG MOUTH, LA GRANDE GUEULE)
Onondaga
fl. 1680s

The French gave Grangula his name (Grande Gueule means "Big Mouth" in French) because of his oratorical abilities and his diplomatic skill. His Iroquois name meant "His Mouth Is Large." Grangula played the English against the French, maintaining Iroquois leverage as he refused French demands that he quit trading with the English in 1684. In 1688, Grangula was a principal organizer of twelve hundred warriors who marched to Montreal to arrange a truce. After a preliminary truce was signed, duplicity by the Huron chief ADARIO caused the Iroquois to mount an attack on Montreal.

Grangula was probably Tadadaho of the Iroquois Confederacy during meetings with the British and French in 1684. At these meetings, he denied both sides' demands for allegiance, saying that the Iroquois had been born free and that they did not depend on the French or the British. "We may go where we please, and carry with us whom we please. If your allies be your slaves, treat them as such." Big Mouth warned against a buildup of armies in the area, saying that it would endanger the "tree of peace," the security of the Iroquois Confederacy. Aggressive moves by either the French or the English could cause the Iroquois to "dig up the hatchet" from under the roots of the Iroquois Great Tree of Peace, Grangula said.

FOR MORE INFORMATION:

Armstrong, Virginia Irving, ed. *I Have Spoken: American History Through the Voices of the Indians.* Chicago: Swallow Press, 1971.

GRASS, JOHN (PEZI)
Blackfoot or Teton Sioux
c. 1837–1918

John Grass's English name came from the Dakota "Pezi," meaning "Field of Grass"; he also was sometimes called Mato Watakpe (Charging Bear). He was a son of Grass, a Sioux leader of the early nineteenth century. He spoke a number of Dakota dialects as well as English, so he was one of the few people in the Dakotas who could communicate with nearly everyone else.

Indian agent Major James ("White Hair") McLaughlin set up Grass, GALL, and other Sioux as rival chiefs to SITTING BULL after the latter had surrendered in 1881, in an attempt to

John Grass. [National Anthropological Archives]

break Sitting Bull's influence over the Sioux. Over Sitting Bull's objections, Grass signed an 1889 agreement that broke up the Great Sioux Reservation. He probably was bowing to threats by Indian agent McLaughlin that the U.S. government would take the land with or without Sioux consent. Even after the land was signed over, the government reduced the food allotments on Northern Plains reservations, intensifying poverty and suffering; this action increased tensions just before the massacre of BIG FOOT's people at Wounded Knee.

For more than three decades, Grass served as head judge in the Court of Indian Offenses of the Standing Rock Reservation. He died at Standing Rock in 1918.

GRATTAN, JOHN LAWRENCE
c. 1830–1854

Early in summer 1854, Lieutenant J. L. Grattan, who had said he thought all Indians were cowards and dogs, invaded a Sioux camp near Laramie, Wyoming, to arrest a Native man who had killed a cow abandoned by an immigrant. Grattan, a brash young man with thirty other men under his command, thought that he could "whip all the Sioux on the Plains and make them run like rabbits." The Sioux killed Grattan and all of his men in fifteen minutes of furious fighting, prompting the army to send Colonel William HARNEY to Laramie with a larger armed force to punish the Sioux.

FOR MORE INFORMATION:
Wiltsey, Norman B. *Brave Warriors.* Caldwell, Idaho: Caxton, 1963.

GREAT SUN (GRAND SOLEIL)
Natchez
fl. 1700–1730

"Great Sun" was a Natchez hereditary title bestowed upon the principal chief or emperor

through the ages. Unfortunately, only one Great Sun has been recorded in the annals of the white man's history. He ruled during the early 1700s when the French first came to the lower Mississippi River. The French established their first mission among the Natchez in 1706; a decade later, to keep the peace and nurture trade and diplomacy between Indians and whites, they also built Fort Rosalie. The French fort overlooked the Mississippi River and the Great Sun's village. Soon after the construction of the fort, the Great Sun began listening to the counsel of the tribe's anti-French faction. Sieur Chepart, recently appointed as governor of Louisiana, demanded the Great Sun's village as the site for his own plantation. When the Great Sun refused, Chepart demanded crops in payment for his concession to the Indians.

As a result of these demands, the Great Sun, his priests, and his warriors plotted a rebellion against the French. The Natchez decided to send out bundles of sticks to other villages, supposedly denoting the number of crops to be tendered to the French but actually charting the time of a planned uprising. On the first autumn frost, November 30, 1729, Natchez's warriors attacked Fort Rosalie and other settlements along the Mississippi; they inflicted more than five hundred casualties. One of those killed was Chepart.

After an army of French soldiers and Choctaw warriors had recaptured Fort Rosalie, the Great Sun agreed to the terms of peace but managed to escape in the night with some of his followers. He led them up the Red River, where the French tracked them down and struck them a year later. French firearms overwhelmed the defending Natchez, and the Great Sun capitulated.

It is thought that the Great Sun and most of his people were subsequently taken to New Orleans and executed by the end of 1730. As a result of French conquest, the Natchez people never recovered their tribal autonomy; many of them were sold into slavery in the Caribbean. Other tribal members became refugees and probably settled among other tribes.

GREENE, GRAHAM
Oneida
1950–

Graham Greene is a well-known actor who played Native American roles in some of the late twentieth century's most popular movies. He was nominated for an Academy Award as best supporting actor in *Dances with Wolves* (1991), in which he worked with Rodney A. Grant, an Omaha. Greene also played major roles in *Clearcut* (1992), *Last of His Tribe* (1992), and *Cooperstown* (1993).

Greene was born on the Six Nations Reserve in Ontario; he began his acting career in 1976 after working in high steel and as a draftsman and a civil technologist. For a time, Greene owned a recording studio in Hamilton, Ontario.

Greene's acting career did not become his major vocation until after he lived in England during the early 1980s and became known for his stage performances there. After returning to Canada, Greene was cast in the British film *Revolution*, starring Al Pacino. In addition to his many movie roles, Greene played in several television series in the United States and Canada and was active in several theatrical productions in Toronto, where he was residing in the 1990s.

FOR MORE INFORMATION:

Johnson, Brian D. "Dances with Oscar: Canadian Actor Graham Greene Tastes Stardom." *Macleans* (March 25, 1991): 60–61.

GUYASUTA
Seneca
c. 1722–1794

Born along the Genesee River shortly after 1720, Guyasuta opposed Euro-American encroachment into the Ohio Valley country. His record was inconsistent, however; at one point, in 1753, he served as a guide for George Washington in his first military campaign.

As the British drove the French from North America shortly after 1760, Native nations struggled to free themselves from British influence. The Senecas were the first to act. As early as 1761, a group of Senecas including Guyasuta, the maternal uncle of HANDSOME LAKE, carried a red wampum belt (a declaration of war) from the Onondaga Council to Fort Detroit.

PONTIAC did not follow the Seneca plan in detail, but it was certainly a factor in fostering his surprise frontier assaults in spring 1763. Pontiac had not intentionally organized a pan-Indian uprising, but several factors helped to further his cause. The prior circulation of the Seneca plan suggested the method of the campaign.

In his later years, Guyasuta became known more as an orator than a warrior. He tried to maintain Seneca neutrality in the American Revolution but reluctantly joined the majority of Senecas who allied with the British. He fought in only one Revolutionary War battle, at Hannastown, Pennsylvania, in 1782. Guyasuta died of smallpox in 1794.

FOR MORE INFORMATION:

Wallace, Anthony. *The Death and Rebirth of the Seneca*. New York: Knopf, 1970.

H

HAGLER (HAIGLER, HAIGLAR, KING HAIGLER; ARATASWA, OROLOSWA)
Catawba
c. 1690–1763

Hagler was probably born along the Catawba River in the northern sector of South Carolina. About 1748, he became a respected principal chief of the Catawba people. At this time, the Catawbas were devastated through conflicts with the Shawnees, Cherokees, and Iroquois. Smallpox also took its toll, especially the epidemic of 1738. In addition, the Catawbas suffered mistreatment by South Carolina traders who squatted on their lands and traded liquor for furs. In the face of such adverse conditions, Hagler's leadership facilitated his people's survival and nurtured their traditional ways.

Hagler maintained cordial relations with the British. He was present at an important peace conference in Albany, New York, in 1751. During the French and Indian War, Hagler and his warriors attacked the French garrison at Fort Duquesne (present-day Pittsburgh) in 1758. With the aid of the British, he battled Cherokee militants in 1759.

Although friendly with the Presbyterian missionary William Richardson, Hagler never converted to Christianity and remained a steadfast advocate of traditional Catawba ways. As a result of his support, the English constructed forts along the Catawba River to bolster the security of the Catawbas. South Carolina raised a statue to memorialize Hagler at Camden in 1826. It is thought to be the first such memorial to an Indian in the United States.

HAIRY MOCCASIN
Crow
fl. 1870s

In late June 1876, Hairy Moccasin was the leader of a group of Crow scouts for George Armstrong CUSTER. He spotted the large camp of up to five thousand Cheyennes, Lakota, and others at the Little Bighorn. Hairy Moccasin tried to persuade Custer not to attack such a sizable camp with 225 men but was rebuffed.

On June 26, Custer attacked and lost his own life and those of all his men at the battle that became known as "Custer's Last Stand."

FOR MORE INFORMATION:

Luce, Edward S., and Evelyn S. Luce. *Custer Battlefield.* Washington, D.C., 1952.

Monoghan, Jay. *Custer.* Lincoln: University of Nebraska Press, 1959.

Rosenberg, Bruce A. *Custer and the Epic of Defeat.* University Park: Pennsylvania State University Press, 1974.

HALF-KING (DUNQUAT, PETAWONTAKAS)
Wyandot (Ohio Huron)
fl. late 1700s

Dunquat was a leader of Hurons who, when they moved to the Ohio country, became known as Wyandots. He was allied with the British in the American Revolution and led several raids on American settlements in the Ohio country during the war. He won the alliance of several bands, including other Wyandots, Shawnees, Delawares, Ottawas, and Chippewas, in the British cause. He also acted as a peace chief in intratribal conflicts; on one occasion, he protected Christianized Delawares from attacks by a more traditional faction of the same tribe.

After the Revolution, Dunquat and his allies joined LITTLE TURTLE, the Miami chief, in his war against Euro-American expansion into the Ohio country, which had been ceded to the United States by the 1783 Treaty of Paris. By about 1800, a flood of immigrants was rolling over the Allegheny Mountains. Dunquat was a signer of the Treaty of Greenville (1795), which effectively ended the insurgency.

HALF-KING (SCAROUDY)
Oneida
fl. 1750s

Scaroudy was military successor to Tanacharison [see HALF-KING (TANACHARISON)] as an ally of the British in the war with the French during the 1750s and early 1760s. When Tanacharison died in 1754, shortly after the war began at the Battle of Great Meadows, Scaroudy, who was known as a great orator, maintained an alliance between the Ohio Valley Iroquois (whom the whites often called Mingos) and the British. Scaroudy was allied with British general Edward Braddock and George Washington, an aide to Braddock, in 1755, as they suffered defeat at the hands of the French near Fort Duquesne (now Pittsburgh).

In October 1753, Benjamin FRANKLIN began his distinguished diplomatic career by watching Scaroudy and a Mohawk, Cayanguileguoa, console the Ohio Indians for their losses against the French. Franklin listened as Scaroudy recounted the origins of the Iroquois Great Law of Peace to the Ohio Indians at a treaty council in Carlisle, Pennsylvania. At this treaty with the Iroquois and Ohio Indians (Twightees, Delawares, Shawnees, and Wyandots), Franklin absorbed the rich imagery and ideas of the Six Nations at close range:

> We must let you know, that there was a friendship established by our and your Grandfathers, and a mutual Council fire was kindled. In this friendship all those then under the ground, who had not yet obtained eyes or faces [that is, those unborn] were included; and it was then mutually promised to tell the same to their children and children's children. [Grinde and Johansen]

Having comforted the Ohio Indians, Scaroudy exhorted the assembled Indians to "preserve this Union and Friendship, which has so long and happy continued among us. Let us keep the chain from rusting." [Grinde and Johansen] The next day, the Pennsylvania commissioners (including Franklin) presented a wampum belt that portrayed the union between the Iroquois and Pennsylvania. The speech echoed Canassatego's words spoken a decade earlier at Lancaster. The speech to the assembled Indians recalled the need for unity and a strong defense.

Cast your eyes towards this belt, whereon six figures are . . . holding one another by the hands. This is a just resemblance of our present union. The first five figures representing the Five Nations . . . [and] the sixth . . . the government of Pennsylvania; with whom you are linked in a close and firm union. In whatever part the belt is broke, all the wampum runs off, and renders the whole of no strength or consistency. In like manner, should you break faith with one another, or with this government, the union is dissolved. We would therefore hereby place before you the necessity of preserving your faith entire to one another, as well as to this government. Do not separate; Do not part of any score. Let no differences nor jealousies subsist a moment between Nation and Nation, but join together as one man. [Grinde and Johansen]

FOR MORE INFORMATION:

Grinde, Donald A., Jr., and Bruce E. Johansen. *Exemplar of Liberty: Native America and the Evolution of Democracy*. Berkeley and Los Angeles: University of California Press, 1991.

HALF-KING (TANACHARISON)
Oneida
c. 1700–1754

Tanacharison was one of a number of Iroquois who lived in the Ohio Valley area during the eighteenth century. Some of these Iroquois, who were often called Mingos by the whites,

held power delegated by the Iroquois Grand Council to conduct diplomacy with local tribes. The whites called such delegates "half-kings," so the designation was more of a title than a personal name.

One such half-king, Tanacharison, born a Catawba, was captured at an early age and raised as a Seneca near the eastern shore of Lake Erie. Tanacharison was a valued ally of the British in the French and Indian War and held councils with several officials, including Conrad Weiser, George Croghan, and a young George Washington, who was then serving in his first combat situation. Tanacharison fought as an ally of Washington in the Battle of Great Meadows (1754), the opening salvo of the final British war with the French in North America, which ended in 1763. As a result of this battle in which Tanacharison killed at least one French officer, Washington surrendered Fort Necessity to the French.

In May 1754, when Washington was trying to find a small party of French under Jumonville in western Pennsylvania, the Virginian commander was completely dependent upon his Indian guides. Before they reached the Indian encampment, the English party was "frequently tumbling over one another, and so often lost that fifteen or twenty minutes search would not find the path again." But when Half-King and his ally Monacatoocha joined the English, Jumonville's hiding place was found in little time. Subsequently, Jumonville was killed and Monsieur La Force was captured.

Tanacharison later moved to Aughwick (now Harrisburg), Pennsylvania, where he died of pneumonia in 1754.

FOR MORE INFORMATION:

Brock, R. A., ed. *The Official Records of Robert Dinwiddie, Lieutenant Governor of Virginia, 1751–1758*. Virginia Historical Society Collections, vol. 3. N.d.

HALL, LOUIS (KARONIAKTAJEH)
Mohawk
c. 1920–1993

Louis Hall, whose Mohawk name was Karoni-aktajeh (meaning "Near the Sky"), is regarded as the ideological founder of the Warrior movement in Mohawk country. The Warriors have played an important role in the recent history of the Mohawk reserves of Akwesasne in upstate New York; Kahnawake, near Montreal; and Kanesatake, near the Quebec hamlet of Oka. Warrior advocacy of armed insurrection on the three reserves played a major role in Akwesasne firefights that killed two Mohawk men on May 1, 1990, and in the standoff with Canadian police and troops at Oka later the same summer (see Doug GEORGE-KANENTIIO).

Hall was a member of the Kahnawake Reserve's Traditional Council in 1971 when it decided to sanction a group of young men who said they wanted to revive a warrior society there. As "keeper of the well," Hall took the young men's request for sanction under advisement and placed it on the council's agenda.

Unlike the Mohawk Nation Council at Akwesasne, the Longhouse at Kahnawake became an advocate of the Warrior cause, so much so that in 1973 its members sought to have non-Indian families evicted from their reserve, a move opposed by the tribal council that Canada recognizes. Following that split at Kahnawake, a group of Mohawks inspired by Hall's beliefs started the settlement at Ganienkeh to carry out their nationalistic vision of Mohawk tradition. The settlement operated farms, a sawmill, cigarette sales, and high-stakes bingo.

Hall maintained that the Warriors hold the true heritage of the Iroquois and that today's traditional council and chiefs at Akwesasne have sold out to elitism, the Quakers, HAND-SOME LAKE, and white interests in general. Hall regarded the religion of Handsome Lake, which began as a series of visions in 1799, as a bastardized form of Christianity grafted onto Native traditions. He regarded its followers as traitors or "Tontos."

Louis Hall called Handsome Lake's visions "the hallucinations of a drunk." Opposition to these teachings is one plank in an intellectual platform that allows the Warriors to claim that the Mohawk Nation Council at Akwesasne and the Iroquois Confederacy Council are enemies of the people and that the Warriors are the true protectors of Mohawk sovereignty.

"What can warrior societies do?" he asked, then answered: "Dump bridges into rivers—which are now sewers—and into the [St. Lawrence] Seaway, canceling all traffic, knock out powerhouses, high-tension power lines, punch holes in the reactors of nuclear power houses." [Johansen]

By such measures, Hall measured the ascendency of Native national liberation. "Legal extermination of the Indians as a distinct people is an act of aggression," he said. "Oppression is an act of war against the people. Legislating Indians into extinction by way of assimilation is an act of war."

Any Iroquois who does not subscribe to Hall's ideology was a racial traitor in his eyes. For following the peace-oriented path, many of the Iroquois chiefs (including the entire Onondaga Council) should be executed. "They should be executing the traitors," Hall said in 1990. "But they will have to do it the way the Mafia do it, in secret and never see the victim again. No body. No case." [Johansen] A year later, Hall backed off this death threat saying that the Warriors would replace the existing grand council by peaceful means.

In 1990, Hall's ideology helped provoke an often emotional debate over the future of the Iroquois Confederacy as a whole. At the heart of this debate were two interpretations of history. One belonged to the Onondaga elders, the Mohawk Nation Council, and many of the other national councils that make up the Iroquois' original political structure. These people rejected violence and looked at the Warriors as illegitimate usurpers of a thousand-year-old history. The other interpretation, espoused by the Warriors (synthesized by Hall), rejected the governing structure as a creation of white-influenced religion (especially that of the Quakers) and advocated a revolution from within to overthrow it.

While some Iroquois have compared him to Adolf Hitler, Hall admired the Jewish people, saying that they have suffered persecution much as American Indians have. Hall was manifestly homophobic, but he was an Indian supremacist who stood the skin-deep aspect of Hitler's ideology on its head, believing for example that white men have hairy chests because they were born in biological union with monkeys. He was also fond of pointing out that jackasses, like white men, have hair on their chests. While Hall was hardly a cardboard cutout of Hitler, many of his adversaries in Mohawk country believe that his ideology is fundamentally fascistic. A June 1991 essay in *Indian Time*, a newspaper serving Akwesasne, analyzed Hall's ideology and carried a small drawing of Hitler, with one difference. One has to look closely to see two Native-style braids dangling from the back of his head.

FOR MORE INFORMATION:

Hornung, Rick. *One Nation Under the Gun: Inside the Mohawk Civil War.* New York: Pantheon, 1991.

Johansen, Bruce E. *Life and Death in Mohawk Country.* Golden, Colo.: North American Press, 1993.

HANCOCK, JOHN
1736–1793

In the midst of the debates over American independence, twenty-one Iroquois Indians came to meet with the Continental Congress in May 1776. The Indians lodged on the second floor of Independence Hall (then called the Pennsylvania State House), observing the debates at the invitation of the delegates.

On June 11, 1776, while independence was being debated, the visiting Iroquois chiefs were invited formally into the hall of the Continental Congress. Speeches were delivered calling them "brothers" and wishing that the "friendship . . . between us . . . will . . . continue as long as the sun shall shine" and the "waters run." The speech also declared that the Americans and the Iroquois be "as one people, and have but one heart."

After this speech, an Onondaga chief asked to give Hancock an Indian name. The Congress graciously consented, and the Onondaga chief gave the "president the name of Karanduawn, or the Great Tree."

FOR MORE INFORMATION:

Grinde, Donald A., Jr., and Bruce E. Johansen. *Exemplar of Liberty: Native America and the Evolution of Democracy.* Berkeley and Los Angeles: University of California Press, 1991.

HANDSOME LAKE (GANEODIYO)
Seneca
c. 1733–1815

Handsome Lake's religion, which began as a series of visions in 1799, combined Quaker forms of Christianity with Native traditions.

Its influence is still strongly felt among the traditional Iroquois, who often call the Code of Handsome Lake "the Longhouse religion." His personal name was Ganeodiyo; Handsome Lake, a reference to Lake Ontario, is one of the fifty chieftainship lines of the Iroquois Confederacy. Handsome Lake was a half brother of the Seneca chief CORNPLANTER and an uncle of RED JACKET.

Handsome Lake was born at Conawagus, a Seneca village near contemporary Avon, New York, on the Genesee River. He and many other Senecas sided with the British in the French and Indian War and the American Revolution. After that war, many Iroquois and other Native Americans who had supported the British were forced into Canada or onto small, impoverished reservations in the United States. Handsome Lake's revival occurred in an atmosphere of dissension within a fractured Iroquois League.

Handsome Lake's early life reflected the disintegration of his people. His birthplace was taken by whites, and Handsome Lake was forced to move to the Allegheny Seneca Reser-

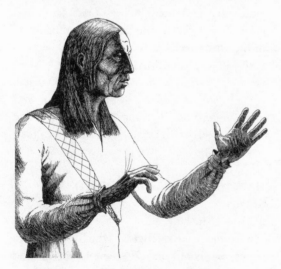

Handsome Lake.
[Courtesy of John Kahionhes Fadden]

vation. The Seneca ethnologist Arthur PARKER characterized Handsome Lake as "a middle-sized man, slim and unhealthy looking . . . [who became] a dissolute person and a miserable victim of the drink."

After four years on his back in a small cabin, Handsome Lake began having a series of visions with which he later rallied the Iroquois at a time when some of them were selling their entire winter harvest of furs for hard liquor, turning traditional ceremonies into drunken brawls, and, in winter, often dying of exposure in drunken stupors. The Iroquois population in upstate New York had declined to roughly four thousand people by this time. By spring 1799, Handsome Lake was experiencing considerable remorse over his alcoholism, but according to Parker he didn't stop drinking until he was nearly dead, "yellow skin and dried bones." During this bout of delirium, Handsome Lake had a series of visions that he later committed to writing as the Code of Handsome Lake.

A nationalistic figure in a religious context, the prophet Handsome Lake finally stopped his own heavy drinking and later committed to writing his code. He persuaded many other Iroquois to give up alcohol. Handsome Lake achieved some political influence among the Senecas, but his popularity slid because of his ideological rigidity. In 1801 and 1802, Handsome Lake traveled to Washington, D.C., with a delegation of Senecas to meet with President Thomas Jefferson and to resist the reduction of their peoples' landholdings.

The Code of Handsome Lake combines European religious influences (especially those practiced by the Quakers) with a traditional Iroquois emphasis on family, community, and the centrality of the land to the maintenance of culture. The largest following for Handsome Lake occurred after his death. Many Iroquois accepted his rejection of alcohol and his concepts of social relationships, as well as his concepts of good and evil (which, again, closely resemble those of Quakerism, studied by Handsome Lake). Handsome Lake also borrowed heavily from the Iroquois Great Law of Peace, popularizing such concepts as looking into the future for seven generations and regarding the earth as one's mother, ideas which have since become part of pan-Indian thought across North America and from there were incorporated into late-twentieth-century popular environmental symbolism.

The Code of Handsome Lake is still widely followed as the Longhouse religion in Iroquois country. By the late twentieth century, roughly a third of the thirty thousand Iroquois in New York State attended Longhouse rites.

FOR MORE INFORMATION:

Deardorff, Merle H. "The Religion of Handsome Lake: Its Origins and Development." Bureau of American Ethnology Bulletin No. 149. Washington, D.C.: Bureau of American Ethnology, 1951.

Parker, Arthur. *The Code of Handsome Lake, the Seneca Prophet.* New York State Museum Bulletin No. 163. Albany, N.Y., 1913.

———. *Parker on the Iroquois.* Edited by William Fenton. Syracuse, N.Y.: Syracuse University Press, 1968.

Wallace, Anthony F. C. *The Death and Rebirth of the Seneca.* New York: Knopf, 1970.

Wright, Ronald. *Stolen Continents.* Boston: Houghton Mifflin, 1992.

HARJO, JOY
Creek
1951–

Born in Tulsa, Oklahoma, Joy Harjo graduated from the Institute of American Indian Arts in Santa Fe, New Mexico, in 1968. She received a bachelor's degree in English from the University of New Mexico in 1976. In 1978, she received a Master of Fine Arts in creative writing from the Iowa Writer's Workshop at the University of Iowa. She has published several books of poems including: *She Had Some Horses* (1983), *Secrets from the Center of the World* (1989), and *In Mad Love and War* (1990). In general, her work commingles the spirituality of Native Americans with realism. In her poetry, she bemoans the violent past and the angst of the present, and she hopes for a better future for American Indian people. She has taught at the University of New Mexico, the University of Colorado at Boulder, and the University of Arizona.

In addition to her poetry, she is a screenwriter and author of children's stories. She gives readings of her poetry across the nation and the world. In her band, Poetic Justice, she plays the saxophone. She has received the Josephine Miles Award for Excellence in Literature from PEN Oakland, the William Carlos Williams Award from the Poetry Society of America, the Delmore Schwartz Award from New York University, and two National Endowment for the Arts Creative Writing Fellowships.

FOR MORE INFORMATION:

Klein, Barry T., ed. *Reference Encyclopedia of the American Indian.* West Nyack, N.Y.: Todd Publications, 1993.

HARNEY, WILLIAM SELBY
1800–1889

Early in the summer of 1853, Lieutenant J. L. Grattan—who had said he thought all Indians were cowards and dogs—invaded a Sioux camp near Laramie, Wyoming, to arrest a Native man who had killed a cow abandoned by an immigrant. The Sioux killed Grattan and all of his men in fifteen minutes of furious fighting, igniting a wave of public anger that led the army to send Harney to Laramie with a larger armed force to punish the Sioux.

By the time Harney interrupted his European vacation to exact retribution from the Sioux and their allies in 1855, he was already a veteran of the war with Mexico (1846–1848), during which he had commanded General Winfield Scott's cavalry units. He had also participated in Black Hawk's War (1832) and in the Second Seminole War (1835–1842).

Harney, who was sometimes called "White Beard" by the Sioux, could not find the Sioux band that had killed Grattan and his men, so he ordered an attack on the friendly village led by Chief YELLOW THUNDER at Ash Hollow, astride the Blue River north of the Northern Platte. Harney said that eighty-six warriors died in the massacre, five were injured, and seventy women and children were captured. The village was laid waste and many horses killed. In his report on the incident, Harney admitted that he had attacked the wrong band of Indians and that he was solely looking for scapegoats.

FOR MORE INFORMATION:

Wiltsey, Norman B. *Brave Warriors.* Caldwell, Idaho: Caxton, 1963.

HARPER, ELIJAH
Cree
1949–

Elijah Harper, the only Native member of Manitoba's legislature, led an effort against ratification of the Canadian Meech Lake Accord by its deadline of June 23, 1990. Harper's vote started a chain of procedural circumstances that kept the accord from going into effect. This rejection of the Meech Lake Accord occurred during a summer of Native protest in Canada during the siege at Oka, Quebec. Less than a month before violence erupted at Oka, Harper killed the Meech Lake Accord by voting "no" during a roll call vote as he held an eagle feather in his hand.

If it had been ratified, the accord would have given Quebec a "special status" designation in the Canadian Confederation, while at the same time refusing to acknowledge Native peoples' original occupancy of Canada. Harper, who was first elected to Manitoba's legislature in 1981 from the northern riding (district) of Rupertsland (which includes his home of Red Sucker Lake), obstructed the accord because Canadian Native people were angered by their omission in it. Manitoba's legislature required unanimous approval of the accord, and Harper, the first Native American to be elected to that body, was in a position to obstruct its passage.

Harper's vote to repeal the Meech Lake Accord occurred during a two-and-a-half-month standoff between Mohawks at Kanesatake, Quebec police, and Canadian army troops at Oka, a suburb of Montreal. At issue was a tract of land that Oka city officials wanted to turn into a golf course but which is part of the Mohawk land grant. The confrontation in Oka ignited many other Native American protests across Canada during the summer of 1990 (see Doug GEORGE-KANENTIIO and Louis HALL).

FOR MORE INFORMATION:

Miller, J. R. *Skyscrapers Hide the Heavens: A History of Indian-White Relations in Canada.* Toronto: University of Toronto Press, 1991.

HARRIS, LADONNA
Comanche
1931–

Born in Temple, Oklahoma, on February 13, 1931, in a traditional Comanche household, LaDonna Harris spoke only Comanche before attending public schools. During the 1960s, Harris became a prominent political figure as the wife of Senator Fred Harris (Democratic senator from Oklahoma). She established, in

1965, a renowned Native American self-help organization, Oklahomans for Indian Opportunity. She has also been a board member or chair of organizations like the Joint Commission on Mental Health, the National Rural Health Conference, the Women's National Advisory Council on Poverty, and the National Association of Mental Health. Harris also established Americans for Indian Opportunity in 1970 and served as its first president. Americans for Indian Opportunity was an organization that aided American Indian tribal groups in their quest for self-determination in social, economic, and political affairs.

Since 1968, Harris has been a strong advocate for world peace and has participated in several international peace conferences. During the 1960s, she traveled in various South American countries, as well as Senegal, Mali, and the Soviet Union as a peace activist. She also served as a representative to the Inter-American Indigenous Institute (an Organization of American States agency) in the 1980s.

LaDonna Harris is well known for her activities fostering Native American equal opportunity nationally. She has also been instrumental in promoting self-determination and economic development for American Indians in the United States.

FOR MORE INFORMATION:

Champagne, Duane, ed. *Native America: Portrait of a People.* Detroit: Gale Research, 1994.

HATATHLI, NED
Navajo
1923–1972

Ned Hatathli was one of the first educated contemporary Navajo leaders. Born at Coalmine Mesa near Tuba City on the Arizona part of the Navajo Reservation on October 11, 1923, Ned

Hatathli had a traditional Navajo childhood until adolescence, when at the urging of an uncle, he went away to boarding school. Eventually, he graduated as valedictorian of Tuba City High School. On a class trip to the California coast, he was amazed by the world outside his reservation, particularly the vastness of the Pacific Ocean. Subsequently, he decided to attend Haskell Institute in Lawrence, Kansas, in the late 1930s, but he left before graduation to join the navy and renew his interest in the ocean at the outbreak of World War II.

After the war, he returned to Flagstaff, Arizona, and attended Northern Arizona University, obtaining B.S. and Ph.D. degrees in education (one of the first Navajos to earn a doctorate). Upon completion of his degrees, Hatathli returned to the Navajo nation and became a leader in the Navajos' movement toward greater social and economic opportunity.

Hatathli helped to found the Navajo Arts and Crafts Guild, feeling strongly that art was an integral part of the Navajo way of life. He improved the quality of Navajo silversmithing and weaving during the early 1950s by establishing standards for quality. In 1955, he was elected to the Navajo Tribal Council and then appointed as director of tribal resources (he believed that people were as important a resource as oil, uranium, coal, or natural gas).

In the mid-1960s, the Navajo Tribal Council decided to improve educational opportunities for the tribe's members through the creation of the Navajo Community College. Ned Hatathli was appointed the first executive vice president. When classes began in 1969, he became Navajo Community College's first president. In 1971, Hatathli saw the U.S. Congress pass a bill that provided significant federal support for construction and operating costs of the college. He died suddenly of an accidental gunshot wound on October 16, 1972, at Many Farms, Arizona, on the Navajo Reservation. He was survived by his wife, Florence, and their four children.

HAWKINS, BENJAMIN
1754–1816

Born in North Carolina, Benjamin Hawkins initially was a farmer. As a young man at the time of the American Revolution, Hawkins was a staff officer to General George Washington. He later served as a delegate to the Articles of Confederation government. Upon the ratification of the U.S. Constitution, Hawkins served one term as one of the first senators from North Carolina (1789–1795). At the beginning of the federal period, military officers maintained most of the governmental relations with Indians; in 1796, with Hawkins's appointment as superintendent of the southern Indians and as agent to the Creeks by Henry Knox, Secretary of War, the federal Indian agency system was initiated. Upon leaving his Senate seat, Hawkins started a twenty-year career in the Indian service.

As agent to the southern Indians, Hawkins tried to change Native peoples' communal ways of life and transform them into farmers with individual plots of land. The 1796 Treaty of Coleraine, which he negotiated with the Creeks, aided in the steadying of Indian relations on the southern frontier for a short time. In establishing schools for Indian children, Hawkins hoped to foster their acculturation into U.S. society.

While an agent, Hawkins encountered uncooperative southern state governments that refused to recognize tribal land claims. With the advent of the War of 1812 and the Creeks' decision to follow the admonitions of TECUM-SEH to fight against the Americans in the Creek War of 1813–1814 under William WEATHER-FORD, Hawkins's policies to assimilate the southeast Indians fell into disrepute, paving the way for the creation of removal policies in the Jacksonian era.

HAYES, IRA HAMILTON
Pima
1923–1955

Born at Sacaton, Arizona, on the Pima Reservation on January 12, 1923, to Joe E. and Nancy W. Hayes (both were Pima farming people), Ira Hayes was a noted World War II hero. Although he had a normal childhood on his reservation, his life changed dramatically when war broke out and he joined the Marine Corps. By the beginning of 1945, he was part of the American invasion force that attacked the Japanese stronghold of Iwo Jima. On February 23, 1945, to signal the end of Japanese control, Hayes and five others raised the U.S. flag atop Mount Suribachi on the island of Iwo Jima (three of the six men were killed while raising the flag). This heroic act was photographed by Joe Rosenthal, and it transformed Hayes's life.

The nation and President Franklin D. Roosevelt called the brave survivors of the flag raising back to the United States to aid a war bond drive. Subsequently, a commemorative postage stamp was created as well as a bronze statue in Washington, D.C. Shuttled from one city to another for publicity purposes with questionable sincerity on the part of the American military, Hayes asked to be sent back to the front lines, stating that "sometimes I wish that guy had never made that picture."

At the conclusion of World War II, he returned to his reservation, disillusioned by what he felt was unwarranted adoration. He began to drink heavily and was arrested fifty-one times in thirteen years (almost every arrest the result of well-meaning friends' offers of drinks in their appreciation of his heroism).

Never able to get his life in balance again, Ira Hayes died of exposure at thirty-three on January 24, 1955. He was memorialized by the Pima people and characterized as "a hero to everyone but himself." He was buried in Arlington Cemetery. He never married.

HENDRICK (TIYANOGA)
Mohawk
c. 1680–1755

Tiyanoga, called Hendrick by the English, was a major figure in colonial affairs between 1710, when he was one of four Mohawks invited to England by Queen Anne, and 1755, when he died in battle with the French as a British ally. In 1754, Hendrick advised Benjamin FRANKLIN and other colonial representatives on the principles of Iroquois government at the Albany Congress.

In reality, Hendrick knew both Iroquois and English cultures well. He converted to Christianity and became a Mohawk preacher sometime after 1700. In England, he was painted by John Verelst and called the "Emperor of the Five Nations." Hendrick was perhaps the most important individual link in a chain of alliance that saved the New York frontier and probably New England from the French in the initial stages of the Seven Years' War, which was called the French and Indian War (1754–1763) in North America.

Well known as a man of distinction in his manners and dress, Hendrick visited England again in 1740. At that time, King George presented him with an ornate green coat of satin, fringed in gold, which Hendrick was fond of wearing in combination with his traditional Mohawk ceremonial clothing.

A lifelong friend of Sir William JOHNSON, Hendrick appeared often at Johnson Hall, near Albany, and had numerous opportunities to rub elbows with visiting English nobles,

sometimes as he arrived in war paint, fresh from battle. According to historian Wilbur R. Jacobs, Thomas Pownall, a shrewd observer of colonial Indian affairs, described Hendrick as "a bold artful, intriguing Fellow and has learnt no small share of European Politics, [who] obstructs and opposes all (business) where he has not been talked to first."

Hector Saint Jean de Crevecoeur, himself an adopted Iroquois who had sat in on sessions of the grand council at Onondaga, described Hen-

Hendrick. [National Anthropological Archives]

drick in late middle age, preparing for dinner at the Johnson estate, within a few years of the Albany Congress:

[He] wished to appear at his very best. . . . His head was shaved, with the exception of a little tuft of hair in the back, to which he attached a piece of silver. To the cartilage of his ears . . . he attached a little brass wire twisted into very tight spirals.

A girondole was hung from his nose. Wearing a wide silver neckpiece, a crimson vest and a blue cloak adorned with sparkling gold, Hendrick, as was his custom, shunned European breeches for a loincloth fringed with glass beads. On his feet, Hendrick wore moccasins of tanned elk, embroidered with porcupine quills, fringed with tiny silver bells. [Grinde]

In 1754, Hendrick attended the conference at Albany that framed a colonial plan of union. By the time Hendrick was invited to address colonial delegates at the Albany Congress, he was well known on both sides of the Atlantic among Iroquois and Europeans alike. Hendrick played a major role in convening the Albany Congress in large part because he wished to see his friend Johnson reinstated as the English superintendent of affairs with the Six Nations. Without him, Hendrick maintained that the covenant chain would rust. It was Johnson himself who conducted most of the day-to-day business with the Indians at Albany.

At the Albany Congress, Hendrick repeated the advice CANASSATEGO had given colonial delegates at Lancaster a decade before. This time the conference was devoted not only to diplomacy but also to drawing up a plan for the type of colonial union the Iroquois had been requesting. The same day, at the courthouse, the colonial delegates were in the early stages of debate over the plan of union.

Hendrick was openly critical of the British at the Albany Congress and hinted that the Iroquois would not ally with the English colonies

unless a suitable form of unity was established among them. In talking of the proposed union of the colonies and the Six Nations on July 9, 1754, Hendrick stated, "We wish this Tree of Friendship may grow up to a great height and then we shall be a powerful people." [Grinde] Hendrick followed that admonition with an analysis of Iroquois and colonial unity when he said, "We the United Nations shall rejoice of our strength . . . and . . . we have now made so strong a Confederacy." In reply to Hendrick's speech on Native American and colonial unity, DeLancey said, "I hope that by this present Union, we shall grow up to a great height and be as powerful and famous as you were of old." [Grinde] Benjamin Franklin was commissioned to compose the final draft of the Albany Plan the same day.

Hendrick died at the Battle of Lake George in late summer 1755 as Sir William Johnson defeated French commander Baron Dieskau. The elderly Mohawk was shot from his horse and bayoneted to death while on a scouting party on September 8.

FOR MORE INFORMATION:

Grinde, Donald A., Jr., and Bruce E. Johansen. *Exemplar of Liberty: Native America and the Evolution of Democracy*. Berkeley and Los Angeles: University of California Press, 1991.

Jacobs, Wilbur R. *Wilderness Politics and Indian Gifts*. Lincoln: University of Nebraska Press, 1966.

Wallace, Paul A. W. *The White Roots of Peace*. Philadelphia: University of Pennsylvania Press, 1946.

HENRY, PATRICK
1736–1799

Patrick Henry, the Virginian revolutionary agitator, advocated state subsidies for Indian-white marriages, believing that intermarriage between European immigrants and Native Americans would blunt conflict as the settlement frontier expanded. In fall 1784, he introduced such a measure into the Virginia House of Delegates. The bill directed the state to pay an unspecified sum for the marriage and an additional sum on the birth of each child. In addition, Henry proposed that Indian-white couples live tax free. Henry pushed the bill with his usual enthusiasm and oratorical flourish as it survived two readings. By the time it reached the third reading, Henry had been elected governor of Virginia. Without his support in the House of Delegates, the intermarriage bill died.

HERRERO GRANDE
Navajo
fl. mid-1800s
Living at Fort Defiance, Arizona, in the 1850s, Herrero Grande received his instruction in blacksmithing from George Carter, a blacksmith brought in by Agent Henry L. (Red Shirt) Dodge to teach the Navajos the trade. Herrero Grande was chiefly known for the fine workmanship of his bridle parts, bits, and knife blades.

In 1861, after a council with American authorities at Fort Fauntleroy, the Navajos chose Herrero as their principal chief. Refusing the order to relocate to Fort Sumner, Herrero eluded the U.S. Army in the early stages of the Navajo War. After being removed to Fort Sumner (Bosque Redondo), Herrero and several other Navajo chiefs endorsed the 1868 treaty that returned the Navajos to lands in the Four Corners region of Utah, Arizona, and New Mexico.

HEWITT, JOHN NAPOLEON BRINTON
Tuscarora
1859–1937
Employed by the Bureau of American Ethnology, J. N. B. Hewitt attempted to separate myth from historical fact in the Iroquois Confederacy's founding epic. Hewitt gathered oral history narratives of the epic involving DEGANAWIDAH and HIAWATHA and published some of them in English.

Born near Lewiston in Niagara County, New York, of a Tuscarora mother and a Scottish father, Hewitt began to collect Iroquois folk history with Mrs. Erminnie A. Smith. He was called to the Smithsonian's Bureau of American Ethnology in 1886 to assume Smith's position there. Hewitt became known in academic circles as a leading authority on the Iroquois. Aside from his contributions to the *Handbook of American Indians North of Mexico* edited by Frederick W. Hodge (1912), most of Hewitt's work (twelve thousand pages of it) remained in manuscript form.

Hewitt worked at the BAE for a half century, becoming fluent in several Native languages. He researched the linguistic relationships between the Cherokees and Iroquois and was one of the founding members of the American Anthropological Association.

FOR MORE INFORMATION:
Hewitt, J. N. B. *A Constitutional League of Peace in the Stone Age of America.* Washington, D.C.: Smithsonian, 1918.
———. *Iroquois Cosmology.* Washington, D.C.: Smithsonian, 1903.
———. *Legend of the Founding of the Iroquois League.* Washington, D.C.: Smithsonian, 1892.

HIAWATHA (AIONWANTHA)
Mohawk
fl. 1100–1150 (?)
The Iroquois Confederacy was formed by the Huron prophet DEGANAWIDAH, who is called "the Peacemaker" in oral discourse among Iroquois. Deganawidah enlisted the aid of a speaker, Hiawatha (sometimes called Aiowan-

tha), to spread his vision of a united Haudenosaunee Confederacy because the prophet himself stuttered so badly he could hardly speak.

Peace among the formerly antagonistic nations was procured and maintained through the Haudenosaunee's Great Law of Peace (Kaianerekowa), which was passed from generation to generation by use of wampum, a form of written communication that outlined a complex system of checks and balances between nations and sexes. A complete oral recitation of the Great Law can take several days; encapsulated versions of it have been translated into English for more than a hundred years and provide one reason why the Iroquois are cited so often today in debates regarding the origins of U.S. fundamental law. (While many other native confederacies existed along the borders of the British colonies, many of the specific provisions of their governments have been lost.)

According to Iroquois oral history, visionaries such as Hiawatha, who was living among the Onondagas, tried to call councils to eliminate the blood feud, but they were always thwarted by the evil and twisted wizard TADADAHO, an Onondaga who used magic and spies to rule by fear and intimidation. Failing to defeat the wizard, Hiawatha traveled to Mohawk, Oneida, and Cayuga villages with his message of peace and brotherhood. Everywhere he went, his message was accepted with the proviso that he persuade the formidable Tadadaho and the Onondagas to embrace the covenant of peace.

Just as Hiawatha was despairing, the prophet Deganawidah entered his life and changed the nature of things among the Iroquois. Together, Hiawatha and Deganawidah developed a powerful message of peace. Deganawidah's vision gave Hiawatha's oratory substance. Through

Hiawatha. [Courtesy of John Kahionhes Fadden]

Deganawidah's vision, the constitution of the Iroquois was formulated.

Historian Charles Hamilton suggests that history presents us with three versions of Hiawatha: the historic Hiawatha, associated with the founding of the Iroquois League; the mythic Hiawatha, described in the oral legends of the Iroquois; and the Hiawatha created by the poet Henry Wadsworth Longfellow, who was a fictional Ojibway, unrelated to the other two except in name.

FOR MORE INFORMATION:

Colden, Cadwallader. *The History of the Five Nations*. 1727 and 1747. Reprint, Ithaca, N.Y.: Great Seal Books, 1958.

Fenton, William N. *Roll Call of the Iroquois Chiefs*. Washington, D.C.: Smithsonian, 1950.

Hale, Horatio. *The Iroquois Book of Rites*. 1883. Reprint, Toronto: University of Toronto Press, 1963.

Hamilton, Charles. *Cry of the Thunderbird.*
Norman: University of Oklahoma Press,
1972.

Henry, Thomas R. *Wilderness Messiah.* New
York: Sloane Associates, 1955.

Hewitt, J. N. B. *A Constitutional League of
Peace in the Stone Age of America.* Washington, D.C.: Smithsonian, 1918.

———. *Iroquois Cosmology.* Washington, D.C.:
Smithsonian, 1903.

———. *Legend of the Founding of the Iroquois
League.* Washington, D.C.: Smithsonian,
1892.

Howard, Helen A. "Hiawatha: Co-founder of an
Indian United Nations." *Journal of the West*
10:3 (1971).

Wallace, Paul. *The White Roots of Peace.* Santa
Fe, N. Mex.: Clear Light, 1994.

White Roots of Peace. *The Great Law of Peace.*
Rooseveltown, N.Y.: *Akwesasne Notes,*
1977.

Wilson, Edmund. *Apologies to the Iroquois.*
New York: Farrar, Straus & Cudahy, 1960.

HIGH HAWK
Brulé Sioux
fl. 1880s–1890s

High Hawk led a Brulé Sioux band that advocated the Ghost Dance in the late 1880s. He
was an ally of several other Sioux chiefs,
including LITTLE WOUND and TWO STRIKE. High
Hawk's band avoided the slaughter at Wounded
Knee Creek in late December 1890. After the
massacre, High Hawk was a member of a Sioux
delegation to Washington, D.C. Officials at the
Interior Department and Bureau of Indian
Affairs told the delegates that they wanted to
solve problems (including nonfulfillment of
treaty obligations) that had caused unrest, but
little actually improved.

*High Hawk (right), with Two Strike (left) and Crow
Dog. [Nebraska State Historical Society]*

High Hawk was especially concerned with
the alienation of Sioux land. According to historian Dee Brown, at one point shortly before
the Wounded Knee massacre, he told General
George Crook: "The land you [the United
States] has now surveyed for us is but a small
piece [of former holdings]. I expect my children
to have children and grandchildren, and get all
over the country, and now you want me to cut
off my 'tool' and not make any more children."
FOR MORE INFORMATION:
Brown, Dee. *Bury My Heart at Wounded Knee.*
New York: Holt, Rinehart, & Winston, 1970.

HIGH HORN (SPAMAGELABE)
Shawnee
c. 1775–1812

Born at Wapakoneta, Ohio, and a nephew of
TECUMSEH, High Horn was captured as a boy by
General James Logan and raised by his family at
their Kentucky home. Shortly before the War of
1812, he was returned to the Shawnees in an
exchange of prisoners; many of his people now
called him "Captain Logan."

High Horn tried unsuccessfully to convince Tecumseh not to make war on the settlers. During the war, he was a scout for the Americans; on one occasion, he evacuated women and children from Fort Wayne before an Indian attack, and he killed Winamac, a Winnebago who had played a part in the Fort Dearborn massacre. High Horn was killed November 24, 1812, while scouting. He was buried with full U.S. Army honors. The town of Logansport, Indiana, was named for him.

FOR MORE INFORMATION:

Eckert, Allan W. *A Sorrow in Our Heart: The Life of Tecumseh.* New York: Bantam, 1992.

HIOKATOO
Seneca
c. 1708–1811

Hiokatoo, husband of Mary JEMISON, became known for his merciless handling of enemies during the French and Indian War. He led a force of Indians who massacred settlers at Cherry Valley on November 11, 1778. Jemison, a white captive who had been adopted by Hiokatoo and the Senecas at thirteen, recalled him as unusually cruel:

He was a man of tender feelings for his friends . . . yet, as a warrior, his cruelties to his enemies perhaps were unparalleled. . . . In [his] early life, Hiokatoo showed signs of thirst for blood . . . [by] practicing cruelties upon every thing that chanced to fall into his hands, which was susceptible to pain. . . . He could inflict the most excruciating tortures upon his enemies.

Hiokatoo died of consumption (probably cancer) in 1811 at the reported age of 103. He is reputed to have been a practicing warrior for three-quarters of a century.

FOR MORE INFORMATION:

Heard, J. Norman. *Handbook of the American Frontier.* Vol. 2, *The Northeastern Woodlands.* Metuchen, N.J.: The Scarecrow Press, 1990.

HOBOMOK
Wampanoag
fl. 1620–1642

One of MASSASOIT's favorite subchiefs, Hobomok played an important role in maintaining an alliance between the English settlers of New England and the Wampanoags until his death. He was delegated by Massasoit to aid the colonists in surviving their first harsh winters in North America.

During the insurrection led by CORBITANT in 1621 against Massasoit and the Pilgrims, Hobomok escaped capture and brought word of the rebellion to Miles Standish and other Pilgrim soldiers. Hobomok allied with Standish in 1622 against the Massachuset people at Wessagusset.

As a spiritual leader and a warrior, Hobomok often carried a supernatural aura into battle. It is said that in 1622 the Massachusets so feared him that they left the field of battle before the engagement began. Hobomok was converted to Christianity late in his life when he became a citizen of the Plymouth colony. He died in 1642.

FOR MORE INFORMATION:

Waters, Frank. *Brave Are My People: Indian Heroes Not Forgotten.* Santa Fe, N. Mex.: Clear Light, 1993.

HOKEAH, JACK
Kiowa
1900–1969

Born in Caddo County, Oklahoma, about 1900, Jack Hokeah was orphaned as a boy and raised by his grandmother. His grandfather was Tsen T'ainte or "White Horse," a renowned Kiowa warrior. As a young adult, Hokeah became one of the Five Kiowa artists who were very prominent in the first half of the twentieth century.

Hokeah was educated at St. Patrick's School and then went to Santa Fe Indian School, where his artistic abilities caused him and several other American Indian artists to be selected for further training at the University of Oklahoma art department under the tutelage of Dr. Oscar Jacobson. Hokeah was also an exceptional dancer and became noted for his dancing as well as his painting. Because of his abilities as a dancer, he did not produce as many paintings as did the other Kiowa artists in his group. Hokeah danced professionally in New York City for a while and then worked for the Bureau of Indian Affairs. His handsome and personable demeanor made him the ideal Indian in the eyes of many Anglos. His dancing had a powerful and exciting effect on both Indians and whites.

His artworks were reproduced in several books, and his mural at Santa Fe Indian School is still touted as an excellent example of early-twentieth-century Kiowa artwork. On December 14, 1969, he died at Fort Cobb, Oklahoma.

HOLE-IN-THE-DAY, ELDER (BUGONEGIJIG)
Chippewa-Ojibway
fl. 1812–1846

Hole-in-the-Day (sometimes called "Hole-in-the-Sky") allied with the United States in the War of 1812 to obtain guns with which to drive the Sioux out of the Lake Superior region. He became a principal war chief of the Chippewas in 1825, and in 1838 he led forces that attacked and massacred Christianized Sioux housed in mission camps along the Chippewa River. Officers at Fort Snelling allowed the Sioux to ambush Hole-in-the-Day on his way from visiting the fort for retaliation, but he won his release by giving them some of his clothing and ornaments.

Hole-in-the-Day (Elder) was a close friend of George COPWAY, who once ran about 270 miles in four days to warn his band of a Dakota attack. He died in 1846.

HOLE-IN-THE-DAY, YOUNGER (BUGONEGIJIG)
Chippewa
1825–1868

Hole-in-the-Day's father, who shared the same name, was also a Chippewa leader; he fought with the Americans against the British in the War of 1812. Hole-in-the-Day's (Younger) principal concern as a Chippewa leader, however, was making war against the Sioux, their traditional enemies. Aided by firearms provided by white traders, Hole-in-the-Day (whose name actually means "Opening in the Sky") played a

Hole-in-the-Day, Younger.
[Nebraska State Historical Society]

major role in pushing the Sioux westward from their former lands near the Great Lakes. At one point, the battles between the Sioux and Chippewa became so violent that the U.S. Army intervened to set boundaries.

The younger Hole-in-the-Day became head chief of the Chippewas' Bear clan in 1846, after his father died. He visited Washington, D.C., several times, and at one point married a white newspaper reporter there. He was known as a bargainer and a person who was not afraid to take his cut of any agreement on behalf of his people. Many Chippewas complained that Hole-in-the-Day was aggrandizing himself at the expense of his people; he did, in fact, become rich. He was politically prudent, however, and distributed benefits to enough people to gain popular support from progressive Chippewas. When his people were compelled to move to the White Earth Reservation in Montana, Hole-in-the-Day at first refused to depart. He relented, however, just before he was murdered by his own people at Crow Wing, Minnesota, because they suspected him of having betrayed them in treaty negotiations.

HOLLOW HORN BEAR (MATIHEHLOGEGO)
Brulé Sioux
c. 1850–1913

Hollow Horn Bear fought with the leading chiefs of the Plains against subjugation until the 1870s; after that, he favored peace with the whites and became something of a celebrity along the East Coast. In his later years, Hollow Horn Bear attended several official functions as a Native representative, including two inaugural parades. His likeness appeared on a fourteen-cent stamp as well as on a five-dollar bill.

Born in Sheridan County, Nebraska, a son of Chief Iron Shell, Hollow Horn Bear earned his early fame as a warrior; he raided the Pawnees at first then aided other Sioux leaders in harassing

Hollow Horn Bear with his two wives and two of his children. [Nebraska State Historical Society]

forts along the Bozeman Trail, between 1866 and 1868, when the Treaty of Fort Laramie was signed. During this time, he gained fame as the chief who defeated Lieutenant William FETTERMAN. Hollow Horn Bear also led raids of Union Pacific Railroad workers' camps.

After his reconciliation to reservation life, beginning in 1873, Hollow Horn Bear was appointed as head of Indian police at the Rosebud Agency, South Dakota; in this role, he arrested CROW DOG for the murder of SPOTTED TAIL. Hollow Horn Bear also became involved in treaty negotiations because of his oratorical abilities.

In 1905, Hollow Horn Bear was invited to take part in the inauguration of President Theodore Roosevelt. In 1913, he led a group of Indians in the presidential inauguration parade for Woodrow Wilson. On that visit, Hollow Horn Bear caught pneumonia and died.

HONAYAWAS (FARMER'S BROTHER)
Seneca
c. 1724–1815

Honayawas was one of the Senecas' principal war chiefs at the turn of the nineteenth century. He acquired the name "Farmer's Brother" from whites in the neighborhood of his Buffalo Creek, New York, home after he forged a friendship with George Washington, a farmer himself. Honayawas signed treaties at Big Tree (1797) and Buffalo (1801). During the War of 1812, he supported the Americans against the British. When Honayawas died, he was buried in Buffalo with U.S. military honors.

HOOKER JIM (HAKAR JIM, "LET ME SEE" JIM)
Modoc
c. 1825–1879

Although little is known of his early life, Hooker Jim's name became a household word throughout the United States when hostilities broke out between the Modocs and the Americans in 1872 and 1873. In the 1850s, the Modocs traded in Yreka, California, and the traders and townspeople there gave the Modoc leaders the colorful and sometimes unflattering names by which they were known. Hooker (from *hakar*, "let me see") Jim opposed the Modoc people's relocation onto the Klamath Reservation in southern Oregon. To oppose U.S. policies, he persuaded his followers to go back to their aboriginal homeland in northern California. In following this course of action, the Mo-docs, led by Hooker Jim, advocated the creation of their own reservation.

In November 1872, the U.S. Army visited CAPTAIN JACK's encampment on the Lost River and ordered the Modocs to go back to the Klam-ath Reservation. Captain Jack opposed the order, and this led to the first battle of the Modoc War. Hooker Jim and his people were living on the opposite side of the river when some ranchers fired on them, killing a woman and a baby and wounding several men. Angered by these actions, Hooker Jim and fellow Modoc, Curly Headed Doctor, raided a neighboring ranch and killed twelve whites. Hooker Jim and his people then fled southward to the Lava Beds of northern California, where Captain Jack and his followers were defending themselves. Captain Jack still believed that a peaceful settlement might be negotiated. However, the Modocs balked at the army's demands to hand over the men who had killed the ranchers. At a peace conference set to discuss matters, Hooker Jim and others told Captain Jack that the only way he could prove that he was not a coward would be to kill General Edward R. S. Canby. On April 11, 1873, as the conference started, Captain Jack shot Canby, wounded the Indian superintendent, Alfred B. Meachum, and killed a minister.

In the weeks after the aborted conference, Hooker Jim and Captain Jack argued about the appropriate course of action. Hooker Jim deserted the fight in the Lava Beds and surren-dered. Subsequently, Hooker Jim showed the army where Captain Jack was holed up. At Cap-tain Jack's trial in July 1873, Hooker Jim gave testimony against Captain Jack to save himself. After the trial and execution of four leaders, Hooker Jim and about 150 other Modocs were sent to Indian Territory. Subsequently, Hooker Jim died at the Quapaw Agency in Indian Terri-tory in 1879.

HOPEHOOD
Abenaki
fl. late 1600s

During and after King Philip's War (1676), Hopehood became one of the most notable raiders of English settlements on New England's northern frontiers. He was taken prisoner at one point and sold into slavery in Boston, but he escaped within a few months to continue his crusade to push the colonists into the sea.

Hopehood made peace with the English for a short time by signing a 1685 treaty wherein the Abenakis, under his leadership, promised to refrain from hostilities if the English would protect them from the Mohawks. This alliance fell apart at the onset of King William's War, during which Hopehood rallied Abenaki forces in alliance with the Frenchman François Hertel at a massacre at Salmon Falls on March 18, 1690. After several other frontier raids that killed roughly two dozen settlers, Hopehood fled to Canada to escape reprisals. Ironically, he was killed there in about 1690 by Native people who mistook him for an enemy.

FOR MORE INFORMATION:

Segal, Charles M., and David C. Stineback. *Puritans, Indians, and Manifest Destiny.* New York: Putnam, 1977.

Slotkin, Richard, and James K. Folsom, eds. *So Dreadful a Judgement: Puritan Responses to King Philip's War 1676–1677.* Middleton, Conn.: Wesleyan University Press, 1978.

Vaughan, Alden T. *New England Frontier: Puritans and Indians, 1620–1675.* Boston: Little, Brown, 1965.

HOPOCAN (CAPTAIN PIPE)
Delaware
c. 1725–1794

Hopocan was one of the Delawares' most influential war chiefs during the French and Indian War and the American Revolution. His Delaware name meant "Tobacco Pipe," and he became known to English-speaking people as Captain Pipe. Hopocan was a hereditary war chief of the Delawares; he sided with the French during the war with Britain. Following that war, his people gave Hopocan the name Konieshguanokee, "Maker of Daylight."

Hopocan was not active in the Revolutionary War until an unprovoked attack by patriot militia on his village along the Shenango River during 1778 killed his brother and wounded his mother. Four years later, Hopocan captured Continental Army colonel William Crawford. The Delaware war chief then avenged his brother's death and his mother's wounding, as well as Crawford's massacre of Christian Indians, by torturing him to death. The tortures were widely reported in the eastern press.

After the Revolution, Hopocan signed several treaties and counseled peace. He died at Captain Pipe's Village on the Upper Sandusky (Ohio). A statue was erected in his memory at Barbertown, Ohio.

HUMP (ETOKEAH)
Miniconjou Sioux
c. 1848–1908

With HOLLOW HORN BEAR, Hump gained notoriety as a war leader among the Sioux during the final years of the Plains Indian wars. Also with Hollow Horn Bear, he led the charge that defeated Colonel William FETTERMAN near Fort Phil Kearney, Wyoming. Hump's birthdate and youth are unrecorded. One indication of how little we know about Hump's life as a young man is the vast range of birthdates from various sources. Some place his birth as early as 1820, others as late as 1850.

Hump was designated as a "no-treaty" chief after he refused to sign the Fort Laramie agreement of 1866; after that he fought beside SIT-

TING BULL, CRAZY HORSE, and other hostile Lakotas. Hump was one of the leaders who rallied the Lakota in the defeat of General George Armstrong CUSTER at the Little Bighorn. For a time in the 1880s, he moved to Canada but returned to the United States as the Ghost Dance swept the Northern Plains. At first Hump advocated the dance but desisted after Captain Ezra Ewers talked him out of it. Hump's people removed themselves from Ghost Dance advocates who were killed at Wounded Knee with BIG FOOT in 1890.

Hump also refused to join Hunkpapa survivors demanding vengeance after the murder of their leader, Sitting Bull, in 1890. After the Wounded Knee massacre, Hump was one of a party of chiefs who visited Washington, D.C.,

to seek better treatment for the reservation-bound Lakota.

Hump died at Cherry Creek, South Dakota, in 1908.

FOR MORE INFORMATION:

Utley, Robert M. *Last Days of the Sioux Nation.* New Haven, Conn.: Yale University Press, 1963.

HUNT, GEORGE
Kwakiutl
1854–1933

As an ethnologist, George Hunt had a major impact on the study of the Kwakiutls. He was a major contributor to the work of Franz Boas, the pioneer ethnologist of the Northwest Coast. During his lifetime, Hunt supplied Boas

Hump was among a Sioux delegation that traveled to Washington, D.C., in the aftermath of the Wounded Knee massacre. [Nebraska State Historical Society]

with more than six thousand pages of ethnographic material. He also appeared as coauthor with Boas on *Kwakiutl Tales* (1905) and *Ethnology of the Kwakiutl* (1921).

Born in 1854 at Fort Rupert, British Columbia, Hunt was a son of Robert Hunt, the Scottish factor for the Hudson's Bay Company in British Columbia. Hunt's mother was Mary Ebbetts, a Tlinget or Tsimhian. Hunt was raised in the traditional manner and had little contact with white immigrants until he was in his twenties. Hunt first came into Anglo-American history as a guide and interpreter for the Adrian Jacobsen expedition along the North Pacific Coast between 1881 and 1883.

Hunt met Franz Boas in 1886, after which he assumed a major role in recording Kwakiutl history and customs into English. Boas taught Hunt to write the Native language in a phonetic script that could be precisely translated into English. To support himself while he did his scholarly work (which began in earnest about the turn of the century), Hunt worked in canneries and as an expedition guide.

As he became an elder, Hunt also became a political leader among his people. He was one

George Hunt (right) *and his wife.*
[American Museum of Natural History]

of few Native informants who maintained the respect of both professional academics and his own people. Hunt also worked as a consultant to the American Museum of Natural History. He died at Fort Rupert.

FOR MORE INFORMATION:

Boas, Franz, and George Hunt. *Kwakiutl Ethnology.* 1921. Reprint, Chicago: University of Chicago Press, 1966.

———. *Kwakiutl Tales.* New York: Columbia University Press, 1910.

IGNACIO (ST. IGNACE, JOHN LYON)
Ute
1828–1913

Born in the San Juan area of southwestern Colorado in 1828, Ignacio was not well known until OURAY's death, at which time he became chief of all the Southern Utes at Cimarron.

Although a quiet man, Ignacio was known to be very resolute and purposeful. When his father, a medicine man, was called to cure a sick person and failed, he was killed by the grieving family (not an unusual practice in those days). Enraged by this behavior, Ignacio killed all twelve members of the family that had killed his father.

He was a large and physically impressive man, weighing about two hundred pounds and standing about six feet, two inches tall. On December 13, 1913, he died on the Ute Mountain Reservation in Colorado. The town of Ignacio, Colorado, derives its name from him.

INKPACHUTA
Wahpekute Sioux
c. 1815–c. 1878

Inkpachuta (Sioux for "Scarlet Point") was among Wahpekute Santee Sioux cast out of the tribe about 1828 after his father, Wamdesapa, had killed principal chief Tasagi. Inkpachuta became the leader of the renegades in 1848, after his father's death. In 1849, he led a raid on the Wahpekutes' principal village, killing their leader Wamundeyakapi and seventeen others.

After his brother was murdered by a white liquor dealer, Inkpachuta turned his rage on settlers. During the Spirit Lake (Iowa) uprising of 1856 and 1857, warriors under Inkpachuta's leadership killed forty-seven colonists and kidnapped four women, only one of whom was later released. Inkpachuta also engaged in skirmishes with other Indians, notably with the Mdewakanton Sioux LITTLE CROW, who killed three of Inkpachuta's warriors in a battle at Lake Thompson.

Inkpachuta may have played a minor role in the Sioux uprising of 1862–1863 in Minnesota, after which reports indicate that he and a few supporters moved westward. Inkpachuta was reported to have allied with the Sioux and Cheyenne at the Battle of the Little Bighorn; he then fled to Canada with SITTING BULL's people. Various accounts place his death date between 1878 and 1882.

IRATEBA (IRATABA, ARATEVA, OR YARATEV)
Mohave
c. 1814–1878

Born in the Mohave lands around Needles, California, Irateba ("Beautiful Bird") was of the Neolge or Sun Fire clan. As a young man, he was a subchief under the principal Mohave chief Cairook. He was tall and cut an impressive figure at about six feet, four inches. Later in life, he became the chief of the Huttoh-pah band from the Mohave Valley. When Lieutenant Joseph C. Ives came to the lower Colorado River area in 1849, Irateba treated the expedition hospitably and even offered his services as a guide. In 1851, he was with Captain Lorenzo Sitgreaves's expedition to San Diego, and he aided Lieutenant Amiel Whipple's journey to Los Angeles in 1854. He also guided Lieutenant Joseph C. Ives's overland exploring party that went up the Colorado from 1856 through 1857. In all of these endeavors, he was a reliable source about the animal life, food resources, topography, and geography of the region.

Between 1857 and 1859, Lieutenant Edward F. Beale established Beale's Crossing at the Colorado River, mapping the wagon roads from Fort Smith, Arkansas, through Fort Defiance, Arizona, and thence to the Colorado River. Beale also experimented with the introduction of camels into the region. All of this activity and the increased frequency of white wagon trains alarmed the Mohaves. In August 1858, Mohave warriors launched an attack on a wagon train. In December 1858, they intimidated some soldiers dispatched to build a fort and forced them to leave.

In spring 1859, more soldiers appeared and constructed Fort Mohave just east of the Colorado River in what is now Arizona. After Fort Mohave was built, the army called a meeting with Irateba and seven other chiefs. At this meeting, the officers insisted on the arrest of the men who had been a part of the December intimidations. The army also wanted the chiefs to be held as hostages at Fort Yuma to ensure that no further attacks would occur. Dismayed and taken aback by these demands, several of the leaders nevertheless went to Fort Yuma, where they were immediately incarcerated. Irateba does not appear to have gone with this group. Because of abusive behavior by the guards, the imprisoned Mohave leaders attempted an escape, during which all of them were killed. As a result, Irateba became chief of the Mohaves. In 1861, he journeyed to Los Angeles to negotiate better conditions for his people, but the discovery of gold there (in 1862) caused tensions to mount once again.

As more and more whites swarmed into southern California, the army had more and more difficulty in maintaining the peace. The situation deteriorated even further when large numbers of area Mormons, wanting to set themselves up as the dominant white group, began stirring up Indians to thwart the army's power. With these political tensions as a backdrop, the U.S. government decided to invite Irateba to tour eastern cities, including New York, Philadelphia, and Washington, D.C., to demonstrate the power of the American government. In Washington, D.C., President Abraham Lincoln presented Irateba with a silver-headed cane.

Upon his return, Irateba advocated peace with the whites. Homoseah Quahorte, a sub-chief who headed a militant faction, opposed his peace policies by saying his tales of powerful and large cities to the east were too fantastic to believe. Subsequently, Irateba was captured and held prisoner by a rival faction. Humiliated by this turn of events, Irateba lost power and prestige among his people.

On June 17, 1878, Irateba died a broken man—no longer powerful and influential. His people were unable to grasp his message that they must compromise with the powerful and ruthless people who were intent on completely taking over their lands if they resisted with arms. The actual cause of his death is uncertain. Some accounts say it was smallpox; others attribute it to old age. According to Mohave custom, he was cremated with the silver cane given to him by President Lincoln as a symbol of his chieftaincy, his papers, belongings, and horses. Irateba tried to walk the political tightrope relating to the internal strife present in his people and the power of the U.S. government. Although he understood what the future held and knew the most prudent course for his people, he was not able to implement his political vision for them.

FOR MORE INFORMATION:

Dockstader, Frederick. *Great North American Indians.* New York: Van Nostrand Reinhold, 1977.

IRON TAIL (SINTE MAZA)
Oglala Sioux
c. 1850–1916

Iron Tail fought under SITTING BULL at the Battle of the Little Bighorn (1876). During the 1880s, he traveled with Buffalo Bill CODY's Wild West Show, visiting Europe with the

Iron Tail. [National Anthropological Archives]

troupe in 1889. Early in the twentieth century, Iron Tail's visage became well known across the United States as one of three models for the Indian head nickel.

FOR MORE INFORMATION:

Rosenberg, Bruce A. *Custer and the Epic of Defeat.* University Park: Pennsylvania State University Press, 1974.

Utley, Robert. *The Lance and the Shield: The Life and Times of Sitting Bull.* New York: Henry Holt, 1993.

ISATAI
Comanche
fl. 1870s

Little is known of Isatai's early life except that he was a child with visions. His Comanche name, Eschiti or Ishatai, meant "Coyote Droppings." He was also sometimes called Little

Wolf. As a young man, Isatai accurately prophesied the arrival of a comet in early 1873; he predicted that it would disappear in five days and that there would be a terrible drought the next summer. After allegedly conversing with the Creator, he asserted that he could make body paint that would stop bullets. He also predicted to the Comanche war chiefs that a united Indian offensive would defeat the whites and bring the buffalo back to the Great Plains in great numbers.

At the Battle of Adobe Walls in Texas in June 1874, the hated buffalo hunters with high-powered Sharps and Remington rifles were attacked by Comanche and Kiowa braves in order to fulfill Isatai's predictions, but the white men drove off the Indian attackers. As a result, Isatai's reputation for powerful medicine was tarnished. Even as late as 1890, however, when Quanah PARKER was leader of the various reservation bands of the Comanche, Isatai was an influential and powerful person in the Comanche community.

ISHI
Yahi/Yana
c. 1862–1916

As a young boy, Ishi saw a flood of whites come into his homeland in the mountainous country of Butte County, California. Soon the ranchers and miners took the good land and made the Indians retreat into the highlands of the Sierra Nevada. After much bitter fighting, whites (in 1868) decided to exterminate Ishi's small band of Yahis, so they attacked his village and killed about thirty-eight people.

About a dozen Yahis escaped this brutal raid. One of them was Ishi, a six-year-old boy. For forty years, these remaining Yahis avoided contact with white people. Occasionally, whites reported seeing unknown Indians; people tried to track them but had little success because the

Yahis left no tracks and cleverly disguised their dwellings.

In 1908, there were only four surviving Yahis: Ishi, his sister (sometimes referred to as a cousin), his mother, and an old man (probably his father). At this time, the Yahis were living by Mill Creek on a narrow stone ledge. After surveyors found their hiding place along the creek in 1908, they fled. The old man and Ishi's sister drowned in their flight; a few weeks later his mother died as well. From 1908 to 1911, Ishi lived alone, hunting for game and gathering wild foods in the untamed lands of Butte County. During this lonely time, he singed his hair off in mourning for his dead relatives. Finally, on August 29, 1911, half-starved and fully expecting to be killed, he wandered into Oroville, California. Some townspeople found him leaning against a fence and wearing only a ragged poncho. The local sheriff put him in jail for a few days, where Ishi refused any food since he was fearful of being poisoned.

Subsequently, Alfred Kroeber, a professor of anthropology at the University of California at Berkeley, and Thomas Waterman, a linguist specializing in American Indian languages, read reports of the unknown Indian in the newspaper. Curious, they made arrangements to see him. When interviewing Ishi in jail, Waterman tried unsuccessfully to communicate with him using a dictionary of the Yana language. At last, when Waterman used the Yana word for "wood" and gestured to the wooden frame on a cot, Ishi inquired of Waterman if he were a member of his tribe. To establish rapport, Waterman replied he was, indeed, a Yahi. Thereafter, with Ishi's prompting, Waterman was able to decipher the Yana Hokan language into the corresponding Yahi dialect.

Kroeber and Waterman took Ishi to the San Francisco Bay area, where he was studied until his death in 1916 of tuberculosis. For the last five years of his life, he was a janitor and groundskeeper at the Anthropological Museum of the University of California; he became good friends with Kroeber's wife, Theodora, and with Dr. Saxton Pope, a physician at the university hospital. His aboriginal habits caused a commotion in the press; he spoke no English and possessed such ancient skills as flint shaping and bow making. As a result of his collaborations with anthropologists, several books were published on Yahi language and culture.

Most Americans became familiar with Ishi's life by reading Theodora Kroeber's book *Ishi in Two Worlds* (1960). For many white people, he was the last noble savage or unspoiled Native American. For California Indians, however, Ishi's lifetime encompasses and symbolizes a terrible time of ethnocide that cannot be forgotten.

FOR MORE INFORMATION:

Kroeber, Theodora. *Ishi in Two Worlds.* Berkeley and Los Angeles: University of California Press, 1961.

ISPARHECHER (ISPAHECHE, SPAHECHA)
Creek
1829–1902

Isparhecher was born in Alabama to the Tiger clan in 1829. His father was Tardeka Tustanugga and his mother was Kecharte; both were Lower Creeks. While he was a young boy, the family was forcibly removed to Indian Territory, but both parents died along the way. When Isparhecher grew up, he became a tribal leader and farmer. He married four times, fathering five children.

At the beginning of the Civil War in 1861, Isparhecher joined the Creek Mounted Volunteers in the Confederate army. By 1863, he and others had become disenchanted with the Confederacy, so they volunteered for the Kansas Infantry Home Guards on the Union side (this group became known as the "Loyal Creek faction").

In 1867, he began a term in the Creek House of Warriors. In this capacity, he was allied with traditionalist Creeks who wanted the reestablishment of tribal customs and political structures. When the conservative leader Lochat Harjo died in 1881, Isparhecher became the undisputed leader of the traditionalist Creeks. In 1882, he became principal chief of the Loyal Creek people, but political pressures led to his impeachment that year. By 1883, violent conflict between the traditionalists and the progressives had broken out into what was called the Green Peach War or Isparhecher's War. After several people were killed in the rebellion, a detachment of troops under the command of Pleasant PORTER, a Progressive Creek, was called in to maintain order in February 1883.

Subsequently, Isparhecher was narrowly elected chief of the Creeks in 1883. After a few weeks he resigned, saying he could not lead such a divided nation. By the early 1890s, the U.S. government had decided to dissolve the large reservations in Indian Territory and redistribute tribally held lands into individual allotments to create the state of Oklahoma. Isparhecher fought the implementation of the General Allotment Act of 1887, which pursued these policies.

After defeats in 1887 and 1891, Isparhecher was selected as principal chief of the Creeks in 1895; he served a four-year term. Throughout his term as principal chief, he tried to stop allotment but to no avail. In 1899, the pro-allotment forces elected Pleasant Porter as chief and allotment was pushed through. Despairing and defeated, Isparhecher died of a massive stroke on December 22, 1902. Buried near Beggs, Oklahoma, he was survived by his fourth wife, Cindoche Sixkiller (Creek).

JACKSON, HELEN HUNT
1830–1885

A wave of compassion for Native people was stirred by the publication of Helen Hunt Jackson's *A Century of Dishonor* in 1881. Jackson, a friend of Emily Dickinson, also wrote a novel, *Ramona* (1884), which put the depredations she had described factually in *A Century of Dishonor* into a novelistic form. The novel, based on the life of RAMONA Lubo Gonzaga Ortega, went through three hundred printings and later inspired several movies. Jackson said at the time that she wanted *Ramona* to raise indignation regarding mistreatment of Indians to the same degree that Harriet Beecher Stowe's *Uncle Tom's Cabin* (1852) had done regarding black slavery.

Despite her intentions as a reformer, Jackson's work was often used to support legislation such as the DAWES Act (passed by Congress in 1887), which would distribute many Native Americans' common landholdings among individuals. Such allotments were often then sold to non-Indians, eroding Native American land base, cultures, and languages. In the late 1800s, there were practically no non-Indian reformers who asserted a Native right to land, language, and culture. Instead, some said they sought to "kill the Indian and save the man" as an alternative to outright extermination. Jackson's work played into the plans of assimilationist reformers who supported allotment.

FOR MORE INFORMATION:

Jackson, Helen Hunt. *A Century of Dishonor.* 1881. Reprint, Minneapolis: Ross and Haines, 1964.

———. *Ramona.* 1884. Reprint, Boston: Little, Brown, 1917.

JAMES, JEWELL (PRAYING WOLF)
Lummi
1953–

Jewell Praying Wolf James became known in the late twentieth century as an advocate of environmental restoration on an international scale. James called for creation of a "world court of the environment" that would publicize "environmentally criminal activity" around the world.

In 1994, James played a major role in convening leaders of more than three hundred Indian tribes at the White House to meet with President Bill Clinton. This was the first time that a pan-tribal summit had been conducted there.

The proposal for a world court of the environment was originally contained in a 1991 declaration of the Group of 100, a group of Native and non-Native writers, scientists, and environmentalists of which James was a member. The Group of 100 seeks to reshape the assumptions of political economy (and, by doing so, the workings of modern life).

James is a lineal descendant of Chief SEATH'TL (after whom the city of Seattle was named). He has been coordinator of the Lummi Tribe's Treaty Protection Task Force. He has extensive experience in law, environment, and politics at the state, national, and international levels. He is the chairman of the board of the Florence R. Kluckhohn Center, founder and director of the Indian-in-the-Moon Foundation, and treasurer of the National Tribal Environmental Council.

Following the 1994 summit at the White House, James and the Lummis' Treaty Protection Task Force were also instrumental in convening a symposium on Native nations and the Constitution in Washington, D.C., early in 1995. However, the proceedings of this conference were never utilized as Clinton had promised.

FOR MORE INFORMATION:

James, Jewell. "Reflections on Common Ground." In *Our People, Our Land: Perspectives on the Columbus Quincentennary*. Bellingham, Wash.: Kluckhohn Center, 1992.

JEMISON, MARY
1743–1833

Mary Jemison, a white woman, was abducted in 1758 by a party of Shawnees and later adopted by the Iroquois. In her biography, published in 1824, Jemison recalled that she had been adopted by two Iroquois women who had lost a brother in the American Revolution.

Once she was assimilated by the Senecas, Jemison married Sheninjee, a Delaware warrior, in an arranged union. Jemison balked at first, but she appreciated Sheninjee's warmth and humor, and she came to love him. Sheninjee died at an unknown date thereafter; later, Jemison and her three-year-old daughter hid in the woods as colonists came calling, demanding the redemption of captives. She later married the Seneca war chief HIOKATOO, with whom she bore six children. Hiokatoo treated Jemison kindly but was notorious for his cruelty against enemies.

Jemison died at the age of ninety, a Seneca grandmother in all but blood, on the Buffalo Creek Reservation in New York.

FOR MORE INFORMATION:

Gangi, Rayna M. *Mary Jemison: White Woman of the Senecas*. Santa Fe, N. Mex.: Clear Light, 1995.

Seaver, James A. *Narrative of the Life of Mrs. Mary Jemison*. 1823. Reprint, Corinth Books, 1961; Norman: University of Oklahoma Press, 1992.

JOHN (OLD JOHN)
Rogue River (Oregon)
fl. 1850s

As principal chief of the Takelma and Tututni peoples (called Rogue River Indians by whites), John fought encroachment by miners during a gold rush in the area during the mid–nineteenth century. He was a leader in the Rogue River War of 1855 and 1856.

By the early 1850s, Old John and his warriors were working as gold miners themselves to accumulate money needed for guns and ammunition with which to arm a rebellion. In 1853, war parties led by Old John were ambushing and sometimes killing miners who had earlier driven the Native peoples from their lands along the Rogue River and into the nearby Sierra foothills.

In 1855, the level of unrest in the Northwest rose with the initiation of the Yakima War, led by KAMIAKIN, in reaction to treaties negotiated by Washington territorial governor Isaac STEVENS. Fearing that the rebellion would intensify violence in the Rogue River area, officers at Fort Lane opened the fort to friendly Indians to better control their movements. Oregon vigilantes killed twenty-three Indians—women, children, and elderly men—before they could get to the fort. In retaliation, the Indians then killed twenty-seven whites.

The Rogue River Indians' leaders realized they didn't stand a chance against a formal army in open combat, so John and his warriors prepared a surprise attack as General John F. Wool arrived in the area with regular troops. They had planned to fake a surrender but were betrayed by two Native women who told General Wool of the plot. Wool's troops waited for reinforcements and then scattered Old John's forces.

Over the next few months, most of Old John's allies surrendered. Old John and a few comrades evaded capture for a month until troops surrounded them. Old John and his son, Adam, were taken as captives by ship to Alcatraz Island. While aboard ship, the two men overpowered guards and killed a sailor before they were again subdued. Both were eventually released from prison; Old John lived out the remainder of his days in the Rogue River Valley.

JOHNSON, EMILY PAULINE (TEKAHIONWAKE)
Mohawk
1861–1913

Emily Johnson, a well-known Mohawk poet, was born on the Six Nations Reserve, Brantford, Ontario. She wrote poetry from a young age, largely in obscurity, until 1892, when a recita-

tion before the Young Liberal Club of Toronto brought her fame across Canada. She gave dramatic performances of her poetry in Native regalia across Canada, the United States, and in England. Her works include *Flint and Feather* and *Legends of Vancouver*, the city in which she died.

FOR MORE INFORMATION:
Johnson, E. Pauline (Tekahionwake). *Flint and Feather.* Toronto: Musson, 1912.
———. *Legends of Vancouver.* 1911. Reprint, Toronto: McClelland & Stewart, 1922.

JOHNSON, GUY
1741–1788

Guy Johnson assumed his Uncle William JOHNSON's role as British Indian agent with the Iroquois and their allies on the elder Johnson's death in 1774. He played a key role in swinging many Iroquois, particularly Mohawks, to the British interest during the American Revolution. After the Revolution, a number of Johnson's Mohawk supporters moved to Canada; today, their descendants live at Kanesatake (Oka), Quebec; Grand River, Ontario; and Kahnasatake, Quebec, as well as in many of Canada's eastern urban areas.

Guy Johnson was well known within the confederacy and had served an ample apprenticeship under Sir William. Johnson inherited from his uncle a problematic policy among the Six Nations. Quintock (Kentucky) was filling with settlers. Harrisburg and Louisville were already firmly established as white settlements on the Ohio in 1773. The Iroquois were alarmed because many of the people from the Six Nations who had been forced from their original lands by the whites were resettling in the Ohio region.

Talk of war grew within the confederacy, and Johnson sought to soften the injury by promising that the king would punish these lawless individuals. Johnson reminded the Iroquois of their covenant with the Crown and asked that they not engage in reprisals. He knew that if the Iroquois joined the Shawnees in resisting the whites in Kentucky, other western tribes would join the resistance movement just as they had done during the rebellion of PONTIAC.

Guy Johnson retained the services of his uncle's personal secretary, the Mohawk Joseph BRANT. In July 1776, Joseph Brant and Guy Johnson returned to America from England just as the spirit of independence was beginning to sweep the eastern seaboard. With the passage of the Declaration of Independence by the Continental Congress, the English felt compelled to press for Iroquois support.

By 1780, after Brant and Guy Johnson had crossed the Atlantic together several times and worked closely for a half-dozen years, they had a falling out. Evidence mounted that Guy Johnson was padding reports to the Crown to swindle large amounts of money in league with several traders at Niagara. For example, Johnson debited the king for 1,156 kettles when the actual number was 156.

Guy Johnson helped direct British campaigns against American revolutionary forces in the Mohawk and Wyoming Valleys as an ally of Joseph Brant. He was at Fort Niagara from 1777 to 1779 and fought in the Battle of Newtown. Before the Revolution, he had built a large mansion at Amsterdam, New York, called Guy Park. In 1779, the New York Assembly confiscated the house and the rest of his holdings in America. After the Revolution, Johnson returned to England, where he engaged in several futile attempts to regain his property. He died in London on March 5, 1788.

FOR MORE INFORMATION:

Edmunds, R. David. *American Indian Leaders: Studies in Diversity.* Lincoln: University of Nebraska Press, 1980.

Graymont, Barbara. *The Iroquois in the American Revolution.* Syracuse, N.Y.: Syracuse University Press, 1972.

Grinde, Donald A., Jr. *The Iroquois and the Founding of the American Nation.* San Francisco: Indian Historian Press, 1977.

JOHNSON, WILLIAM
1715–1774

Sir William Johnson was probably the single most influential Englishman in relations with the Iroquois and their allies during the French and Indian War. From his mansion near Albany, Johnson forayed on Indian war parties, painted himself like an Indian, and took part in ceremonial dances. He was a close friend of the elderly HENDRICK, with whom he often traveled as a warrior. Joseph BRANT fought beside Johnson at the age of thirteen. Hendrick was killed making war on the French with Johnson against Baron Dieskau's forces at Lake George in 1755.

William Johnson learned the customs and language of the Mohawks. He had a number of children by Mohawk women and acknowledged them as such. He had several children by Mary BRANT, a Mohawk clan mother and granddaughter of Hendrick. Johnson was well liked particularly among the Mohawks. Hendrick had a high regard for the Englishman and expressed his regard when he said, "he has Large Ears and heareth a great deal, and what he hears he tells us; he also has Large Eyes and sees a great way, and conceals nothing from us." [Grinde] Because he successfully recruited a sizable number of Iroquois to the British interest, Johnson was made a baronet, Sir William Johnson, with a £5,000 award.

In June 1760, in the final thrust to defeat the French in North America, Johnson called for men to attack Montreal. About six hundred warriors responded. Many of the tribesmen living in the Montreal area also responded to his call. Sir William reported he was sending gifts to "foreign Indians" who were switching their allegiance from the sinking French empire. By August 5, 1760, the Native contingent had reached 1,330. Johnson reported to William Pitt, "Thus Sir, we became Masters of the last place in the Enemy's possession in these parts and made those Indians our friends by a peace, who might otherwise have given us much trouble." [Sullivan]

The defeat of the French and their departure from Canada at the end of the war upset the balance that the Iroquois had sought to maintain. Reluctantly, they attached themselves to the British, but they could no longer play one European power against another. The English now occupied all the forts surrounding Iroquois country. Johnson played a key role in pressing the Crown to limit immigration west of the Appalachians, but land-hungry settlers ignored the royal edicts, intensifying conflicts over land. In the meantime, Johnson became one of the richest men in the colonies through land transactions and trade with Indians.

In his later years, Johnson agonized over whether to side with the British Crown or the revolutionary patriots. The aging Sir William died at a meeting with the Iroquois on July 11, 1774, at his mansion near Albany. For two hours, Johnson had addressed the Iroquois in the oratorical style he had learned from them, summoning them to the British cause in the coming American Revolution. Suddenly, Johnson collapsed. He was carried to his bed, where he died two hours later. The assembly of chiefs was stunned by his sudden death, but Guy JOHNSON, Sir William's nephew and son-in-law, stepped in to fill the breach left by his elder.

FOR MORE INFORMATION:
Flexner, James Thomas. *Mohawk Baronet.* New York: Harper & Row, 1959.

Graymont, Barbara. *The Iroquois in the American Revolution.* Syracuse, N.Y.: Syracuse University Press, 1972.

Grinde, Donald A., Jr. *The Iroquois and the Founding of the American Nation.* San Francisco: Indian Historian Press, 1977.

Sullivan, James, et al., eds. *The Papers of Sir William Johnson.* Albany, N.Y., 1921–65.

JOLLY, JOHN (OOLOOTESKEE, OOLOOTEKA, AHULUDEGI)
Cherokee
fl. early 1800s

Growing up on Hiwassee Island, where the Hiwassee River joins with the Tennessee River, John Jolly met young Sam Houston in eastern Tennessee about 1806. Houston, during his boyhood, spent three years with the Cherokees there. Accordingly, John Jolly made him his son and inducted him into the Cherokee tribe. Later, Houston married one of Jolly's nieces.

In 1818, Jolly and his group of three hundred members, acting on the advice of Houston, removed to the West, carrying their belongings in four keelboats and thirteen flatboats. After crossing the Mississippi, they relocated along the Arkansas River, where they were reunited with an Arkansas band of Cherokees headed by Tahlonteskee (Jolly's brother). Tahlonteskee was a principal chief of the Western Cherokees along with BOWL. When his brother died, Jolly assumed the principal chieftaincy of the Western Cherokees.

JOSEPH, ELDER (TUEKAKAS)
Nez Perce
c. 1788–1871

Joseph (elder) led a Nez Perce band that fought restriction to reservation life during early years of contact with European immigrants in the Pacific Northwest. His son Joseph (usually referred to as Chief Joseph or JOSEPH, YOUNGER) led remnants of the Nez Perce on a fifteen-hundred-mile march to escape detention by the U.S. Army.

An 1855 sketch of Joseph, Elder.
[Washington State Historical Society]

The elder Joseph's early life portended little of the turmoil that surrounded the Nez Perce at his death. He was born near Wawawai on the Snake River. His father was a Cayuse chief and his mother a Nez Perce. During his childhood, the family migrated around the inland Northwest, living a generally peaceful life. In 1836, they greeted missionaries Henry Spalding and his wife. In 1839, Spalding gave Tuekakas, as he was called among the Nez Perce, the Christian name Joseph.

The Nez Perce became steadfast U.S. allies as settlers moved into the Pacific Northwest in the face of opposition from Great Britain. They even rescued a body of U.S. troops from attack by other Indians in 1858. Nevertheless, during the same year, the United States signed a treaty with Nez Perce treaty commissioners who did not represent the nation. The treaty ceded the Nez Perces' Wallowa Valley to the United States and opened it for settlement. The elder Joseph protested that the treaty was illegal, a violation of the Treaty of Walla Walla, which had been signed with Washington territorial governor Isaac STEVENS only three years earlier.

The betrayal embittered Old Joseph. He tore up his copy of the agreement and his New Testament. The Nez Perce in Joseph's band stayed in the valley despite the 1858 treaty. They continued to tend their large herds of prize horses even as settlers moved in around them. At first, the Nez Perces welcomed the settlers, figuring that (as young Joseph remarked later) there was plenty of land for all and the Indians would learn useful things from the whites. The situation became complicated in 1860, when gold was discovered in the area. It was not a large gold strike but large enough to bring to the Nez Perces' territory several thousand non-Indians with no enduring stake in the land and whose presence sparked several violent incidents.

In 1871, Joseph senior died and the leadership of his band passed to Hin-mah-too-yah-laht-ket, whom English-speakers at first called Young Joseph and later Chief Joseph. On his deathbed, Old Joseph asked his son never to sell or otherwise cede the Nez Perces' homeland, an admonition that led the younger Joseph to resist removal to a reservation even as his dwindling band was being pursued fifteen hundred miles through the northern Rockies in 1877.

FOR MORE INFORMATION:

DeVoto, Bernard. *Across the Wide Missouri.* Cambridge, Mass.: Harvard University Press, 1947.

JOSEPH, YOUNGER (HINMATON YALATIK; HIN-MAH-TOO-YAH-LAHT-KET; CHIEF JOSEPH)

Nez Perce
1841–1904

JOSEPH, ELDER died in 1871, passing the leadership of his Nez Perce band to his son Hin-mah-too-yah-laht-ket ("Thunder Rolling over the Mountains"), whom English-speakers at first called Young Joseph and later Chief Joseph. Like his father, Young Joseph refused to surrender to reservation life. His people's struggles to retain their freedom on a fifteen-hundred-mile march became a metaphor for the end of the Indian wars in the late nineteenth century.

Chief Joseph. [National Anthropological Archives]

As Young Joseph assumed leadership of his Nez Perce band, government emissaries continued to press the Nez Perce to move to a reservation where they would be allocated a plot of land for each head of a household (as defined in the European sense)—far too little land to run the prized blue Appaloosas that the Nez Perce used for hunting and war.

In 1871, under pressure from the United States, Joseph and his band signed the last treaty negotiated by any Native nation with the United States. Under the treaty terms, the Nez Perce agreed to move to Lapwai, Idaho. As the logistics of the move were being worked out, settlers stole hundreds of the Nez Perces' prized horses. A renegade band of young Nez Perce—led by young Wahlitis, whose father had been murdered by whites two years earlier—retaliated by killing eighteen settlers. The army was brought in to arrest the hostiles. Instead of surrendering, the entire band of about five hundred men, women, and children decamped and marched into the mountains.

Even though Joseph and his people had agreed to the treaty, they did so without pleasure. In reply to an Indian agent's proposal that he and his people move to a reservation and become farmers, Chief Joseph had said, "The land is our mother. . . . She should not be disturbed by hoe or plow. We want only to subsist on what she freely gives us." [Josephy, *Nez Perce Indians*]

During the next several months, the vastly outnumbered Nez Perce led troops on a fifteen-hundred-mile trek through some of the most rugged country on the continent, north almost to Canada then south again. Joseph, with at most two hundred warriors, fought over a dozen engagements with four army columns, evading capture several times. In one night raid, the Nez Perce made off with the pursuing army's pack animals. At other times, the Nez Perce so skillfully evaded army pincer movements that the two closing columns ran into each other without capturing a single Indian. The army did inflict casualties on the Nez Perce at other times. Eighty-nine were killed in one battle, fifty of them women and children. Despite the deaths, the Nez Perce continued to fight.

Chief Joseph instructed his warriors not to take scalps, and the Nez Perce earned praise for their military acumen from General William Tecumseh Sherman, who said the Indians went to great lengths to avoid killing innocent settlers. General Nelson A. Miles, whose troops brought the Nez Perces' Long March to an end, echoed Sherman's opinion: "In this skillful campaign, they have spared hundreds of lives and thousands of dollars worth of property that they might have destroyed." [Josephy, *Nez Perce Indians*]

Through the Bitterroot Mountains and what is now Yellowstone National Park, to the headwaters of the Missouri, to the Bear Paw Mountains, Joseph's band fought a rear guard action with brilliance. They traveled through four present-day states (Washington, Oregon, Idaho, and Montana) and crossed the Continental Divide twice. Near the end of the march, the survivors suffered immensely according to army accounts: "The Indians, wounded, hungry, and cold, suffered intensely. Using hooks, knives, and pans, the people tried to dig crude shelters in the sides of the hollows. One dugout was caved in by a hit from [General Nelson A.] Miles' howitzer . . . and a woman and child were buried alive."

Exhausted, the Nez Perce surrendered October 5, 1877, at Eagle Creek, roughly thirty miles south of the Canadian border. Many of the Nez Perce were starving. Several also had been maimed and blinded. Joseph handed his rifle to General Miles, and said he was "tired of fighting. . . . My people ask me for food, and I have none to give. It is cold, and we have no blankets, no wood. My people are starving to death. Where is my little daughter? I do not know. Perhaps, even now, she is freezing to death. Hear me, my chiefs. I have fought, but from where the sun now stands, Joseph will fight no more

forever." [Josephy, *Nez Perce Indians*] Chief Joseph then drew his blanket over his face and walked into the army camp, a prisoner. Of roughly 650 Nez Perce who had begun the long march, about 400 had survived—87 warriors, 40 of whom were wounded; 184 women; and 147 children. Most of them were sick, nearly starved, and freezing. About 275 warriors had died during the Long March, as they held off 2,000 army troops in eleven engagements, killing 266 soldiers.

In 1879, Joseph appealed to Congress (speaking in person to a full chamber) to let his people return home. "It has always been the pride of the Nez Perces that they were the friends of the white men," he began, recounting how the Indians helped support the first few immigrants. "There was room enough for all to live in peace, and they [Joseph's ancestors] were learning many things from the white men that appeared to be good. . . . Soon [we] found that the white men were growing rich very fast, and were greedy to possess everything the Indian had." He recalled how his father had refused to sign a treaty with Washington territorial governor Isaac Stevens: "I will not sign your paper. . . . You go where you please, so do I; you are not a child; I am no child; I can think for myself. . . . Take away your paper. I will not sign it." [Josephy, *Nez Perce Indians*] Joseph said that the Nez Perce had given too much and that they had gone to war only when the whites forced them off their cherished homeland.

The War Department refused Chief Joseph's request to let his people resettle in their homeland. Instead, they were imprisoned at Fort Leavenworth, Kansas, where many who had survived the Long March died of malaria. In 1885, the 268 surviving Nez Perce were moved to Indian Territory (later Oklahoma), where still more died.

The Nez Perce were provided no supplies as they arrived at the onset of winter. They experienced profound suffering yet again. Lieutenant H. Clay Wood, who had witnessed Chief Joseph's surrender speech and later wrote a narrative of the Nez Perces' Long March, said, "I think that, in his long career, Joseph cannot accuse the Government of the United States of one single act of justice." [Josephy, *Nez Perce Indians*] Later, roughly 140 survivors were finally allowed to return to the Northwest—some to Lapwai, Idaho, and others to the Colville Reservation in eastern Washington. Joseph died at Colville in 1904, his heart still yearning to go home to the land where he had buried his father.

FOR MORE INFORMATION:

Beal, Merrill D. *I Will Fight No More Forever.* Seattle: University of Washington Press, 1963.

Chalmers, Harvey. *The Last Stand of the Nez Perce.* New York: Twayne, 1962.

Davis, Russell, and Brant Ashabranner. *Chief Joseph: War Chief of the Nez Perce.* New York: McGraw-Hill, 1962.

DeVoto, Bernard. *Across the Wide Missouri.* Cambridge, Mass.: Harvard University Press, 1947.

Fee, Chester. *Chief Joseph: The Biography of a Great Indian.* New York, 1936.

Howard, Helen A., and Dan L. McGrath. *War Chief Joseph.* Caldwell, Idaho: Caxton, 1952.

Howard, O. O. *Nez Perce Joseph.* Boston, 1881.

Jackson, Helen Hunt. *A Century of Dishonor.* 1881. Reprint, Minneapolis: Ross and Haines, 1964.

Joseph, Chief [In-mut-too-yah-lat-lat]. "An Indian's View of Indian Affairs." *North American Review* 128 (April 1879): 415–433.

Josephy, Alvin M., Jr. *The Nez Perce Indians and the Opening of the Northwest.* New Haven, Conn.: Yale University Press, 1965.

———. *The Patriot Chiefs.* New York: Viking, 1961.

Lavender, David. *Let Me Be Free.* San Francisco: HarperCollins, 1992.

Nabokov, Peter. *Native American Testimony.* New York: Viking Penguin, 1991.

Waters, Frank. *Brave Are My People: Indian Heroes Not Forgotten.* Santa Fe, N. Mex.: Clear Light, 1993.

Wood, H. Clay. *The Status of Young Joseph and His Band of Nez Perce Indians.* Portland, Ore., 1876.

JOSEPHY, ALVIN M., JR.
1915–

Alvin Josephy, a leading twentieth-century author and Native rights activist, was born in Woodmere, New York, and attended Harvard University between 1932 and 1934. During World War II, Josephy served in the U.S. Marine Corps and earned a Bronze Star. Between 1951 and 1960, he worked as an associate editor at *Time;* in 1960, he became editor of *American Heritage.* After writing several books on soldiering themes drawn from his World War II experience, Josephy began to contribute notably on American Indian subjects with his *American Heritage Book of Indians* and *The Patriot Chiefs,* both first published in 1961. *The Nez Perce Indians and the Opening of the Northwest* (1965) was another of his notable early works in this field. He also wrote *The Indian Heritage of America* (1968), *Red Power* (1971), and *Now That the Buffalo's Gone* (1982).

FOR MORE INFORMATION:

Josephy, Alvin M., Jr. *American Heritage Book of Indians.* New York: Dell, 1961.

———. *The Indian Heritage of America.* Reprint, Boston: Houghton Mifflin, 1991.

———. *The Nez Perce Indians and the Opening of the Northwest.* New Haven, Conn.: Yale University Press, 1965.

———. *Now That the Buffalo's Gone.* New York: Random House, 1982.

———. *The Patriot Chiefs.* New York: Viking, 1961.

———. *Red Power: The American Indians' Fight for Freedom.* New York: American Heritage Press, 1971.

JOURNEYCAKE, CHARLES (NESHAPANASUMIN)
Delaware
1817–1894

Charles Journeycake, one of the founders of Bacone College, an Indian school in Oklahoma, took the white man's road but not always willingly and always with a searing knowledge of what had been inflicted upon his people.

Born in the Upper Sandusky region of Ohio to Delaware chief Solomon Journeycake and a French-Indian mother named Sally, Charles Journeycake was baptized in 1833 at the age of sixteen. He learned English as a young man and moved with ease between the two worlds. He served at the same time as a preacher and as head of the Wolf clan. He was a strenuous opponent of liquor sales to Indians.

Journeycake led his people during a number of relocations—to Kansas, then to land formerly allocated to the Cherokees in northeastern Oklahoma. He was also a principal figure in the Indian Defense Association. He told a meeting of that group in 1886:

> We have been broken up and moved six times. We have been despoiled of our property. We thought when we moved across the Missouri River, and had paid for our homes in Kansas, [that] we were safe. But in a few years, the white man wanted our country. We had good farms [and had] built comfortable houses and big barns. We had schools for our children and churches where we listened to the same gospel the white man listens to. The white man came into our country from Missouri, and drove our cattle and horses away. . . . If our people followed them, they were killed.

Journeycake died in 1894.

FOR MORE INFORMATION:

Armstrong, Virginia Irving, ed. *I Have Spoken: American History Through the Voices of the Indians.* Chicago: Swallow Press, 1971.

JUH
Nednhi Apache
c. 1830–1883

Little is known about Juh's early life. By the 1870s, he had become the principal chief of the Nednhi Apache, a small group of Chiricahuas who refused to be relocated to the San Carlos Reservation when the Chiricahua Reservation was eliminated in 1876. Eschewing U.S. control, Juh's group hid in the wilderness of the Sierra Madre of Mexico and southern New Mexico. During this time, Juh's followers merged with Chiricahuas from the Warm Springs (Ojo Caliente) Reservation in New Mexico as well as other dissident groups. Juh's band, along with GERONIMO and his followers, raided Mexican settlements repeatedly in the late 1870s. In April 1882, the Nednhi Apaches participated in the LOCO Outbreak, a foray to the San Carlos Reservation.

In 1883, Juh died in northern Mexico allegedly from a heart attack. When he was stricken, it is said that he fell off his horse into some water and died. Some sources claim he was intoxicated at the time and drowned.

JUMPER (OTE EMATHLA, OTEE AMATHLA)
Seminole
c. 1790–1838

After participating in the Creek War of 1813–1814 as a Red Stick Creek, Jumper (whose Native name means "He Makes Sense") emigrated southward and settled in Florida with the Seminoles. During the First Seminole War in 1818, Jumper opposed troops led by General Andrew Jackson. In the Second Seminole War in the 1830s, he fought against removal to Indian Territory. He was MICANOPY's aide and fought with ALLIGATOR and Micanopy in the ambush of Major Francis L. Dade's unit as it left Tampa Bay en route to reinforce a detachment at Fort King. Subsequently, these Seminoles (including Jumper) combined with OSCEOLA to strike a contingent commanded by General Duncan L. Clinch. Upon his capitulation in December 1837, Jumper was to be removed to Indian Territory, but he died en route in 1838.

JUMPER, JOHN (OTEE EMATHLA, HEMHA MICCO)
Seminole
c. 1820–1896

Born in Florida about 1820, John Jumper was removed with other Seminoles in 1840–1841. A young man, he apparently participated in just a few of the Seminole skirmishes resisting removal. In spite of his physical prowess (he was six feet, four inches and weighed over two hundred pounds), he was a lifelong advocate of peace with the white man.

In the 1850s, the Seminoles and Creeks sought to dissolve the union forced upon them during removal by the U.S. government. To resolve this problem, a treaty signed in Washington in 1856 finally created two distinct nations with separate lands and annuities. At the beginning of the Civil War in 1861, John Jumper decided to ally with the South after Confederate general Albert Pike visited Indian Territory. Subsequently, Jumper and the Cherokee STAND WATIE forced pro-Union American Indians under the command of the Creek OPOTHLEYAHOLO to move into Kansas. From 1862 through 1863, a campaign led by Union general James G. Blunt defeated Jumper and other Confederate Indian regiments.

After the war, reconstruction came to Indian Territory, and the Seminoles were forced to sell two million acres for about fifteen cents an acre and then purchase about two hundred thousand acres of Creek land for about fifty cents an acre. Jumper protested such machinations but with little success.

A devout Christian throughout most of his adult life, he resigned as chief of the Southern Seminoles and became the pastor of the Spring Baptist Church in 1877. In 1881, he was elected chief of the united Seminole nation. Jumper also continued in his capacity as a Baptist minister until 1894. He died two years later in 1896.

JUNALUSKA
Cherokee
c. 1795–c. 1858

During the Creek War, Junaluska commanded Cherokee men on the side of the United States in the campaign against Creek Red Sticks led by William WEATHERFORD. In March 1814 at the Battle of Horseshoe Bend, Junaluska is reputed to have slain a Creek warrior who was about to strike General Andrew Jackson with a tomahawk. Junaluska and the Cherokees swam the Tallapoosa River and charged the Creek forces at their rear—a bold action that saved the day for the Americans. Junaluska allegedly got his name (which in Cherokee means "He Tries Many Times but Does Not Succeed") when he swore that he would see to the annihilation of the Creeks during the Creek War. For his service in the U.S. cause, he was granted a large tract of land.

JUNEAU, JOSEPH
Menominee
fl. 1880s

Joseph Juneau, after whom Juneau, Alaska, was named, moved to the Alaska Panhandle from Milwaukee, Wisconsin, where his father, French Canadian Solomon Juneau, was that city's founder and first mayor. Juneau traveled to Alaska seeking gold and found it in 1880 while prospecting with a party of Tlingets. Several hundred miners followed him to the area, and Juneau, Alaska, was incorporated there in 1900.

KAMIAKIN
Yakima
c. 1798–c. 1877

Kamiakin was a major leader of the Yakimas during a wave of resistance (in the middle 1850s) to treaties negotiated by Washington territorial governor Isaac STEVENS. Like Chief Joseph (see JOSEPH, YOUNGER), whose band lived nearby, Kamiakin was a friend of the first whites to settle in eastern Washington. Their increasing numbers and their depredations on Native people sent him and his people to war.

Born near the current site of Tampico, Washington, Kamiakin inherited his chieftainship among the Yakimas from his mother; his father was Nez Perce. Shortly after reaching maturity, Kamiakin began to build a considerable estate of horses and other livestock in the Yakima Valley. He was described as a tall man with a domineering personality. While he welcomed the earliest settlers, Kamiakin became concerned over the destruction of Native peoples and cultures by increased immigration in the wake of reports that gold had been discovered in

Washington Territory. He worked to have the treaties signed with Stevens nullified. Kamiakin's Yakimas did not sign the 1855 treaty over which they waged the Yakima War (1857–1858).

The Yakima chief used his oratorical skills to unify a number of tribes in the region, including the Paloose, Cayuse, and Walla Walla. He raised an army of two thousand warriors, some of whom came from as far away as southern Alaska. The combined warrior force won an early battle near The Dalles, but a defeat in Seattle and the hanging of Chief LESCHI, along with another defeat (1858) at Four Legs, sealed the end of the Yakima War. While many other leaders of the rebellion were shot or hanged, Kamiakin escaped to British Columbia for a time then returned to Idaho where he settled with the Paloose people. He rejected annuities from the United States until his death in about 1877. Shortly after he was buried, Kamiakin's grave was vandalized. His head was removed and publicly exhibited to the settler community.

Early in the twentieth century, the Yakima chief MENINOCK cited a conversation Kamiakin held with Stevens in 1855 to support the Yakimas' claim of treaty fishing rights. Meninock was arrested in 1878 for fishing illegally despite the treaties' preservation of their right to fish. Meninock's trial was the opening salvo in a struggle over fishing rights in the Pacific Northwest, which continued to the end of the century.

FOR MORE INFORMATION:

Emmons, Della Gould. *Leschi of the Nisquallies.* Minneapolis: T. S. Denison, 1965.

KANCAMAGUS
Pennacook
fl. late 1600s

During King Philip's War (1675–1676) the Pennacook federation split. Paugus, son of Wannalancet, allied with METACOM, while Kancamagus argued against war with the colonists. The Plymouth colonists sabotaged Kancamagus's peace initiative by inviting several peaceful Indians to a Dover sporting match that was used as cover for an ambush. The Indians were captured and sold into slavery.

Kancamagus then turned against the colonists and plotted revenge. In 1689, at the beginning of King William's War—the first of several wars between Britain and France that continued until 1763—Kancamagus sent Indian women to sleep in the stockade at Dover. They opened the gates at night and allowed access to a warrior party that killed several men and babies then kidnapped a number of women and children to be sold into slavery. A majority of the women and children were recovered by British troops, but a few were taken to French Quebec.

The British then urged the Mohawks to attack the Pennacooks, who retreated from their homes, escaping to Quebec, to live among the Abenakis. Kancamagus moved with them, but little is known of his later life.

KATERI TAKAWITA (KATERI TEKAWITHA)
Mohawk
1656–1680

Born in Caughnawaga (now Auriesville), New York, of a Mohawk father and a Christian white woman captured by the Algonquians, Kateri Takawita became the first Native American nun. In the late twentieth century, efforts mounted inside the Vatican to raise her to sainthood.

Kateri's parents died of smallpox very early in her life; she was raised by an uncle, a Mohawk. When she was about ten, a party of Jesuit priests visited her adoptive father's home, after which she decided to become a Christian against her uncle's strong objections. After Kateri was baptized in 1675, her uncle abused her and other villagers ostracized her. Later, she moved to a community of Christian Indians near Montreal, where she served the people as a nun. Kateri's health had always been frail, and she died at twenty-four. After her death, she became such a strong example of Catholic devotion that many people claimed to have been cured of physical ailments after receiving visions involving her. She was recommended for canonization in 1844 and beatified in 1980.

KATLIAN
Tlinget
fl. 1800

Katlian led his people in a sporadic war with Russian freebooters and colonists in the present-day Alaska Panhandle. The Russians had arrived in the Aleutian chain after the exploratory voyage of Vitus Bering (1741); there they made a practice of forcing the Aleuts to trap furs for export.

Born in Sitka, Katlian led a Native raid there which destroyed the first Russian fort in America (1799). The Tlingets held the fort with great tenacity until 120 Russians and about 1,000

Aleuts retook it. The Tlingets retreated from the fort in the face of cannon fire and armed assault, but they attacked the Russian fort at Yakutat in 1805. Raids continued after that; by 1818, a Russian warship was delegated to patrol Sitka harbor, after traders there appealed for protection.

KAUFFMAN, HATTIE
Nez Perce
1955–

Hattie Kauffman became known to millions of Americans in the late twentieth century as a national correspondent for *CBS This Morning* and as a feature reporter for ABC's *Good Morning America*. For her earlier television news reporting at KING-TV in Seattle, Kauffman, of German and Nez Perce ancestry, won four Emmy awards.

Hattie Kauffman. [CBS News]

Kauffman began her professional broadcasting career in Seattle at KING in 1981, following study for a bachelor's degree at the University of Minnesota, where she worked in Minneapolis radio. Since March 1990, Kauffman has been consumer affairs reporter for *CBS News*, a job that has taken her to a Hawaiian leper colony, to an interview of deep-sea treasure hunters, and to a women's shooting range. Kauffman is a frequent substitute anchor on *CBS This Morning*, and she reports regularly for CBS's *48 Hours*.

KAYATENNAE (KAAHTENEY, KAYTENNAE, KE-E-TE-NA, KAYATENNA, KOW-TINNE, JACOB)
Mimbreno Apache
fl. 1880s

While little is known of Kayatennae's early life, he did become a noted warrior, leader, and army scout in his later years. Although Kayatennae was a hereditary chief, he became prominent among the Apaches because of his courage and aggressiveness during war. While ensconced in Mexico in the Sierra Madre, he joined with NANA's band in raids on American and Mexican outposts.

In 1883, he laid down his arms and reported to San Carlos, Arizona, even though he had never experienced reservation life. Other Mimbrenos and Chiricahuas continued to resist U.S. controls. At San Carlos in 1884, Kayatennae was arrested for an assault on Lieutenant Britton Davis. Sentenced to three years at Alcatraz for this attack, he was freed after about eighteen months by General George Crook, who agreed to use him as a scout. In 1886, Kayatennae as well as the scouts CHATO, ALCHESAY, and Mickey FREE aided the U.S. Army in tracking GERONIMO, and thus were present to witness his surrender in Mexico at Canyon de los Embudos.

KENNEKUK (KICKAPOO PROPHET)
Kickapoo
c. 1788–1852

Kennekuk ("Putting His Foot Down") was also known as Pakala, "the Kickapoo Prophet," a spiritual leader who led a settlement along the Osage River in Illinois. He urged Native people to adopt Euro-American ways on an agricultural model and to reject alcohol. In so doing, Kennekuk was bucking a history of aggression against settlers by many other Kickapoos. The Kickapoos were to move west of the Mississippi from Illinois under terms of a treaty signed in 1819. Many of Kennekuk's people did not want to leave their farms, so he became a master of delaying tactics. For a decade and a half, Kennekuk told officials that he was preparing to leave but was not quite ready. In 1833, Kennekuk's band, consisting of three hundred to four hundred people, finally moved to Kansas.

Kennekuk died of smallpox in 1852.

KENNY, MAURICE
Mohawk
1929–

One of Native America's best-known poets of the twentieth century, Mohawk Maurice Kenny won the 1984 Before Columbus Foundation American Book Award for *The Mama Poems.* Kenny's work has been nominated for a Pulitzer Prize, and he has won an American Book Award for poetry. He has also authored several other collections of poetry while working as professor of English or poet in residence at several eastern and midwestern universities and colleges. Kenny's collections include *North: Poems of Home* (1977), *Dancing Back Strong the Nation* (1979), *I Am the Sun* (1979), *Blackrobe: Isaac Jogues* (1982), *Boston Tea Party* (1982), *Is Summer This Bear?* (1985), *Rain and Other Fictions* (1985), *Between Two Rivers* (1987), and *Last Mornings in Brooklyn* (1991).

Literary critic Craig Womack has written, "Contemporary poet Maurice Kenny's unique combination of historic and poetic faculties is an excellent addition to . . . tribal histories as well as to American poetry in general."

FOR MORE INFORMATION:

Kenny, Maurice. *On Second Thought: A Compilation.* Norman: Oklahoma University Press, 1995.

Womack, Craig. "The Spirit of Independence: Maurice Kenny's Tekanwatonti/Molly Brant: Poems of War." *American Indian Culture & Research Journal* 18:4 (1994): 95–118.

KEOKUK (WATCHFUL FOX)
Sauk
c. 1783–1848

Keokuk was a Sauk chief recognized by U.S. officials after he refused to support BLACK HAWK during the years before and after Black Hawk's War (1832). Born in the village of Saukenuk to a mother who was half French, he could not be a hereditary chief. He obtained his position among the Sauk through merit, notably bravery against the Sioux as well as political intrigue with invading whites.

A contemporary of Black Hawk, Keokuk debated with him the efficacy of opposing Euro-American expansion with armed force. The division between the two split the Sauk and Fox tribes before Black Hawk's War. Keokuk, attempting to maintain peace, moved his supporters from present-day Illinois into Iowa in 1820. In the early 1830s, Keokuk, with Fox treaty chiefs POWESHEEK and WAPELLO, signed a cession of the Rock River country for $20,000 in annuities and a tract of land in Iowa. In 1845, the land in Iowa was exchanged for a tract in Kansas.

Keokuk. [Nebraska State Historical Society]

After Black Hawk's War, President Andrew Jackson recognized Keokuk, instead of Black Hawk, as chief of the Sauk and Fox. The news came to Black Hawk and Keokuk as they stood together with army officers. Angry and frustrated, Black Hawk removed his breechclout and slapped Keokuk in the face.

Keokuk died in Kansas during 1848, probably of dysentery. He was buried in Keokuk, Iowa, under a statue erected in his honor. Keokuk's leadership role among the Sauk was then taken by Moses Keokuk, a Baptist preacher.

FOR MORE INFORMATION:

Beckhard, Arthur J. *Black Hawk*. New York: Julian Messner, 1957.

Drake, Benjamin F. *The Life and Adventures of Black Hawk*. Cincinnati: 1838.

Hagan, William T. *The Sac and Fox Indians*. Norman: University of Oklahoma Press, 1958.

Jackson, Donald, ed. *Black Hawk: An Autobiography*. Champaign: University of Illinois Press, 1964.

Stevens, Frank E. *The Black Hawk War*. Chicago, 1903.

Thwaites, Reuben Gold. *The Story of the Black Hawk War*. Madison: University of Wisconsin Press, 1892.

KICKING BEAR
Miniconjou/Oglala Sioux
1853–1904

Kicking Bear, an Oglala by birth, was a close friend and first cousin of CRAZY HORSE and fought with him in many of the battles of the Plains wars, including George Armstrong CUSTER's defeat at the Little Bighorn in 1876.

Kicking Bear. [Nebraska State Historical Society]

Kicking Bear married the niece of a Miniconjou Sioux chief and so became a minor chief himself. He paid the bride-price in horses stolen from the Crow, traditional enemies of his people. Kicking Bear's father was named Black Fox and his mother's name was Woodpecker, but his place of birth is not known.

During the winter of 1889, Kicking Bear was among a small group of Sioux traveling to Nevada to meet with WOVOKA and to witness the Ghost Dance. Upon his return, Kicking Bear advocated the dance at the Standing Rock Agency with permission of his uncle, SITTING BULL. He said that the dance foretold the coming of a Native messiah who would free Indians from the dominance and corrupting influences of the invading Euro-Americans. The Ghost Dance religion held that the Indian messiah would return the buffalo and the Indians' ancestors and restore their lives as they had been. Military officials and settlers around the Sioux reservations saw the Ghost Dance as a barbaric, threatening ritual; Agent James McLaughlin called it "an absurd craze . . . demoralizing, indecent, and disgusting." [Vanderwerth]

At a council of Sioux leaders at which no whites were present, Kicking Bear advocated the Ghost Dance with a mixture of Native and Christian imagery. This version of Kicking Bear's speech was related to Indian Agent James McLaughlin through SHORT BULL, a Sioux who was present at the meeting.

My brothers, I bring to you the promise of a day in which there will be no white man to lay his hand on the bridle of the Indian's horse; when the red man of the prairie will rule the world and not be turned from the hunting grounds by any man. I bring you the word from your fathers the ghosts, that they are now marching to join you, led by the Messiah who came once to live on earth with the white men, but was cast out and killed by them. I have seen the wonders of the spirit land, and have talked with the ghosts. I have traveled far and am sent back with a message to tell you to make ready for the coming of the Messiah and return of the ghosts in the spring. [Vanderwerth]

James McLaughlin, Indian agent at Standing Rock and a longtime adversary of Sitting Bull, forced Kicking Bear to leave the reservation a few days after his return. Intensive ghost dancing continued anyway, leading to the incidents that sparked the December 29, 1990, massacre of BIG FOOT's band at Wounded Knee. After the massacre, a group including Kicking Bear continued the Ghost Dance at White Clay, a settlement at Pine Ridge, into early January. General Nelson A. Miles ordered the White Clay encampment surrounded but was able to negotiate a peaceful surrender. Kicking Bear gave up his rifle to Miles's forces on January 15, 1891. Kicking Bear's surrender, involving about five thousand Sioux and others, is significant to history as the last formal subjugation of Native Americans by the U.S. Army.

Following the massacre at Wounded Knee, Kicking Bear was among a number of Sioux who joined Buffalo Bill CODY's Wild West Show to tour the urban areas of the East Coast and Europe.

FOR MORE INFORMATION:

Jensen, Richard E., et al. *Eyewitness at Wounded Knee.* Lincoln: University of Nebraska Press, 1991.

Utley, Robert M. *The Last Days of the Sioux Nation.* New Haven, Conn.: Yale University Press, 1963.

Vanderwerth, W. C. *Indian Oratory.* Norman: University of Oklahoma Press, 1971.

KICKING BIRD
Kiowa
1835–1875

Although little is known of Kicking Bird's early life, it is reported that one of his grandfathers was a Crow Indian captive who had been adopted into the Kiowa nation. The Kiowa called him Watohkonk, meaning "Black Eagle," as well as Tene-Angpote, "Eagle Striking with Talons," or simply "Kicking Bird."

Kicking Bird became a noted warrior while still a young man. His one wife was called Guadalupe. As he grew older, he began to accept the counsel of Little Mountain, principal chief of the Kiowas, who asserted that a peaceful approach to relations with the whites was better than military actions. In 1865, Kicking Bird signed the Little Arkansas Treaty, which set up a Kiowa Reservation that was elaborated in the Treaty of Medicine Lodge in 1867.

With the demise of Little Mountain in 1866, Kicking Bird became the proponent of the peace party, while SATANTA represented the war faction. In 1866, to resolve this split, the Kiowas turned to LONE WOLF as the compromise choice for principal chief. However, Lone Wolf was unable to unite the opposing forces in his nation. By 1870, Kicking Bird was being called a coward at a Sun Dance on the north fork of the Red River. To disprove such allegations, he commanded a war party of about a hundred men against a detachment of U.S. troops in Texas. At the resulting battle, Kicking Bird proved his valor by personally charging into a unit of fifty-four soldiers, slaying one with his lance.

Because of SATANK's death while trying to escape his captors, bad feelings were present in all Kiowa factions about U.S. policies. In 1872, STUMBLING BEAR and Kicking Bird went to Washington, D.C., to seek peace, but they met with little success. When hostilities flared up again during the Red River War of 1874–1875, Kicking Bird kept followers at Fort Sill in western Oklahoma, where he was made principal Kiowa chief by U.S. authorities. At the conclusion of the Red River War, he had to decide which Kiowas would be jailed at Fort Marion in Florida. Kicking Bird chose Lone Wolf and MAMANTI. About a week later, on May 3, 1875, Kicking Bird died at Cache Creek in Indian Territory—some say he was poisoned, but Kiowa lore alleges that Mamanti used his medicinal powers to kill his old adversary. (Mamanti himself died shortly after hearing of Kicking Bird's death.) Kicking Bird is buried at Fort Sill. At the time of his death, he had become a staunch proponent of education and had persuaded Thomas C. Battey, Kiowa Indian agent, to build a school for Kiowa children.

KINACHE
Seminole-Miccosukee
c. 1750–c. 1819

During the American Revolution, Kinache allied with the English in the American Revolution. At that time, he resided near the forks of the Apalachicola River. At the end of the Revolution, he emigrated to a Miccosukee village on the west side of Lake Miccosukee in western Florida. At various times in his life, Kinache also was known as Kinhega, Kinheja, Kinhijah, Opie Mico, Kapitca Mico, Capichee Micco, Tom Perryman, and Lye Drop Mico, meaning "Far-off Warrior."

From 1800 through 1802, Lake Miccosukee was also BOLEK's operations site. In 1815, at the Battle of New Orleans, it was reported that Kinache fought with the English against General Andrew Jackson. In 1816, Kinache defended Negro Fort (later named Fort Gadsden) against an attack by U.S. troops who were pursuing runaway African American slaves.

In 1818, the Creeks, allied with General Jackson and commanded by William MCINTOSH, mounted an offensive against the Miccosukees. Initially, Kinache was reputed to have been killed during this campaign. However, it appears that he fled to the Bahamas and then returned, in 1819, to Florida. He died in his homeland that same year.

KLAH, HOSTEEN
Navajo
1867–1937

Klah was born at Bear Mountain near Fort Wingate in New Mexico. Klah's father was Hoskay Nolyae and his mother was Ahson Tsosie of the Tsithahni clan. As a youth, he was called Ahway Eskay, a common name for pre-pubescent Navajo boys. *Hosteen*, in Navajo, is an appellation of respect for men and *Klah* means "Left Handed."

During his youth, Klah fell off a pony and had to use crutches. An uncle who was a medicine man decided to aid the boy's recovery by performing the Wind Chant over his body. After "singing over him" during this five-day ceremony, the Fire Ceremony was also performed. Fascinated by the ancient ceremonies, the impressionable young lad sought out knowledgeable Navajo traditionalists to learn more about his people's ways.

During this time, it was discovered that he was a hermaphrodite—an honorable state, in Navajo tradition, for its combination of the admirable traits of both sexes. Klah was chosen in the early 1890s to be a male weaver at the World Columbian Exposition in Chicago in 1893, although women usually did the weaving. In later years, he became an outstanding weaver.

In the meantime, he continued his studies of Navajo traditional ways and collaborated with Dr. Washington Matthews on *The Night Chant*, a classic anthropological work, in the early twentieth century. After his work with Matthews, Klah focused on learning the Winter or Yeibichai Ceremony. By 1917, he had completed his lengthy spiritual apprenticeship; he became an honored medicine man when he was able to fully perform his first Night Chant (a nine-day curing rite).

As a medicine man, Klah realized that sand-painting was an important component in the Yeibichai ritual. The art of creating designs with finely ground earth on hogan floors intrigued Klah. Usually, the sandpaintings are scattered outside the hogan when the ceremony is completed. In an attempt to preserve some of these designs, Klah began to weave some of the important images into rugs. In 1916, he finished a Yeibichai dancer rug. By 1919, his rugs were becoming more detailed in their representations of designs in the ritual life of the Navajo. Although many Navajo traditionalists censured his work as sacrilegious, Klah appeared to experience no injuries for his artistic representations of Navajo ceremonies.

During the latter part of his life, the rugs that he wove recorded over two dozen ceremonial motifs. Mary Cabot Wheelwright, a friend of Klah's, memorialized his work in the Wheelwright Museum at Santa Fe, New Mexico. On February 27, 1937, he died at the age of seventy; he is buried on the grounds of the Wheelwright Museum. Through his abilities as a medicine man and the artforms that he developed, he was able to introduce the non-Navajo world to the vitality, beauty, dignity, and harmony of Navajo ritual art.

FOR MORE INFORMATION:

Dockstader, Frederick. *Great North American Indians*. New York: Van Nostrand Reinhold, 1977.

KONAPOT, JOHN
Mahican
c. 1700–1775
Konapot, who was christened "John," invited Moravian missionaries into his village to convert fellow Mahicans to Christianity. They became known as the Stockbridge Indians. He held a commission as a captain in a colonial militia (granted in 1734) and became a principal sachem of the Mahicans in 1744.

L

LADUKE, WINONA
Mississippi Band Anishinabe
1959–

Winona LaDuke became one of the foremost environmental advocates in Native America during the last quarter of the twentieth century. She lectured, wrote, and pressed authorities for answers on issues from the Navajo uranium mines to Hydro-Quebec's construction sites at James Bay to toxic waste sites on Native Alaskan and Canadian land along the Arctic Ocean.

LaDuke was a daughter of Vincent LaDuke, an Indian activist in the 1950s, and Betty LaDuke, a painter. She was educated at Harvard University in the late 1970s, and in the early 1980s moved to the White Earth Ojibwa Reservation at Round Lake, Minnesota. LaDuke became involved in protests of environmental racism and in the recovery of a Native American land base. With a $20,000 grant from the first Reebok Human Rights Awards, she founded the White Earth Land Recovery Program, which took action to regain land ownership on her home reservation. (In the early 1990s, the land area of the thirty-six-mile-square reservation was 92 percent owned by non-Indians.)

For much of the late twentieth century, LaDuke publicized her findings in numerous newspaper and magazine articles and as a founder of the Indigenous Women's Network, director of the White Earth Recovery Project, and board member of Greenpeace.

FOR MORE INFORMATION:
Bowermaster, Jon. "Earth of a Nation." *Harper's Bazaar* (April 1993).

LAFLESCHE, FRANCIS (ZHOGAXE, "WOODWORKER")
Omaha
c. 1867–1932

Son of Omaha chief Joseph LaFlesche and Elizabeth Esau, Francis LaFlesche was an interpreter, lawyer, and ethnologist who, with his sister, Susette LaFlesche, was involved in the Poncas' struggle to regain their homeland in the late 1870s and 1880s.

Francis traveled with Ponca chief STANDING BEAR and Omaha journalist Thomas H. TIBBLES on a tour of several eastern cities to advance the Poncas' cause after they had been given shelter by the Omahas. He worked as an interpreter on the tour. Afterward, Francis attended National University Law School in Washington, D.C., graduating in 1892. While there, he began working with anthropologist Alice C. FLETCHER, collaborating with her on *A Study of Omaha Music* (1893). Fletcher and LaFlesche also collaborated on *The Omaha Tribe* (1911), published a year after he joined the Bureau of American Ethnology. Francis LaFlesche also authored *Middle Five: Indian Boys at School* (1900), a play titled *Da-o-ma* (1912), *Who Was the Medicine Man?* (1904), and *A Dictionary of the Osage Language* (1932).

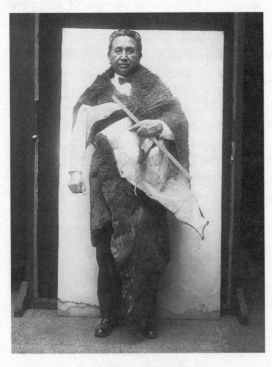

Francis LaFlesche.
[National Anthropological Archives]

FOR MORE INFORMATION:

LaFlesche, Francis. *The Osage and the Invisible World.* Edited by Garrick A. Bailey. Norman: University of Oklahoma Press, 1995.

LAFLESCHE, JOSEPH (ESTAMAZA, IRON EYE)
Omaha
c. 1820–1888

Joseph LaFlesche was the son of a French father and an Omaha or Ponca mixed-blood mother. He succeeded the second BIG ELK as principal chief of the Omahas. He was a leader of the Progressive Party, which adopted Christianity and advocated the allotment of Omaha lands for farming and the construction of roads. He also advised Omahas to move out of their traditional earth lodges (which settlers had adapted as sod huts) in favor of frame homes. LaFlesche believed in retaining Native culture and history but adapting to technology brought by the whites. He advised his ten children (by several wives) to be educated in white schools and colleges.

The Omahas were split between traditionalists and progressives; LaFlesche's two-story frame house stood in a settlement that the traditionals scorned as "the home of the make-believe white men." LaFlesche harbored a lifelong loathing for liquor, one aspect of Euro-American culture he did not adopt. As a young man, LaFlesche had watched a drunken Omaha beat another to death. Under his tribal chieftainship, the Omaha police administered corporal punishment to any Indian found drunk on the Omaha Reservation; as a result, alcohol became very scarce there. LaFlesche passed his aversion to alcohol on to his children, the most prominent of whom was Susan LAFLESCHE. She carried on an anti-drunkenness campaign during her years as tribal physician.

LaFlesche steadfastly maintained that the white man's road was the way of the future; he

Joseph LaFlesche.
[Nebraska State Historical Society]

forbade his daughters to have the traditional tattoos and did not want his sons to have their ears pierced out of concern that such marks would disadvantage them in the future.

The Omahas became U.S. citizens under the DAWES (Allotment) Act in 1887 and became one of the first Native American peoples to divide their lands under that law. A year before he died, Joseph LaFlesche proudly led a group of his people to the polls on election day. Later, Susan would complain that politicians defiled her father's memory by trading liquor for Omahas' votes.

FOR MORE INFORMATION:

Fletcher, Alice C., and Francis LaFlesche. *The Omaha Tribe.* Lincoln: University of Nebraska Press, 1972.

LaFlesche, Francis. *The Middle Five: Indian Schoolboys of the Omaha Tribe.* Madison: University of Wisconsin Press, 1963.

LAFLESCHE, SUSAN PICOTTE
Omaha
1865–1915

Daughter of Omaha principal chief Joseph LAFLESCHE, Susan LaFlesche became a government doctor on the Omaha Reservation during a time when cholera, influenza, tuberculosis, and other diseases were reaching epidemic proportions. She blazed a career of genius through a number of white schools and then nearly worked herself to death serving the Omahas as a government physician from 1889 until her death in 1915.

In 1884, after two and a half years at the Elizabeth Institute for Young Ladies in Elizabeth, New Jersey, LaFlesche enrolled at the Hampton Normal and Agricultural Institute in Hampton, Virginia. This vocational school had been started by General Samuel C. Armstrong to educate freed slaves. (A number of Indians also attended, and the school played a role in the designs of Lieutenant Richard Henry PRATT, who started Carlisle Indian School.) LaFlesche graduated from Hampton on May 20, 1886, at the top of her class. Between 1886 and 1889, she attended the Women's Medical College of Pennsylvania on a scholarship raised by her friends, many of whom were non-Indian, again graduating at the top of her class.

LaFlesche thus became one of a handful of Native American physicians in the nineteenth century, including Charles EASTMAN and Carlos MONTEZUMA. She was the only Native American woman to become a medical doctor during that century. For five years, LaFlesche fought pervasive disease on the Omaha Reservation, making some progress.

In December 1891, LaFlesche wrote that influenza "raged with more violence than during the two preceding years. Some families were rendered helpless by it. . . . Almost every day I was out making visits. . . . Several days the temperature was 15 to 20 degrees below zero, and I had to drive [a horse-drawn buggy] myself." During that winter, she treated more than six hundred patients.

By 1892, the intensity of her work was costing LaFlesche her health. She was beset by a number of debilitating illnesses for the rest of her life as she ministered to the ever-present ills of the Omahas. At one point she wearily departed for Washington, D.C., to appear in Congress, but only because her fellow Omahas had threatened to convey her there bodily, her mission was of such importance to them. There LaFlesche testified about the dire straits of the Omahas, including the raging epidemics, and reminded federal officials of the government's treaty obligations to her people.

Back on the reservation, LaFlesche waged a tireless campaign against alcoholism, recounting stories of how Indians craving liquor used their rent money and even pawned their clothes in winter to obtain it. She wrote of Harry Edwards, who on a winter's night in 1894, "fell from a buggy, was not missed by his drunken companions, and in the morning was found frozen to death." From a medical point of view, LaFlesche believed that alcoholism was at the

root of many of the physical, mental, and moral ills facing the Omahas and other American Indians.

In 1894, her health improving, LaFlesche married Henri Picotte, who was part French and part Sioux; she also began a new medical practice for Indians and whites at Bancroft, Nebraska. LaFlesche practiced medicine there for the rest of her life as her own health permitted. After LaFlesche's death on September 18, 1915, the *Walthill Times* added an extra page to its September 24 issue filled with warm eulogies to her. Friends recalled that hundreds of people in that area, Indian and Euro-American, owed their lives to her care.

The hospital that Susan LaFlesche built at Walthill has since been declared a national historic landmark. Since 1988, her memory has been celebrated at an annual festival there.

FOR MORE INFORMATION:

Mathes, Valerie Sherer. "Dr. Susan LaFlesche Picotte: The Reformed and the Reformer." In *Indian Lives,* edited by L. G. Moses and Raymond Wilson. Norman: University of Oklahoma Press, 1985.

LAFLESCHE, SUSETTE TIBBLES (BRIGHT EYES, INSHTA THEAMBA)
Omaha
1854–1903

Susette LaFlesche became a major nineteenth-century Native rights advocate through the case of the Ponca STANDING BEAR.

LaFlesche was born near Bellevue, Nebraska, the eldest daughter of Joseph (Iron Eye) LA-FLESCHE and Mary Gale LaFlesche, daughter of an army surgeon. Like her sister Susan LAFLESCHE, Susette attended the Presbyterian mission school on the Omaha Reservation. She also studied art at the University of Nebraska. In the late 1870s, she traveled with her father to Indian Territory to render rudimentary medical

A 1922 Omaha camp at Macy, Nebraska.
[Nebraska State Historical Society]

Susette LaFlesche.
[National Anthropological Archives]

among the public. In 1882, Susette, who often used the name Bright Eyes in public, married Tibbles. She also coauthored a memoir with Standing Bear, *Ploughed Under: The Story of an Indian Chief* (1882). During the ensuing years, LaFlesche and Tibbles also toured the British Isles. Later, the couple lived in Washington, D.C., but eventually Susette returned to Lincoln, Nebraska, where she died in 1903 and was buried in Bancroft, Nebraska.

In 1994, Susette LaFlesche was inducted into the National Women's Hall of Fame.

FOR MORE INFORMATION:

Massey, Rosemary, et al. *Footprints in Blood: Standing Bear's Struggle for Freedom and Human Dignity.* Omaha: American Indian Center of Omaha, 1979.

Tibbles, Thomas Henry. *The Ponca Chiefs: An Account of the Trial of Standing Bear.* Lincoln: University of Nebraska Press, 1972.

Wilson, Dorothy Clarke. *Bright Eyes: The Story of Susette LaFlesche.* New York: McGraw-Hill, 1974.

attention to the Poncas under Standing Bear, whose people had been forced to move there from their former homeland along the Niobrara in northern Nebraska. When the Poncas attempted to escape their forced exile and return to their homeland, they marched for several weeks in midwinter, finally eating their moccasins to survive and arriving at the Omaha Reservation with bleeding feet. The Omahas, particularly the LaFlesche family, granted them sanctuary and sustenance.

Susette accompanied her brother Francis LaFlesche and Standing Bear on a lecture tour of eastern cities during 1879 and 1880 to support the Poncas' case for a return of their homeland. Newspaper articles about the Poncas' forced exile by Omaha journalist Thomas H. Tibbles helped ignite a furor in Congress and

LAME DEER (TACHA USHTE)
Miniconjou Sioux
fl. 1860s–1870s

An ally of SITTING BULL, Lame Deer was principal chief of the Miniconjous during the battles over the Bozeman Trail in the late 1860s, the CUSTER battle in 1876, and the final phases of the Plains wars in the late 1870s.

Following the Battle of the Little Bighorn (1876), troops under the command of General Nelson A. Miles tracked Lame Deer's band to Muddy Creek, Montana, on May 7, 1877, where HUMP, a Miniconjou chief who had already surrendered, tried to induce Lame Deer to do the same. Communications seem to have been confused: Miles's soldiers charged Lame Deer's camp before Hump could begin negotiations. Nevertheless, Hump persuaded Lame Deer and

Iron Star, a war chief, to surrender. Lame Deer placed his rifle on the ground to demonstrate friendly intent to Miles, just as a cavalryman charged and tried to shoot him. Lame Deer then retrieved his rifle and shot at another soldier as a third killed Iron Star. By the time the Battle of Muddy Creek ended, a dozen Indians, including Lame Deer himself, and three soldiers had died. Most of Lame Deer's band surrendered, but his son, Fast Bull, escaped with a few other men, whom Miles's troops pursued for several months before forcing their surrender and settlement at the Cheyenne River Reservation, South Dakota.

FOR MORE INFORMATION:

Utley, Robert M. *The Lance and the Shield: The Life and Times of Sitting Bull.* New York: Henry Holt, 1993.

LAME DEER, JOHN FIRE
Oglala Lakota
1900–1970

John Lame Deer, an Oglala Lakota spiritual leader, recalled the suffering among the reservation-bound Lakota early in the twentieth century. In an interview with historian Peter Nabokov, he agonized over his inability as a medicine man to cope with the new maladies affecting his people:

There were twelve of us, but they are all dead now, except one sister. Most of them didn't even grow up. My big brother, Tom, and his wife were killed by the flu in 1917. I lost my own little boy thirty-five years ago. I was a hundred miles away, caught in a blizzard. A doctor couldn't be found for him soon enough. I was told it was the measles. Last year I lost another baby boy, a foster child. This time they told me it was due to some intestinal trouble. So in a

lifetime we haven't made much progress. We medicine men try to doctor our sick, but we suffer from many new white man's diseases, which come from the white man's food and white man's living, and we have no herbs for that. [Nabokov]

A great-grandson of the elder LAME DEER, he wrote a book, published in 1972, called *Lame Deer: Seeker of Visions,* about his own experiences as a spiritual leader.

FOR MORE INFORMATION:

Nabokov, Peter. *Native American Testimony.* New York: Viking Penguin, 1991.

LAPOWINSA
Delaware
fl. 1680s

Lapowinsa led a band of Delawares who occupied land between the Delaware and Lehigh Rivers north of Bethlehem, Pennsylvania, which became the subject of the Walking Purchase Treaty signed with William Penn in 1686. The treaty stipulated that the Indians would cede land as far north of present-day Bethlehem as a man could walk, round-trip, in three days. Penn, a man who was considerate of the Indians' need for land, took only as much as a slow stroll netted him. In 1737, another generation of Pennsylvanians forced a renegotiation of the treaty and took as much land as a swift runner could cover, thereby laying claim to nearly all of the land occupied by Lapowinsa's people.

LAWYER
Nez Perce/Flathead
c. 1795–1876

Lawyer negotiated treaties in the name of the Nez Perce that were repudiated by Chief JOSEPH, YOUNGER before his Long March in 1877. Chief Joseph gave Lawyer that name because (as Joseph noted in a speech to Congress in 1879) "he talked too much" and gave away land that did not belong to him.

Lawyer was a son of Twisted Hair, a Nez Perce chief who had greeted Lewis and Clark's expedition, and his Flathead wife. Lawyer often worked as a guide and interpreter for missionaries and traders and became well known for his oratorical skill in both the English and Nez Perce languages.

Lawyer was designated as a representative of all the Nez Perces by Washington territorial governor Isaac STEVENS at a treaty council in 1855. The outcome of that council was bitterly protested by Old Joseph (see JOSEPH, ELDER), his son Chief Joseph, Younger, and other non-treaty Nez Perces. During the ensuing Yakima War of 1855–1856, Lawyer's band protected Stevens from attack by warriors seeking revenge for the death of PEOPEOMOXMOX. In 1863, Lawyer signed another treaty and ceded even more land that Old Joseph insisted was not his to give. By 1868, Lawyer himself was upset at the number of treaties that had been broken and traveled to Washington, D.C., to protest. He died in 1876, one year before the Long March of the non-treaty Nez Perces under Chief Joseph, Younger.

FOR MORE INFORMATION:

Josephy, Alvin M., Jr. *The Nez Perce Indians and the Opening of the Northwest.* New Haven, Conn.: Yale University Press, 1965.

LEAN BEAR (AWONINAHKU)
Cheyenne
c. 1813–1864

Lean Bear was the most influential leader of a band of Cheyennes camped near Ash Creek, Nebraska Territory, in 1864, who were slaughtered without provocation by Colorado militia under the command of Lieutenant George Eayre. Eayre's troops were marching from Denver to Fort Larned with orders to kill Indians on sight.

As the troops approached, Lean Bear and several other Cheyennes emerged from the village to greet them. Noting that they were positioned for battle and wishing to give a sign of his peaceful intentions, Lean Bear approached Eayre alone to show him the peace medal he had been given on a visit to Washington, D.C., two years earlier. Eayre ordered his men to fire at Lean Bear, who was blown off his pony. As he writhed in pain on the ground, soldiers shot him several times.

LEATHERLIPS (SHATEYARONYAH)
Wyandot/Huron
c. 1732–1810

While the derivation of the name "Leatherlips" is not known, this Sandusky Wyandot chief's Native name Shateyaronyah means "Two Equal Clouds." A signatory of the Treaty of Greenville (1795), Leatherlips was widely distrusted by other Native leaders because of his accommodation of invading whites. As TECUMSEH erected his confederacy against white advancement, Leatherlips became a major rival. In 1810, Tecumseh and his brother "the Prophet" accused Leatherlips of witchcraft and sentenced him to die. The sentence was served to Leatherlips in the form of a drawing of a tomahawk etched into birch bark.

Leatherlips accepted the verdict and the punishment, singing his death song as Chief Roundhead, a Huron, prepared to flay Leatherlips's brain with a tomahawk. The execution was staged in front of several witnesses near Leatherlips's home not far from present-day Columbus, Ohio. One of the witnesses, a white justice of the peace, tried and failed to dissuade the others from killing him. Leatherlips was said to have clung to life for several hours after a number of surely fatal blows to the head and

despite his advanced age—evidence to some of
his murderers that they had indeed put a witch
to death. In 1888, a granite memorial to
Leatherlips was placed on the site of his execution by the Wyandot Club of Columbus.

LE FLORE, GREENWOOD
Choctaw
1800–1865

Greenwood Le Flore's father was Louis Le Flore,
a French trapper. His mother was a Choctaw
woman named Nancy Cravat. In the mid-1820s,
Le Flore became one of the wealthiest Choctaws; he owned large tracts of land and a considerable number of African American slaves. In
1826, he ousted Robert Cole as chief of the
Choctaw northwestern district on the grounds
that Cole had little education and could not stop
land cessions. Subsequently, he and other Choctaw leaders wrote a new Choctaw constitution.
This group of leaders also championed the adop-
tion of agriculture, Christianity, and education
as ways to stop U.S. demands for more Choctaw
lands. In 1828, U.S. superintendent of Indian
affairs Thomas McKenney appointed Le Flore to
head a Choctaw expedition to inspect lands for
the Choctaw in Indian Territory.

In January 1830, Le Flore became principal
chief of the Choctaws. At this time, the old tri-
partite government was deemed ineffective in
resisting U.S. territorial expansion. Although
Le Flore viewed removal as inevitable, he and
David FOLSOM felt that the Choctaws should
strive for a good removal agreement. (The traditionalist faction led by Mushalatubbee flatly
opposed removal and Le Flore's negotiating
policies.) Holding out for what he thought was
the best deal, Le Flore proposed a Choctaw
removal compromise agreement to President
Andrew Jackson that became the Treaty of
Dancing Rabbit Creek (1830). Oddly enough, Le
Flore never relocated to Indian Territory with

the Choctaw people because he gained special
agreements that allowed him to remain on his
plantation along the Yazoo River in Mississippi. Later in life, he served in the Mississippi
state legislature.

LESCHI
Nisqually
c. 1825–1858

Chief Leschi was one of the principal leaders in
the Yakima War, the armed resistance in 1855
and 1856 to treaties negotiated by Washington
territorial governor Isaac STEVENS. The guerrilla war at one point spilled westward over the
Cascades in a raid on the Puget Sound settlement of Seattle, after which Leschi was caught
and hanged.

Beginning in 1843 and continuing until the
middle 1850s, Stevens negotiated at least half a
hundred heavy-handed treaties with the Native
peoples of the Pacific Northwest. Many of the
Native peoples felt insulted by the treaties,
which cajoled and threatened them into signing
away 157 million acres.

The 1855 Walla Walla Treaty galled them the
worst. The Yakimas, claiming that Stevens had
bought off their leaders, recruited allies from
several other tribes and waged a guerrilla war
against the U.S. Army that spread over the
mountains to the Pacific Coast. The army
brought the rebellion under control after three
years of occasionally bloody fighting. During
the rebellion, Dr. Marcus Whitman (who, it
was said, had come to the Walla Walla area to
civilize the Indians with a Bible in one hand
and a whip in the other) was murdered, along
with his wife and twelve other whites. A freelance posse formed immediately and hanged
five captured Cayuse in retribution.

Leschi attacked the newly established settlement of Seattle on February 29, 1856, with
about one thousand warriors. The warriors

Leschi. [Washington State Historical Society]

FOR MORE INFORMATION:

Emmons, Della Gould. *Leschi of the Nis-quallies.* Minneapolis: T. S. Denison, 1965.

LITTLE
Oglala Lakota
fl. 1880s, 1890s

Little was a band leader who became a fervent advocate of the Ghost Dance in the months before the Wounded Knee massacre of 1890. On November 12, 1890, Lieutenant Thunder Bear of the Pine Ridge Indian Police tried to arrest Little on a warrant for cattle theft. Instead of complying, Little waved a butcher knife in Thunder Bear's face as more than two hundred of his supporters gathered and shouted death threats to whites at Pine Ridge. AMERICAN HORSE tried to calm the crowd but had scant

might have overrun the settlement, except that a navy ship that happened to be stationed in the harbor opened fire on them. After his force was defeated, Leschi surrendered to the U.S. Army. Initially, Leschi was offered amnesty, but Governor Stevens, who was determined to bring Leschi to trial for deaths occurring during the raid on Seattle, took up his case as a personal matter. He is said to have bribed one of Leschi's warriors with fifty blankets to betray him. Leschi was tried twice and then sentenced to hang on January 22, 1858. Some whites contended that he had committed no crimes, but others sought to have Leschi hanged before their opponents could obtain a pardon from the federal government. After an intense struggle between these two groups, which included a number of postponements of the hanging date, Leschi was put to death on February 19.

Little. [Nebraska State Historical Society]

success. During the confrontation, Jack RED
CLOUD, son of Chief Red Cloud, pulled a gun on
American Horse and called him a traitor to his
people.

Following this incident, an army buildup
began at Pine Ridge and resulted in the Wounded
Knee massacre of BIG FOOT and his people a
month and a half later. Daniel F. Royer, the
Indian agent whose warrant had provoked the
incident, retreated twenty-eight miles to Rush-
ville, Nebraska, and sent a telegram requesting
more troops because, he said, "Indians are dancing in the snow and are wild and crazy."
FOR MORE INFORMATION:
Smith, Rex Alan. *Moon of the Popping Trees.*
    Lincoln: University of Nebraska Press, 1975.

LITTLE BIG MAN
Oglala Lakota
fl. 1870s
Little Big Man was a shirt-wearer in CRAZY
HORSE's band. Like Crazy Horse himself, Little
Big Man was known for his sense of drama. In
September 1875, during negotiations at Red
Cloud Agency regarding the future ownership
of the Black Hills, he led a mock charge at the
white commissioners by a large group of war-
riors. Firing their guns and shouting ritual war
chants, they badly scared everyone but did no
physical damage.
FOR MORE INFORMATION:
Clark, Robert A. *The Killing of Crazy Horse.*
    Lincoln: University of Nebraska Press, 1976.

LITTLE CROW (CETAN WAKAN)
Santee or Mdewakanton Sioux
c. 1815–1863
Little Crow was a principal figure in an effort
by Sioux in Minnesota to break out of concentration camp–like conditions during 1862. The
breakout, which resulted in widespread death
and destruction on both sides, was often called

the Great Sioux Uprising. The resubjugation of
the Sioux by settlers included the largest mass
hanging in U.S. history.

Throughout the Midwest in the last half of
the nineteenth century, defeated Indians were
forced into camps and promised supplies that
often did not arrive. Despite occasional exposés
in the press, "Indian rings" made graft a fine art
in the bureaucracy, siphoning goods and money
meant to purchase supplies. The Indians, now
cut off from their traditional hunting economy,
had no other means of survival. Some of the
camp-bound Indians ate their horses, many of
which also were starving. When they had finished with the emaciated horses, the Indians
gnawed the bark of trees. When the bark gave
out, they starved to death, sometimes hundreds
at a time.

The Minnesota Sioux (Santee) signed a treaty
in 1851 and moved onto reservations. By the
early 1860s, the outbreak of the Civil War
caused the government to fall so far behind on
providing food supplies and annuity payments

Little Big Man. [Nebraska State Historical Society]

that many Santees were starving. By August 1862, the situation was so desperate that Santees from the Upper Agency (the northern part of the reservation) broke into a government warehouse and took enough pork and flour to feed their families. Santees under the jurisdiction of the Lower Agency, who also were starving, requested emergency rations. Indian agent Thomas Galbraith flatly refused to supply the food, telling the Santees to "eat grass or their own dung." [Tebbel] The desperation of hunger, combined with Galbraith's insult, initiated the Great Sioux Uprising of 1862.

Little Crow, then about sixty years old, led the uprising, which began during the early hours of August 18, 1862, with strikes on outlying farms. The Indians quickly killed several hundred settlers. Individuals with whom the Indians had specific grievances (such as the

Little Crow. [Nebraska State Historical Society]

Indian trader Andrew Myrick) were found slain with grass stuffed in their mouths. After three days of intensive raiding, reinforcements joined army troops in the area, driving the Sioux back slowly, under orders from President Lincoln to quell the uprising at any cost. "Necessity knows no law," Lincoln reportedly told army commanders in the area. [Tebbel] Colonel Henry Hopkins Sibley took command of fourteen hundred men of the Third Minnesota Volunteer Regiment and issued orders to "destroy everything they own and drive them out into the plains. . . . They are to be treated as maniacs or wild beasts," Sibley said.

The Santees killed more than seven hundred settlers and one hundred soldiers before the army drove them into the Plains. A large number of Santees who had not taken a direct role in the uprising stayed in Minnesota. Many Christianized Indians had risked their own lives to protect white settlers. They expected to be treated as neutrals, but the settlers' wrath fell on them as well. "Exterminate the wild beasts," clamored Jane Swisshelm, editor of the *St. Cloud Democrat.* After the uprising was quelled, a military court condemned 303 of 392 imprisoned Santees to death by hanging. President Lincoln demanded a review of the sentences and cut the number to be executed to thirty-eight. Lincoln asserted that each of these had taken part in the massacre, raped women, or both. The thirty-eight Santees died on a single scaffold at Fort Mankato on December 26, 1862, in the largest mass hanging in U.S. history. William J. Dudley, who lost two children to the Santees' scalping knives during the massacre, cut the rope that hung the Santees.

The bodies of the executed men were removed from their mass grave after nightfall by medical doctors, who used them as laboratory specimens. Army units trailed the Santees who had escaped Minnesota to the Badlands of

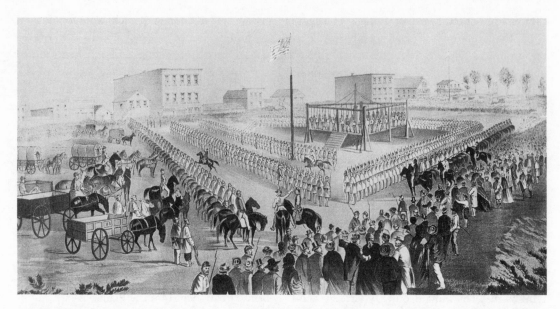

An artist's rendering of the largest mass execution in U.S. history: the hanging of thirty-eight Sioux at Fort Mankato, Minnesota, in the wake of the 1862 Great Sioux Uprising. [Nebraska State Historical Society]

South Dakota, which Sibley called "hell with the fires out." On August 4, 1864, Sibley's forces killed more than five hundred Santee warriors in a single day. A dwindling number of survivors moved westward and took shelter with the Cheyennes. They forged an alliance which General George A. CUSTER, whom they would face at the Little Bighorn a dozen years later.

Little Crow escaped Sibley's raids. He was later shot by a farmer (some say the farmer's son fired the fatal shot) while foraging for berries. The farmer did not know until later that he had ended the life of the chief who started the Great Sioux Uprising. The Minnesota legislature voted the farmer a $500 honorarium. On May 4 and 5, 1863, thirteen hundred neutral Santees, most of them women and children, boarded two steamboats and went into exile from their homelands. Settlers on shore threw rocks at them.

FOR MORE INFORMATION:

Anderson, Gary C. *Little Crow: Spokesman for the Sioux*. St. Paul: Minnesota Historical Society Press, 1986.
Tebbel, John. *The Compact History of the Indian Wars*. New York: Hawthorn Books, 1966.

LITTLE HILL
Winnebago
fl. mid-1800s

Little Hill, a nineteenth-century leader of the Wisconsin Winnebago, testified before Congress in 1865 that his people had been subjected to seven treaties that forced them to move six times. In the 1820s, the group was evicted from its land along the Wisconsin River; they were forced to wander about for four decades, until they settled in Minnesota, only to find local settlers coveting their land in the wake of the Great Sioux Uprising of 1862. The Winnebagos

fled to the Crow Creek Reservation in South
Dakota. Most fell into poverty there, and some
secretly moved back to Wisconsin; others took
refuge with the Omahas in Nebraska. Later, Little Hill's unwilling nomads were given a tract of
land neighboring the Omahas in northeastern
Nebraska, which they occupy to this day.

At the 1865 congressional hearings into fraud
among Indian agents, Little Hill told of his people's travails in South Dakota and how some
agents fed them food that killed.

It was not good country. It was all dust.
Whenever we cooked anything, it would be
full of dust. We found out after a while that
we could not live there. There was not
enough to eat. . . . Before the first agent left
us, he had a cottonwood trough made, and
put beef in it, and sometimes a whole barrel of flour and a piece of pork, and let it
stand the whole night. . . . We tried to use
[eat] it, but many of us got sick on it and
died. They also put in the unwashed
intestines of the beeves and the liver. After
dipping out the soup, the bottom [of the
pot] would be very nasty and offensive.
Some of the old women and children got
sick on it and died. [Nabokov]

FOR MORE INFORMATION:

Nabokov, Peter. *Native American Testimony.*
New York: Viking Penguin, 1991.

LITTLE TURTLE (MICHIKINIKWA)
Miami/Mohican
1752–1812

Little Turtle was one of the principal chiefs
among a coalition of Shawnees, Miamis,
Delawares, Potawatomis, Ottawas, Chippewas,
and Wyandots in the Old Northwest (Ohio
country). This coalition defeated fourteen hun-

Little Hill (seated, far right) *and other Winnebago
chiefs meet with Indian agent Robert Furnas*
(standing, second from left) *and his delegation.*
[Nebraska State Historical Society]

dred soldiers under General Arthur St. Clair on
November 4, 1791. Little Turtle's twelve hundred warriors, aided by the element of surprise,
killed roughly nine hundred of St. Clair's men,
the largest single battlefield victory by an American Indian force in history. The victory was
short-lived, however; in 1794, "Mad Anthony"
Wayne's forces defeated Little Turtle and his
allies at the Battle of Fallen Timbers. On August
3, 1795, the Indians gave up most of their hunting grounds west of the Ohio River following
the defeat by signing the Treaty of Greenville.

Little Turtle was known as a master of battlefield strategy. The son of a Miami chief and a
Mohican mother, Little Turtle became a Miami
war chief because of his extraordinary personal
abilities; under ordinary circumstances, the
matriarchal nature of the culture would have
prohibited a leadership role for him.

In 1787, the hunting grounds of the Miamis
and their allies had been guaranteed in perpetuity by the U.S. Congress. The act did not stop
an invasion of settlers, however, and by the
early 1790s, Little Turtle had cemented an
alliance that foreshadowed the later efforts of

Little Turtle. [National Anthropological Archives]

TECUMSEH. Little Turtle's principal allies in this effort were the Shawnee BLUE JACKET and the Delaware BUCKONGAHELAS. This alliance first defeated a one-thousand-man American force under Josiah Harmer during October 1790. Harmer dispatched an advance force of 180 men, who were drawn into a trap and annihilated. Harmer then dispatched 360 more men to punish the Indians; they were drawn into a similar trap, and about a hundred of them were killed. The remainder of Harmer's force then retreated to Fort Washington, or present-day Cincinnati.

Harmer's defeat stunned the army, whose commanders knew that the Old Northwest would remain closed to settlement as long as Little Turtle's alliance held. General St. Clair, who had served as president of the Continental Congress in the middle 1780s, gathered an army of two thousand men during the summer of 1791 and marched into the Ohio country.

About a quarter of the men deserted en route, and to keep the others happy, St. Clair permitted about two hundred soldiers' wives to travel with the army. On November 4, 1791, Little Turtle and his allies lured St. Clair's forces into the same sort of trap that had defeated Harmer's smaller army near St. Mary's Creek, a tributary of the Wabash River. Thirty-eight officers and 598 men died in the battle; 242 others were wounded, many of whom later died. Fifty-six wives also lost their lives, bringing the total death toll to about 950—the largest defeat of a U.S. Army force in all of the Indian wars, a death toll higher than any inflicted on the United States by the British in the American Revolution. After the battle, St. Clair resigned his commission in disgrace.

Dealing from strength, Little Turtle's alliance refused to cede land to the United States. In 1794, "Mad Anthony" Wayne was dispatched with a fresh army, which visited the scene of St. Clair's debacle. According to Wayne, "Five hundred skull bones lay in the space of 350 yards. From thence, five miles on, the woods were strewn with skeletons, knapsacks, and other debris." Little Turtle had more respect for Wayne than he had for Harmer or St. Clair; he called Wayne "the chief who never sleeps." Aware that Wayne was unlikely to be defeated by his surprise tactics, Little Turtle proposed that the Indian alliance talk peace. A majority of the warriors rebuffed Little Turtle, so he relinquished his command to Blue Jacket. On August 29, 1794, Wayne's forces defeated the Native alliance. When the time to talk peace came a year later, the defeated Indians were forced to give up most of their lands.

For almost two centuries, local historians placed the site of the Battle of Fallen Timbers along the Maumee River floodplain near U.S. Highway 24. A monument was erected at the site, even as Native Americans contended that the battle had really occurred a mile away in what is today a soybean field. In 1995, to settle the issue, G. Michael Pratt, an anthropology professor at Heidelberg College in Tiffin, Ohio, organized an archaeological dig in the soybean field. He organized teams that included as many as 150 people who excavated the site, which yielded large numbers of battlefield artifacts, indicating conclusively that the Native American account of the site was correct.

In 1802, Little Turtle addressed the legislatures of Ohio and Kentucky, urging members to pass laws forbidding traders to supply Indians with whiskey. He said that whiskey traders had "stripped the poor Indian of skins, guns, blankets, everything—while his squaw and the children dependent on him lay starving and shivering in his wigwam." Neither state did anything to stop the flow of whiskey, some of which was adulterated with other substances, from chili peppers to arsenic.

Little Turtle died on July 14, 1812, at his lodge near the junction of the St. Joseph River and St. Mary Creek. He was buried with full military honors by army officers who knew his genius. William Henry Harrison, who had been an aide to Wayne and who later defeated Tecumseh in the same general area, paid Little Turtle this tribute: " 'A safe leader is better than a bold one.' This maxim was a great favorite of [the Roman] Caesar Augustus . . . who . . . was, I believe, inferior to the warrior Little Turtle."

FOR MORE INFORMATION:

Hamilton, Charles. *Cry of the Thunderbird.* Norman: University of Oklahoma Press, 1972.

Porter, C. Fayne. *Our Indian Heritage: Profiles of Twelve Great Leaders.* Philadelphia: Chilton, 1964.

Winger, Otho. *Last of the Miamis: Little Turtle.* N.p.: Lawrence W. Shultz, 1935.

LITTLE WARRIOR
Creek
c. 1780–1813

Little Warrior and his warriors allied with the English during the War of 1812. In January 1813, he was a party to the Raisin River massacre of Americans in Michigan. While returning to their Creek homelands in the south, Little Warrior's band launched an attack that killed several settlers near the confluence of the Ohio and Mississippi Rivers. The U.S. Indian agent, Benjamin Hawkins, sought punishment for Little Warrior's deeds when he learned of this raid.

Consequently, the Creek Council condemned Little Warrior and his men to death for their transgressions. William MCINTOSH, with a posse, tracked down and killed five of Little Warrior's men on the Tallahoosa River at Red Warrior's Bluff. Meanwhile, Captain Isaacs, Alexander MCGILLIVRAY's son-in-law, pursued the remaining warriors. He apprehended them in a swamp outside of Wetumpka and killed Little Warrior and two of his men. This episode caused deep divisions in the Creek nation and led to the Creek Civil War, in which the Red Sticks, commanded by William WEATHERFORD, fought McIntosh and his White Sticks, who allied with the United States and the forces of General Andrew Jackson.

LITTLE WOLF (OHKOM KAKIT)
Northern Cheyenne
c. 1818–1904

Little Wolf was a principal chief of the Northern Cheyennes during early contact with Anglo-American traders, settlers, and troops. With DULL KNIFE, Little Wolf led the Cheyennes from exile in Indian Territory (now Oklahoma) back to their homeland in present-day eastern Montana during the late 1870s. This diaspora, completed in direct contradiction to orders by the U.S. Army, is chronicled in Mari Sandoz's *Cheyenne Autumn* (1953). Little Wolf was the bearer of the Sacred Chief's Bundle of the Northern Cheyennes and therefore carried the highest personal responsibility for the preservation of the people.

Little Wolf was reputed to have been a notable warrior as early as the middle 1830s, probably his late teenage years. In 1851, along with other Cheyennes, Little Wolf ceased warfare against encroaching whites in exchange for an Indian agency and annuities. The agency was not established, and annuity payments arrived only rarely, but Little Wolf counseled peace with the European Americans, with one exception. In 1865, he took part in an attack on U.S. Army troops to avenge the unprovoked murder of BLACK KETTLE's band of Cheyennes at the Sand Creek massacre in 1864.

By 1876, in his late fifties, Little Wolf could still outrun all of the younger Cheyenne warriors. He had two sons, who were called Pawnee and Woodenthigh by whites. He also had a daughter, Pretty Walker, and two wives, Quiet One and Feather on Head. Little Wolf's Cheyennes did not take part in the battle against George Armstrong CUSTER's troops at the Little Bighorn on June 25, 1876, but were caught up in waves of U.S. Army retribution afterward. Little Wolf's people came to the aid of Dull Knife's Cheyennes as their village on the Powder River was destroyed by the U.S. Army. Little Wolf was shot seven times but survived.

Little Wolf and Dull Knife's bands escaped into the Yellowstone country during the winter of 1876–1877 but surrendered because they were hungry and because General Nelson Miles and General George Crook both promised them a reservation in their homeland and an Indian agent to conduct business with the federal government, including delivery of annuities. After the surrender, all of the generals' promises were broken. Little Wolf had even enlisted as a scout for Crook when he was told that his people would get no more food unless they accepted the army's orders to move to Indian Territory. The Cheyennes departed only when they realized that the alternative was starvation, because the buffalo had become too scarce to hunt.

In the middle of August 1878, Dull Knife and Little Wolf pleaded with Indian agent John A. Miles to let them return home. Half the band had died, mostly of disease, during a year in Oklahoma. Dull Knife himself was shaking with fever as they talked. Miles asked for a year to work on the problem, and Little Wolf told him the Cheyennes would be dead in a year. Three weeks later, ten young Cheyennes left the reservation in the night, and Agent Miles demanded that Little Wolf give up ten hostages

Little Wolf (left) *with Dull Knife.*
[Nebraska State Historical Society]

until troops could locate the runaways. After Little Wolf refused, Miles said that rations would be withheld. Little Wolf became angry and told Miles that his people were already starving. "Last night I saw children eating grass because they had no food. Will you take the grass from them?" Little Wolf asked. [Sandoz]

The Cheyennes then left Oklahoma on their own with army troops in pursuit. They evaded recapture as they fought off the troops in several rear guard actions during the fall, but they suffered many casualties. The complex sequence of battles and the Cheyennes' suffering is described in detail in Sandoz's book. Near present-day White Clay Creek, Nebraska, the Cheyennes split into two groups. Dull Knife and 150 others went into Red Cloud Agency to surrender. Little Wolf and a roughly equal number headed into the Nebraska Sand Hills, where they spent the winter in hiding.

The next March, Little Wolf's band moved out of the Sand Hills to the mouth of the Powder River, where they encountered Lieutenant W. P. Clark and an army unit of Cheyenne and Lakota scouts. Clark persuaded Little Wolf and his followers to surrender to General Miles (whom Little Wolf knew as "Bear Coat") at Fort Keough. This time, the survivors of Little Wolf's band were allowed to remain near their homeland on the Northern Plains.

During the first reservation winter, 1879–1880, Little Wolf, who had been drinking, shot and killed the Cheyenne Thin Elk, who had been an antagonist of Little Wolf since he had made advances on Little Wolf's wives almost a half century earlier. Thin Elk's relatives then ransacked Little Wolf's lodge, which was held as a traditional Cheyenne right of a family aggrieved by murder. Little Wolf's role as a leader of his people ended with that murder. After a quarter century of quiet reservation life, Little Wolf died in 1904.

FOR MORE INFORMATION:

Llewellyn, K. N., and E. Adamson Hoebel. *The Cheyenne Way*. Norman: University of Oklahoma Press, 1941.

Sandoz, Mari. *Cheyenne Autumn*. New York: Hastings House, 1953.

Wiltsey, Norman B. *Brave Warriors*. Caldwell, Idaho: Caxton, 1963.

LITTLE WOUND
Oglala Lakota
fl. 1860s–1890s

Little Wound was a political and war leader among the Oglala and had a long record of distrusting whites and asserting Sioux land claims. On the eve of the Wounded Knee massacre, however, he counseled peace despite his advocacy of the Ghost Dance.

Little Wound came to the attention of the U.S. Army during RED CLOUD's War (1866–1868); he was active in several raids and resisted pressure to settle on a reservation. By 1883, however, Little Wound had surrendered to reservation life. He told a congressional committee chaired by Senator Henry DAWES that the Sioux were being swindled of their lands.

Little Wound became an Episcopalian in the 1880s before he was converted again, this time to WOVOKA's Ghost Dance. Little Wound described how he went into a trance, died, and was born again into a world in which the whites had vanished and Indians again lived in peace and prosperity. Little Wound and his band resisted pressure, including an elimination of rations, and continued to dance well into fall 1890, when increasing numbers of U.S. Army troops arrived at Pine Ridge following LITTLE's abortive arrest on November 12. On November 26, Little Wound surrendered and tried to convince other Sioux to do the same.

Following the massacre of BIG FOOT's band at Wounded Knee a month later, Little Wound

Little Wound. [Nebraska State Historical Society]

was one of a number of Sioux who made up a delegation to Washington, D.C., in an attempt to address the problems that had provoked the conflict. Several Sioux leaders told officials at the Interior Department of mistreatment, illegal taking of land, and rotten rations as they posed for their photographs in suits purchased at Saks', an early department store which later became Saks' Fifth Avenue.

FOR MORE INFORMATION:

Jensen, Richard E., R. Eli Paul, and John E. Carter. *Eyewitness at Wounded Knee.* Lincoln: University of Nebraska Press, 1991.

Smith, Rex Alan. *Moon of the Popping Trees.* Lincoln: University of Nebraska Press, 1975.

LOCO
Mimbreno Apache
c. 1840–1905

In 1880, Loco became the leader of the peace faction of the Warm Springs Apaches (a group that also contained a significant number of Mimbrenos) who had relocated from New Mexico to Arizona upon VICTORIO's death. At about this time, NANA became chief of the militants. On April 19, 1882, a war party led by GERONIMO, NAICHE, CHATO, JUH, and others who had left San Carlos in 1881 returned for a raid in the United States that is sometimes called the Loco Outbreak. The militant Apaches coerced Loco and his people into going with them into Mexico. Loco engaged in hit-and-run tactics with the Chiricahuas until General George Crook cornered the militants in Mexico in 1883. After an assault on Chato's contingent, Loco decided to lay down his arms. Loco did not participate in Geronimo's 1885 escape from the San Carlos Reservation in New Mexico. However, he journeyed with ALCHESAY, Chato, and others to Washington, D.C., in 1886 for peace talks. Although he advocated peace, Loco was imprisoned in Florida with more militant Apaches in 1886. He was released from prison in 1894, and he died in 1905.

LOGAN, JAMES (TAHGAHJUTE)
Cayuga
c. 1728–1780

The son of a Cayuga mother and French father, Tahgahjute took the name "James Logan" after James Logan, secretary to William Penn. The Cayuga Logan was born at Shamokin, Pennsylvania, and supported the colonists throughout his adult life. He rallied to the English cause in the war with the French and the British interest in PONTIAC's Rebellion. His friendship was strained severely in 1774, when at least one of Logan's relatives was murdered in an unprovoked attack.

A gang of white squatters massacred a camp of peaceful Indians at the mouth of Yellow Creek, Ohio, in spring 1774. According to contemporary reports, the victims included Logan's entire family. The local Indians retaliated with a number of attacks. After that, Logan refused to attend a peace conference but sent a speech via an interpreter. Thomas Jefferson later compared the speech to the great orations of ancient Greece. "I may challenge the whole orations of Demosthenes and Cicero, and of any more eminent orator, if Europe has furnished more eminent, to produce a single passage, superior to the speech of Logan," wrote Jefferson. Logan's speech was popularized during the nineteenth century in millions of copies of *McGuffy's Reader*.

Logan's speech read, in part:

I appeal to any white man to say, if he ever entered Logan's cabin hungry, and he gave him not meat; if he ever came cold and naked, and he clothed him not. During the course of the last long and bloody war, Logan remained idle in his cabin, an advocate for peace. Such was my love for the whites, that my countrymen pointed as they passed, and said, "Logan is the friend of the white man." I had even thought to have lived with you, but for the injuries of one man, Colonel Cresap, the last spring, in cold blood and unprovoked, murdered all the relations of Logan, not sparing even my women and children. There runs not a drop of my blood in any living creature. . . . Who is there to mourn for Logan?—not one. [Hamilton]

According to Charles Hamilton in *Cry of the Thunderbird: The American Indian's Own Story* (1972), Logan's speech contained some factual errors. It was a man named Greathouse, not Cresap, who initiated the massacre. Logan had no wife or children, though his sister was killed. Nevertheless, Logan was infuriated by the incident and stricken with grief. That summer he attacked several white families located on Indian land and killed many of them. By late summer, the Ohio frontier was raging in conflict.

Virginia called out the militia to punish Logan. Several thousand Indians and whites met at the Battle of Point Pleasant. The Indians (Shawnee, Mingo, Delaware, Wyandot, Cayuga, and Seneca) were outnumbered and were defeated by the militia. The Iroquois League at Onondaga refused to sanction the war and chose to ignore the Shawnee who were trying to form their own western confederacy.

As the war waned, Logan became increasingly addicted to alcohol and may have lost his sanity. He was murdered by his nephew in 1780 as they returned from a trip to Detroit.

FOR MORE INFORMATION:

Hamilton, Charles. *Cry of the Thunderbird*. Norman: University of Oklahoma Press, 1972.

Jefferson, Thomas. *Notes on the State of Virginia*. Edited by William Peden. Chapel Hill: University of North Carolina Press, 1955.

Seeber, Edward D. "Critical Views on Logan's Speech." *Journal of American Folklore* 60 (1947): 130–146.

Wallace, Anthony. *The Death and Rebirth of the Seneca*. New York: Knopf, 1970.

LONE DOG
Sioux
fl. late 1800s

Lone Dog was a Sioux artist who created *winter counts*, annual pictorial histories of his people, done on buffalo hide. These and other winter counts were created between 1800 and 1871 and served as a major medium of history-keeping. The contents of the winter counts illustrate the relative importance of various events in Lone Dog's village. For example, a horse-raiding party might be recalled, but a treaty with the whites might not.

LONE WOLF (GUIPAGO)
Kiowa
c. 1820–1879

Lone Wolf was one of the most respected warriors and chiefs in the Kiowa nation. He thought that the peace policy of KICKING BIRD was inappropriate. In general, he supported the more militant tactics of SATANK, BIG TREE, and SATANTA.

After the death of Satank and the jailing of Big Tree and Satanta, Lone Wolf assumed the principal chieftainship of the Kiowas that were located around Fort Sill, Indian Territory. Essentially, he was the compromise choice, over Kicking Bird, as principal chief of the peace faction and Satanta of the militant faction. It is alleged that Lone Wolf had great medicine powers. During a thunderstorm, for example, his tepee was struck by a lightning bolt that killed his wife and child but left him unscathed. In 1867, Lone Wolf, along with eight other leaders, agreed to the Medicine Lodge Treaty, which set up the confines of the combined Kiowa and Comanche Reservations in the western part of Indian Territory. Afterward, when the Kiowas refused to adhere to the tenets of the treaty and settle on the reservation, General Philip H. Sheridan directed that Satanta and Lone Wolf be used as hostages.

In 1872, Lone Wolf traveled to Washington, D.C., to negotiate a peace agreement and secure the release of some Kiowa prisoners. Later in the same year, angered by the army's killing of his son and nephew as they journeyed through Texas after raiding in Mexico for horses, Lone Wolf led a group of Kiowas south to retrieve their bodies and exact retribution.

In the resulting Red River War of 1874–1875, Lone Wolf, BIG BOW, and MAMANTI, as well as the Comanche Quanah PARKER, saw action against the Texas Rangers and the regular army commanded by Colonel Nelson A. Miles and Colonel Ranald S. MacKenzie. In June 1874, he also took part in the attack on the buffalo hunters at Adobe Walls. On August 22, 1874, he fought the army to a standstill at the Anadarko Agency in western Oklahoma. In September 1874, he also participated in the defense of Palo Duro Canyon against Mackenzie's units. Since the battle at Palo Duro Canyon devastated Indian supplies and livestock, Lone Wolf and Mamanti laid down their arms in spring 1875 at Fort Sill, Indian Territory. Subsequently, Kicking Bird, appointed principal chief of the Kiowas

Lone Wolf. [Nebraska State Historical Society]

by the whites, decided that Lone Wolf and about seventy-five of his men should be imprisoned at Fort Marion, Florida.

While in exile in Florida, Lone Wolf caught malaria. Consequently, he was released from Fort Marion in Florida and returned to Indian Territory in May 1878. He died in 1879, a year after his release. He was buried on Mount Scot in Indian Territory.

LONG, WILL WEST ("WILI WESTI")
Cherokee
c. 1870–1947

Born in Big Cove, North Carolina, around 1870, Will West Long was the son of John Long, a Cherokee Baptist preacher, and Sally Terrapin, a Cherokee woman. Growing up in the North Carolina hills in a traditional Cherokee household, Long collected a vast store of knowledge about Cherokee ways. Although his father was a Christian, the Longs were essentially traditionalists; his mother taught her children Cherokee customs from an early age. Long's first experience with schooling in High Point, North Carolina, lasted only a few days. However, he did eventually learn English and the Cherokee syllabary. These linguistic and written skills enabled him to become an interpreter and translator.

In 1887, James Mooney, an ethnologist from the Smithsonian, began to study Cherokee life, and Long collaborated with him. Mooney persuaded the young Long to attend Hampton Institute and then spend several years in Massachusetts, where he learned more of the white ways.

In 1904, he came back to his community upon his mother's death and found that the traditional way of life held great meaning for him. While in the white world, he had suffered ill health; however, the North Carolina environment and Cherokee medicinal practices restored both his health and his faith in his people's culture. His friendship with Mooney became deeper, and they worked together until about 1920. Throughout the first half of the twentieth century, Long was an interpreter and informant for some of the United States' leading anthropologists.

In the early twentieth century, the Cherokees of North Carolina experienced some pronounced changes in their political and social life. Disease also took its toll on this isolated group of American Indians. Indeed, their very isolation retarded the Eastern Cherokees' ability to improve their conditions on their homeland. Will West Long wanted his traditional knowledge to survive, and that is why he allowed it to be recorded in books, museums, and documents. He devoted much of his adult life to this work of cultural preservation, even though he had doubts about the efficacy of his work and even though it was often interrupted by the needs of his farm.

Long worked hard on cultural preservation projects that related to medicine and curing. He also carved wooden ceremonial masks—a craft he had learned from his cousin, Charley Lawson. On March 14, 1947, he succumbed to a heart attack at Qualla, North Carolina, at the age of seventy-seven.

LOOKING GLASS
(ALLALIMYA TAKANIN)
Nez Perce
c. 1822–1877

As a war chief with JOSEPH YOUNGER's band of Nez Perce, Looking Glass led the band through much of its Long March in 1877. At first, Looking Glass was the principal chief of a Nez Perce band that was not allied with Joseph. Looking Glass's village was attacked by U.S. troops looking for Joseph's hostiles, after which his people joined them.

Born in the Wallowa country, Looking Glass was a son of Apash Wyakaikt (Flint Necklace), chief of the Asotin Nez Perce. His father was sometimes called Looking Glass because he had obtained a small mirror in trade and hung it around his neck. The son took the mirror and the name after his father's death in 1863.

Like Chief Joseph, Looking Glass refused to sign treaties with the invading whites; both repudiated the treaties signed with Washington territorial governor Isaac STEVENS that precipitated the Yakima War. When General O. O. Howard told the non-treaty Nez Perce to move to a reservation or be forced there by the army, tensions intensified. After a series of incidents, the Long March began.

During July 1877, Looking Glass persuaded Joseph and the rest of the fleeing Nez Perce to take refuge with the Crows in Montana. He was convinced that the army would not follow them into Crow land and that they would be free to pursue their traditional way of life there. Unexpectedly, the army and allied militia attacked the Nez Perce at Big Hole River. The Nez Perce escaped the attack but suffered some casualties. Looking Glass suffered a loss of prestige because of his mistaken advice and lost his leadership role.

The Nez Perce next fled to Canada but were again attacked on September 30 as they stopped to rest thirty miles south of the border. Most of those who had survived the months-long march died in this attack during which Joseph prepared to surrender. Looking Glass was in favor of continuing the battle, but according to most accounts, he was struck in the head by a bullet and killed. Others, however, maintain that he was shot October 5, the day that Joseph and the rest of the survivors surrendered.

FOR MORE INFORMATION:

Josephy, Alvin M., Jr. *The Nez Perce Indians and the Opening of the Northwest.* New Haven, Conn.: Yale University Press, 1965.

LOOKING HORSE, ARVOL
Cheyenne River Sioux
1954–

Late in the twentieth century, Arvol Looking Horse became the nineteenth Keeper of the Sacred Pipe of the Lakota, Nakota, and Dakota, the peoples that Europeans often call the Sioux. It is believed that the pipe was handed to the Lakota, Dakota, and Nakota four centuries ago by White Buffalo Calf Woman.

Looking Horse believes that while he holds the pipe, in the seventh generation after the subjugation of the Sioux and other Plains peoples, "the sacred hoop will be mended." He is referring to the Lakota, Dakota, and Nakota metaphor for life, creation, and cultural continuity, the same sacred hoop that BLACK ELK maintained had been broken during the conquest. Looking Horse cites the resurgence

Looking Glass. [National Anthropological Archives]

of Native American languages and cultures as evidence that the sacred hoop is being mended.

Looking Horse has lectured at Berkeley, Stanford, Dartmouth, and Harvard and has led prayer ceremonies at the United Nations. In 1992, he married Carole Anne Heart. He played a leading role in tribal leaders' meetings with President Bill Clinton in April 1994, the first time that all tribal leaders had been invited to a single meeting with a U.S. president. Looking Horse also travels frequently to Europe to appear before U.N. agencies and private groups.

LOOKOUT, FRED (WAHTSAKE TUMPAH)
Osage
c. 1860–1949

Fred Lookout was born about 1860 outside of Independence, Kansas. His mother was an Osage named Metsahelum and his father was the Osage chief Wahkasetompahpe. (His Osage name means "The Eagle Who Sits Thinking.") He attended the Osage Boarding School at Pawhuska, Oklahoma, as a youth and then went to Carlisle Indian School in Pennsylvania. In 1896, he was elected to the Osage Tribal Council. When his father died in 1913, Lookout became head chief of the Osage nation. By the end of the nineteenth century, he proved to be very able in dealing with the whites on their own terms.

With the discovery of oil on Osage lands near Pawhuska, the influx of speculators, fortune hunters, and prospectors in Oklahoma seemed overwhelming. Boomtowns were created overnight, and the Osages became very prosperous. By 1935, the average Osage family had a yearly income of over $50,000. Throughout this economic expansion, Lookout and his tribal council held on to the mineral rights of the Osages and prevented many Osages from being cheated

by unscrupulous whites. He was reelected principal chief for nine terms. He traveled to Washington, D.C., many times to lobby for Osage rights.

Lookout was also a devout member of the Native American Church and very knowledgeable about peyote ceremonies. He was married to Julia Pryor Mosecheche of Pawhuska, and she bore him a daughter and two sons. He was a kindly and well-liked man, known widely in Oklahoma for his integrity, dignity, and generosity. On August 28, 1949, he died at about eighty-eight at his home in Pawhuska.

LOWRY, GEORGE (MAJOR LOWREY, LOWERY, OR LOWRY; AGILI)
Cherokee
fl. 1820s–1830s

In 1817, George Lowry (whose Cherokee name Agili means "He Is Rising") and others agreed to a land cession ceding one-third of the remaining Eastern Cherokee lands in preparation for removal to Arkansas lands between the Arkansas and White Rivers. According to this treaty, removal to the west was still optional and not mandatory. In 1839, after the forced removal of the Cherokee and the Trail of Tears, Lowry became chief of council of the emigrants that initiated the development of the new Western Cherokee government.

LOWRY, HENRY BERRY (LOWERY OR LOWRIE)
Lumbee
c. 1846–1872

In 1953, the Lumbee Indians, a triracial people who are descendants of several southeastern Indian tribes, whites, and African Americans, named themselves after the Lumber River, which flows through their homeland in North Carolina. According to the Lumbee historian Adolph Dial, they are also descended from the "lost" Roanoke colonists, who took up residence with American Indians farther inland.

During the Civil War, Southern whites abused the Lumbees by forcing them to work on Confederate military positions under awful circumstances where they experienced short sleeping periods, little food, and lengthy exposure to bad weather conditions. To avoid this forced labor, some hid out in the swamps and piney woods, while others coped by fleeing from the labor camps. The North Carolina Confederate Home Guard retaliated by menacing the entire American Indian community in Robeson County, North Carolina.

Faced with these oppressive measures, a teenager by the name of Henry Berry Lowry created a resistance movement of African Americans, Lumbees, and at least one white person in 1864. His brother-in-law, Boss Strong, became one of his lieutenants even though Strong was only fourteen at the time. The guerrilla band looted plantations and gave their spoils to the poor of Robeson County. Even after the Civil War, the group clashed with white vigilante groups like the Klu Klux Klan. Their raids also involved attacks on federal troops after the Civil War. In 1866, 1868, and 1869, Lowry narrowly eluded capture by authorities. By this time he was becoming a legend among his people.

In 1871, while Lowry was paddling his canoe, eighteen militiamen attacked him from the banks of the Lumber River. Using the canoe as a shield from the barrage of bullets, he slipped into the river and counterattacked with his rifle. Gradually moving toward the riverbank and the militiamen, he managed to force them to run. In 1872, Lowry vanished; rumor had it that he had been murdered; however, the price on his head was never claimed. Even into the 1930s, some Lumbees vowed he was living quietly in the backwoods as an old man.

LOWRY, JOHN (COLONEL LOWREY OR LOWRY)
Cherokee
fl. early 1800s

John Lowry commanded about fourteen hundred Cherokee warriors who allied with General Andrew Jackson in the campaign against William WEATHERFORD's Creek Red Sticks. In November 1813, Lowry and Colonel Gideon Morgan stormed and took the village of Hillabee, Alabama. In March 1814, he and his forces were instrumental in the American victory at the Battle of Horseshoe Bend. Cherokee warriors under Lowry's command decimated Creek battle ranks when they swam the Tallapoosa River and charged the Creeks from behind.

LYONS, OREN (JOAGQUISHO)
Onondaga
1930–

Oren Lyons became known worldwide during the last half of the twentieth century as a spokesman for the Iroquois Grand Council at Onondaga, as well as an author, publisher, and crisis negotiator. Lyons was lead author of the 1992 study of Native American constitutionalism, *Exiled in the Land of the Free: Democracy,*

Oren Lyons (center), *speaking as faithkeeper of the Iroquois Grand Council. [Courtesy of Marcia Keegan]*

Indian Nations, and the U.S. Constitution (1992).

Lyons enjoyed a successful career as a commercial artist in New York City before returning home to Onondaga, where he was condoled (selected) as faithkeeper of the Iroquois Grand Council. He edited the Native American newspaper *Daybreak* in the early 1990s. Lyons is also an artist of note and a member of the Syracuse Sports Hall of Fame for his activities as an all-American lacrosse player for Syracuse University in the 1950s. In 1990, Lyons organized an Iroquois national team that played in the world lacrosse championships in Australia.

Lyons was also part of an Iroquois Confederacy negotiating team that helped resolve the 1990 standoff between Mohawks and authorities at Kanesatake (Oka), Quebec. The confederacy's negotiators came to occupy a crucial middle ground between the Warriors and Canadian officials during the months of negotiations that preceded the use of armed force by the Canadian army and police at Kanesatake and Kahnawake. The Iroquois negotiators urged both sides (see Doug GEORGE-KANENTIIO and Louis HALL) to concentrate on long-term solutions to problems brought to light by the summer's violence. They recommended a fair land rights process, the creation of viable economic bases for the communities involved in the crisis, and the recognition of long-standing (but often ignored) treaty rights, including border rights.

FOR MORE INFORMATION:

Lyons, Oren, et al. *Exiled in the Land of the Free.* Santa Fe, N. Mex.: Clear Light, 1992.

Nabokov, Peter. *Native American Testimony.* New York: Viking Penguin, 1991.

$\mathcal{M}$

MACDONALD, PETER
Navajo
1928–

Born at Teec Nos Pos on the Navajo Reservation, Peter MacDonald's first language was Navajo. His father died when he was only two and he was forced to leave school after the seventh grade to work and herd sheep. At the age of sixteen, he enlisted in the Marine Corps and became a Navajo Code Talker (their coded Navajo messages confused the Japanese cryptographers during World War II). After being discharged from the Marine Corps, MacDonald attended Bacon Junior College in Oklahoma and earned a degree in electrical engineering from the University of Oklahoma in 1957. After working for several years in Southern California, MacDonald returned to the Navajo Reservation in 1963 to serve on the New Mexico Economic Development Advisory Board. At this time, he also became Director of the Office of Navajo Economic Opportunity (ONEO). As a result of his aggressive management style, he

brought in more than $20 million in federal grants from 1965 to 1968. This record led to his being elected Navajo Tribal Chairman in 1970.

During his three terms of office, MacDonald aggressively renegotiated mineral leases on the Navajo Reservation. He also tried to gain more favorable policies for the control of Colorado River rights. He always worked to keep industrial development under tribal control and encouraged a broader cross section of people to participate in tribal elections. MacDonald has been a vocal critic of the Bureau of Indian Affairs. Throughout his administrations, he faced serious problems such as the Navajo-Hopi land dispute. Although he was also subject to charges of favoritism and fraud, his achievements in fostering Navajo self-determination and energy use management are exemplary. MacDonald has served on numerous advisory boards and received many honorary awards. As a notable American Indian leader, MacDonald has been the subject of many news features in the U.S. media.

FOR MORE INFORMATION:

Klein, Barry T., ed. *Reference Encyclopedia of the American Indian.* West Nyack, N.Y.: Todd Publications, 1993.

MCCLOUD, JANET (YET SI BLUE)
Tulalip
1935–

A descendent of Chief SEATH'TL, McCloud is one of several Puget Sound–area Native people who defended their treaty rights to fish the rivers despite an assault by state game and fishing officials in the 1960s. She and others engaged in "fish-ins," which the state maintained were illegal. In 1974, a federal court decision by Judge George BOLDT led to implementation of the treaties.

Alvin M. JOSEPHY, Jr., described McCloud as "an energetic and forceful traditionalist, [who] believed in brotherhood between Indians and whites, but fought to get Indians to maintain pride in their Indianness as well." McCloud demanded that teachers and administrators in the Yelm, Washington, school district where she lived act to reduce prejudice against Indians. She advocated inclusion of a Native role in general history long before the multicultural movement in this century and has continued to be active in Native rights issues, especially fishing rights.

FOR MORE INFORMATION:

Josephy, Alvin M., Jr. *Now That the Buffalo's Gone.* New York: Alfred A. Knopf, 1982.

McCloud, Janet. "Fisher Indians in Fight for Treaty but State Refuses Recognition." *The Indian Historian* (San Francisco) 4:2 (May 1967).

MCGILLIVRAY, ALEXANDER (HIPPO-ILK-MICO)
Creek
1759–1793

In 1759, Alexander McGillivray (whose Creek name means "The Good Child King") was born at his father's trading post in the Creek village of Little Tallassie on the Coosa River in Elmore County, Alabama. His mother was Sehoy Marchand, the daughter of a French army captain and a Creek matron of the powerful Wind clan; his father was a Scottish trader by the name of Lachlan McGillivray. At about fourteen, the young Alexander went to Charleston, South Carolina, where he was taught by the Reverend Farquahar McGillivray. After completing his education, he served briefly as a clerk in a merchant house in Savannah, Georgia. On the eve of the American Revolution, Alexander became head chief of the Creeks because of his training and leadership talents.

As the Revolution's battles drew closer, his father, a devout loyalist, returned to Scotland while Alexander stayed behind. Consequently, he became a British agent with the rank and pay of a colonel. When Georgia officials seized his property during the Revolution, McGillivray allied with the English. During this time, it was said that he led a force of over ten thousand warriors in campaigns against American settlers in the Cumberland Valley and eastern Tennessee. His chief advisor and war chief was a Frenchman by the name of Louis Le Clerc Milfort.

At the conclusion of the war, McGillivray strived to build a united Indian front to fight against growing settler expansion. He also sought to promote his own trade ventures. In 1784, he negotiated a military and trade agreement with the Spanish in Florida as the "emperor of the Creeks and the Seminoles" and became a colonel in the Spanish army. Also, McGillivray and his partner, William Panton, secured a Spanish monopoly on trade with the Creeks. With arms supplied by the Spanish, McGillivray continued to wage a war of attrition against white settlers on the Cumberland River and in Georgia. Seeking to placate McGillivray, Georgia officials negotiated a $100,000 settlement to compensate him for property confiscated during the American Revolution. Although McGillivray was not considered a great warrior, he was a respected diplomat, trader, and leader.

In 1790, he journeyed to New York City to negotiate the Treaty of New York, which ceded some disputed Creek territory and made him a brigadier general in the U.S. Army with a $1,200 annual salary. But two years later, he repudiated the treaty and repledged his support to the Spanish in Florida for a salary of $2,000 and later $3,500. Over the years, he maintained very contradictory roles as emperor and chief of the Creeks, British general, Spanish colonel, and brigadier general in the U.S. Army; he was consistent only in using these positions to further the interests of his people while amassing personal wealth. A tall, dark, and handsome man, McGillivray was reputed to have the "polished urbanity of the Frenchman, the duplicity of the Spaniard, the cool sagacity of the Scotsman, and the subtlety and inveterate hatred of the Indian."

Never a very healthy person, he spent the last few years of his life suffering from various illnesses. On February 17, 1793, he died while visiting William Panton's home in Pensacola, Florida. McGillivray's assets at the time of his death were quite large. He had a home, Little Tallase, outside of Wetumpka, Alabama; several plantations; sixty slaves; and a large quantity of livestock. He was twice married. His first wife was Joseph Curnell's daughter, while his second wife was the mother of his son, Alexander, and two daughters. Throughout his rather short life, McGillivray corresponded with many friends and numerous public officials. After his death, the leadership of the Creek nation in the Southeast would never again be so adroit.

MCINTOSH, CHILLY (ROLLY MACINTOSH or MCINTOSH)
Creek
fl. 1820s–1830s
With the execution of his half-brother William MCINTOSH in 1825, Chilly McIntosh assumed leadership of the White Stick Creeks; thus, he became the chief of the Creeks' minority faction, which gave tacit approval to the cession of Creek lands in Georgia and their subsequent removal to Indian Territory. During his tenure as a Creek leader, he traveled to Washington, D.C., several times to bargain with U.S. authorities about removal and land cessions.

MCINTOSH, WILLIAM (WILLIAM MACINTOSH)
Creek
1775–1825
Born at Coweta, Carroll County, Georgia, William McIntosh was the son of a Creek woman and a Scottish captain in the British army, William McIntosh, who served as an English agent to the Creeks. He obtained a good education and became a tribal leader of the White Sticks (the pro-U.S. faction) of the Lower Creek villages. Although many Creeks were unhappy with American land cessions before the War of 1812, McIntosh sensed British weakness at the time of the war and allied with the United States and General Andrew Jackson. He was made a brigadier general during the War of 1812 and fought against William WEATHERFORD's Red Sticks from 1813 through 1814.

In 1811, at the Broken Arrow Council, McIntosh witnessed Creek elders enact a law that forbade the further sale of Creek lands. However, McIntosh and Creek leaders under his authority sold more lands in the treaties at Fort Jackson, Alabama (1814); Creek Agency, Georgia (1818); and Indian Springs, Georgia (1821).

In 1823, there was another proposal to cede fifteen million acres, so the Creek elders decided to enforce the Broken Arrow Law. By 1824, McIntosh and his followers had ceded about fifteen million acres of the twenty-five million acres that the Creek nation had originally held. In 1825, when McIntosh and other chiefs agreed to the Treaty of Indian Springs, he endorsed earlier cessions and included ten million additional acres to be transferred to the state of Georgia. Seeing no other course for McIntosh's perfidy, the Creek Council sentenced McIntosh to death for his crimes.

On the morning of May 1, 1825, MENEWA led a contingent that shot McIntosh and a companion as they attempted an escape from his house. Buried near Whitesburg, Georgia, on the banks of the Chattahoochee River, he was survived by his third wife, Eliza Hawkins, and a son, David. Previously, McIntosh was married to Susanna Coe (Creek) and Peggy (a Cherokee woman). After his death, Chilly McINTOSH (a half-brother) became chief of the White Sticks.

MCNICKLE, D'ARCY
Flathead/Salish/Kootenai
1904–1977

Born at St. Ignatius, Montana, on the Flathead Reservation, D'Arcy McNickle, who would become one of America's best-known Native authors, attended a Bureau of Indian Affairs boarding school at Chemawa, Oregon, in his boyhood. He then attended the University of Montana, Oxford University, and the University of Grenoble. McNickle also worked as a freelance writer and editor.

In 1935, McNickle joined the Works Progress Administration of the Franklin D. Roosevelt administration; a year later he joined the staff of Bureau of Indian Affairs (BIA) commissioner John Collier. McNickle then worked with the BIA until 1952. He was a cofounder of the National Congress of American Indians and was awarded a Guggenheim Fellowship in 1963–1964. He also worked as executive director of American Indian Development, Inc. In 1966, McNickle became a professor of anthropology at the University of Saskatchewan/Regina; he also served a year as program director at the Newberry Library's Center for History of the American Indian.

McNickle authored several books, including *The Surrounded* (1936); *They Came Here First* (1949); *Runner in the Sun* (1954); *Indians and Other Americans* (with Harold E. Fey, 1959); *The Indian Tribes of the United States—Ethnic and Cultural Survival* (1962); and *Native American Tribalism* (1973), a revision of his earlier title *The Indian Tribes of the United States*. He also wrote *Wind from an Enemy* (1978), a novel, and *The Hawk Is Hungry and Other Stories* (1992).

FOR MORE INFORMATION:

McNickle, D'Arcy. *Indian Man: A Life of Oliver LaFarge*. New York: Twayne, 1972.
———. "The Indian Tests the Mainstream." *The Nation* 203:9 (September 26, 1966): 275–279.

MCQUEEN, PETER
Creek-Seminole
c. 1780–1818

Peter McQueen was probably born on the lower Tallapoosa River in central Alabama. He opposed U.S. Army forces under the command of General Andrew Jackson in two separate wars. His activities worked to cause the Creek War, because he led a group of Red Sticks to Pensacola to gain guns and ammunition from the Spanish in Florida. Subsequently, in July 1813, he raided a party of settlers at Burnt Corn Creek.

After the end of the Creek War and the defeat of the Red Sticks, McQueen went south into Florida so he could join forces with the Seminoles. In 1818, Jackson overran Florida and seized St. Marks during the Second Seminole War. Fleeing Jackson's invasion, McQueen drifted farther southward; he is reputed to have died destitute on one of the Florida Keys.

MADOKAWANDO
Penobscot
c. 1630–1698

Madokawando, a sachem in the Abenaki Confederacy, was initially neutral in the British struggle with France in North America; but he allied with the French through one daughter's marriage to Frenchman Jean Vincent de l'Abadie (Baron de St. Castin), who founded a trading post at Castine, Maine. Madokawando also was angered at the spread of English settlement onto Penobscot lands. After British troops plundered the trading post, Madokawando joined the French cause. He and his supporters raided several British settlements, including York, Maine, where they killed seventy-seven people in 1691. For a short time, most white settlers were driven out of Maine by these and other raids.

Madokawando was respected as an enemy because he was humane. In 1689, during the siege of Pemaquid, he was responsible for sparing the lives of Lieutenant James Weems and six other soldiers. By 1693, he realized that despite his distaste for the English, they would eventually overwhelm the French, so he negotiated a peace at Pemaquid as other chiefs continued to raid English settlements and in spite of the objections of the French and younger Penobscot warriors. Madokawando's decision seems to have been influenced most strongly by Boston's growing appetite for furs.

MAGNUS (MATANTUCK)
Narraganset/Niantic
fl. 1670s

Magnus, a sister of Chief NINIGRET, was a principal chief of the Narragansets during King Philip's War (1675–1676). Magnus was married to a son of the powerful sachem CANONICUS. Her home village was near Exeter, Rhode Island.

Magnus, one of six Narraganset chiefs, allied with METACOM, a Wampanoag, and CANONCHET, a fellow Narraganset, in fighting the English colonists encroaching on what remained of their lands. Magnus was captured by colonial troops on July 2, 1676, after a battle near Warwick, Rhode Island, then executed. After her death, Magnus's chieftainship was assumed by MRIKSAH, who late in the century became a major leader from her village at Queen's Fort.

MAHASKAH
Iowa
c. 1790–1834

Mahaskah ("White Cloud"), one of the Iowas' most influential leaders in the early nineteenth century, probably was born near the mouth of the Iowa River. As a young man, Mahaskah moved with his father Mauhawgaw ("Wounding Arrow") from tribal homelands in the Great Lakes area to the western bank of the river that settlers would later call the Iowa.

After his father was killed by Sioux raiders, Mahaskah refused to assume leadership of his Pauhoochee band of Iowas until he had been tested in battle. Shortly after that, he brought home the scalp of a Sioux chief and claimed the chief's title. From then on, Mahaskah became well known as a warrior, taking part in at least eighteen battles, mostly against the Osages.

While attending treaty talks in Washington, D.C., during 1824, Mahaskah accidently stepped out of a second-floor hotel room window and broke his arm in the fall. He had been chasing one of his seven wives, Female Flying Pigeon, with a chair leg. According to an account by Thomas L. McKenney, Mahaskah was tired of his wives' squabbling. Female Flying Pigeon died shortly after that in a riding accident back in Iowa country.

Mahaskah was killed in 1834 by an Iowa that he had turned over to white authorities after they raided an Omaha Native settlement. He had several children by his seven wives; one of his sons, Mahaskah the Younger, assumed the chieftainship after his father was killed.

MALACA
Patwin
c. 1780–1817

In 1817, Don Jose Arguello, commander of the presidio at San Francisco, was ordered by the Spanish governor of Alta California, Vicente de Sola, to subdue the militant Indians north of San Francisco. Don Jose Sanchez crossed the Carquinez Straits under orders from Arguello and engaged Malaca and six hundred of his Patwin warriors in battle. After this bloody encounter, Malaca withdrew to the village of Suisun. As the Spanish approached the village, Malaca and most of his followers decided to burn their village and kill themselves rather than continue a life of slavery and oppression. A few people survived the holocaust and escaped to a neighboring village on the west bank of the Sacramento River.

MAMANTI (MAMAN'TE)
Kiowa
c. 1840–1875

Mamanti ("Walks in the Sky"), along with BIG TREE, SATANK, and SATANTA, decided to ambush wagons on the Butterfield Southern Route in Texas in 1871. Mamanti had prophesied that a very large wagon train would come by their path, so the Kiowas allowed a small army ambulance train past the ambush unharmed. Since the raid was based on Mamanti's shamanic vision, he was the leader of the ambush. When the larger Warren wagon train crossed the Kiowas' path, they attacked it, slew seven of the twelve defenders, and sacked the wagons. Unbeknownst to the militant Kiowas, General William T. Sherman had been a passenger in the earlier ambulance wagons. Consequently, when he received news of the ambush on the Warren wagon train following his route, he directed that military forces be redoubled against Kiowa and Comanche rebels. These orders caused the Red River War of 1874–1875.

As Mamanti and other Native American leaders (such as Quanah PARKER of the Comanches) entered the conflict, the locus of the war became the Staked Plain of Texas. At the Battle of Palo Duro Canyon in September 1874, Mamanti's group lost most of its horses and effects because of the efforts of a unit commanded by Colonel Ranald S. MacKenzie. In February 1875, Mamanti and LONE WOLF, as well as their followers, laid down their arms at Fort Sill in western Oklahoma.

KICKING BIRD, the chief of the peace party among the Kiowas, told the Americans to imprison Mamanti at Fort Marion, Florida. Consequently, Mamanti prayed that Kicking Bird should die. Within a week, Kicking Bird was dead—some say from poison, but others maintain it was due to Mamanti's powers as a medicine man. Shortly after his removal to Florida in 1875, Mamanti died also. Kiowa lore has it that he willed his own death immediately after receiving word of Kicking Bird's death, because he had used his shamanic abilities to end the life of another Kiowa.

MAN AFRAID OF HIS HORSES, YOUNGER (TASUNKKAKOKIPAPI)
Oglala Lakota
c. 1828–1900

Man Afraid of His Horses was an important leader of the Sioux during the 1860s and 1870s, at a time when RED CLOUD's people forced the United States to abandon its forts along the Bozeman Trail en route to the gold rush country of eastern Montana. The colloquial English translation of Man Afraid's name is really the opposite of its original Lakota meaning, which is "He Whose Horses Inspire Fear in Others." He is also sometimes called Old Man Afraid of His Horses because his son was named after him.

A hereditary chief among the Oglala Lakota, Man Afraid of His Horses was a war chief under Red Cloud during the war for the Bozeman Trail

Man Afraid of His Horses.
[National Anthropological Archives]

in 1866–1868. His son was a member of the Southern Cheyenne Warrior Society Crooked Lances and was allied with Red Cloud and his father. After the Oglalas' surrender and confinement to reservations, Man Afraid of His Horses served as president of the Pine Ridge Indian Council. He also made several trips to Washington, D.C., to advocate for the Oglalas. At the time of the Wounded Knee massacre (1890), Man Afraid of His Horses was working with AMERICAN HORSE for peace, against SHORT BULL's and KICKING BEAR's advocacy of resistance via the Ghost Dance.

MANGAS COLORADAS
Mimbreno Apache
c. 1791–1863

Born in New Mexico about 1791, Mangas Coloradas's people originally inhabited the Mimbres Mountains of southwestern New Mexico. The Spanish name *Mangas Coloradas* meant "Red Sleeves." He was also known as Mangos, Mangus, Magnas, or Magnus Colorado, Colorados, or Coloradus. He has also been called Dasoda-hae, "He Just Sits There." It is believed that he was married to a woman named Carmen who bore him three sons and three daughters.

Due to incessant Apache raiding on Mexican settlements, officials in the state of Chihuahua, Mexico, put a $100 bounty on Apache scalps (regardless of sex or age) in the early nineteenth century. Although the Mimbrenos' initial relations with Americans were friendly, this soon changed. In 1837, a group of American trappers invited the Mimbrenos to a great feast at Santa Rita then began to slaughter them for their scalps. To retaliate for such greedy and inhumane actions, Mangas Coloradas and his men killed most of the miners and trappers and raided nearby settlements.

In 1846, when the United States took possession of the New Mexico Territory, Mangas pledged friendship to the Americans and negotiated a peace treaty with General Stephen Watts Kearny. However, the Mimbrenos became upset when a boundary commission at Santa Rita forced them to return some Mexican captives while a Mexican who had murdered an Apache went unpunished. Tensions mounted as the Mimbreno Apaches retaliated by stealing livestock from the boundary commission.

In spite of these problems, Mangas signed another peace treaty in 1852. A few days after the treaty signing, some miners from the Pinos Altos mines seized Mangas and beat him with a bullwhip until his back was in ribbons. Subsequently, the miners released Mangas saying it was a warning for Indians to stay away from whites. Incensed by such barbaric treatment and convinced that whites were unable to keep their word with Indians, Mangas began raiding settlers in his homeland and travelers along the Butterfield Southern Route.

Mangas joined forces with COCHISE, who had received similar treatment at the hands of whites in Arizona. By the early 1860s, the U.S. Army had abandoned the forts in Apache country due to the Civil War, and the Apaches had a free hand in the Southwest. To secure the routes to California, Governor John Downey of California dispatched two columns east: one unit to Utah under the command of Colonel Patrick E. Connor, the other to the Southwest under Colonel James Henry Carleton. In July 1862, five hundred of Cochise's Chiricahua Apaches and Mangas's Mimbrenos stopped Carleton's advance company, headed by Captain Thomas Roberts, at Apache Pass in southern Arizona until Carleton moved his artillery up. Although the Apaches were powerless against the artillery, they still attacked small units.

While attacking an American platoon, Mangas was shot in the chest. The warriors carried him one hundred miles on a litter to Janos, Mexico, where a surgeon lived. Cochise told the surgeon at gunpoint that if Mangas died, the town would die. Mangas recovered from his wound and returned to the Mimbreno Mountains.

Although an old man in his seventies, Mangas responded to General Joseph West's offer of a flag of truce for negotiations in January 1863 near Pinos Altos. But when Mangas arrived, West's men captured him and took him to Fort McLane on the Mimbres River. While Mangas was imprisoned, West let it be known that he wanted the old chief dead. A witness reported that two guards put their bayonets in a fire and then placed the hot bayonets on the sleeping Mangas's feet and arms. Jumping up in pain and shouting at his tormentors in Spanish, Mangas was killed by the guards, who claimed he had tried to escape. After an inquiry, West later cleared all the soldiers implicated in the deed.

Upon Mangas's death, the Mimbreno VICTORIO and the Chiricahua GERONIMO assumed the leadership in what came to be known as the later Apache Wars.

MANGUS (MANGAS, CARL)
Mimbreno Apache
fl. 1860s–1900s

With the death of his father, MANGAS COLORADAS, in 1863, Mangus lost political influence to his father-in-law, VICTORIO, even though he was the hereditary chief. In 1880, he was in Mexico at the Battle of Tres Castillos when Victorio died. At this juncture, LOCO became head of the Warm Springs band. Throughout the early 1880s, Mangus remained hidden with other Chiricahua militants in the Sierra Madre of Mexico, only emerging to raid for supplies. But in November 1883, he decided to lay down his arms and was followed in early 1884 by CHATO and GERONIMO.

Dismayed about conditions on the reservation, Geronimo, Mangus, and Chato took their followers off the San Carlos Reservation and fled again to Mexico in 1885. Although Mangus stayed in the Sierra Madre region of Mexico after all the other Apache leaders had given up, he was finally seized without resistance near the Mexican border in October 1886. Subsequently, Mangus and his followers were shipped to Fort Marion, Florida, to join the other Apache prisoners already there. By the end of the 1890s he had returned to Oklahoma, where he died.

MANKATO
Mdewakanton Sioux
fl. 1850s–1860s

In 1853, Mankato ("Blue Earth") succeeded his father Tacankuwashtay as head chief of a village eight miles up the Minnesota River, near the contemporary site of Minneapolis-St. Paul. He signed the Washington Treaty (1858). During the Sioux uprising of 1862–1863, Mankato assumed command of the insurgents after the wounding of LITTLE CROW on August 22, 1862. He led Sioux forces at the Battle of Birch Coulee on September 2. A month later, he was killed as a cannonball struck his back at the Battle of Woodlake. The city of Mankato, Minnesota, was named for him.

MANKILLER, WILMA P.
Western Cherokee
1945–

Born in the Indian Hospital at Tahlequah, Oklahoma, Wilma Mankiller spent her early life in Rocky Mountain, Oklahoma (Adair County). When she was eleven, her family emigrated to California as a part of the relocation program of the Bureau of Indian Affairs. Her father obtained employment in California that barely provided for his large family of eleven children. Mankiller had firsthand experience with poverty in the city.

In the late 1960s and early 1970s, Mankiller became involved in urban Indian issues in San Francisco. She also acquired skills in community organization and program development during these years. In 1979, she completed a master's degree in Community Planning at the University of Arkansas.

After finishing her education she returned to Oklahoma in 1979. In 1983, Mankiller became the first woman elected deputy chief of the Cherokee nation. When the principal chief resigned in December of 1985, Mankiller became the first woman Cherokee principal chief and was subsequently elected to that office in the historical tribal election of 1987. In the late 1980s, Mankiller attracted media attention for her efforts on behalf of the Cherokee nation; Mankiller insisted throughout this time that her achievements in office could not have been possible without the support and hard work of many people.

Mankiller is married to Charley Soap, a Cherokee, who shares her interests in community development. In 1996 after ending her service as principal chief, she became Visiting Professor of Native American Studies at Dartmouth College.

FOR MORE INFORMATION:
Mankiller, Wilma. *Mankiller*. New York: St. Martin's Press, 1993.

MANUELITO
Navajo
c. 1818–1894

Born into the Bit'ahni (Folded Arms People) clan near Bear Ears Peak in southeastern Utah about 1818, Manuelito was not well known until he was elected headman after the death of Zarcillas Largas (Long Earrings). He was a noted warrior and married the war chief Narbona's daughter. Later, he took a second wife after a raid on a Mexican settlement.

Manuelito is Spanish for "Little Manuel." His Navajo names included Hastin Ch'ilhajinii or Childjajin, meaning "The Man of the Black Weeds"; Ashkii Dighin, or "Holy Boy," which he was called as a youth; and Hashkeh Naabah, or "The Angry Warrior," his war name.

At the beginning of the Mexican War in 1846, the United States quickly occupied New Mexico. To punish the Navajo for stealing livestock, Colonel Alexander W. Doniphan led his Missouri volunteers into the Navajo homelands. Since each Navajo headman was responsible only for the acts of members of his group and there were no centralized head chiefs, there was much misunderstanding between the Navajos and the whites. Hiding in their rugged terrain, and particularly in the recesses of their sacred place, Canyon de Chelly, the Navajos avoided any major military conflicts with the Americans. In 1846 and 1849, Navajo headmen negotiated treaties with the American government, but they avoided U.S. control.

During the 1850s, Navajo leaders such as Manuelito had become wealthy through agricultural pursuits, livestock raising, and raids. But disputes emerged over grazing rights at the mouth of Canyon Bonito near Fort Defiance between the Navajos and the U.S. soldiers. Although the Navajos had grazed their livestock for generations on this land, the army wanted it as a pasture for its horses. The Americans killed some Navajo horses; the Navajos took army horses to compensate for their lost mounts. At this point, Zarcillas Largas stepped down as headman, stating that he could no longer command the respect of his men, and Manuelito was elected as the new headman. In 1859, as a consequence of the continuing unease, Manuelito's home, crops, and livestock were destroyed by U.S. soldiers in a punishment raid for his people's past transgressions.

In 1860, Manuelito and BARBONCITO retaliated in an attack on Fort Defiance. Although the Navajos came very close to capturing it, they were driven back in a valiant defense by the Americans. Colonel Edward R. S. Canby unsuccessfully pursued the Navajos into the Chuska Mountains; Manuelito and his warriors used guerrilla tactics to wear Canby down.

In January 1861, Manuelito, Barboncito, HERRERO GRANDE, DELGADITO, and ARMIJO met with Canby at Fort Fauntleroy (later Fort Wingate) to discuss peaceful solutions. During this period, Herrero Grande was made principal chief and spokesman of all the Navajo bands.

Over the next few years, tensions remained high in New Mexico. In September 1861, fighting broke out over a horse race at Fort Fauntleroy. Navajos claimed that a soldier had cheated them by cutting Manuelito's bridle rein; officials decided to cancel the race. In 1862, Union troops drove the last of the Confederate troops out of New Mexico. In 1863, General James Henry Carleton became the new commander of the Department of New Mexico and made Colonel Christopher "Kit" CARSON his field commander with orders to confine all Indians to a reservation at Fort Sumner, New Mexico (a desolate area also called Bosque Redondo). When the Navajos refused the order to surrender, Carson and his troops began to destroy their homes, livestock, and crops. The devastation was enormous, and Navajo chiefs began to surrender in the fall of 1863, beginning with Delgadito in October. Shrewdly, Carleton supplied Delgadito well for the 350-mile trek to Fort Sumner. Delgadito then returned and persuaded other chiefs to follow on the Long Walk. By spring 1864, Navajos were surrendering by the thousands, but Manuelito held out. In February 1865, Carleton told Manuelito to surrender for the sake of his starving people, but Manuelito said no, and stated, "I have nothing to lose but my life, and they can come and take that whenever they please. . . . If I am killed innocent blood will be shed." Finally, in September 1866, he and his twenty-three remaining men laid down their arms; they were starving and in rags.

The plight of the Navajos at Fort Sumner was no better. While over two hundred Navajos had died on the Long Walk to Fort Sumner in the barren flats of the Pecos River, the survivors at Bosque Redondo fared even worse. With no food and clothing, over two thousand men, women, and children died of disease and starvation. Carleton's policies were deemed excessive by his superiors and he was relieved of his command. On June 1, 1868, the Navajos agreed to a treaty granting them 3.5 million acres and returning them to their homeland adjacent to Fort Defiance. From 1870 through 1884, Manuelito served as head chief of the Navajos. In 1872, Manuelito was also elected head of the Indian police force.

Although Henry Chee Dodge succeeded him as principal chief in 1885, Manuelito continued to be a strong force among the Navajos. When he died in 1894 at the age of seventy-five, he was one of the most respected people in Navajo history.

MARIN
Pomo
fl. 1820s

In the early nineteenth century, Marin became a chief of the Pomo Indians (Gallinomero band). In 1815 and 1816, he was defeated in battle by the Spanish; he was then seized and transported to San Francisco. However, he was able to escape his captors by crossing San Francisco Bay on a raft made from reeds.

Upon Marin's return, he kept the Spanish out of Pomo Territory by instigating more attacks.

In 1824, after Mexico took the rule of California from Spain, a Mexican army detachment commanded by Lieutenant Ignacio Martinez with Indian auxiliaries campaigned against the Pomos. Marin, with his warriors and the subchief QUINTIN, took a defensive posture near the mouth of San Rafael Inlet on two islands and held that position against the Mexican soldiers for several days before finally capitulating. Imprisoned for a year, Marin embraced Christianity and took up residence at Mission San Rafael in Pomo Territory. His death at the mission took place somewhere between 1834 and 1848. Present-day Marin County, California, was named for him.

MARSHALL, JOHN
1755–1835

John Marshall, as chief justice of the United States Supreme Court, was the author of several decisions that still define Native rights in the United States, most notably *Worcester* v. *Georgia*, which upheld limited sovereignty for the Cherokee nation in 1832. President Andrew Jackson, surrendering to states' rights interests in the South, ignored the decision and proceeded with his plans to remove the Cherokees to Indian Territory (later Oklahoma). Jackson's actions resulted in the Cherokees' Trail of Tears.

While Marshall's opinions were ignored by President Jackson, they shaped the relationship of the United States to Native nations within its borders through the end of the twentieth century. The 1934 Indian Reorganization Act and legislative efforts promoting self-determination after the 1960s were based on Marshall's opinion that the rights of "discovery" did not extinguish the original inhabitants' "legal as well as . . . just claim to retain possession [of their land] and to use it according to their own jurisdiction." Marshall defined Indian nations not as totally sovereign, nor as colonies, but as "domestic dependent nations."

Marshall had long-running political differences with President Jackson, and he agonized over the conflicts between states' rights and Native sovereignty. In 1831, in *Cherokee Nation* v. *United States,* Marshall held that the Cherokees had no standing at court to appeal Georgia's seizure of their lands. This situation troubled Marshall so deeply, he said at one point, that he thought of resigning from the Supreme Court over it. A year later, in *Worcester* v. *Georgia,* Marshall held unconstitutional the imprisonment by Georgia of a Congregationalist missionary, Samuel Austin Worcester (1798–1859), who had tried to advise the Cherokees on their rights. Historians disagree over whether President Jackson actually made the famous comment "John Marshall has made his decision, now let him enforce it." Whether Jackson expressed himself in those words is a moot point; his implementation of removal flew in the face of the law as interpreted by Marshall in *Worcester* v. *Georgia.*

In the decision, Marshall wrote, in part:

The Constitution, by declaring treaties already made, as well as those to be made, to be the supreme law of the land, has adopted and sanctified the previous treaties with the Indian nations. . . . The words "treaty" and "nation" are words of our own language, selected in our diplomatic and legislative proceedings, by ourselves, having each a definite and well-understood meaning. We have applied them to Indians, as we have applied them to the other nations of the earth; they are applied to all in the same sense.

FOR MORE INFORMATION:

Cherokee Nation v. *Georgia* 5 Peters 1 (1831).
Johnson v. *MacIntosh* 8 Wheaton 543 (1823).

McNickle, D'Arcy. *Native American Tribalism.* New York: Oxford University Press, 1973.
Worcester v. *Georgia* 31 U.S. 6 Peters, 515, 560 (1832).

MARTIN, MUNGO (NAQUAPENKIM)
Kwakiutl
c. 1880–1962

Like many other outstanding Northwest Coast artists, Mungo Martin also served as a chief. Born at Fort Rupert, British Columbia, Martin spent much of his time restoring totem poles that had fallen into disuse after the initial Euro-American occupancy of the Northwest Coast.

During the first half of the twentieth century, appreciation of Northwest art declined to the point that Martin and other artists had to work as fishermen to earn a living. By 1950, however, interest was reviving. The University of British Columbia hired Martin to restore old, decaying totem poles. He did that and also carved several originals himself. Martin used forty-foot cedar logs and carved them using traditional methods and interweaving traditional styles with his own. In 1956, the city of Victoria commissioned Martin to carve the tallest totem pole known, 127½ feet high. He also carved a one-hundred-foot pole for Queen Elizabeth of England in 1958.

Martin died at eighty-three near Victoria while fishing.

MARTINEZ, CRESCENSIO (TE E)
San Ildefonso Pueblo
c. 1890–1918

Crescensio Martinez was born at San Ildefonso Pueblo around 1890. His uncle was the noted artist Awa Tsireh. Martinez was married to Maximiliana Montoya, the sister of Maria Martinez (see Julian MARTINEZ). Martinez began his career painting pottery but turned to watercolors by 1910. With new artistic materials available, talented artists like Crescensio Martinez influenced many of his peers. He even signed the works of friends and colleagues so that they could fetch a better price.

Edgar Lee Hewett, Ph.D., of the Museum of New Mexico first gave Martinez paper and watercolors after observing him trying to draw on a piece of cardboard. Soon afterward, Hewett gave Martinez a commission to paint Summer and Winter ceremonial dances for the museum's collection. Martinez also did a series of paintings for the School of American Research in Santa Fe. In 1918–1919, his work was showcased at the Society of Independent Artists in New York City. In 1920, writer Mary Austin sponsored an exhibit of his works at the American Museum of Natural History in New York.

Martinez died at twenty-eight of complications accompanying pneumonia on June 20, 1918, during an influenza epidemic. During his short career, his vibrant colors, sharp detail, and two-dimensional representations of Pueblo ceremonial life revolutionized Pueblo Indian art. Euro-Americans had never appreciated American Indian painting until his shows at the close of World War I drew the attention and the enthusiastic support of Hewett, Austin, and a small group of devoted artists in Santa Fe.

MARTINEZ, JULIAN (POCANO or "COMING OF THE SPIRITS")
San Ildefonso Pueblo
c. 1883–1943

Born at San Ildefonso Pueblo in New Mexico in the early 1880s, Julian Martinez and his famous wife Maria Montoya had an enormous influence on ceramic art in the American Southwest. Julian painted on paper and animal hides until his marriage to Maria in 1904. They honeymooned at the St. Louis World's Fair, where he aided in the organizing of the Indian village

exhibit. Upon his return to New Mexico, Julian abandoned farming and found a job as a laborer at an archaeological excavation, where he was able to study prehistoric artifacts. Both he and his wife repaired and copied the designs on the excavated pottery.

Subsequently, Martinez was offered a job as janitor at the New Mexico State Museum in Santa Fe, and he and his wife went to the museum to live. Maria soon became homesick for San Ildefonso. Although they only stayed three years at the state museum, they made significant artistic progress there. Julian continued to paint and had several commissions for government buildings in the area. Both Maria and Julian enjoyed considerable success in selling their artwork in Santa Fe. This success convinced them that they could make a living at San Ildefonso from their art alone. In their experiments with ancient pueblo artforms, the couple rediscovered, about 1919, the process of creating a satiny black finish on pottery; this finish became their hallmark. Although it was also developed by neighboring potters at Santa Clara and Nambe, it soon began to bring the San Ildefonso Pueblo more income than its farm produce.

About this time, Drs. Kenneth Chapman and Edgar Lee Hewett urged the pair to sign their pieces for the benefit of museums and collectors. During the 1920s, the couple toured the United States and abroad, educating many about the nature of Pueblo Indian art. In 1933, they displayed their works at the Century of Progress Exhibit in Chicago, where they were awarded many honors. The couple had several children who also made a reputation for themselves in the art world.

Elected governor of the San Ildefonso Pueblo in the late 1930s, Julian Martinez continued his artistic successes in spite of alcohol problems. In 1943, he wandered away from his pueblo and was discovered dead of exposure on March 6.

MASSAI (BIG FOOT)
Chiricahua Apache
fl. 1880s–1910

In 1886, Massai, GERONIMO, and other Apache dissidents surrendered to the U.S. Army. Subsequently, Massai became one of the Apache prisoners scheduled to be taken to Fort Marion, Florida. In Kansas, while en route to Florida, he escaped from the train and made his way back to Arizona. There he seized a Mescalero Apache woman and engaged in raids on Mexican and white settlements for supplies and food.

For over twenty years, he eluded the army and the law in Arizona and Mexico. Mickey FREE, the noted army scout, pursued him unsuccessfully during this time. Massai Canyon and Massai Point in the Chiricahua National Monument in Arizona derive their names from him.

MASSASOIT (CUSAMEQUIN)
Wampanoag
c. 1580–1661

Massasoit was among the first Native American leaders to greet English settlers in what would become Puritan New England. His people, the Wampanoags, assisted the Puritans during their first hard winters in the new land and took part in the first Thanksgiving. Massasoit allied with the Pilgrims out of practical necessity; many of his people had died in an epidemic shortly before the newcomers arrived, and he sought to forge an alliance with them against the more numerous Narragansets. In 1621, Massasoit was described by William Bradford, governor of the Massachusetts colony, as "lustie . . . in his best years, an able body grave of countenance, spare of speech, strong [and]

tall." The father of METACOM, he favored friendly relations with the English colonists when he became the Wampanoags' most influential leader about 1632.

Massasoit also became a close friend of the dissident Puritan Roger WILLIAMS and provided Williams life-sustaining lodging through a blizzard during his flight from Boston to found the new colony of Providence Plantations, now Rhode Island. Williams met Massasoit when the latter was about thirty years of age and, in Williams's words, became "great friends" with the sachem. Williams also became close to CANONICUS, elderly leader of the Narragansets. With both, Williams traveled in the forest for days at a time.

By January 1635, the Puritans' more orthodox magistrates had decided Williams must be exiled to England, jailed if possible, and shut up. They opposed exiling Williams in the wilderness because they feared that he would begin his own settlement, from which his "infections" would leak back into Puritania.

About January 15, 1636, Captain Underhill was dispatched from Boston to arrest Williams and place him on board ship for England. Arriving at Williams's home, Underhill and his deputies found that he had escaped. No one in the neighborhood would admit to having seen him leave. Aware of his impending arrest, Williams had set out three days earlier in a blinding blizzard, walking south by west to Massasoit's lodge at Mount Hope. Walking eighty to ninety miles during the worst of a New England winter, Williams suffered immensely and likely would have died without Indian aid. Half a century later, nearing death, Williams wrote: "I bear to this day in my body the effects of that winter's exposure." Near the end of his trek, Williams lodged with Canonicus and his family. He then scouted the land that had been set aside for the new colony.

A statement of Massasoit's has served for more than three centuries to illustrate the differences in conception of the earth and property ownership between many Native American and European-derived cultures. In *Brave Are My People*, historian Frank Waters describes a "purchase" by Miles Standish and two companions of a tract of land fourteen miles square near Bridgewater, for seven coats, eight hoes, nine hatchets, ten yards of cotton cloth, twenty knives, and four moose skins. When Native people continued to hunt on the land after it was purchased and were arrested by the Pilgrims, Massasoit protested. "What is this you call property? It cannot be the earth. For the land is our mother, nourishing all her children, bears, birds, fish, and all men. The woods, the streams, everything on it belongs to everybody and is for the use of all. How can one man say it belongs to him only?" [Waters]

While Standish and his companions thought they had carried away an English-style deed, Massasoit argued that their goods had paid only for use of the land in common with everyone.

As he aged, Massasoit became disillusioned with the colonists as increasing numbers of them pressed his people from their lands. Upon Massasoit's death, ALEXANDER briefly served as grand sachem of the Wampanoags until his own death. Metacom, whom the English called King Philip, became grand sachem after Alexander.

In 1921, a statue memorializing Massasoit was erected at Plymouth Rock.

FOR MORE INFORMATION:

Brockunier, Samuel H. *The Irrepressible Democrat: Roger Williams*. New York: Ronald Press, 1940.

Covey, Cyclone. *The Gentle Radical: A Biography of Roger Williams*. New York: Macmillan, 1966.

Guild, Reuben Aldridge. *Footprints of Roger Williams*. Providence, R.I.: Tibbetts & Preston, 1886.

Waters, Frank. *Brave Are My People: Indian Heroes Not Forgotten*. Santa Fe, N. Mex.: Clear Light, 1993.

MASSE HADJO
Dakota
fl. 1890

After the *Chicago Tribune* printed an editorial that said that "If the United States Army would kill a thousand or so of the [Ghost] dancing Indians there would be no more trouble," Masse Hadjo defended the religion in a reply to the newspaper. It read, in part:

> I judge [that] you are a "Christian". . . . You are doubtless a worshipper of the white man's Savior, but are unwilling that the Indians should have a "Messiah" of their own. . . . You are anxious to get hold of our Messiah, so you can put him in irons. This you may do—in fact, you may crucify him as you did that other one, but you cannot convert the Indians to the Christian religion. . . . The white man's heaven is repulsive to the Indian nature, and if the white man's hell suits you, why, you keep it. I think there will be white rogues enough to fill it. [Moquin]

FOR MORE INFORMATION:

Moquin, Wayne, ed. *Great Documents in American Indian History*. New York: Praeger, 1973.

MATONABBEE
Chippewa
c. 1736–1782

Born near Fort Prince of Wales on the western shore of Hudson's Bay near the mouth of the Churchill River, Matonabbee gained notice as the Native guide who conducted Samuel Hearne of the Hudson's Bay Company on his unsuccessful search for a Northwest Passage between the Atlantic and Pacific Oceans.

Between 1769 and 1772, Matonabbee led three expeditions coordinated by Hearne, all of which were seeking deposits of copper in the Far North. Hearne found only trace amounts.

In 1782, Matonabbee hanged himself after a prolonged period of despair following the deaths of many in his family by smallpox.

MATO TOPE, ELDER (FOUR BEARS)
Mandan
c. 1795–1837

Mato Tope, Elder, was second chief of the Mandans when George CATLIN visited in 1832 and painted his portrait. Catlin said at the time that the elder Mato Tope was one of his favorite artistic subjects and one of his closest Native American friends. Karl Bodmer also painted the elder Mato Tope when he visited the Mandans two years after Catlin.

The elder Mato Tope was selected head chief in 1837, just as a smallpox epidemic was sweeping in with an influx of transient whites. On July 30, 1837, the day he died, an embittered Four Bears described the smallpox epidemic that was killing him and many of his people. The smallpox descended on the Mandans with a virulence that ultimately killed all but thirty-one of sixteen hundred people.

Mato Tope, Elder.
[National Anthropological Archives]

> Ever since I can remember, I have loved the whites. . . . I have always protected them from the insults of others. I have done everything that a red skin could do for them, and how they have repaid it! . . . They have deceived me! I do not fear death, my friends. You know it, but to die with my face rotten, that even wolves will shrink in horror from seeing, and say to themselves[:] that is the Four Bears, the friend of the whites.
>
> Listen well what I have to say, as it will be the last time you will hear me. Think of your wives, children, brothers, sisters, friends, and in fact all that you hold dear, are all dead, or dying, with their faces all rotten, caused by those dogs the whites, think of all that, my friends, and rise all together and leave not one of them alive. [Armstrong]

While some historians have questioned the validity of this account, the fact remains that Mato Tope, like most of the Mandans, died horribly.

FOR MORE INFORMATION:

Armstrong, Virginia Irving, ed. *I Have Spoken: American History Through the Eyes of the Indians.* Chicago: Swallow Press, 1971.

MATO TOPE, YOUNGER
Mandan
fl. 1850s–1860s

Mato Tope, Younger, inherited a Mandan chieftainship from his father, who also was called Mato Tope. He and leaders of several allied bands decided to isolate themselves from further contact with immigrating whites. They built a fortified stronghold at Like-a-Fishhook, a bend on the Missouri River in present-day North Dakota. This stockade later became a reservation as well as the site of Fort Berthold. Mato Tope, Younger, signed the 1851 Treaty of Fort Laramie in an attempt to establish a peace that was later broken by the Plains wars. He died at his stockaded village in 1861.

MAYUINNA
Nootka
fl. early 1800s

Mayuinna led an attack on the trading ship *Boston* in 1803 along the North Pacific Coast. The ship had sailed from England to Vancouver Island, where sea otter furs were traded from the Nootkas for sale in China. During the attack, Mayuinna and his warriors killed the captain and twenty-five crew members but allowed the survival of two men who they thought had skills useful to them. One was named Thompson, a sail maker, and the other was John Jewitt, a blacksmith. Both were held for more than two years and became partially assimilated as Nootkas. In 1806, both men escaped on the fur-trading vessel *Lydia*.

MEANS, RUSSELL
Oglala Lakota
1939–

In 1968, Russell Means was one of the founders of the American Indian Movement (AIM). Having graduated from Arizona State University in 1967 with a degree in accounting, Means moved to Cleveland on a Bureau of Indian Affairs relocation program. With Sarge Old Horn, a Crow, he formed the Cleveland American Indian Center. At about the same time, Means met with activists in Minneapolis; together they formed AIM, initially as a Native American effort to combat brutality and the selective law enforcement policies of the Minneapolis police. Their first action was the establishment of an Indian patrol to follow the police as they traveled through Native American neighborhoods. Arrest rates of Native Americans fell to the general average of the city just nine months after the AIM patrols were introduced.

Means, along with Dennis BANKS, served as a spokesman for AIM as it led one thousand to fifteen hundred American Indians and others into Gordon, Nebraska, to protest the murder of Raymond YELLOW THUNDER by a group of white toughs. Protests over the death of Richard OAKES (a leader of the 1969 Alcatraz occupation) at the hands of a prison guard in California also flared up in 1972. A new militancy began to emerge, and many AIM leaders believed that 1972 would be a year for change because of the presidential election and AIM's ability to focus national attention on American Indian issues.

During the summer of 1972, Means was among a group of Native leaders who planned the Trail of Broken Treaties caravan, which marched across the United States from Seattle and from San Francisco to Washington, D.C. Upon arriving there on November 3, 1972, the protesters found that lodging for them had not been arranged. They elected to stay in the BIA building, which they peacefully occupied for several hours until security guards sought to forcibly remove them. At that point, events turned violent. The protesters seized the building for six days as they asserted their demands that tribal sovereignty be restored and immunity from prosecution be granted to all protesters. Files were seized and damage was done to the BIA building. (AIM leaders claimed that federal agents who had infiltrated the movement had done most of the damage.)

After the occupation of BIA national headquarters in 1972, Means and many other AIM members returned to the Pine Ridge Reservation in South Dakota, where they organized the 1973 protest of Yellow Thunder's murder in Gordon, Nebraska. Shortly thereafter, AIM and its supporters occupied the tiny hamlet of Wounded Knee, site of the 1890 massacre that killed more than two hundred Native people. During the seventy-one-day siege, the site became a focus of prolonged media attention, and reservation residents became bitterly divided between supporters of AIM and those of Tribal Chairman Richard WILSON.

The struggle, which resulted in so many violent deaths, was also taking place within the realm of tribal politics. When Wilson sought reelection in 1974, Means challenged him. In the primary, Wilson trailed Means, 667 votes to 511. Wilson won the final election over Means by fewer than 200 votes in balloting that the U.S. Commission on Civil Rights later found to be permeated with fraud.

Following the occupation of Wounded Knee, the federal government made 562 arrests, which produced only fifteen convictions; five of those came on charges of "interfering with federal officers" while the convicted were trying to get through a federal roadblock at Wounded Knee. Means, for example, was charged with thirty-seven felonies and three misdemeanors after Wounded Knee. The forty charges came from seven state and five federal indictments. He was exonerated in thirty-nine of the forty charges.

After the confrontation at Wounded Knee, Means played a leading role in establishing Yellow Thunder camp in the Black Hills, a memorial to Raymond Yellow Thunder. The camp was also maintained by AIM and its allies as a source of pressure on the federal government to return the Black Hills to the Lakotas.

During the 1980s, Means supported the indigenous peoples of Nicaragua's eastern coast in their struggle for autonomy in Sandinista Nicaragua. In January 1986, Means was among a group of non-Nicaraguan Native people who accompanied dissident Brooklyn Rivera into Nicaragua. The group's campsite near Puerto Cabezas was bombed on orders from Tomas Borge, Nicaraguan interior minister.

In 1992, Means launched an acting career with a starring role in the movie *The Last of the Mohicans* (1992), based on the James Fenimore Cooper novel. In 1995, he provided the voice of Powhatan in the animated Disney film *Pocahontas*.

In early 1993, in an interview with *Indian Country Today*, Means recalled the role of AIM: "The part I am most proud of is [that] Wounded Knee was a catalyst for the rebirth of our self-dignity and pride in being Indians. The second part is, it alerted the entire world that American Indians are still alive and well with traditional beliefs and we are still resisting colonization." [Little Eagle]

FOR MORE INFORMATION:

Churchill, Ward, and Jim Vander Wall. *Agents of Repression*. Boston: South End Press, 1988.

Johansen, Bruce E., and Roberto F. Maestas. *Wasi'chu: The Continuing Indian Wars.* New York: Monthly Review Press, 1979.

Little Eagle, Avis. "Looking Back at Wounded Knee: Means Reminisces." *Indian Country Today* (February 25, 1993).

Means, Russell. *Where White Men Fear to Tread.* New York: St. Martins, 1995.

MECINA
Kickapoo
fl. 1820s

In 1813, Mecina refused to leave his people's homeland between the Illinois and Wabash Rivers when William Clark ordered the Kickapoos to remove west of the Mississippi in accordance with the Edwardsville Treaty. Mecina told Clark that he believed, with TECUMSEH, that one Native tribe could not be dispossessed without the approval of all Native peoples.

Mecina's band of Kickapoos resisted removal for more than a decade as warriors raided white settlements for stock, which was traded to renegade whites or other Indians for guns. Some of Mecina's warriors eventually allied with BLACK HAWK, while others faded slowly into other Kickapoo bands.

MENATONON
Chowanoke
fl. 1580s

As chief of the Chowanokes, Menatonon resided with his people on the Chowan River in what is now northeast North Carolina. In 1585–1586, he was taken prisoner by a group of English colonists under the command of Ralph Layne, one of Sir Walter Raleigh's first Roanoke colonists. As a result, Menatonon provided the colonists with information about the geography, indigenous inhabitants, flora, and fauna of the area. Since the English respected him for his demeanor and intelligence,

they released Menatonon within several days of his capture. Subsequently, Menatonon convinced the Weapemeoc chief Okiska to aid the Roanoke colonists. When the Englishman John White reported on the disappearance of the Roanoke colony in 1587, he mentioned Menatonon's wife. Little else is known of him from the historical record.

MENEWA (MENAWA)
Creek
c. 1765–1865

Born about 1765 on the Tallapoosa River in central Alabama, Menewa quickly gained notoriety among his people for his daring and numerous horse raids on white settlements in Tennessee. His Creek name meant "Great Warrior"; as a youth he was also known as Hothlepoya, "Crazy War Hunter."

As Menewa's wealth increased, his great rival became William McINTOSH, a chief of the White Stick Creeks, who instigated a murder for which Menewa was blamed. In retaliation, whites laid a Creek village to the torch, and tensions mounted along the Georgia frontier just before the War of 1812.

About this time, TECUMSEH came to Creek country seeking allies, and Menewa joined him and William WEATHERFORD against the forces of General Andrew Jackson in the Creek War of 1813–1814. In March 1814, at the Battle of Horseshoe Bend, Menewa was shot seven times while commanding the Red Stick forces. Of the one thousand warriors at Horseshoe Bend, over eight hundred were killed and most of the remaining two hundred were wounded. As he lay wounded on the field of battle, Menewa observed an American soldier looting the possessions of dead Creeks. Angered at this behavior, he took a rifle and shot the looter. In retaliation, the soldier wounded him again. Somehow, Menewa crawled to a camp hidden in the swamps, where Creek women and children awaited the outcome of the battle. Upon his recovery, he laid down his arms. However, his village was destroyed and he lost all his lands and personal effects to whites.

Menewa was opposed to removal to Indian Territory. In 1825, when Creek elders condemned William McIntosh to death for his illegal land cessions, Menewa was appointed to lead the execution party. The next year, Menewa journeyed to Washington, D.C., with OPOTHLEYAHOLO and Paddy CARR. Through complex negotiations, Menewa enabled some Creeks to retain some parcels of land. Before he left Washington, he posed for a portrait for the art gallery of the War Department.

A decade later, Menewa and many of his Creek warriors served with federal troops in the Second Seminole War of 1835–1842. For his loyal service, he was promised that he would not be removed to Indian Territory. In spite of this promise, Menewa was removed to Indian Territory in 1836 along with others of the Creek nation. Always feeling out of place in Indian Territory, Menewa died at his home there in 1865.

MENINOCK
Yakima
fl. 1910s

In 1915, a group of Yakima Indian fishermen were arrested by state officials for fishing in accordance with the terms of a treaty signed with Washington territorial governor Isaac STEVENS in 1855. Meninock thus became the first twentieth-century Native American to legally challenge the state's unilateral abrogation of the treaties' fishing rights.

The treaties had ceded much of the land but retained for Indians the right to fish "in common with" other residents of Washington. The Yakimas at first lost in state court but later

began a series of legal steps that ultimately led to the landmark 1974 ruling by Judge George BOLDT that enforced the treaties with regard to fishing rights.

After they were arrested, Meninock and Wallahee, another Yakima leader, recalled for the court the words of Stevens through the oral history of the Yakimas. They cited a conversation that KAMIAKIN had had with him. Stevens's pledge, echoed in the treaties, retained for Indians the right to fish at their usual and accustomed places.

MERCREDI, OVIDE
Cree
1945–

Educated as an attorney and as an expert in constitutional law, Ovide Mercredi served as National Chief of the Assembly of First Nations during the early 1990s. He was a leading voice for pluralism in Canada's efforts to adopt a new constitution. Mercredi was reelected to the office in 1994, after a contentious election in which his major rival was Akwesasne Mohawk Mike MITCHELL. The national chief represents 533,000 status (enrolled) Native Americans on 633 reserves.

Mercredi first became politically active in his home community of Grand Rapids, Manitoba, as he organized Native people against hydroelectric development that would ruin their way of life. He earned a law degree at the University of Manitoba (1977) and then practiced law for several years in The Pas, Manitoba. Step by step Mercredi became involved in efforts to recognize First Nations' rights in Canada's constitution. In 1990, during the crisis at Oka, Mercredi advised Elijah HARPER, a Native member of Manitoba's legislature whose negative vote defeated the Meech Lake Accord. This proposal gave special recognition to Quebec but not to the First Nations. Mercredi also became known for his work with the United Nations, including measures to protect the rights of children as well as those of Native peoples worldwide.

Mercredi pointed out that sixteen million people in Canada are neither English nor French. He believes that the "two pillars" of Canada, the English and the French, should be joined by a third, Native Canadians. Had that happened earlier, he said, "Your grandchildren and mine would have grown up with a different view of this country."

Mercredi also wrote a book, *In the Rapids: Navigating the Future of First Nations*, published by Viking in 1993. The book alleges that Canada has been negligent in addressing the problems of its indigenous peoples. In the early 1990s, unemployment on Native reserves in Canada rose to 70 percent. Alcoholism and abuse of other drugs was rampant, and as Mercredi's book was released, a wave of teenage suicides swept through Davis Inlet, Ontario.

In the early 1990s, Mercredi was living in Orleans, Ontario, with his wife, Shelly, and a daughter.

METACOM (KING PHILIP)
Wampanoag
c. 1637–1676

In 1662, the mantle of leadership among the Wampanoags fell to Metacom, who was called King Philip by the English. About twenty-five in 1662, Metacom distrusted nearly all whites, with Roger WILLIAMS, founder of the colony of Providence Plantations (Rhode Island) being one of the few exceptions. Metacom was known as a man who did not forgive insults easily. It was said that he chased a white man named John Gibbs from Mount Hope to Nantucket Island after Gibbs had insulted his father.

Throughout his childhood, Metacom had watched his people dwindle before the English advance. By 1671, about forty thousand people

Metacom. [National Anthropological Archives]

of European descent lived in New England. The native population, double that of the Europeans before the Pequot War (1636), was then about twenty thousand. European farms and pastures were crawling toward Metacom's home at Mount Hope, driving away game, creating friction over land that the Indians had used without question for so many generations they had lost count. By 1675, the Wampanoags held only a small strip of land at Mount Hope, and settlers wanted it.

Metacom grew more bitter by the day. He could see his nation being destroyed before his eyes. English cattle trampled Indian cornfields; farming forced game animals farther into the wilderness. He was summoned to Plymouth to answer questions, while other people in his nation were interrogated by Puritan officials.

Traders fleeced Indians, exchanging furs for liquor. The devastation of alcohol and disease and the loss of land destroyed families and tradition. These were Metacom's thoughts as he prepared to go to war against the English.

As rumors of war reached Williams, he again tried to keep the Narragansets out of it. This time he failed. Nananawtunu, son of Mixanno (the Narraganset sachem who had succeeded CANONICUS), told his close friend Williams that although he opposed going to war, his people could not be restrained. They had decided the time had come to die fighting rather than to expire slowly. Williams's letters of this time were pervaded with sadness as he watched the two groups he knew so well slide toward war.

Shortly after hostilities began in June 1675, Williams met with Metacom, riding with the sachem and his family in a canoe not far from Providence. Williams warned Metacom that he was leading his people to extermination. He compared the Wampanoags to a canoe on a stormy sea of English fury. "He answered me in a consenting, considering kind of way," Williams wrote. " 'My canoe is already overturned.' "

Metacom's Confederation (which included all of the Indians in the area, with the exception of UNCAS's Mohegans) ripped a trail of fire through New England's ninety settlements. Over half were attacked and a dozen destroyed. At one point, Metacom's warriors charged into Plymouth, the hub of Puritania. At the height of his victories, however, Metacom watched his confederacy crumble in intertribal squabbling.

In August 1676, the war ended. The Mohawks and Mohegans opted out of their alliance with the Wampanoags, leaving after the English had exterminated the Narragansets. Nearly all of Metacom's warriors, their families, and their friends had been killed or driven into hiding.

Metacom himself fled toward Mount Hope then hid in a swamp. When English soldiers found him, they dragged Metacom out of the mire then had him drawn and quartered—each limb was tied to a horse, after which all four horses were set off in different directions. His head was sent to Plymouth on a gibbet, where it was displayed much as criminals' severed heads were shown off on the railings of London Bridge. Metacom's hands were sent to Boston, where a local showman charged admission for a glimpse of one of them. The remainder of Metacom's body was hung from four separate trees. Metacom's head remained on display in Plymouth for a quarter century thereafter.

In terms of deaths in proportion to total population, King Philip's War was among the deadliest in American history. About one thousand colonists died in the war; many more died of starvation and war-related diseases. Every Native nation bordering the Puritan settlements was reduced to ruin, including all those whose members, in happier days, had offered the earliest colonists their first Thanksgiving dinner. Many of the survivors were sold into slavery in the West Indies. By doing this the colonists accomplished two purposes: removing them from the area and raising money to help pay their enormous war debts. Philip's son was auctioned off with about five hundred other slaves.

FOR MORE INFORMATION:

Church, Thomas. *Diary of King Philip's War, 1676–77.* Edited by Alan and Mary Simpson. Chester, Conn.: Pequot Press, 1975.

———. *Entertaining Passages Relating to King Philip's War.* Boston, 1716.

Cook, Sherburne F. "Interracial Warfare and Population Decline Among the New England Indians." *Ethnohistory* 20:1 (Winter 1973).

Drake, Samuel G. *The History of King Philip's War.* Exeter, N.H.: J & B Williams, 1829.

Ellis, George W., and John E. Morris. *King Philip's War.* New York: Grafton Press, 1906.

Howe, George. "The Tragedy of King Philip." *American Heritage* (December 1958).

Labaree, Benjamin L. *America's Nation-Time: 1607–1789.* Boston: Allyn and Bacon, 1972.

Leach, Douglas Edward. *Flintlock and Tomahawk.* New York: Norton, 1959.

Mather, Increase. *A Brief History of the War with the Indians in New England.* Boston, 1676.

Segal, Charles M., and David C. Stineback. *Puritans, Indians, and Manifest Destiny.* New York: Putnam, 1977.

Slotkin, Richard, and James K. Folsom, eds. *So Dreadful a Judgement: Puritan Responses to King Philip's War 1676–1677.* Middleton, Conn.: Wesleyan University Press, 1978.

Vaughan, Alden T. *New England Frontier: Puritans and Indians, 1620–1675.* Boston: Little, Brown, 1965.

METOYER-DURAN, CHERYL
Cherokee
1947–

Born in 1947 at Los Angeles, California, Cheryl Metoyer-Duran obtained a bachelor's degree in English (1968) and a master's degree in Library Science from Immaculate Heart College in Los Angeles, California. In 1976, she completed her Ph.D. in Library Science at Indiana University.

Upon the completion of her terminal degree, she did significant work developing and planning American Indian library services in reservation and urban institutions. She is the author of *Gatekeepers in Ethnolinguistic Communities* (1992) and was the recipient of the prestigious Rupert Costo Chair of American Indian Studies at the University of California, Riverside. She is the assistant dean of the Graduate School of Library and Information Science at the University of California, Los Angeles.

FOR MORE INFORMATION:

Champagne, Duane, ed. *Native North American Almanac.* Detroit: Gale Research, 1994.

MIANTINOMO
Narraganset
c. 1600–1643

A nephew of Chief CANONICUS, Miantinomo became the Narragansets' principal chief about 1632. He maintained an alliance with the colonists of Massachusetts Bay and with Roger WILLIAMS's new colony at Providence Plantations (later Rhode Island), begun in 1635 with Narraganset aid. Miantinomo even attended church with some of the colonists.

Despite his evidences of friendship, Miantinomo was suspected of provoking Indian hostility toward the New England colonies, largely because of statements made by UNCAS, the founder of the Mohegan tribe, who made a specialty of betraying hostile Indians to the Puritan authorities. In 1642, Miantinomo was imprisoned briefly by the Puritans, who scolded and then released him. After that incident, Miantinomo attempted to build an anticolonial alliance among the Indians. When word of the attempt got to Uncas, he turned Miantinomo over to the English, who sentenced him to die at the hands of Uncas' brother Wawequa in September 1643.

MICANOPY (MICCO-NUPPE, MICHENOPAH)
Seminole
c. 1780–1849

Although there is little known of his early life, Micanopy seems to have been born near St. Augustine, Florida, about 1780. His Seminole name meant "Chief of Chiefs," "Head Chief" or "the Governor," or "Pond Governor." He was also occasionally known as Halputta Hadjo or "Crazy Alligator."

When the head chief of the Seminoles, BOLEK (who was the successor to King PAYNE), died in about 1819, Micanopy became the hereditary leader. As a mature adult, he acquired large tracts of land and cattle. Like many other Seminoles, he employed over one hundred runaway African American slaves to till the soil and tend his livestock in the early nineteenth century. Through intermarriage, these African Americans gained influence in Seminole councils and some rose to the rank of war chief.

After the United States purchased Florida from Spain in 1819, Andrew Jackson became governor in 1821. As Euro-American settlers streamed into northern Florida through the next decade, conflict rose. Slowly the Seminoles withdrew from the coastal areas of Florida into the swampy hinterlands. Also, white slaveholders in Florida and in neighboring states began to press for the return of the runaway African American slaves among the Seminoles.

Pressures for removal mounted until, on May 9, 1832, a group of Seminole chiefs signed the Treaty of Payne's Landing, which ceded Seminole lands in Florida for lands in Indian Territory. Although Micanopy steered a peaceful course initially, he soon supported the younger leaders like ALLIGATOR, OSCEOLA, and WILD CAT, who forcefully opposed removal. After the slaying of General Wiley Thompson (the Seminole Indian agent) by Osceola, Micanopy in late 1835 attacked Major Francis Langhorne Dade's and General Duncan Lamont Clinch's units. With these events, the Seminole Wars began.

By June 1837, an aging Micanopy had decided to relocate to Indian Territory; however, Osceola kidnapped Micanopy in an attempt to stop his removal. Later that year, Micanopy was captured under a flag of truce when he came to sign a treaty with General Thomas S. Jesup. This breach of honor helped to create sympathy for the Seminoles among urban Americans. Micanopy was imprisoned at Charleston, South Carolina, and then sent to Indian Territory with about two hundred other Seminoles.

Although he sought to reestablish his position as head chief in Indian Territory, Micanopy never regained his previous power. In 1845, he was one of the signers of a treaty that gave the Western Seminoles some independence from the Creek nation. However, full self-government for the Seminoles did not come until 1855. Micanopy died at his home in Indian Territory in 1849 before Seminole independence could be fully realized.

MILLS, BILLY
Oglala Lakota
1938–

After entering the race as a virtual unknown, Billy Mills won the 10,000-meter run at the 1964 Olympic Games in Tokyo. His victory, the first by an American in an Olympic long-distance track event, is often recalled as one of the most astounding upsets in the history of the games.

Mills was born on the Pine Ridge Reservation and attended government Indian schools through high school. He then accepted an athletic scholarship at the University of Kansas, where he was a member of a track team that twice won national championships. Mills himself won the Big Eight Conference cross-country championship. He tried out for the 1960 U.S. Olympic Team but did not make the cut.

After college, Mills quit running competitively and joined the U.S. Marine Corps on an officer's commission. Fellow officers urged Mills to begin running again, and he won a 10,000-meter run in interservice competition. The Marines then sent Mills to the Olympic trials for the 1964 games, and he made the team.

In Tokyo, Mills's name did not arise in pre-race speculation over medal winners. After his surprising victory, some sports reporters did not even know Mills's name. He returned to the United States a hero but four years later was disqualified from competition because of an error on his application form. Later in his life, Mills became a businessman in Sacramento, California. He also remained active in causes benefiting Native Americans, particularly athletes.

MILLS, SIDNEY
Yakima/Cherokee
1950–

One of the first Native Americans in the Pacific Northwest to heed the call for fishing rights activism in the 1960s, Sid Mills arrived at that battlefront after service in Vietnam. He said in 1968, "We have already buried Indian fishermen returned dead from Vietnam, while Indian fishermen live here without protection and under steady attack from the power processes of this Nation and the State of Washington." Mills, a paratrooper, had been returned to the United States for treatment of injuries, but he became so upset over the treatment of Indian fishing people that he went absent without leave.

By 1972, Mills was coordinator for the Northwest for the Trail of Broken Treaties, in which the Survival of American Indians Association, which he helped form, joined with the American Indian Movement and other activist groups to march across the United States to Washington, D.C. Mills coordinated a portion of the march that began in Seattle. Mills often spoke for the caravan alongside Dennis Banks and Russell Means as it crossed the northern United States to protest treatment of Native peoples and for the need to enforce existing treaties.

FOR MORE INFORMATION:
American Friends Service Committee. *Uncommon Controversy: Fishing Rights of the Muckleshoot, Puyallup, and Nisqually Indians.* Seattle: University of Washington Press, 1970.
Moquin, Wayne, ed. *Great Documents in American Indian History.* New York: Praeger, 1973.

MITCHELL, MIKE
Mohawk
1947–

As violence at Akwesasne escalated to its 1990 peak, when the shooting deaths of Mathew Pyke and Junior Edwards provoked a massive police invasion, Mitchell was serving as grand chief of the Mohawk Council of Akwesasne, which governed parts of the reservation under Canadian jurisdiction. He was a key figure among the "antis," who were opponents of commercial gambling and Louis Hall's paramilitary Warrior Society at Akwesasne. Mitchell has also been a longtime treaty rights activist.

On March 22, 1988, about six hundred Mohawks accompanied Mitchell in a demonstration of Mohawk treaty rights that allow free passage over the border. They drove across the International Bridge in a blue pickup truck loaded with a washing machine, clothes, motor oil, and Bibles. Canadian authorities did not arrest him, even though they maintained that he was engaging in an illegal act. Mitchell said that Canadian authorities restricted border-crossing rights to crimp smuggling and thereby threatened legitimate crossings. The smugglers had tried to stop the march because it would bring attention to them.

Mitchell's position on the gambling issue was clear: "Our traditions are breaking down. Greed, money. It's hitting us like a disease. We need education, to be doctors, nurses, and lawyers. You don't need an education to pass out bingo cards. The gambling people tell me it's about time we gave it back to the white man. We got slapped; let's slap them back. They tell me you can't eat honor. And I look back at them and say, 'But you can live it.' " [Johansen]

On March 6, 1990, two months before the crisis reached its peak, Grand Chief Mitchell challenged the Warrior Society: "If you're going to kill someone, kill me." During a press conference, Mitchell showed reporters bullet holes in the Canadian Akwesasne police station house, as well as an assortment of shotguns, assault rifles, and ammunition the Canadian Mohawk police had confiscated from members of the Warriors over the previous eighteen months. He said that the reservation police force was outgunned by the Warriors. Mitchell also played a tape recording of a telephone conversation he said was made by two Warriors: "Mike is trying to get the people to get us to lay down our arms," one voice said on the recording. "We'll lay down our arms if he cuts his head off," said the second voice. "Ten-four," responded the first. [Johansen]

On June 22, 1991, Mitchell was reelected as grand chief on Akwesasne's Canadian side. Supporters of gambling turned out six "antis," however, splitting the council down the middle. After almost three years of struggling with a bitterly divided council, Mitchell resigned the head chieftainship on February 18, 1994. After ten years in the job, he said he was frustrated and worn out by increasing infighting. "Now those who have opposed me will have a chance to govern the reserve," he said. Later the same year, Mitchell made a run for the presidency of the Assembly of First Nations, which represents about five hundred thousand status (enrolled) Native people in Canada. He lost to Ovide MERCREDI, the incumbent.

FOR MORE INFORMATION:

Johansen, Bruce E. *Life and Death in Mohawk Country.* Golden, Colo.: North American Press, 1993.

Vesilind, Pritt J. "Common Ground, Different Dreams: The U.S.-Canada Border." *National Geographic* (February 1990).

MOHAWK, JOHN
Seneca
1945–

John Mohawk, professor of Native American studies at the State University of New York at Buffalo, has gained national recognition as a coauthor of *Exiled in the Land of the Free* (1992); he has also figured importantly in the recent history of the Iroquois Confederacy.

Mohawk compiled several reports for the confederacy during the 1990 crises at Akwesasne and Kanesatake (Oka). He wrote that frustration among the present generations of Mohawks and other Iroquois that gave rise to the Warrior Societies began during the 1950s, when the governments of the United States and Canada ignored Native protests against construction of the St. Lawrence Seaway. Mohawk traced frustrations running from the first contact with Europeans intent on imposing their languages, cultures, and religions as they took Native lands.

Mohawk served on an Iroquois Confederacy negotiating team that played an important role in mediating the armed standoffs at Kanesatake (Oka) and Kahnawake in the summer of 1990 (see Doug GEORGE-KANENTIIO and Louis HALL). The crises at Akwesasne, Kahnawake, and Kanesatake caused the Iroquois Grand Council to examine its procedures and the way it was perceived by its constituents. A year after the two deaths at Akwesasne, the Grand Council issued a complex report on its own operations, authored by Mohawk. It advocated establishment of full-time administrative offices at Onondaga and Grand River, Ontario, the site of the Canadian Grand Council. Representatives of other Native nations, as well as non-Indian officials and journalists, would thereby have greater access to Council chiefs, who often had been difficult to locate in the past.

FOR MORE INFORMATION:

Mohawk, John. *Exiled in the Land of the Free.* Santa Fe, N. Mex.: Clear Light, 1992.

MOMADAY, NAVARRE SCOTT
Kiowa and Cherokee
1934–

Momaday was born in Lawton, Oklahoma, on February 27, 1934, and was influenced by his Kiowa father's storytelling traditions and his Cherokee mother's love of English literature. Having lived in both American Indian and non-Indian communities as a boy, he attended reservation, public, and parochial schools. He received a B.A. in political science from the University of New Mexico in 1958, an M.A. in English from Stanford University in 1960, and a Ph.D. in English from Stanford in 1963.

He has taught in the English departments at the University of California, Santa Barbara; the University of California, Berkeley; and Stanford University. He was awarded a Guggenheim Fellowship in 1966 and a Pulitzer Prize for fiction in 1969 for *House Made of Dawn* (1968). His second novel, *The Way to Rainy Mountain,* was published in 1969. His other books are *Angle of Geese and Other Poems* (1973), *The Gourd Dancer* (1976), *The Names* (1976), and *Ancient Child* (1985). The themes that recur in Momaday's works include the celebration of imagination, oral traditions and memory, land as a fundamental part of Native American identity, recognition of the power of Native American concepts like harmony, beauty, and sacredness, and a respect for lan-

guage that engenders wonder, delight, economy, and power.

While non-Indians know him mostly through his novels, Momaday prefers to write poetry because he believes that American Indians express themselves more naturally in poetic and artistic terms. Although Momaday thinks that the general public does not know enough about the creative and intellectual accomplishments of Native Americans, he hopes that his acclaim will promote a greater awareness of the diverse abilities and talents of Native American people.

MONCACHTAPE
Yazoo
fl. mid-1800s

In the mid-1800s, Le Page du Pratz, a Frenchman, befriended a Yazoo Indian in Louisiana and obtained from him details concerning his travels through North America. Upon the demise of his spouse and children, the grieving Moncachtape ("Killer of Pain and Fatigue") decided to journey through Shawnee country along the Ohio River to Haudenosaunee (Iroquois) country in New York, and finally the land of the Abenakis in northern New England and southern Quebec. Back in the lower Mississippi Valley region, Moncachtape asserted that he had witnessed a group of local Indians attack and slay eleven Euro-American males. Although his travels and the ambush were never documented, Moncachtape's accounts showed a capacity for quite a number of diverse Indian languages.

MONTEZUMA, CARLOS (WASAJAH, WASAGAH, WASSAJA)
Yavapai
c. 1867–1923

Carlos Montezuma was born in the Superstition Mountains of central Arizona about 1867 of Yavapai Indian parents. His father was called Cocuyevah, but there is no record of his mother's name. At the age of five (about 1871), a group of Pima Indians seized him during a raid. Among the Yavapai he was known as Wassaja, meaning "Gesturing" or "Beckoning."

For a brief period, he resided with the Pimas on the Gila River, but a photographer-prospector by the name of Carlos Gentile soon bought him for about thirty dollars. At about this time, his mother, defying the Indian agent's admonitions not to leave her reservation, went out to search for her son, but she was shot by an Indian scout in the nearby mountains. In the meantime, Gentile took the young Wassaja to the East, where he was baptized as a Christian and given the name of Carlos Montezuma. Young Carlos received a good education in Chicago and then went to Carlisle Indian School. When Montezuma was about twenty-five, Carlos Gentile's photography venture failed and his depressed adoptive father took his own life in 1893. Before his death, however, Gentile gave the boy to a Baptist missionary, George W. Ingalls, who soon turned him over to the Reverend W. H. Stedman of Urbana, Illinois.

For two years, Montezuma received private tutoring and then entered a prep school for the University of Illinois; after just one year, he was ready to enroll at the University of Illinois. In 1884, Montezuma received a bachelor of science degree (cum laude). Subsequently, he went to the Chicago Medical College at Northwestern University with a partial scholarship and also worked as a pharmacist. In 1889, he received his medical degree.

Montezuma briefly tried private practice in Chicago, but he soon took a one-year appointment at the Fort Stevenson Indian School in North Dakota as physician-surgeon. After this appointment, he worked at Indian agencies in Washington and Nevada. In 1894, he accepted an appointment at the Carlisle Indian School and became a good friend of

its head, Colonel Richard Henry Pratt. He also befriended Zitkala-sa—Gertrude Simmons BONNIN—a Sioux woman who was a famous writer and Indian rights activist.

Montezuma returned to Chicago in 1896 and started a very successful private practice. He specialized in gastrointestinal disorders and was eventually invited to teach at the College of Physicians and Surgeons as well as in its Postgraduate Medical School. Throughout his adult life, Montezuma opposed the reservation system and its administration by the Bureau of Indian Affairs. He remembered the humiliation of his mother having to ask the Indian agent's permission to leave her homeland to hunt for her son. Governmental caprice and insensitivity to American Indians fueled Montezuma's fight for Indian rights. Montezuma considered it an insult that African Americans were made U.S. citizens after the Civil War while America's Native inhabitants were still legally regarded as aliens. Although he encouraged citizenship and assimilation, he also advocated pride in being an American Indian.

In 1906, President Theodore Roosevelt offered Montezuma the post of commissioner of Indian Affairs, but he refused. He authored Let My People Go (1914) and two other books on Indian affairs. He also established the Indian rights magazine Wassaja in 1916. In 1917, he was jailed for opposing the drafting of American Indians in World War I. President Woodrow Wilson released him and then reoffered him the position as head of the Bureau of Indian Affairs. Once again he declined, knowing that it would compromise his crusade for Indian rights and the abolition of the BIA.

Montezuma became a Mason in the latter part of his life and achieved the rank of Master Mason. Due to his taxing Indian rights activities and complications as a result of diabetes and tuberculosis, Montezuma returned to Arizona in 1922 with his second wife, Marie Keller. On January 23, 1923, he died at the Fort McDowell Reservation and was buried in the Fort McDowell Indian Cemetery in Arizona. By then *Wassaja* had ceased publication; but in 1972, the name was given to a new magazine by Rupert COSTO and Jeannette Henry to honor Carlos Montezuma's Indian rights activities.

MONTOUR, ART (KAKWIRAKERON)
Mohawk
1943–

Art Montour played a key role in the Mohawk Warrior Society (see Louis HALL) during the 1990 crisis at Akwesasne.

On July 21, 1989, New York State Police arrested Montour, a frequent Warrior spokesman, and charged him with using a gun to hold off state troopers and FBI agents during gambling raids the previous day. Montour, forty-seven, a former ironworker, called himself by his Mohawk name Kakwirakeron, as he said that the raid was a declaration of war. "It's upsetting when you're invaded by a foreign nation. You're on our land and our territory. You are the aggressor." [Johansen] Montour was charged with

Art Montour confronts New York State Police officers on June 6, 1989. [Akwesasne Notes]

forcibly impeding execution of a search warrant through the use of a deadly weapon.

On July 10, 1990, almost a year after the gambling raid that had prompted his arrest, Montour (Kakwirakeron) was sentenced to ten months in prison for conspiracy and obstruction of a federal search warrant. "It's not criminal to stand up and defend our people," Montour told U.S. District Judge Neal McCurn in Syracuse during his emotional fifteen-minute final statement. "You can't arrest the spirit that is in me, and all Native American peoples. . . . People in our community tried to find an economy to help us survive. You condemned it. You criminalized it."

Kakwirakeron continued: "You may be able to arrest my physical body. You may be able to injure my body. You may be able to incarcerate me. You may even be able to terminate me. But the spirit that lives in me and all Mohawk people who sincerely believe we have a right to exist here as equals, you cannot extinguish that spirit. The spirit of sovereignty will not be quashed by this court." [Johansen]

Montour's appeal for freedom on bond pending appeal was denied. He was led away by federal marshalls as his supporters shouted curses at the judge. "You are the criminal," Lorraine Montour shouted at Judge McCurn. "Don't let me see your face on the reservation again," she yelled at Jack McEligot, an FBI agent assigned to investigate gambling at Akwesasne.

Montour walked out of Allenwood Federal Prison, free after a ten-month sentence, one year to the day after Mathew PYKE and Junior EDWARDS had died by gunfire in violence related to his ideas and mission.

FOR MORE INFORMATION:

Johansen, Bruce E. *Life and Death in Mohawk Country*. Golden, Colo.: North American Press, 1993.

MOOTZKA, WALDO (MOOTSKA)
Hopi
1910–1940

Born at New Oraibi, Arizona, in 1910, Waldo Mootzka was the son of Tom Mootzka; his mother was a member of the Badger clan. As a youth, he attended schools in Albuquerque and subsequently took up residence in Santa Fe. Like many Pueblo artists of his time, he taught himself how to paint.

Although Fred Kabotie, another Hopi painter, strongly influenced his work, Mootzka's art had European influences as well. Mootzka's paintings have a broad array of colors and a profound sense of detail. Hopi kachinas were a major source of inspiration and creative sensibilities for him. By the 1930s, he had become a major Hopi artist.

Chronic tuberculosis sapped his strength, however, and limited the production of his art. Toward the end of his life, he took up silversmithing. In 1940, he died in a car accident and was buried at Oraibi, Arizona.

MOPOPE, STEPHEN (QUED KOI)
Kiowa
1898–1974

Born on August 27, 1898, on the Kiowa Reservation in Oklahoma, Stephen Mopope achieved prominence as one of five Kiowa artists under the mentorship of art teacher Susie Peters and Professor Oscar Jacobsen of the University of Oklahoma in the 1930s and 1940s. As a child, he was taught Kiowa ways by his grandmother. He also developed an interest in art at a young age. (His Kiowa name means "Painted Robe.") As a result of his artistic talents, his great-uncle, Silverhorn, educated him in the techniques of painting on hides. This process proved invaluable to him in later years.

He was such a promising talent that Peters and another art teacher, Edith Mahier, appealed to Professor Jacobsen to train him formally in art. As a result of his training and creative skills, Mopope became an artist whose works were exhibited throughout the country. He also was commissioned to do murals for the federal government, local governments, and businesses. He was known to be an accomplished dancer as well.

Toward the end of his life, he became less active as a painter and spent much of his time farming. In 1966, he was given a certificate of appreciation by the Indian Arts and Craft Board. His wife was the former Janet Berry; she bore him two daughters. Mopope died at Fort Cobb, Oklahoma, on February 3, 1974. Today his works can be found in many public and private collections.

MORGAN, LEWIS HENRY
1818–1881

A pioneer ethnologist who is regarded as the father of American anthropology, Lewis Henry Morgan provided the first detailed ethnographic account of the Iroquois in his book *League of the Ho-de-no-sau-nee, or Iroquois* (1851). While Morgan's was not the first detailed account of the Iroquois—Cadwallader COLDEN did one more than a century before him—Morgan's studies set standards for generations of scholars and inspired Friedrich Engels in his *Origin of Property, Private Property and the State* (1884).

Morgan was born at Aurora on Cayuga Lake in New York State. He attended Union College and later became wealthy as a corporate lawyer in Rochester, New York. Morgan was elected to the New York State legislature as he developed his interest in the Iroquois and his friendship with Ely PARKER, the Seneca who would later serve as Ulysses S. Grant's secretary and the first Native American commissioner of Indian affairs.

Together with other citizens of upstate New York, Parker and Morgan participated in the Gordian Knot, later known as the Grand Order of the Iroquois, an intellectual and social club.

In the middle 1840s, Morgan began publishing his research under the pen name "Skenandoah" in the *American Review*. Between the publication of his *League of the Iroquois* in 1851 and *Ancient Society* in 1877, Morgan became arguably the most important social scientist in nineteenth-century North America. Morgan also published *Systems of Consanguinity and Affinity of the Human Family* (1870). The effect of Morgan's work on the developing field of ethnology has been compared with that of his contemporary Charles Darwin on biology. Francis Parkman, the historian, admired Morgan; and Karl Marx read Morgan's *Ancient Society* a few years before his death, making copious notes. The notes were inherited by Engels and used to produce *The Origin of Private Property and the State*, which analyzes Iroquois political and social systems. Engels also held out hope that future societies based on a communist model would embrace Iroquois notions of social and economic equality.

After the Battle of the Little Bighorn in 1876, the elderly Morgan wrote in *The Nation* that the Sioux and Cheyenne who had obliterated George Armstrong CUSTER's army at the Little Bighorn were merely defending their birthright. Morgan's point of view was not popular among whites, however. And the army retaliated against the Lakota, Cheyenne, and others.

FOR MORE INFORMATION:

Morgan, Lewis Henry. *Houses and House-life of the American Aborigines*. Edited by Paul Bohannon. Chicago: University of Chicago Press, 1965.

———. *League of the Iroquois*. 1851. Reprint, Seacaucus, N.J.: Citadel Press, 1962.

Resek, Carl. *Lewis Henry Morgan: American Scholar*. Chicago: University of Chicago Press, 1960.

MOSES (QUELATICAN, BLUE HORN, HALF-SUN)
Sinkiuse Salish
c. 1830–1899

Moses (Quelatican) was an early leader of an Indian coalition that reacted to Washington territorial governor Isaac STEVENS's ruthless treaty negotiations in the Yakima War of 1855–1856. The name Moses was given to Quelatican by Stevens; the name Blue Horn was associated with the ornamentation of his headdress.

Moses was born at Wenatchee Flat in what would become Washington Territory, about 1830. He was a son of a major Salish leader. Moses led Native forces in a major battle at the Yakima River in 1858. After the war, however, he became a peace advocate and a personal friend of Major General O. O. Howard, the army officer who would later lead the army's chase of Chief Joseph (see JOSEPH, YOUNGER) and other non-treaty Nez Perces in 1877. During the 1870s, Moses declined several entreaties to ally with the non-treaty Nez Perces.

Howard, who came to know Moses so well that he once bailed him out of jail after Moses had been taken hostage by unruly white settlers, recalled him this way: "He was a very handsome man, tall and straight, and always well-dressed. He usually wore a buckskin coat and trousers, and handsome beaded moccasins, and a broad, light felt hat with a thin veil encircling it. He always had a leather belt around his waist, in which he carried long knife and pistol holster, the ivory pistol knob in plain sight.

"By his simple word," said Howard, "[Moses] kept many hundred Indians at peace." With

Howard's aid, Moses' band was given a reservation along the Columbia River.

FOR MORE INFORMATION:

Howard, O. O. *Famous Indian Chiefs I Have Known*. 1908. Reprint, Lincoln: University of Nebraska Press, 1989.

Ruby, Robert H., and John A. Brown. *Half-Sun on the Columbia: A Biography of Chief Moses*. Norman: University of Oklahoma Press, 1995.

MOUNTAIN CHIEF (NINASTOKO)
Blackfoot
1848–1942

Mountain Chief, the Blackfoot's last hereditary leader, was born on Old Man River in southern Alberta. Mountain Chief began his career as a

Mountain Chief.
[National Anthropological Archives]

warrior leader in 1866 at age eighteen, when he led a Blackfoot war party against the Crows at Cypress Hills. In 1867, he went to war against the Kutenai and survived a hand-to-hand fight with the Kutenai leader Cut Nose. In an 1873 battle against the Crow, he was badly wounded in one of his legs. Mountain Chief limped for the rest of his life.

Although aggressive in the face of the Blackfoot's traditional Native enemies, Mountain Chief was more accommodating to immigrating Euro-Americans. He made several trips to Washington, D.C., as a representative of the Blackfoot. He signed the Treaty of 1886 ceding the Sweet Grass Hills, and in 1895 signed away the land that now composes Glacier National Park. During his work as a negotiator, Mountain Chief met four U.S. presidents—McKinley, Taft, Theodore Roosevelt, and Wilson. He also worked with General Hugh L. Scott for several years to record Plains Indians' sign languages.

In his later years, Mountain Chief frequently assisted tourists at the Glacier National Park. He went blind late in life and died in 1942 at age ninety-four at his home near Browning, Montana.

MOUNTAIN WOLF WOMAN
Winnebago
1884–1960

The autobiography of Mountain Wolf Woman was initiated by anthropologist Nancy O. Lurie as a companion volume to Paul Radin's 1926 biography of her brother CRASHING THUNDER. Mountain Wolf Woman provides details of Winnebago life during a time of forced assimilation, when many Winnebagos traveled as migrant workers throughout the Midwest. Her story also details her conversion and that of several other Winnebagos to the Native American Church and its peyote rituals. As Ruth

Underhill points out in her foreword to *Mountain Wolf Woman: Sister of Crashing Thunder* (University of Michigan Press, 1961), this account fills in gaps in a history where the affairs of diplomacy, war, and other events recorded by historians concentrate on the lives of men, omitting the lives of Native American women.

MOXUS
Penobscot
fl. 1690–1717

Moxus, one of the most influential leaders among the Penobscots at the turn of the eighteenth century, led some of the most destructive raids on the northern frontiers of early New England. In 1689, he and the Baron de St. Castin routed English settlers at Pemaquid, Maine, capturing several dozen colonists. In July 1694, Moxus, his warriors, and their French allies killed more than one hundred English colonists in the Battle of Oyster River, near the site of present-day Durham. Several other deadly raids on a smaller scale followed.

Between raids Moxus professed a desire for peace as he signed various usually ineffectual treaties with numerous New England officials in 1689, 1699, 1702, 1713, and 1717.

MOYTOY (MOTOY)
Cherokee
fl. 1720s–1730s

During the early eighteenth century, Moytoy became the chief of Tellico village in eastern Tennessee. While seeking to secure the aid of all seven of the Cherokee villages against the French, the British emissary, Sir Alexander Cumming, turned to a Cherokee leader that he thought he could manipulate. In a ceremony in 1730, Cumming made Moytoy the emperor of the Cherokees. Despite Cumming's machinations, Moytoy continued to act independently and even spearheaded attacks against English outposts throughout the 1730s.

MRIKSAH
Narraganset
fl. 1640s–1670s

Mriksah was the eldest son of CANONICUS, the principal Narraganset chief who had helped Roger WILLIAMS establish Providence Plantations (Rhode Island). Mriksah assumed his father's role as principal chief in 1647. He married MAGNUS, a sister of Chief NINIGRET and a tribal leader in her own right. Mriksah also allied with METACOM, the Wampanoag leader, in King Philip's War (1676).

NAICHE (NACHI, NACHE, NATCHEZ)
Chiricahua Apache
c. 1857–1921

As a young man, Naiche (meaning "the Mischief Maker" or "Meddlesome One") led many raids against white settlers. When his older brother TAZA died of pneumonia in 1876, he became chief of the Chiricahua Apaches.

In 1879, Naiche resisted relocation to the San Carlos Apache Reservation and went to Mexico with GERONIMO's band. While ensconced in the Sierra Madre south of the Rio Grande, Naiche and Geronimo attacked American and Mexican communities with relative impunity. While Naiche was certainly the hereditary chief of the Chiricahua Apaches at this time, it appears that Geronimo was viewed as the great leader and probably persuaded Naiche, the younger man, to submit to his leadership during these campaigns. During the early 1880s, the U.S. Army relentlessly tracked the rebellious Chiricahua Apaches until Naiche surrendered on May 25, 1883, to General George Crook.

For a while, Naiche and Geronimo languished at the San Carlos Reservation, but in 1885, the two leaders left with over one hundred men in a last attempt to avoid American control. By September 1886, Apache scouts and detachments of the U.S. Army were able to force their surrender in the inhospitable terrain of Mexico. Soon after the Chiricahuas were captured, Naiche and Geronimo and their men were incarcerated first at Fort Marion, Florida, and then at Mount Vernon Barracks in Alabama.

Although Naiche and his men wanted to return home to Arizona, angry white settlers there prevented it. After Kiowa and Comanche leaders invited the Chiricahua Apaches to share their reservation, Naiche and 295 other Apaches relocated to Fort Sill, Oklahoma, on October 4, 1895. Naiche remained in Oklahoma until 1913. He eventually returned to the Southwest, where he lived in peace for eight years, dying of influenza at Mescalero, New Mexico, in 1921.

NAILOR, GERALD (TOH YAH)
Navajo
1917–1952

Gerald Nailor was one of the most talented artists of his era. Born at Pinedale (near Crownpoint, New Mexico) in 1917 of Navajo parents, he went to the Santa Fe Indian School where he was encouraged to develop his artistic capabilities. Later, Olaf Nordmark at the University of Oklahoma mentored him as well. In 1942, Nailor was commissioned to paint the mural in the Navajo Tribal Council House in Window Rock, Arizona; he was also selected to paint several murals in Washington, D.C.

While making a living as a rancher, he married a Picuris woman, Santana Simbola, who bore him three children. Nailor died at thirty-five when he tried to stop a Picuris man from beating his wife near his home at San Lorenzo, Picuris, New Mexico. Nailor was beaten severely, and he died from his wounds in a Taos Hospital on August 13, 1952. His premature death cut short an already stellar artistic career before its time.

NAKAI, R. CARLOS
Navajo/Ute
1946–

Born in Flagstaff, Arizona, and reared on the Navajo Reservation, Nakai is a noted composer and musician. He is a prominent Native American flautist and has worked to keep this form of music alive through his recordings.

In the 1960s, Nakai played the trumpet at first and then took up the Native American flute in 1972 when he failed to gain admission to the Juilliard School of Music in New York City. In 1979, he received a bachelor's degree in music from Northern Arizona University. Encouraged by elders to pursue the flute, Nakai met Ray Boley, the head of Canyon Records in 1982. As a result, he made his first recording, *Changes.* Subsequently, he has recorded numerous albums on the Canyon label including: *Winter Dreams, Carry the Gift, Spirit Horses, Natives,* and *Migrations.* In 1985, he played at the Magic Flute Festival in St. Paul, Minnesota. Presently, he is developing a theory and methodology that relates to the Native flute in its own context. Frequently, he collaborates with ethnomusicologists, composers, musicologists, and instrumentalists in his work.

FOR MORE INFORMATION:

Klein, Barry T., ed. *Reference Encyclopedia of the American Indian.* West Nyack, N.Y.: Todd Publications, 1993.

NAKAIDOKLINI (BARDUDECLENNY, BOBBY-DOK-LINNY, NAKAYDOKLUNNI, NOCADELKLINNY, NOCAKY-DELKLINNE)
White Mountain Apache (Coyotero)
c. 1845–1881

In the early 1880s, Nakaidoklini proclaimed a new and revitalizing spiritual message that focused on a dance that allegedly brought dead warriors back to life to aid in the resistance to white domination. White leaders, dismayed by his religious message, demanded that he be arrested.

On August 30, 1881, a contingent of army troops and Apache scouts sent out to arrest him approached Nakaidoklini's village at Cibecue Creek. After some tense moments, Nakaidoklini submitted to his arrest, but his adherents followed the army down the valley. When violence ensued, the Coytero scouts revolted and Nakaidoklini was slain in the resulting fracas. Subsequently, five of the Apache scouts were tried for mutiny; three of them were executed and the others were jailed for long terms.

Incensed by the army's treachery, Nakaidoklini's proponents struck Fort Apache but were driven back. Some of his adherents went to the San Carlos Reservation for sanctuary with the

Chiricahua Apaches. When more U.S. troops were summoned, Chiricahua leaders such as GERONIMO became alarmed and escaped San Carlos for Mexico to start a new revolt. The Coyotero Apache leader NATIOTISH led the remaining warriors against U.S. forces in the Battle of Big Dry Wash in July 1882.

NAMONTACK
Powhatan
c. 1585–1610

In 1608, Thomas Savage went to live with the Powhatan Indians to learn the languages and customs of the nations of the Powhatan Confederacy. Namontack, on the order of POWHATAN, went to live with the English at Jamestown to learn their ways. The English captain Christopher Newport helped to negotiate this important exchange. Soon, Namontack proved invaluable to the British by securing necessary supplies and averting hostile Indian attacks. Subsequently, he journeyed to the British Isles with Newport and became an able student of British ways. When he was returning to Virginia in 1610, a fellow Indian killed him in an argument on board ship.

NAMPEYO (TCU-MANA, NAMPAYU, NAMPAYO)
Hopi-Tewa
c. 1859–1942

Born at Hano, Arizona, about 1859, Nampeyo ("Snake Girl") was the daughter of Qotsvena, a Snake clan man and Qotcakao, a Tobacco clan woman. As a young girl, she watched her grandmother make the large *ollas* (water pots) and other vessels used in traditional Hopi village life. Her village was adjacent to Walpi on the first mesa and was set up by Tewa people fleeing Spanish oppression in the Rio Grande valley after POPE's Rebellion. Although the Tewas intermarried with the Hopis, they still retained much of their language and distinctive ceremonies into the nineteenth century.

Nampeyo was a stunningly beautiful young woman. In 1879, she married her first husband, Kwivioya, who left her soon after their marriage because he felt that he could not keep other men away from her. In 1881, she was married for a second time, to Lesou, from the neighboring village of Walpi.

About 1892, she began to revive the designs and forms of ancient Hopi pottery, which she felt were superior to contemporary styles. Initially, her Hopi neighbors scorned her work, but when they saw that her pottery commanded higher prices, they began to copy her designs and techniques. When the archaeologist Jesse Walter Fewkes employed Lesou in excavations at Sikyatki (an early Pueblo ruin) in 1895, the old pottery shards unearthed by her husband provided her with even more classical designs. Subsequently, she visited archaeological sites at nearby Awatovi, Payupki, and Tsukuvi to expand her knowledge of ancient styles. Using these broken bits of pottery, she created her own motifs rooted in ancient Hopi forms. As her pottery improved, it took on the fluid, bold style that distinguishes her work.

By the end of the nineteenth century, Nampeyo had become a prominent Indian artist. In 1898 and 1910, she journeyed to Chicago to promote her work. In 1904 and 1907, she was employed by the Fred Harvey Company (a western hotel company) at their Grand Canyon lodge. Her partnership with Fred Harvey made her a figure of international renown. The Smithsonian Institution began to collect her work as well.

Through Nampeyo's efforts, Hopi pottery was elevated to an art form. When she began her work, few Hopi women still produced pots, but she single-handedly revived the craft and enhanced its esthetics. In the early 1930s, she began to go blind; she could no longer create the remarkable, precise, fine, and fluid decorations that were her hallmark. For a while her husband helped her create her art in her declining years, but he died in 1932. Her four daughters (Annie, Cecilia, Fannie, and Nellie) were also renowned potters in their own right. Nampeyo died at her home on July 20, 1942.

NANA (NANAY or NANE)
Mimbreno Apache
c. 1810–c. 1895

Nana's military pursuits encompassed the period from the 1860s to the 1880s. He fought throughout the Apache Wars from the 1860s to 1880s with most of the famous Apache leaders, including MANGAS COLORADAS, VICTORIO, and GERONIMO. In 1880, when Victorio died in Mexico, Nana became chief of the more militant Apaches, while the moderates supported the leadership of LOCO.

In summer 1881, an aging Nana with about fifteen Mimbrenos and two dozen Mescaleros began raids on settlers and attacked an army wagon train. Traversing more than twelve hundred miles, Nana's band engaged in eight battles

Nana (seated center, in shadow), with Geronimo seated to his right, meets with U.S. Army representatives. [Nebraska State Historical Society]

that summer, slaying seventy-five to one hundred whites and seizing several hundred head of livestock. As a result of these depredations, the Ninth Cavalry under Colonel Edward Hatch and several citizen's posses were dispatched to subdue Nana and his followers. Fleeing back across the Rio Grande into the Sierra Madre of Mexico, he combined his forces with Geronimo, Loco, JUH, NAICHE, and CHATO. All had recently left the San Carlos Apache Reservation in Arizona. In 1882, Nana was captured and forced to settle on the San Carlos Reservation, but in 1885 he fled San Carlos for the Sierra Madre once again with Geronimo, Naiche, and several other chiefs. After eluding capture for about a year, he surrendered for the last time in March 1886.

Initially, Nana and many other militant Apache war chiefs were shipped to Florida. Eventually, he ended up at Fort Sill in Indian Territory, where he was given some land. It was at Fort Sill, while in his eighties and still resisting white control, that Nana died around 1895. He is buried in the Apache cemetery outside of Fort Sill.

NATIOTISH (NANTIATISH, NANTIOTISH)
White Mountain Apache (Coyotero)
fl. 1880s

Angered by the slaying of NAKAIDOKLINI near Fort Apache, Arizona, and the carnage at Cibecue Creek in 1881, many White Mountain Apaches kept up their resistance to American domination (these events helped Geronimo to renew his opposition to the U.S. government). Natiotish became the leader of these militant Coyotero Apaches.

On July 6, 1882, a White Mountain Apache contingent slew four Indian agency policemen. Among the dead was "Cibecue Charley" Colvig, chief of police. With about fifty men, Natiotish attacked settlers all along the Tonto Mogollan Rim. He set up an ambush on July 17,

1882, but Albert Sieber, a scout, saw the trap and alerted a force commanded by Major Andrew Evans. Evans formed a battle column at the edge of the canyon, pinning the Apaches down. Next, Evans sent two flanking actions around the canyon. The resulting attacks mortally wounded at least twenty-seven warriors and Natiotish seems to have been one of the casualties. The remaining Apaches dispersed and then filtered back onto the White Mountain Reservation in the ensuing weeks.

This skirmish, called the Battle of Big Dry Wash, was a stinging setback for the Apaches and one of the few military confrontations in which Apache men set aside their guerrilla tactics to engage in a pitched battle. As a result, most militant Apache bands abandoned their resistance to U.S. control and settled on government reservations. Only the Chiricahuas and Mimbrenos continued their resistance after this defeat.

NAWKAW (WALKING TURTLE)
Winnebago
c. 1736–1833

Born near present-day Green Bay, Wisconsin, Nawkaw rallied significant numbers of Winnebagos to the British cause in the War of 1812, in which he fought with TECUMSEH at the Battle of the Thames. After that war ended, he made peace with white immigrants, signing several treaties, as he refused BLACK HAWK's call to war in 1832. He also helped negotiate peace between immigrants and RED BIRD's followers.

NEAMATHLA (INNEMATHLA, NEAH EMARTHLA, NEHE MARTHLA)
Miccosukee/Seminole
fl. 1800s

Though born a Creek, Neamathla achieved historical note as a Miccosukee leader among the

Nawkaw. [National Anthropological Archives]

Seminoles. By 1817, it is reported that he demanded that Anglos cease their encroachment on Native American lands in the Southeast. Defying Neamathla's admonitions, soldiers from Georgia, in the service of General Edmund Pendleton Gaines, sacked his settlement (Fowltown) in the Florida Panhandle. This brutal attack helped to cause the First Seminole War (1817–1818).

After the war was over and some Seminoles resettled near Tallahassee, the U.S. government in 1821 made Neamathla a principal Seminole chief. In spite of this edict by federal authorities, many traditional Seminoles still acknowledged MICANOPY as their leader. In September 1823, Neamathla and thirty-two other signatories agreed to the Treaty of Moultrie Creek (Camp Moultrie), which relinquished around five million acres in Florida to the Americans. In 1826, however, he declined the U.S. government's $1,000 payment to construct an academy for Seminole children; he felt that his nation should develop its own schools. Furthermore, Neamathla opposed Seminole relocation to Indian Territory, so he was relieved of his principal chief duties by federal officials. As a result, he relocated to southern Alabama and became a member of the Creek Tribal Council, where he rejected removal from the Southeast and raided white settlements in the area. In 1836, Alabama militiamen seized him and sent him west to Indian Territory in shackles. Like many Creek leaders of the time, he was known as an able and persuasive orator.

NEAPOPE
Sac
fl. 1820s

Neapope was a spiritual leader consulted by BLACK HAWK about 1820 when he was deciding whether to make war against encroaching Euro-Americans or move his supporters, with his fellow Sauk chief KEOKUK, from Illinois into Iowa. Neapope advised Black Hawk that other tribes, specifically the Potawatomis and Winnebagos, would help defend his land, a promise that drew few supporters to Black Hawk's cause.

During the ensuing war, Neapope served as one of Black Hawk's top military leaders. Neapope also distinguished himself as a warrior as he led Native forces during the Battle of Wisconsin Heights, near contemporary Sauk City, Wisconsin. His strategy was credited with holding off a large enemy militia while Indians allied with him crossed the Wisconsin River to temporary safety. As the war wound down, Neapope was captured by Keokuk, Black Hawk's rival, who was cooperating with the immigrating whites. Neapope was imprisoned briefly with Black Hawk; they rejoined the Sauks in Iowa several weeks later after their release by President Andrew Jackson.

NEMACOLIN
Delaware
fl. mid-1700s

Nemacolin was hired by explorers Christopher Gist and Thomas Cresap to establish a trail across the Appalachian Mountains from the headwaters of the Potomac River to the source of the Monongahela. The trail, called Nemacolin's Path, was used in cross-mountain forays by George Washington in 1754 and by the English general Edward Braddock in 1755 during the early years of the French and Indian War. Later it became a leg of the United States' National Road.

NIMHAM
Wappinger
fl. mid-1700s

Nimham was a leader of a Wappinger band in Westenhuck, New York, who allied with Sir William JOHNSON and the British against the French in the last of several colonial wars in North America (1754–1763). He took part in the Battle of Lake George on September 8, 1755, at which HENDRICK was killed.

As the war with France neared its conclusion, Nimham traveled to England with other Native leaders, principally Connecticut Mohegans, to seek the return of lands they contended had been illegally taken by English colonists. The American Revolution intervened, and the legal actions filed by Nimham and others never were heard in court. Nimham joined the patriots during the Revolution and was killed fighting on their behalf at Kingsbridge, New York, on August 3, 1778.

NINIGRET
Niantic
c. 1600–1678

Ninigret became a chief at Wekapaug (now Westerly), Rhode Island, in the early seventeenth century and waged a delicate diplomatic balancing act between enemy tribes and English settlers that allowed his people to retain their lands until his death.

Like the Narraganset MIANTINOMO, his cousin and ally, Ninigret was implicated by the Mohegan leader UNCAS as a conspirator against the English colonies during the 1640s and 1650s. After Uncas executed Miantinomo in 1643, Ninigret declared war on Uncas and his English collaborators but was forced to admit defeat and sign a treaty in 1647. Rumors that he wanted to revive a hostile Pequot Confederacy persisted, however. Uncas insisted that Ninigret was plotting to kill him and to bring the Mohawks into war against the English and Mohegans.

While he resisted English encroachment, Ninigret was also an enemy of the powerful Wampanoag chief METACOM and refused to ally with him in King Philip's War. Ninigret also rebuffed several English attempts to convert him to Christianity; he insisted that he would adopt Christianity only when the English began to follow Christ's teachings in their relationships with Native peoples.

A statue in memory of Ninigret stands at Watch Hill, Rhode Island.

NOCONA, PETA (NOKONI)
Comanche
c. 1815–c. 1861

Knowledge of Peta Nocona's birth and parentage is nonexistent, but it is known that his Comanche name meant "the Wanderer" or "Lone Camper." He was reported in 1836 to be a leader of the Quahadi Comanche that raided Fort Parker, Texas. During that raid, several white settlers were taken, including Cynthia Ann Parker, aged nine. Subsequently, Cynthia Parker was adopted into the Comanche nation and named Preloch. Several years after her capture, Cynthia Parker married Nocona and bore him several children, including Quanah PARKER. Apparently, Nocona and Cynthia Parker loved each other very deeply, because Nocona took no other wives during the rest of his life (traditionally, Comanche men took more than one wife). Nocona and his family had a traditional Comanche life with the men hunting, raiding, and frequently moving their camp.

A group of Texas Rangers led by Captain Sul Ross brutally attacked Nocona's camp in December 1860, while many of the men were away hunting. While most of the Comanche women and children were killed by the Rangers immediately, a few, including Cynthia Parker Nocona, survived the awful slaughter. Consequently, the Rangers returned her to the Parker family (who tried unsuccessfully to convince her to adopt white ways again), and she was held there as a virtual prisoner. After unsuccessfully trying to escape to her Comanche husband and children, she died at her parents' house about a year later, it was said, of a broken heart. Peta Nocona never saw his wife again after she was taken from him. He died in 1861 at Antelope Hills, a year after his wife's capture, from an infected wound. The lost love of Cynthia Parker and Peta Nocona and their tragic deaths so soon after their forced separation became part of the romantic lore of the frontier.

OACPICAGIGUA, LUIS
Pima
fl. 1750s

Luis Oacpicagigua was a captain general in a Spanish campaign against the Seri Indians. When he saw the enormous growth of mining on Pima lands and the effects of coerced labor on Indian workers, he clandestinely devised a revolt among the Papagos, Sobaipuris, Apaches, and Pimas.

On the evening of November 20, 1751, Oacpicagigua and his insurgents killed eighteen people. During the ensuing weeks of the uprising, the Indians struck and laid waste a number of missions and rancherias (Caborca, Sonoita, Bac, and Guevavi). However, the Apaches and Sobaipuris did not join the insurrection. Fearing Spanish retaliation, many Papagos and Pimas also refused to enter the revolt.

Subsequently, Spanish leaders pressed presidio captains and their contingents into the field, and they managed to defeat the rebel groups within a few months. They seized and killed many militants (one a close relative of Oacpicagigua). Oacpicagigua bargained for his own freedom by promising to supervise the reconstruction of war-ravaged churches; however, he did not follow through with these promises after the end of the revolt.

OAKES, RICHARD
Mohawk
1942–1972

Richard Oakes was among the leaders of the occupation of Alcatraz Island (1969) and was murdered shortly thereafter under mysterious circumstances. His death helped inspire plans for the 1972 cross-country march called the Trail of Broken Treaties.

As a leader of the Iroquois traveling troupe White Roots of Peace in the late 1960s, Oakes's visit to San Francisco with the group in 1969 had an electrifying effect on local Native Americans (out of which sprang plans to occupy Alcatraz under a century-old law that gives Indians first option on U.S. government land that has been declared surplus). Oakes also played an important role in establishing early

Native American studies programs at several California colleges and universities. Oakes worked to restore ancestral lands to the Pitt River and Pomo Indians of California.

Oakes was shot to death while walking along a dirt road near a YMCA camp outside Santa Rosa, California. Michael Oliver Morgan, a camp caretaker, was charged with manslaughter in Oakes's death but acquitted by a district court jury on March 16, 1973. Defenders of Oakes asserted that he was murdered for his advocacy of treaty rights, while Morgan's attorney said Oakes had jumped his client from a bush.

A week after Oakes's murder sent shock waves through Native American activist circles, in late September 1972, about fifty people met in Denver to formulate plans for the cross-country trek they named the Trail of Broken Treaties (see Russell MEANS), which reached Washington, D.C., in early November and occupied the Bureau of Indian Affairs' head office.

FOR MORE INFORMATION:

Johansen, Bruce E., and Roberto F. Maestas. *Was'chu: The Continuing Indian Wars.* New York: Monthly Review Press, 1979.

OCCUM, SAMSON
Mohegan
c. 1722–1792

Samson Occum, the first Native American to preach Christianity in English, traveled to England in 1765 on behalf of Dr. Wheelock's Indian Charity School in Connecticut. He dined with Lord Dartmouth and met King George III as he raised £12,000 sterling for the charity school—enough funds to turn it into Dartmouth College.

Born near New London, Connecticut, Occum was ordained in 1759 and served as a missionary to the Oneidas from 1759 to 1763. As he matured, Occum developed intense personal

differences with Wheelock; he opposed the establishment of Dartmouth College and the move to New Hampshire. Occum's relationship with Wheelock ended in 1768.

Following the breakup with Wheelock, Occum continued his mission to various Indian peoples, preaching a gospel that upheld Native rights. He established Brothertown, a community of Christianized New England Indians who were determined to live outside of white influence. Occum published an Indian hymnal and authored two hymns himself. At New Haven, he delivered an anti-alcohol sermon that was published in nineteen editions. Occum served as pastor at Brothertown until his death in 1792.

FOR MORE INFORMATION:

Blodgett, Harold W. *Samson Occum.* Hanover, N.H., 1936.

Love, W. D. L. *Samson Occum and the Christian Indians of New England.* Boston, 1899.

Occum, Samson. *Sermon at the Execution of Moses Paul.* New Haven, Conn., 1788.

Szasz, Margaret Connell. "Samson Occum: Mohegan as Spiritual Intermediary." In *Between Indian and White Worlds,* edited by Margaret Connell Szasz. Norman: Oklahoma University Press, 1994.

OCONOSTOTA
Cherokee
c. 1710–1785

In 1730, Oconostota ("The Groundhog Sausage") met with King George II in England. At this time, he was a war chief. During the 1750s, as white settlers pressured the Cherokees in South Carolina, violent acts increased as Cherokee warriors sought to stem the tide. As a result, Oconostota and others went to Charleston, South Carolina, for peace talks. When the Cherokees would not turn over the men suspected of attacking settlers, Oconostota and several other chiefs were arrested on the order of Governor William Lyttleton. Subsequently, ATTAKULLAKULLA negotiated the ransoming of Oconostota and some of the chiefs.

Once freed, Oconostota saw violence as the only viable path. Allying with the Creeks, he mounted a siege in 1760 of Fort Prince George, South Carolina. For three years, war raged on the southern frontier. In 1763, a peace was signed that brought more encroachment on Cherokee lands. During the American Revolution, Oconostota allied with the English; but after many defeats, he stepped down as chief. He died shortly thereafter in 1783.

OH-NEE-YEATH-TON NO PROW
Mohawk
fl. early 1700s

The three Mohawks who accompanied HENDRICK to Queen Anne's court in 1710 had very short historical careers. Oh-Nee-Yeath-Ton No Prow's Christian name was John. During the royal visit, he was often called "King of Ganajahhore," which suggests that many English, in 1710, were still not quite past Columbus's geographical error. He signed with the wolf, his clan. History has left us nothing more about him. Two other Native Americans rounded out the visiting delegation: SA GA YEAN QUA PRAH TON, whom the English called "King of the Maquas," and ELOW-OH-KAOM, called "King of the River Nation" during the visit.

No Mohawk or Iroquois Council had appointed the four "American kings" as ambassadors to Queen Anne's court. They had been chosen more or less at the convenience of Peter SCHUYLER, British Indian agent, from the Iroquois he knew. The fact that all four were Mohawks was not coincidental, for to the English the Mohawks were the best known of the five Iroquois nations, the keepers of the eastern door of the longhouse, which opened at the British trading post of Albany.

FOR MORE INFORMATION:
Bond, Richmond P. *Queen Anne's American Kings.* Oxford: Clarendon Press, 1952.

OLD BRITON (LA DEMOISELLE)
Miami
fl. 1750s

Convinced of the superiority of British trade goods over those of the French, Old Briton was a major force behind the establishment of a large trading center at Pickawillany, on Ohio's Miami River. As many as fifty traders did business out of Pickawillany, swaying many Ohio River tribes to the British interest in the cold war with France that preceded the armed hostilities in 1754. Small French forces attacked the trading village from time to time but were repulsed with British aid. In 1750, the French tried to bribe Old Briton without success.

After a raid in January 1752, Old Briton ordered the execution of three French soldiers and cut off the ears of a fourth man. The ears were sent to the governor of New France as a warning. In May 1752, a larger French force attacked Pickawillany with Ottawa and other Indian allies. The town was nearly empty; most of the traders were doing business elsewhere, and most allied Indians were on their summer hunt. Old Briton and five traders who remained in the settlement were easily defeated by the French and their Indian allies. Old Briton was killed in the battle.

ONE BULL
Hunkpapa Sioux
fl. 1880s–1890s

One of SITTING BULL's closest allies, One Bull was a major force in keeping discipline among the Hunkpapas during the difficult years of exile in Canada. This was often carried out under the auspices of *akicita,* a form of discipline in which people who had offended the consensus of the tribe had to atone for their actions under a cloud of public dishonor. In one incident while in Canada, Gray Eagle, Sitting Bull's brother-in-law, stole 150 Métis horses, causing trouble with Canadian officials. Sitting Bull summoned the culprits with One Bull and his akicita (police troupe), who fired over their heads as they returned the stolen horses to Sitting Bull's camp.

In 1880, One Bull rode back into the United States, stopping at Fort Buford to determine what sort of welcome would be awaiting Sitting Bull's band if they were to return to the United States. He was told that the Hunkpapas would have to give up their weapons and horses and accept life at a reservation agency. Despite the stringent conditions, One Bull returned convinced that surrender was the only alternative.

Once Sitting Bull had surrendered, One Bull, like GALL, was used by the Anglos to under-

mine the chief's authority. One Bull joined Agent James McLaughlin's agency police force and signed agreements ceding Sioux land for settlement in the late 1880s. He fades from the historical record after Sitting Bull's assassination in 1890.

FOR MORE INFORMATION:

Dugan, Bill. *Sitting Bull*. San Francisco: Harper-Collins, 1994.

ONEKA (OWANECCO)
Mohegan
c. 1640–1710

Like his father, UNCAS, whom Oneka succeeded as chief of the Mohegans about 1683, Oneka allied staunchly with New England colonists against METACOM in King Philip's War (1676). He personally led fifty warriors into Boston to volunteer for battle. Oneka participated in the destruction of the Narragansets'

One Bull. [Nebraska State Historical Society]

main stronghold in the Great Swamp Fight of December 19, 1675; his warriors came close to capturing Metacom as he fled into swamps near the end of King Philip's War.

OPECHANCANOUGH
Powhatan
c. 1545–1644

In the early 1600s, Opechancanough, as head of the Pamunkey band of Powhatans, opposed the land expansion and attempted controls of the Jamestown colonists. In 1607, Opechancanough pursued and attacked Captain John Smith's forces with three hundred Native American men. Smith was the only white man to escape death during the battle. Opechancanough captured and took Smith to his brother's village on the York River where POCAHONTAS allegedly spared Smith's life. Released in 1608, Smith retaliated by leading his men to Opechancanough's village and seizing him as a hostage. The Powhatans regained Opechancanough from Smith by ransoming him with food.

When POWHATAN died in 1618, Opechancanough became the moving force in the confederacy. The English, greedy for land because of the profitability of tobacco, tricked the Indians into ceding huge tracts of it, ruining the Indian economy. This frustrated and angered the Powhatans, but Opechancanough was uncertain whether his men could defeat the treacherous colonists. After some thought, he ordered a surprise military assault on March 22, 1622. Despite a warning by an Indian informer, 347 men, women, and children out of about 1,400 Euro-Americans were killed. The English started military operations against the Powhatans, burning crops and dwellings and forcing the Indians farther into the interior. Intermittent warfare continued for many years.

In 1632, a peace treaty was finally signed to end the conflict. But on April 18, 1644, the one-hundred-year-old Opechancanough ordered another military strike. His men killed almost five hundred whites. Soon after, the Virginians launched a counterattack. Governor William Berkeley seized Opechancanough and brought the aged chief to Jamestown. Taunted by the Virginians as he entered the city, he was shot and killed by one of his guards while incarcerated.

OPOTHLEYAHOLO (APOTHLEYAHOLA, OPOTHLEYOHOLA, HOPOTHLEYCHOLO, HUPUEHELTH YAHOLO)
Creek
c. 1798–1862

Born in Georgia, Opothleyaholo (which means "Good Shouting Child" in Creek) was a veteran of the Creek War of 1813–1814; he served under Red Eagle (see William WEATHERFORD) and fought against General Andrew Jackson. Since he was an able orator, he was speaker of the Upper Creek towns and participated in many of the negotiations over land.

At Indian Springs, Georgia, in 1825, Opothleyaholo told federal agents that the Upper Creek leaders would not agree to land cessions negotiated by William MCINTOSH. Angry with McIntosh's machinations, the Creek Council mandated his death for ignoring the ban on land cessions to the whites.

During the 1820s, the Upper Creeks still wanted to remain in Georgia and Alabama after the removal of the Lower Creeks. In 1832, Opothleyaholo met with President Andrew Jackson in Washington and endorsed the second Treaty of Washington, which removed the Creeks. From 1834 through 1835, he sought to buy land in Texas but was stopped by the Mexican government. He also led a contingent of Seminoles against OSCEOLA's forces in 1836.

In 1862, while fleeing to Kansas from the ravages of the Civil War, he died near Leroy Creek, Kansas. He was survived by his wife, a son, and two daughters.

OREHAOUE
Cayuga
fl. late 1600s

Early in his life, Orehaoue was violently opposed to the conversion of Indians by missionaries and kept them out of Cayuga Territory while he was influential there. In 1687, Orehaoue was captured by the Denonville Expedition and sold into slavery. He traveled to France as a galley slave and remained there two years.

Returning to America in 1689, Orehaoue became a strong French ally and a Christian, a faith he had come to hold so strongly that he was fond of saying that if he had witnessed the crucifixion of Christ, he would have sought the scalps of those who killed him.

ORONHYATEKHA
Mohawk
1841–1907

One of the earliest Native Americans to practice western medicine, Oronhyatekha began his education at a mission school near Brantford, Ontario, near his birthplace on the Six Nations Reserve. He studied at Wesleyan Academy (Wilbraham, Massachusetts), Kenyon College, and Toronto University, often paying his educational expenses by organizing Wild West shows in which he recruited whites to play Indians.

In 1860, Oronhyatekha delivered an address on behalf of the Canadian Six Nations to the Prince of Wales (soon to be King Edward VII). The prince invited the Mohawk to continue his education at Oxford University. Oronhyatekha studied medicine at Oxford and returned to Toronto to practice, his medical knowledge accompanied by a definite upper-class English touch to his clothes and manners. Oronhyatekha married a granddaughter of the Mohawk leader Joseph BRANT, another Mohawk who had traveled to England and been shaped there.

ORTIZ, SIMON
Acoma Pueblo
1941–

Born in Albuquerque, New Mexico, on May 27, 1941, Ortiz attended Indian schools during his elementary and high school years. From 1961 to 1962 he matriculated at Fort Lewis College, and he did a stint in the U.S. Army from 1963 to 1966. From 1966 to 1968, he attended the University of New Mexico and then enrolled at the University of Iowa from 1968 to 1969.

In the late 1960s, he was strongly influenced by James Welch, N. Scott Momaday, and several other American Indian authors who were forging a new American Indian literature. Consequently, Ortiz's motive for writing changed from self-expression to a need to express an American Indian nationalistic literary voice. Raised in a traditional household at Acoma Pueblo, Ortiz gained an appreciation for the integrity and power of language from his father. His poetry is intended to be oral and often is narrative since he feels that people experience life through songs and poetry. Another theme in Ortiz's work is Native American peoples' urge to fashion an identity (communally and individually) by instilling a sense of place. He believes that Anglo society has been disconnected from the land and that Euro-American society has sought to glorify this alienation through an expansionistic ideology relating to the frontier. Ortiz's major poetry works include *Going for the Rain* (New York, 1976) and *Fight Back: For the Sake of the People* (Albuquerque, 1980).

FOR MORE INFORMATION:

Klein, Barry T., ed. *Reference Encyclopedia of the American Indian.* West Nyack, N.Y.: Todd Publications, 1993.

OSCEOLA (ASI-YAHOLA, BILL POWELL, TALCY)
Seminole
c. 1803–1838

Osceola, whose name was derived from *asi-yahola* (meaning "Black Drink Crier"), was born on the Talapoosa River near the border of Alabama and Georgia. His mother was Polly Copinger, a Creek woman; she married William Powell, a white man. As a result of his mother's marriage to Powell, Osceola was sometimes called Bill Powell, but he considered Powell his stepfather and asserted that he was a full-blood.

As a boy, Osceola moved with his mother to Florida and took up residence along the Apalachicola River about 1814. As a young man, he is believed to have fought in the First Seminole War of 1817–1818. Indeed, some reports during the war assert that he was captured in 1818 along the Enconfino River by troops under General Andrew Jackson and then released because of his youth.

In 1823, Seminole leaders such as NEA-MATHLA agreed to the Treaty of Moultrie Creek, which ceded tribal lands and created reservations for the Seminoles. Later, as a result of U.S. removal policies, the Treaty of Payne's Landing of 1832 required all Seminoles to leave Florida within three years for Indian Territory. According to the treaty, Seminoles with African American blood were to be sold into slavery. In 1833, seven Seminole chiefs, including Charley EMATHLA and FOKE LUSTE HAJO, endorsed the Treaty of Fort Gibson, which created a homeland in Oklahoma near the Creeks. However, most Seminoles did not comply readily with the requirements of the treaty. At this time, Osceola became a noted antiremoval leader. He urged various bands to remain in Florida.

At Fort King in April 1835, Wiley Thompson, the Indian agent, dictated a new treaty with the Seminoles, forcing their removal to Oklahoma. Several chiefs declined to endorse the treaty or to deal with white officials. Seminole tradition has it that Osceola angrily slashed the treaty with his knife. Subsequently, Osceola was seized and jailed. Although he continued to protest, in the end he agreed to the terms of the treaty. After his release, however, he slipped into the marshes with many Seminole people following him.

During preparation for removal, Osceola ambushed Charley Emathla. Osceola allegedly threw the money the whites gave Emathla on his dead body. Osceola attacked and killed Wiley Thompson on December 28, 1835. On the same day, ALLIGATOR, MICANOPY, and JUMPER, with about three hundred men, attacked Major Francis Langhorne Dade's detachment of 108 soldiers and killed all but three soldiers. On New Year's Eve 1835, Osceola's men won a battle against General Duncan Lamont Clinch's force of eight hundred men on the Withlacoochee River. Four infantrymen were killed and only three Indians died. Osceola was injured but eluded capture.

While waging a guerrilla war for two years, Osceola devastated the countryside. Finally Micanopy and other rebel chiefs stopped fighting in the spring of 1837. Osceola forced Micanopy to flee with him into the swamps, but Micanopy stopped fighting again later in the year. In October 1837, General Thomas Jesup seized Osceola through subterfuge. Under a flag of truce, Osceola attended a peace council at Fort Augustine in fall 1837. Despite the flag of truce, Osceola was captured, bound, and incarcerated at Fort Moultrie outside of Charleston, South Carolina.

There are varying accounts of Osceola's demise: poisoning, malaria, or abuse in prison may have been the causes. In any case, the whites were excoriated by public opinion for their treachery and his tragic death. On January 30, 1838, Osceola died at Fort Moultrie in full battle regalia. Even in death, Osceola did not escape white exploitation. Dr. Frederick Weedon, the military surgeon, kept his head in a medical museum until it was destroyed by a fire in 1866.

In spite of the death of their renowned leader, many Seminoles continued to resist removal to Oklahoma for many years, using the Florida swamps as a base for their operations.

OSHKOSH (OISCOSS)
Menominee
1795–1858

Oshkosh, namesake of a city in present-day Wisconsin, was born at Old King's Village on the Fox River, son of a Menominee chief. Oshkosh first went to war at seventeen in support of British troops in the War of 1812. He took part in the attacks on Fort Mackinaw, Wisconsin, and Fort Stephenson, Ohio. After he was recognized by the United States as treaty chief for the Menominees, Oshkosh switched allegiance to the American side in BLACK HAWK's War with the Sacs and Fox.

His support of the American cause did not keep the federal government from diplomatically forcing Oshkosh's hand in 1848, when he signed the Treaty of Lake Powahekone, ceding much of the Menominees' land base in Wisconsin. Oshkosh became alcoholic with age; it was once said that he murdered a man without provocation while drunk. Oshkosh died in a drunken brawl with another Native man at Keshena, Wisconsin, in 1858. In 1911, a statue depicting a slim, sober Oshkosh at the prime of

Oshkosh. [State Historical Society of Wisconsin]

his life (about thirty-five) was erected in Oshkosh, Wisconsin.

FOR MORE INFORMATION:

Nichols, Phebe Jewell. *Oshkosh the Brave.* Menominee Indian Reservation, 1954.

OTHERDAY, JOHN
Wapeton Sioux
1801–1871

Born the son of Red Bird (Zitkaduta) and a Sioux woman at Swan Lake, Minnesota, John Otherday was first called Angpetu Tokecha ("Other Day"). As a young man, he was known for his drunken brawls; in one of them he killed two other Indians.

The immigration of settlers and the onset of adulthood seemed to sober Otherday, who became a firm friend of the whites. He married a white woman and refused to join INKPACHUTA in the Spirit Lake uprising (1857). Otherday also warned colonists of the Great Sioux Uprising in 1862 and guided several dozen of them to safety. He volunteered as a U.S. Army scout to track down LITTLE CROW, the leader of the rebellion.

Otherday became something of a celebrity among whites because of his daring rescues. In 1867, he was honored by Congress and granted $2,500, which he used to buy a farm near Henderson, Minnesota. The farm failed, and Otherday sold it. He then moved to the Sisseton Sioux Reservation in South Dakota. He died of tuberculosis shortly thereafter.

OURAY (U-RAY, U-RE; WILLY)
Ute-Apache
c. 1820–1880

Ouray ("The Arrow") was born in Taos, New Mexico, about 1820. His father, Guera Murah, was actually a Jicarilla Apache adopted by the Utes, while his mother was a Tabeguache Ute. During most of his youth, Ouray worked for Mexican sheepherders, from whom he learned Spanish. As a young man, he became a noted warrior among the Tabeguache Utes (later called the Uncompahgres) during raids against the Sioux and Kiowas. Ouray also learned English and several Indian languages, skills that helped make him a key figure in many negotiations in the American Southwest.

Ouray's son by his first wife was taken by a Sioux raid on a Ute hunting camp and was never returned. When his first wife died in 1859, Ouray married Chipeta, a Tabeguache woman. In 1860 when his father died, Ouray was appointed chief of his band and government interpreter. This appointment occurred in Washington, D.C., where he was awarded medals, titles, and a $1,000 annuity.

In 1863, Ouray aided in negotiating the Treaty of Conejos, in which the Utes ceded all lands east of the Continental Divide. In 1867, he helped Christopher "Kit" CARSON quell a Ute uprising lead by Chief Kaniatse. By 1872, Ouray was spearheading resistance to government takeovers of lands permanently reserved for the Ute people. Although he was generally patient, he did lose his temper during these negotiations when a government official accused the Utes of laziness. Incensed at such a characterization, Ouray replied, "We work as hard as you do. Did you ever try skinning a buffalo?"

In 1873, Ouray and other tribal representatives met with a federal commission headed by Felix Brunot and were forced to compromise on the issue of land cessions. Pressured by the influx of miners and cattlemen, the Utes ceded an additional four million acres (the San Juan cession) for an annual payment of $25,000.

In 1876, when Colorado became a state, mining companies attempted to oust three White River Ute bands from their lands. "The Utes must go" became a political watchword in spite of the fact that Utes served as scouts for the U.S. Army and state militia in operations against other Indians. These tensions were compounded by the policies of a new Indian agent, Nathan Meeker, who arrived in 1878. In September 1879, Meeker decreed that a segment of Ute land would be used for farming. Canalla, brother-in-law of Ouray and a Ute shaman, protested this conversion of grazing lands to agricultural lands. He challenged Meeker's decision and told him to leave the agency. Meeker asked federal officials to send a detachment of 150 troops under Major Thomas T. Thornburgh against the rebellious Utes. Shortly after this call for aid, the Utes killed Meeker and seven other whites. Despite some subsequent bloody altercations, Ouray was able to secure a peaceful settlement because both sides respected him.

On August 27, 1880, soon after his return from Washington, D.C., Ouray died of Bright's disease near Ignacio, Colorado. In 1925, he was reburied at Montrose, Colorado.

OWHI
Yakima
fl. 1850s

Father of QUALCHIN, Owhi led a village of Yakimas on the Yakima River. Unlike his son, Owhi did not take a major role in the Yakima War (1855–1856). In 1858, Owhi met with U.S. Army colonel George Wright on the assumption that peace negotiations would commence. Instead, Owhi was taken prisoner and placed in irons. Colonel Wright was hoping that Qualchin, whom he considered to be dangerous, would come to his father's rescue. When Qualchin appeared, Wright's men executed him in a summary fashion. Owhi then escaped Wright's party as it was crossing the Snake River. Troops shortly caught up with Owhi and shot him to death.

PACOMIO
Chumash
fl. 1820s

Raised and educated at La Purisima Mission near Lompoc, California, Pacomio had a talent for carpentry. Chafing under Spanish domination, he fomented a revolt that sought to drive the Spanish out of Alta California. He journeyed to other missions to advance his plot and beseeched neighboring groups, like the Yokuts, to relocate closer to the missions to facilitate surprise attacks.

On March 19, 1824, Pacomio dispatched envoys to tell his confederates that the day of rebellion had arrived. Some runners made it to Santa Barbara and Santa Inez Missions, but others were captured on their way north. Nonetheless, Pacomio declared himself general-in-chief of the Alta California Indians and attacked La Purisima Mission with about two thousand Indians, overwhelming the Spanish soldiers and then putting them in jail. Indians at Santa Barbara and Santa Inez Missions revolted as well. But since many other mission Indians failed to

participate in the attack, Spanish counterattacks gradually quelled Pacomio's Rebellion. Pacomio himself fades from the historic record after its end.

PAINE, THOMAS
1737–1809

Writer and revolutionary, Thomas Paine displayed a fascination with Native American societies after arriving in America from England shortly before the Revolutionary War. Paine worked the examples of Native societies into his writings on occasion; in particular, his image of the Indians helped to shape some of the ideas in his famous revolutionary tract "Common Sense" (1776).

Paine attended a treaty council at Easton, Pennsylvania, in 1777, in order to negotiate the Iroquois' support, or at least neutrality, in the Revolution. According to Paine's biographer, Samuel Edwards, he was "fascinated by them." Paine quickly learned some of the Iroquois language. Soon Paine was comparing Native societies to Europe's in his writing. He especially admired their lack of poverty. "Among the Indians," wrote Paine in 1795, "there are not any of those spectacles of misery that poverty and want present to our eyes in the towns and streets of Europe." To Paine, poverty was a creation "of what is called civilized life. It exists not in the natural state. . . . The life of an Indian is a continual holiday compared to the poor of Europe." As one who sought to mold the future in the image of the natural state, Paine admired the Indians' relatively equal distribution of property, but he believed it impossible "to go from the civilized to the natural state."

An Englishman whose 1774 visit to America was sponsored by Benjamin FRANKLIN, Paine's ideas are a good example of the transference of New World ideas to the Old. "Common Sense" illustrated how imbued Americans were with the self-evident truths of natural rights. Its major point—that civil and religious liberties stemmed from governments in a natural state—captured the essence of the American spirit.

Paine—his prominent nose, lofty forehead, ruddy complexion, and eyes that author Charles Lee said shone with genius—was particularly well known among the Senecas. John Hall, who emigrated from Leicester, England, to Philadelphia in 1785, recorded in his journal for April 15, 1786: "Mr. Paine asked me to go and see the Indian chiefs of the Sennaka Nation. I gladly assented. . . . Mr. Paine . . . made himself known . . . as Common Sense and was introduced into the room, addressed them as brothers, and shook hands cordially[.] Mr. Paine treated them with 2s. bowl of punch." [Grinde and Johansen]

FOR MORE INFORMATION:

Foner, Philip S., ed. *The Complete Writings of Thomas Paine.* New York: Citadel Press, 1945.

Grinde, Donald A., Jr., and Bruce E. Johansen. *Exemplar of Liberty: Native America and the Evolution of Democracy.* Berkeley and Los Angeles: University of California Press, 1991.

Paine, Thomas. "Common Sense." In *The Political Writings of Thomas Paine.* New York: Peter Eckler, 1892.

PALMA (SALVADOR PALMA)
Quechan
fl. 1780s

In 1774, Chief Palma of the Yuman-speaking Quechans lived with his people along the Colorado River in southern California and Arizona. In 1774, he met with the Spanish expedition of Juan De Anza. The Spanish had built two missions in his area by 1780. Usually, the Spanish constructed a presidio with a garrison to defend the missions and stationed about ten soldiers at each mission. However, these missions ran short of supplies and gifts for the Indians in 1781. Consequently, the Indians moved to regain control of their lands. On July 17 and 18, 1781, Chief Salvador Palma and Ygnacio Palma (Salvador's brother) mounted an attack on the missions. They slew about one hundred priests, soldiers, and settlers and took about seventy-six women and children as prisoners. During 1781 and 1782, the Spanish tried unsuccessfully to regain control of the land of the Quechans. As a result of this resistance, the Quechans kept control of their Colorado homeland for many years.

PARKER, ARTHUR (GAWASOWANEH)
Seneca
1881–1955

Arthur Parker, whose Iroquois name means "Big Snowsnake," became one of history's leading Native Americans in anthropology and museum directorship. Born on the Cattaraugus Seneca Reservation, the one-quarter-blood Parker was a great-nephew of Ely S. PARKER, secretary to Ulysses S. Grant, as well as a distant relative of the Iroquois prophet HANDSOME LAKE. After studying at Dickinson Seminary in Pennsylvania, Parker came to know Dr. Frederick Ward Putnam, a leading museum director, while studying at Harvard.

Parker never finished his degree at Harvard, but he became a field archaeologist for Harvard's Peabody Museum in 1903. Parker also worked part-time at the American Museum of Natural History before he was appointed state archaeologist for the New York State Museum, Albany, in 1906. Parker took the lead in excavating several Iroquois sites and organized the New York State Archaeological Survey as he built the state museum into a major center for archaeological study. In the meantime, Parker also authored several books.

In 1911, a great fire struck the west end of the capitol in Albany, destroying Native art and artifacts collected by Parker, as well as an older collection that had belonged to Lewis Henry MORGAN, founder of American anthropology and a friend of Ely Parker. The fire occurred as Parker was assuming a broader national role as founder of *American Indian Magazine* and as a presidential adviser on Indian affairs. In 1925, Parker was appointed director of the Rochester Museum of Arts and Sciences, a role that he filled for almost two decades as he added to a personal bibliography that eventually included fourteen books, including *Erie Indian Village* (1913), *Code of Handsome Lake* (1913), *Life of General Ely S. Parker* (1919), *Seneca Myths and Folk Tales* (1923), and *Last of the Senecas* (1952). Parker died in Naples, New York, in 1955.

FOR MORE INFORMATION:

Parker, Arthur. *The Code of Handsome Lake, the Seneca Prophet.* New York State Museum Bulletin No. 163. Albany, N.Y.: New York State Museum, 1913.

————. *The History of the Seneca Indians.* 1926. Reprint, Port Washington, N.Y.: Ira J. Friedman, 1967.

————. *Parker on the Iroquois.* Edited by William N. Fenton. Syracuse, N.Y.: Syracuse University Press, 1968.

————. *Red Jacket, Last of the Senecas.* New York: McGraw-Hill, 1952.

————. *Seneca Myths and Folk Tales.* 1923. Reprint, Lincoln: University of Nebraska Press, 1989.

PARKER, ELY (DONEHOGAWA)
Seneca
1828–1905

Colonel Ely Parker was secretary to General Ulysses S. Grant; he wrote the surrender ending the Civil War that General Robert E. Lee signed at Appomattox. After the Civil War, Parker became the United States' first Native American commissioner of Indian affairs when Grant was elected president.

Parker, planning on a legal career, passed the necessary examinations but was denied certification because he was Indian and therefore not a U.S. citizen. Parker then switched to civil engineering but also had a considerable background in ethnology. He helped to inspire Lewis Henry MORGAN's pioneering Iroquois studies that founded the academic discipline of anthropology in the United States. Parker became an early member of the Grand Order of the Iroquois, a fraternal society established by Morgan.

Parker's tenure in the Indian Bureau coincided with investigations by Congress under Senator James B. Doolittle regarding corruption on the frontier. The Doolittle report received considerable publicity; it found that "in a large number of cases, Indian wars are to be traced to the aggressions of lawless white men, always to be found upon the frontier." Parker came into

Ely Parker. [National Anthropological Archives]

office under the aegis of a peace policy initiated by Congress after the publicity attending the Doolittle report. After that, the special interests that had done so much to corrupt the system made his life miserable.

Parker was driven from the office of Indian commissioner by the corrupt Indian rings that had profited so handsomely from government contracts for services paid for but rarely delivered. During Parker's tenure as Indian commissioner, however, he helped orchestrate considerable public outrage over the treatment of Indians nationwide, particularly those on the Plains who were being ruthlessly pursued as he served in the office. After Parker was hounded out of office by established interests and racial intolerance, he expressed his disgust: "They made their onslaught on my poor,

innocent head and made the air foul with their malicious and poisonous accusations. They were defeated, but it was no longer a pleasure to discharge patriotic duties in the face of foul slander and abuse. I gave up a thankless position to enjoy my declining years in peace and quiet." [Nabokov]

Parker had overseen a brief interlude in the destructive Indian policies of the nineteenth century, a time during which RED CLOUD and his allies had forced the U.S. Army to disassemble its forts in the Powder River country and sign the Treaty of 1868, guaranteeing the Black Hills to the Lakota. In June 1870, Parker had hosted Red Cloud and a companion chief, Red Dog, as they visited Washington, D.C., and spoke at the Cooper Union. This was Parker's evaluation of U.S. Indian policies:

The white man has been the chief obstacle in the way of Indian civilization. The benevolent measures attempted by the government for their advancement has been almost uniformly thwarted by the agencies employed to carry them out. The soldiers, sent for their protection, too often carried demoralization and disease into their midst. The agent appointed to be their friend and counselor, business manager, and the [manager] of government bounties, frequently went among them only to enrich himself in the shortest possible time, at the cost of the Indians, and spend the largest available sum of the government money with the least ostensible beneficial result. [Armstrong, *I Have Spoken*]

During his later years, Parker made a large amount of money playing the stock market but was ruined when he was forced to pay the bond of another man who had defaulted. After retiring from service with the U.S. government, Parker was appointed New York City building superintendent in 1876. He held the post until he died in 1905. Parker was buried in Buffalo, New York, in a common plot with his grandfather RED JACKET.

FOR MORE INFORMATION:

Armstrong, Virginia Irving, ed. *I Have Spoken: American History Through the Voices of the Indians.* Chicago: Swallow Press, 1971.

Armstrong, William N. *Warrior in Two Camps: Ely S. Parker.* Syracuse, N.Y.: Syracuse University Press, 1978.

Nabokov, Peter. *Native American Testimony.* New York: Viking Penguin, 1991.

Parker, Arthur C. *The Life of General Ely S. Parker.* N.p., 1919.

Prucha, Francis Paul, ed. *Documents of United States Indian Policy.* Lincoln: University of Nebraska Press, 1975.

PARKER, QUANAH
(QUANA, KWAINA, KWAHNAH)
Comanche
c. 1845–1911

Born at Cedar Lake, Texas, in May 1845, Quanah ("Fragrant or Sweet Smelling") Parker was a strong and brave leader of the Comanches. His mother, Cynthia Ann Parker, was captured on May 19, 1836, during a raid on white settlements by Comanches; she was nine years old at the time. Adopted by the Comanches and renamed Preloch, a teenaged Cynthia Ann Parker married the Comanche chief Peta NOCONA of the Quahadi band. As a young adult, she preferred Comanche ways over white ways.

Growing up as the son of Cynthia and Peta, Quanah adhered to Comanche traditions as well. Throughout his childhood, he excelled in the arts of war and hunting as well as showing leadership skills. With the death of his parents, he grew to hate the whites. His mother was

captured in 1860 and returned to her white family, dying a year after her separation from the Comanches. Subsequently, his father died of a wound during combat with the whites. Quanah's brother also succumbed to a white disease. As a result of his father's death, Quanah became a leader of the powerful Quahadi Comanche band in the Texas Panhandle. He had became one of their war chiefs by 1867.

After the Civil War, the U.S. Army attempted to subdue the Southern Plains Indians. Under the Medicine Lodge Treaty of 1867, the Comanches and Kiowas were given a reservation in the southern part of Indian Territory between the Washita and Red Rivers. But Quanah's band

Quanah Parker. [Nebraska State Historical Society]

did not accept the terms of the treaty and refused to settle on the reservation assigned to them, preferring to hunt and raid in their accustomed manner. For seven years, Quanah Parker's band raided white settlements and frontier towns. When General Philip H. Sheridan's southern column under Major Andrew Evans attacked Comanches and Kiowas at the Battle of Soldier Spring on December 25, 1868, the army burned Indian tepees and destroyed their food supply but failed to get a decisive victory.

By May 1871, SATANTA, SATANK, BIG TREE, and MAMANTI were leading Kiowa attacks against whites on the Butterfield Southern Route (also known as the Southern Overland Trail). As a result, General William T. Sherman ordered the Fourth Cavalry to move against the Comanches and Kiowas. After scouring the reservation in 1871, the Fourth Cavalry moved onto the Staked Plain of the Texas Panhandle, and Quanah led two attacks against them. In the first assault, Comanche warriors stampeded and captured many of the Fourth Cavalry's horses. In the second sortie, Quanah commanded an offensive against a scouting party. He scalped and killed the only casualty. With the winter of 1871–1872 coming, the Fourth Cavalry withdrew from the Staked Plain but not before defeating some Comanches at McClellan Creek on September 29, 1872. Thirty Comanche men were killed there and another 124 were captured. But Quanah's band still eluded the grasp of the U.S. Army.

In spite of their early successes against the army, other events would eventually defeat the Comanches. Before the early 1870s, white hunters shot the buffalo only in the winter when the fur on the hides was still long. However, a new tanning process developed in the 1870s made shorthaired hides workable for tanning also. Thus, year-round hunting of the buffalo became profitable. In addition, by the 1870s,

white hunters were armed with new high-powered Sharps rifles with a range of six hundred yards. As a result, the buffalo herds were rapidly decimated by the whites. When white hunters set up camp on the Staked Plain at the abandoned trading post of Adobe Walls on the South Canadian River, Quanah and seven hundred warriors attacked the twenty-eight buffalo hunters there on June 27, 1874. Although they clearly outnumbered the buffalo hunters, the Indians were turned back by the hunters' repeating rifles and a cannon. Although Quanah's band continued to resist subjugation by the army, he was forced to surrender two years later in June 1876.

After his surrender, Quanah's life changed dramatically. He became a prosperous and settled farmer in Indian Territory, quickly adapting to his new life. He started to use his mother's last name and he learned Spanish and English. Although he believed in his father's traditions, he urged his people to adopt the white man's ways. Through his leadership, tribal lands began to be leased to cattlemen to increase tribal revenues.

From 1886 to 1898, Parker was one of three judges on the Court of Indian Offenses until his polygamy caused his dismissal. By 1890, he was head of all the Comanche bands. He represented his people in negotiations with the Jerome Commission in 1892 (formed in 1889 to implement the General Allotment Act) and gained significant concessions for his people.

Parker also helped the spread of the Native American Church, or peyotism. After raids on Mexico, Comanches brought the use of the hallucinogen peyote northward. Subsequently, Parker developed what is known as the Peyote Road in the 1890s after the collapse of the Ghost Dance religion founded by WOVOKA. His spiritual work along with other peyotists like the Kiowa Big Moon spread American Indian peyote use throughout North America.

Quanah Parker had seven wives, two of whom survived him. He also had three sons and four daughters. He died on February 21, 1911, at the age of sixty-four. He was buried next to his mother at Cache, Oklahoma (he had earlier reinterred her at this site). Over fifteen hundred people attended his funeral.

PASSACONAWAY (BEAR CUB)
Pennacook
c. 1568–c. 1666

During early colonization of New England, Passaconaway was the principal chief of a number of Pennacook bands in the area that the colonials called southern New England. His influence spread westward to the fringes of Mohawk country and southward toward the expanding British settlements. Passaconaway fought British encroachment as his warriors made occasional small-scale attacks. In 1642, colonial troops moved on his village of Pennacook near contemporary Concord. Passaconaway was not in the village at the time, but his wife and son were taken prisoner. He negotiated their release, and in 1644 pledged a cessation of hostilities. Later in his life, Passaconaway claimed to have had visions instructing him to seek peace with the whites because anyone opposing them would be destroyed.

Passaconaway was known as a sorcerer, as well as a political leader. He lived to be about a hundred years old. On Passaconaway's death in 1666, his son, WANNALANCET, assumed the Pennacook chieftainship.

PAWNEE KILLER
Oglala Lakota
fl. 1860s

As his name indicates, Pawnee Killer was known for his exploits against the Pawnees, traditional enemies of the Lakota. With the arrival of white immigrants, the Pawnees often acted

Pawnee Killer. [Nebraska State Historical Society]

as scouts for the U.S. Army as it sought to destroy Sioux power.

Pawnee Killer was one of a number of Lakota who migrated southward from the Dakota country into the Platte River valley of Colorado and Nebraska during the 1850s, at the beginning of the Plains Indian wars. Pawnee Killer became an ally of TALL BULL and other Southern Cheyennes in battles with the invading whites. At one point, he played a role with the Cheyenne Dog Soldiers in routing George Armstrong CUSTER at the Little Bighorn. Pawnee Killer also took part in the 1868 Battle of Beecher's Island, during which the Southern Cheyenne chief ROMAN NOSE was killed. Very little is known of Pawnee Killer after his band settled at Red Cloud Agency in Nebraska.

PAXINOSA
Shawnee/Delaware
fl. 1750s

Paxinosa became the most influential chief of several Delaware bands in contemporary northern New Jersey and eastern Pennsylvania. His influence peaked during the first half of the eighteenth century. During the mid-1750s, Paxinosa and many of his people migrated to the Ohio country and became attached to the French cause in the French and Indian War. He also befriended several Moravian missionaries. Later in the decade, Paxinosa maintained relations with William JOHNSON, the British Indian superintendent, despite his off-and-on alliance with the French. He died in about 1758.

PAYEPOT
Cree
1816–1908

Payepot ("He Who Knows the Secrets of the Sioux"), who would lead Native resistance to railroad construction on the Canadian prairies, was raised by his grandmother after both his parents died of smallpox. As a young man, Payepot was captured by the Sioux with his grandmother. After fourteen years with the Sioux, a Cree war party recaptured him. Afterward, as a Cree leader, Payepot played a leading role in raids on the Sioux and their allies. In 1870, Payepot led about seven hundred warriors who were defeated by the Blackfoot in present-day Manitoba. Five years later, under duress, Payepot signed Canadian Treaty No. 5, ceding Cree lands in the Qu'appelle Valley of Manitoba. Payepot's Crees were then forced to move to new lands in what later became Saskatchewan.

In the early 1880s, Payepot became known for his band's resistance to construction of the Canadian Pacific Railway. Warriors pulled up surveyors' stakes and camped in the path of construction crews before the Royal Canadian Mounted Police forced them away from the area near Moose Jaw. Payepot resented white incursions but kept his people out of the Second RIEL Rebellion. He was deposed as chief by

Canadian authorities after he sanctioned an illegal Sun Dance late in the century, but his people continued to consider him their leader.

PAYNE (KING PAYNE)
Seminole
fl. 1800–1812

In the early nineteenth century, and particularly at the start of the War of 1812, many Seminoles and Creeks of northern Florida engaged in raids on Spanish territory. In one of these skirmishes, King Payne, a principal chief of the Seminoles, was slain. BOLEK, his brother, was injured in the same battle. The next year, Colonel John Williams commanded some Tennessee militiamen and U.S. regulars on a raid into Florida. Williams laid waste to hundreds of Indian houses and crops and seized many Indian horses and cattle. These frequent border incidents aided in instigating the Creek War of 1813–1814 and the First Seminole War of 1817–1818.

PELTIER, LEONARD
Anishinabe
1944–

An activist in the American Indian Movement during the 1973 confrontation at Wounded Knee, Peltier was caught in a shootout with FBI agents and state police at the Jumping Bull compound on the Pine Ridge Indian Reservation in June 1975. He was later convicted of killing two FBI agents there, Jack Williams and Ronald Coler. The trial, held in the Fargo, North Dakota, Federal District Court in 1977, has since become the focus of an international protest movement aimed at getting Peltier a retrial.

Before Peltier's trial opened in March 1977, the prosecution's case began to fall apart. Discovery proceedings produced an affidavit, signed by government witness Myrtle Poor Bear and dated February 19, 1976 (before two others known to the defense, dated February 23 and March 31), which said that the woman had not been on the scene of the June 25, 1975, gun battle in which the two FBI agents had been shot to death. This information, contained in an affidavit not sent to Canada by the U.S. government during Peltier's extradition hearing there, contradicted the other two statements attributed to Poor Bear.

More importantly, Poor Bear herself recanted. On April 13, out of earshot of the jury, Poor Bear told the court (having been called by the defense) that she had never seen Peltier before meeting him at the trial, that she had not been allowed to read the three affidavits bearing her name, and that FBI agents David Price and Bill Wood had threatened physical harm to her and her children if she did not sign them.

Judge Paul Benson refused to let the jury hear Poor Bear's testimony, ruling it irrelevant to the case. The next day the judge changed his mind and ruled the testimony relevant but still would not let the jury hear it. He ruled this time that Poor Bear's testimony was prejudicial to the government's case and, if believed, would confuse the jury.

Prosecution testimony, which occupied the first five weeks of the trial, ranged far afield from what happened on the day of the shootings. The prosecution was allowed to bring up extraneous charges against Peltier on which he had not been tried and testimony that ran counter to the federal rules of evidence. The defense's planned two weeks of testimony were shaved to two and one-half days by Judge Benson, who limited defense testimony to events directly connected with the shootings themselves.

The only evidence directly linking Peltier to the killings of Coler and Williams (other than that fabricated in Poor Bear's name) came from Frederick Coward, an FBI agent, who said he had recognized Peltier from half a mile away through a seven-power rifle sight. The defense team replicated the sighting and found that the feat was impossible through such a sight at such a distance, even for a person with excellent vision. In court, defense attorneys offered to duplicate their experiment for the jury so that its members could judge for themselves the veracity of the FBI agent's statement. Judge Benson refused the request. "Finally," said Bruce Ellison, a member of the defense team, "we brought in someone from a gun shop, who said that an idiot could tell you that it is impossible to recognize someone, even someone you know, from a half-mile away through a seven-power sight."

Three Indian juveniles also testified that they had seen Peltier at the scene. Each of them also testified under cross-examination that their testimony had been coerced by the FBI. Mike Anderson testified that he had been threatened with beating. Wish Draper said that he had been tied and handcuffed to a chair for three hours to elicit his statement. Norman Brown swore that he was told that if he did not cooperate he "would never walk the earth again."

The prosecution, its eyewitness testimony impeached, linked Peltier to the use of an AR-15, a semiautomatic weapon, which was not introduced as evidence because it had been blown apart during a Kansas freeway explosion on September 10, 1975. The prosecution also asserted that Peltier's thumbprint had been found on a bag containing a gun belonging to one of the dead agents. The bag and the gun were found on November 14, 1975, after two men police described as Peltier and Dennis BANKS had escaped their dragnet near Ontario, Oregon.

Following his conviction, Peltier became the object of a growing popular movement demanding a new trial. Peltier's request for a new trial was turned down by U.S. Circuit Court (St. Louis) in 1978; his appeal was also declined by the U.S. Supreme Court in 1978 and 1986. In the meantime, support for Peltier spread to the Soviet Union and Europe. By 1986, an estimated seventeen million people in the Soviet Union had signed petitions on his behalf. Peter Matthiessen's book *In the Spirit of Crazy Horse*, which made a case for Peltier's innocence, was published in 1983, but its publisher, Viking, withdrew the book from the market after former South Dakota governor William Janklow threatened to sue for libel over passages linking him to the rape of a young Native American woman. Bootlegged copies of the book nonetheless began to circulate, and it was officially republished in 1991. *In the Spirit of Crazy Horse* presents, in an epilogue appended after the book had been suppressed eight years, an interview with a Native man known only as "X," who confesses to the murders. In the meantime, the FBI had withheld from the public six thousand pages of documents on the case for reasons the agency characterized as national security.

During the 1980s and 1990s, as Peltier's appeals for a new trial were denied, he served two life terms, first at Marion Federal Penitentiary, Illinois, and later at Leavenworth Federal Penitentiary, Kansas. He developed his talents as an artist, including posters, paintings, and designs for a line of greeting cards that were sold nationwide. His case also became the focus of a feature film (*Thunderheart*, 1992) and a documentary (*Incident at Oglala*, 1992). His case has come to the attention of Amnesty International and the government of Canada, from which Peltier was extradited to face trial on the basis of the Poor Bear affidavits.

Peltier's appeals were directed by several well-known legal personalities, including former U.S. Attorney General Ramsey Clark and Attorney William Kunstler. His third appeal for a new trial was turned down by the Eighth Circuit Court of Appeals (St. Paul, Minnesota) in 1993, finally exhausting his remedies within the U.S. court system. During the first half of 1994, Banks helped organize a five-month Walk for Justice across the United States on behalf of Peltier. About four hundred people took part in the march, and twenty-eight walked the entire three-thousand-mile distance. The Walk for Justice ended in Washington, D.C., on July 15, at a rally calling on President Bill Clinton to free Peltier.

FOR MORE INFORMATION:

Ewen, Alexander. "Crazy Horse Rides Again." *Native Nations* (June/July 1991).

Johansen, Bruce E. "Peltier and the Posse." *The Nation* (October 1, 1977).

——. "The Reservation Offensive." *The Nation* (February 25, 1978).

——, and Roberto F. Maestas. *Wasi'chu: The Continuing Indian Wars*. New York: Monthly Review Press, 1979.

Matthiessen, Peter. *In the Spirit of Crazy Horse*. New York: Viking, 1983, 1991.

Weisman, Joel. "About That 'Ambush' at Wounded Knee." *Columbia Journalism Review* (September/October 1975).

PENA, TONITA (QUAH AH)
San Ildefonso Pueblo
1895–1949

Tonita Pena was born on June 13, 1895, at San Ildefonso Pueblo and was the daughter of Ascension Vigil and Natividad Pena. Since her mother died when she was young, Tonita was brought up by her aunt, Martina Vigil, of Cochiti Pueblo. She was educated at San Ildefonso Pueblo and then at St. Catherine's School in Santa Fe. Her early life appears to be like that of most other Pueblo children of her era.

In 1909, at fourteen, she married a Cochiti man, Juan Rosario Chavez; however, he died two years later in 1911. Subsequently, she wed Felipe Herrera and had three children.

Coming from an artistic family, Tonita Pena started to paint at an early age. By the time she was twenty-one, she was selling her works throughout the Southwest. Although she had little formal training, she was encouraged by Dr. Edgar Lee Hewitt and Dr. Kenneth Chapman, who saw much talent in her art. Very early in her career, she threw off traditional stylistic restrictions and advanced quickly beyond casual experimentation in her works.

Her determination and perseverance caused her to make significant contributions to American Indian art. While teaching at the Santa Fe Indian School and the Albuquerque Indian School, she encouraged her students to strive for excellence while insisting that they must not copy their teacher's techniques.

Her works were reproduced in many publications, and her pieces can be found in many private collections throughout the world. In addition to her noted paintings, she was also a talented muralist.

Later in life she married Epiotacio Arquero and had three children by him. At the time of her death in September 1949, she was the most prominent female Pueblo artist on the scene and was known fondly as the "Grand Old Lady of Pueblo Art."

PEOPEOMOXMOX (YELLOW BIRD)
Wallawalla
fl. 1850s

Peopeomoxmox was one of the principal leaders in the Yakima War (1855–1856), when Indians from western Washington to Idaho rose up against land cessions signed with treaty chiefs and Isaac STEVENS, territorial governor of Wash-

ington. The war climaxed with a raid on Seattle led by the Nisqually LESCHI, who was later captured and hung. At a treaty council on June 2, 1855, held on the Chehalis River, Peopeomoxmox told Stevens that a promise of annuities could not replace the land that his people used. They refused to retreat to a reservation.

Despite his opposition to Stevens's treaties, Peopeomoxmox advised his people against joining in the Yakima War of 1855–1856. In December 1855, a party of Oregon volunteers under Colonel James Kelly advanced into the Walla Walla Valley, attacking a number of Umatilla, Cayuse, and Wallawalla villages. Peopeomoxmox and five other men from his village approached the volunteers under a flag of truce. The chief and the other five men were murdered without provocation and then mutilated. Peopeomoxmox's scalp and ears were put on display by the volunteers. Other Indians used the incident as a reason not to trust the whites, leading to an escalation of the Yakima War.

PESHEWAH (THE LYNX)
Miami
c. 1760–1841

Son of Joseph Drouet de Richardville, a wealthy French Canadian trader, Peshewah became head chief of the Miamis in 1814, after the death of Pacanne, who had taken the place of LITTLE TURTLE in 1812. Peshewah had inherited a small fortune from his parents and augmented his wealth throughout his adult life as a diplomat, businessman, and as a dealer in other Indians' lands. He preferred business deals to military alliances.

Peshewah advised his people to avoid confederation with TECUMSEH and alliance with either the Americans or the English in the War of 1812. Instead, he preferred to accommodate and extract pledges of land and presents from both sides. Peshewah was fluent in English and French and lavishly entertained people from both sides at his home.

At his death, Peshewah was said to have been the richest Native person in North America. He had accumulated titles to land worth more than $1 million. He signed many land cessions but somehow managed to postpone the westward removal of his own people for over a decade. In 1840, however, Peshewah signed the Forks of the Wabash Treaty, which compelled all the Miamis except himself to move west of the Mississippi. Many of his fellow tribesmen thereafter disowned Peshewah.

FOR MORE INFORMATION:

Eckert, Allan W. *A Sorrow in Our Heart: The Life of Tecumseh.* New York: Bantam, 1992.

Edmunds, R. David. *The Shawnee Prophet.* Lincoln: University of Nebraska Press, 1983.

———. *Tecumseh and the Quest for Indian Leadership.* Boston: Little, Brown, 1984.

PETALESHARO ("MAN CHIEF")
Pawnee
c. 1797–c. 1874

"Petalesharo" seems to have functioned as a title as well as a personal name during the early eighteenth century among the Pawnee. Several outstanding warriors used the name, and it is sometimes difficult to attribute biographical details to one individual.

The best-known person to claim the title not only distinguished himself as a warrior but also as a humanitarian. He aggressively curtailed the Pawnee use of human sacrifice in certain rituals. Until his time, the Pawnees had raided other tribes for girls of about thirteen years of age, who would be treated well until their sacrifice in the Morning Star Ceremony, which had some parallels to Aztec rites. During one

such ceremony, which occurred in the late 1820s, Petalesharo is said to have protested by rescuing a young woman from the sacrifice. Petalesharo cut the bonds that held the woman to a sacrificial cross, carried her to a horse to escape, then fed and protected the woman before sending her home.

During the fall and winter of 1821, Petalesharo toured the urban areas of the Northeast, including Washington, D.C., where he spoke at a conference attended by president James Monroe and secretary of war John Calhoun. He also attended a New Year's reception at the White House.

FOR MORE INFORMATION:

Hyde, George E. *The Pawnee Indians.* Norman: University of Oklahoma Press, 1974.

One of the line of outstanding Pawnee leaders who bore the name Petalesharo. [National Anthropological Archives]

PIERCE, MARIS BRYANT
(HA-DYA-NO-DOH)
Seneca
1811–1874

Following the American Revolution, the Senecas who remained in the United States were faced with reconstructing lives shattered by the punitive raids of American troops under General John Sullivan in 1779. The destitution of the area contributed to the rise of HANDSOME LAKE's prophecy and to the land rights activities of Maris Bryant Pierce. Pierce fought efforts to convince Senecas to cede all of their lands in New York and move westward. His primary focus was the 1838 Treaty of Buffalo Creek.

Pierce (whose name, Ha-dya-no-doh, means "Swift Runner") was born on the Allegheny Seneca Reservation, a tract of forty-two square miles left from Seneca landholdings that once covered much of western New York. He was converted to Christianity as a teenager and attended Dartmouth College, entering as a freshman in 1836. While a college student, Pierce spent much of his time researching and speaking on issues affecting Seneca land tenure.

Pierce explained why the Senecas should oppose emigration from New York to Missouri or Kansas:

> The right of possession of our lands is undisputed, so with us it is a question dealing directly to our interest. . . . Our lands are fertile, and as well situated for agricultural pursuits as any we shall get by a removal. The graves of our fathers and mothers and kin are here, and about them still cling our affections and memories. . . . We are situated in the midst of facilities for physical, intellectual, and moral improvement. . . . In this view of facts surely there is no inducement for removing.

Removal was stipulated in the Buffalo Creek Treaty of 1838, which the Senecas had signed after considerable coercion. The federal government paid for 750 gallons of whiskey meant to keep the Senecas inebriated during the negotiations.

Pierce, with fourteen other Seneca chiefs, mobilized opposition to the Buffalo Creek Treaty among Senecas and some non-Indians, leading to a renegotiation in 1842. The Senecas had hoped to have their property reinstated on lines existing before 1838; instead, they were left with even smaller reservations. Pierce's birthplace was slated to be turned over to non-Indian settlers. Pierce and his wife, Mary Jane Carroll, were forced to move from Buffalo Creek in 1845. Reluctantly the Senecas agreed to the terms because the new treaty permitted them to stay in New York State.

During his later years, Pierce acted as secretary of the Seneca nation. He also played a role in bringing an elective form of government to the Senecas in 1848.

FOR MORE INFORMATION:

Pierce, Maris Bryant. "Address on the Present Condition and Prospects of the Aboriginal Inhabitants of North America." Philadelphia, 1839. In *Indian Lives*, edited by L. G. Moses and Raymond Wilson. Norman: University of Oklahoma Press, n.d.

Vernon, H. A. "Maris Bryant Pierce: The Making of a Seneca Leader." In *Indian Lives*, edited by L. G. Moses and Raymond Wilson. Norman: University of Oklahoma Press, n.d.

PIOMINGO (MOUNTAIN LEADER)
Chickasaw
fl. late 1700s

During Piomingo's leadership, the Chickasaws of northern Mississippi and western Tennessee were being pressed by other American Indian nations for their lands. The Creek leader, Alexander McGILLIVRAY, attempted to force the Chickasaws into joining a Spanish-Indian alliance, but the Chickasaws spurned their overtures and rebuffed Creek war parties at Piomingo's request. Due to Piomingo's entreaties during the 1790s, Tennessee leaders gave the Chickasaws much arms and ammunition. Subsequently, Chickasaw villages along the Mississippi River functioned as headquarters for American agents. Piomingo was a key figure in this pro-American diplomacy during the late eighteenth century.

PITCHLYNN, PETER PERKINS (HA-TCHOO-TUC-KNEE, "THE SNAPPING TURTLE")
Choctaw
1806–1881

Born at the Choctaw tribal village of Hushookwa in Noxubee County, Mississippi, on January 30, 1806, Peter Perkins Pitchlynn was the son of Sophia Folsom (a member of an influential Choctaw family) and John Pitchlynn, a white interpreter for the federal government and PUSHMATAHA. His Choctaw name, Hatchoo-tuc-knee, means "The Snapping Turtle." As a boy, Pitchlynn saw someone writing a letter and decided to secure both an Indian and a white education. Returning from his first term of school, young Pitchlynn witnessed his people negotiating what he felt was an unfair treaty with the U.S. government. He was so upset by this that he refused to shake the hand of General Andrew Jackson when he first met him. After attending an academy at Columbia, Tennessee, he then went to Nashville University.

Upon his graduation, Pitchlynn settled down to farming and married Rhoda Folsom, a Choctaw woman. Having natural leadership skills, he soon became immersed in tribal politics and was elected to the Choctaw Council in 1824. Pitchlynn, along with David FOLSOM, was a key

figure in the founding of several English-language schools. He was also instrumental in helping to end the practice of polygamy among the Choctaws.

In 1828, Pitchlynn was one of the Choctaw leaders who selected suitable lands for resettlement along the Arkansas River. He also made peace with the Osage tribe in Oklahoma in preparation for his people's relocation. Although he opposed removal, Pitchlynn bargained for what he thought were the best possible lands for his people when he signed the Treaty of Dancing Rabbit Creek in September 1830.

After the Choctaws completed their removal in 1834, Pitchlynn started a new farm on the Arkansas River and became a major figure in reorganizing the Choctaw tribe and reestablishing new schools. He often journeyed to Washington, D.C., to address the president and congressional committees. In 1860, the Choctaws elected Pitchlynn as their principal chief.

Although Pitchlynn remained neutral during the Civil War, three of his sons joined the Confederate cause. When the Civil War was over, he began to lobby in Washington for his people's land claims. After Pitchlynn's first wife died, he married Caroline Lombardy in 1869. He also became a Mason and a member of the Lutheran Church. He befriended many notables of his generation, including Charles Dickens and Henry Clay.

PLENTY COUPS (ALEEK-CHEA-AHOOSH)
Crow
1848–1932

Plenty Coups, whose Crow name meant "Many Achievements," was the principal chief of the Crows during the latter stages of the Plains wars. He spearheaded the Crow strategy to cooperate with the U.S. Army in its pursuit of the Cheyennes, Sioux, Arapahoes, and other hostiles. Plenty Coups's Crows provided scouts for

George Armstrong CUSTER in his loss at the Little Bighorn in 1876; he mourned Custer's death.

Plenty Coups was groomed for chieftainship from an early age and was paid uncommon attention as a child by the Crows. His boyhood was detailed in a biography, *Plenty Coups: Chief of the Crows* (1930), by Frank Linderman. When Plenty Coups was nine years of age, one of his brothers was killed by the Sioux, creating in the boy a lifelong enmity. The Sioux had earlier pushed the Crows westward into the Little Bighorn country from the Black Hills area. Their new homeland was located in the midst of one of the last surviving large buffalo runs on the Plains and became a site of competition between the Crows and their traditional enemies.

In boyhood, Plenty Coups was beset by harrowing dreams in which the buffalo disappeared from the Plains and white men's cattle replaced them. He told the dreams to the Crows' spiritual leaders, who concluded that the tribe would suffer less if they cooperated with the invaders. Plenty Coups did not appear to be reacting out of fear but out of pragmatism. He had a healthy taste for battle and joined the warriors of the Crow by taking his first scalp (and capturing two horses) at age fifteen.

Following Plenty Coups's vision, 135 Crow warriors volunteered to serve as scouts for General George Crook in the 1876 campaign that resulted in the deaths of Custer and 225 of his men at the Little Bighorn. Plenty Coups worried that Crook was not prepared for CRAZY HORSE's Lakotas and WASHAKIE's Shoshonis when they met in battle on June 16, 1876. He was correct; Crazy Horse routed Crook and his Indian allies in a battle that presaged Custer's Last Stand nine days later.

After the Custer battle, the Crows under Plenty Coups continued to support the U.S. Army as it drove the Cheyennes and Sioux into

Plenty Coups. [National Anthropological Archives]

subjugation. Crow warriors aided in the pursuit of SITTING BULL into Canada, the hounding of the Northern Cheyennes, and the surrender of Crazy Horse. Plenty Coups urged his people to become farmers and ranchers, and he abandoned his tepee for a log farmhouse. He also opened a general store so that the Crows could buy trade goods at fair prices.

Plenty Coups traveled to Washington, D.C., several times after 1880 to assure trade and aid for the Crows. He was noted for his sagacity in business dealings. Not all of the Crows supported him, however; like other Native American tribes and nations, they had been sickened and killed by smallpox and other diseases. Many young warriors also resented being confined to a reservation.

Nearly three hundred Crow opponents of Plenty Coups joined forces in fall 1887 with the young firebrand SWORD BEARER, who sought to prove his acumen as a warrior by leading a horse raid on the neighboring Blackfoot. On their return, Sword Bearer and his companions paraded through Crow Village with their captured horses and confronted the local Indian agent, H. E. Williamson, who sent to Fort Custer for troops. Sword Bearer's group then galloped into the mountains and spurred a rash of rumors of an alliance with the Cheyennes and Sioux that would decimate white settlements and Plenty Coups' "good Indians." Plenty Coups eventually persuaded Sword Bearer to lay down his arms.

While Plenty Coups was a longtime ally of the whites, he was often critical of their character.

> We made up our minds to be friendly with them, in spite of all the changes they were bringing. But we found this difficult, because the white men too often promised to do one thing and then, when they acted at all, did another. They spoke very loudly when they said their laws were made for everybody; but we soon learned that although they expected us to keep them, they thought nothing of breaking them themselves. [Hamilton]

During World War I, Plenty Coups encouraged young Crow men to leave the enforced idleness and alcoholism of the reservation and join the U.S. Army. After the war, in 1921, he was chosen to represent all American Indians at the dedication of the Tomb of the Unknown Soldier in Arlington, Virginia. In 1928, his health failing, Plenty Coups willed his personal real estate, about two hundred acres, to the U.S. government for the future use of the Crow people. Plenty Coups died March 3, 1932. The Crow Council at the time so revered him that

its members refused to name another principal chief in his place.

FOR MORE INFORMATION:

Hamilton, Charles. *Cry of the Thunderbird.* Norman: University of Oklahoma Press, 1972.

Linderman, Frank. *Plenty Coups: Chief of the Crows.* 1930. Reprint, Lincoln: University of Nebraska Press, 1962.

PLENTY HORSES
Oglala Lakota
fl. 1890s

After five years at Carlisle Indian School, Plenty Horses returned to the Pine Ridge Indian Reservation angry and alienated, just in time to witness the 1890 massacre of BIG FOOT's people at Wounded Knee. A few days after the massacre, on January 7, 1891, he shot Lieutenant Edward W. Casey in the back, hoping to be hanged for his bravery. Plenty Horses' wife, Roan Horse, was killed in the ensuing melee.

After his arrest, Plenty Horses said that he killed Casey because

> I am an Indian. Five years I attended Carlisle and was educated in the ways of the white man. When I returned to my people, I was an outcast among them. I was no longer an Indian. I was not a white man. I was lonely. I shot the lieutenant so I might make a place for myself among my people. I am now one of them. I shall be hung, and the Indians will bury me as a warrior. They will be proud of me. I am satisfied. [Jensen]

Plenty Horses was jailed at Fort Meade and tried in Sioux Falls, South Dakota. But instead of convicting Plenty Horses and sentencing him to hang, a judge threw the case out because a state of war had existed on the Pine Ridge Reservation—the same state of war that the army was using as a reason not to prosecute the soldiers who had taken part in the massacre. (Instead, the army awarded them medals of honor.) Plenty Horses was sent home to Rose-bud still confused and alienated.

He died at Pine Ridge in the 1930s.

Witnesses in the trial of Plenty Horses: from left, Thompson, White Moon, Rowland (interpreter), and Rock Road. [Nebraska State Historical Society]

FOR MORE INFORMATION:

Jensen, Richard E., et al. *Eyewitness at Wounded Knee.* Lincoln: University of Nebraska Press, 1991.

POCAHONTAS
Powhatan
c. 1595–1617

As the favorite daughter of POWHATAN (Wahun-sonacock), Pocahontas enjoyed considerable power. Her father was the chief of the Powhatan Confederacy, which consisted of about thirty-two different Algonquian bands and two hundred villages in the Virginia tidewater. In Algonquin, the name Pokahantes or Pokahantesu meant "She Is Playful"; in the Pamunkey language, she was called Matoaka, Mataoaka, Matowaka, Matoka, Matoax, and Matsoaks'ats, all of which mean "She Plays with Things."

Although the incident is shrouded in ambiguity, the thirteen-year-old Pocahontas allegedly saved the life of Captain John Smith in 1608. As the leader of the Jamestown settlement, Smith had been taken captive by Pocahontas's uncle, OPECHANCANOUGH. Just before Chief Powhatan was to behead Smith, Pocahontas supposedly intervened on Smith's behalf. (Smith, in his later published account of the incident, never mentioned Pocahontas's largesse.)

When Smith departed for England the next year, Indian-white relations deteriorated. Poca-hontas was coaxed onto an English ship on the Potomac in 1612 and then taken as a hostage to Jamestown to bargain for the release of Virginia captives held by the Powhatans. During her detention at Jamestown, she became a convert to Christianity and was baptized with the name Rebecca. At this time, the widower John Rolfe courted Pocahantas. With her father's consent—though he did not attend the ceremony—she married Rolfe in April 1613. The union facilitated a period of peaceful relations between the Powhatans and the Virginians.

In 1616, Pocahontas and Rolfe journeyed to Great Britain with Sir Thomas Dale and several Indians (including her brother-in-law, Utta-matomac). In England, she was received as the daughter of an emperor. King James I and Queen Anne met Pocahontas at court. Her portrait was painted and still exists today. She saw John Smith again.

While at Gravesend, England, en route to return to Virginia in 1617, she died of a European disease while waiting to board her ship. Pocahontas was buried in the yard of St. George's Parish Church at Gravesend, and memorials were built to her there as well as in Jamestown. Powhatan, her father, passed away the next year. In 1622, Opechancanough made war with the colonists, and John Rolfe was killed in that conflict.

Pocahontas's son, Thomas Rolfe, was educated in London and then returned in 1641 to North America. He became a successful entrepreneur. As a result of tensions between whites and American Indians, Thomas Rolfe had to plead with Virginia authorities to allow him to visit his Indian relations. Today, some prominent Virginia families trace their ancestry to Thomas Rolfe, Pocahontas, and Powhatan. Pocahontas remains a part of American folklore: in 1995 the Walt Disney Company released *Pocahontas*, an animated film *very* loosely based on her life.

POKAGON, LEOPOLD (POCAGIN, RIB)
Potawatomi/Chippewa
c. 1775–1841

Leopold Pokagon sold the site of Chicago to the United States in 1832 as part of the Treaty of Tippecanoe. He was a Chippewa who was captured and raised by Potawatomis in contemporary Michigan. Pokagon was converted to Catholicism by Jesuits as a young man. Once he became a chief, Pokagon asked for a Jesuit to live in his village along the St. Joseph River where Michigan borders Indiana. Father Stephen Badin soon took up residence there.

Pokagon worked to keep his people out of TECUMSEH's uprising and the War of 1812. Twenty years later, he also rebuffed BLACK HAWK's urgings to ally for war. Despite his alliance with white settlers, Pokagon was forced to relocate his village to Dowagiac, Michigan, before his death.

POKAGON, SIMON
Potawatomi
1830–1899

Simon Pokagon was a son of Leopold POKAGON. His father died when Simon was eleven years of age. Leopold was succeeded in the chieftainship by his son Paul, who died; another son, Francis, then became chief until his death. Younger brother Simon then inherited the office of chief.

Simon spoke only Potawatomi until age fourteen, but later studied English at Notre Dame and Latin and Greek at Oberlin College. He eventually mastered five languages and became an accomplished organist. Pokagon used his education to his advantage when meeting with presidents Lincoln and Grant on behalf of the Potawatomis. He spoke at the Chicago World Exposition (1893) and composed poetry and several articles on Native American customs and beliefs. He also wrote an autobiographical romance in the Potawatomi language, which he later translated into English, *O-Gi-Maw-Kwe Mit-I-Gwa-Ki* (Queen of the Woods). The book was published in 1899, the year Pokagon died.

After a sixty-year struggle, the Pokagon band of Potawatomis, then numbering about fifteen hundred people, was granted federal recognition in 1994 by the U.S. House of Representatives.

FOR MORE INFORMATION:

Buehner, "Pokagons." *Indiana Historical Society Publications* 10:5 (1933).

Pokagon, Simon. *The Red Man's Greeting.* Hartford, Mich., 1893.

POKER JOE (LEAN ELK, WAHWOOKYA WASAAW)
Nez Perce
fl. 1870s

Poker Joe, a name given Lean Elk by whites, was known for his skill at buffalo hunting; he was also a war chief. He took over the military command of non-treaty Nez Perces who fled on the Long March with Chief Joseph (see JOSEPH, YOUNGER) during 1877 after tactical errors by LOOKING GLASS. Poker Joe was killed during the last military engagement of the Long March on September 30, 1877, shortly before Chief Joseph's surrender.

FOR MORE INFORMATION:

Howard, Helen A., and Dan L. McGrath. *War Chief Joseph.* Caldwell, Idaho: Caxton, 1952.

Josephy, Alvin M., Jr. *The Nez Perce Indians and the Opening of the Northwest.* New Haven, Conn.: Yale University Press, 1965.

PONTIAC (PONTEACH)
Ottawa
c. 1720–1769

Historian Frank Waters characterized Pontiac as "a man of steel pounded between a British hammer and a French anvil." Pontiac, after whom General Motors named a long-lived automobile model, tried to erect a Native confederacy that would block Euro-American immigration into the Old Northwest.

Pontiac was a man of medium build and dark complexion who highly valued personal fidelity. If Pontiac owed a debt, he would scratch a promissory note on birch bark with his sign, the otter. The notes were always redeemed. He was an early ally of the French in 1755, at Fort Duquesne, now the site of Pittsburgh, along with an allied force of Ottawas, Ojibwas, Hurons, and Delawares. He played a major role in the French defeat of English general Braddock in 1755 during the opening battles of what came to be known as the French and Indian War.

Pontiac was probably born along the Maumee River in northern Ohio of an Ottawa father and a Chippewa mother. He married Kantuckeegan and had two sons, Otussa and Shegenaba. Pontiac held no hereditary chieftainship among the Ottawas, but by about 1760, his oratorical skills and reputed courage as a warrior had raised him to leadership. By 1763, Pontiac had also formed military alliances with eighteen other Native peoples from the Mississippi River to Lake Ontario.

After the British defeat of the French in 1763, Pontiac found himself faced on the southern shore of Lake Erie with an English force that included Robert ROGERS's legendary Rangers, who were self-trained as forest warriors. Rogers told Pontiac that the land he occupied was now British, having been ceded by France, and that his force was taking possession of French forts. Pontiac said that while the French might have surrendered, his people had not. After four days of negotiations, Rogers agreed with Pontiac's point of view. Rogers was allowed to continue to the former French fort on the present-day site of Detroit. Power was transferred as hundreds of Indians watched. Rogers and Pontiac became friends.

Pontiac now looked forward to peaceful trade with the British, but when Rogers left the area, fur traders began swindling the Indians, getting them addicted to cheap liquor. Pontiac sent a belt of red wampum—signifying the taking up of arms—as far east as the Iroquois Confederacy then southward along the Mississippi. He appealed for alliance, telling assembled chiefs of each nation he visited that if they did not unify and resist colonization, the English would flood them like waves of an endless sea.

By spring 1763, a general uprising had been planned by the combined forces of the Ottawa, Huron, Delaware, Seneca, and Shawnee. On May 9, each tribe was to attack the closest English fort. Pontiac's plan was betrayed to the commander of the British fort at Detroit by an Ojibwa woman named Catherine. Pontiac laid siege to Fort Duquesne at Detroit, and other members of the alliance carried out their respective roles. An appeal to the French for help fell on deaf ears, since they had been defeated. After a siege that lasted through the winter and into the spring of 1764, the fort received outside reinforcements, tipping the balance against Pontiac after fifteen months.

After the rebellion ended, settlers swarmed into the Ohio Valley in increasing numbers, and the prestige of the old leader began to disintegrate. Pontiac now counseled peace. The younger warriors were said to have shamed him, possibly beating him physically in their frustration. With a small band of family and friends, Pontiac was forced to leave his home village and move to Illinois.

On April 20, 1769, Pontiac was murdered in Cahokia, Illinois. According to one account, he was stabbed by a Peoria Indian who may have been bribed with a barrel of whiskey by an English trader named Williamson. A statue memorializing Pontiac now stands in the lobby of City Hall in Pontiac, Michigan.

FOR MORE INFORMATION:

Blackbird, Andrew J. *History of the Ottawa and the Chippewa Indians of Michigan.* Ypsilanti, Mich., 1887.

Carver, Jonathan. *Travels Through the Interior Parts of North America.* Dublin: S. Price, 1779.

Hays, Wilma P. *Pontiac: Lion in the Forest.* Boston: Houghton Mifflin, 1965.

Parkman, Francis. *History of the Conspiracy of Pontiac.* 1868. Reprint, New York: Collier Books, 1962.

Peckham, Howard H. *Pontiac and the Indian Uprising.* Chicago: University of Chicago Press, 1947.

Rogers, Robert. *A Concise Account of North America.* 1765. Reprint, New York: Johnson, 1966.

Waters, Frank. *Brave Are My People: Indian Heroes Not Forgotten.* Santa Fe, N. Mex.: Clear Light, 1993.

POPE
Tewa
c. 1633–1690

When the Spanish first arrived in the upper Rio Grande valley under Francisco Vasquez De Coronado in 1540, the Pueblos initially accepted them as new deities. But they soon found that the Spanish were abusing them. As the repartimiento system decreed and the Spanish soldiers enforced, the Pueblo Indians paid Spain tribute through cotton, forced labor, and various crafts products. At this time, the Catholic Church's missionaries also demanded the suppression of Pueblo Indian spiritual ways and rituals. Colonial officials started to punish spiritual leaders through public floggings. As a result, the conduct of the Pueblo kachina religion became more secretive in the underground ceremonial chambers known as *kivas.* However, fierce power struggles between colonial civil and religious leaders undermined the authority of the Spanish over the Indians. Also, severe droughts starting in 1660 convinced many Indian converts that the Christian religion was not for them.

In this turmoil, Pope, a San Juan Pueblo spiritual leader, forged a traditionalist resistance movement. (His name derives from a Tewa word meaning "Pumpkin Mountain.") As his prominence rose, he revealed Nicolas Bua, his son-in-law, as a Spanish spy and allowed Bua's execution by his irate supporters to prove his adamant resistance to Spanish domination.

As tensions mounted in 1675, Pope and about fifty other Pueblo medicine men were arrested and taken to Santa Fe. The Spanish hanged three of the men, and the remainder were whipped and jailed. They were released only after seventy Indian leaders warned the Spanish of violence if the captives remained in custody. Upon his release, Pope did not return to San Juan Pueblo. Instead, he hid at Taos Pueblo and organized a rebellion. Soon other pueblo leaders joined Pope's movement. Pueblo leaders far to the west, such as the Hopis, became part of the rebellion.

To thwart Spanish informants, Pope kept news of the revolt from anyone suspected of being sympathetic to the Spanish. Messengers carried maguey fiber cords to leaders to denote the number of days until the revolt was to begin. August 13, 1680, was the date set for the initial attack on the Spanish, but Pope pushed the date up to August 10, fearing that the Spanish might get word of it through Christian informants. Before dawn on August 10, Pueblo warriors attacked Spanish outposts along the Rio Grande as well as ranchers living on isolated haciendas.

After overwhelming the Spanish in outlying settlements, five hundred Pueblo men began to lay siege to Santa Fe. A garrison of fifty Spanish soldiers, plus civilians at the governor's palace there, mounted a defense of the city on August 14. The Spanish held their ground at the palace under the leadership of Governor Antonio de Otermin. After several days of skirmishing, the Indians succeeded in diverting the town's water supply and stormed the chapel. After considerable casualties, the Indians urged Otermin to retreat southward to El Paso. On August 21,

Otermin moved out of Santa Fe. During ten days of warfare, about four hundred of the twenty-five hundred Spanish settlers were killed (twenty-one out of a total of thirty-three missionaries were dead). About 250 Indians died during the conflict.

With Spanish far to the South in Juarez, the Pueblo Indians regained control over their spiritual and temporal lives. Pope mandated that all elements of Spanish culture—churches, livestock, plants, tools—be destroyed. The Spanish language and names were prohibited. Baptized Christian Indians were bathed with suds from the yucca plant to eliminate all vestiges of Christianity.

But Pope became autocratic. He adopted many of the habits of the Spanish, using the governor's carriage, for example. He also began to execute many of his opponents. A drought aggravated tensions, as did Ute and Apache raids on the Rio Grande Pueblos. Unable to resolve political conflicts, Pope was ousted, though he later recovered power. When he died in 1690, his union of Pueblo peoples had all but disappeared. Spanish power along the upper Rio Grande was reinstituted by 1692. However, Spanish rule would never again seek to repress traditional religious practices.

After 1692, the Pueblo Indians were ruled by Spain until the Mexican Revolution of 1821. Mexican rule continued until 1848, when the United States acquired the area as a result of the Mexican War.

POPOVI DA (TONY MARTINEZ)
San Ildefonso Pueblo
1923–1971

Born April 10, 1923, into the Summer phratry of his mother, Tony Martinez was the eldest son of Julian and Maria Martinez. Since both of his parents were talented artists, young Tony was encouraged to express himself and soon showed promise. Initially, he directed his creative efforts toward painting, following in the footsteps of his father. However, with his father's death in 1943, he began working with his mother to fashion beautifully designed symbolic and geometrical figures on her pottery.

He was educated like most other Pueblo children of the period at the San Ildefonso School and then at St. Catherine's School in Santa Fe. When he attended the Santa Fe Indian School, he enrolled in art classes and excelled. He graduated from the Santa Fe Indian School in 1939. He served in the army during World War II (first in Tennessee and then in Los Alamos, New Mexico). After he was discharged at the end of the war, he opened an arts and crafts studio in 1948 in San Ildefonso Plaza. At this time, he legally changed his name to Popovi Da, meaning "Red Fox."

In the post–World War II years, San Ildefonso Pueblo was a stimulating center for Pueblo art of all kinds. Working with his mother, he continued to experiment in ceramic designs, eventually developing a distinctive black-and-sienna matte ware. He also began to produce some excellent silver jewelry. His prominent role in Southwestern Indian art was reinforced by his being chosen as the Pueblo art representative at many international and national conferences on American Indian art. Peers, collectors, and museum curators recognized his innovative and gifted craftsmanship.

In 1952, Popovi Da was elected governor of San Ildefonso Pueblo and served in that position until 1960. He was also elected to the All-Indian Pueblo Council. He was married to a Santa Clara Pueblo classmate from his Santa Fe school days, Anita Cata Montoya. During the course of their marriage, they had two daughters, Janice and Joyce, and two sons, Bernard and Tony. On October 17, 1971, following a short illness, Popovi Da died in Santa Fe.

PORTER, PLEASANT (TALOF HARJO)
Creek
1840–1907

Pleasant Porter was born on September 26, 1840, near Clarksville, Alabama. He was the son of Benjamin Edward Porter and Phoebe Porter. His mother was the daughter of Tulope Tustunugee, an important Creek chief. (His Creek name means "Crazy Bear.") Even though he had a limited education, Pleasant Porter's extensive reading and his leadership skills helped him to rise quickly within the leadership ranks of the Creeks. Since he was over six feet tall, he had a commanding presence that reinforced his amiable personality. At the onset of the Civil War, Porter became a lieutenant in the Confederate Second Creek Regiment and was wounded while in battle (he walked with a slight limp for the rest of his life).

After the war, he returned home and took an active part in tribal affairs. He supported the faction consisting of Progressive mixed-bloods that favored acculturation to white society and a constitutional form of government as prescribed by the Creek Constitution of 1876. Many others of Creek–African American ancestry supported the mostly full-blood faction favoring traditional tribal government. During these tense times in the Creek nation, Porter was appointed general of the Progressive warriors. Although the split over the nature of tribal government was settled without bloodshed, the two factions were at odds again when a railroad was built through part of their land and white entrepreneurs sought to capitalize on opportunities caused by these investments. The U.S. government intervened on the side of the Progressives to bolster the Creek constitution.

In the post–Civil War era, Porter served his people in a variety of capacities. As school superintendent, he created the modern Creek educational system. In 1889, he was one of the leaders that ceded lands to the United States under the DAWES Commission. During the allotment era, he also acted as a tribal emissary to Washington, D.C. He was the Creeks' principal chief when the Indian Territory became the state of Oklahoma in 1907. He was married to Mary Ellen Keys, a Cherokee woman. In 1907, while traveling to a meeting in Missouri, he had a stroke and died on September 3. He was buried at Wealaka, Oklahoma.

PORTER, TOM
Mohawk
1944–

Tom Porter played a central role in the Akwesasne Mohawks' traditional council, the Mohawk Nation Council, before and during the violence that led to the deaths of Mathew PYKE and Junior EDWARDS there on May 1, 1990. Porter also was a leader in the spiritual and cultural revival of Akwesasne and an advocate of environmental cleanup there.

In the early 1990s, Porter played a major role in acquiring Mohawk Valley land that would host Mohawks migrating from Akwesasne—refugees from pollution, smuggling, and gambling. Proposals for a migration to the Mohawk Valley were being aired while violence at Akwesasne hit its height in 1990. Porter, with Doug GEORGE, was one of the moving forces behind the proposal, which called the settlement Kanatshiohare ("The Clean Pot" in Mohawk), and envisioned it as an agriculturally based settlement that would also offer traditional spiritual teaching and combine the old ways with modern energy-conserving technology.

FOR MORE INFORMATION:

Porter, Tom. "Crisis at Akwesasne." Testimony presented at the New York State Assembly hearings, Fort Covington, N.Y., July 24, 1990.

POSEY, ALEXANDER LAWRENCE (CHIN-NUBIE HARJO)
Creek
1873–1908

Born on August 3, 1873, near Eufala, Oklahoma, Posey was raised steeped in the traditions of his Creek mother, Nancy Phillips (his father was Lewis H. Posey, of Scots-Irish ancestry). His native name, Chinnubie Harjo, was derived from a legendary character in Creek mythology. Although he spoke only Creek until he was twelve, Posey quickly learned English when he became a student at Bacone Indian University in Oklahoma. At Bacone, he set type for a paper entitled *The Instructor* and also acted as a librarian at the school. While helping to produce *The Instructor*, Posey became interested in literature.

When he graduated from Bacone in 1895, the Creek people recognized his leadership abilities by electing him to the House of Warriors. He also became the Creek nation's superintendent of public instruction. Politically, he was considered a Progressive Creek leader because he favored a written constitutional government for his people. In 1901, Posey resigned his leadership position so that he could dedicate more time to his writing. Subsequently, he became editor of the *Indian Journal*; his popular "Fux Fixico Letters" were first published there. The "Fux Fixico Letters" were a series of humorous and satirical dialogues within an ensemble of Creek personages who commented on the politics of the white population.

In the early twentieth century, he continued his political life by representing American Indian interests in the plans for Oklahoma statehood. He worked for the DAWES Commission to enroll Creeks, even though many traditional Creeks wanted to ignore the policies of the U.S. government. In 1905, he served as a major figure in the writing of the new Creek constitution at the Sequoyah Constitutional Convention at Muskogee, Oklahoma (he was elected secretary to the convention).

Among the Creek people, Posey is most remembered as a poet and writer of major importance. On May 27, 1908, at the age of thirty-four, he drowned in the Oktahutchee River while traveling from Muscogee to Eufala, Oklahoma.

POUNDMAKER (OPETECA HANAWAYWN)
Cree
1842–1886

Poundmaker, whose followers included Plains Cree and some Assiniboines, pledged to assist Louis David RIEL and other Métis in the Second Riel Rebellion. Poundmaker had initially urged peace, but his young warriors pushed him into raids on settlements and a brief (but successful) battle with three hundred Canadian soldiers. The uprising was short-lived, however, because the newly constructed railroad allowed the Canadian government to transport a large number of troops into the area in a short time. Riel's second rebellion was crushed in a few days; Poundmaker was arrested and sent to prison.

FOR MORE INFORMATION:

Flanagan, Thomas. *Louis "David" Riel: Prophet of the New World.* Toronto: University of Toronto Press, 1979.

POWESHEEK (AROUSED BEAR)
Fox Mesquaki
c. 1810–1844

Born in the vicinity of present-day Davenport, Iowa, Powesheek (or Pawishik: "He Who Shakes Something Off Himself") was a son of full-blooded Fox parents; Powesheek's grandfather was Black Thunder, a Fox chief. Powesheek became an ally of KEOKUK and white settlers in BLACK HAWK's War.

At the beginning of the Black Hawk War (1832), Powesheek fought with the insurgents as part of a Sauk-Fox Confederation. Later, Powesheek left the alliance. Known for his personal integrity, Powesheek was reported to have foiled an Indian agent's plot to defraud the Fox people of $20,000 due them. Powesheek also spurned a bribe from Keokuk, opponent of Black Hawk. He declined Joseph Smith's efforts to convert him to Mormonism in the late 1830s.

Powesheek died at Des Moines, Iowa.

FOR MORE INFORMATION:

Beckhard, Arthur J. *Black Hawk.* New York: Julian Messner, 1957.

Hagan, William T. *The Sac and Fox Indians.* Norman: University of Oklahoma Press, 1958.

POWHATAN (WAHUNSONACOCK)
Powhatan
c. 1547–1618

Powhatan is actually a place name meaning "Hill of the Pow-Wow" or "Falls in a Current." It is derived from the Algonquian word *pau't-hanne* or *pauwau-atan.* The chief usually called Powhatan was also known by his given name—Wahunsonacock, also Wahunsonacook or Wa-hun-sen-a-cawh.

Powhatan's father had been forced north from Florida by the Spanish. As a result, he founded a powerful alliance of over thirty Algonquian-speaking tribes, with over one hundred villages and over nine thousand people in what would become tidewater Virginia. Powhatan strengthened this alliance system into a confederacy that included the Pamunkey (Powhatan's people), Mattaponi, Chickahominy, Nansemond, Potomac, and Rappahanock peo-

ples. His confederacy stretched from the Potomac River in northern Virginia to Albemarle
Sound in North Carolina. Powhatan's main village was located on the York River. It is estimated that he had eleven wives, over twenty
sons, and at least eleven daughters. POCAHONTAS
was reputed to be his favorite child.

Although Powhatan was deeply suspicious of
the English, he fostered an awkward peace
between the Jamestown colonists and his people, allowing them to establish the first permanent English colony in North America. Some of
Powhatan's followers, like his son NAMONTACK,
provided the English colonists with food and
taught them to plant maize.

Pocahontas, Powhatan's daughter, became
fond of the colonists and later married one of
them, thus furthering the peaceful relationship
between the two groups. It is reported that Captain John Smith, leader of the Virginia colony,
and Powhatan had an uneasy regard for each
other. When Smith was captured by Powhatan
in the fall of 1608, he was released unharmed—
as legend has it, at the request of Pocahontas.
The next year, Smith ceremonially crowned
Powhatan as emperor of the area in a political
exercise to court his favor, though Powhatan
was unimpressed by the honor.

In 1610, the Virginians tried unsuccessfully
to capture and imprison Powhatan. Reacting to
these machinations, Powhatan removed farther
inland. In spite of this precaution, in 1613 the
Virginians did take Pocahontas as a hostage. As
a result, Powhatan had to ransom her with
some English captives. During her captivity,
Pocahontas and a young widower, John Rolfe,
had developed a romantic interest in each
other. In 1614, Pocahontas and Rolfe were married, but Powhatan did not attend the wedding.
However, he did restrain his people from any
further attacks on the Jamestown settlement
during his lifetime. He died in 1618.

PRATT, RICHARD HENRY
1840–1924

Pratt coined the phrase "Kill the Indian, save
the man" during the 1870s to express non-
Indian reform sentiments late in the nineteenth century. Pratt was a proponent of
education as a means by which to assimilate
Indians and dissolve the tribal bonds that kept
them on reservations. He founded Carlisle
Indian School.

Pratt's educational experiment began in the
1870s with seventy-two Native men, most of
them Cheyenne, who were imprisoned in an old
Spanish fort at St. Augustine, Florida. In 1878,
this class graduated, and Pratt approached Congress for an appropriation to begin an Indian
industrial school on an abandoned army post at
Carlisle, Pennsylvania.

To recruit students for his new school, Pratt
visited the Sioux of the high Plains. One hundred and sixty-nine students traveled eastward
in 1879 to form Carlisle's first class. Included
was Luther STANDING BEAR, who later became a
well-known author. Standing Bear recalled his
days at Carlisle in the book *My Indian Boyhood*
(1930).

The Carlisle Indian School was run on an
army model. Students were strictly regimented
and forced to divest themselves of all vestiges
of Indian identity. They wore uniforms, their
hair was cut, and they were forbidden to speak
Native languages. Missionaries were brought in
to teach them Christianity. Runaways were
punished severely; many students died of disease or other causes. This system produced a
notable amount of alienation among some
Native young people, such as PLENTY HORSES. It
also produced some notable success stories,
such as those of Charles EASTMAN and Jim
THORPE.

By the turn of the century, this type of assimilation had become national government pol-

icy. Carlisle formed the prototype for twenty-five Indian industrial schools in thirteen states, most of which closed after enactment of reform legislation under Franklin Delano Roosevelt in the 1930s.

Pratt wrote a book, *Battlefield and Classroom: Four Decades with the American Indian, 1867–1904.*

FOR MORE INFORMATION:

Pratt, Richard. *Battlefield and Classroom.* Edited by Robert M. Utley. New Haven, Conn.: Yale University Press, 1964.

PRETTY EAGLE
Crow
c. 1840–1903

Pretty Eagle was a principal chief of the Crows during the first organized incursions into their territory by the U.S. Army. As he aged, Pretty Eagle began to defer to PLENTY COUPS, who counseled the Crows to aid the invaders against their traditional enemies, the Sioux, Cheyenne, and Arapaho.

Pretty Eagle married nineteen times and was known for hard bargaining with the Indian Bureau when Crow lands were threatened. (In the late 1880s, Charles Barstow, head BIA clerk at Crow Agency, said he kept a loaded revolver in his desk drawer while negotiating with Pretty Eagle.) He resented the incursions of the whites but came to agree with Plenty Coups that they could not be defeated or driven out. As early as the 1880s, Plenty Coups and Pretty Eagle grew and sold hay to the U.S. government to demonstrate Crow financial independence.

Following his death, Pretty Eagle's body was placed in a wagon (in lieu of a burial scaffold) about sixteen miles south of Hardin, Montana. Sometime later, an employee of the county sanitarium removed the body and sold it to the

Pretty Eagle. [National Anthropological Archives]

Museum of Natural History in New York City. In 1994, the museum returned Pretty Eagle's remains to the Crows.

PUSHMATAHA (THE INDIAN GENERAL)
Choctaw
1764–1824

Born June 1764 along Noxubee Creek, Mississippi, Pushmataha became, as a young adult, a Choctaw chief of the Kinsahahi clan. The identity of his parents is unknown; Pushmataha said of himself that he had no parents and that the lightning struck a "living oak, and Pushmataha sprang forth." His name is derived from the Choctaw words *apushim-alhtaha*, meaning "Sapling Is Ready for Him" or "Oak Tree."

In his youth, Pushmataha was a brave warrior and was known as Hochifoiksho (a term connoting no appellation until one had earned a name). While on an expedition against the Osage, he mysteriously disappeared from the war party. When he returned, the other warriors questioned his courage. He replied quietly to their mockery by dropping five scalps on the ground and stating, "Let those laugh who can show more scalps than I can." As a result, he was given the name of Eagle. During this time, his accounts of his exploits won him the name Ishtilawata, or "The Boastful One."

In 1805, Pushmataha was elected principal chief of the Choctaws. He then took the name Pushmataha, which he always claimed meant "Oak Tree." Shortly after his election, he signed a treaty at Mount Dexter in 1805 ceding large tracts of Choctaw lands in Mississippi and Alabama. When the agreement was endorsed, he received $500 in cash and a $150 annuity for life. After this treaty, he became quite friendly with the Americans. When TECUMSEH came south to admonish the southern tribes to join him in his Indian Confederacy against the Americans in 1811, Pushmataha, a persuasive orator, spoke against the designs of Tecumseh and urged a continuation of the Choctaw alliance with the Americans.

During the ensuing Creek War of 1813–1814, Pushmataha remained loyal to the United States. Under General Andrew Jackson, he commanded about five hundred Choctaw warriors at the Battle of Horseshoe Bend and thus was instrumental in the defeat of the traditionalist Creek Red Sticks led by William WEATHERFORD. For his service in this campaign, he was commissioned a brigadier general in the U.S. Army and given a full-dress uniform.

After the Creek War, Pushmataha signed several treaties ceding more Choctaw lands. At the Treaty of Doak's Stand in 1820, it is said

that he demonstrated as much negotiation skill, aplomb, and diplomacy in his demeanor as Andrew Jackson. At this time, he became an advocate of education and invested considerable amounts of tribal money as well as his own personal fortune in educating numerous Choctaw children. Thus, he spearheaded the development of a Choctaw educational system using white methods.

In 1824, alarmed by pressures to cede much of the remaining Choctaw lands in Mississippi, Pushmataha went to Washington, D.C., to lobby against any more land cessions. While in Washington, he met with President James Monroe, the Marquis de Lafayette, and other influential white leaders. During his stay in Washington, he developed a throat infection on December 23, 1824, and died the next day. Since he died in Washington, he was given a full military funeral and buried in the National Cemetery. He was survived by one son, Johnson Pushmataha, also known as Mingo.

PYKE, MATHEW
Mohawk
1968–1990

Mathew Pyke was one of two Mohawk men killed during escalating violence at the Akwesasne Mohawk Reservation on May 1, 1990. Pyke had been an outspoken opponent of commercial gambling at Akwesasne, the issue most immediately responsible for the violence.

Pyke was cut down about three hundred yards roughly east of a house occupied by Davey George, his brother Doug GEORGE, and several other Mohawks who had been under assault for several nights. Doug George said that Pyke had parked about a quarter mile from the house and was killed by gunfire as he walked toward it. The occupants of the car in which Pyke was riding were forced to stop short of the George house and scatter for cover because rifle fire began to hit their car. Some of them returned .22 and shotgun fire as they ran.

Funeral services for Mathew Pyke began at 2 P.M. on May 4 at the St. Regis Catholic Church in St. Regis after several hundred mourners had marched, arm in arm, one mile from the home of Pyke's parents to the church's limestone sanctuary along the river bank. During the hour-long walk, mourners sang "Give Peace a Chance," the John Lennon song that had been Pyke's favorite.

FOR MORE INFORMATION:

Johansen, Bruce E. *Life and Death in Mohawk Country*. Golden, Colo.: North American Press, 1993.

QUALCHIN
Yakima
fl. 1850s

Qualchin, son of OWHI, led a band in the Yakima War (1855–1856). In 1858, Owhi met with Colonel George Wright on the assumption that peace negotiations would commence. Instead, Owhi was taken prisoner and placed in irons. Colonel Wright was hoping that Qualchin, whom he considered to be dangerous, would come to his father's rescue. When Qualchin appeared, Wright's men executed him in a summary fashion. Owhi then escaped Wright's party as it was crossing the Snake River. Troops quickly caught up with Owhi and shot him to death.

FOR MORE INFORMATION:

Brown, Bruce. *Mountain in the Clouds.* New York: Simon & Schuster, 1982.

Stevens, Hazard. *The Life of Isaac I. Stevens.* 2 vols. Boston: Houghton Mifflin, 1900.

QUEEN ANNE
Pamunkey
c. 1650–1725

As the wife of Totopotomoi, a Pamunkey chief in mid–seventeenth-century tidewater Virginia, the young Queen Anne became the head of the Pamunkeys upon the death of her husband in about 1656. The Pamunkeys, who resided at the confluence of the Mattapony and Pamunkey Rivers in present-day Virginia, were a major ally of the English colonists in Virginia; Totopotomoi's death probably occurred while he was fighting with the English against inland tribes. The nation was a member of the Powhatan Confederacy. As a result of her esteemed position, she was always called Queen Anne by the Virginians.

At the beginning of Bacon's Rebellion in 1675, the Virginia colonial government requested that Queen Anne provide warriors to fight the rebellious whites led by Nathaniel Bacon. This request is the first mention of her in the historical record. Queen Anne's appearance before the colonial council to refuse the request for warriors created great tension in Virginia. Her rejection was based on the grounds that the whites had neglected, for twenty years, the old alliance between the Pamunkeys and the Virginians. When the whites gave firm assurances of better treatment for the Pamunkeys, Queen Anne relented and gave assistance to the Virginia colonial government.

After Nathaniel Bacon and his rebels were defeated, the English king Charles II presented Queen Anne with a silver coronet, inscribed "Queen of the Pamunkey," as a token of appreciation for her efforts. After these events, Queen Anne lapsed into historical obscurity until 1715, when she visited the Virginian authorities and renewed her requests for better treatment of her people.

FOR MORE INFORMATION:

Dockstader, Frederick. *Great North American Indians.* New York: Van Nostrand Reinhold, 1977.

QUINAPEN
Narraganset
c. 1630–1676

Quinapen and his supporters allied with METACOM in King Philip's War (1675–1676). He was married to WEETAMOO, who had been widowed after the death of ALEXANDER, Metacom's brother. In 1676, after a brief and bloody rebellion, the Indian alliance was broken by the colonists. Quinapen was captured, tried, and convicted then fatally shot by colonial authorities.

FOR MORE INFORMATION:

Segal, Charles M., and David C. Stineback. *Puritans, Indians, and Manifest Destiny.* New York: Putnam, 1977.

Slotkin, Richard, and James K. Folsom, eds. *So Dreadful a Judgement: Puritan Responses to King Philip's War 1676–1677.* Middleton, Conn.: Wesleyan University Press, 1978.

QUINNEY, JOHN W. (WAUN-NA-CON)
Stockbridge or Mahican
1797–1855

An adroit negotiator on behalf of the Stockbridge [New York] Iroquois, John W. Quinney accepted pressure to relocate to Wisconsin but lobbied the New York legislature to pay market value for the land his people would be leaving. Quinney and the rest of the Stockbridge people obtained land near the southern end of Green Bay, Wisconsin, from the Menominees. Local whites and some Winnebagos objected to the Stockbridges' immigration, and the United States eventually took the land from Quinney's people, but not before he had convinced Congress to pay them $25,000 for improvements they had made to it.

Quinney was willing to negotiate and agree to payment of a fair settlement, but he ran into trouble with the U.S. government when, after accepting a treaty promising a new home west of the Mississippi, he insisted on maintaining tribal sovereignty in a constitution he wrote in 1833. For twenty years, until the middle 1850s, the government was not able to find a new home for Quinney and his people. In 1854, Quinney proposed to Congress that the band move back to their original home in New York. Congress then passed a law allocating 460 acres for that purpose. Quinney died shortly afterward as one of very few Indian leaders who defeated the United States at the bureaucratic politics of relocation.

FOR MORE INFORMATION:

Dictionary of Indians of North America. St. Clair Shores, Mich.: Scholarly Press, 1978.

QUINTANA, BEN (HA-A-TEE)
Cochiti Pueblo
c. 1925–1944

Ben Quintana was born at Cochiti, New Mexico. Little is known of his parents and his early childhood. As a boy, he was taught by Tonita PENA, another Cochiti artist. Subsequently, his career was nurtured by Po-tsunu (or Geronimo Montoya), another noted artist and art teacher from his area.

In 1940, Quintana, at about fifteen, won first prize in the New Mexico State Coronado Quadricentennial Competition. This prize established him as a prodigy in American Indian art. In 1942, his poster entry was selected for first prize in a contest sponsored by the *American Magazine*. During this time, he also painted murals for the Santa Fe Indian School and Cochiti Day School in his native New Mexico.

Like other young artists of the time, he served in the armed forces during World War II. Quintana was killed in action in the Philippines, November 9, 1944. He was awarded the Silver Star, posthumously, for his heroism. In his short life, Quintana's paintings demonstrated his great talent and promise as a gifted artist. His works were acquired by museums and collectors throughout the world. Had he lived, he would probably have become one of the greatest American Indian artists of his generation.

QUINTIN (QUENTIN)
Pomo
fl. 1820s

Little is known of Quintin's early life as a California Mission Indian. As an adult, Quintin became a subchief under MARIN, a noted Pomo chieftain. As one of Marin's lieutenants, Quintin was a major leader in the 1824 Mission Indian Rebellion against the Mexican army. Quintin was taken to the San Francisco Presidio after his surrender and incarcerated there for two years. When he was freed, the priests of Mission Dolores employed him on a trading ship as a pilot in San Francisco Bay. It is said that the town of San Quentin, California, was named to commemorate him.

RAIN-IN-THE-FACE (IROMAGAJA)
Hunkpapa Sioux
c. 1835–1905

As with a number of other Northern Plains leaders who drew their names from natural phenomena, Rain-in-the-Face's name suffers somewhat in translation. Actually, his Dakota name meant "His Face Is Like a Storm."

In 1866, Rain-in-the-Face took part in the destruction of a force led by Captain William FETTERMAN outside Fort Phil Kearny, Wyoming. During the years of Sioux resistance to the opening of the Bozeman Trail, Rain-in-the-Face led a number of raids. He settled for a time at the Standing Rock Agency but was accused of murdering a white man and jailed. A friendly guard freed Rain-in-the-Face, and he joined SITTING BULL after raiding several Union Pacific Railroad crews.

Rain-in-the-Face was one of several Lakota and Cheyenne military leaders who defeated George Armstrong CUSTER's Seventh Cavalry at the Little Bighorn in 1876. After the battle, some reports indicated that Rain-in-the-Face had killed Custer; this assertion was the central theme in Henry Wadsworth Longfellow's poem "The Revenge of Rain-in-the-Face." Subsequent events, described by historian Stanley Vestal in his book *Sitting Bull: The Champion of the Sioux*, indicate that WHITE BULL, not Rain-in-the-Face, took Custer's life. Robert Utley, in his Sitting Bull biography *The Lance and the Shield* (1993), repudiates Vestal's case for White Bull in this regard.

Rain-in-the-Face was badly wounded in the Custer battle and walked with a limp the rest of his life. After joining Sitting Bull's exiles in Canada until 1880, Rain-in-the-Face surrendered to General Nelson Miles at Fort Keough, Montana. Reservation life did not agree with Rain-in-the-Face. He was married seven times, and his last wife was found with her throat cut. He died at Standing Rock and was buried at Aberdeen, South Dakota.

FOR MORE INFORMATION:

Stannard, David. *American Holocaust: Columbus and the Conquest of the New World.* New York: Oxford University Press, 1992.

Utley, Robert M. *The Lance and the Shield: The Life and Times of Sitting Bull.* New York: Henry Holt, 1993.

Rain-in-the-Face.
[National Anthropological Archives]

RAMONA (RAMONA LUBO or LUGO; RAMONA GONZAGA ORTEGA or ORTEGNA)
Cahuilla (Kawia)
c. 1865–1922

Ramona was the California Indian woman whose life was the basis of Helen Hunt JACK-SON's novel *Ramona* (1884). Before the publication of *A Century of Dishonor*, Jackson's polemic against the Bureau of Indian Affairs, the reformer and author, during a trip to south-ern California, met and interviewed Ramona (there is some debate over her parents' last name), a Cahuilla Indian who lived near Mis-sion San Diego. Ramona probably was born about 1865 in a cave on the Carey Ranch at Anza, California. As a result of their conversa-tions, Jackson used the broad outlines of Ramona's life as the story line for her novel.

Like Jackson's earlier work, *Ramona* sought to criticize the inept and capricious Indian poli-cies in the late nineteenth century through the life story of a southern California Mission Indian. Jackson fashioned a literary work that was part truth and part invention. (For in-stance, the novel included an elopement with Alessandro, a totally fabricated event and char-acter.) As a result of the popularity of the book and the subsequent movie based on it, the real Ramona was celebrated and lionized—from a distance—by southern California society. Un-like Jackson, it appears that Ramona herself did not reap much in the way of financial gain from all of the publicity surrounding the book and the movie. For years after the book's publica-tion, she made a living by selling photographs of herself and her finely crafted baskets at a sou-venir stand near Mission San Diego.

In spite of this attention, Ramona lived a rel-atively modest life. She was married to Juan Diego, a California Indian. On July 21, 1922, near Hemet, California, she died. She was buried at the side of her beloved husband in the old Cahuilla Cemetery west of Anza.

RED BIRD (WANIG SUCHKA)
Winnebago
c. 1790–1828

Following a surge in illegal immigration of lead miners into Winnebago country in what would later become southwestern Wisconsin, Red Bird led a brief insurgency in 1827 that resulted in his offering himself to be hanged to save his people. He was never executed but instead languished in jail and died of dysentery in 1828.

The Winnebagos had supported TECUMSEH and the British in the War of 1812, as their mixed-blood chief DECORA (Konoka) led Winnebago warriors in British campaigns at Sandusky River and the Battle of the Thames. Following the war, most Winnebagos remained under British influence and did not make friends with the Americans who began to flood their territory.

The Winnebagos' anger rose when U.S. officials forbade their sale of lead to traders—the same trade that whites were carrying out illegally on their land. This, the widespread abuse of Winnebago women by white frontiersmen, and the long-term incarceration of many Winnebagos in American jails led the Winnebagos' headmen to seek vengeance.

Red Bird was selected to take revenge for the offenses. Red Bird, accompanied by WEKAU and CHICKHONSIC, entered the trading town of Prairie du Chien on June 26, 1827. In an unplanned incident, Red Bird shot trader Registre Gagnier in his cabin. Chickhonsic killed Solomon Lipcap, another trader, during the fray. Wekau had his rifle taken from him by Gagnier's wife. Enraged, he scalped her eleven-month-old infant, who somehow survived the incident.

Red Bird and other Winnebago chiefs urged a number of neighboring Native peoples to rise up with them, but few responded. The area was flooded with U.S. troops, as well as a militia composed of white miners. American Indian agents separated friendly Winnebagos from hostiles; 450 tribesmen under principal chief Four Legs agreed to cease hostilities. On September 3, 1827, Red Bird and Wekau surrendered to American authorities, expecting to be put swiftly to death. Instead, they were incarcerated while the case languished in the courts. At the same time, the number of white miners on Winnebago land increased dramatically. On February 16, 1828, Red Bird died in prison of dysentery and a general lack of will to live.

In September 1828, the other two leaders of the raid were found guilty of being accomplices to Red Bird in the murder of Gagnier: Wekau was convicted of assault and battery with intent to kill the Gagnier infant, and Chickhonsic was convicted of murdering Lipcap the same day that Red Bird had killed Gagnier. They were sentenced to hang but were later pardoned by President John Quincy Adams, who was seeking peace with a delegation of Winnebagos in Washington, D.C., in late 1828.

FOR MORE INFORMATION:

Edmunds, R. David. *Tecumseh and the Quest for Indian Leadership.* Boston: Little, Brown & Co., 1984.

RED CLOUD (MAKHPIYA-LUTA)
Oglala Lakota
c. 1820–1909

Red Cloud, whose Oglala name Makhpiya-luta literally means "Scarlet Cloud," was a major leader of the Oglala Lakota during the late phases of the Plains Indian wars. At one point, during the 1860s, Red Cloud and his allies forced the United States to concede considerable territory in and around the Black Hills, borders of which were outlined in the Fort Laramie Treaty of 1868.

His name refers to an unusual formation of crimson clouds that hovered over the western horizon as he was born. As a young man, Red Cloud learned to fight and hunt like most other Sioux boys. Very quickly he proved himself adept at both. Red Cloud was especially known as a fierce warrior who was always ready to personally take an enemy's scalp.

In 1865, Red Cloud and his allies refused to sign a treaty permitting passage across their

*Red Cloud poses with a young boy, Freddie Davis,
in about 1900. [Nebraska State Historical Society]*

lands from Fort Laramie, along the Powder
River, to the gold fields of Montana. Red
Cloud was angered by the rapid and ruthless
encroachment of Euro-Americans on the lands
of his people. In about 1820, when he was born
"at the forks of the Platte," only a few whites
lived on the plains and prairies of North America; when he died in 1909, his people had been
pushed onto a tiny fraction of their former
land, imprisoned in concentration camp conditions, famished, and impoverished. Born
into the heyday of the Plains horse culture,
Red Cloud died in the era of the vanishing
race.

Red Cloud advised trading with whites but
otherwise avoiding them. His valor as a warrior
was legendary. He had counted more than
eighty coups and once returned from battle
against a contingent of Crows with an arrow
through his body. In the late 1860s, when Red
Cloud was about forty-five years old, the Sioux
dominated the Northern Plains. When U.S.
Army troops built forts in the Sioux Territories
without their permission, war parties cut off
food supplies to Fort Phil Kearney in northern
Wyoming and laid siege to the outpost for two
years. In 1868, with the wagon road still closed,
the government signed a treaty at Fort Laramie
that caused the forts to be dismantled. The
Powder River country as well as the Black Hills
were reserved for the Lakotas forever—or so the
treaty said.

During the 1870s and 1880s, Red Cloud
fought the army and the reservation system,
but at the same time he provided aid to Yale
professor Othniel C. March, who was searching the area for dinosaur bones. In exchange,
March said he would take Sioux allegations of
mistreatment to the highest levels of government. March and his crew dug two tons of
bones during the midst of the war for the Black
Hills. March investigated Red Cloud's complaints of rotten food and unmet promises.
The Yale professor uncovered massive profi-
teering by Indian rings in the Grant administration, sparking a congressional investigation
and several newspaper exposés. At one point,
March confronted Grant personally. March
and Red Cloud became friends for the rest of
their lives, into the twentieth century. Red
Cloud said that he appreciated the fact that
March did not forget his promise after he got
what he wanted.

Once Red Cloud was asked by a trader at
Wolf Point why he continued to pursue dimin-

ishing herds of buffalo rather than settle on a reservation despite cold and near starvation. Red Cloud answered,

> Because I am a red man. If the Great Spirit had desired me to be a white man, he would have made me so in the first place. He put in your heart certain wishes and plans, in my heart he put other and different desires. Each man is good in his sight. It is not necessary for eagles to be crows. Now we are poor but we are free. No white man controls our footsteps. If we must die[,] we die defending our rights. [Vanderwerth]

As the Plains wars ended, Red Cloud settled at Red Cloud Agency, Nebraska, but later moved to Pine Ridge. He counseled peace and was even accused of selling out by some younger Oglalas. He later was moved to the Great Sioux Reservation, where, in 1881, Indian agent V. T. McGillycuddy stripped Red Cloud of his chieftainship.

Red Cloud's biographer, George E. Hyde, characterizes him in old age as "wrinkled, stooped, and almost blind." Red Cloud was sometimes given to ironic bitterness over what had become

Red Cloud's home at the Pine Ridge Agency.
[Nebraska State Historical Society]

of him and his people: "I, who used to control 5,000 warriors, must tell Washington when I am hungry. I must beg for that which I own." Red Cloud spent his final years in retirement, having little to do with his people's affairs. He died December 10, 1909. Red Cloud had five children and perhaps as many as six wives.

FOR MORE INFORMATION:

Armstrong, Virginia Irving, ed. *I Have Spoken: American History Through the Voices of the Indians.* Chicago: Swallow Press, 1971.

Brininstool, E. A. *Fighting Indian Warriors.* New York: Bonanza Books, 1953.

Hyde, George E. *Red Cloud's Folk: A History of the Oglala Sioux Indians.* Norman: University of Oklahoma Press, 1967.

Milner, Richard. "Red Cloud." In *The Encyclopedia of Evolution.* New York: Henry Holt Reference Books, 1990.

Olson, James C. *Red Cloud and the Sioux Problem.* Lincoln: University of Nebraska Press, 1965.

Powers, William K. *Indians of the Northern Plains.* New York: G. P. Putnam's Sons, 1969.

Vanderwerth, W. C. *Indian Oratory.* Norman: University of Oklahoma Press, 1971.

RED CLOUD, JACK
Oglala Lakota
c. 1858–1918

Jack Red Cloud, son of Chief RED CLOUD, was an early advocate of WOVOKA's Ghost Dance among the Sioux but later counseled peace. Red Cloud was among the advocates of the Ghost Dance before the massacre at Wounded Knee in December 1890. He was among roughly two hundred Sioux who prevented Indian police from arresting LITTLE, a Sioux, for practicing the dance after the massacre. At one point during the confrontation, AMERICAN HORSE tried to calm the combatants. Jack Red

Jack Red Cloud. [Nebraska State Historical Society]

Cloud drew his pistol and aimed at American Horse. Red Cloud said that peacemakers such as American Horse were responsible for the Sioux subjugation.

Later, Jack Red Cloud aided Father John Jutz, a Catholic missionary, in attempts to obtain the surrender of militant ghost dancers at the Stronghold, an area to which they had retreated after the Wounded Knee massacre. Jack Red Cloud had initially retreated to the Stronghold with the other militant ghost dancers after the massacre but was among the first to open discussions for surrender. He was being practical, it appeared, and not ready to abandon his long-held belief that Indians should be allowed the same religious freedoms enjoyed by whites. He had told the *Omaha World-Herald* (November 23, 1890): "White men [have] religions and religious celebra-

tions. Why shouldn't an Indian be treated just the same?"

FOR MORE INFORMATION:

Jensen, Richard E., et al. *Eyewitness at Wounded Knee.* Lincoln: University of Nebraska Press, 1991.

RED HORSE
Sioux
fl. 1870s

Red Horse's drawings of the 1876 Battle of the Little Bighorn are now being used, more than a century after their creation, to compose a Native American perspective on the event.

Carole Barrett, a professor of American Indian studies at the University of North Dakota, said that the Native historical records were contained not in narratives but in drawings, including forty-one visual images that Red Horse drew shortly after the battle at the request of the U.S. Army. While little is known of Red Horse's personal life, his drawings have become an important record of the battle.

The drawings depict the large camp of Lakota, Cheyenne, and other Indians at peace as the soldiers advanced. The forty-five-minute battle is depicted by Red Horse as brutal, confusing, and one-sided. "Custer's soldiers became foolish, many throwing away their guns and raising their hands, saying 'Sioux, pity us, take us prisoner.' The Sioux did not take a single soldier prisoner but killed all of them," said Professor Barrett. Red Horse's drawings show a battlefield littered with horses and dead soldiers as the victorious Indians took some of the soldiers' clothing and horses that remained alive. The Lakota side of the record indicates that 130 Indians died in the battle and 160 were wounded. They killed between 210 and 225 men of the Seventh Cavalry, Custer included.

One of Red Horse's depictions of the battle at the Little Bighorn. [National Anthropological Archives]

FOR MORE INFORMATION:

Harrison, Eric. "To Sioux, Wounded Knee Seems Like Only Yesterday." *Los Angeles Times*, 26 December 1990, sec. A, p. 1.

RED JACKET (SAGOYEWATHA)

Seneca

c. 1755–1830

Red Jacket, a nephew of HANDSOME LAKE, was a major Iroquois leader during the late eighteenth and early nineteenth centuries. He was probably best known as a British ally in the American Revolution. Red Jacket's first name was Otetiani, meaning "He Is Prepared." Later he took the name Sagoyewatha, meaning "He Causes Them to Be Awake." The name Red Jacket came from a scarlet coat given to him by the British for fighting with them during the American Revolutionary War.

Red Jacket's skills lay more in diplomacy than in the waging of war. After he fled the Battle of Oriskany in 1777, avoided battle at Wyoming Valley in 1778, and made an early exit at the Battle of Newtown in 1779, Red Jacket got a reputation as a coward. At another point during the American Revolution, Red Jacket killed a cow and smeared his tomahawk with blood to convince other Iroquois that he had killed a white man. Instead, Joseph BRANT and CORNPLANTER ridiculed Red Jacket as a "cow killer."

After the war, Red Jacket reconciled his differences with the Americans (unlike Brant, who moved to Canada). In 1792, Red Jacket was among a number of Iroquois chiefs invited to

Red Jacket. [National Anthropological Archives]

Philadelphia to parlay with George Washington. In the War of 1812, he fought on the American side against the British. Regardless of his allegiances, Red Jacket believed that Indians should retain their own lands and cultures. He sought and sometimes got extensive legal protection for reservation lands. His speeches in defense of Native rights have been cited by generations of Iroquois. One famous speech, given in 1828, was addressed to a representative of the Boston Missionary Society named Mr. Cram, who was requesting approval to recruit Iroquois to his faith.

Brother, listen to what we say. There was a time when our forefathers owned this great island. Their seats extended from the rising to the setting sun. The Great Spirit had made it for the use of Indians. He had created the buffalo, the deer, and other animals for food. He had made the bear and

the beaver. Their skins served us for clothing. He had caused the earth to produce corn for bread. All this he had done for his red children because he loved them. If we had some disputes . . . they were generally settled without shedding much blood.

But an evil day came upon us. Your forefathers crossed the great water and landed on this island. Their numbers were small. They found friends and not enemies. They told us they had fled from their own country for fear of wicked men. . . . They asked us for a small seat. We took pity on them, granted their request, and they sat down among us. We gave them corn and meat; they gave us poison in return. . . .

They wanted more land; they wanted our country. . . . Wars took place. . . . You have got our country, but you are not satisfied. You want to force your religion upon us. . . . [But] we also have a religion which has been given to our forefathers and handed down to us, their children. . . . Brother, we do not wish to destroy your religion or take it from you. We only want to enjoy our own.

On another occasion, Red Jacket sarcastically told a "black-coat" (clergyman), "If you white people murdered 'The Savior,' make it up yourselves. We had nothing to do with it. If he had come among us, we would have treated him better."

In 1821, Red Jacket sent a letter to De Witt Clinton, governor of New York, enumerating the problems that the Iroquois were having with white settlers, including illegal cutting of timber on Indian lands, poaching of livestock, the death of fishing stocks because of dam building, and the decrease in hunting animals. "The greatest source of all our grievances is, that the white men are among us," Red Jacket concluded.

In his last years, Red Jacket became an alcoholic and was deposed as an Iroquois chief in 1827. The chieftainship was restored shortly before he died on January 20, 1830, in Seneca Village, New York. He was memorialized with a statue erected in 1891 by the Buffalo Historical Society near the graves of Cornplanter and Ely S. PARKER.

FOR MORE INFORMATION:

Armstrong, Virginia Irving, ed. *I Have Spoken: American History Through the Voices of the Indians.* Chicago: Swallow Press, 1971.

Hamilton, Charles. *Cry of the Thunderbird.* Norman: University of Oklahoma Press, 1972.

Red Jacket. *A Long Lost Speech of Red Jacket.* Edited by J. W. Sanborn. Friendship, N.Y., 1912.

Stone, William L. *The Life and Times of Say-go-ye-wat-ha, or Red Jacket.* Albany, N.Y.: Munsell, 1866.

Waters, Frank. *Brave Are My People: Indian Heroes Not Forgotten.* Sante Fe, N. Mex.: Clear Light, 1993.

RED SHOES (SHULUSH HOMA or SHULUSH HUMMA)

Choctaw

c. 1700–1748

Red Shoes, Choctaw war chief and ally of the English, was born Choctaw, probably with some Chitimacha lineage as well. In his early years, he was allied with the French; however, in 1734, when a Frenchman raped one of his wives, he switched to the British side and favored the development of new trade relations with James ADAIR of South Carolina. Red Shoes also led a Choctaw faction that advocated peace with the Chickasaws and the British.

Angered by the actions of Red Shoes, Pierre Rancois Rigaud, the French governor of Louisiana, ordered him to be executed by his own people to demonstrate Choctaw loyalty to the French Crown. As a result, pro-French Choctaw warriors killed him as he was returning home one day in 1748. Red Shoes's assassination led to a civil war between rival Choctaw factions that was called the Choctaw Revolt. Edmond Atkin, the first English superintendent of Indian affairs for the Southern Department, wrote in detail of this bitter battle among the Choctaw.

RED TOMAHAWK (TACANHPI LUTA)

Miniconjou Sioux

c. 1853–1931

Red Tomahawk, who assassinated SITTING BULL, shared with BULLHEAD the command of a column of forty-three Indian police sent to arrest Sitting Bull at the Standing Rock Agency on December 15, 1890, only a few days before the massacre at Wounded Knee. Bullhead, Red Tomahawk, and the other police faced off with a similar number of Sitting Bull's supporters, who were armed and ready for a fight. Sitting

Red Tomahawk.
[National Anthropological Archives]

Bull refused to go, and shooting broke out. Bull-head shot Sitting Bull in the back as he was falling from a bullet wound. Red Tomahawk also shot Sitting Bull as he fell from Bullhead's wound.

The death of Sitting Bull was the culmination of a rivalry with Indian agent William ("White Hair") McLaughlin, who had used the Indian police to harass Sitting Bull and had appointed four recognized chiefs to undermine his authority among the Sioux.

FOR MORE INFORMATION:

Utley, Robert M. *The Lance and the Shield: The Life and Times of Sitting Bull.* New York: Henry Holt, 1993.

REIFEL, BEN
Brulé Sioux
1906–1990

Ben Reifel, who would become a U.S. congressman from South Dakota, was born in Parmelee, South Dakota, the son of a German father and a Sioux mother. Reifel did not pass the eighth grade until he was sixteen and did not go to high school because his father could see no reason for it. The elder Reifel told Ben he was needed on the farm, so the young man read whatever he could find. His passion for education grew until Reifel at last ran away from home, hiking 250 miles to enroll in high school.

Despite his late start in formal education, Reifel earned a bachelor's degree from South Dakota State University in 1932. Reifel joined the U.S. Army reserves as a commissioned officer while in college and was called to duty in World War II. At the end of the war, he was appointed Bureau of Indian Affairs superintendent at the Fort Berthold Agency, North Dakota. Reifel returned to college at Harvard University for a master's degree in public administration and then became one of the first

Ben Reifel. [Nebraska State Historical Society]

American Indians to earn a Ph.D., also at Harvard. Reifel then returned to the Dakotas and held several BIA posts, including the superintendency at Pine Ridge, where he was the first Indian agent of Native ancestry. His career at the BIA culminated as Reifel was appointed area director of the office in Aberdeen, South Dakota.

In 1960, Reifel retired from the BIA to run for Congress. He won on his first run for public office (as a Republican) and served five terms before retiring in 1970. On his retirement, Reifel, who had fought so hard to get a formal education, was awarded an honorary degree from the University of South Dakota.

Reifel died of cancer in January 1990 in Sioux Falls, South Dakota, at the age of eighty-three.

FOR MORE INFORMATION:

Paulson, T. Emogene. *Sioux Collections.* Vermillion: University of South Dakota Press, 1982.

REVERE, PAUL
1735–1818

Paul Revere, whose "midnight rides" became legend in the hands of Henry Wadsworth Longfellow, played a crucial role in forging a sense of American identity, contributing to the Revolutionary cause a set of remarkable engravings that cast as America's first national symbol an American Indian woman—long before Brother Jonathan or Uncle Sam came along.

Revere was one of the earliest Sons of Liberty, a clandestine society in the American colonies that agitated against the British. The Boston Tea Party was only one of its many acts of agitation, propaganda, and creative political mischief. The use of American Indian imagery as a counterpoint to British tyranny ran through the group's activities. Some of the Sons of Liberty's units had named themselves after native peoples long before they dressed as Mohawks at the Tea Party. The "Mohawk River Indians" were the most notable.

Revere was among the "Mohawks" who instigated the Boston Tea Party. As the first group of "Mohawks" boarded the tea ship *Dartmouth* and began to rip open thirty-five thousand pounds of symbolic oppression, others boarded the *Beaver* and *Eleanor*. Several thousand people gathered along the waterfront in the cold, drizzly December day, cheering as each tea chest hit the water. During the three hours they took to lighten the three ships of £10,000 sterling worth of tea, the "Mohawks" exchanged words in a secret sign language using Indian hand symbols and sang:

Rally Mohawks, and bring your axes
And tell King George we'll pay no taxes
   on his foreign tea;

His threats are vain, and vain to think
To force our girls and wives to drink
   his vile Bohea!

Then rally, boys, and hasten on
To meet our chiefs at the Green Dragon!

Our Warren's here, and bold Revere
With hands to do and words to cheer,
   for liberty and laws;

Our country's "braves" and firm defenders
shall ne'er be left by true North Enders
   fighting freedom's cause!
Then rally, boys, and hasten on
To meet our chiefs at the Green Dragon.
      [Grinde and Johansen]

Within hours, Paul Revere had stripped off his Mohawk disguise and begun the first of his "midnight rides," carrying news of the Boston Tea Party to other cities: Springfield, Hartford, New Haven, New York City, and Philadelphia. In Philadelphia, on December 27, more than eight thousand people gathered at the State House to hear Revere.

Between the Boston Tea Party and his most famous "midnight ride" on April 18, 1775, Revere created a remarkable series of engravings that carried messages akin to modern political cartoons. The engravings were meant to galvanize public opinion against the British. Many of them used the Indian (usually a woman) as a symbol of independent American identity, much as the "Mohawk" disguise had been used in the Tea Party.

Revere's engravings used an Indian woman as a patriotic symbol and often were sharply political. One of them, titled "The Able Doctor, or America Swallowing the Bitter Draught," portrays the Indian woman being held down by British officials, forced to drink "the vile Bohea." Lord Mansfield, in a wig and judicial robe, holds America down as Lord North, with the Port Act in his pocket, pours the tea down her throat. Lord Sandwich occupies his time peering under "America's" skirt.

Lord Bute stands by with a sword inscribed "Military Law." The bystanders (Spain and France) consider aid for the colonies. In the background, Boston's skyline is labeled "cannonaded"; a petition of grievances lies shredded in the foreground, symbolic of the British government's failure to provide justice for America. This engraving was published in the *Royal American Magazine*'s June 1774 edition.

In 1780, three years before the Revolution was concluded by treaty, Massachusetts' provisional government felt confident enough of its sovereignty to commission creation of a state seal. Paul Revere engraved the seal, according to instructions given him:

An Indian dressed in his shirt, moggosins, belted proper—in his right hand a bow—in his left, an arrow, its point toward the base . . . on the dexter [right] side of [the] Indian's head, a star for one of the United States of America—on the wreath a dexter arm clothed and ruffled proper, grasping a broad sword, the pommel and hilt with this motto: "Ense petit placidam sub Libertate quietem." And around the seal: "Sigillum republicae Massachusetts." [Grinde and Johansen]

Few better graphic examples exist of the fusion of Native American and European civilizations that Revere and other colonists were shaping into a new nation in their adopted homeland.

FOR MORE INFORMATION:

Forbes, Esther. *Paul Revere and the World He Lived In*. Boston: Houghton Mifflin, 1969.

Goss, Eldridge Henry. *The Life of Col. Paul Revere*. Boston: G. K. Hall & Co./Gregg Press, 1972.

Grinde, Donald A., Jr., and Bruce E. Johansen. *Exemplar of Liberty: Native America and the Evolution of Democracy*. Berkeley and Los Angeles: University of California Press, 1991.

Honour, Hugh. *European Visions of America*. Cleveland: Cleveland Art Museum, 1975.

Johansen, Bruce E. "Mohawks, Axes and Taxes." *History Today* (London) 35 (April 1985): 18–24.

RIDGE, JOHN (GANUN'DALEGI)
Cherokee
1803–1839

Born at Rome, Georgia, in 1803, John Ridge (Ganun'dalegi or Gahna Tahtlegi, meaning "One Who Follows the Ridge") was the son of Major RIDGE and Princess Schoya (Susie Wickett). As a youth, he was sent by his father to the Cornwall Foreign Mission School in Connecticut with his cousin, Elias BOUDINOT. While in Connecticut, Ridge met and married a white woman, Sarah Bird Northrup. This marriage caused racial hatred and bitterness in her small New England town of Cornwall, Connecticut. They later had a son, John Rollin Ridge.

When he returned to Georgia with his new bride, Ridge became a prominent tribal leader. He wrote articles for the *Cherokee Phoenix* and was an interpreter and secretary to several tribal groups that journeyed to Washington, D.C., seeking justice for the Cherokee people. By 1835, John Ridge, Elias Boudinot, and Major Ridge had accepted the removal policy of federal government as inevitable, so they negotiated and signed the Treaty of New Echota. Since the Cherokee Council had decreed in 1829 that anyone selling Cherokee lands without the consent of the people would be executed, the Treaty Party knew that they were signing their own death warrants. John ROSS, as principal chief of the Cherokees, opposed the treaty.

In 1836, Ridge wrote to President Andrew Jackson complaining about the brutal treatment of his people by the unscrupulous Georgians. After the Trail of Tears, Ridge, his father, and Boudinot were killed on June 20, 1839, in Indian Territory for their role in signing the removal treaty.

FOR MORE INFORMATION:

Foreman, Grant. *The Five Civilized Tribes.* Norman: University of Oklahoma Press, 1936.

RIDGE, MAJOR (NUNNA HIDIHI)
Cherokee
c. 1770–1839

Nunna Hidihi (also Nungo Hattarhee), "Man on the Mountaintop" or "The Ridge," was born at Hiwassee in the old Cherokee nation (present-day Tennessee), but his family soon moved to what would become northern Georgia. He was the son of a Cherokee man named Ogonstota and Susannah Catherine, a Scot-Cherokee woman of the Deer clan. Having little formal education, Ridge gained most of his academic skills from his parents and neighbors. He would become an American ally in the Creek War, as well as speaker of the Cherokee Council and leader of the Treaty Party. He was the father of John RIDGE and uncle to Elias BOUDINOT and Stand WATIE.

As a young man, Ridge's considerable oratorical skills facilitated his election to the Cherokee Council when he was only twenty-one, and he became speaker of the Cherokee Council within a few years. Ridge also became a prosperous farmer. In 1792 he married Princess Schoya (Susie Wickett), a full-blooded Cherokee woman.

Although he received the title "major" during the Creek War of 1813–1814 while serving under General Andrew Jackson, Ridge was unhappy with the way the Georgia legislature was treating his people. Spurred by racial hatred and contempt, white settlers treated the Cherokees as mere animals to be driven back into the woods in the face of white settlement. Early in the 1830s, Major Ridge, his son, and Boudinot became leaders in the Treaty Party. In 1835, the three men signed the Treaty of New Echota. They were killed by their opponents in Indian Territory in 1839.

FOR MORE INFORMATION:

Foreman, Grant. *Indian Removal: The Emigration of the Five Civilized Tribes.* Norman: University of Oklahoma Press, 1939.

RIEL, LOUIS (ELDER)
Métis/Cree
c. 1810–1864

Louis Riel, who would lead the first organized Native resistance to Euro-American colonization of the Canadian prairies, tried to start a woolens factory in the Red River area of present-day Manitoba during the mid–nineteenth century. His project was scuttled by the Hudson's Bay Company, which did not want Métis to compete with its own manufactures. When the Hudson's Bay Company tried to restrict commerce between Métis and people in the United States, Louis Riel organized resistance. In 1849, as the company brought charges against Guillaume Sayer for smuggling furs into the United States, Riel led three hundred armed Métis who encircled the courthouse at Fort Garry (later Winnipeg, Manitoba). Sayer was found guilty but released. The courthouse rebellion served as an inspiration for another, broader Métis uprising later in the century, in which Riel's son, Louis David RIEL, played a leading role.

FOR MORE INFORMATION:

MacEwan, Grant. *Métis Makers of History.* Saskatoon, Sask.: Western Producer Prairie Books, 1981.

RIEL, LOUIS DAVID (YOUNGER)
Métis/Cree
1844–1885

Louis David Riel was the leader of the most substantial Native uprising on the Canadian frontier, a clash that illustrated the complexities of
clashing cultures. Riel was only one-eighth
Native but was representative of a large number
of Canadians: the offspring of French traders,
usually men, and Native American women.
These mixed-bloods, called "Métis," form a
substantial part of Canadian Native popula-
tions. Many Métis adopted Native American
families and lifeways as the settlement frontier
engulfed them. During the nineteenth century,
a large Métis community grew near the site of
contemporary Winnipeg, Manitoba, reaching
southward to the junction of the Minnesota and
North Dakota borders with Canada.

Louis David Riel.
[National Archives of Canada/Neg. no. C06688]

Riel was born at Saint Boniface of a French
mother and a mixed-blood father, Louis RIEL.
He was exceptionally intelligent from an early
age, leading a priest to urge him to attend the
College of Montreal in 1864 and to become the
first Métis priest. Riel attended the college for
two years but declined to take the path into the
priesthood. He traveled for a while and then
returned to his homeland to find his fellow
Métis worried that the British-dominated government of Canada would favor Protestant settlers over the Catholic Métis. By 1870, Riel had
become a Métis spokesman; he allied with
other Indians to block surveyors from entering
the Red River country. Riel and his allies prevented a newly assigned governor from taking
up residence in the area; they also seized Fort
Garry, a Hudson's Bay Company outpost near
St. Boniface. After that, the Métis and their
allies established a provisional government.
Two attempts to retake the fort were fought off
as the Métis sent a delegation to Ottawa to
argue their case for independence.

In May 1870, Canada promised amnesty for
the rebels as part of the formation of Manitoba
as a province. After authorities discovered that
the Métis had killed an English-speaking captive, the amnesty was revoked (along with a
plan to allow Métis to purchase land), and a
military force was sent to retake Fort Garry.
The Métis dispersed, some taking refuge with
other native peoples in Canada. Riel was
harassed for several years and finally took up
residence in the United States.

In 1884, a delegation of Métis asked Riel to
lead their campaign for provincial status. Riel
accepted, believing that God had chosen him to
lead a great Métis-Native Confederacy. He con-
tacted SITTING BULL and other Native leaders on
the Plains, most of whom were cool to his plan
and suspicious of his claims of divine inspiration. One chief, POUNDMAKER, whose followers

included Plains Cree and some Assiniboines, pledged to assist Riel and his followers. The uprising was short-lived because the newly constructed railroad allowed the Canadian government to transport a large number of troops into the area in a short time. Riel's second rebellion was crushed in a few days; Poundmaker was arrested and sent to prison.

Riel was tried for sedition and hanged November 16, 1885. Afterward he became a martyr and folk hero to many Métis and French Canadians.

FOR MORE INFORMATION:

Davidson, William McCartney. *Louis Riel: 1844–1885.* Calgary: Alberton Publishing, n.d.

Flanagan, Thomas. *Louis "David" Riel: Prophet of the New World.* Toronto: University of Toronto Press, 1979.

ROCK, HOWARD
Inuit
1911–1976

As editor and publisher of the *Tundra Times*, Howard Rock became the first Native American newspaper owner among the Inuit of Alaska.

Rock was born in Point Hope, Alaska, and attended St. Thomas Mission School as a young man. He later worked his way to the Pacific Northwest and studied art at the University of Washington, before starting a career as a jewelry designer. In World War II, Rock served in the U.S. Army Air Force in North Africa between 1943 and 1945.

Returning to Alaska after the war, Rock became involved in community affairs and began to seek an effective communication medium for the area. He found financial backing and began publishing the *Tundra Times* in 1962. As editor, Rock was known for his tenacity and his advocacy of Native self-determination. A

year before he died, Rock was nominated for a Pulitzer Prize.

ROCKY BOY (STONE CHILD)
Chippewa
1860–1914

Rocky Boy was a leader of the Chippewa nomads, who were left out of treaties in both the United States and Canada. During the nineteenth century, roughly 350 Chippewas had left the main group in Wisconsin and gone off to hunt in Montana. They evaded settlement on any reservation and thus were omitted from all treaty negotiations. As more land was fenced, the nomads' life became untenable; by 1900, many had been reduced to a life of begging.

Rocky Boy and his family.
[Nebraska State Historical Society]

Stone Child, who was often called "Rocky Boy" by settlers, emerged as a leader as the nomads' situation became desperate. He lobbied the Bureau of Indian Affairs, and after a number of years of bureaucratic backing and filling, "Rocky Boy's Band" was granted a tract of land on the Fort Assiniboin military reserve in Montana. The land grant came in 1914, the same year that Rocky Boy died.

FOR MORE INFORMATION:

Dockstader, Frederick J. *Great North American Indians*. New York: Van Nostrand Reinhold, 1977.

ROGERS, ROBERT
1731–1795

An Anglo colonist, Robert Rogers headed the famed Rogers' Rangers, who adapted guerrilla warfare methods in the French and Indian War of the mid–eighteenth century. He was a friend of PONTIAC and wrote a play called *Ponteach*, which outlined the treachery that had caused Pontiac's Rebellion.

Born in Methuen, Massachusetts, Rogers lived in the frontier regions of New Hampshire as a young man. His first fight with Indians occurred near his home when he was fifteen. In 1755, Rogers escaped charges in a counterfeiting incident by volunteering for a colonial militia in the French and Indian War (1754–1763). In the militia, Rogers became a scout under William Johnson and was present at the 1755 attack on Crown Point, near Lake Champlain. After that battle, Rogers was promoted to captain and given command of a company that he molded into frontier guerrilla fighters who did not need the supply lines required by most European armies.

Rogers' Rangers took part in several campaigns during the war against the French, as well as raids on Indian allies of the French. In one such engagement against the Abenakis in early fall 1759, he lost about half of his 350-man force. As hostilities wound down, Rogers worked as a frontier trader, a job in which he accumulated a very large personal debt.

After the defeat of the French in 1763, Rogers was sent to take forts that were to be surren-

dered by the French. He told Pontiac that the land his people occupied was now British, having been ceded by France. Pontiac retorted that while the French might have surrendered, his people had not. After four days of negotiations, Rogers agreed with Pontiac's point of view. Rogers was allowed to continue to a fort on the present-day site of Detroit. Power was transferred as hundreds of Indians watched. Rogers and Pontiac became friends.

In 1765, Rogers traveled to London and there published his journals and *A Concise Account of North America*. His stage play *Ponteach, or the Savages of America* was written and produced in 1766. Rogers returned to America in 1767 as an Indian trader in Michigan, but his shady business practices caused his removal by Sir William Johnson. Rogers was imprisoned for debt in England on another visit there in 1769.

In 1776, Rogers found himself back in the colonies just as the American Revolution broke out. With the advent of war, he was suspected of being a spy by General George Washington. Residing in New Hampshire at the time, Rogers accepted a commission in the British army and raised the Queen's Rangers. He was also suspected of spying by the British, who imprisoned him during a visit to England. In 1778, he was ordered proscribed and banned by the British government. Because of this banishment, his subsequent history is sketchy. The circumstances of his death in 1795 are not known.

FOR MORE INFORMATION:

Peckham, Howard H., ed. *The Journals of Major Robert Rogers*. N.p.: Corinth Books, 1961.

ROGERS, WILL
Cherokee
1879–1935

Born William Penn Adair Rogers near Oologah, Indian Territory (now Oklahoma), Will Rogers was widely known as a humorist and actor.

Rogers was a son of Clement Vann Rogers, a former Confederate army officer, banker, and rancher who was also a leading figure in Cherokee political circles.

Rogers was famous for using rope tricks that he learned as a cowboy on his father's ranch. The rope served him well in Wild West shows and in vaudeville acts. In 1902, Will Rogers sold a number of livestock given him by his father then used the money to travel to England and South Africa. In South Africa, he became the rope-twirling "Cherokee Kid" in a Wild West show.

Rogers first appeared on a New York City vaudeville stage at Hammerstein's Roof Garden in 1903; in 1914, he joined Ziegfeld's Follies. During 1915, Rogers began to introduce political commentary into his act. In 1922, Rogers began writing a nationally syndicated weekly newspaper column of satire and contemporary political commentary. Four years later, the column began running daily, reaching a peak audience of thirty-five million people.

Rogers wrote several books of political humor and commentary, including Rogerisms—*The Cowboy Philosopher on Prohibition* (1919), *Illiterate Digest* (1924), and *There's Not a Bathing Suit in Russia* (1927). Rogers's acting career included major roles in *A Connecticut Yankee* (1931), *State Fair* (1933), and *David Harum* (1934). He starred in seventeen major motion pictures.

Rogers died August 15, 1935, near Barrow, Alaska, on a flight to the Orient piloted by Wiley Post.

ROMAN NOSE (WOQINI, HOOK NOSE)
Southern Cheyenne
c. 1830–1868

Well known to both Cheyennes and non-Indians in his time, Woqini (Hook Nose) stood six-foot-three. He was a fierce warrior who refrained from attacking railroad workers and passing wagon trains until after the Sand Creek Massacre of 1864 (see BLACK KETTLE). But in 1866, Roman Nose bitterly opposed the construction of a Union Pacific railway through his people's hunting grounds. Roman Nose was a chief of the Pointed Lance Men Society, a leading Southern Cheyenne Dog Soldier Society.

Roman Nose was said to be invincible in battle—a quality rumored to be guaranteed if he wore a special headdress of forty red and black eagle feathers. The headdress was so long that it almost reached the ground even when Roman Nose was mounted on his favorite horse. The donning of this headdress was accompanied by many rituals and taboos, one being that Roman Nose must never eat anything with an iron eating utensil, such as a knife or fork. If this taboo was broken, a lengthy purification ceremony was required to restore the war bonnet's medicine. He proved the story time and again by loping at a slow pace in front of the enemy on his horse. Young Cheyennes idolized his exploits.

During September 1868, Roman Nose accidentally ate with iron utensils. A day or two later, allies came to summon Roman Nose to battle against a group of fifty-two scouts headed by Colonel G. A. Forsyth. This was too soon for the required purification of his war bonnet. Roman Nose, who had declined to go into battle until his warriors urged him, donned his war bonnet and prepared to die. He rode into battle at Beecher's Island, Colorado, and was quickly shot from his horse. He died the evening of September 17, 1868.

FOR MORE INFORMATION:

Brown, Dee. *Bury My Heart at Wounded Knee.* New York: Holt, Rinehart & Winston, 1970.

Hoig, Stan. *The Sand Creek Massacre.* Norman: University of Oklahoma Press, 1961.

ROSE, EDWARD (FIVE SCALPS, NEZ COUPE, "CUT NOSE")
Cherokee
c. 1780–1832 or 1833

Edward Rose's father was a white trader and his mother was Cherokee and African American. As a youth, Rose lived with the Crow people in what is now southern Montana and northern Wyoming. He quickly acquired their customs as well as their language. According to the historical record, Wilson Price Hunt, a prominent fur trader, employed Rose in 1811 as a guide through Crow Territory; Rose was dismissed, however, when he was suspected of leading the traders into an ambush.

By the early 1820s, Rose had also learned the Arikara language and was residing with them in North Dakota. In 1823, while serving as a guide and interpreter for William Henry Ashley's expedition up the Missouri River, Ashley disregarded Rose's warnings about an impending Arikara attack. As a result of Arikara depredations, Colonel Henry Leavenworth mounted his 1823 campaign against the Arikara, and Rose served under Leavenworth as interpreter and envoy to the Native Americans in the region. By September 1823, Rose had joined Jedidiah Smith's expedition journeying from the Black Hills to the Rocky Mountains. In 1825, Rose was Colonel Henry Atkinson's interpreter during his Yellowstone expedition.

Shortly after this expedition, Rose resumed residency among the Crows and became a famous war chief. The Crows named him "Nez Coupe," meaning "Cut Nose," because his nose was scarred. Rose was sometimes called "Five Scalps" because he killed five Blackfoot single-handedly in battle. Although the exact date of Rose's death is unclear, some say that he died on the Yellowstone River along with two mountain men as a result of an Arikara attack in 1832 or 1833.

FOR MORE INFORMATION:
Littlefield, Daniel F. *Cherokee Freedmen.* Westport, Conn.: Greenwood Press, 1978.

ROSE, WENDY
Hopi, Chowchilla, and Miwok
1948–

Born in Oakland, California, in 1948, Wendy Rose grew up in the San Francisco Bay area during the post–World War II boom era. In an environment of urban sprawl, she came to terms with her gender, ethnicity, and an American Indian's place in an urban context.

In 1974, she married Arthur Murata when she was an anthropology undergraduate at the University of California at Berkeley. Upon completion of her master's degree in Cultural Anthropology in 1978 at Berkeley, she taught in the Native American Studies and Ethnic Studies programs at the University of California at Berkeley from 1979 to 1983. From 1983 to 1984, she taught at Fresno State University and then became Coordinator of the American Indian Studies Program at Fresno City College from 1984 to the present.

She serves on the Modern Languages Association Commission on Languages and Literature of America and is active in a wide variety of Native American community programs. Wendy Rose is one of the foremost American Indian poets in the latter part of the twentieth century. Her work is widely anthologized and her poems are a bridge between the traditional American Indian narrative and song traditions and modern literary styles. Her major works include *Hopi Roadrunner Dancing* (Greenfield Center, New York, 1973), *Long Division: A Tribal History* (New York, 1976), *Academic Squaw: Reports to the World from the Ivory Tower* (Marvin, South

Dakota, 1977), *Builder Kachina: A Home-Going Cycle* (Marvin, South Dakota, 1979) and *What Happened When the Hopi Hit New York* (New York, 1982).

FOR MORE INFORMATION:

Bataille, Gretchen M., and Kathleen Mullen Sands, eds. *American Indian Women: Telling Their Lives*. Lincoln: University of Nebraska Press, 1984.

ROSS, JOHN (COOWESCOOWE or "THE EGRET")
Cherokee
1790–1866

Born along the Coosa River at Tahnoovayah, Georgia (near Lookout Mountain), John Ross, who would become the founder of a constitutional government among the Cherokees, was the third of nine children. His father was Daniel Ross, a Scot, and his mother was Mary (Molly)

John Ross. [Nebraska State Historical Society]

McDonald, a Scot-Cherokee woman. As a youth he was called Tsan-usdi or "Little John."

Although brought up with other Cherokees, Ross was educated at home by white tutors, continuing his education at Kingston Academy in Tennessee. Although he was only about one-eighth Cherokee, Ross always identified himself as Cherokee and was married in 1813 to "Quatie" or Elizabeth Brown Henley, a full-blooded Cherokee. They had five children.

Ross began his political career in 1809 when he went on a mission to the Arkansas Cherokees. By 1811, he was serving as a member of the standing committee of the Cherokee Council. In 1813–1814, he was an adjutant in a Cherokee regiment under the command of General Andrew Jackson and saw action with other Cherokees at Horseshoe Bend in 1813 against the Red Sticks commanded by William WEATHERFORD. Ross led a contingent of Cherokee warriors in a diversionary tactic and thus was an important factor in Jackson's success at Horseshoe Bend.

In 1814, shortly after his marriage, Ross set up a ferry service and trading post at Ross's Landing. In 1817, he became a member of the Cherokee National Council; he served as president of the national council from 1819 to 1826. In 1820, the Cherokee people instituted a republican form of government similar in structure to that of the United States. As an advocate of education and missionization among his people, Ross thought that the Cherokees might become a state in the union with its own constitution. When New Echota became the Cherokee national capital in 1826, he moved there with his family. In 1827, he became president of the Cherokee Constitutional Convention, which drafted a new constitution. From 1828 to 1839, Ross served as principal chief of the Cherokee nation under this new constitution.

During Ross's years as chief, he opposed federal and state encroachments on tribal lands. He resisted Georgia's contention that the Cherokees were mere tenants on state lands. When Georgia stripped the Cherokees of their civil rights between 1828 and 1831, Ross took their case to the Supreme Court and won, but President Andrew Jackson violated his oath of office by defying the Supreme Court when he refused to enforce its decision. With the discovery of gold near Dahlonega, Georgia, in the 1820s, white officials pressed for the relocation westward of the Cherokees along with other eastern American Indians. Jackson also signed the Indian Removal Act of 1830, which provided for the relocation of eastern tribes in an area west of the Mississippi that would become Indian Territory.

Although Ross continued to resist removal policies as principal chief of the Cherokees, a dispirited minority of Cherokee leaders called the Treaty Party (including Major RIDGE, John RIDGE, Elias BOUDINOT, and Stand WATIE) consented to removal by signing the Treaty of New Echota in 1835. Ross and a majority of the Cherokees sought to have the treaty reversed and sent a letter to Congress in 1836 asking for an investigation into its legality.

Although Ross continued to protest removal for three more years, Georgia started to coerce the Cherokees into selling their lands for a fraction of their real value. Marauding whites plundered Cherokee homes and possessions and destroyed the *Cherokee Phoenix*'s printing press because it opposed removal. The army forced Cherokee families into internment camps to prepare for the arduous trek westward. As a result of unhealthy and crowded conditions in these hastily constructed stockades, many Cherokees died even before the Trail of Tears began. While failing in his efforts to stop removal, Ross managed to gain additional federal funds for his people.

During the internment of the Cherokees in Georgia and the two disastrous trips along the Trail of Tears, over four thousand Cherokees died of exposure, disease, and starvation—about a quarter of the total Cherokee population. Quatie, Ross's wife, was among the victims of this forced emigration. After removal, the miserable conditions did not cease; many Cherokees died after they arrived in Indian Territory as epidemics and food shortages plagued the new settlements.

Upon his arrival in Indian Territory, Ross joined the Western Cherokees who had moved several years earlier. He aided in the drafting of the constitution for the United Cherokees and served as its head from 1839 until his death in 1866. In 1839, with the assassination of the Ridges and Boudinot in retaliation for their role in signing the removal treaty, tribal factions became polarized, and some of the proponents of the Treaty Party claimed that Ross had a role in the assassinations, but they never produced any evidence. SEQUOYAH, the originator of the Cherokee alphabet, and other peacemakers sought to reconcile the factions within the tribe. In 1844, Ross married a Quaker woman named Mary Bryan Stapler and they had three children. Between 1839 and 1856, he went to Washington five times seeking justice for his people.

Although Ross was a large slaveholder when the Civil War began, he opposed a Cherokee alliance with the Confederacy. Instead, he advocated Cherokee neutrality. Many of Ross's supporters were nonslaveholding Cherokees. By summer 1861, many influential leaders, including Stand Watie, favored joining the Confederacy. Ross convened a national conference and was overruled by the pro-Confederacy

Running Antelope.
[Nebraska State Historical Society]

forces. By 1862, federal troops had regained control over most of Indian Territory, so Ross moved his wife and family to Kansas. As a result, Ross was deposed from office and the Cherokees repudiated their ties to the Confederacy in 1863. But the Southern Cherokees under Stand Watie formed a separate government that still allied with the Confederacy. Faced with such tragic divisions, Ross went to Washington to tell President Abraham Lincoln about the rebellious Southern Cherokees.

At the end of the Civil War, the Cherokees were deeply split. Ross, at seventy-five and in bad health, journeyed to Washington as the head of the Northern Cherokees for new treaty negotiations that sought to protect the Cherokees and their constitution. He died while in Washington on August 1, 1866, during negotiations. His body was returned to Indian Territory and he was buried at Park Hill, Oklahoma.

RUNNING ANTELOPE
Hunkpapa Sioux
fl. 1860s–1880s

Running Antelope was one of four Hunkpapa Sioux principal chiefs who were close advisors to SITTING BULL during the Plains Indian wars. Well known for his bravery in war, his oratory, and his talents at diplomacy, Running Antelope believed that compromise with the whites was in the Sioux's best interests. Gradually, he moved away from Sitting Bull, who maintained an independent posture throughout his life.

FOR MORE INFORMATION:

Vestal, Stanley. *Sitting Bull: Champion of the Sioux.* 1932. Reprint, Norman: University of Oklahoma Press, 1957.

S

SACAJAWEA (SACAGAWEA, BIRD WOMAN)
Shoshoni
c. 1784–c. 1811 or c. 1880

For nineteen months, Sacajawea guided Lewis and Clark over the Rocky Mountains toward the Pacific Coast near present-day Astoria, Oregon. Without her, the expedition probably would have halted for lack of direction. She also guaranteed friendly relations with Native peoples along the way.

Known as Boinaiv (meaning "Grass Maiden") in her youth, Sacajawea was captured around 1800 by Hidatsa warriors who attacked her people's camp at the Three Forks of the Missouri River in Montana. The warriors killed four men, four women, and several boys before taking several other Shoshoni captives. The name Sacajawea (or Sacagawea) was given to her by the Hidatsas. Her name, spelled "Sacajawea," may have meant "Boat Launcher" in the Shoshoni language; spelled "Sacagawea," it may have meant "Bird Woman." At some point between 1800 and 1804, Toussaint CHARBONNEAU, who

was residing among the Hidatsa, either won Sacajawea in a gambling match or bought her from her captors and made her his wife.

Lewis and Clark's expedition began at St. Louis with a party of forty-five men on May 14, 1804. By late October, the party passed near Mandan and Hidatsa villages near the mouth of the Knife River in North Dakota. They decided to stop there for the winter. On November 4, according to Clark's journal, Toussaint applied to become an interpreter for the expedition. He was hired along with Sacajawea, who interpreted Native American languages for Toussaint, who then passed her words to French-and-English-speaking members of the expedition. These men in turn passed the messages to Lewis and Clark in English.

Sacajawea provided more than help with languages. She had expert knowledge of edible plants that supplemented the explorers' diets for the rest of the journey. She also performed feats of uncommon valor. At one point, she saved a large store of the expedition's provisions from being swept into the Yellowstone

River during a storm. Lewis and Clark watched from shore; her husband was unable to swim.

Little was known of Sacajawea by whites other than Lewis and Clark until 1811, when she and Charbonneau traveled to St. Louis, where Clark had become a regional superintendent of Indian affairs. Sacajawea and her husband were visiting St. Louis to accept an offer by Clark to educate their son Pomp (see Jean Baptiste CHARBONNEAU), of whom Clark had become fond during the expedition. Clark's papers note that Sacajawea died shortly after that visit, but some argue that Sacajawea returned to the Shoshonis and lived to be almost a hundred years old. The source of the confusion seems to be the fact that Charbonneau had two Shoshoni wives, a fact unknown to Clark. An argument has been made that the wife who died was not Sacajawea but Otter Woman, Charbonneau's other wife. Various historians cite accounts of Sacajawea into old age; others assert that Clark knew Sacajawea well enough not to mistake her for another woman.

Sacajawea is memorialized with statues in several places, notably on the capitol grounds at Bismarck, North Dakota. A five-hundred-foot likeness of her was constructed during the 1960s outside the same city and near the site of a former Mandan village.

FOR MORE INFORMATION:

Bryant, Martha F. *Sacajawea: A Native American Heroine.* New York: Council for Indian Education, 1989.

Edmonds, Della, and Margot Edmonds. *Sacajawea of the Lewis and Clark Expedition.* Berkeley and Los Angeles: University of California Press, 1979.

Frazier, Neta L. *Sacajawea: The Girl Nobody Knows.* New York: McKay Co., 1967.

Harold, Howard. *Sacajawea.* Norman: University of Oklahoma Press, 1971.

Nebard, Grace R. *Sacajawea.* Glendale, Calif.: Arthur H. Clark, 1932.

Seymour, Flora W. *Sacajawea: American Pathfinder.* New York: Macmillan, 1991.

Thwaites, Reuben Gold. *The Original Journals of Lewis and Clark.* New York, 1904–1905.

SADEGANAKTIE
Onondaga
c. 1640–1701

Sadeganaktie was probably *tadadaho* (speaker) of the Iroquois Grand Council late in the seventeenth century. He was known in Iroquois, British, and French circles as a spellbinding orator. In 1693, he became ill on the eve of an important conference in Albany; he was carried bodily from Onondaga (near contemporary Syracuse, New York) to Albany by his people on whose behalf he would speak. Upon Sadeganaktie's death in 1701, the antlers of office were bestowed on Sadeganaktie's son, who shared the same name.

SAGAUNASH (BILLY CALDWELL)
Potawatomi
c. 1780–1841

Born in Ontario of an Irish father (an officer in the British army) and a Potawatomi mother, Sagaunash mastered English and French while attending Catholic schools. During his younger years, Sagaunash earned his living as a fur trader. He also spoke several Algonquian dialects. He was an interpreter and negotiator and served as personal secretary to TECUMSEH during the War of 1812. Tecumseh charged Sagaunash with preventing Indians under his command from committing atrocities during battle. After the War of 1812, Sagaunash remained in Canada for a period of years; the British gave him the title of captain of the Indian Department.

In 1820, Sagaunash swore allegiance to the United States and moved to Chicago. In 1826, he was elected as a justice of the peace there. He was asked by white officials to negotiate the Winnebago uprising (1827) and BLACK HAWK's War (1832), for which he was paid in cash and land. During Black Hawk's War, Sagaunash was the head of U.S. Army scouts. He later moved with the Potawatomis when they were relocated to Iowa. He died in Council Bluffs just as the town was being founded as a possible terminus for the Union Pacific Railroad.

FOR MORE INFORMATION:
Eckert, Allan W. *A Sorrow in Our Heart: The Life of Tecumseh.* New York: Bantam, 1992.

SA GA YEAN QUA PRAH TON (BRANT)
Mohawk
fl. early 1700s

Sa Ga Yean Qua Prah Ton was one of four Mohawks invited to the court of Queen Anne in 1710 by British Indian agent Peter SCHUYLER as part of a diplomatic effort to win Iroquois allegiance from the French.

Sa Ga Yean Qua Prah Ton's Christian name was Brant, and he would later become known as the grandfather of Joseph BRANT, a prominent figure in Iroquois history later in the century. The elder Brant, who also signed with the wolf, died shortly after returning to America from London. During the visit, the English called him "King of the Maquas."

FOR MORE INFORMATION:
Bond, Richmond P. *Queen Anne's American Kings.* Oxford: Clarendon Press, 1952.

SAINTE-MARIE, BUFFY
Cree
1942–

Folksinger Buffy Sainte-Marie was born on the Piapot Reserve at Craven, Saskatchewan. Sainte-Marie earned a bachelor's degree in phi-

Sa Ga Yean Qua Prah Ton.
[National Anthropological Archives]

losophy from the University of Massachusetts in 1963 after having become a U.S. citizen.

After playing her music in several Greenwich Village clubs, Sainte-Marie turned professional. By 1965, she was performing at Carnegie Hall and the Newport (Rhode Island) Folk Festival. She had no formal voice training until after the beginning of her professional career. She recorded several albums of popular and American Indian music, often mixing traditional and modern themes. Her singing career included the hit singles "Universal Soldier" and "Until It's Time for You to Go"; she won an Academy Award for the song "Up Where We Belong," which she cowrote with Jack Nitzche for the film *An Officer and a Gentleman.*

Sainte-Marie has acted in several movies, including the Turner Network's *The Broken Chain* (1993). She has also produced writing and poetry for several American Indian publications and served as an associate editor of *The Indian Voice* (Vancouver, B.C.). By the 1990s, Sainte-Marie had toured in most of the world's larger countries and in major urban areas of the United States and Canada. In 1992, she released a collection of recordings, "Confidence and Likely Stories," which departed from her earlier folk and pop music in that it contained more complex instrumental arrangements. Sainte-Marie has also authored a children's book on Native themes, *Nokosis and the Magic Hat* (1986).

FOR MORE INFORMATION:

Bataille, Gretchen M. *Native American Women.*
    New York: Garland Publishing, 1993.

SAKARISSA
Tuscarora
c. 1730–c. 1810

Sakarissa (meaning "Spear Dragger") represented the Tuscaroras in several treaty negotiations following their migration from the Carolina country to western New York, where they were taken in as the sixth nation of the Iroquois Confederacy. He is a signatory on the Treaty of Fort Stanwix (1768). As an elderly man, Sakarissa helped found the Tuscarora Congregational Church in 1805.

SAMOSET
Pemaquid Abenaki
c. 1590–c. 1653

In the early years of the seventeenth century, Samoset, whose name means "He Who Walks Over Much" in the Abenaki language, made contact with English fishermen near the home of his band, the Pemaquid Abenakis, on Mon-

hegan Island off the coast of Maine. Samoset had had enough contact so that by the time the Pilgrims reached the area in 1620, he was able to greet them in English. On March 21, 1621, Samoset surprised the English immigrants by walking into Plymouth Plantation and announcing, "Welcome, Englishmen!" Samoset was nearly naked despite freezing weather; the settlers gave him clothing and food, and they became friendly.

Samoset returned to the settlement on March 22 in the company of SQUANTO, who also had learned English. Squanto had been taken hostage by Europeans and taken to Spain and later to England before the Pilgrims reached America. Samoset and Squanto arranged a meeting between the colonists and the Wampanoags' principal chief, MASSASOIT, which took place later the same day. This meeting was the beginning of Massasoit's long-term friendship with the New England settlers. During the first years of settlement, Samoset sold large tracts of land at the Pilgrims' behest. He acknowledged the first such deed in 1625 for twelve thousand acres of Pemaquid territory.

FOR MORE INFORMATION:

Apess, William. *On Our Own Ground.* 1836.
    Reprint, Amherst: University of Massachusetts Press, 1992.

SANDS, OKTARSARS HARJO
Creek
1830–1872

During the U.S. Civil War, Oktarsars Harjo Sands (whose name means "Sandy Place") supported the Union. After the war was over, he opposed the Creek Reconstruction Treaty in which federal authorities appropriated half the Creeks' lands in the Indian Territory. Like OPOTHLEYAHOLO before him, Sands sought a return to traditional Creek ways. The ongoing struggle between the traditionalist full-blooded Creeks and the progressive mixed-bloods who supported acculturation caused much violence and devastation of property. Other full-blooded leaders allied with Sands and carried on the struggle for traditional ways in Indian Territory. These included CHITTO HARJO and ISPARHECHER.

SASSACUS
Pequot
c. 1560–1637

Sassacus, the last Pequot grand sachem and a leader in the Pequot War (1636–1637), was a son of Pequot grand sachem Wopigwooit. As a young man, Sassacus (or "Wild One") joined other Pequot warriors in campaigns that expanded their territory from contemporary Connecticut and Rhode Island to the Hudson River valley and Long Island. He was so successful in battle that at least some of the Pequots thought he had supernatural powers.

Wopigwooit was killed by the Dutch in 1832, after which Sassacus became grand sachem of the Pequots. He governed twenty-six villages.

Sassacus led his people into war with the colonists in 1636. They were the major victims of the Battle of Mystic, during which colonial forces laid siege to a Pequot stockade then burned it, killing about seven hundred people on July 5, 1637. Sassacus escaped the carnage with about twenty other warriors, but he was killed by Mohawks a year later. They presented his scalp to the governor of Massachusetts.

The defeat of the Pequots altered the demographic balance in New England. Before the Pequot War, Native peoples were demographically dominant; after the carnage, the English took the upper hand in the area.

SASSAMON, JOHN
Wampanoag
fl. 1670s

Sassamon was a Christianized Indian who served as secretary to METACOM and whose murder in 1675 helped precipitate King Philip's War.

Sassamon was converted to Christianity early in his life and educated by missionaries. He then studied for a short time at Harvard. A few days before he was found murdered in a pond near Plymouth in January 1675, Sassamon had related to colonial governor Josiah Winslow plans that were being formulated by Metacom for a general uprising against the English. The colonists believed the murder to have been Metacom's work, and they rounded up three Wampanoags, including one of Metacom's closest advisors, and placed them on trial. The Wampanoags, already angry over several years of mistreatment, became even angrier as they protested that Indians should not be tried in colonial courts for crimes against each other. The three men were found guilty and then hanged on June 8, setting the spark that culminated in war.

SATANK (SETANGYA, SITTING BEAR)
Kiowa-Sarci
c. 1810–1871

Born in the Black Hills, Satank had a mother who was part Sarci and a father who was Kiowa. He was for many years the principal war chief of the Kiowas, leader of the Kiowa Dog Soldier Society or the Principal Dogs (sometimes called Ten Bravest) military society. About 1840, he aided in negotiating the peace between the Cheyennes and the Kiowas. In 1846 during a battle with the Pawnee, an arrow wounded him in the upper lip, causing a bad scar for the rest of his life.

Along with SATANTA, STUMBLING BEAR, and KICKING BIRD, Satank was one of the signers for the Kiowas of the Treaty of Medicine Lodge in 1867. This treaty granted the Kiowas lands in Indian Territory if they lived in peace, but the Kiowas did not give up raiding. In 1870, after his son was slain by Anglos during a raid in Texas, Satank journeyed to Texas and collected his son's bones in a buckskin bundle. From that day on, he carried the bones on a separate horse in all of his travels. Despairing, he became a staunch proponent of war with the Americans.

With the southern buffalo herds vanishing and treaties being broken, it was impossible for the Kiowas to remain on their shrinking lands in Indian Territory. In May 1871, Satank accompanied MAMANTI, Satanta, BIG TREE, and other noted Kiowa chiefs and warriors when they launched an attack on a wagon train on the Butterfield Southern Route just outside of Fort Richardson, Texas. In the resulting fracas, the Kiowas killed seven teamsters and captured forty-one mules.

Returning to Fort Sill, Indian Territory, Satank boasted of the raid to Lawrie Tatum, the Indian agent. The army quickly arrested Satank as well as Big Tree and Satanta. En route to his trial in Texas, Satank sang his death song, slipped the handcuffs from his wrists, and then attacked a guard with a knife. In the ensuing struggle, he was shot and killed. Subsequently, he was interred at Fort Sill's military cemetery.

FOR MORE INFORMATION:

Dockstader, Frederick. *Great North American Indians.* New York: Van Nostrand Reinhold, 1977.

SATANTA (SET-TAINTE)
Kiowa
1830–1878

Born on the Northern Plains, Satanta ("White Bear Person") was the son of Red Tepee, who was the keeper of the Tai-me, the Kiowa medicine bundles. During his boyhood, he was known as Guaton-bain or "Big Ribs." He was a young man when a prominent warrior, Black Horse, presented him with a war shield that he used while raiding in Texas and Mexico. During the early days of the Civil War, he conducted many raids along the Santa Fe Trail. He would later become a principal chief in the Kiowa Wars of the 1860s–1870s and was known as "The Orator of the Plains."

When Little Mountain died in 1866, Satanta became the leader of the war faction of the Kiowas. His rival was KICKING BIRD of the peace faction. As a result of this rivalry, LONE WOLF became the compromise choice for the position of principal chief. Meanwhile, Satanta and his warriors continued raiding in Texas. Famed for his eloquence, Satanta spoke at the Medi-

Satanta. [Nebraska State Historical Society]

cine Lodge Treaty of 1867 where the Kiowas ceded their lands in the valleys of the Canadian and Arkansas Rivers and agreed to settle on a reservation within Indian Territory. However, some of the Kiowas were slow to move onto their lands in Indian Territory. When Satanta came under a flag of truce to tell the U.S. Army that he had not been with Black Kettle at the Battle of the Washita, General Philip H. Sheridan held him and several other leaders as hostages until their bands had relocated to Indian Territory.

In May 1871, Satanta was in a war party that attacked the Warren wagon train with SATANK, BIG TREE, and MAMANTI. Later, Big Tree, Satank, and Satanta were seized for trial after bragging openly about their exploits. Satank tried to escape on the road to Texas; he was fatally shot. Big Tree and Satanta went to trial and were sentenced to death. Indian rights groups objected to the harsh penalties, however. The Bureau of Indian Affairs even contended that they should be released because their actions were associated with war and not murder. In 1873, they were paroled on a pledge of good behavior for themselves and the entire Kiowa tribe. However, Kiowa, Comanche, Cheyenne, and Arapaho war parties renewed their raids on white settlers under the Comanche leader Quanah PARKER. These actions started the Red River War of 1874–1875. Satanta tried to prove to army officials that he was not a party to the raids. In September 1874, Big Tree appeared at the Cheyenne Agency at Darlington to state that Satanta wished to surrender peacefully. True to his word, Satanta surrendered the next month.

Although it appears that he had not violated the terms of his parole, Satanta was taken into custody and then imprisoned at Huntsville, Texas. On October 11, 1878, sick, tired, and despairing that he would ever be released, Satanta jumped off the upper floor of the prison hospital and committed suicide. The proud and dignified warrior was buried in Texas. His grandson, James Auchiah, received permission in 1963 to bring Satanta's remains to Fort Sill, Oklahoma, so that he could be interred with other Kiowa chiefs.

FOR MORE INFORMATION:

Champagne, Duane, ed. *Native North American Almanac*. Detroit: Gale Research, 1994.

SAVANNAH JACK (JOHN HAGUE or HAIG)
Shawnee or Yuchi
fl. late 1700s through early 1800s

Although Savannah Jack's precise lineage is unknown, he was probably of either Shawnee or Yuchi blood through his mother. He may have been the son of John Haig, an English trader (though other sources hold that he was the younger half brother or son of Simon Girty, a loyalist trader). On the eve of the American Revolution, Savannah Jack, who would become a leading Shawnee war chief, resided near Augusta, Georgia.

By 1789, he was living in Pensacola, Florida, where he was sought by Spanish authorities for the slaying of a cattleman. Around 1800, it appears that he had taken up residence at Miccosukee in Florida, where he headed a small contingent of Shawnee warriors. At this time, he was allied with William Bowles, an Englishman who was the Creek nation's director general. In the Creek War of 1813–1814, Savannah Jack joined forces with William WEATHERFORD and saw action at the Battle of Horseshoe Bend in Alabama. When those hostilities ended, he returned to Florida and settled there permanently. Throughout the American Southeast he was renowned as an able chief and courageous warrior.

SAYENQUERAGHTA
Seneca
c. 1707–1786

During the French and Indian War and the American Revolution, Sayenqueraghta (whose name means "Old Smoke") was one of the most respected of all the chiefs in the Iroquois Confederacy. He was also said to have presented a commanding physical presence that complemented his booming voice.

Sayenqueraghta spoke for the Six Nations at several treaty councils with the English between 1758 and 1775; he signed the Treaty of Easton in 1758, treaties at Johnson Hall in 1759 and 1764, and one at Fort Stanwix (1759). Although he was nearly seventy during the American Revolution, Sayenqueraghta led Seneca forces in several battles, including Oriskany, Wyoming Valley, and Newtown, on behalf of the British.

In council, Sayenqueraghta had voiced doubts about Joseph BRANT's alliance with the British. But in the debates regarding the Iroquois alliance with England, Molly BRANT reminded Sayenqueraghta that his family had been loyal to the Crown since the time of Queen Anne. Molly also talked, with tears in her eyes, of the friendship between Sayenqueraghta and Sir William Johnson. The Iroquois Grand Council was deeply touched by her eloquent plea, and Sayenqueraghta decided to continue supporting the Crown.

Joseph Brant and Sayenqueraghta mapped strategy for the coming spring campaign. Sayenqueraghta decided to move against the Pennsylvanians and cut off the Wyoming Valley. Brant centered his activities in the Mohawk Valley region. Before the winter set in, the Senecas had sent war parties to the Virginia and Pennsylvania frontiers to harass settlers. The Senecas were becoming more keenly aware of the fact that the Americans could be expected to cheat Indian people out of their land.

As the American War for Independence was coming to a close, pressure for westward expansion grew. The frontiersmen knew that the British were restraining their Indian allies, so they flocked into the Ohio region, staking out claims, clearing land, and building cabins. At this time also, a force of Americans attacked a lower Shawnee village at Standing Stone. While the Indian men were away hunting, the invaders killed the women and children. The Iroquois were furious about this attack on their younger brothers in the confederacy, so they called a council at Niagara to ask for British aid in retaliating against the frontiersmen. Sayenqueraghta reported there that the Americans "gave us great Reason to be revenged on them for their cruelties to us and to our Friends, and if we had the means of publishing to the World the many Acts of Treachery and Cruelty committed by them on our Women and Children, it would appear that the title of Savages wou'd with much greater justice be applied to them than to us." [Wallace]

FOR MORE INFORMATION:

"Anecdotes of Brant." Claus Papers, Buffalo Publications, IV. Buffalo Historical Society, n.d.

Wallace, Anthony. *The Death and Rebirth of the Seneca.* New York: Knopf, 1970.

SCARFACED CHARLEY (CHIKCHACKAM LILALKUELATKO)
Modoc
c. 1837–1896

Born on the Rogue River in northern California about 1837, Modoc war chief Scarfaced Charley may have gotten his name from a traumatic childhood ordeal. When he was about ten years old, he and his father, Tipsoe Tyee, met four brutal white men on a road near their home. The boy fled and hid in a lava cave, but the whites seized his father, shackled him by the feet to a wagon, and then hauled him behind the wagon for eight miles until he died. Some accounts assert that the child scarred his face while emerging from his hiding place in the cave. However, another story suggests that he was accidentally run over and scarred by a wagon. The Modoc form of his name supports the latter explanations of its derivation: Chikchackam Lilalkuelatko means "Wagon Scarface" or "Run Over by a Wagon and Scarred."

During the late 1860s, sporadic hostilities broke out between the Modocs and U.S. authorities over their relocation to the Klamath Reservation in Oregon. Scarfaced Charley was one of the Modocs who supported Kintpuash (also known as CAPTAIN JACK) in his resistance to this policy. When the army, in November 1872,

Scarfaced Charley.
[Nebraska State Historical Society]

finally caught up with the Modocs who had left the Klamath Reservation and commanded them to return, Scarfaced Charley would not lay down his sidearm. As he laughed at the order to disarm by Lieutenant Frazier Boutelle, both men drew their pistols and fired at each other. Although neither was injured in the exchange of gunfire, this incident became the opening volley of the Modoc War. As Scarfaced Charley and other Modocs quickly snatched their guns from the cache of surrendered firearms, the skirmishing continued until the soldiers backed down. This action allowed Scarfaced Charley and his comrades to retreat into the remote but highly defensible Lava Beds of northern California. When the fighting ended that day, one American soldier was killed and seven were wounded.

At about the same time, another band of Modocs led by HOOKER JIM also escaped into the Lava Beds after killing a dozen settlers in revenge for a vigilante attack on their people. Although he respected Captain Jack's arguments for peace to avoid further bloodshed, Scarfaced Charley thought this was a foolhardy course and advocated continued armed resistance. On one occasion he almost attacked two white emissaries, but Captain Jack was able to stop him. On April 26, 1873, Modoc warriors under Scarfaced Charley ambushed sixty-three soldiers under Captain Evan Thomas. These soldiers were on a reconnaissance mission and were caught resting in an indefensible position. In a devastating attack, the Modocs killed all five officers as well as twenty enlisted men; sixteen more soldiers were wounded. During a lull in the battle, Scarfaced Charley is said to have yelled to the surviving men that they had better beat a hasty retreat so that the rest of the soldiers would not be slain by his Modoc forces.

After he laid down his arms with the main Modoc contingent at the end of the war, Scarfaced Charley became a witness for Captain Jack's defense. Having no part in the slaying of Eleasar Thomas and General Edward Canby or in the injuring of Alfred B. Meacham, he was allowed to leave with the 152 Modocs sent initially to Wyoming, then to Nebraska, and finally to Indian Territory in 1874. From 1874 to 1881, he traveled in the East participating in a successful drama, *Winema*, which detailed the events of the Modoc War and the wounding of Meacham. Other actors in the play included Meacham, Winema, and several other Modocs.

Although Scarfaced Charley could sometimes be impetuous, he was widely regarded as the best military strategist among the Modocs. Largely through Scarfaced Charley's efforts, Captain Jack was able to withstand vastly superior white forces during the Modoc War. His knowledge of the Lava Beds made pursuit of the rebellious Modocs virtually impossible. Also, he was never accused of disgraceful acts against his adversaries.

After the Modoc removal to Indian Territory, Scarfaced Charley became their principal chief. On December 3, 1896, he succumbed to tuberculosis at Seneca Station in Indian Territory.

FOR MORE INFORMATION:

Dockstader, Frederick. *Great North American Indians*. New York: Van Nostrand Reinhold, 1977.

SCHOLDER, FRITZ
Luiseno
1937–

Scholder was born in Breckenridge, Minnesota, in 1937. His grandmother was a member of the Luiseno nation of southern California. Scholder characterizes himself as a "non-Indian Indian." In 1960, he received a Bachelor's degree in art from Sacramento State College. In 1964, he received a Master of Fine Arts from the University of Arizona. Subsequently, he taught art history and painting for five years at the Institute of the American Indian Arts. While Scholder grew up on the fringes of American Indian life, his art gave him a focus to explore his ethnic background. His paintings are often an eclectic blending of Native American mysticism and pop images in a surrealistic fashion. They frequently address the contradictory aspects of contemporary American Indian existence (the degrading of Native American ways, alcoholism, and assimilation into the mainstream society). Scholder has been criticized for trivializing American Indian culture to the point where it has little aesthetic value. Also, though some American Indian leaders have tried to convince Scholder to promote their causes, he resolutely prefers to communicate through his artwork.

In 1980, Scholder stated that he would no longer paint American Indian themes. In 1992, he broke this promise in order to create a lithograph entitled *Indian Contemplating Columbus*. This sixty-by-forty-inch lithograph reflects Scholder's ambiguity about Columbus, depicting an American Indian person sitting in a chair —facing a corner; the only clue that the figure in the work is a Native American is a brightly colored moccasin that the silhouetted figure is wearing. Fritz Scholder continues to be a leading modern artist in the United States; his work is displayed prominently in national and international galleries.

FOR MORE INFORMATION:

Klein, Barry T., ed. *Reference Encyclopedia of the American Indian*. West Nyack, N.Y.: Todd Publications, 1993.

SCHONCHIN JIM
Modoc
c. 1815–1873

As a young man, Schonchin (from the Modoc *skonches*, or "He Goes with His Head Thrust

Out") Jim defended his people and their lands against the invasion of the Americans during the California gold rush of 1849. He would later defend them to his death in the Modoc War more than two decades later.

History records that Schonchin Jim was a head chief as early as 1846, but he was not a hereditary chief and thus had to obtain his title through exemplary actions. When the forty-niners came into Modoc lands in northern California, he fought bravely and fiercely against their depredations with about six hundred men.

By the 1860s, Schonchin Jim came to the realization that he could fight and face genocide or adjust to white domination. Choosing peace, he became a signatory to an unpopular 1864 treaty that ceded traditional tribal lands for a reservation in Oregon. Many Modocs opposed this treaty because they knew that the Klamath Indians in Oregon had no intention of being hospitable to their distant relatives, the Modocs. When CAPTAIN JACK, SCHONCHIN JOHN, and others left the Oregon Reservation in 1872, he advised against this suicidal course but did not deter them from leaving. While Schonchin Jim remained at peace in Oregon, a war raged in the Lava Beds and tunnel-like caves of northern California against the rebellious Modocs that had left the reservation. In 1873, Schonchin Jim died.

SCHONCHIN JOHN
Modoc
c. 1820–1873

As the younger brother of SCHONCHIN JIM, a principal chief of the Modocs, Schonchin (from the Modoc *skonches*, or "He Goes with His Head Thrust Out") John advocated armed resistance during the Modoc War in spite of his older brother's admonitions of peace. On April 11, 1873, during the Modoc assault on the peace commissioners of President Ulysses S.

Grant, it was Schonchin John who wounded Alfred B. Meacham. As a result of WINEMA's intervention, Meacham's life was saved and he later recovered from his gunshot wounds. At the conclusion of the Modoc War, Schonchin John laid down his arms with CAPTAIN JACK, SCARFACED CHARLEY, and Black Jim. After a trial, Schonchin John was hanged with the three other leaders with whom he had surrendered. Peter Schonchin, his son, who served with his father, subsequently became an important historical source on the conduct of the Modoc War.

SCHUYLER, PETER (QUIDER)
1657–1724

Peter Schuyler was one of Britain's foremost Indian agents ("Quider," a Mohawk mispronunciation of his first name, was what the Iroquois called him). He was born in Albany when it was under Dutch control and had the name Beverwyck. In 1678, he was appointed British representative to the Iroquois Confederacy. Schuyler kept the Iroquois from uniting against the English in support of the French in King William's War, 1689–1697. Schuyler was Albany's first mayor after it was incorporated in 1686. He also served as acting governor of New York in 1719 and 1720, shortly before his death.

In 1710, Schuyler invited four Mohawks, including HENDRICK, to the court of Queen Anne in London as part of a diplomatic offense to win Iroquois alliance from the French. The fact that all four were Mohawks was not coincidental, for to the English the Mohawks were the best known of the five Iroquois nations, the figurative keepers of the eastern door of the Iroquois longhouse, which opened at the British trading post of Albany.

FOR MORE INFORMATION:

Bond, Richmond P. *Queen Anne's American Kings.* Oxford: Clarendon Press, 1952.

SCHUYLER, PHILIP
1733–1804

Grandnephew of Peter Schuyler and the first British Indian agent to the Iroquois, Philip Schuyler was born into a family that had become one of the wealthiest in America and probably the richest in Albany after Peter Schuyler was appointed its first mayor in 1686. Philip Schuyler fought in the French and Indian War (1754–1763) and became a major general in the Continental army during the American Revolution. He was a member of the Board of Indian Commissioners and campaigned for Native neutrality in the war with England.

Schuyler was present on August 15, 1775, at an important meeting between colonial representatives and Iroquois leaders at German Flats, near Albany, New York. He attended this meeting as part of a delegation from the Continental Congress, which was seeking Iroquois alliance during the coming American Revolution. As part of the proceedings, the colonial delegation recalled for the Iroquois CANASSATEGO's advice that the colonists unite in a union similar to that of the Iroquois. The advice, made at a treaty council in Lancaster, Pennsylvania, on July 4, 1744, was quoted from an account published by Benjamin FRANKLIN's press:

> Brethren, We the Six Nations heartily recommend Union and a good agreement between you our Brethren, never disagree but preserve a strict Friendship for one another and thereby you as well as we will become stronger. Our Wise Forefathers established Union and Amity between the Five Nations . . . we are a powerful Confederacy, and if you observe the same methods . . . you will acquire fresh strength and power.

After the Battle of Saratoga, General Schuyler sent a wampum belt to the Six Nations, telling them of the great victory over Burgoyne and asking them to make peace with Congress. As the wampum belt made its way westward, pro-American Iroquois rejoiced and pro-English factions began to waver.

Under the Treaty of Paris (1783), Great Britain ceded to the United States a large area of land west of the Appalachians, which was still largely occupied by Native peoples. Schuyler argued (agreeing with George Washington) that a pellmell rush of settlement should be restrained to forestall problems with the Native peoples in the area. This policy led to the negotiation of several treaties that were subsequently broken; the most famous of those treaties was the Treaty of Fort Stanwix (1784) with the Iroquois.

Schuyler served as U.S. representative from New York in 1789–1791 and 1797–1798; his daughter Elizabeth married the prominent New York federalist Alexander Hamilton.

FOR MORE INFORMATION:

Graymont, Barbara. *The Iroquois in the American Revolution.* Syracuse, N.Y.: Syracuse University Press, 1972.

SEATH'TL (SEATTLE)
Duwamish/Suquamish
c. 1788–1866

Seath'tl, probably born on Blake Island in Puget Sound, was the principal chief of the Duwamish, whose original homeland today comprises an industrial area immediately south of downtown Seattle. This city was named with an anglicized version of the chief's name. In 1833, he was described by William Fraser Tolmie, a Hudson's Bay Company surgeon, as "a brawney Suquamish with a Roman countenance and black curley hair, the handsomest Indian I have ever seen." David Denny, one of

Seattle's first white settlers, said that Seath'tl's voice could be heard a half-mile away when he spoke and that he commanded his people by the force of his intellect.

Son of the Duwamish chief Schweabe, Seath'tl was about seven when George Vancouver sailed the H.M.S. *Discovery* into Puget Sound and met briefly with the Duwamish and their allies, the Suquamish. Seath'tl later aided his father and other Duwamish in the construction of the Old Man House, a community longhouse one thousand feet long that housed forty families. The Duwamish and the Suquamish formed an alliance that ringed central Puget Sound. Seath'tl took a wife, La-da-ila, and became chief of the Duwamish-Suquamish alliance at the age of twenty-two. La-da-ila had died by 1833, when the Hudson's Bay Company established a trading post at Nisqually, in southern Puget Sound. In 1841, the first "Bostons," as the Duwamish called whites, sailed into central Puget Sound in Seath'tl's

Seath'tl. [Washington State Historical Society]

territory. Ten years later, the schooner *Exact* delivered the first settlers in what later became the city of Seattle.

From the beginning, Seath'tl resolved to cooperate with the settlers, but when they proposed naming their city after him, he protested that his spirit would be disturbed if his name was said after he died. The settlers retained the name anyway. Seath'tl had been a Catholic since the 1830s, when he was converted by missionaries. He adopted the biblical name Noah at his baptism and began regular morning and evening prayers among his people.

Seath'tl and his band moved westward across Puget Sound after signing the Treaty of Point Elliot with Washington territorial governor Isaac STEVENS in 1854. As his people prepared to move, Seath'tl delivered a haunting farewell speech that has come to be recognized as one of history's great pieces of Native American oratory. The speech was given in Salish and translated by Dr. Henry Smith, who published it in 1887. Seath'tl's speech has been published several times after that and sometimes embellished.

Environmental conservation was not a subject of general debate and controversy in the mid–nineteenth century as Euro-American settlement sped across the land mass of the United States. Yet from time to time, the records of the settlers contain warnings by Native leaders whose peoples they were displacing describing how European-bred attitudes toward nature were ruining the land, air, and water. Perhaps the most famous warning of this type came in Chief Seath'tl's farewell speech.

> Our dead never forget the beautiful world that gave them being. They still love its verdant valleys, its murmuring rivers, its magnificent mountains, sequestered vales and verdant-lined lakes and bays. . . . Every part of this soil is sacred in the estimation

of my people. Every hillside, every valley, every plain and grove has been hallowed by some sad or happy event in days long vanished. Even the rocks, which seem to be dumb and dead as they swelter in the sun along the silent shore, thrill with memories of stirring events connected with the lives of my people. [Anderson]

In the development of an environmental philosophy today, Chief Seath'tl's words are often cited as evidence that many Native Americans practiced a stewardship ethic toward the earth long before such attitudes became popular in non-Indian society. The debate ranges from acceptance of several versions of Seath'tl's speech to a belief that the original translator, Smith, as well as many people who followed him, put the ecological concepts into the chief's mouth.

Regardless of the exact wording of Seath'tl's speech, it did contain environmental themes. Seath'tl was not telling the immigrants what they wanted to hear, because they displayed no such ideological bent. The farewell speech also touched on fundamental differences between cultures.

Your God is not our God. . . . We are two distinct races with separate origins and separate destinies. . . . To us, the ashes of our ancestors are sacred and their resting place is hallowed ground. You wander far from the graves of your ancestors, seemingly without regret. Your religion was written on tables of stone by the iron fingers of your God so that you cannot forget it. The Red Man could never comprehend nor remember it. Our religion is the tradition of our ancestors—the dreams of our old men, given to them in the solemn hours of the night by the Great Spirit, and

the visions of our sachems; and it is written in the hearts of our people.

Your dead cease to love you and the land of their nativity as soon as they pass the portals of the tomb and wander away among the stars. They are soon forgotten and never return. Our dead never forget the world that gave them being. . . . It matters little where we pass the remnants of our days. They will not be many. A few more moons, a few more winters—and not one of the descendants of the mighty hosts that once moved over this broad land . . . will remain to mourn over the graves of a people once more powerful and hopeful than yours. But why should I mourn the untimely fate of my people? Tribe follows tribe, and nation follows nation, like the waves of the sea. It is the order of nature, and regret is useless. Your time of decay may be distant, but it will surely come, for even the white man . . . cannot be exempt from the common destiny. [Anderson]

In the middle 1850s, when the Yakima War spilled over the Cascades into Seattle under Chief LESCHI, Seath'tl and his people looked on from their retreat on the western shores of Puget Sound. He died there in 1866. In 1912, a statue memorializing Seath'tl was dedicated in the city named for him.

FOR MORE INFORMATION:

Anderson, Eva Greenslit. *The Life Story of Chief Seattle.* Caldwell, Idaho: Caxton Publishers, 1950.

Vanderwerth, W. C., ed. *Indian Oratory: Famous Speeches by Noted Indian Chieftains.* Norman: University of Oklahoma Press, 1971.

Waters, Frank. *Brave Are My People: Indian Heroes Not Forgotten.* Santa Fe, N. Mex.: Clear Light, 1993.

SENACHWINE
Potawatomi
fl. 1830s

Senachwine was among Potawatomis who refused to ally with BLACK HAWK in his war against white encroachment in early 1830s Illinois. After Senachwine spoke at a council in Indiantown, Illinois, in June 1830, Black Hawk is said to have risen and left the meeting in anger. Senachwine said, in part:

> No one is more attached to his home than myself, and none among you is so grieved to leave it. But the time is near at hand, when the red men of the forest will have to leave the land of their nativity, and find a home toward the setting sun. The white men of the east, whose numbers are like the sands of the sea, will overrun . . . this country . . .
>
> Resistance to the aggression of the whites is useless; war is wicked and must result in our ruin. Therefore, let us submit to our fate, return not evil for evil, which would offend the Great Spirit. . . . Do not listen to the words of Black Hawk. He is trying to lead you astray. Do not imbrue your hands in human blood; for such is the work of the evil one, and will only lead to retribution upon our heads. [Armstrong]

FOR MORE INFORMATION:

Armstrong, Virginia Irving, ed. *I Have Spoken: American History Through the Voices of the Indians.* Chicago: Swallow Press, 1971.

SEQUOYAH (GEORGE GIST, GUESS, GUEST)
Cherokee
1776–1843

Sequoyah, the inventor of Cherokee syllabary, was born in Taskigi near Fort Loudon, Tennessee, of a Cherokee mother of the Paint clan named Wurtee and (some say) the Revolutionary soldier and trader Nathaniel Gist, although this lineage is not clear. His name is derived from the Cherokee word *sikwaji* or *sogwili,* meaning "Sparrow" or "Principal Bird."

Clearly, Sequoyah is one of the most remarkable figures in American history. As a boy of twelve living with his mother near Willstown, Alabama, Sequoyah learned to tend dairy cattle and make cheese. He also broke horses, planted corn, and gained skills in hunting and trading furs. During a hunting trip, he sustained an injury to his leg that developed into arthritis. Consequently, Sequoyah walked with a limp and was given the nickname "the Lame One."

With a quick mind and active imagination, he became intrigued by the "talking leaves," or written language of the whites. Perhaps out of frustration with his disability and its effects on his hunting, Sequoyah developed a drinking habit as a young man. Realizing what alcohol was doing to him, he turned away from the habit and sought a new way of life. As a result, Sequoyah became an excellent silversmith. In the Creek War of 1813–1814, he served under General Andrew Jackson. In 1815, he married Sarah (Sally), a Cherokee woman, and they had several children. Three years later, he and his family decided to leave for what would become Pope County, Arkansas, as part of Chief John JOLLY's band.

As early as 1809, Sequoyah started his work on a written version of the Cherokee language using pictorial symbols, but he abandoned this method as untenable after he had created more than one thousand symbols. Next, Sequoyah reduced the Cherokee language to two hundred and then finally to eighty-six characters that represented all the syllables or sounds in the language. He derived the resulting syllabary in part from English, Greek, and Hebrew characters in mission schoolbooks. At first he was thought by some to be engaging in witchcraft, and his home was burned down along with his notes.

Undaunted by these allegations, Sequoyah completed his writing system in 1821. He is the only human being in history to invent an entire syllabary or method of writing by himself. In 1821, before an assembly of Cherokee leaders, he proved the viability of his system by writing messages to his six-year-old daughter that she understood and answered independently. The Cherokee Tribal Council formally adopted his syllabary soon after this demonstration. Within months, thousands of Cherokees were able to communicate across long distances through the use of his writing methods. By 1824, white missionaries had translated parts of the Bible into Cherokee. In 1828, the Cherokee Tribal Council started in north Georgia a weekly newspaper called the *Cherokee Phoenix and Indian Advocate.* It enjoyed great success until it was suppressed in 1835 by the state of Georgia for advocating Cherokee rights to their lands in Georgia.

In 1829, Sequoyah moved with his wife and children to Indian Territory in what would become Sequoya County, Oklahoma. He also helped to unite uneasy Eastern and Western Cherokee factions in 1839. In 1841, the Cherokee National Council granted him a pension; Sequoyah became the first member of any Indian tribe to be rewarded in this manner.

In 1842, Sequoyah launched an expedition to find a group of Cherokees who had gone West during the American Revolution. The trip through Texas exacerbated Sequoyah's failing health. Suffering from dysentery, he died in August 1843 near San Fernando, Tamaulipas, Mexico. He was buried there along with his treasured papers in an as yet undiscovered grave. Later, Oklahoma would memorialize Sequoyah by placing his statue in the Capitol's

Statuary Hall. His homestead was also designated as an Oklahoma state historical site. As a testimony to his remarkable genius, Stephen Endilicher, the Hungarian botanist, named a species of giant coastal redwood trees after him.

FOR MORE INFORMATION:

Champagne, Duane, ed. *Native North American Almanac.* Detroit: Gale Research, 1994.

SHABONA (SHABONEE, CHAMBLY)
Potawatomi
c. 1775–1859

Shabona was a grandnephew of PONTIAC. He was born an Ottawa but married into the Potawatomis and became a peace chief in the Three Fires Confederacy, comprising the Ottawa, Potawatomi, and Chippewa. Shabona was a longtime friend and ally of TECUMSEH and fought at the Battles of Tippecanoe and the Thames, where Tecumseh was killed. After that, he became an ally of the Americans and saved several whites during the Fort Dearborn massacre. One of more than fifty warriors (including twenty chiefs) who mustered duty for the United States, he kept many Potawatomis from joining the Winnebago War (1827) and BLACK HAWK's War. Shabona also often warned settlers of Native attacks and once barely escaped with his life when a Sauk and Fox war party attempted to ambush him.

Despite his friendliness to settlers, Shabona's people were removed west of the Mississippi in 1836; he alone was given two sections (320 acres) in the old homeland. The double standard was rationalized as Shabona's reward for his help to the United States. Speculators later stole the land from Shabona, contending that he had abandoned it. Since his claim to ownership clouded the title, the United States eventually paid Shabona $1,600 for the land. Later, citizens of Ottawa, Illinois, bought Shabona a twenty-acre farm. When Abraham Lincoln and

Shabona.
[State Historical Society of Wisconsin]

Stephen Douglas held one of their now-famous debates in Ottawa, Shabona witnessed it. He occupied his Ottawa farm until his death in 1859. After a day of hunting in the rain, he passed away at the age of about seventy-five.

SHAIKES (Tlinget family name)
Tlinget
c. 1800–1944

The name *Shaikes* was used by several succeeding Tlinget chiefs who lived along the Stikine River, Alaska, between 1800 and 1944. The first chief of this lineage to become known to Europeans met Sir George Simpson during the latter's expedition of 1841 and 1842. Simpson remarked on the hierarchical nature of Tlinget society and at the cruelty with which Shaikes treated his slaves. According to Simpson,

Shaikes once ordered five slaves killed to dedicate his new house. Once, Shaikes shot another slave to enhance his own prestige as a man who was rich enough to dismiss another's life without concern.

The chiefs carrying the name *Shaikes* lived in Wrangell, Alaska, and grew rich during the early years of the fur trade. In line with general practice of many Northwest Coast societies, Shaikes demonstrated his wealth to enhance his social and political status. Shaikes obtained promises from the United States for schools and economic development, which did not occur. He resisted the incursion of missionaries.

The last of the Shaikes line established a Museum of Indian Curiosities. He also dealt in Tlinget artifacts to such an extent that possessions of the elder Shaikes may today be found in several museums. The youngest Shaikes died at Wrangell in 1944.

SHAKOPEE (LITTLE SIX)
Mdewakanton Sioux
fl. 1850s–1860s

The name *Shakopee* (or "Six") was shared by several Mdewakanton Sioux leaders in the nineteenth century whose village was located along the Minnesota River at the site on which Shakopee, the town, was later constructed. Shakopee the Elder died in 1862 on the eve of the Great Sioux Uprising after having spent his life trying to promote peace between Indians and immigrating whites. He had signed the Traverse des Sioux Treaty (1851) and in 1858 had traveled to Washington, D.C., seeking reconciliation.

Shakopee's son of the same name (who was often called "Little Six" by colonists) joined LITTLE CROW in the Great Sioux Uprising and fled to Canada after the rebellion was crushed. Shakopee escaped the mass hanging at Mankato that followed the uprising, but in 1864, he and Medicine Bottle were kidnapped

Shakopee (Little Six).
[National Anthropological Archives]

You love your country—you love your people—you love the manner in which they live, and you think your people brave. I am like you. . . . I love my country—I love my people—I love the manner in which we live, and think myself and warriors brave. So, spare me then . . . and let me enjoy my country. . . .

Before our intercourse with the whites, who have caused such a destruction in our game, we could lie down to sleep, and when we awoke we would find the buffalo feeding around our camp—but now we are killing them for their skins and feeding the wolves with their flesh, to make our children cry over their bones. [Armstrong]

Sharitarish died of cholera at the age of thirty-two.

FOR MORE INFORMATION:

Armstrong, Virginia Irving, ed. *I Have Spoken: American History Through the Voices of the Indians.* Chicago: Swallow Press, 1971.

SHAVEHEAD
Potawatomi
fl. early 1800s

from Canada by Major Edwin Hatch (acting on orders from General Henry Hastings Sibley). Both men were returned to the United States, quickly tried, sentenced to death, and hanged.

In the 1980s, the Mdwekanton Sioux established a prosperous casino and named it Little Six after Shakopee the Younger.

SHARITARISH (ANGRY CHIEF)
Pawnee
c. 1790–1822

Sharitarish was one of the first Pawnee chiefs to encounter white expansion. In 1806, he also assisted the explorations of Zebulon Pike along the Republican River in present-day Nebraska. As brother of the Pawnee chief Tarecawawaho, Sharitarish was appointed to meet with President James Monroe and Secretary of War John C. Calhoun in 1822. On February 22, he gave a speech that subsequently became famous as he tried to explain why his people did not want to become "civilized."

A warrior noted for glorifying the brutality of battle, Shavehead was a leader in the Fort Dearborn massacre and an ally of TECUMSEH. He was the type of warrior that Tecumseh's secretary SAGAUNASH was charged with keeping from committing atrocities. According to accounts of his atrocities, some of which were doubtlessly embellished, Shavehead wore enemy scalps as personal adornments and fashioned his victims' tongues (ninety-nine of them) into a neck chain. After the War of 1812, Shavehead demanded money to let whites pass across the St. Joseph River on a ferry. The date and circumstances of his death are unknown, but one story has it that an enraged survivor of the Fort

Dearborn massacre shot him to death. Another account says that he crossed paths, and tongues, with a white hunter in the forest and was killed by him in a fistfight.

FOR MORE INFORMATION:

Heard, J. Norman. *Handbook of the American Frontier: Four Centuries of Indian-White Relationships.* Vol. 1, *The Northeastern Woodlands.* Metuchen, N.J.: Scarecrow Press, 1990.

SHENANDOAH, JOANNE
Oneida
1957–

Late in the twentieth century, Joanne Shenandoah became a major presence in Native American folk music, fusing traditional songs with contemporary styles such as western, pop, and new age. In 1986, she was honored with two awards, the Native American Woman's Recognition Award and Native American Woman of Hope. In 1994, she was recognized by the First Americans in the Arts Foundation as its "Musician of the Year," and was listed among *Who's Who Among Native Americans.*

Shenandoah married Mohawk editor and activist Doug GEORGE-KANENTIIO and, with him, formed Round Dance Productions, Inc., a nonprofit foundation for the preservation of Native American culture. George and Shenandoah produced films, books, and other media that combined entertainment with themes emphasizing Native American philosophy, culture, music, birthrights, and history.

Shenandoah is a daughter of Maisie Shenandoah, a clanmother, and the late Clifford Shenandoah, an Onondaga chief and jazz guitarist. Clifford Shenandoah was one of a line of Iroquois chiefs reaching back to Shenandoah (or SKENANDOAH; the two names are variants of the same, meaning "Deer") who organized the Oneidas to carry hundreds of bushels of corn to

Joanne Shenandoah.
[Courtesy of Joanne Shenandoah]

feed General George Washington's Continental Army during a bitter winter at Valley Forge, Pennsylvania, in the midst of the Revolutionary War.

Joanne Shenandoah was urged to study music from a young age and to make use of her voice. For fourteen years she made her living as a computer systems architectural engineer, but a rediscovery of her people's stories, songs, and respect for the earth prompted Shenandoah to begin a music career.

As she matured, Shenandoah's voice was likened to a "Native American trance." By the middle of the 1990s she had released four albums in the United States (one of which received a four-star review from Knight Ridder International News), as well as one single

("Nature Dance" in Germany). She had also been a guest artist on ten albums, including the CD-ROM version of the major motion picture *Indian in the Cupboard.*

Most notably, Shenandoah opened the 1994 concert at Woodstock and Earth Day on the Mall in Washington, D.C., before audiences, in each place, of more than 250,000 people. She also contributed to an album in defense of Leonard PELTIER and performed a concert at the White House. Her music was featured on documentaries such as *The War Against the Indians, How the West Was Lost, Indian Time II—Fly with Eagles,* and on numerous national public broadcast stations. Her original compositions were used in the commercial television series *Northern Exposure.* Cable News Network's *Larry King Live* aired a song she wrote about the repatriation of Native American remains. "Hopefully," Shenandoah said after the song was played on the talk show, "my listeners, Indian or not, can begin to see the human side of Indian problems."

FOR MORE INFORMATION:

O'Brien, Jill. "Full-time Fun for Shenandoah." *Indian Country Today,* February 9, 1995, C-1.

SHENANDOAH, LEON
Onondaga
1915–1996

Leon Shenandoah served as *tadadaho* (speaker) of the Iroquois Confederacy during much of the late twentieth century, from his initiation into the office in 1969 to his death of kidney failure July 22, 1996. He was the contemporary occupant of the oldest political office in North America, and one of the oldest in the world. The Iroquois Confederacy has seated a tadadaho since at least about A.D. 1400, and perhaps longer. According to Iroquois oral historians, Shenandoah was the 235th tadadaho of the confederacy.

When he first assumed office, Shenandoah visited the Museum of the American Indian in New York City. When a receptionist asked "May I help you," he said: "Yes. You can give us back our wampum belts." For almost three decades, Shenandoah worked to have Iroquois wampum belts returned from several museums and from the State of New York. In his last official act, on July 4, 1996, he presided over the return of seventy-four wampum belts from the Museum of the American Indian.

Shenandoah was a steadfast opponent of gambling on Iroquois land: he maintained that the culture of money and greed had no place among traditional Iroquois. He was also a frequent spokesman for the Iroquois, having twice addressed the United Nations. He spoke at the Earth Summit in Brazil in 1992 and participated in the affairs of the Green Cross, an international environmental group led by Mikhail Gorbachev, the former president of the Soviet Union.

At home, Shenandoah's demeanor belied his international celebrity. He smoked a corn-cob pipe and drove an old, donated Pontiac. His home was heated with a wood stove. Shenandoah was born at Onondaga on May 18, 1915, and grew up in a cabin on Hemlock Creek, the

Leon Shenandoah (right) meets with a Tibetan lama. [Courtesy of Marcia Keegan]

youngest of five brothers and sisters. His formal education ended at the eighth grade. Shenandoah was fluent in the Onondaga language, and was a long-time devotee of the Code of Handsome Lake. He and his wife, Thelma, raised seven children.

FOR MORE INFORMATION:

Austin, Alberta. *Ne'Ho Niyo' De:No': That's What It Was Like.* Lackawanna, N.Y.: Rebco Enterprises, 1986.

SHICKSHACK
Winnebago
fl. early 1800s

After his birth in present-day Wisconsin, Shickshack lived in Illinois early in his life, shortly after 1800. An outgoing man, he was friendly to settlers and was probably one of the Indians responsible for capturing BLACK HAWK and ending the Black Hawk War in 1832. Later in his life, Shickshack's followers were removed to Kansas, where he died. Shickshack was succeeded as chief by Kabay Noden, his son.

FOR MORE INFORMATION:

Beckhard, Arthur J. *Black Hawk.* New York: Julian Messner, 1957.

Carter, Harvey Lewis. *The Life and Times of Little Turtle.* Urbana: University of Illinois Press, 1987.

SHIKELLAMY (ONGWATEROHIATHE)
Oneida
fl. 1720s–1740s

Shikellamy, "the Enlightener," is known to history mainly as the Iroquois governor of relations with Shawnees and Delawares in Pennsylvania who were allied with the Iroquois. He was probably born of a Cayuga mother and a French father then was captured at the age of two, adopted, and raised by Oneidas.

About 1727, Shikellamy moved into the Susquehanna Valley and began working as an intermediary between the Pennsylvania tribes and the whites. He became a leader by combating the liquor trade to Indians. In 1736, Shikellamy helped organize an Iroquois delegation of more than a hundred chiefs and their families to visit Philadelphia for treaty negotiations. During that treaty council, colonial land dealers wheedled a deed for much of the Delawares' and Shawnees' land from a minority of the chiefs. For two decades after that, conflict over who owned this land, which comprised a large part of Pennsylvania, caused sporadic armed conflict.

In 1745, the Iroquois Grand Council appointed Shikellamy, who lived at Shamokin, Pennsylvania, as their ambassador to the tribes in Pennsylvania. As a political leader and ambassador, Shikellamy conducted the affairs of the Iroquois not only among Indians in Pennsylvania but with the colony as well. He died in 1748. Shikellamy is memorialized with a statue near Womelsdorf, Pennsylvania.

FOR MORE INFORMATION:

Grinde, Donald A., Jr., and Bruce E. Johansen. *Exemplar of Liberty: Native America and the Evolution of Democracy.* Berkeley and Los Angeles: University of California Press, 1991.

SHORT BULL
Brulé Sioux
c. 1846–1915

In fall 1889, GOOD THUNDER, Brave Bear, and as many as four other Sioux slipped away from the Pine Ridge Agency without the agent's permission to investigate WOVOKA's claims to have seen the Messiah in the Ghost Dance. They returned to Pine Ridge convinced that the Ghost Dance could restore their old lives as they were before the coming of the European Americans. In spring 1890, a larger delegation of Indians from the Pine Ridge, Cheyenne River, and Rosebud Agencies visited Wovoka in

Short Bull (left) with Joseph Horn Cloud.
[Nebraska State Historical Society]

Nevada with sanction from some of the leading chiefs on the Northern Plains. This delegation included Good Thunder, Short Bull, and KICK-ING BEAR, all of whom became leading advocates of the Ghost Dance during the months before the massacre at Wounded Knee in late December 1890.

The Ghost Dance was quickly outlawed (along with other Native rituals) by the Bureau of Indian Affairs, making its performance a statement of resistance to the Euro-American invasion. According to a report from Major General Nelson Miles to the secretary of war on September 14, 1891, Short Bull told Lakotas that "Soldiers [may] surround you, but pay no attention to them, continue the dance. If the soldiers surround you

four deep . . . some of them will drop dead, the rest will start to run. . . . Then you can do as you desire with them. Now you must know this[:] that all the soldiers and that [white] race will be dead."
FOR MORE INFORMATION:
Brown, Dee. *Bury My Heart at Wounded Knee.*
    New York: Holt, Rinehart & Winston, 1970.

SILKO, LESLIE MARMON
Laguna Pueblo
1948–

Born in Albuquerque, New Mexico, Silko grew up on the Laguna Indian Reservation in the house where her father, Lee H. Marmon, was born. Her mother, Virginia, worked, so Silko spent her preschool years next door at her great-grandmother's house. During her childhood at the Laguna Pueblo in eastern New Mexico, she attended Bureau of Indian Affairs schools and was surrounded by the lore and culture of the Keres and Laguna peoples. After graduating from high school in Albuquerque, she attended the University of New Mexico and graduated *magna cum laude* with a degree in English in 1969. After a brief stint in law school, she decided to devote herself to her writing. Silko has taught at Navajo Community College, the University of New Mexico, and the University of Arizona.

She was formerly married to John Silko, an attorney. She has two sons, Robert, born in 1966 and Cazimir, born in 1972. The Silko family lived in Alaska in the mid-1970s while she was writing *Ceremony* (1977), the first published novel by an American Indian woman. Although *Storyteller* (1977) is set in Alaska, most of Silko's poetry and fiction is set at Laguna Pueblo. She was awarded a "genius" fellowship from the MacArthur Foundation, which allowed her to work on her seven-hundred-page novel, *Almanac of the Dead* (1991). This novel contrasts an apocalyptic and declining Western society with the sacred traditions of Native American peoples. An underlying theme in Silko's work is the anger and tragedy that she feels for the humiliation and violation that Native Americans have experienced since 1492. Silko believes that one's identity is created through stories that one hears while growing up. She asserts that literature locates us in the family, community, and universe that we are a part of. Silko's prose has the "feel" of ancient American Indian storytelling interwoven with her own personal experiences. She is considered one of the foremost American Indian writers of the late twentieth century.

FOR MORE INFORMATION:

Champagne, Duane, ed. *Native North American Almanac*. Detroit: Gale Research, 1994.

SILVERHEELS, JAY
Mohawk
c. 1912–1980

Born as Harry Smith around 1920, the Mohawk who acquired the stage name "Jay Silverheels" became well known as the Lone Ranger's television sidekick Tonto on the long-running series *The Lone Ranger*. Silverheels also acted in a film version of the same plot, as well as in other films, including *The Prairie* (1947), *Broken Arrow* (1950), and *War Arrow* (1953). In 1979, Silverheels became the first Native American to have a star set on Hollywood Boulevard's Walk of Fame.

FOR MORE INFORMATION:

Corneau, Ernest N. *The Hall of Fame of Western Film Stars*. North Quincy, Mass.: Christopher Publishing, 1969.

SITTING BULL (TATANKA YOTANKA)
Hunkpapa Sioux
c. 1830–1890

Sitting Bull, whose Lakota name is more accurately translated as "a Large Bull Buffalo at

Jay Silverheels (left) *plays Tonto in a scene with Clayton Moore as the Lone Ranger. [The Lone Ranger publicity photo]*

Rest," was one of the principal war chiefs who negotiated the Fort Laramie Treaty of 1868, which forced the United States to abandon several forts and to respect the Lakotas' claim to their sacred Paha Sapa, or Black Hills, "the Heart of Everything That Is." Sitting Bull was known among the Lakota as an outstanding warrior as a young man; in later years, he was best known as a spiritual leader—a visionary and a dreamer. Before the 1876 battle with George Armstrong CUSTER's forces at the Little Bighorn, Sitting Bull had a vision that portended a Native victory.

Captain Edmund Fechet, who observed Sitting Bull's influence after he surrendered to reservation life during the 1880s, later wrote: "Since the days of PONTIAC, TECUMSEH, and RED JACKET, no Indian has had the power of drawing to himself so large a following . . . and molding it and wielding it against the authority of the United States."

Born at a site the Hunkpapas called Many Caches along the Grand River in Dakota country, Sitting Bull's first childhood name was "Slow." He apparently resented the stigma and both a great warrior and a Wichasha Wakan—a man of mystery, a medicine man.

Sitting Bull was reluctant to engage the U.S. Army in war until the Hunkpapas' land was invaded. After that happened, he allied with other Sioux bands, as well as Cheyenne, to stem the flood. Sitting Bull and his allies closely watched the invasion of the Black Hills by Custer in 1874 and played a key role in rallying the Lakota and Cheyenne to defeat Custer in 1876 at the Little Bighorn. Just as PLENTY COUPS's visions had played a key role in the Crows' decision to accommodate the whites, Sitting Bull's dreams foreshadowed the defeat of Custer. In June 1876, a great Sun Dance was held on the west bank of the Rosebud. Sitting Bull performed the dance thirty-six hours straight, after which he had a vision of U.S. Army soldiers without ears falling into a Sioux village, upside down. The lack of ears signified ignorance of the truth, and the upside-down positioning indicated that they would die.

The allied camp of the Sioux, Cheyenne, and others, as many as five thousand people, including as many as two thousand warriors, followed the Little Bighorn River for about three miles. The elite Seventh Cavalry under Custer had expected only a thousand. Even after he discovered that the camp was much larger than he had expected, Custer decided to attack the Indians on their home ground on June 25, 1876. That decision resulted in the deaths of Custer and his entire force of about 225 men. The news of Custer's defeat reached the East Coast in July in time to spoil the United States' centennial celebrations. Sitting Bull said of the battle, "Let no man say that this was a massacre. They came to kill us and got killed themselves."

The Custer battle occurred as Dakota country was filling with white people. In 1870, fewer than five thousand whites had lived in the Dakota Territory. By 1880, the non-Indian

Sitting Bull. [Nebraska State Historical Society]

worked to prove himself from a very early age. At ten, he killed a buffalo. At fourteen, Sitting Bull counted coup on an enemy and received his adult name. He also showed promise as a medicine man by undertaking a vision quest. Shortly after that, he was initiated into the Strong Heart Warrior Society. Sitting Bull assumed leadership in the society in 1856, after he killed a Crow in combat and sustained a bullet wound that forced him to limp for the rest of his life. Sitting Bull was conscious of his leadership role from early in his life—first in battle, first in the buffalo hunt. WHITE BULL remarked, "Wherever he was, and whatever he did, his name was great everywhere." Sitting Bull's enemies held his name in such awe that Hunkpapa warriors could intimidate enemies by shouting "Tatanka-Iyotanka tahoksila," meaning "We are Sitting Bull's boys." Sitting Bull grew to be population had grown to 134,000, some 17,000 of whom were digging gold in the Black Hills.

Later in the 1870s, Sitting Bull and about two hundred other Lakota escaped the Great Sioux Reservation and took refuge in Canada. In Canada, Sitting Bull was afforded the deference due a visiting head of state. He received visitors from around the world. In 1881, Sitting Bull and his band returned to the United States and surrendered. By this time, his once vast following had dwindled to 44 men and 143 women and children. Sitting Bull was taken to the Standing Rock Agency where he ridiculed efforts to sell Indian land. "Take a scale and sell it by the pound!" he is said to have shouted satirically. On the Great Sioux Reservation, millions of acres were being sold to non-Indians, and epidemics were spreading. Sitting Bull staunchly opposed any form of allotment. Although he adopted farming and sent his children to reservation schools, Sitting Bull maintained until his death that "I would rather die an Indian than live a white man."

In September 1886, Sitting Bull joined a hundred other Lakota in a journey to Crow Territory. Within sight of the monument erected to the slain General Custer at the Little Bighorn, the longtime enemies "buried the hatchet." In the meantime, Indian agent Major James ("White Hair") McLaughlin tried to break Sitting Bull's influence. He appointed Indian police to spy on Sitting Bull and named GALL of the Hunkpapas and John GRASS of the Blackfeet Sioux as recognized chiefs. By 1890, the remaining Lakota were corralled into concentration camp–like conditions on the Plains. The Ghost Dance religion arrived at their lowest ebb. Spawned by the prophet WOVOKA, a Paiute, the Ghost Dance spread among the destitute Native peoples of the West, from

Oregon to Nebraska into the Dakotas, where Sitting Bull endorsed its vision of Native restoration. The Sioux took to the Ghost Dance with a frenzy that Wovoka had not anticipated; Sioux medicine men also said that special "Ghost Shirts" would shield the Sioux from soldiers' bullets. Driven by hunger, desperation, and a determined desire to escape from their new, brutal reality, many Sioux ghost dancers worked themselves into a frenzy during which they said they had seen the return of the buffalo and spoken with dead relatives.

By late 1890, an estimated thirty-five hundred Indians were gathered against their will in the hills near Wounded Knee Creek, which bisects the Pine Ridge Indian Reservation. Many of them demanded the right to practice the Ghost Dance religion. The rules of the reservation laid down by the Indian Bureau forbade practice of the religion. Anglo settlers demanded protection from what they regarded as a revolutionary movement. Several thousand troops converged on the reservation from surrounding forts in anticipation of renewed conflict. Troops with itchy trigger fingers were spurred by settlers eager to extinguish the Indian threat. L. Frank Baum, who would later author *The Wonderful Wizard of Oz*, penned these words as editor of the Aberdeen, South Dakota, *Saturday Pioneer* a week and a half before the fatal confrontation:

The nobility of the Redskin is extinguished, and what few are left are a pack of whining curs who lick the hand that smites them. The Whites, by law of conquest, by justice of civilization, are masters of the American continent, and the best safety of the frontier settlements will be secured by the total annihilation of the few remaining Indians. Why not annihilation? Their glory has fled, their spirit broken, their manhood effaced; better that they should die than live [as] the miserable wretches that they are. [Stannard]

Baum's beliefs contrasted with those of Sitting Bull at about the same time:

What treaty that the whites have kept has the red man broken? Not one. What treaty that the whites ever made with us red men have they kept? Not one. When I was a boy, the Sioux owned the world. The sun rose and set in their lands. They sent 10,000 horsemen to battle. Where are the warriors today? Who slew them? Where are our lands? Who owns them? [Utley]

Tension intensified between McLaughlin, who was pressuring the Sioux to sign new treaties ceding more of their territory, and Sitting Bull, who had campaigned all his life against signing away Native homelands. At one point, Sitting Bull's old friend Buffalo Bill CODY tried to intercede to negotiate but failed. Cody had been one of Sitting Bull's very few white friends.

Sitting Bull's log cabin, the site of his assassination in 1890. [Nebraska State Historical Society]

Sitting Bull was killed on December 15, 1890, a few days before the massacre of BIG FOOT's band at Wounded Knee, as forty-three tribal police tried to arrest him. Accounts of Sitting Bull's assassination vary, but it appears that BULLHEAD, a police officer employed by the Indian agency, served a warrant on Sitting Bull, who protested. Bullhead then shot him in the thigh as his partner, Sergeant RED TOMAHAWK, shot Sitting Bull in the head. A riot ensued during which six policemen and eight of Sitting Bull's followers, including his son CROW FOOT, were also killed.

FOR MORE INFORMATION:

Dugan, Bill. *Sitting Bull.* San Francisco: Harper-Collins, 1994.

Edmunds, R. David, ed. *American Indian Leaders: Studies in Diversity.* Lincoln: University of Nebraska Press, 1980.

Giago, Tim. "Book Lacks Lakota View." *Indian Country Today,* August 4, 1993.

Hamilton, Charles. *Cry of the Thunderbird.* Norman: University of Oklahoma Press, 1972.

Hyde, George E. *A Sioux Chronicle.* Norman: University of Oklahoma Press, 1956.

McLaughlin, James. *My Friend, the Indian.* 1910. Reprint, New York: Houghton-Mifflin, 1926.

Stannard, David. *American Holocaust: Columbus and the Conquest of the New World.* New York: Oxford University Press, 1992.

Utley, Robert M. *The Lance and the Shield: The Life and Times of Sitting Bull.* New York: Henry Holt, 1993.

Vestal, Stanley. *Sitting Bull: Champion of the Sioux.* 1932. Reprint, Norman: University of Oklahoma Press, 1957.

Waters, Frank. *Brave Are My People: Indian Heroes Not Forgotten.* Santa Fe, N. Mex.: Clear Light, 1993.

SITTING BULL, "THE MINOR"
Oglala Lakota
1841–1876

As a young man, the Oglala Lakota Sitting Bull was named Drum Packer. He became an avid student of the printed word and learned to read and write English from an Overland Trail telegrapher named Oscar Collister. As an adult, he became chief of LITTLE WOUND's band. His accomplishments as a warrior were often confused with those of the more famous Hunkpapa SITTING BULL.

Sitting Bull (Minor) displayed an affinity for white people until the Sand Creek massacre of BLACK KETTLE's people in 1864, after which he joined with CRAZY HORSE in answering the Cheyennes' call for help. He participated in the Battle of Julesburg, Colorado, to avenge Sand Creek. Sitting Bull (Minor) also participated in the FETTERMAN affair. Fighting under the command of Little Wound, in alliance with RED CLOUD, Sitting Bull (Minor) attacked Overland Trail stations and other manifestations of Euro-American expansion until the Fort Laramie Treaty was signed in 1968.

By 1870, Sitting Bull (Minor) had enrolled at Red Cloud Agency, breaking with Crazy Horse, who remained outside agency jurisdiction. His Hunkpapa namesake was still defined by the U.S. Army as hostile. At twenty-nine, Sitting Bull (Minor) set about improving the lot of his people by traveling with a delegation of Lakota to Washington, D.C., to negotiate.

In 1875, Sitting Bull (Minor) returned to Washington with SPOTTED TAIL and Red Cloud to protest the thousands of miners who had swarmed into the Black Hills following Custer's announcement, a year before, of gold in the hills. Sitting Bull (Minor) found that the Indian commissioners were interested only in buying the Black Hills, not in addressing cuts in rations at the agencies or the general destitution of the Indians. Disregarding the lack of progress at the 1875 meeting, Sitting Bull (Minor) was presented with a Winchester carbine that was engraved "[To] Sitting Bull, from The President, for Bravery and True Friendship."

Following the annihilation of Custer's small army at the Little Bighorn in 1876, U.S. negotiators visited South Dakota seeking legal title to the Black Hills with a new degree of vigor. To begin, Sitting Bull (Minor) and other negotiators for the Lakota were taken to a stockade and held in protective custody as they talked. They were told to sell the Black Hills or suffer a complete cutoff in rations and a forced march to Indian Territory (now Oklahoma). Insulted, Sitting Bull (Minor) ran out of the stockade carrying the rifle that the President had given him. He ran to the war camp of Crazy Horse, who was but months from surrendering, and became discouraged at the destitution of the people there. Sitting Bull (Minor) then returned to the negotiations at the stockade only to find that the other treaty chiefs had signed an agreement (later annulled) that would have given the Black Hills to the United States.

In 1877, Sitting Bull (Minor) played a leading role in persuading Crazy Horse to surrender. Returning from that mission and carrying a white flag given to him by General George Crook on December 17, 1876, Sitting Bull (Minor) and four companions passed a group of Crow scouts who killed all five as both Crazy Horse and General Nelson Miles watched. They were close enough to see the altercation but too far away to offer help.

FOR MORE INFORMATION:

Hyde, George E. *Red Cloud's Folk: A History of the Oglala Sioux Indians.* Norman: University of Oklahoma Press, 1967.

Olson, James C. *Red Cloud and the Sioux Problem.* Lincoln: University of Nebraska Press, 1965.

SKENANDOAH (SHENANDOAH)
Oneida
c. 1710–1816

Skenandoah ("Deer"), who lived at Oneida Castle, New York, supported the British in the French and Indian War (1754–1763) but switched his allegiance to the patriots in the American Revolution. Little is known of his early life or the early years of his chieftainship except that he became a committed campaigner against alcohol after he got drunk and was robbed while sleeping on a street in Albany. As an adult, Skenandoah was exceptionally tall (about six feet, three inches) and known for his graceful manner.

Although Skenandoah asserted the Oneidas' official neutrality at the beginning of the American Revolution, he supplied warriors and intelligence to the patriots along with the Tuscaroras. As Washington's army shivered in the snow at Valley Forge, Skenandoah's Oneidas carried baskets of corn to the starving troops. Washington later named the Shenandoah Valley after the Oneida chief in appreciation of his support. Most of the Mohawks, Oneidas, Senecas, and Cayugas sided with the British, causing the Iroquois League to split. During September 1778, Skenandoah supplied a key warning to residents of German Flats, near Albany, that their settlements were about to be raided by the British with their Iroquois allies under Joseph BRANT. The settlers were thus able to get out of the area in time, though their home and farms were burned and their livestock captured.

After the Revolution, Skenandoah continued to serve as a principal chief of the Oneidas and signed several treaties on their behalf. Skenandoah was a close friend of the missionary Samuel Kirkland and was buried, at Skenandoah's request, next to Kirkland at the Hamilton College cemetery in Clinton, New York, after having lived to the extraordinary age of about 110. One of Skenandoah's descendants, the Oneida folksinger Joanne SHENANDOAH, became prominent in the late twentieth century.

FOR MORE INFORMATION:

Grinde, Donald A., Jr. *The Iroquois and the Founding of the American Nation.* San Francisco: Indian Historian Press, 1977.

SKY CHIEF (TIRAWAHUT LASHAR)
Pawnee
fl. 1870s

During the Plains Indian wars, the Pawnees allied with the United States against their traditional enemies, the powerful Sioux Confederacy. Sky Chief was one of the main architects of the Pawnees' policy of accommodation; he provided scouts for the U.S. Army and guards for crews building the transcontinental railroad. In 1873, Sky Chief was leading one of the last Pawnee buffalo hunts in southern Nebraska when his party was ambushed by a large body of Sioux warriors. Sky Chief and about 150 other Pawnees were killed by the Sioux before the army came to the rescue of a few survivors. The site of the ambush later became known as Massacre Canyon.

SLOCUM, JOHN
Squakson/Coast Salish
fl. 1880s

John Slocum, creator of the Indian Shaker religion, was one of a number of Native American religious figures who combined elements of Christianity with Native spiritual practices to form new religions. Like HANDSOME LAKE and WOVOKA, among others, Slocum had contact with Christianity (he was converted by missionaries in the Puget Sound area) but wished to retain Native cultural and religious values.

Similar to other Native prophets, whose designs for the new faith came to them in a series of visions, Slocum said that he had been transported to heaven. In 1881, he outlined Tschadam, the Indian Shaker religion. Adherents were said to twitch or shake as they meditated and "brushed" their sins away. The Indian Shaker religion also became a political issue at a time when white officials sought to outlaw all Indian religious practices. Indian Shakerism spread to several tribes in western Washington, and many of its devotees were arrested for participating in church rites before and after Wovoka's Ghost Dance played a role in the massacre of BIG FOOT and his people at Wounded Knee, South Dakota, in December 1890.

DE SMET, PIERRE JEAN
1801–1873

Pierre Jean de Smet, a Jesuit priest, enjoyed access to many Plains tribes that was unrivaled by any other non-Indian during the Indian wars in that region. U.S. officials sometimes called on de Smet to act as a diplomat as well as a priest. De Smet played a key role in gathering between eight thousand and twelve thousand Indian people at a key treaty council in 1851 at the junction of Horse Creek and the North Platte River in present-day Morrill County, Nebraska. The 1851 Fort Laramie (or Horse Creek) Treaty presaged the Plains Indian wars later in the century.

De Smet emigrated to the United States from Belgium in 1821. After serving his novitiate in Florissant, Missouri, de Smet was ordained in 1827. In 1838, de Smet began his missionary career on the site that would later be called Council Bluffs, Iowa. In 1840, he began his exploration of the upper Missouri Valley in the company of two Flathead Indians who had come to St. Louis in search of a "blackrobe," or Jesuit priest. De Smet then opened missions throughout the Pacific Northwest as well as in

present-day Montana. De Smet also traveled frequently to Europe to raise funds for his and other Jesuits' missions in North America.

During 1867 and 1868, de Smet accepted an appointment as "envoy extraordinary" of the U.S. government to negotiate with SITTING BULL and other Sioux leaders who were raiding U.S. forts that had been erected, contrary to treaty terms, in the Powder River country. His first object was to stop anti-U.S. hostility; his ultimate aim was to bring hostile Indians to agencies where they could be taught to live like whites.

At a historic conference at the confluence of the Yellowstone and Powder Rivers, de Smet reported that Sitting Bull put the blame for hostilities on the United States.

> Black-robe[:] I hardly sustain myself beneath the weight of white men's blood that I have shed. The whites provoked the war. Their injustices, their indignities to our families . . . shook all the veins which bind and support me. I rose, tomahawk in hand, and I have done all the hurt to the whites that I could. Today, thou art among us, and in thy presence my arms stretch to the ground as if dead. I will listen . . . and as bad as I have been to whites, just so good I am ready to become toward them. [Chittenden]

Although de Smet and other missionaries converted some Indians and taught them to farm, in the long run, according to Alvin M. Josephy, Jr., they "undermined tribal institutions and stability and created bitter factionalism that weakened the tribes and paved the way for their eventual loss of power and lands." Killoren, by contrast, depicts de Smet as a defender of Native rights, comparing him at times to Dr. Martin Luther King, Jr.

FOR MORE INFORMATION:

Chittenden, Hiram Martin, and Alfred Talbot Richardson, eds. *Life, Letters, and Travels of Father Pierre Jean DeSmet, 1801–73.* 4 vols. New York: Frances P. Harper, 1905.

Josephy, Alvin M., Jr. *The Indian Heritage of America.* New York: Bantam, 1969.

Killoren, John J. *"Come, Blackrobe": De Smet and the Indian Tragedy.* Norman: University of Oklahoma Press, 1993.

Peterson, Jacqueline. *Sacred Encounters: Father de Smet and the Indians of the Rocky Mountain West.* Norman: University of Oklahoma Press, 1993.

de Smet, Pierre-Jean, S. J. *Letters and Sketches.* 1843. Reprint, Cleveland: A. H. Clark, 1906.

———. *New Indian Sketches.* New York: D. & J. Sadlier, 1865.

———. *Oregon Missions and Travels Over the Rocky Mountains in 1845–1846.* New York, 1847.

———. *Western Missions and Missionaries: A Series of Letters.* New York: P. J. Kenedy, 1859.

SMITH, NIMROD JARRETT (TSALATIHI)
Cherokee
c. 1838–1893

Born near what would become Murphy, North Carolina, to a Cherokee father and mother, Nimrod Jarrett Smith was in the Confederate army during the Civil War. He served as a sergeant in an Eastern Cherokee company under the command of Colonel W. H. Thomas, a Cherokee trader, and married Mary Guthrie, a white woman. In the 1870s, Smith became principal chief of the Eastern Cherokees, a position he held until his death in 1893. During his tenure as principal chief, Smith secured the Eastern Cherokees' title to their lands in North Carolina and created a modern educational system.

SMITH, REDBIRD
Cherokee
1850–1918

Born on July 19, 1850, near Fort Smith, Arkansas, Redbird Smith would become a principal chief and a Cherokee traditionalist who resisted allotment and Oklahoma statehood. His Cherokee father was called Pig Redbird Smith (so named because he was a blacksmith); his mother was a Cherokee named Lizzie Hildebrand. Redbird Smith's family felt strongly about their Cherokee traditions and the threat to their continuance.

After the Civil War, traditionalist families such as the Smiths rallied around the Keetowah Society (named after the Cherokee word *kituwha,* meaning "key") to protect themselves against capricious land appropriation by Union armies in Indian Territory. Originally organized by Evan Jones and his son John, the Keetowah Society became less active during the 1870s and 1880s when federal threats to Native American power in Indian Territory ebbed.

In the 1890s, however, a new challenge to the Cherokee land base surfaced. When the DAWES Commission came to Indian Territory in 1893, it wanted to regain control over lands that were ceded to the Five Civilized Tribes (Cherokee, Creek, Choctaw, Chickasaw, and Seminole) when they were removed from the East. White settlers or "sooners" had been coming into Indian Territory, and they were pressuring the federal government to legitimize their claims and lands.

The resulting General Allotment Act or Dawes Severalty Act of 1887 called for the abolition of communal landholdings and the allotment of parcels of land in 160-acre tracts to tribal members. It also provided that such allottees become citizens in due course and that a new state, Oklahoma, be created. Many traditionalist Cherokees resisted such land and statehood plans through the Keetowah Society. They lobbied the U.S. Congress to exempt the Five Civilized Tribes from such allotment policies. In 1893, the federal government voided the exemption of the Five Civilized Tribes from allotment policies and established the Dawes Commission to dispense with tribal lands.

To the further chagrin of the traditionalists, Congress enacted the Curtis Act in 1898, which abolished tribal governments and created civil governments in Indian Territory. Under these circumstances, Redbird Smith and other traditionalists revitalized the Keetowah Society to stop federal assaults on tribalism. But there soon developed a split in the ranks of the Keetowahs, with one faction resigning itself to losing autonomy while the other group opposed any capitulation to governmental policies. Redbird Smith sought to reconcile the two groups so that united they could become stronger. He also reached out to traditionalists in all of the Five Civilized Tribes through the Four Mothers Society that he founded in 1912.

The Keetowahs collected monthly dues to hire lawyers, lobby Congress, and travel to Washington. With powerful economic interests arrayed against them, it appeared that no one could keep the land speculators, oil men, and railroads from gaining what they wanted in Congress. In this heated environment, Redbird Smith's adherents were known as the Nighthawk Keetowahs because they met at night in order to keep their political strategies secret. The Keetowahs encouraged many Cherokees to refuse enrollment during the U.S. census of 1900. Such disruptive activities caused much bureaucratic confusion. In 1902, Redbird Smith was arrested for refusing to enroll. Although he continued to resist enrollment, the government enrolled him by force.

Protesting enrollment and allotment in Washington, Redbird Smith stated, "I can't stand and live and breathe if I take this allotment." However, his protests in Washington were futile. In despair, he returned to Indian Territory and told his people that any more resistance was hopeless. In 1905, under federal pressure, the Cherokees became the last tribe to sign the allotment agreement.

In 1907, the former Indian Territory became the state of Oklahoma. Smith became principal chief of the Cherokees in 1908; many of Smith's followers withdrew to the Cookson Hills of northeastern Oklahoma, hoping to preserve their way of life and avoid white interference in their affairs. Late in life he was active in preserving traditional ways among the Five Civilized Tribes through the Four Mothers Society. On November 8, 1918, he died in Oklahoma. He was survived by his wife, Lucy Fields Smith.

FOR MORE INFORMATION:

Dockstader, Frederick. *Great North American Indians.* New York: Van Nostrand Reinhold, 1977.

SMOHALLA
Wanapam
c. 1818–c. 1907

Smohalla (or Smoqula, "The Preacher") was one of a core of leaders among the Nez Perce who resisted U.S. attempts to place them on reservations. This resistance culminated in the fifteen-hundred-mile Long March in 1877. Smohalla was also a spiritual leader who fused aspects of Christianity and Native tradition into the Dreamer religion, which swept the Northwest United States before the better-known Ghost Dance took hold of the Plains.

Early in his adult life, Smohalla distinguished himself in battle despite his physical deformity of a hunchback. He incurred the personal enmity of MOSES, leader of the neighboring

Sinkiuses. The two men met in hand-to-hand combat, after which Moses left Smohalla for dead. Smohalla was not dead, however. He made his way to a nearby river and floated downstream in a boat, beginning a journey that eventually took him down the Pacific Coast to Mexico, then back to Wanapam country through Arizona and other inland points.

Smohalla's reappearance among his people caused a degree of awe that was impressive for a spiritual leader. Smohalla came bearing teachings said to be acquired on a visit to the Spirit World: that all Native peoples should reject the whites' beliefs and artifices. He counseled Native peoples to stay away from reservations and to restore traditional ways of life. The Dreamer religion included dances done in hypnotic rhythm to bells, drums, and other musical instruments. Frustrated with the duplicity of the whites, JOSEPH YOUNGER (also known as Chief Joseph) of the Nez Perce turned to Smohalla's Dreamer religion.

Smohalla also figures in the treaty literature as he used an ecological motivation for wishing to escape the new life the United States sought to force on him and his people.

In 1877, Chief Joseph replied to an Indian agent's proposal that he and his people move to a reservation and become farmers. Chief Joseph said: "The land is our mother. . . . She should not be disturbed by hoe or plow. We want only to subsist on what she freely gives us." Smohalla said at the same meeting:

> You ask me to plow the ground? I should take a knife and tear my mother's bosom? Then when I die, she will not take me to her bosom to rest. . . . You ask me to dig for stone! Shall I dig under her skin for her bones? Then when I die I cannot enter her body to be born again. You ask me to cut grass and make hay and sell it, to be rich

like white men! But how dare I cut off my mother's hair? [Waters]

Smohalla survived the Long March and lived until 1907. He was buried at the Satus graveyard in Washington State, and his nephew Puckhyahtoot ("The Last Prophet") carried on his Dreamer religion.

FOR MORE INFORMATION:

Josephy, Alvin M., Jr. *The Indian Heritage of America.* New York: Bantam, 1969.

———. *The Nez Perce Indians and the Opening of the Northwest.* New Haven: Yale University Press, 1965.

Waters, Frank. *Brave Are My People: Indian Heroes Not Forgotten.* Santa Fe, N. Mex.: Clear Light, 1993.

SNAKE, REUBEN
Winnebago
1937–1993

Reuben Snake synthesized an extraordinary range of life experience into a personal force for commitment and consensus that served his Winnebago people as well as Native Americans on a national and international level. Snake served twenty-eight years in Winnebago tribal governance, first as a tribal council member, later as vice chairman and chairman, before he became president of the National Council of American Indians. He was a lifelong member of the Native American Church and a pipe carrier, and he lectured to many diverse audiences around the world.

Snake began adulthood as a member of the U.S. Army Green Berets between 1954 and 1958. He was educated at Northwestern College, Orange City, Iowa; the University of Nebraska at Omaha; and Peru (Nebraska) State College. Noted for humor that kept him in demand as a conference speaker, Snake often signed personal letters "Your humble serpent."

He was active in efforts to broaden the scope of Native American religious freedom, as well as tribal economic development, and was a member of several national boards of directors.

Snake often used humor to drive home the point that Native American philosophy, especially the idea that all natural phenomena move in cycles and that all things are related, could help ameliorate European man's alienation from nature, his fellows, and himself. During a speech in Seattle, October 1991, at an event sponsored by the Lummi tribe, Snake proposed that "every Indian person in this nation of ours . . . go out and adopt two hundred and fifty white people. Bring them into the family. Teach them the right way to do things."

After he died of a heart attack and complications from diabetes on June 28, 1993, a report in *Indian Country Today* said: "A warm-hearted bear of a man noted for his leadership in spiritual circles and the political arena was called home by his creator June 28. . . . Reuben Snake will be mourned by people across the nation who remember his booming voice, his ever-present wit, and his dauntless dedication to Indian people of many tribal nations."

Snake's forte was consensus building and conflict resolution. "Three things that characterized Reuben were strength, clarity, and patience," said Susan Harjo, director of the Morning Star Institution. "He always had a very good way of bringing people to consensus. No matter how long it took, how contentious the issue was, he was prepared to stay for however long it took."

"Reuben always imparted a message of respect, describing a faithful vision of a loving world—'a world of relatives,' " said the editors of *Akwe:kon Journal*, published by Cornell University's American Indian Program. "Reuben Snake could explain things better than anyone, and he was very funny and pleasant to be with. . . . [He] encouraged communications that were not normally possible."

One of Snake's six children and sixteen grandchildren, Abigail Snake, said that shortly before his death, Reuben Snake had a vision in which a long-deceased brother came to him burning sage and smudging him with its residue, a Winnebago rite of passage. "I'm not afraid," he told Abigail. "I'm ready." [Little Eagle]

FOR MORE INFORMATION:

"In Memoriam." *Akwe:kon Journal* (Summer 1993)

Little Eagle, Avis, and Jerry Reynolds. "Tribute to Reuben Snake: 'Humble Serpent' Journeys On." *Indian Country Today*, June 30, 1993, A-1.

Snake, Reuben. In *Our People, Our Land*, edited by Kurt Russo. Bellingham, Wash.: Kluckhohn Center, 1992.

———. *Your Humble Serpent*. As told to Jay C. Fikes. Santa Fe, N. Mex.: Clear Light, 1995.

SOHAPPY, DAVID
Wanapam
1925–1991

Many Native people along the Columbia River and its tributaries in eastern Washington had fished for a livelihood long before Euro-Americans migrated to their land, but they had no treaties protecting their right to do so. The 1974 BOLDT decision restored recognition of treaty rights at least regarding salmon fishing west of the Cascades. East of the Cascades, during the 1980s, the fishing rights battle continued in a form that reminded many people of the Frank's Landing "fish-ins" of the 1960s (see Billy FRANK, Jr.). For years, David Sohappy, his wife, Myra, and their sons erected a riverbank shelter and fished in the traditional manner.

The Sohappys' name came from the Wanapam word *souiehappie*, meaning "shoving something under a ledge." David Sohappy's ancestors had traded fish with members of the Lewis and Clark expedition. The Wanapams never signed a treaty; they wished only to be left in peace to live as they had for hundreds if not thousands of years. By the early 1940s, Sohappy's family was pushed off its ancestral homeland at Priest Rapids and White Bluffs, which became part of the Hanford Nuclear Reservation, in the middle of a desert that Lewis and Clark characterized as the most barren piece of land that they saw between St. Louis and the Pacific Ocean. Still, David Sohappy fished, even though his father, Jim Sohappy, warned him that if he continued to live in the old ways, "The white man is going to put you in jail someday."

During the 1950s, development devastated the Celilo Falls, one of the richest Indian fishing grounds in North America. Most of the people who had fished there gave up their traditional livelihood and moved to the nearby Yakima Reservation or into urban areas. David and Myra Sohappy moved to a sliver of federal land called Cook's Landing, just above the first of several dams along the Columbia and its tributaries. They built a small longhouse with a dirt floor. Sohappy built fishing traps from driftwood. As the "fish-ins" of the 1960s attracted nationwide publicity, Sohappy fished in silence until state game and fishing officials raided his camp, beat his family members, and put Sohappy in jail in 1968 on charges of illegal fishing. He then brought legal action; the case, *Sohappy* v. *Smith*, produced a landmark federal ruling that was supposed to prevent the states of Washington and Oregon from interfering with Indian fishing, except for conservation purposes.

The states ignored the ruling and continued to harass Sohappy and his family. Usually under cover of darkness, state agents sank their boats and slashed their nets. In 1981 and 1982, the states of Washington and Oregon successfully (but quietly) lobbied into law a federal provision that made the interstate sale of fish taken in violation of state law a felony—an act aimed squarely at Sohappy. Eight months before the law was signed by President Reagan, the state enlisted federal undercover agents in a fish-buying sting expressly to entrap Sohappy. The press called it "Salmonscam." He was later convicted in Los Angeles (the trial had been moved from the local jurisdiction because of racial prejudice against Indians) of taking 317 fish, and he was sentenced to five years in prison. During the trial, testimony about Sohappy's religion and his practice of conservation measures was not allowed.

Sohappy became a symbol of Native rights across the United States. Myra Sohappy sought support from the U.N. Commission on Human Rights to have her husband tried by a jury of his peers in the Yakima nation's tribal court. The new trial was arranged with the help of U.S. Senator Daniel Inouye, chairman of the Senate Select Committee on Indian Affairs. The Yakima court found that the federal prosecution had interfered with Sohappy's practice of his Seven Drum religion. Shortly thereafter he was released from prison.

During twenty months of incarceration, Sohappy had aged rapidly. Confinement and the prison diet had sapped his strength. Sohappy suffered several strokes during the months in prison, when he was denied even the use of an eagle prayer feather for comfort (it was rejected as contraband by prison officials). Back at Cook's Landing, Sohappy found that vindictive federal officials had tacked an eviction notice to his small house. Sohappy took the eviction notice to court and beat the government for what turned out to be his last time. He died in a nursing home in Hood River, Oregon, on May 6, 1991.

A few days later Sohappy was buried as his Wanapam relatives gathered in an old graveyard. They sang old songs and lowered his body into the earth, having wrapped it in a Pendleton blanket. He was placed so that the early morning sun would warm his head, facing west toward Mount Adams. Tom Keefe, Jr., an attorney who had been instrumental in securing Sohappy's release from prison, stood by the grave and remembered:

> And while the sun chased a crescent moon across the Yakima Valley, I thanked David Sohappy for the time we had spent together, and I wondered how the salmon he had fought to protect would fare in his absence. Now he is gone, and the natural runs of Chinook that fed his family since time immemorial are headed for the Endangered Species Act list. "Be glad for my dad," David Sohappy, Jr., told the mourners. "He is free now, he doesn't need any tears."

FOR MORE INFORMATION:

Keefe, Tom, Jr. "A Tribute to David Sohappy." *Native Nations* (June/July, 1991).

SPOKANE GARRY
Spokane
1811–1892

Spokane Garry was the head chief of the confederated Spokane bands during the middle of the nineteenth century, before Anglo settlers pushed his people off their land to found the city that they named for his people. Spokane Garry was also the first person (Indian or not) to use the *Book of Common Prayer* in public worship in the Pacific Northwest.

Spokane Garry was born in 1811 near the junction of Latah Creek and the Spokane River. He was a son of Illim Spokane, a chief of the Central Spokanes. He was educated in missionary schools, where he was given the Christian name Garry. He traveled the Northwest preaching Christianity and was selected as chief of his band because of his education, his organizational skills, and his ancestry. Spokane Garry married twice; Lucy, his first wife, died shortly after bearing him a daughter. Spokane Garry's second wife, Nina, had two sons and a daughter with him.

For all his efforts to be the model Indian for missionaries, Spokane Garry's appeals for a mission teacher were ignored. Gradually, Spokane Garry began to distrust the growing numbers of whites who were immigrating to the area. His family was driven from their farm in 1888 by land-hungry whites, and the central village of his band was dispossessed two years later to make way for the city of Spokane. Spokane Garry died impoverished in 1892, bitter at the whites' treatment of him and his people. A statue of him was dedicated in Seattle, Washington, in 1961.

FOR MORE INFORMATION:

Howard, O. O. *Famous Indian Chiefs I Have Known.* 1908. Reprint, Lincoln: University of Nebraska Press, 1989.

Jessett, Thomas E. *Chief Spokan Garry.* Minneapolis: 1960.

SPOTTED TAIL (SINTE GALESHKA)
Brulé Sioux
1823–1881

Spotted Tail, a major Sioux leader in the Plains Indian wars, was born along the White River of South Dakota (or, as some accounts have it, near Laramie, Wyoming) to a father named Cunka

(Tangled Hair) and a mother named Walks with Pipe. Known as Jumping Buffalo in his youth, Spotted Tail got his adult name from a striped raccoon pelt that was given him by a trapper.

Spotted Tail won his laurels as a chief by merit in battle and diplomacy. His title was not hereditary. He came to be known as an extremely valiant man. On one occasion, about 1855, Spotted Tail and two other men gave themselves up at Fort Laramie to spare the rest of the tribe after an unidentified Brulé was charged with murder. During his imprisonment for a crime he did not commit, Spotted Tail learned to read and write English.

During the early 1860s, after his release, Chief Little Thunder died; the tribal council ignored the hereditary line and selected Spotted Tail to succeed him. He refused to sign a treaty with the United States in 1865 but did sign the 1868 Fort Laramie Treaty. In 1871, Spotted Tail

Spotted Tail. [Nebraska State Historical Society]

served as guide on a buffalo hunt with the Grand Duke Alexis of Russia.

In 1875, Spotted Tail was among Lakota chiefs who traveled to Washington, D.C., to negotiate the sale of the Black Hills. Following General George Armstrong CUSTER's expedition into the Black Hills in 1874, which violated the terms of the 1868 Fort Laramie Treaty, Spotted Tail played a central role in negotiations with government officials in which all offers to buy the Black Hills were refused. The Sioux have still refused to sell, even though one of the Black Hills' tallest mountains was turned into a shrine to four U.S. presidents and is known as Mount Rushmore. It was Spotted Tail who declined the original offer. Even as he spoke, more than ten thousand miners were swarming into the hills in search of the gold that Custer's expedition had found there.

As the Sioux were confined on reservations following the Custer battle, dissension rose among some of their leaders. Spotted Tail was an unusually strong-willed administrator; he maintained a police force to keep whiskey merchants off the reservation, and he deplored threats by the army to relocate the Lakota to Indian Territory (now Oklahoma). Spotted Tail forbade young warriors to raid white settlements, and when a white man was murdered, he turned the perpetrator over to white authorities, then hired a lawyer to represent the man and paid for the defense out of his own pocket.

Throughout the 1870s, Spotted Tail was accused by RED CLOUD of pocketing the proceeds from a sale of tribal land. Possibly as part of this dissension, Spotted Tail was shot to death by CROW DOG, a Sioux subchief, on August 5, 1881.

FOR MORE INFORMATION:

Hyde, George E. *Spotted Tail's Folk: A History of the Brulé Sioux.* Norman: University of Oklahoma Press, 1961.

SQUANTO (TISQUANTUM)
Wampanoag
c. 1580–1622

Squanto, one of the first Indians to aid English colonists, was kidnapped from his native land (the area immigrants called New England) in 1614 by English explorers. They sold him and twenty Patuxent companions on the slave market at Malaga, Spain. A Christian friar smuggled Squanto to England, where he worked for a rich merchant as he learned the English language. Squanto obtained passage back to America on a trading ship not long before the arrival of the Pilgrims, who came ashore in 1620.

Squanto surprised the Pilgrims by greeting them in English; he and other Native Americans helped the new immigrants survive their first American winter. Squanto showed the immigrants how to plant corn—since their seeds of English wheat, barley, and peas would not grow—in hillocks using herring as fertilizer. Squanto also taught them how to design traps to catch fish and acted as a guide and interpreter. He died of "an Indian fever" in November or early December 1622.

FOR MORE INFORMATION:

Vaughan, Alden T. *The New England Frontier: Puritans and Indians, 1620–1675.* Boston: Little, Brown, 1965.

STANDING BEAR (MO-CHU-NO-ZHI)
Ponca
c. 1830–1908

Standing Bear gained national notoriety in the late 1870s during a time of forced removal for the Ponca and other Native peoples on the Great Plains. He led some of the Poncas on a forty-day, five-hundred-mile march from Indian Territory (now Oklahoma) back to Nebraska. In Omaha, Standing Bear became engaged in the first court case to result in a declaration that American Indians are to be treated as human beings under U.S. law. Thus, the army could not legally relocate an Indian by force without cause. The army promptly ignored the court order.

Before they were forcibly removed from their homeland along the Niobrara River in northern Nebraska, the Poncas had gone to great lengths to maintain friendly relationships with the United States. In 1858, they ceded part of their homeland along the Niobrara in exchange for a homeland in the same area that was then said to be theirs in perpetuity. Ten years later, the United States, in a classic example of sloppy bureaucracy, signed the Poncas' land over to the Sioux, their traditional enemies, in the Laramie Treaty of 1868. It took a dozen years for the United States to acknowledge its error; in the meantime, many of the Poncas died in Oklahoma and on forced marches.

During 1877, federal troops removed 723 Poncas from three villages along the Niobrara

Standing Bear. [Nebraska State Historical Society]

River to Indian Territory. The tribe was moved at bayonet point after eight of their leaders had inspected and refused to accept the arid land that the government wanted the Poncas to occupy in Oklahoma. During their march to Indian Territory, several of the Poncas died of starvation and disease.

A year after their removal, a third of the Poncas had died. One of the dead was a son of Standing Bear, who, determined to bury the boy's bones in the lands of his ancestors, escaped northward toward the Niobrara with thirty other Poncas. Standing Bear recalled: "It was winter. We started for home on foot. We barely lived [un]til morning, it was so cold. We had nothing but our blankets. We took the ears of corn that had dried in the fields; we ate it raw. The soles of our moccasins wore out. We went barefoot in the snow." [Massey]

After two months of walking, including a ten-day stop among the Otoes, the group led by Standing Bear took shelter on land owned by the Omahas, their bloody feet leaving tracks in the snow.

The following spring, U.S. Army troops arrived at the Omaha camp and began to force the Poncas southward again. They camped for a time outside Omaha, where local citizens obtained a writ of habeas corpus and brought the army into the federal court of Judge Elmer S. DUNDY, who ruled: "An Indian is a person within the meaning of the law, and there is no law giving the Army authority to forcibly remove Indians from their lands." [Massey] Ironically, the case was prepared with the help of the old Indian fighter George Crook, who was swayed by the manifest injustice of the Poncas' case. The harsh treatment of the Poncas also received publicity in Omaha newspapers, which wired to larger newspapers on the East Coast and caused a storm of protest letters to Congress.

Shortly after Judge Dundy denied the army's presumed power to forcibly relocate Indians in the case of Standing Bear, his brother BIG SNAKE tested the ruling by moving roughly one hundred miles in Indian Territory from the Poncas' assigned reservation to one occupied by the Cheyennes. He did not know that Dundy had restricted the ruling to Standing Bear's party. He was arrested by troops. On October 31, 1879, Ponca Indian agent William H. Whiteman called Big Snake a troublemaker and ordered a detail to imprison him. When Big Snake refused to surrender, contending he had committed no crime, he was shot to death. Later, the U.S. Senate called for an investigation of the shooting and other aspects of the Poncas' tragedy.

Following the Senate investigation, Standing Bear's band was allowed to go home. Standing Bear died in his homeland along the Niobrara in 1908.

In 1990, the Poncas were restored to tribal status by an act of Congress, signed by President George Bush, twenty-five years after the tribe's termination in 1965. Across the United States, several dozen Native nations were following the same path. In 1992, the Poncas moved into new tribal offices at Niobrara. During the restoration, a new generation of Poncas, standing above the Niobrara Valley near the unmarked grave of Standing Bear, recalled how their elders had held a requiem for the old ways in 1962.

In 1995, Ponca City, Oklahoma, commissioned a twenty-foot statue of Standing Bear.

FOR MORE INFORMATION:

Massey, Rosemary, et al. *Footprints in Blood: Standing Bear's Struggle for Freedom and Human Dignity*. Omaha: American Indian Center of Omaha, 1979.

Nabokov, Peter. *Native American Testimony*. New York: Viking Penguin, 1991.

Tibbles, Thomas Henry. *The Ponca Chiefs: An*

Account of the Trial of Standing Bear. Lincoln: University of Nebraska Press, 1972.

STANDING BEAR, LUTHER
Oglala Lakota
1868–1939

Luther Standing Bear was one of the founders of a remarkable Sioux literary tradition that includes Charles EASTMAN, Gertrude BONNIN, and Vine DELORIA, Jr. Recognition of Standing Bear's works, which range from social commentary to autobiography, grew toward the end of the twentieth century, when he was often seen as voicing concerns salient to a pan-Indian sense of identity.

As a young man on leave from Carlisle Indian School, Standing Bear attended a speech in Philadelphia given by the legendary Hunkpapa Sioux chief SITTING BULL in 1884. Sitting Bull's speech stressed the need for education and detailed how he was about to talk peace with the Great Father in Washington. The white translator told the audience that Sitting Bull was recounting the Battle of the Little Bighorn in lurid detail. "He [the translator] told so many lies that I had to smile," Standing Bear wrote later.

During his own life, Standing Bear was not as well known as Eastman or Bonnin. Standing Bear often survived from job to job; he worked with Buffalo Bill's Wild West Show for a time. Standing Bear was an unabashed Native traditionalist during a time when the dominant ideology in non-Indian society was "kill the Indian, save the man," the slogan invented by U.S. Army general R. H. PRATT, founder of Carlisle Indian School, to describe assimilation.

Standing Bear's father had participated in the CUSTER fight and later represented his people at a conference in Washington, D.C. Standing Bear's father returned from that conference

Luther Standing Bear.
[Nebraska State Historical Society]

dressed in a Prince Albert coat and other formal trappings, including a silk top hat later used to carry water. Standing Bear was at first called Ota Kre ("Plenty Kill") because of his father's reputation as a warrior. The young Standing Bear was trained traditionally to become a hunter and warrior just as increasing Euro-American presence was making the old ways impossible. He was among the first class to attend Carlisle Indian School, one of 147 Indian young people, mainly Sioux, recruited by Pratt in 1879. Later, Standing Bear recounted how the young students were lined up in front of a blackboard with symbols on it that they didn't understand. Each was told to choose a white man's name. Standing Bear choose "Luther."

Standing Bear turned to writing late in his life and wrote four books intended to describe his people. The first was *My People, the Sioux* (1928), a memoir describing the debate over allotment among the Lakotas. In 1931, Standing Bear published an autobiographical work, *My Indian Boyhood*, followed by *Land of the Spotted Eagle* (1933) and *Stories of the Sioux* (1934).

Standing Bear also played leading roles in several motion pictures, beginning with *White Oak* (1921) and including *Santa Fe Trail* (1930). Standing Bear died as he was working on the film *Union Pacific* in 1939.

Standing Bear was an early critic of the whites' attitudes toward nature.

I know of no species of plant, bird, or animal that were exterminated [in America] until the coming of the white man. For some years after the buffalo disappeared, there still remained huge herds of antelope, but the hunter's work was no sooner done in the destruction of the buffalo than his attention was attracted toward the deer. They are plentiful now only where protected. The white man considered natural animal life just as he did natural [human] life upon this continent, as "pests." Plants which the Indian found beneficial were also "pests." There is no word in the Lakota vocabulary with the English meaning of this word. [Hamilton]

Standing Bear was also critical of Euro-American society in general.

The white man does not understand the Indian for the reason that he does not understand America. He is too far removed from its formative processes. The roots of the tree of his life have not yet grasped the rock and soil. The white man is still troubled with primitive fears; he still has in his consciousness the perils of this frontier continent. . . . He shudders still with the memory of the loss of his forefathers upon its scorching deserts and forbidding mountain-tops. The man from Europe is still a foreigner and an alien. And he still hates the man who questioned his path across the continent. [Standing Bear]

In 1933, Standing Bear wrote to President Franklin Roosevelt suggesting that a bill be drawn up to require the teaching of American Indian history and culture in non-Indian schools, a prescient idea that foreshadowed the establishment of Native American studies programs around the United States after 1970.

FOR MORE INFORMATION:

Hamilton, Charles. *Cry of the Thunderbird.* Norman: University of Oklahoma Press, 1972.

Standing Bear, Luther. *My People, the Sioux.* Lincoln: University of Nebraska Press, 1975.

STANISLAUS (ESTANISLAO)
Mission Indian (probably Yokuts)
fl. 1820s

Captured in his childhood and taken to the San Jose Mission in California, Stanislaus grew up as a neophyte in the California mission system. Later, he would play a leading role in the Mission Indian Rebellion of 1828 and 1829. As a youth, however, he was one of the Franciscan priests' better students. He became a ranch foreman or majordomo on the mission's lands. Although he was a model convert, he still resented the harsh treatment that he and his people received at the missions, so he fled from this oppressive environment in 1827 or 1828.

Shortly after his escape, Stanislaus and another dissident neophyte leader, Cipriano, started an insurgent movement against the missions. These two leaders organized California Indians in the northern San Joaquin Valley into a widespread uprising, causing turmoil at both the Santa Clara and the San Jose Missions. As a result of their depredations, the priest at Mission San Jose sought military aid from the presidio at San Francisco. In 1828, responding to this appeal, Mexican army sergeant Antonio Sota and a small detachment of men were deployed into the field against the Mission Indians led by Stanislaus. In the ensuing battle, the rebellious California Indians defeated the Mexican force and fatally wounded Sota.

The next year, in 1829, another Mexican expedition of about forty men lead by Lieutenant Jose Sanchez stormed the Indian stronghold, but this force failed to breach the Indian fortress. Subsequently, a third expedition, which numbered about one hundred soldiers and some Indian auxiliaries, was launched from the presidio. This campaign successfully used artillery to dislodge Stanislaus and his followers from the stockade.

After this defeat, Stanislaus fled to Mission San Jose, where the head of the mission, Father Narcios Duran, gave him sanctuary from the Mexican military authorities. As a result of Father Duran's largesse, Stanislaus returned to mission life. Subsequently, Spanish authorities pardoned him for his rebellious actions. Little is known of his later life; it is assumed that he lived his remaining years at Mission San Jose.

STANTON, ELIZABETH CADY
1815–1902

Historian Sally Roesch Wagner asserts that "nineteenth century radical feminist theoreticians, such as Elizabeth Cady Stanton and Matilda Joslyn Gage, looked to the Iroquois for their vision of a transformed world."

Stanton quoted the memoirs of the Reverend Asher Wright, who wrote of Seneca home life:

Usually the females ruled the house. The stores were in common, but woe to the luckless husband or lover who was too shiftless to do his share of the providing. No matter how many children, or whatever goods he might have in the house, he might at any time be ordered to pick up his blanket and budge; and after such an order it would not be healthful for him to attempt to disobey. The house would be too hot for him, and unless saved by the intercession of some aunt or grandmother he must retreat to his own clan, or go and start a new matrimonial alliance with some other. [Wagner, *Iroquois Confederacy*]

According to Stanton, Wright also noted that Iroquois women alone could "knock off the horns" of a sachem who had abused his office, as well as make the original nominations for sachemships. In early treaty negotiations, representatives of the United States, all male, often found themselves face-to-face with Iroquois women. Many of the treaties negotiated before 1800 are signed by both male sachems and their female advisors.

In her 1891 speech before the National Council of Women, "The Matriarchate or Mother-age," Stanton surveyed the research of Lewis Henry MORGAN and others that indicated that "among the greater number of the American aborigines, the descent of property and children were in the female line. Women sat in the councils of war and peace and their opinions had equal weight on all questions." In this regard, she mentioned the Iroquois' councils specifically. After surveying tribal societies in other parts of the world as well, Stanton closed her speech with a case for sexual equality:

In closing, I would say that every woman present must have a new sense of dignity and self respect, feeling that our mothers, during long periods in the long past, have been the ruling power and that they used that power for the best interests of humanity. As history is said to repeat itself, we have every reason to believe that our turn will come again[.] It may not be for woman's supremacy, but for the as yet untried experiment of complete equality, when the united thought of man and woman will inaugurate a just government, a pure religion, a happy home, a civilization at last in which ignorance, poverty and crime will exist no more. Those who watch already behold the dawn of the new day.

FOR MORE INFORMATION:

Allen, Paula Gunn. *The Sacred Hoop: Recovering the Feminine in American Indian Traditions.* Boston: Beacon Press, 1986.

Anthony, Susan B., Elizabeth Cady Stanton, and Matilda Joslyn Gage. *History of Woman Suffrage.* Reprint, Salem, N.H.: Ayer Co., 1985.

Brown, Judith K. "Economic Organization and Position of Women Among the Iroquois." *Ethnohistory* 17: 3–4 (Summer/Fall, 1970).

Carr, Lucien. *The Social and Political Position of Women Among the Huron-Iroquois Tribes.* Salem, Mass.: Salem Press, 1884.

Gage, Matilda Joslyn. *Woman, Church and State.* 1893. Reprint, Watertown, Mass.: Persephone Press, 1980.

Stanton, Elizabeth Cady. "The Matriarchate or Mother-age." *National Bulletin* [National Council of Women] 1:5 (February 1891).

Wagner, Sally Roesch. "The Iroquois Confederacy: A Native American Model for Non-sexist Men." *Changing Men* (Spring/Summer, 1988).

———. "The Root of Oppression Is the Loss of Memory: The Iroquois and the Early Feminist Vision." *Akwesasne Notes* (Late Winter, 1989).

STEVENS, ISAAC INGALLS
1818–1862

Washington became a territory of the United States on March 2, 1853. Isaac Stevens was appointed governor and superintendent of Indian affairs for the territory. As governor, Stevens wished to build the economic base of the territory; this required the attraction of a proposed transcontinental railroad, which in turn required peace with the Indians. Stevens worked with remarkable speed; in 1854 and 1855 alone, he negotiated five treaties with six thousand Indian people west of the Cascades.

Stevens was born in Andover, Massachusetts, and was graduated from West Point Military Academy in 1839. He served in the U.S. Army as an engineering officer after graduating from West Point; during the war with Mexico (1846–1847), he served on the staff of General Winfield Scott. After that, still an army officer, Stevens was named Indian agent for Washington Territory. His main charge at the time was to survey the area as a prospective route for a new transcontinental railroad. In 1853, President Franklin Pierce appointed Stevens governor of the territory.

After 1853, Governor Stevens wrested from the Indians most of the present-day states of Montana, Idaho, and Washington. In all the treaties, Stevens drove an extremely tough bargain, but the Indians, who had relied on fishing for a livelihood, would not relent on their continued right to fish. Stevens said, "It was also thought necessary to allow them to fish at all accustomed places, since this would not in any manner interfere with the rights of citizens and was necessary for the Indians to obtain a subsistence." He said these words after emerging from the signing of the Medicine Creek Treaty on

December 26, 1854. The treaty, signed on a small island surrounded by salt marshes not far from the present-day state capital, Olympia, guaranteed the Indians the right to fish at their usual and accustomed places "in common with" citizens of the territory. By signing the treaty, the Indians ceded to the United States 2,240,000 acres of land, an immense sacrifice, in exchange for the right to fish (see George BOLDT).

Many Native peoples refused to sign Stevens's treaties, including the Nez Perce under Old Joseph (see JOSEPH, ELDER), father of Chief Joseph (see JOSEPH, YOUNGER). Other non-treaty Indians pointed to unlawful invasions of land set aside for Indians in the treaties by miners and settlers as they began armed resistance in the Yakima War of 1855 and 1856.

While settlement of the coastal Northwest began temporally in tandem with that of California, accelerating about 1850, most of the people who traversed the continent along the Oregon Trail were not looking for gold or other quick riches. Most sought to set up farms; some planned utopian communes.

Some of the white settlers aided Indians who were being pursued by Stevens's militia. When his white opponents sought the protection of local courts, Stevens called up a militia of a thousand men, declared martial law, closed the courts, and arrested the chief justice of the territory—a rare example of government by fiat in the face of settlers' resistance to ill treatment of Indians. A brief but bloody Native uprising, the Yakima War, followed and ended with the hanging of Chief LESCHI, the leader of the Native people opposing the treaties. By that time, whites were flooding the area around Puget Sound while the Duwamish (led by Chief SEATH'TL, after whom Seattle is named) abandoned their home grounds peacefully as the urban area approached.

Stevens's militia also arrested several settlers suspected of aiding renegade Indians. Lion A. Smith, Charles Wren, Henry Smith, John McLeod, Henry Murray, and another man asserted that they were taken from their land claims in Pierce County "without process of law, and without any complaint or affidavit being lodged against them." The men were escorted against their wills to Fort Steilacoom (near Tacoma), where they were held, at Stevens's request, on charges of treason. Following complaints by attorneys for the men, Stevens issued a martial law declaration suspending civil liberties in Pierce County, accusing the arrested settlers of giving "aid and comfort to the enemy." A few days later, Stevens ordered the men back to Olympia, out of Pierce County, because a judge there had issued a writ of habeas corpus on their behalf.

Later, the case was taken up in the court of the Honorable Edward Lander, chief justice of the territory. When Judge Lander convened court to hear the case, a column of militiamen filed into his courtroom and arrested him, leading the judge and the clerk of the court from the bench. The arrests occurred on May 6; by May 9, the judge was released. A few days later, Stevens extended martial law to Thurston County, including Olympia, the territorial capital.

A legal ballet ensued in which Governor Stevens refused to honor the writ of habeas corpus. Members of the militia stood outside the house in which Chief Justice Lander was holding court. "The marshal, being ordered to keep the room clear of armed men, was compelled to lock the door. . . . The counsel engaged inside could distinctly hear the men [outside] cocking their rifles," said a contemporary statement. An officer of the militia called on Judge Lander to surrender once again.

He refused. Finally, the armed men barged into the courtroom, seized the judge and clerk, and transported them to the office of Governor Stevens. An observer said the judge was kidnapped. The judge was told that he would be freed if he stopped issuing orders contrary to the decree of martial law. The judge flatly refused. Stevens had violated his oath of office by refusing to respect a writ of habeas corpus, an act that the U.S. Constitution says may be suspended only by Congress.

Stevens served as Washington's territorial delegate to Congress in 1857 then returned to active duty with the Union army during the Civil War. During that war he was promoted to major general before he was killed at the Battle of Chantilly (Virginia) in 1862.

FOR MORE INFORMATION:

"A Brief Notice of the Recent Outrages Committed by Isaac Stevens, May 17, 1856," cited in W. H. Wallace, "Martial Law in the Washington Territory," *The Annals of America*, 1856, pp. 3–16.

American Friends Service Committee. *Uncommon Controversy: A Report on the Fishing Rights of the Muckleshoot, Puyallup, and Nisqually Indians*. Seattle: University of Washington Press, 1970.

Brown, Bruce. *Mountain in the Clouds*. New York: Simon & Schuster, 1982.

Stevens, Hazard. *The Life of Isaac I. Stevens*. 2 vols. Boston: Houghton Mifflin, 1900.

STRUCK BY THE REE
Yankton Sioux
1804–1888

Struck by the Ree, who would become a principal chief of the Yankton Sioux, was born in August 1804, the same week that Lewis and Clark passed through his village. It is said that Lewis swaddled the young man in a U.S. flag and baptized him as an American. Later, he earned his adult name in combat with the Arikas, who were also called "Rees." In 1837, Struck by the Ree visited Washington, D.C., on behalf of his people.

During the 1862 Great Sioux Uprising in Minnesota, Struck by the Ree positioned his warriors to protect innocent white settlers from raiding Indians. Regardless of their aid, his people were run out of Minnesota with other Native peoples after the uprising.

In 1865, Struck by the Ree testified at hearings of the Doolittle Commission, which was looking into fraud among Indian agents. He told the hearing commissioners that Indian agents routinely siphoned goods from stockpiles purchased with Indian annuity money and that Native people were often forced to pay for meals prepared with their treaty money, while agents ate for

Struck by the Ree.
[National Anthropological Archives]

free. Agents routinely paid themselves out of money meant to buy supplies for Indians under treaty agreements. He said that it was also common for frontier soldiers to routinely force sexual favors from Indian women. "Before the soldiers came along, we had good health, but . . . the soldiers go to my squaws, and they want to sleep with them, and the squaws being hungry will sleep with them in order to get something to eat, and will get a bad disease, and then the squaws turn to their husbands and give them the bad disease." [Nabokov]

FOR MORE INFORMATION:

Nabokov, Peter. *Native American Testimony.* New York: Viking Penguin, 1991.

STUMBLING BEAR (SETIMKIA)
Kiowa
c. 1832–1903

During his youth, Stumbling Bear became an influential war chief noted for leading raids against the Sac and Fox, Pawnees, and Navajos as well as against white settlers. A cousin of KICKING BIRD, he would become well known among the Kiowas as a warrior, chief, and advocate of peace. The name by which he is widely known is a mistranslation of his Kiowa name, Setimkia, which really means "Charging Bear" or "An Animal Pressing Down."

In 1854, he sought to avenge his brother's death by leading a raid against the Pawnee. Failing to engage the Pawnee, his men met up with some Sac and Fox warriors who defeated him with better firearms. As a result of this incident, the Kiowas decided that they needed superior firepower to continue their role as one of the predominant raiders on the Southern Plains, so they began to raid white wagon trains to gain better arms. In 1856, Stumbling Bear raided the Navajos and secured a large

booty. In the early 1860s, he was the scourge of the Southern Plains when U.S. forces there were weakened by the advent of the Civil War in the East.

In November 1864 at the Battle of Adobe Walls, Stumbling Bear fought U.S. forces led by Kit CARSON. Soon after the signing of the Treaty of Medicine Lodge, however, both Stumbling Bear and Kicking Bird became ardent advocates of peaceful accommodation with the whites. In 1872, he journeyed to Washington, D.C., with a delegation of Kiowa chiefs who sought peace. When the Comanches under Quanah PARKER started the Red River War in 1874, Stumbling Bear advocated peace with whites and was a rival of the more militant LONE WOLF.

As a result of his actions for peace, the federal government built a home for Stumbling Bear in 1878 on the Kiowa Reservation in Indian Territory. He lived there until his death in 1903. At the time of his death at Fort Sill, Stumbling Bear was the last surviving Kiowa chief from the old raiding days on the Southern Plains.

SWAMP, JAKE (TEKARONIANEKEN)
Mohawk
1941–

During the late years of the twentieth century, Jake Swamp became known to many people around the world as a chief spokesman of the Tree of Peace Society, which planted great white pines, the principal symbol of the Iroquois Confederacy, in public and private places from Australia to France, including several locations in the United States and Canada. One of the trees, planted in 1988, stands near Independence Hall in Philadelphia.

Swamp was born at Akwesasne and by the early 1990s had served two decades as a subchief of the Mohawk Wolf clan. Jake Swamp is married to Judy Swamp, who often travels with him to public appearances around the world. Together they have had seven children. The Swamps also have eleven grandchildren. Jake Swamp was present at the 1973 Wounded Knee occupation (see Dennis BANKS and Russell MEANS) and has represented the Iroquois Confederacy at the United Nations. At Akwesasne, Swamp has directed the Akwesasne Freedom School and CKON, Akwesasne radio. He has developed curricula in the Mohawk language and introduced aquaculture to the community.

Swamp, a member of Akwesasne's traditional Mohawk Nation Council, was a principal figure in the Akwesasne crisis that culminated in the deaths of Mohawks Mathew PYKE and Junior EDWARDS on May 1, 1990. As a member of the traditional Mohawk Nation Council, Swamp stood strongly against commercial gambling and the influence of Louis HALL's Warrior Society. His family's home was shot at several times during the crisis.

FOR MORE INFORMATION:

Johansen, Bruce E. *Life and Death in Mohawk Country.* Golden, Colo.: North American Press, 1993.

Jake Swamp. [Courtesy of Jake Swamp and Tree of Peace Society]

SWAN, YVONNE (YVONNE WANROW)
Sinixt/Arrow Lakes Nation
fl. 1970s–1990s

In 1972, a reputed child molester broke into the home of Yvonne Swan (then known as Yvonne Wanrow) in Spokane, Washington. She killed him to protect her children and was later charged with murder by state prosecutors. After an initial conviction, the case was appealed to the state supreme court and later to the U.S. Supreme Court. In 1979, the high court used the case to frame the so-called "Wanrow instruction," which expanded women's right to self-defense.

The Washington State Supreme Court overturned the initial conviction because it ruled that the trial judge had not adequately explained a woman's right of self-defense to the jury. The court ordered Wanrow retried, but she plea-bargained a guilty plea to a manslaughter charge rather than undergo another ordeal. She received a suspended sentence and was ordered to do community service, which grew into a career as a Native and women's activist. The court case ended in 1984, a dozen years after the incident that spawned it. In the early 1990s, Swan was affiliated with the San Francisco office of the International Indian Treaty Council.

FOR MORE INFORMATION:

Johansen, Bruce. "Mother or Murderer: Yvonne Wanrow Is Waiting for Supreme Court to Decide." *Seattle Times,* 8 May 1976.

SWORD BEARER (CHEEZTAHPAEZH)
Crow/Bannock
1863–1887

Sword Bearer was one of the Crows who did not support PLENTY COUPS's accommodation of white settlement. Like other Native American tribes and nations, the Crows had been sick-

ened and killed by smallpox and other diseases. Many young warriors resented being
confined to a reservation; nearly three hundred of them joined forces in fall 1887 with the
young firebrand Sword Bearer, who sought to
prove himself as a warrior by leading a horse
raid on the neighboring Blackfoot. On their
return, Sword Bearer and his companions
paraded through Crow Village with their captured horses and confronted the local Indian
agent, H. E. Williamson, who sent to Fort
Custer for troops. Sword Bearer's group then
galloped into the mountains and spurred a
rash of rumors of a Cheyenne and Sioux
alliance that would attack white settlements
and Plenty Coups's good Indians. Plenty
Coups persuaded Sword Bearer to lay down his
arms later that same year.

T

TADADAHO
Onondaga
fl. 1100–1150 (?)

In the founding epic of the Iroquois Confederacy, Tadadaho was HIAWATHA's half brother and an evil wizard who tried to frustrate his and DEGA-NAWIDAH's designs to unify the Iroquois in a league of peace. At one point, to frustrate the unification of the Iroquois, Tadadaho is said to have killed Hiawatha's wife and three daughters.

After the founding of the confederacy, Tadadaho became the name of the office held by the speaker of the league, who is always an Onondaga; the story of Tadadaho is an allegory for the conversion of evil by good.

FOR MORE INFORMATION:

Wallace, Paul. *The White Roots of Peace.* Santa Fe, N. Mex.: Clear Light, 1994.

TAHCHEE (TATSI; DUTCH)
Cherokee
c. 1790–1850

Born about 1790 at Turkey Town on the Coosa River (present-day Alabama) of Cherokee par-ents, Tahchee spent his boyhood learning the fighting and hunting methods of the Southern Plains Indians. As a young man, he took part in raids on the Osages. When a peace was negotiated with the Osages, Tahchee lived with them for fourteen months—thus enhancing his raiding abilities. When hostilities were renewed, he led Cherokee raids against the Osages.

Angry over the 1828 treaty between the Cherokees and the U.S. government, Tahchee forded the Red River into Texas and launched raids against the Osages and the Comanches. Declared an outlaw by the U.S. Army with a reward of $500 on his head, he became a leg-endary figure on the Southern Plains. To defy the army, Tahchee attacked a group of Osages at a trading post near Fort Gibson. Although a bullet scarred his cheek, he was able to escape. This was to be his only wound during many years of raiding.

Subsequently, Tahchee became an army scout against the Comanches. He also hunted for the army. In his later years, Tahchee took up residence and farmed along the Canadian River near Fort Gibson.

TAHOMA, QUINCY (TOHOMA)
Navajo
1920–1956

Quincy Tahoma was one of the most successful artists to be trained at the Santa Fe Indian School Studio in New Mexico. After his birth in 1920, Tahoma was raised on the Navajo Reservation near Tuba City, Arizona. As a youth, he became familiar with many of the traditional Navajo religious chants and rituals. During this time, he also became an accomplished sand painter. Later in life, he drew much of his artistic inspiration from his boyhood experiences.

After studying art in Santa Fe from 1936 to 1940, Tahoma joined the armed forces and served in the signal corps during World War II. After the war, he returned to the Navajo Reservation and became a successful artist. His brilliant colors and precise lines along with the two-dimensional disposition of his work reflected the nature of American Indian painting in the American Southwest at that time. His imaginative style and elegant designs distinguished him from his peers. Rather than posing his subjects in a static manner, for example, Tahoma painted them in action.

As a successful American Indian artist, he created a studio for young American Indians that fostered many famous artists. Although most of Tahoma's subjects were traditional Indian pursuits such as riding, fishing, and hunting, he also painted distinctive landscape scenes.

This gifted Navajo artist died of alcoholism in November 1956 in Santa Fe. He left behind a tremendous legacy of art that is still remembered and cherished by those familiar with the field.

TAIMAH
Fox/Mesquaki
c. 1790–1830

Taimah ("Thunder") gained some notoriety on the frontier as the man who saved the Indian agent at Prairie du Chien from an attempted murder by an Indian. He straddled both cultures and was known among the Fox not only for his political leadership but also for his shamanistic powers, especially his reputed ability to cure the physically ill.

Taimah. [National Anthropological Archives]

TALL BULL (HOTOAKHIHOOIS)
Cheyenne
c. 1830–1869

Son of a Sioux mother, Tall Bull became known as the leader of the Cheyennes' largest society of Dog Soldiers during the early phases of the Plains wars. The Dog Soldiers haunted wagon trains and settlers on the High Plains; Tall Bull's band consisted of a hundred lodges, or about five hundred people, Cheyenne and Sioux.

Tall Bull was among Cheyenne leaders who attended the Medicine Lodge Treaty of 1867, but the Dog Soldiers continued to raid frontier settlements after that. On July 11, 1869, during a series of Dog Soldier raids along the border of Colorado and Kansas, Pawnee scouts under General E. R. Carr stung the Dog Soldiers with major casualties. Tall Bull was among the dead.

TAMAHA (ONE EYE)
Mdewakanton Sioux
c. 1776–1860

Born near Winona, Minnesota, Tamaha lost an eye in an accident as a child so the French called him Le Borgne, or "One Eye." The English picked up the name as "the One-eyed Sioux."

In 1806 and 1807, Tamaha became a friend of U.S. Army lieutenant Zebulon M. Pike and was one of the very few Sioux leaders who supported the United States in the War of 1812. He retained his loyalty even after his capture by the British, during which he refused to divulge information about the Americans on pain of death (a threat which turned out to be a bluff).

Tamaha was known as a powerful orator and a diplomat of unusual ability. Wearing his trademark stovepipe hat, he managed to maintain amicable relations between whites and Indians until his death at age eighty-five in Wabasha, Minnesota, two years before the peace was shattered in 1862 by the Great Sioux Uprising.

TARHE
Wyandot
1742–1818

An ardent opponent of TECUMSEH, Tarhe was a spiritual and political leader of the Porcupine Wyandot during the second half of the eighteenth century.

Born in Detroit, Tarhe fought at the 1774 Battle of Mount Pleasant in present-day West Virginia. He also fought with BLUE JACKET at the Battle of Fallen Timbers. He signed the 1795 Treaty of Greenville with a dozen other principal chiefs, who chose him as one of their principal speakers.

Tarhe was a leading opponent of Tecumseh's plans to forge an Indian Confederacy against continued white encroachment, which he seemed to consider inevitable. On the eve of the War of 1812, Tarhe called a council of pro-U.S. chiefs at Brownstown on the Detroit River. Tecumseh then called his own council on the river's opposite shore and prepared to raid the opposing camp. Tecumseh pressed many of Tarhe's allies into joining him as Tarhe himself escaped the attack. He later joined William Henry Harrison's forces in the war and helped defeat Tecumseh at the 1813 Battle of the Thames.

After the war, Tarhe returned to Cranetown, near Upper Sandusky, Ohio, where he died.

FOR MORE INFORMATION:

Clark, Peter (Dooyentate). *Origin and Traditional History of the Wyandotts.* Toronto, 1870.

Eckert, Allan W. *A Sorrow in Our Heart: The Life of Tecumseh.* New York: Bantam, 1992.

TASCALUSA (TUSCALOOSA, TASZALUZA, TASCALUCA, TASTALUCA)
Alabama
fl. 1540s

Although the first contacts between the Alabama (or Alibamu) Indians and the men of Hernando De Soto's 1540 expedition were amicable, this uneasy peace would not last. Tascalusa ("Black Warrior") welcomed De Soto to his domain on a raised dais with his son at his side and with tribal dignitaries surrounding him. The Spanish attempted to intimidate the Alabamas with a show of their horsemanship. After the riding display, De Soto demanded provisions and bearers from the Alabamas. Tascalusa resisted these demands initially. When De Soto threatened violence, he assented to his orders. While pretending to cooperate, Tascalusa sent word to his warriors from outlying villages and ordered them to come and defend his stockaded home.

Although the Alabamas entertained their guests with dancing at Mabila, the Spanish discovered concealed arms among the Indians. Fearing a revolt, De Soto's soldiers attempted to seize Tascalusa and fighting commenced. In the ensuing battle, the Alabamas released the bearers from other tribes. These men joined in the fighting and drove the Spanish from the town; however, the fighting continued outside the town. Eventually, the conquistadores set the village on fire. Indians who were not slain by sword or pike were forced into the flames. Some Indians took their own lives rather than be captured by the Spanish. An estimated 2,500 Indians died while only 20 Spaniards were killed and 150 wounded, including De Soto.

Tascalusa's fate in this incident is unknown; his son was found dead, skewered by a Spanish pike.

TAVIBO (TAB-BE-BO, THE PAIUTE PROPHET)
Paiute
c. 1810–1870

Born around 1810 in the Mason Valley near Walker Lake in what would become Nevada, medicine man Tavibo ("Sun Man"), father of WOVOKA, and his people were forced out of their traditional lands by a steady stream of armed and dangerous whites. With only a few exceptions, the Paiutes tried to adjust to white presence or to retreat into more remote areas. Witnessing the passing of their way of life, the

Paiutes turned to their religious leaders for solace and counsel.

During this time, Tavibo had a vision of a giant earthquake that would swallow up the whites and leave the Indians as survivors to inherit the earth. But this vision seemed fantastic, so Tavibo sought another explanation. Eventually, he revised his vision, saying that the earthquake would destroy all people but that Indians would be resurrected while the whites would remain dead. With this modification, he attracted many Paiute believers desperate for a better life.

Although Tavibo became a respected medicine man after the vision, many people lost faith in his abilities when the earthquake did not materialize. Perhaps as a result, Tavibo had another vision about a devastating earthquake in which only his followers would be saved. Although he managed to maintain a small band of followers, Tavibo never regained prominence among his people. He died in 1870 with his prophesies remaining more fantasy than reality. Tavibo was survived by his teenage son, Wovoka. He was probably unaware that his son would carry on his mystical, visionary, and apocalyptic messages within the next twenty years.

TAWANIMA, LOUIS
Hopi
c. 1879–1969

Born into the Sand clan at Shungopovi, Second Mesa, Arizona, on the Hopi Reservation around 1879, Tawanima was one of the first American Indians to participate in modern Olympic competition. Little is known of his early life. At the Carlisle Indian School, he was coached by football legend Glenn S. "Pop" Warner. Tawanima and Jim THORPE participated in many track and field events while at Carlisle. In the 1908 London Olympic Games, he ran in the marathon;

he took a silver medal in the 1912 Stockholm Olympics in the 10,000-meter run.

Tawanima also ran in races in the United States. He won a twelve-mile run in New York City in 1910. He also won the "Bunion Derby" from New York to California in 1925 but was disqualified by the promoter for running too fast and endangering profits. At the end of his career in track, Tawanima returned to his reservation and farmed. In 1957, he was inducted into the Arizona Hall of Fame for his athletic abilities.

Blind in his old age, Tawanima misjudged his footing on a narrow path and fell to his death from a mesa cliff at Shungopovi while returning from a religious rite on January 18, 1969.

TAWAQUAPTEWA
Hopi
c. 1882–1960

Tawaquaptewa was born at Oraibi, Third Mesa, Arizona, on the Hopi Reservation. His father was Cheauka ("Clay" or "Adobe") of the Bear clan. His own name means "Sun on the Horizon." Until Tawaquaptewa was selected as village chief in 1902, he was not prominent in Hopi politics. Until that time, Tawaquaptewa had paid more attention to women than politics because he did not believe that he would ever become a chief. But when the previous village leader—his uncle, Lololoma—died of smallpox in 1901, he sought to lead his people to the best of his abilities.

The early twentieth century was a troubled time for the Hopi, however. Isolated from white domination until the late nineteenth century, the Hopis had been unscathed by the white world that was slowly engulfing them. By the early twentieth century, however, white influence in traditional Hopi life became unavoidable. This influence divided the Hopis between those who were militantly opposed to white ways and those who sought to accommodate themselves to the new ways.

At first, Tawaqueptewa welcomed the whites, while his rival YOUKIOMA opposed any outside influences. Slowly this conflict between the two leaders increased and was exacerbated by the interference of missionaries and government agents. With the village split in 1906, a "Shoving War" occurred between the two factions; the losers, those hostile to the whites, left Oraibi to form a new village, Hotevilla. This "Shoving War" is one of the few recorded civil wars in history where a disagreement was solved with no resulting bloodshed.

After the "Shoving War" was won, misguided white authorities decided to send Tawaquaptewa to Riverside Indian School in California to learn white ways in October 1906. This left his people at Oraibi without a strong leader. Indeed, his rival, Lomahongyoma, tried to return to Oraibi and make himself chief. Failing to gain their confidence at Oraibi, Lomahongyoma eventually left in 1907 to create still another village at Babaki.

When Tawaquaptewa returned to Oraibi in 1910, he was resentful of efforts to depose him. He also became distrustful of the whites, who had sent him off to school against his wishes. This bitterness manifested itself through subsequent divisions in his people. He changed from a kind and paternal leader to a suspicious man who often took out his frustrations upon village residents. Many of the people at Oraibi turned against him, became Christian, and moved to the lower village, Kiaktsomovi (New Oraibi); this weakened the cohesion in the old village. Still other traditionalist Hopis decided they could better stay Hopi by moving to the Hopi satellite village at Moenkopi, near Tuba City, Arizona. As a result of these splits, Old Oraibi declined from about six hundred people in 1900 to about one hundred in 1950; but it could still claim to be the oldest continually occupied site in the United States.

In his later years, Tawaquaptewa became renowned as an accomplished carver of kachina dolls. Initially, he remained faithful to traditional kachina designs, but over the years he developed an individual style of his own invention. He died on April 30, 1960, at Oraibi. His wife, Naninonsi, of the Parrot clan, had died five years earlier in 1955. They had an adopted daughter called Betty.

TAX, SOL
1907–

In 1962, voices of protest were raised at the American Indian Chicago Conference, which brought together more than five hundred Native people from more than ninety groups. At the behest of President Kennedy, the conference was organized by Sol Tax, professor of anthropology at the University of Chicago, as a forum to enable Native people to express their views regarding their own futures. It occurred as Kennedy was repudiating the policies of the termination era; it has been described as the opening call for the Indian activism that grew later in the 1960s and 1970s.

Tax was born in Chicago and educated at the University of Wisconsin (Ph.D., 1931) and at the University of Chicago (Ph.D., 1935). Beginning in 1948, he worked as a professor of anthropology at the University of Chicago. Tax wrote or edited several books, including *Heritage of Conquest* (1952); *Indian Tribes of Aboriginal America* (1952); *Acculturation in the Americas* (1952); *Penny Capitalism: A Guatemalan Indian Economy* (1953); the three-volume *Evolution After Darwin* (1960); and *Horizons of Anthropology* (1963).

The Chicago conference adopted a "Declaration of Indian Purpose," which shaped the char-

acter of later protest movements. The declaration emphasized retention of cultural identity at a time when federal policy was just emerging from an era of termination, which sought to eradicate Native lands and tribal values in the United States.

In the wake of Tax's conference, the National Indian Youth Council organized in the early 1960s. By 1964, the first modern civil disobedience by Native Americans was taking place on Puget Sound salmon streams as Indian "fish-ins" dramatized Native assertion of treaty rights to harvest fish. In 1968, the American Indian Movement started its first chapter in Minneapolis. This group, with the assistance of many other Native organizations, helped organize the siege of Alcatraz Island shortly afterward.

TAZA (TAZI)
Chiricahua Apache
c. 1835–1876

As the first son of COCHISE, Taza became the leader of his father's group when Cochise died in 1874. Taza, who was also brother of NAICHE and grandson of MANGAS COLORADAS, strove to honor his father's peace agreement with the army. In 1876, he agreed to relocate his people from the Chiricahua Reservation at Apache Pass, Arizona, to the San Carlos Reservation. However, he could not unite the various Apache bands under his leadership as Cochise had done. Consequently, GERONIMO and his followers crossed the Mexican border into the Sierra Madre of Mexico. This remote area became their base camp. In the summer of 1876, Taza joined the Apache delegation to Washington, D.C., to sue for peace. During this trip, Taza succumbed to pneumonia and was buried in the Congressional Cemetery. As a result of Taza's death, Naiche became more militant.

TEBBEL, JOHN
Ojibwa
1912–

John Tebbel has been a major contributor to twentieth-century literature in the histories of journalism and American Indians. Born in Boyne City, Michigan, as a descendant of an Ojibwa chief, Tebbel was educated at Central Michigan University (B.A., 1935, and Litt. D., 1948). He was also awarded an M.S. in journalism from Columbia University in 1937. Tebbel worked as a journalist at *Newsweek*, the *Detroit Free Press*, and the *New York Times* before returning to Columbia as a faculty member in 1943. From 1954 to 1965, Tebbel chaired the journalism department at New York University. After 1965, he continued to teach journalism there.

In the field of American Indian history, Tebbel wrote *The American Indian Wars* (1960). In addition, he was one of the nation's most prolific journalism historians, as well as a contributor to several national magazines.

TECUMSEH (TECUMTHA)
Shawnee
c. 1768–1813

Tecumseh ("Crouching Tiger" or "Shooting Star") was a major military leader and alliance builder who sought to stop Euro-American expansion into the Ohio Valley area early in the nineteenth century.

Tecumseh was born about 1768 near present-day Oldtown, Ohio. He was raised from birth to make war on the encroaching whites by his mother, Methoataske, whose husband, the Shawnee Puckeshinwa, was killed in cold blood by settlers when Tecumseh was a boy. Tecumseh and his mother found him dying. As he watched his father die, Tecumseh vowed to become like "a fire spreading over the hill and valley, consuming the race of dark souls."

Tecumseh. *[National Anthropological Archives]*

[Josephy] A few years later, Tecumseh's hatred for the whites was compounded by the murder of CORNSTALK, a Shawnee chief who had been a mentor to the young man.

As Euro-American settlement began to explode across the Appalachians into the Ohio Valley and Great Lakes shortly after 1790, Native resistance expressed itself in attempts at confederation along lines of mutual interest. A confederation that included elements of the Shawnees, Delawares, Wyandots, Miamis, and Ottawas told the United States in 1790 that settlers were not to transgress beyond the Ohio River. Thousands of settlers were surging into the area, ignoring governmental edicts from both sides. The settlers, who were squatters in the Indians' eyes, sought military help after members of the Native confederacy began attacking their settlements. Military expeditions were sent into the Ohio country during 1790 and 1792, but the Native confederacy remained unbowed and unmoved. In 1794, a force under the command of General "Mad Anthony" Wayne defeated the confederacy's warriors at Fallen Timbers (a battle in which a young Tecumseh fought). In 1795, most of present-day Ohio and parts of Indiana were surrendered at the Treaty of Greenville.

Native resistance surged again shortly after the turn of the century under the aegis of Tecumseh. As he came of age after the American Revolution, his influence grew rapidly not only because of his acumen as a statesman and a warrior, but because he forbade torture of prisoners. Both settlers and his Native allies trusted Tecumseh. By the turn of the century, as the number of settlers grew, Tecumseh began to assemble the Shawnees, Delawares, Ottawas, Ojibwas, Kickapoos, and Wyandots into a confederation with the aim of establishing a permanent Native state that would act as a buffer zone between the United States to the east and English Canada to the north. One white observer recalled Tecumseh as a commanding speaker. His voice was said to have "resounded over the multitude . . . his words like a succession of thunderbolts." He advanced the doctrine that no single Native nation could sell its land without the consent of the entire confederacy that he was building.

Rallying Native allies with an appeal for alliance about 1805, Tecumseh said, "Let us unite as brothers, as sons of one Mother Earth. . . . Sell our land? Why not sell the air. . . . Land cannot be sold." He tried to unite the southern tribes by appealing to history:

Where today are the Pequot? Where are the Narraganset, the Mohican, the Pocanet, and other powerful tribes of our people? They have vanished before the avarice and oppression of the white man, as snow before the summer sun. . . . Will we let ourselves be destroyed in our turn, without an effort worthy of our race? Shall we, without a struggle, give up our homes, our lands, bequeathed to us by the Great Spirit? The graves of our dead and everything that is dear and sacred to us? . . . I know you will say with me, never! Never! [Armstrong]

Tecumseh told the southern tribes that they faced extinction:

Our broad domains are fast escaping from our grasp. Every year our white intruders become more greedy, exacting, oppressive, and overbearing. . . . Before the palefaces came among us, we enjoyed the happiness of unbounded freedom, and were acquainted with neither riches, wants, nor oppression. How is it now? Wants and oppression are our lot. . . . Dare we move without asking, by your leave. Are we not being stripped, day by day, of the little that remains of our ancient liberty? Do they not even kick and strike us as they do their black-faces? How long will it be before they will tie us to a post and whip us, and make us work for them. . . . Shall we wait for that moment or shall we die fighting before submitting to such ignominy? [Vanderwerth]

Territorial governor William Henry Harrison (who would later popularize his coming battle with Tecumseh at Tippecanoe in a successful campaign for the presidency with the campaign slogan "Tippecanoe and Tyler Too") tried to undermine the growing strength of Tecumseh's Indian union by negotiating treaties of cession with individual tribes. Since only a portion of each tribe or nation's warriors elected to follow Tecumseh, Harrison found it easy enough to find "treaty Indians" among those who did not elect to fight. By 1811, Harrison negotiated at least fifteen treaties, all of which Tecumseh repudiated. Harrison's wariness of Tecumseh's power sprang from a deep respect for him.

> The implicit obedience and respect which the followers of Tecumseh pay to him is really astonishing and more than any other circumstance bespeaks him [as] one of those uncommon geniuses, which spring up occasionally to produce revolutions and to overturn the established order of things. If it were not for the vicinity of the United States, he would, perhaps, be the founder of an Empire that would rival in glory Mexico or Peru. No difficulties deter him.

For his part, Tecumseh was particularly galled by the fact that Harrison had chosen as his territorial capital the village of Chillicothe, the same site (with the same name) as the Shawnees' former principal settlement. (The name itself is corrupted Shawnee for "Principal Town.") At one treaty council, Tecumseh refused to meet Harrison's terms. Finding himself seated next to Harrison on a bench, Tecumseh slowly but aggressively pushed him off its edge then told Harrison that that was what was happening to his people. During his last conference with Tecumseh, Harrison bid the chief to take a chair. "Your father requests you take a chair," an interpreter told Tecumseh, to which the chief replied, "My father! The sun is my father and the earth is my mother. I will repose upon her bosom." He then sat crosslegged on the ground.

Tecumseh was also angry over Harrison's treaty of September 30, 1809, with the Delaware, Potawatomi, Miami, Kickapoo, Wea, and Eel River peoples. For $8,200 in cash and $2,350 in annuities, Harrison had laid claim for the United States to roughly three million acres of rich hunting land along the Wabash River, in the heart of the area in which Tecumseh wished to erect his Native confederacy. When Tecumseh and his brother, also a Shawnee war chief, complained to Harrison that the treaty terms were unfair, Harrison at first rebuked Tecumseh by saying that the Shawnees had not even been part of the treaty. The implicit refusal to recognize Tecumseh's alliance angered the Indians even more. Realizing that Tecumseh's influence made it politic for him to do so, Harrison agreed to meet with him. At a meeting on August 12, 1810, each side drew up several hundred battle-ready warriors and soldiers. Harrison agreed to relay Tecumseh's complaints to the president, and Tecumseh said that his warriors would join the Americans against the British if Harrison would annul the treaty.

Nothing came of Harrison's promises, and in 1811, bands of warriors allied with Tecumseh began ranging out of the settlement of Tippecanoe to terrorize nearby farmsteads and small backwoods settlements. Harrison said he would wipe out Tippecanoe if the raids did not stop; Tecumseh said they would stop when the land signed away under the 1810 treaty was returned. Tecumseh then journeyed southward to bring the Creeks, Chickasaws, and Choctaws into his alliance. He carried the message that he had used to recruit other allies.

> Brothers—When the white men first set foot on our grounds, they were hungry. They had no place on which to spread their blankets, or to kindle their fires. They were feeble; they could do nothing for themselves. Our fathers commiserated with their distress, and shared freely with them whatever the Great Spirit had given his red children. They gave them food when hun-

gry, medicine when sick, spread skins for them to sleep on, and gave them ground so that they might hunt and raise corn.

Brothers—the white people are like poisonous serpents: when chilled, they are feeble, and harmless, but invigorate them with warmth, and they sting their benefactors to death. [Moquin]

For the most part the trip failed to bring new allies. During this time, the command of the existing alliance fell to Tecumseh's brother Tenskwatawa, who was called the Prophet.

On September 26, 1811, Harrison decamped at Vincennes with more than nine hundred men, two-thirds of them Indian allies. He built a fort and named it after himself on the present-day site of Terre Haute, Indiana. Harrison then sent two Miamis to the Prophet to demand the return of property Harrison alleged had been stolen in the raids, along with the surrender of Indians he accused of murder. The Miamis did not return to Harrison's camp. The governor's army marched to within sight of Tippecanoe and met with Tenskwatawa, who invited them to make camp, relax, and negotiate. Instead, Harrison's forces set up in battle configurations, and the Prophet's warriors readied an attack. Within two hours of pitched battle, Harrison's forces routed the Indians and burned the village of Tippecanoe as Tenskwatawa's forces scattered into the woods.

Returning to the devastation from his travels, Tecumseh fled to British Canada, where, during the War of 1812, he was put in command of a force of whites and Indians as a British brigadier general. Harrison's forces met Tecumseh at the Battle of the Thames in Kentucky. During the battle, Tecumseh was killed on October 5, 1813. After it, some of the Kentucky militia who had taken part found a body they thought was Tecumseh's and cut strips from it

for souvenirs. (His warriors, who had dispersed in panic when Tecumseh died, said later that they had taken his body with them.) Having committed twenty thousand men and $5 million to the cause, the United States had effectively terminated armed Indian resistance in the Ohio Valley and surrounding areas.

A statue called "Tecumseh" plays a major role in traditions at the U.S. Naval Academy. The statue was originally the figurehead of the ship *Delaware* and, as such, was said to portray Tammerund (Saint Tammany), a Delaware chief who befriended William Penn. The figure was renamed "Tecumseh" in 1891 and installed at the academy in Annapolis, Maryland, where its supernatural aid is often requested to help midshipmen pass their exams.

FOR MORE INFORMATION:

Armstrong, Virginia Irving, ed. *I Have Spoken: American History Through the Voices of the Indians.* Chicago: Swallow Press, 1971.

Britt, Albert. *Great Indian Chiefs.* 1938. Reprint, Freeport, N.Y.: Books for Libraries Press, 1969.

Clark, Peter (Dooyentate). *Origin and Traditional History of the Wyandotts.* Toronto, 1870.

Drake, Benjamin. *The Life of Tecumseh and His Brother the Prophet.* Cincinnati, 1841.

Eckert, Allan W. *A Sorrow in Our Heart: The Life of Tecumseh.* New York: Bantam, 1992.

Edmunds, R. David. *The Shawnee Prophet.* Lincoln: University of Nebraska Press, 1983.

———. *Tecumseh and the Quest for Indian Leadership.* Boston: Little, Brown, 1984.

Eggleston, Edward, and Lillie Eggleston-Seelye. *Tecumseh and the Shawnee Prophet.* New York, 1878.

Esarey, Logan, ed. *Messages and Letters of William Henry Harrison.* Indianapolis, 1922.

Gurd, Norman S. *The Story of Tecumseh.* Toronto, 1912.

Josephy, Alvin M., Jr. *The Patriot Chiefs.* New York: Viking, 1961.

Nabokov, Peter. *Native American Testimony.* New York: Viking Penguin, 1991.

Oskinson, John M. *Tecumseh and His Times.* New York, 1838.

Tebbel, John, and Keith Jennison. *The American Indian Wars.* New York: Bonanza Books, 1960.

Tucker, Glenn. *Tecumseh: Vision of Glory.* Indianapolis: Bobbs-Merrill, 1956.

Vanderworth, W. C. *Indian Oratory.* Norman: University of Oklahoma Press, 1971.

Waters, Frank. *Brave Are My People: Indian Heroes Not Forgotten.* Santa Fe, N. Mex.: Clear Light, 1993.

TEEDYUSCUNG
Delaware
c. 1700–1763

Teedyuscung was principal chief of a dissident group of Delawares who shunned accommodation with the immigrant Europeans in the mid–eighteenth century. Teedyuscung was elderly—about fifty-five—when he assumed a leadership role. Despite his animosity toward the English, Teedyuscung was a baptized Moravian who lived as a Christian at Fort Allen on the Lehigh River. Despite his acceptance of Christianity, he was adamantly opposed to Euro-American usurpation of Native land. On April 19, 1763, Teedyuscung's cabin was destroyed by fire, immolating him. Some reports said he was drunk at the time of the fire, but others maintained that jealous Iroquois had plotted his death.

TENAYA
Miwok
fl. 1850s

In 1850, the Yokuts and Miwoks of the San Joaquin Valley and Sierra Nevada foothills in present-day California united under Tenaya in a rebellion against the miners and settlers who had come into the gold fields. A state militia, known as the Mariposa Battalion, was organized against them. The militia chased the rebels into the highlands of the Sierra Nevada. There the Indians and whites engaged in a number of inconclusive skirmishes. As a result of this increased military pressure, Tenaya's Rebellion gradually faded.

TEN BEARS (PARIA SEMEN, PARIASEA-MEN, PARRYWASAYMEN, PARYWAHSAY-MEN, PAROOWAY SEMEHNO)
Comanche
1792–1873

Ten Bears of the Yamparika band of Comanches spent an uneventful childhood on the Southern Plains. Although he was never considered a great warrior, Ten Bears became noted among whites and Indians for his compelling speeches, adroit leadership, and poetic language. Although he visited Washington, D.C., in 1863 as a Comanche leader, he failed to get any major concessions for his people from the U.S. government.

Two years later, Ten Bears signed the 1865 treaty at the Little Arkansas River in Kansas, which created a reservation for the Comanches in the southwestern area of Oklahoma. Although he advocated peace, Ten Bears was always suspicious of the whites and resented their intrusions. At the 1867 Medicine Lodge Conference, Ten Bears gave an eloquent speech during which he asserted that he disliked being put on a reservation and "was born where there were no enclosures and where everything drew a free breath. . . . I want to die there and not within walls." The whites were in no mood for negotiation, however, and dictated that the Comanches give up most of their lands and freedom for their small reservation. In

Ten Bears. [Nebraska State Historical Society]

1872, Ten Bears revisited Washington along with TOSAWI of the Peneteka Comanche band and leaders from other tribes, but the hope that promises would be kept was futile. Despairing and spurned by his own people for his part in negotiating unpopular treaties, Ten Bears died in 1873 at Fort Sill.

TENDOY
Bannock
c. 1834–1907

When his father Kontakayak, a Bannock war chief, died in combat with the Blackfoot, Tendoy ("the Climber") became war chief of the Lemhi Bannock band. An ally of WASHAKIE, to whom his mother was related, Tendoy believed in accommodating white immigration to the highlands of what would become Wyoming.

Unlike many Bannocks, who became destitute with the destruction of their hunting economy, Tendoy and his band prospered by supplying white settlers, miners, and others through a trading relationship. Even during the

Nez Perce War (see JOSEPH, YOUNGER), he maintained that his people would prosper by seeking accommodation. In February 1875, President Grant issued an order allowing the Lemhi Bannocks to remain on their ancestral lands. In 1892, however, they were removed to Fort Hall, Idaho. Tendoy died there, after which local residents built a monument in his honor.

FOR MORE INFORMATION:
Crowder, David L. *Tendoy: Chief of the Lemhis.* Caldwell, Idaho: Caxton, 1969.

TENSKWATAWA ("THE PROPHET")
Shawnee
c. 1770–1837

Tenskwatawa was a major spiritual and military leader among the Shawnees early in the nineteenth century as his brother TECUMSEH assembled an alliance to repel Euro-American migration into the Ohio Valley country. Tenskwatawa's religion preached rejection of imported ways and borrowed on an earlier movement inspired by Neolin, "the DELAWARE PROPHET." Tenskwatawa's religious interpretations shared a tradition which included not only Neolin but also HANDSOME LAKE, the Iroquois revivalist, and WOVOKA, prophet of the Ghost Dance.

Born in the Ohio country, possibly as the twin brother of Tecumseh, Tenskwatawa early acquired an aura of mysticism, which developed into a religious resistance to white domination. He was charismatic and sometimes overbearing; he was blind in one eye. Some reports indicate that Tenskwatawa was an alcoholic as a youth but stopped drinking as part of his religious experience. He took seriously the meaning of his Native name, "the Open Door," as a path to revelation.

Tenskwatawa was in command of Shawnee and allied forces at the Battle of Tippecanoe (1811) as forces under the command of William

Henry Harrison attacked while Tecumseh was away on a mission to recruit new allies among the Creeks, Choctaws, and Chickasaws. Harrison later parlayed his victory into a successful presidential campaign under the slogan "Tippecanoe and Tyler [his vice president], too."

Tenskwatawa's prestige suffered measurably after the defeat at Tippecanoe. He moved to Canada until 1826 then lived for a time in Missouri and Kansas. Late in his life (in 1832) he was interviewed and painted by George CATLIN.

FOR MORE INFORMATION:

Eckert, Allan W. *A Sorrow in Our Heart: The Life of Tecumseh.* New York: Bantam, 1992.

Edmunds, R. David. *The Shawnee Prophet.* Lincoln: University of Nebraska Press, 1983.

THOMAS, JAKE
Cayuga
c. 1915–

In the late twentieth century, Jacob Thomas was the only living person who could recite the entire Iroquois Great Law of Peace in its original Iroquoian language. To maintain the oral tradition, Thomas recited the entire Great Law to the Iroquois Grand Council at Onondaga once every five years.

The Great Law of Peace is available in English translation but usually in vastly condensed versions that lead many to forget that a complete oral recitation can take as long as a week. The recitation takes place in a simple log building that today functions as the heart of the traditional confederacy on the Onondaga nation, near Nedrow, New York, a few miles south of Syracuse.

Thomas utilizes wampum belts returned to the Iroquois in 1989 after a century of possession by the state of New York. Thomas deciphers the symbols on the ancient beaded belts in the Onondaga language, reciting the law, tenet by tenet, until his feet ache and his voice cracks. He recalls the ancient story of the Iroquois League's founding as a union of Native nations that previously had waged vicious war against each other. It says, in part:

> I am going to uproot the tree which is a symbol of life and peace. And when I uproot the tree there is a cavity that goes deep into the earth. And at the bottom of that tree there is a swift river. All the generations that you have cried because of the war clubs, the spears and the weapons that killed and injured your fellow men left you in grief. So, therefore, it has been proven that that is not the answer to peace. . . . Now I call upon all the men. All the war leaders come forth and bring your spears and your clubs and all your weapons of war. . . . And I ask you now to throw them in that hole. . . . And they all put their weapons of war [into] that swift water that took the weapons to the unknown regions. . . . There can be no peace unless there is logic and there is reason. Peace cannot be attained through intimidation. Peace cannot be attained with fear and threats. [Johansen]

FOR MORE INFORMATION:

Johansen, Bruce E. *Life and Death in Mohawk Country.* Golden, Colo.: North American Press, 1993.

Thomas, Jake. "The Great Law Takes a Long Time to Learn." *Northeast Indian Quarterly* 4:4 (Winter 1987): 13–17.

THORPE, JAMES FRANCIS (WATHOHUCK)
Sac and Fox/Potawatomi
1888–1953

Born near Prague, Oklahoma, of Irish, French, and Potawatomi descent, Jim Thorpe (whose Native name, Wathohuck, means "the Bright

Path") was an outstanding college and professional football player and an Olympic gold medal athlete. Some sports historians have called him one of the greatest athletes of any era. Thorpe's mother was a granddaughter of the Sauk leader BLACK HAWK.

Thorpe was an all-American college football player in 1911 and 1912, as Coach Glenn S. ("Pop") Warner turned Carlisle Indian School into a national football power. Thorpe won letters in ten sports besides football while at Carlisle: baseball, track, boxing, wrestling, lacrosse, gymnastics, swimming, hockey, handball, and basketball. He was also a prize-winning marksman and excelled at golf. Thorpe represented the United States at the 1912 Olympics in Stockholm, where he won both the decathlon and the pentathlon, the first time the same person had ever won both events in an Olympic games. King Gustav of Sweden called him the greatest athlete in the world.

Thorpe played professional baseball between 1913 and 1919 for the New York Giants and Boston Braves. In the 1920s, he began another professional sports career in football with the Chicago Cardinals and other teams. Thorpe also recruited an all-Indian team (the Oorang Indians) for the fledgling National Football League. The team played two seasons. In 1921, the team won two games and lost six; in 1922, before the team was disbanded, the Oorang Indians of Marion, Ohio, won one game and lost ten.

In the 1930s, Thorpe's sports career declined. He made celebrity appearances, played bit parts in a few movies, and returned to Oklahoma for a time to delve into tribal politics. During World War II, Thorpe joined the Merchant Marine; after that, in 1950 and 1951, he took part in the filming of the movie *Jim Thorpe—All-American*. Thorpe died in Lomita, California, in 1953. The next year two villages in Pennsylvania, Mauch Chunk and East Mauch Chunk, merged and named the new town for him.

Thorpe was named the best athlete of the first half of the twentieth century in a 1950 poll of sports writers by the Associated Press. He has been inducted into the college and professional football halls of fame.

His gold medals were taken from Thorpe later when it was discovered that he had played professional baseball for a short time in 1911, violating Olympic rules. In 1982, the Jim Thorpe Foundation was established to work for restoration of his Olympic medals. Replicas of the medals were presented to Thorpe's family in 1983. A year later, Dennis BANKS and other members of the American Indian Movement helped organize The Longest Run, during which Indian runners saluted Thorpe with a relay across North America. The run began at Onondaga, New York, and ended at the site of the 1984 Summer Olympics in Los Angeles, where the return of his medals was celebrated.

FOR MORE INFORMATION:

Hirschfelder, Arlene, and Martha Kreipe de Montano. *The Native American Almanac.* New York: Prentice-Hall, 1993.

Thorpe, James, and Thomas F. Collinson. *Jim Thorpe's History of the Olympics.* Los Angeles, 1932.

THUNDER HAWK
Oglala Lakota
fl. 1860s–1870s

Thunder Hawk was an ally of CRAZY HORSE in several important battles during the Plains Indian wars. One of them was the so-called FETTERMAN fight, in which Captain William Fetterman claimed he could ride through territory occupied by the Sioux, Cheyennes, and allied peoples with eighty men. Thunder Hawk helped arrange the decoy maneuver that enabled more

Thunder Hawk.
[National Anthropological Archives]

than two thousand warriors to kill all eighty of Fetterman's men in 1866.

FOR MORE INFORMATION:

Sandoz, Mari. *Crazy Horse: Strange Man of the Oglalas.* New York: Alfred A. Knopf, 1942.

TIBBLES, THOMAS HENRY
1840–1928

Thomas Henry Tibbles was an assistant editor at the *Omaha Herald* in the late 1870s, as STANDING BEAR and his band of Poncas tried to return to their homeland along the Niobrara River in northern Nebraska. Tibbles's publicity rallied support for the Poncas. Later, Standing Bear was engaged in a landmark trial during 1879 in which federal Judge Elmer DUNDY said that American Indians were protected under U.S. civil rights law. The ruling meant that the army could not legally apprehend Indians who had left their reservations and committed no other crimes.

Tibbles's advocacy for the Poncas later led to a tour of eastern cities in the company of several members of the Omaha LaFlesche family as well as congressional hearings into the army's treatment of the Poncas. Tibbles lived with the Poncas for several months during which he took part in flesh-piercing rituals that accompanied his initiation into their Soldiers Lodge, a warrior society.

Tibbles's first wife, Amelia Owen Tibbles, died in 1879. In 1882, he married Susette LAFLESCHE (Bright Eyes). Through most of the 1880s, they traveled widely, including a trip to England and Scotland, lecturing on Native issues.

Tibbles returned to Lincoln, Nebraska, and began a newspaper, *The Independent,* in 1895. He became involved in politics with populist causes and ran as People's Party candidate for U.S. vice president with candidate Thomas Watson in 1904. Tibbles wrote an autobiography in 1905, *Buckskin and Blanket Days,* which was published in 1957, almost three decades after his death.

FOR MORE INFORMATION:

Tibbles, Thomas Henry. *The Ponca Chiefs: An Account of the Trial of Standing Bear.* Lincoln: University of Nebraska Press, 1972.

TIGER, JEROME RICHARD (KOCHA)
Seminole/Creek
1941–1967

Jerome Richard Tiger was a remarkably talented artist whose career was cut short by his death at the age of twenty-six. He was born July 8, 1941, at Tahlequah, Oklahoma; his father was the Reverend John M. Tiger (Seminole) and his mother was Lucinda Lewis (Creek). After attending the public schools in Muskogee and Eufala, he went for a year to the Cleveland Engineering Institute in Ohio. From 1958 to 1960 he served in the U.S. Naval Reserves. In

1962, he began to paint and submitted several of his works to the Philbrook Indian Art Annual. His style was quite original in its delicacy, strong colors, and precise detail. His work also had remarkable depth perception. His depictions of traditional scenes and mythology were very popular and his works were highly sought after.

In 1960, he and Margaret (Peggy) Lois Raymond were married. They had three children. On the night of August 13, 1967, while playing with a revolver, he was accidentally shot and killed.

TILGHMAN, TENCH
1744–1786

Tench Tilghman served several years as George Washington's secretary. As part of his duties, he served on diplomatic assignments among the Iroquois before and during the war. He was adopted by the Onondagas on the eve of the American Revolution and given the Iroquois name Teahokalonde.

TILOUKAIKT
Cayuse
fl. 1840s

Tiloukaikt was among Cayuse leaders who permitted construction of a Presbyterian mission in the Walla Walla Valley of Oregon Territory. Students attending the school and taught by missionary Marcus Whitman and his wife, Narcissa, began to contract measles, scarlet fever, and other illnesses that were brought into the settlement by visiting whites. Whitman, also a medical doctor, treated the children; many of them died anyway. The Cayuse suspected him of poisoning them.

Visiting the mission on November 29, 1847, to request medicine to combat measles, which was by then spreading from children to Cayuse adults, Tiloukaikt got into an argument with Whitman. During the course of the argument another Cayuse, TOMAHAS, tomahawked Whitman in the back, killing him. Other Cayuses rose up in anger, killing twelve whites and taking more than fifty hostages.

Captured after ensuing hostilities, Tiloukaikt was sentenced to hang after a summary trial in 1849.

TINKER, CLARENCE LEONARD
Mixed Osage
1887–1942

Clarence Tinker was born one-eighth Osage on November 21, 1887, near Elgin, Kansas. Clarence Tinker's father was George Ed Tinker (who was part Osage) and his mother was Rose Jacobs Tinker. As a boy, he attended Wentworth Military Academy in Lexington, Missouri. In 1908, he became an officer in the Philippine constabulary. In 1913, he became a regularly commissioned officer in the U.S. Army. After serving in World War I, Tinker became interested in the Air Force. In short order, he earned his wings and by 1927 was serving on the army air corps staff. Between 1927 and 1939, he served as the commander of several air bases and advanced in rank.

Seven months after the attack on Pearl Harbor, Major General Tinker commanded all of the army air forces in Hawaii. On June 7, 1942, six months after the attack on Pearl Harbor, Tinker was shot down at the Battle of Midway. He was the highest ranking officer to die in combat during World War II. His body was never recovered. He also was the highest ranking officer of Indian ancestry in U.S. military history. He was married and had one daughter and two sons. In October 1942, Tinker Air Force Base near Oklahoma City was named in his honor.

TOMAH
Menominee
c. 1752–1817

Born near present-day Green Bay, Wisconsin, Tomah became known as an adroit negotiator on behalf of his people while still a young man. He was tapped to take the place of a hereditary chief who was regarded as incompetent.

In 1805, Tomah worked as a guide for the explorer and U.S. Army lieutenant Zebulon Pike, who described him as a superlative hunter and scout. Tomah refused to join TECUMSEH's bid for a Native alliance against white encroachment. He sided with the British during the War of 1812, hoping that they would drive American settlers from his people's lands. Before the British were defeated, Tomah lent aid in the capture of Forts Sandusky and Mackinaw. He led a force of about a hundred, including his understudy, OSHKOSH.

According to witnesses of his funeral, Tomah died in 1817, although his tombstone was later inscribed "1818."

FOR MORE INFORMATION:

Eckert, Allan W. *A Sorrow in Our Heart: The Life of Tecumseh.* New York: Bantam, 1992.

TOMAHAS
Cayuse
fl. 1840s

Tomahas tomahawked missionary Marcus Whitman in the back on November 28, 1847, killing him. Other Cayuses rose up in anger, killing twelve whites and taking more than fifty hostages in response to the spread of diseases in the Walla Walla area.

In response, settlers in the area raised a volunteer militia headed by Cornelius Gilliam, a fundamentalist preacher and professional Indian fighter. Gilliam attacked Cayuse villages that had had nothing to do with the Whitman massacre, prompting Indian retaliation on a broader scale. Gilliam was killed (by accidental discharge of his own gun), and the rest of his private army decided to end the offensive in the face of superior Indian numbers. The war continued in intermittent fashion for several years, but after two years in hiding, TILOUKAIKT and Tomahas surrendered. Both were tried very quickly and sentenced to die on the gallows.

TOMOCHICHI
Creek
c. 1650–1739

Tomochichi was born about 1650 at the Creek village of Apalachukla along the Chattahoochee River in what would become Alabama. His name derived from the Creek term *tomochee-chee,* meaning "the One Who Causes to Fly Up." He also was called "the King of Yamacraw." His name may characterize his charismatic personality, since it may be loosely translated as "Causing a Stir Wherever He Goes." He would become best known as a chief or "Mico" of the Yamacraw Creeks, a tribal emissary to London, and an advocate of trade.

Around 1700, he relocated to Yamacraw Bluff on the Savannah River, near the future site of Savannah, Georgia. When Georgia was founded in 1733, he met the English colonists led by Sir James Oglethorpe and signed a peace treaty with them. Subsequently, he negotiated another treaty with the Lower Creeks on the Georgians' behalf.

In 1734, Tomochichi; his nephew, Toonahowi; his wife, Scenanki; and several other influential Creek leaders sailed to England with Oglethorpe. Upon their arrival, the Indian delegation headed by Tomochichi was treated like royalty; he and his entourage were received by King George II and Queen Caroline and were introduced to the Archbishop of Canterbury. Although the Creek Indians became curiosities to the crowds of London, Tomochichi sought to capitalize on this interest by seeking most-favored nation status, fair trade agreements, free repair of traded weapons, prohibition of the rum trade, and standardized prices. Although he was not successful in getting these terms at the time, Tomochichi's aplomb made a lasting impression on the British public and officials. After his visit, the British government became more sensitive to the Indian position on trade matters.

As a result of Tomochichi's encouragements, English traders came to the American Southeast and established a long-standing trading relationship with the Creek people. The resulting trade created an era of prosperity in the Southeast for the English and the Creeks that lasted throughout most of the eighteenth century. Tomochichi lived to be an old man and remained loyal to the English. After his death on October 15, 1739, the people of Savannah, Georgia, gave Tomochichi an elaborate funeral, burying him in a city square in the vicinity of a monument in his honor, which remains to this day.

TOSAWI (TOSHAWAY, TOSHUA)
Comanche
fl. 1860s–1870s

As a leader of the Penetaka band, Tosawi ("Silver Brooch") engaged in many raids in the American Southwest in the 1860s. When the U.S. Army retaliated for these depredations in 1867–1868, Tosawi was the first Comanche leader to surrender to the military at Fort Cobb in the Indian Territory. When he spoke to General Philip H. Sheridan, saying "Tosawi, good Indian," the general responded with an oft-misquoted statement: "[T]he only good Indians I ever saw were dead." (Sheridan's infamous reply is often mistakenly restated as "The only good Indian is a dead Indian.")

Tosawi and TEN BEARS of the Yamparika band of the Comanches journeyed to Washington, D.C., in 1872 along with other tribal leaders seeking peace.

TOYPURINA
Gabrielino
fl. 1780s

A renowned religious leader among the Gabrielino Indians, Toypurina and Nicolas Jose, a Mission Indian convert to Christianity, fomented an insurrection in 1785 against the San Gabriel Mission near what would become Los Angeles, California. The two leaders persuaded six Indian villages in the area to mount an offensive against Spanish rule. Under the cover of darkness on October 25, 1785, an attack was launched against the mission. Toypurina's supernatural powers were supposed to slay and subdue the Spanish, but the padres and military men were forewarned of the rebellion and thwarted it, subsequently arresting the dissidents involved. During the ensuing trial, Toypurina chided the Spanish for seizing and exploiting the Gabrielino ancestral lands. Her comrade in arms, Nicolas Jose, also harangued the Spanish interlopers for prohibiting traditional ceremonies. Many of the insurgent Indians received twenty lashes for their efforts. Two headmen as well as Nicolas Jose were incarcerated in San Diego at the presidio. For her role in the rebellion, Toypurina was exiled to San Carlos Mission in the north. She later married a Spaniard.

TRUDELL, JOHN
Santee Sioux
1947–

John Trudell, who spent his early years on the Santee Sioux Reservation and in Omaha, was one of a core of American Indian activists identified with the founding of the American

Indian Movement (AIM) in 1968 and its turbulent years in the early 1970s. Trudell came to national prominence in 1969 as a spokesman for the Native Americans who were occupying Alcatraz Island. Later in his life, Trudell became a nationally known poet and singer.

Trudell participated in many of AIM's initiatives during the early 1970s, including the Trail of Broken Treaties (1972) and the occupation of Wounded Knee in 1973. Beginning in 1976, he coordinated AIM's work on behalf on Leonard PELTIER.

In 1979, Trudell's wife, Tina, their three children, and his mother-in-law were killed in an arson fire at their home on the Duck Valley Reservation, Nevada. The arson was never solved, but many Native American activists believed it was in retribution for Trudell's outspoken stands on issues affecting Native America. The fire had occurred within hours after Trudell burned a U.S. flag on the steps of the FBI headquarters in Washington, D.C., to protest its treatment of Peltier.

Trudell's poetry and musical compositions with his Grafitti Band on the album "AKA Grafitti Man" mix the spoken word, rock-and-roll, and Northern Plains musical traditions. Trudell appeared in the documentary film *Incident at Oglala* (1992) and performed the role of Jimmy Looks Twice in the feature film *Thunderheart* (1992). Both films examine the incidents surrounding the trial of Peltier.

Trudell continued to be active in AIM through the 1990s and was one of the key organizers of a protest march that forced the cancellation of Denver's Columbus Day Parade in 1992, the five-hundredth anniversary of Columbus's first voyage to the Americas.

FOR MORE INFORMATION:

Matthiessen, Peter. *In the Spirit of Crazy Horse.* New York: Viking, 1983.

TSALI
Cherokee
c. 1795–1838

His life shrouded in legend, Tsali is said to have lived at Valley Town in the Great Smokey Mountains of North Carolina with his relatives. Like others of his tribe, he farmed and hunted in the Cherokee manner until the fateful spring of 1838, when the U.S. Army came to his cabin to take him and his family to a stockade in preparation for removal. En route to the stockade in May 1838, his wife stumbled and a soldier goaded her with his bayonet. Angered by this egregious act, Tsali told his sons and his brother-in-law, Lowney, in Cherokee (so the soldiers could not understand what he was planning), to be ready for action when he pretended to be injured. As planned, he soon faked a hurt ankle. When the troopers tried to aid him, Tsali pounced on one of them while Ridges (one of Tsali's sons) and Lowney attacked the other. In the ensuing fracas, the first soldier's gun was discharged and he fell dead. The second man fled into the forest.

Hiding out all summer at the top of Clingman's Dome in the Great Smokey Mountains, Tsali was soon joined by about three hundred other Mountain Cherokees opposed to removal. In the autumn, U.S. Army general Winfield Scott sent word to Tsali through William Thomas, an adopted Cherokee, that if the people responsible for the soldier's death were to turn themselves in, the military would end its quest for the other Cherokees resisting removal. Tsali, Lowney, and Ridges surrendered, were subjected to a military trial, and were executed by firing squad at the stockade at Bushnell.

Specific circumstances in the story remain unknown. For instance, there is no certainty as to the course of events leading to the soldier's death, and there is no clear understanding of the precise role that the adopted Cherokee William Thomas played in the bargaining. Also, there is some question about whether Tsali surrendered or was seized by Cherokees who favored removal. Indeed, some people doubt that white authorities would have borne the expense of ferreting out the Mountain Cherokees even if Tsali had not surrendered. At any rate, Tsali's descendants and the other non-removed Cherokees today constitute the Eastern Cherokees of North Carolina. Tsali's martyrdom is a centerpiece of the tribal history of the Eastern Cherokees. His tale of self-sacrifice is recounted to this day in Eastern Cherokee lore and festivals.

TSATOKE, MONROE
Kiowa
1904–1937

Born on September 29, 1904, near Saddle Mountain, Oklahoma, of mixed-blood Kiowa parents, Monroe Tsatoke went to local schools and attended Bacone College. After leaving Bacone, he settled down to farming like his father Tsa-To-Ke, who had also been a scout for General George A. CUSTER. However, Tsatoke liked to draw and sketch, so he spent a great deal of his spare time improving his technique. He became a noted artist.

Tsatoke's formal art instruction began in the early 1920s, when Mrs. Susie Peters started a Fine Arts Club at Anadarko, Oklahoma, for American Indian men and boys. During this period of informal instruction, Mrs. Peters noticed that several of the students had great artistic potential. As a result, Peters persuaded Dr. Oscar J. Jacobson (head of the University of Oklahoma art department) to unofficially instruct five of the Kiowa male artists. Although they were not enrolled as regular students, the arrangement allowed them to continue their artistic training in a more rigorous setting under an excellent teacher.

From this unique situation, a distinct form of artistic expression materialized. Monroe Tsatoke was considered the most talented of the group. Immersing himself in his work, he developed quickly into an important Native American painter. Tsatoke's paintings were vibrant and dynamic, energized by the Kiowa lifestyle and stories that he knew so well.

While working diligently at his art, Tsatoke contracted tuberculosis; he ignored the seriousness of the disease until it caused his general health to decline. Tsatoke was a chief singer at Kiowa rituals; some of his art reflects his interest in music. Particularly because of his ability to attract patronage from wealthy collectors, he became a significant figure in Plains Indian art in the early twentieth century.

Tsatoke became a member of the Native American Church in his youth, an experience that amplified his religious passions. Using his spiritual experiences, he tried to develop a series of paintings that captured the depth of his religious visions. However, he did not complete the series before he died of tuberculosis at the age of thirty-two in 1937. His wife, Martha Koomsataddle (Kiowa), and four children survived him. Tsatoke is buried in Oklahoma near his birthplace at Saddle Mountain.

TUHULKUTSUT
Nez Perce
c. 1810–1877

Tuhulkutsut was one of the principal leaders of Nez Perce who, under Chief Joseph (see JOSEPH, YOUNGER), helped lead non-treaty Nez Perce who maintained their independence as the United States tried to force them onto a reservation. Their defiance culminated in the Long March, a fifteen-hundred-mile trek across the rugged northern Rocky Mountains, during which Tuhulkutsut died.

As a young man, Tuhulkutsut lived near Pikunan on the Snake River, south of the mouth of the Salmon. He was said to be an accomplished hunter and warrior and so strong he could carry a deer over each of his shoulders. As a Dreamer—a follower of the visionary SMOHALLA—Tuhulkutsut possessed a vitriolic hatred of the white invaders in his homeland. His ample distrust of the U.S. government flared into anger in an 1877 meeting with General Oliver O. Howard in which the army officer all but ordered the non-treaty Nez Perce to take up reservation life. Howard jailed Tuhulkutsut briefly after the exchange but ordered his release when tempers cooled.

Tuhulkutsut described his resistance to reservation life with ecological metaphors at this meeting, which Chief Joseph and Smohalla also attended: "The earth is part of my body. I belong to the land out of which I came. The earth is my mother." Howard is recorded to have protested, "Twenty times over [you] repeat that the earth is your mother. . . . Let us hear it no more, but come to business."

The vastly outnumbered Nez Perce led U.S. troops on a chase through some of the most rugged country on the continent, north into Canada then south again. Through the Bitterroot Mountains and what is now the Yellowstone National Park, to the headwaters of the Missouri, to the Bear Paw Mountains, Joseph's band fought a rear guard action with unquestioned brilliance. At one point, the Indians were harbored briefly by SITTING BULL's Lakotas. But many of the Nez Perce were starving. Tuhulkutsut was killed during the Nez Perces' last battle with the army, only days before Chief Joseph's surrender on October 5, 1877.

FOR MORE INFORMATION:

Josephy, Alvin M., Jr. *The Nez Perce Indians and the Opening of the Northwest.* New Haven, Conn.: Yale University Press, 1965.

Waters, Frank. *Brave Are My People: Indian Heroes Not Forgotten.* Santa Fe, N. Mex.: Clear Light, 1993.

TWO GUNS WHITE CALF
Blackfoot
1872–1934

Also known as John Two Guns and John Whitecalf Two Guns, this Blackfoot chief provided one of the most readily recognizable images of a Native American in the world after an impression of his portrait appeared on a common coin, the Indian head nickel.

Two Guns White Calf.
[National Anthropological Archives]

Two Guns White Calf was born near Fort Benton, Montana, son of White Calf, who was known as the last chief of the Pikuni Blackfoot. His visage was used along with those of John Big Tree (Seneca) and IRON TAIL (Sioux) in James Earl Fraser's composite design for the nickel.

After the coin's release around the turn of the century, Two Guns White Calf became a fixture at Glacier National Park, where he posed with tourists. He also acted as a publicity spokesman for the Northern Pacific Railroad, whose public relations staff came up with the name "Two Guns White Calf."

He died of pneumonia at the age of sixty-three and was buried in a Catholic cemetery at Browning, Montana.

TWO LEGGINGS
Crow
c. 1844–1923

For many Crow warriors during the Plains wars, it was a small jump from stealing Sioux horses to scouting for the U.S. Army against them. Two Leggings, like CURLY and WHITE-

MAN-RUNS-HIM, became a well-known scout for General George Armstrong CUSTER.

Born along the Bighorn River in Montana, Two Leggings was a member of the Crows' Uxarache clan. His life story was told to William Wildschut, a Montana businessman, between 1919 and 1923. This manuscript was edited by Peter Nabokov and published as *Two Leggings: The Making of a Crow Warrior* in 1967. Two Leggings died at home in Hardin, Montana.

TWO MOON (ISI'EYO NISSI)
Northern Cheyenne
fl. 1860s

The uncle of TWO MOONS, Two Moon led Cheyenne warriors in several battles with white invaders as well as against traditional foes. In 1866, Two Moon led Cheyenne forces in an attack on

Two Leggings. [National Anthropological Archives]

Fort Phil Kearney, Wyoming, one of the battles preceding the Fort Laramie Treaty of 1868.

TWO MOONS (ISHI'EYO NISSI)
Northern Cheyenne
1847–1917

The nephew of TWO MOON, this Cheyenne leader led his people in the Battle of the Little Bighorn. Later, in 1898, his account of the battle appeared in *McClure's* magazine. After the battle with CUSTER, General Nelson A. Miles convinced Two Moons to surrender. He later became a U.S. Army scout. In this role, Two Moons conducted LITTLE CROW's Cheyenne band to Fort Keough. Two Moons later served as chief of the reservation Northern Cheyenne and traveled to Washington, D.C., to advance their cause. He met with President Woodrow Wilson in 1914. Two Moons died three years later at his home in Montana.

Two Moons' camp on Rosebud Creek, Montana, 1880. [Nebraska State Historical Society]

Two Moons. [Nebraska State Historical Society]

TWO STRIKE (NOMKAHPA)
Brulé Sioux
1832–c. 1915

Also called Two Strikes, this war chief's Brulé Sioux name, Nomkahpa, meant "Knocks Two Off." The name was earned in battle after Two Strike knocked two Utes off their horses with a single blow of his war club. Two Strike figured prominently in the history of the Brulés late in the nineteenth century up to and including the closing of the frontier at Wounded Knee in 1890.

Born near the Republican River in what would become Nebraska, Two Strike played an important role in raids on the Union Pacific Railroad during RED CLOUD's War (1866–1868). During the 1870s, Two Strike allied with SPOTTED TAIL and tried to insulate his people from the Euro-American invasion. In the 1880s, Two Strike

Two Strike. [National Anthropological Archives]

became an advocate of the Ghost Dance. A month before the massacre at Wounded Knee, however, Two Strike heeded whites' advice to give up the dance and its promised delivery from Euro-American domination. After the slaughter of Native people under BIG FOOT at Wounded Knee in late December 1890, Two Strike led his people on an angry rampage with other Sioux. He desisted again after General Nelson Miles promised fair treatment for his people. Two Strike's people surrendered for a second time on January 15, 1891.

General Miles was generally regarded as credible by the Sioux because he rarely broke his promises. Two Strike was a member of a Sioux delegation to Washington, D.C., a month after the Wounded Knee massacre. The Sioux asked that Miles be allowed to negotiate for them with the Interior Department and Bureau of Indian

Affairs, but the general was excluded by white officials who thought of him as too pro-Indian.

After the turn of the century, Two Strike lived quietly at Pine Ridge, where he was buried after his death, about 1915.

TYHEE
Bannock
c. 1825–1871

Tyhee resisted early white incursions into the Pacific Northwest but later became an advocate of peace. History has left little detail of Tyhee's early life, which was undisturbed by Euro-American immigration. By the 1850s, however, the tide of settlement was destroying the Bannocks' hunting resources. In 1869, the Bannocks were forced to sign the Treaty of Fort Bridger.

Tyhee died two years after signing the 1869 treaty.

TYHEE, YOUNGER
Bannock
fl. late 1800s

Tyhee (Younger) led the Bannocks after the death of the elder man of the same name in 1871. During Tyhee's (Younger) tenure as chief, most of the Bannocks who had survived the wars of the 1860s moved onto reservations. Tyhee himself became a successful farmer as he struggled to have treaties enforced both at home and in trips to Washington, D.C.

In 1878, dissatisfied with reservation life, several thousand Bannocks moved without U.S. Army permission to the Camas prairie in search of sustenance and freedom. The move was headlined in some eastern newspapers as "the Bannock War" because General Oliver O. Howard's troops rounded up most of the people and moved them against their wills back to the reservation. The roundup was marred by a slaughter of several defenseless women and children at Clark's Ford on September 5, 1878.

$\mathcal{U}$

UNCAS
Mohegan
c. 1605–1682

Uncas was the founder of the Mohegans as a band of dissident Pequots who were allied with the English of Massachusetts Bay during the early days of colonization. Uncas' name (which means "Fox" in Pequot) became synonymous with betrayal among many New England Native Americans because he told lies to ingratiate himself with the English. By the time he died, fat and alcoholic, Uncas had probably sold the colonists more of other Indians' land than anyone else in New England's history. In 1826, James Fenimore Cooper used the names of Uncas and the Mohegans in his fictional *Last of the Mohicans*. In point of historical fact, Uncas was "the first of the Mohegans."

Uncas married a daughter of Chief SASSACUS, who led the Pequots. Uncas then became jealous of Sassacus' power and broke away from the Pequot Confederacy. He allied with the colonists of Massachusetts Bay and worked to subvert the interests of the Pequots, often with lies and other forms of political intrigue.

Following the Pequot War, during which many of Sassacus' supporters were killed, Uncas assumed leadership over the remnants of the Pequot Confederacy. He toadied to the English colonists by ceding to them the lands of other tribes. In 1642, Uncas contended to colonial authorities that MIANTINOMO, a Narraganset chief, was plotting to kill him. Miantinomo was jailed for a time, after which he attacked Uncas' village for revenge. Miantinomo was then captured by the Mohegans and sentenced to die at Uncas' hand in September 1643, an event that hardened the long-standing hatred of the Narragansets for the Mohegans.

Uncas was so enthusiastically anti-Indian that the Puritans told him to desist in spreading rumors about his Native neighbors. He continued, however, and curried favor with the colonists by supplying them with real and imagined intelligence. During King Philip's War, he supplied warriors, led by his own son,

Oweneco, to support the colonials against METACOM's alliance.

Uncas did not want his people converted to Christianity. As he got older he was known for insulting men of the cloth. Uncas became increasingly alcoholic and lost some of his popular support before he died in 1683.

Four centuries later, a settlement of a few hundred Mohegans live at Uncasville, Connecticut.

FOR MORE INFORMATION:

Voight, Virginia Frances. *Uncas: Sachem of the Wolf People.* New York: Funk & Wagnalls, 1963.

VICTORIO (BIDU-YA, BEDUIAT)
Mimbreno Apache
c. 1825–1880

Victorio, who would become a leader in the Apache Wars, was born about 1825 in Chihuahua, Mexico. In his youth, he served with distinction under MANGAS COLORADAS and became renowned as a brave man and skilled strategist. With the death of Mangas Coloradas in 1863, Victorio assumed leadership of the Ojo Caliente or Warm Springs band and battled Mexicans and Americans with equal force.

In 1877, Victorio and his band ceased their raids and were granted a permanent reservation at Warm Springs in southwestern New Mexico. The agreement fell through because the U.S. government unilaterally decided in May 1877 that Victorio's band would be required to resettle on the San Carlos Reservation in Arizona. Reacting to this turn of events, Victorio slipped away with three hundred followers in September 1877. Within a month, many of the Mimbrenos had surrendered at

Fort Wingate, New Mexico, but Victorio and eighty men remained in the Mimbres Mountains and continued to raid the surrounding countryside until the army convinced them that they would be settled on their Warm Springs Reservation. Soon after this agreement, in April 1878, the Mimbrenos were told that they would be relocated to the Mescalero Reservation. As a result of this duplicity, many of the Mimbrenos under Victorio again slipped away and resumed raiding.

In early 1879, the raiding stepped up, but Victorio tried again to settle at Warm Springs. In June he agreed to settle at the Mescalero Reservation. In July 1879, he was indicted on an old charge of murder and horse stealing. Fearing a trial, Victorio fled with his men. Many Mescaleros also followed him. His war party attacked a cavalry horse camp, killed eight guards, and ran off with forty-six horses. Next, Victorio's band headed into Mexico, then into Texas, and even returned to New Mexico before finally going into Arizona for raids. Both the

United States (under Colonel Edward Hatch in New Mexico) and Mexico (under General Geronimo Trevino in Chihuahua, Mexico) mounted campaigns against Victorio. During this campaign, American troops were allowed by Mexico to routinely cross the international border, but Victorio eluded both the Mexicans and the Americans in spite of many military engagements.

On October 14, 1880, Victorio, while being pursued by American forces, was cornered by a force of 350 Mexicans and Tarahumara Indians under Colonel Joaquin Terrazas. In the ensuing two-day battle in the Tres Castillos Mountains, about eighty warriors died and the rest of the band (about eighty women and children) was captured. Although thirty warriors escaped, Victorio turned up among the dead. The historical record is unclear whether he died in battle or took his own life when his forces were overwhelmed by the Mexican army. One thing is clear: his bravery, tactics, endurance, and tenacity in the face of huge odds gained him the respect of all his adversaries.

VIZENOR, GERALD
White Earth Chippewa
1934–

Gerald Vizenor, professor of Native American literature in the ethnic studies department at the University of California at Berkeley, is the author of many fictional works, including *The Heirs of Columbus* (1991), *Landfill Meditation* (1991), *Griever: An American Monkey King in China* (which won an American Book Award for 1987), and *Dead Voices: Natural Agonies in the New World* (1994), as well as an autobiography, *Interior Landscapes*, published in 1990. Vizenor also wrote *Wordarrows: Indians and Whites in the New Fur Trade* (1978).

Vizenor was born in Minneapolis. He served in the U.S. Army between 1952 and 1955 and later worked as a guidance director at the Minnesota Department of Corrections. Some of his early poems appeared in *Summer in the Spring: Ojibway Lyric Poems* (1965), *Seventeen Chirps* (1964), *Raising the Moon Vines* (1964), *Empty Swings* (1967), *New Voices from the People Named the Chippewa* (1971), and many others.

WABAN
Nipmuc
c. 1610–c. 1677

Born on the site of contemporary Concord, Massachusetts, Waban was probably the first influential Native American to become a Christian when he was converted by the Reverend John Eliot in 1646. Five years later, Waban founded a town of "praying Indians" in Natick, Massachusetts; he served as the town's justice of the peace. In 1676, Waban warned colonial officials of the onset of King Philip's War but was confined with his followers because some Puritans suspected him of complicity with METACOM.

WAFFORD, JAMES (TSUSKWANUN-NAWATA)
Mixed Cherokee
1806–1896

James Wafford, born near what is now Clarkesville, Georgia, became a noted research informant and political leader among the Cherokees. His grandfather, a Revolutionary War colonel with the same name, settled in 1785 in northern Georgia. In 1804, when the Wafford settlement was ascertained to be on Cherokee Territory, his grandfather was ceded about one hundred acres through a special treaty. James Wafford's mother was SEQUOYAH's cousin and was said to be of Cherokee, Natchez, and European descent. His Cherokee name, Tsuskwanun-nawata, means "Worn-out Blanket."

While attending the mission school in Valleytown, Wafford helped translate a Cherokee speller. He obtained extensive information about the Cherokees and their lands in southern Appalachia while working for the U.S. census in 1824. As a result of this knowledge, he became an important anthropological informant about Cherokee ways. He headed a party of Cherokee emigrants during the Trail of Tears. Wafford became a member of the tribal council of the Western Cherokees after their removal to Indian Territory. James Mooney of the Bureau of American Ethnology interviewed him in 1891 at his residence in Tahlequah in the Indian Territory.

WALKER, WILLIAM
Wyandot/Huron
c. 1800–1874

William Walker's father was a white man who had been captured and adopted by the Wyandots (as the Hurons of Ohio were called). Walker's father married a mixed-blood wife and became a chief of the Wyandots. Walker was raised with an Anglo-American education and studied languages at Kenyon College. He served for a time as interpreter for Lewis Cass while the latter was governor of Michigan Territory. He also served as an informant for ethnologist Henry Rowe Schoolcraft.

In 1824, Walker's father died, and Walker assumed leadership of his band. He was known as an adroit negotiator as his people were pressed to move from the Ohio country to Kansas in the early 1840s. In 1853, Walker served briefly as governor of Nebraska Territory.

WALKS-IN-THE-WATER
Wyandot/Huron
c. 1775–1825

Walks-in-the-Water was one of TECUMSEH's principal allies in his bid to erect a unified American Indian state as a buffer zone between British land claims and the United States. Treaties were signed between the Americans and the Hurons, among others, but increasing colonization caused friction, which peaked in Tecumseh's Rebellion (1809–1811) as well as the War of 1812.

During January 1813, Walks-in-the-Water and his Huron ally Roundhead led a Native force that defeated an American military unit on the Raisin River south of Detroit. Walks-in-the-Water was instrumental in the defeat of the Americans at Fort Madden. He was also present at the final British defeat, the Battle of the Thames, in which Tecumseh was killed.

Walks-in-the-Water was one of the principal chiefs who sued for peace. After the war, he migrated to a small reservation near Brownstone, Michigan, where he died about 1825, having generally avoided the public limelight for more than a decade.

FOR MORE INFORMATION:

Clark, Peter (Dooyentate). *Origin and Traditional History of the Wyandotts.* Toronto, 1870.

Eckert, Allan W. *A Sorrow in Our Heart: The Life of Tecumseh.* New York: Bantam, 1992.

WANETA
Yankton Sioux
c. 1795–1848

"He Who Rushes On," a steadfast ally of the British in the War of 1812, was born about 1795 on the Elm River in northern South Dakota. He was the son of the Shappa Indian Red Thunder. Both men enlisted in the British army for the War of 1812 and fought with storied bravery. Waneta was badly injured at the Battle of Sandusky. The British later commissioned Waneta a captain and invited him to London.

By 1825, Waneta had allied with the Americans and rejected the British. He signed the Treaty of Fort Pierre (1825) and the Treaty of Prairie du Chien (1825). George CATLIN painted Waneta's portrait in 1832. Waneta died at fifty-three years of age near the present-day Standing Rock Indian Reservation in North Dakota.

WANNALANCET
Mahican
c. 1625–1695

Like his father PASSACONAWAY, Wannalancet tried his best to maintain peace with the English colonists of Massachusetts Bay. Despite his people's noncombatant status, many of them were imprisoned during King Philip's War, during which Wannalancet's village was burned to the ground by Puritan vigilantes who were devastating friendly Indians as well as the allies of METACOM. Roughly two hundred of Wannalancet's people were sold into slavery after they arrived at Dover to seek refuge from the war. A band of about two hundred survivors escaped to Canada, where Wannalancet died.

FOR MORE INFORMATION:

Leach, Douglas Edward. *Flintlock and Tomahawk*. New York: Norton, 1958.

Segal, Charles M., and David C. Stineback. *Puritans, Indians, and Manifest Destiny.* New York: Putnam, 1977.

WAPASHA
Mdewakanton Sioux
c. 1718–1806

Wapasha, or "Red Leaf," was the name of several important Mdewakanton Sioux chiefs between roughly 1750 and 1870. The eldest known to the historical record was born about 1718 in present-day Minnesota. As a chief, he spent much of his time making war or negotiating peace with the Chippewas. Later in his life, Wapasha made contact with the English, who withdrew trading relations after the murder of a merchant. Wapasha captured the culprit and set off to deliver him to his accusers. The man escaped, but Wapasha offered himself in his place. The English refused that offer but made an ally. He died near Hokah, Minnesota.

WAPASHA
Mdewakanton Sioux
c. 1763–1836

Son of the elder Wapasha, the younger leader was born in Winona, Minnesota. He met Zebulon Pike's 1805 expedition in search of the Mississippi River's source. He was generally an ally of immigrating Americans, and while the British claimed his loyalty in the War of 1812, Wapasha was regarded as suspect to the point of court-martial. He died of smallpox and was succeeded by his brother (some accounts say nephew), Joseph WAPASHA.

WAPASHA, JOSEPH
Mdewakanton Sioux
c. 1825–1876

Joseph Wapasha became the Mdewakanton Sioux's principal chief in the mid–nineteenth century. He continued the accommodationist policies of his two forebears of the same name. By the 1840s, however, white immigration in Minnesota had reached unprecedented levels, and friendliness was becoming more difficult to maintain without abject surrender. Wapasha reluctantly surrendered to pressure to join in the Great Sioux Uprising that began in 1862 under LITTLE CROW. He and his people did their best to stay out of the hostilities, but after the war they were caught in the colonists' general fervor to rid the state of all Indians. Vigilantes drove Wapasha and his people to a reservation on the upper Missouri. They later moved to the Santee Agency in Nebraska, where Joseph Wapasha died.

WAPELLO
Fox
1787–1842

Wapello, who was born at Prairie du Chien in contemporary Wisconsin, was a principal ally of KEOKUK, the Fox leader who opposed BLACK HAWK in Black Hawk's War (1832). Like Keokuk, Wapello accommodated white expansion and agreed to removal of Fox peoples west of the Mississippi River. In 1837, he traveled to Washington, D.C., for treaty making with a delegation of Fox leaders. He died near the site of present-day Ottumwa, Iowa.

WARD, NANCY (NANYE-HI)
Cherokee
c. 1738–c. 1824

Nanye-hi ("One Who Goes About") was born into the Wolf clan at Chota, the old Cherokee capital near Fort Loudon, Tennessee. She was nicknamed as a youth Tsistunagiska, or "Wild Rose," for her rose petal–like skin. Ward's father was Fivekiller, a Cherokee-Delaware, and her mother was Tame Doe (also known as Catherine), the sister of the acclaimed Cherokee chief ATTAKULLAKULLA, and a cousin of DRAGGING CANOE. While still a teenager, Nanye-hi married Kingfisher, a Cherokee of the Deer clan. She had two children by him.

At the Battle of Taliwa with the Creeks, Nanye-hi helped her husband from behind a bulwark by chewing on the bullets to make them more lethal. When her husband was slain, she took up his musket and aided in turning the tide of battle for the Cherokees. For her bravery in battle, she was given the lifetime title of Ghighau or Agigau, "Beloved Woman." Hence, she became head of the Woman's Council and also voted on the Chief's Council. One of her prerogatives was the pardoning of condemned captives.

In this powerful role, Nanye-hi avoided being vindictive and was known as a peace advocate. At the beginning of the American Revolution, she warned the white settlers in the Holston and Wautauga Valleys in 1776 of the planned attack by pro-English Cherokees under the leadership of her cousin Dragging Canoe. Many times she used her position as "Beloved Woman" to save white captives. When the whites mounted a stinging counterattack in 1780, she implored U.S. troops to cease their attacks on her people. Although she failed in this entreaty, American forces did spare the town of Chota from devastation. At the conclusion of the American Revolution, she advocated forgiveness and friendship in the treaty negotiations. Although many persons on both sides of the conflict thought her policies of peace to be foolhardy and even perilous, there were few people, Indian or white, who did not respect her.

After the American Revolution, she married her second husband, an Irish trader by the name of Brian (Bryant) Ward, and had three children, Catherine, Fivekiller, and Elizabeth. She also opened a successful inn at Womankiller Ford along the Ocowee River. At this time, she became known as "Nancy," an abridgement of her Cherokee name, Nanye-hi.

As more white settlers came into Tennessee, Nancy Ward became disenchanted with her views about friendship toward the whites. She told the Cherokee Council of 1817 to cede no more tribal lands to the Americans. In the early 1820s, she advised her people against any more land cessions and opposed relocation to the West.

Despite these difficulties, her inn continued to prosper, and she was a wealthy woman at the time of her death in the spring of 1824. Among the Cherokee people, she is still deeply revered for her kindness, friendship, power, beauty, and wisdom. Ward's acclaim is well known among whites in Tennessee as well; the Nancy Ward chapter of the Daughters of the American Revolution paid homage to her with a monument at her gravesite inscribed: "Princess and Prophetess of Tennessee. The Pocahontas of Tennessee and the Constant Friend of the American Pioneer."

WARREN, WILLIAM WHIPPLE
Chippewa/Ojibway
1825–1853

William Warren's birth represented the synthesis that became America—his father, Lyman Warren, was an English blacksmith and a descendant of one of the Pilgrims who sailed on the *Mayflower*; his mother, Mary Cardotte, was part Chippewa and part French. He was educated in Anglo-American schools and became fluent in English. Meanwhile he also became conversant with the language and lifeways of his Native American ancestors.

In 1850, Warren was elected to the Minnesota state legislature from his home in Crow Wing. He also composed a history of the Ojibways. He died at twenty-eight of tuberculosis after having traveled to New York in an unsuccessful attempt to get his book published. At the time of his death, Warren was designing two other major publishing projects on the Ojibways. His first book was published in 1885, more than three decades after his death, as *History of the Ojibways, Based upon Traditions and Oral Statements.*

WASHAKIE
Shoshoni
c. 1802–1900

Washakie's Shoshonis allied with PLENTY COUPS's Crows to assist the U.S. Army against the Cheyennes, Sioux, and others who were defined by the United States as hostile during the final phases of the Plains wars, beginning in the 1870s. Washakie's accommodation helped him bargain for a sizable, fertile reservation in the Shoshonis' homeland, while hostiles were assigned arid reservations and treated miserably after their surrenders.

Various accounts place Washakie's birth between 1798 and 1804. His father, Pasego, was of mixed blood; his mother was Shoshoni. Pasego was killed by Flatheads when Washakie was a child. As a young man, Washakie developed his skills as a warrior by riding for several years with a band of Bannocks. He stood six feet tall, married several women, and had twelve children. His reputation was mainly as a war-

Washakie. [Nebraska State Historical Society]

rior (although he was rarely aggressive after his youth), but he was also known among the Shoshonis as an excellent singer.

By the 1840s, large numbers of gold seekers on their way to California passed through the Shoshonis' homeland in present-day Wyoming, but few settled in the area. A few years later, a large party of Mormons under Brigham Young settled on the southern edge of the Shoshoni homeland at the Great Salt Lake. In 1851, Washakie rejected terms of a proposed treaty that would have diminished Shoshoni lands and allied for a time with the Mormons before the federal government asserted authority over them as part of Utah's bid for statehood. In 1869, Washakie negotiated the Treaty of Fort Bridger, which set apart three million acres for the Shoshonis in their traditional homeland.

By the middle 1870s, the Plains wars were drawing to a close. Washakie allied with the Crows and the U.S. Army at the Little Bighorn. Plenty Coups worried that General George Crook was not prepared for CRAZY HORSE's Lakotas when they met in battle along with

Washakie's Shoshonis on June 16, 1876. He was correct; Crazy Horse routed Crook and his Indian allies in a battle that presaged Custer's Last Stand nine days later.

Oliver O. Howard, best known as the army commander who pursued Chief Joseph (see JOSEPH, YOUNGER) and other non-treaty Nez Perces on their Long March in 1877, recalled Washakie as "a tall, big man with fine eyes and a great deal of hair. He spoke broken English, but could make himself understood. He was a great eater.... He ate very politely, but was like a giant taking his food." Howard said that Washakie was famous for his skill as a buffalo hunter.

Despite his support for the immigrants, Washakie and his people had their share of troubles with broken treaties. In 1870, land that had been set aside for the Shoshonis and Bannocks by a treaty signed in 1864 was demanded for white settlement. Many young Shoshoni warriors called for war, but Washakie forbade it.

Washakie allied with the whites out of necessity, not choice. He chafed at being confined on a reservation. In 1878, at a meeting called by the governor of Wyoming, Washakie said,

The white man, who possesses this whole vast country from sea to sea, who roams over it at pleasure and lives where he likes, cannot know the cramp we feel in this little spot, with the undying remembrance of the fact, which you know as well as we, that every foot of what you proudly call America, not very long ago belonged to the Red Man. The Great Spirit gave it to us, [and] there was room enough for all his tribes; all were happy in their freedom. [Armstrong]

The whites had superior tools and weapons, said Washakie, and "hordes of men" to use

them against the Indians. He continued: "We . . . sorry remnants of tribes once mighty, are cornered on little spots of the earth, all ours by right—cornered like guilty prisoners, and watched by men with guns who are more than anxious to kill us off."

When Washakie was an elderly man, his eldest son (also called Washakie) was killed in a drunken brawl with a white man. The elder Washakie was grieved by the fact that his son had passed on to the Spirit World in disgrace, "like an Arapaho." (The Shoshonis and Arapahoes were bitter enemies, even in the face of overwhelming white encroachment.) Washakie also opposed the Ghost Dance, but he urged his people to continue the Sun Dance, which they had borrowed from the Sioux.

Despite his doubts, Washakie was such a source of support for the U.S. Army that in 1878 it named a frontier fort after him in the Wind River valley. Washakie died in his sleep on February 20, 1900. He was buried with the honors accorded a captain in the post cemetery at Fort Washakie.

Two statues in the Salt Lake City area memorialize Washakie. The most notable is downtown, where his likeness is part of the Brigham Young Monumental Group, along with other people (all European Americans) who gave great aid to initial Mormon settlement in the Salt Lake valley.

FOR MORE INFORMATION:

Armstrong, Virginia Irving, ed. *I Have Spoken: American History Through the Voices of the Indians.* Chicago: Swallow Press, 1971.

Hebard, Grace Raymond. *Washakie: Chief of the Shoshones.* Lincoln: University of Nebraska Press, 1995.

Howard, O. O. *Famous Indian Chiefs I Have Known.* 1908. Reprint, Lincoln: University of Nebraska Press, 1989.

WASHUNGA
Kansa
c. 1830–1908

Washunga was the leader of the Kansa tribe during the allotment period and had a distrust for white intentions during this time. As a non-Christian conservative, he gained prominence when he was made tribal chief councilor about 1885. During this time, Charles CURTIS, a mixed-blood Kansas politician from the Kaw tribe, convinced his friend Washunga that the best course for Indians was to seek citizenship through individualized land allotments.

In 1902, Washunga and several Kansa chiefs arrived in Washington to sign an allotment treaty that Curtis had drawn up several months before. Each individual was supposed to receive

Washunga. [Nebraska State Historical Society]

450 acres. Although already an old man, Washunga made sure that negotiations for the treaty were completed. After the treaty was signed, he retired from tribal politics. He died at the age of about seventy-eight in 1908.

WATIE, STAND
(DEGATAGA, TAKERTAWKER)
Cherokee
1806–1871

Stand Watie was born at Coosawalee in the Cherokee nation near what would become Rome, Georgia, on December 2, 1806. He was a member of the Deer clan and his father, David Oowatie (Uwati), was an important leader. His mother was Susannah Reese, the daughter of the British trader Charles Reese and a Cherokee woman. He was the younger brother of Buck Watie, better known as Elias BOUDINOT, a cousin of John RIDGE, and nephew of Major RIDGE. By the end of his accomplished life, Stand Watie had been a Confederate general, a principal chief, and an ethnological source.

Stand Watie attended school at Brainerd Mission in eastern Tennessee like his older brother Elias. Upon completion of his schooling, he returned to his people to work with his brother on the newspaper the *Cherokee Phoenix*. Perceiving resistance to white encroachment as hopeless, he took an active role in the Treaty Party, a proremoval faction. Stand Watie's uncle and cousin, Major and John Ridge, were prominent leaders of this faction, which opposed the antiremoval faction led by John ROSS. He was one of the signers of the Treaty of New Echota (1835), which sought to sanction Cherokee removal. After the Trail of Tears, Stand Watie, his brother Elias, and both Ridges were to be killed by members of the Ross faction. However, he was warned and was the only one of the four men who managed to escape assassination. Seeking revenge, he torched John Ross's house. After these events, he helped to reorganize Cherokee tribal affairs. From 1845 to 1861, Stand Watie was a member of the Cherokee Council, and he served as speaker of the council from 1857 to 1859.

With the coming of the Civil War, he decided to support the Confederacy. He took command of two Cherokee Mounted Rifles regiments, which served with distinction. These regiments served in more battles west of the Mississippi than any other unit. Stand Watie was promoted to brigadier general. On March 6–8, 1864, at the Battle of Pea Ridge, Arkansas, his men seized the Union artillery batteries that were causing severe damage to the Confederates. After this strategic blow, the valiant Cherokees then protected their allies' retreat. Also in 1864, he was made principal chief of the southern band of Cherokees. Throughout this time, the Cherokee contingent under Stand Watie continued to lay waste to the federals' lands in the Missouri-Kansas area. When he finally laid down his arms at Doaksville in the Choctaw nation, he was credited with being the last Confederate general to surrender.

After the Civil War, Stand Watie helped to negotiate the 1866 Cherokee Reconstruction Treaty. He also took up farming on the Grand River near Bernice in Indian Territory. He was married to Sarah Caroline "Betsy" Bell, with whom he had three sons and two daughters. Since he had a very sound knowledge of Cherokee culture, Stand Watie also served as an ethnological source for Henry Rowe Schoolcraft's *Information Respecting the History, Condition, and Prospects of the Indian Tribes of the United States* (1851–57).

Although small in stature, he was a personable, vibrant, and dignified man. When he felt he was right, he was "Immovable," as his name

connotes, but he is reputed to have always been open to opposing arguments. On September 9, 1871, Stand Watie died at his house on Honey Creek. He was buried in Delaware County, Oklahoma, at the Ridge Cemetery.

WA-WA-CHAW (BENITA NUÑEZ)
Luiseno
1888–1972
Born on December 25, 1888, at Valley Center in the Tule River area of California, Wa-Wa-Chaw ("Keep from the Water") became an artist, writer, and feminist with an international reputation. Two New Yorkers, Dr. Cornelius Duggan and his sister Mary Duggan, took her to New York City as an infant and raised her as their own child. She was a child prodigy—her medical and scientific sketches of early radium and cancer experiments conducted by Pierre and Marie Curie demonstrated her artistic talents. As an activist for Indian and feminist causes, she gave a lecture as a teenager at the Astor Hotel sponsored by Carrie Chapman Catt.

During the course of her career, Wa-Wa-Chaw expressed herself on huge canvases with oils, and many of her portraits were of the important people of her times. She also painted studies of social problems that were of deep concern to her. She was a close friend to Dr. Carlos MONTEZUMA and a fund-raiser for his Wassaja project. She spoke out on many of the same topics as he did and planned many of Montezuma's campaigns for Indian rights.

Throughout her life, Wa-Wa-Chaw was known as a colorful, outspoken person who was loved by all who knew her. She knew many white intellectuals of the early twentieth century, including Arthur Conan Doyle, Arthur C. PARKER, General Richard H. PRATT, and Sir Oliver Lodge. She was as much an influence upon these people as they were upon her. Although quite proud of her art, she was modest about her social activities and herself. She was a prolific writer until her death. Although she frequently sold her artworks at sidewalk sales in Greenwich Village, she was even more interested in furthering the equality of American Indian women.

After her marriage to Manuel Carmonia-Nuñez (a businessman and organizer of the Cigar Worker's Union), she assumed the name of Benita Nuñez. They had one child, who died in infancy. During the first part of the twentieth century, Wa-Wa-Chaw was a familiar figure on the lecture circuit and prominent among American Indian leaders of the time. She died at the age of eighty-three on May 12, 1972, in New York City.

WEATHERFORD, WILLIAM (LUMHE CHATI)
Mixed Creek
1780–1822

Although there is no agreement as to his parentage, it seems likely that William Weatherford was the son of Charles Weatherford (a Scottish trader) and Sehoy, Alexander McGILLIVRAY's half sister. He spent his early years on the Alabama River near present-day Montgomery, Alabama. According to some accounts, Charles Weatherford offered his two sons, William and John, a choice between the Native American and Euro-American ways of life. William chose the life of the Creek Indian and John chose life in white society. William's Creek name means "Red Eagle."

On the eve of the War of 1812, Weatherford realized that the American Indians must fight white domination or lose their autonomy, so he embraced TECUMSEH's call for united action and an American Indian barrier state from the

Great Lakes to the Gulf of Mexico. In fall 1811, Tecumseh spoke before a conference of more than five thousand Creeks and Indians of other tribes. He envisioned a confederation of Indian nations and a military coalition to maintain independence from U.S. rule. His idea was unpopular with the White Sticks, the people of peace, from the Lower Creek villages in southern Alabama, but it resonated with many of the young Red Sticks, the traditionalist warriors, from the Upper Creek towns. William Weatherford was one of the Red Stick leaders.

Although the Creek War did not begin until 1812, months after Tecumseh's forces began their resistance in the north, it was the hardest fought. On August 30, 1813, Weatherford's force of one thousand Creek warriors attacked American forces at Fort Mims near the confluence of the Alabama and Tombigbee Rivers, killing over five hundred soldiers and civilians. Although African American slaves warned Major Daniel Beasley, the garrison commander, about Creeks that were crawling toward the fort in the high grass, Beasley disregarded the slaves' advice and continued to leave the fort's outer gate wide open. In the initial attack, Beasley was slain. Although the settlers defended themselves behind the fort's inner perimeter and repulsed the Creek warriors for several hours, eventually flaming arrows allowed the Indians to penetrate the defenses. Only thirty-six whites escaped, but the Red Sticks spared the African American slaves, allowing them to go free.

In the "Thirty Battles" that followed, both sides saw thousands of casualties. Both state and federal troops were called into action. Tennessee raised a volunteer militia of about thirty-five hundred, including Cherokee forces led by John Ross, Major RIDGE, SEQUOYAH, John LOWRY, Junaluska, and WHITE PATH. William

COLBERT commanded a Chickasaw detachment;
the Choctaws were headed by PUSHMATAHA and
Mushalatubbee; the Yuchi forces were spearheaded by Timpoochee BARNARD. Even the
White Stick Creeks marched against Weatherford and his men.

General Andrew Jackson—or "Sharp Knife,"
as the Indians called him—assumed command
of the forces against Weatherford. After many
indecisive engagements, the final battle was
joined at the Horseshoe Bend of the Tallapoosa
River on March 29, 1814. Jackson's forces advanced into positions around the Red Sticks'
barricades, seized their canoes, and struck at
Weatherford's forces. The Red Sticks maintained their position from behind log barricades they had erected on a peninsula. The
battle raged all day. Although the log defenses
deflected artillery fire, Jackson's forces eventually managed to set the barricades on fire and
rout the Red Sticks. Because he had left to
inspect other defenses, Weatherford did not
surrender that day. Instead, he walked into
Jackson's camp at Fort Toulouse several days
later, identified himself, and then surrendered.
Weatherford expected to be executed because of
the hatred that many whites had for him, but
Jackson pardoned him and admonished him to
work for peace.

Later, in August 1814, Jackson forced peaceful and hostile Creek leaders to sign the Treaty
of Fort Jackson, which ceded twenty-three million acres of Creek land. As a result of the harsh
terms, many embittered Creeks resettled in
Florida among the Seminoles and became combatants in the First Seminole War of 1817–
1818. Subsequently, Weatherford settled on a
plantation with his large family. He became a
respected member of both the white and Indian
communities. He kept his word and always
worked for peace between Creeks and whites.
He died on March 9, 1822, at his home in Polk
County, Tennessee, before the removal of the
Creeks to Indian Territory.

WEAVER, PAULINO (PAULINE WEAVER)
Mixed Cherokee
fl. mid-1800s

Paulino Weaver was a fur trader who worked
out of Taos, New Mexico, during the 1820s and
1830s. He explored the Casa Grande Mountains
of central Arizona in 1832. Settling later in
southern California, he became a friend of the
Cahuilla leader Juan ANTONIO. As a result of
Weaver's efforts in southern California, the
uprising of 1851–1852 led by the Cupeno Antonio GARRA was thwarted.

WEETAMOO
Pocasset
c. 1650–1676

Born near present-day Fall River, Massachusetts, Weetamoo ("Sweetheart") was one of a
number of female principal chiefs who lived in
the vicinity of the early English colonies in
New England. She allied with METACOM and
died in hostilities attending King Philip's War
in 1676.

Weetamoo was linked by family ties to many
of the leaders who joined Metacom. Her sister,
Wootenekauske, was married to him. Weetamoo herself was the widow of ALEXANDER,
Metacom's brother; after his death, she married
QUINAPEN, another chief allied with Metacom.
Contemporary sources describe her as tall, well
muscled, and generally able to hold her own
with men in battle. She affected the trappings
of royalty on occasion and was called "The
Squaw Sachem" by many of the English.

Near the end of King Philip's War, after the
defeat at the Great Swamp Fight, Weetamoo
took to the swamps to evade colonial troops. As
they followed her, she drowned while crossing
the Teticut River. The whites took Weetamoo's

body out of the river, cut off her head, and mounted it for display at Taunton.

FOR MORE INFORMATION:

Segal, Charles M., and David C. Stineback. *Puritans, Indians, and Manifest Destiny.* New York: Putnam, 1977.

Slotkin, Richard, and James K. Folsom, eds. *So Dreadful a Judgement: Puritan Responses to King Philip's War 1676–1677.* Middleton, Conn.: Wesleyan University Press, 1978.

WEKAU
Winnebago
c. 1790–1828

Following a surge in illegal immigration of lead miners to what would become southwestern Wisconsin, the Winnebago leader Wekau ("The Sun") instigated a brief insurgency in 1827 with RED BIRD and CHICKHONSIC. After the insurgency, Wekau offered himself to be hanged to spare his people. He was never executed but languished in jail and died of dysentery in 1828.

Earlier in the 1820s, the Winnebagos' anger had risen when U.S. officials forbade their sale of lead to traders—the same trade that whites were carrying out illegally on their land. This, the widespread abuse of Winnebago women by white frontiersmen, and the long-term incarceration of many Winnebagos in American jails led the Winnebagos' headmen to seek vengeance. With this intention, Red Bird, accompanied by Wekau and Chickhonsic (or Little Buffalo), entered the trading town of Prairie du Chien on June 26, 1827. During an argument, Red Bird shot trader Registre Gagnier; Chickhonsic killed Solomon Lipcap, another trader, during the fray. Wekau had his rifle taken from him by Gagnier's wife. Enraged, he scalped her eleven-month-old infant, who somehow survived the incident. On June 30, a party of Winnebagos drunk on whiskey ambushed the keelboat *O. H. Perry* near the mouth of the Bad Axe River, killing two whites. The whites on the keelboat said they killed a dozen Winnebagos in the incident.

In response, the area was flooded with U.S. troops as well as a militia composed of white miners. On September 3, 1827, Red Bird and Wekau surrendered to American authorities, expecting to be put swiftly to death; Chickhonsic was apprehended as well. All three were incarcerated as the case languished in the courts. On February 16, 1828, Red Bird died of dysentery and a general lack of will to live. In September 1828, the other two leaders were found guilty of being accomplices to Red Bird in the murder of Gagnier; Wekau was convicted of assault and battery with intent to kill the Gagniers' infant, and Chickhonsic was convicted of murdering Lipcap. They were sentenced to hang but were pardoned late in 1828 by President John Quincy Adams as a gesture of peace toward a delegation of Winnebagos visiting Washington, D.C. The pardon came too late for Wekau, who had by then died in prison.

WELCH, JAMES
Blackfoot
1940–

James Welch gained fame among Native Americans and reading audiences at large in the second half of the twentieth century by writing a series of critically acclaimed novels and collections of poetry.

Welch attended schools on the Blackfoot and Fort Belknap Indian Reservations and studied writing at the University of Montana (where he later held a faculty position) with Richard Hugo. Welch's better-known novels and collections of poetry include *The Death of Jim Loney* (1979), *Fools Crow* (1986), *Winter in the Blood* (1974), *Riding the Earthboy 40* (1971), and *The Indian Lawyer* (1990). *Fools Crow* won a Los Angeles Times Book Prize, an American Book

Award, and the Pacific Northwest Booksellers Award. Welch also edited Hugo's autobiography, *The Real West Marginal Way* (1986).

WESTERMAN, FLOYD RED CROW
Sisseton-Wahpeton Sioux
1936–

An outstanding Native singer and actor in the late twentieth century, Floyd Red Crow Westerman played important roles in the films *Dances with Wolves* (1990) and *Clearcut* (1992) as well as in two television series, *Northern Exposure* and *L.A. Law*. Before beginning his career as an actor for mass audiences, Westerman was known in Native America as a folksinger and activist. His recordings included "Custer Died for Your Sins," "Indian Country," and "The Land Is Your Mother."

FOR MORE INFORMATION:

Paulson, T. Emogene. *Who's Who Among the Sioux*. Vermillion, S.D.: Institute for Indian Studies, 1982.

WHITE BIRD (PEOPEO KISKIOK HIHIH)
Nez Perce
c. 1805–1882

An ally of Chief Joseph (see JOSEPH, YOUNGER), White Bird was among non-treaty Nez Perces who tried to live peacefully with encroaching settlers until the center of their homeland was threatened. He was among the shamans and chiefs (he was both) who refused to sign the Treaty of 1863 that would have forced the non-treaty Nez Perces to move to Lapwai, Idaho. His name literally meant "White Goose," from the white goose-wing fan that he carried when acting as a shaman. White Bird was also known for the acuity of his marksmanship in battle.

White Bird, TUHULKUTSUT, and ALOKUT were among Chief Joseph's top aides during the Long

March in 1877. White Bird led a group of Nez Perce marksmen who were famed for their accuracy and for extricating the Nez Perce from several skirmishes with army troops as the band of 650 people marched roughly fifteen hundred miles through the Rocky Mountains.

During the final engagement of the Long March in the Bear Paw Mountains, just before Joseph surrendered, White Bird and Joseph were the only surviving chiefs. The night of the final battle, White Bird and a small band escaped the army's siege and made their way to Canada to join SITTING BULL's exiled band. White Bird later returned to the United States. He was killed in 1882 by a Native man who was enraged after White Bird's medicine failed to cure his two sons.

FOR MORE INFORMATION:

Josephy, Alvin M., Jr. *The Nez Perce Indians and the Opening of the Northwest*. New Haven, Conn.: Yale University Press, 1965.

WHITE BULL
Hunkpapa Sioux
1847–1947

The identity of the slayer of George Armstrong CUSTER at the Little Bighorn in June 1876 has been a matter of conjecture. RAIN-IN-THE-FACE first claimed to have taken "Yellow Hair's" life; his claim was asserted in Henry Wadsworth Longfellow's poem "The Revenge of Rain-in-the-Face." In his book *Sitting Bull: Champion of the Sioux* (1932), historian Stanley Vestal makes a case that White Bull killed Custer. Vestal says that White Bull did not claim Custer's life after the battle for fear that the whites would take revenge on him but disclosed it to Vestal in 1932. Vestal kept the secret until White Bull died, disclosing it in a 1957 article for *American Heritage*. Vestal pointed out that in 1926, on the fiftieth anniversary of the battle, eighty surviving Cheyennes and Sioux picked White Bull to lead their column across the site. However, in neither his SITTING BULL biography nor his White Bull biography (*Warpath: The True Story of the Fighting Sioux*, 1934) did Vestal claim that White Bull killed Custer.

Robert Utley, in his biography of Sitting Bull (*The Lance and the Shield*, 1993), contends that the assertion of White Bull's responsibility for the Custer slaying was not contained in Vestal's notes. "No serious student of the Little Bighorn today believes that he was responsible," writes Utley.

FOR MORE INFORMATION:

Utley, Robert M. *The Lance and the Shield: The Life and Times of Sitting Bull.* New York: Henry Holt, 1993.

White Bull. [Nebraska State Historical Society]

WHITE CLOUD (WABOKIESHIEK)
Winnebago/Sauk
c. 1795–c. 1840

White Cloud, a spiritual leader in BLACK HAWK's War, was born near contemporary Prophetstown, Illinois, on the Red Rock River about thirty miles from the Mississippi. White Cloud is described as having been a tall man, about six feet, with a moustache and a paunch; he smoked a pipe with a long stem. His first leadership role came in the Winnebago uprising of 1827, during which White Cloud sought peace. By the time of Black Hawk's revolt in 1832, White Cloud claimed to have had visions of a united Native revolt. KEOKUK later claimed that without White Cloud's endorsement, Black Hawk could not have gathered enough popular support to wage war in 1832.

White Cloud was consulted by the Sauk Black Hawk about 1820, when he was considering whether to make war against encroaching Euro-Americans, or like Keokuk, to move his supporters westward from Illinois into Iowa. White Cloud told Black Hawk that the Potawatomis and Winnebagos would help his people defend their homeland. Other leaders of the Winnebagos refused to join White Cloud's efforts in aid of Black Hawk.

Despite the lack of Winnebago and Potawatomi support, White Cloud fought with Black Hawk until the revolt was suppressed at Prairie du Chien, Wisconsin, August 27, 1832. White Cloud was arrested and imprisoned with Black Hawk and later met President Andrew Jackson with him. After his release from prison, White Cloud lived for a time with the Sacs in Iowa.

FOR MORE INFORMATION:

Beckhard, Arthur J. *Black Hawk.* New York: Julian Messner, 1957.

WHITE EAGLE
Ponca
fl. 1870s

White Eagle was the principal chief of the Poncas who remained in Indian Territory (now Oklahoma) in 1877 when STANDING BEAR and other Poncas journeyed north to bury Standing Bear's deceased son in their homeland along the Niobrara River in northern Nebraska. As Standing Bear and his band waged a publicity campaign to retain their homeland, White Eagle's band made the best of their lot in Oklahoma; he reported to a congressional committee in 1880 that they would elect to stay there.

White Eagle left to history a narrative of the U.S. Army's removal of the Poncas from their traditional lands along the Niobrara River in northern Nebraska. White Eagle said, in part,

> The soldiers came to the borders of the village and forced us across the Niobrara to the other side, just as one would drive a herd of ponies. . . . And so I reached the Warm Land [Oklahoma]. We found the land there was bad and we were dying, one after another, and we said, "What man will take pity on us?" And our animals died, and, oh, it was very hot. "This land is truly sickly, and we'll be apt to die here, and we hope the Great Father will take us back [home] again." That is what we said. There were one hundred of us died there. [Yenne]

White Eagle, chief of the Poncas in exile.
[Nebraska State Historical Society]

FOR MORE INFORMATION:

Yenne, Bill, and Susan Garratt. *North American Indians.* Hong Kong: Ottenheimer Publishers, 1993.

Zimmerman, Charles Leroy. *White Eagle: Chief of the Poncas.* Harrisburg, Pa.: Telegraph Press, 1941.

WHITE EAGLE
Pawnee
fl. mid-1800s

White Eagle was a principal chief of the Skidi Pawnees in the mid–nineteenth century. His leadership of the Pawnee buffalo hunt was described in detail by Gene Weltfish in his classic study of the Pawnees, *The Lost Universe: Pawnee Life and Culture* (1965). As chief of the hunt, White Eagle was also in charge of the considerable logistics of moving camps of several hundred people. He was a shaman (or "deer doctor") and called upon supernatural aid for success in the hunt.

White Eagle, principal chief of the Pawnees.
[Nebraska State Historical Society]

White Eagle was a leader of the Pawnee just as they were making contact with Europeans and their diseases—smallpox, cholera, and measles—which destroyed several Pawnee bands within two decades at mid-century. Between 60 and 120 Pawnees were massacred by the Sioux in 1873. After that, White Eagle and other Pawnee chiefs reluctantly accepted exile in Oklahoma. White Eagle built his last earth lodge near the present-day town of Pawnee, Oklahoma, where he died in 1879.

WHITE EAGLE (WANBLI SKA)
Rosebud Sioux
1951–1995

A tenor who acquired a national reputation in the late twentieth century, White Eagle discov-ered in 1989 that he had Acquired Immune Deficiency Syndrome (AIDS). His theme song, "The Impossible Dream," became an anthem of survival to many AIDS patients.

A native of Mission, South Dakota, White Eagle was the son of a minister. Inspired by recordings of Mario Lanza, he sang his first solo at the age of five. His singing career began in the church run by his father and mother, Marrles and Frances Moore. White Eagle studied music in New York and San Francisco, where he met music teacher Franco Iglesias, a major influence in his professional life. White Eagle began to sing professionally in 1971; in 1973, he began touring for eight years as musical director and soloist in Re-Generations, a fourteen-member musical group. During the 1980s, he developed his tenor as a classical soloist. In 1985, White Eagle graduated from the Merola Program of the San Francisco Opera.

In 1989, White Eagle sang the finale at the presidential inaugural gala for George Bush and was backed by the Mormon Tabernacle Choir. During 1993, he also performed in the Weil Recital Hall at Carnegie Hall, New York City. Shortly after that performance, White Eagle's declining health ended his career as a soloist. Even in his weakened condition, however, White Eagle brought an Omaha Symphony audience of fourteen hundred to its feet in May 1994 with his rendition of "America the Beautiful."

White Eagle struggled with alcoholism much of his life and appeared to be recovering from it when he was found to have AIDS. "From . . . early in my life, I knew I wanted to sing and I have lived a dream come true. . . . I will fight for every breath I have left," White Eagle said in 1994. He died in Sioux Falls, South Dakota, on July 7, 1995.

FOR MORE INFORMATION:

LeMay, Konnie. "Scholarship Fund Established to Honor White Eagle." *Indian Country Today*, November 2, 1994.

———. "White Eagle Is Instrument of Hope for Those with AIDS." *Indian Country Today*, April 20, 1994.

WHITE EYES (KOQUETHAGECHTON)
Delaware
c. 1730–1778

Named for his light-colored eyes, White Eyes played a diplomatic role in the American Revolution after becoming a friend of Colonel George Morgan, Indian agent of the Continental Congress. In 1778, he signed a treaty designed to incorporate the Delaware nation as the fourteenth state of the United States.

White Eyes became principal chief of the Ohio Delawares in 1776. At the beginning of the American Revolution, he counseled neutrality but took up the patriot cause after the Delaware leader HOPOCAN sided with the British. White Eyes thought that the conflict would destroy the Delawares and was reported to have said that he would prefer to die during the conflict than see his people torn apart choosing sides.

In 1778, White Eyes was a party to the first treaty negotiated by the new United States at Fort Pitt. The treaty was notable because it outlined a plan for a Delaware state with representation in Congress. The plan never materialized.

Two months after signing that treaty, White Eyes was acting as a guide for General Lachlin McIntosh in his expedition against Fort Sandusky. During the expedition, White Eyes was killed by American troops under confusing conditions, possibly by friendly fire. To cover up the death of an ally, the soldiers reported that Whites Eyes had died of smallpox.

FOR MORE INFORMATION:

Grinde, Donald A., Jr. *The Iroquois and the Founding of the American Nation.* San Francisco: Indian Historian Press, 1977.

WHITE HAIR (WHITE HAIRS, CHEVEUXBLANCS, TESHUMINGA, GREDAMANSE, PAHUSKA)
Osage
c. 1755–1808

White Hair was probably born on the Little Osage River in present-day Missouri. He is supposed to have received his name among the Euro-Americans when he grabbed General Arthur St. Clair's white wig in 1791 during LITTLE TURTLE's War. It is said that he wore it often thereafter.

White Hair befriended French trader Jean Pierre Chouteau, supporting Chouteau's trading endeavors with the Osages. Both men traveled to Washington, D.C., in 1804, when White Hair met president Thomas Jefferson. By 1806, when Zebulon Pike explored what is now western Missouri, White Hair had become principal chief of the Big (or Great) Osages. The Little Osages had lived to the north along the Missouri River during the 1700s for a time before rejoining their kinsmen along the Osage River at the end of the eighteenth century. Another Osage band, led by CLERMONT, left the Big Osages in the early 1800s and moved into the Arkansas River valley in what is presently northeastern Oklahoma.

A second White Hair, probably his son, relocated the Osages from the Little Osage River west to the Neosho sometime before 1822. Ten years after the move, he died. Later, George CATLIN painted a third White Hair, presumably a relative of the other two men.

WHITE-MAN-RUNS-HIM (MIATASHEDEKAROOS)
Crow
c. 1855–1925

White-Man-Runs-Him inherited his adult name from his father, who had once been chased by a white man firing a rifle. In later years, as White-Man-Runs-Him became a prominent scout for the U.S. Army, the name was applied to him by the Sioux with a sneer, meaning "the white man controls him." The Sioux knew White-Man-Runs-Him from his youth as a wily thief of their horses.

White-Man-Runs-Him led Crow scouts who spotted the Native camp at the Little Bighorn and then were ordered to the rear of the lines as George Armstrong CUSTER and his

White-Man-Runs-Him.
[National Anthropological Archives]

men were killed. White-Man-Runs-Him became a source of popular accounts of the battle for many years afterward, until his death in 1925.

FOR MORE INFORMATION:

Monoghan, Jay. *Custer.* Lincoln: University of Nebraska Press, 1959.

Rosenberg, Bruce A. *Custer and the Epic of Defeat.* University Park: Pennsylvania State University Press, 1974.

WHITE PATH (NUNNATSUNEGA)
Cherokee
1763–1835

White Path was probably born near Turniptown, close to present-day Ellijay, Georgia. During the American Revolution, under DRAGGING CANOE'S leadership, he raided American settlements. In the Creek War of 1813–1814, however, he allied with the Americans against William WEATHERFORD and the Creek Red Sticks.

White Path worked a small farm and was a headman at Turniptown. He also served as a member of the Cherokee National Council. In November 1825, he counseled against rapid acculturation. Because he disliked the great number of laws that tribal leaders were imposing on the Cherokee people and the presence of missionaries, he was ejected from his seat on the nation's council.

In February 1827, White Path and other traditional Cherokees formed an alternative council at Ellijay that opposed the drafting of the Cherokee constitution under the leadership of John Ross. By June 1827, White Path's Rebellion lost momentum when certain accommodations by the mixed-bloods were put in the constitution on July 26, 1827. Although he remained a maverick, White Path was reelected to the Cherokee National Council on August 28, 1827.

WHITE PIGEON
Potawatomi
fl. early 1800s

Near Detroit, in 1812, White Pigeon, a Potawatomi chief, learned of a pending Indian massacre of settlers in the village that was later
named for him (White Pigeon, Michigan). He
warned the settlers and enabled them to escape.
White Pigeon also signed the Treaty of Greenville (1795) and the Treaty of Brownstown
(1808). He died at about thirty and was buried in
White Pigeon, Michigan. A monument to him
was installed there in 1909.

FOR MORE INFORMATION:

Winger, Otho. *Last of the Miamis: Little Turtle.*
   Lawrence W. Shultz, 1935.

WILD CAT (COACOOCHEE, COWACOOCHEE)
Seminole
c. 1810–1857

Born about 1810 in the Seminole village of
Yulaka along the St. Johns River in northern
Florida, Wild Cat was said to have had a twin
sister who died soon after birth. Since he was a
twin he was thought to have special gifts. Wild
Cat would grow up to become a major leader in
the Second Seminole War (1835–1842). He was
a nephew of MICANOPY.

When Florida became a U.S. territory in 1822,
tensions between the Seminoles and the U.S.
government intensified. With the United States
desiring Indian land, the Seminoles developed a
policy of welcoming runaway slaves into their
midst. At the beginning of the Second Seminole
War, the young Wild Cat, about nineteen years
old, led a band of Seminoles and runaway slaves
(mostly from Georgia). In 1837, his father, King
Philip, or Ee-mat-la, was seized by American
forces and held at Fort Marion.

In October 1837, Wild Cat emerged from the
Florida swamps as an emissary of OSCEOLA. He
carried a pipe decorated with a white feather of
peace and said that Osceola was ready for peace
talks. At the ensuing meeting, General Thomas
S. Jesup captured all the Seminoles and African
Americans present, including Osceola, under a
flag of truce. Wild Cat and eighteen of his followers fasted for six days so they could fit
through the bars of their cell window and make
a daring escape from Fort Marion. Osceola
would remain behind and perish in prison.

In retaliation for Jesup's perfidy, Wild Cat
became a major figure in the Second Seminole
War. On Christmas Day 1837, he fought with
ALLIGATOR and ARPEIKA in the Battle of Lake
Okeechobee against troops under Colonel (soon
to be general) Zachary Taylor. Although the
army technically won the "ground," it was a
qualified draw because the Indians had fewer
casualties before their retreat into the Everglades. Wild Cat's father, Ee-mat-la, died in
1839 while removing to Indian Territory. In
1841, Wild Cat agreed to come and talk at Fort
Pierce on the Indian River, where he was met
by then-Lieutenant William T. Sherman. There,
Wild Cat and his two hundred followers agreed
to remove to Fort Gibson in Indian Territory.
Depressed by his defeat, he stated, "I was in
hopes I should be killed in battle, but a bullet
never reached me."

In 1843, Wild Cat and Alligator led a Seminole delegation to Washington, D.C., asking
financial help for their impoverished people.
They were unsuccessful. The situation in the
Indian Territory deteriorated because of devastating floods and Creek slavers who were kidnapping Wild Cat's African American friends
for slave markets. In 1849, Wild Cat and a band
of about a hundred followers (African Americans and Seminoles) left for Texas. They were
joined by about a thousand Kickapoos in their
attempt to form a new community. Eventually
the Mexican government granted the Semi-

noles a tract of land because of their military service against Apache and Comanche raiders. For his efforts, Wild Cat gained a commission as a colonel in the Mexican army. He fell ill of smallpox in 1857 and died at Alto, near the town of Muzquiz in Coahuila, Mexico. His son, who took on the leadership of the exiled group, was called Gato Chiquito, or "Young Wildcat."

WILLIAMS, ROGER
c. 1603–1683

Roger Williams is known today simply as the founder of Rhode Island. During his own life, Williams was excoriated as a spreader of intellectual infections. Afterward, he was hailed as the first flower of Enlightenment's spring. Roger Williams was the first North American revolutionary, or at least the first of European extraction.

Although they were couched mainly in a religious context, Williams's ideas also engaged debates regarding political liberty that would fire the American Revolution more than a century later. Like many U.S. founders, Williams often used his perceptions of American Indians and their societies as a reference point by which to hone his preexisting desires for an alternative to the European status quo. As the founder of Providence Plantations (now called Rhode Island), Williams tried to implement his ideas of "soul liberty," political freedom, and economic equality. His experiment presaged the later revolution of continental scope.

Within a few months of Williams's arrival in Boston during 1631, he was learning the Algonquian language. He would master the dialects of the Showatuck, Nipmuck, Narraganset, and others. Williams met MASSASOIT, a sachem among the Wampanoags (also called Pokanokets), when the latter was about thirty years of age, In Williams's words, he became "great friends" with the sachem. Williams also became close to CANONI-

CUS, the elderly leader of the Narragansets. With both, Williams traveled in the forest for days at a time, learning what he could of their languages, societies, and opinions, drinking in experiences that, along with his prior European life, would provide the intellectual groundwork for the model commonwealth Williams sought to establish in Providence Plantations.

By January 1635, the Puritans' more orthodox magistrates had decided Williams must be exiled to England, jailed if possible, and shut up because he was preaching that the Indians, not the Puritans, held title to the land under Boston. They opposed exiling Williams in the wilderness, fearing that he would begin his own settlement from which his "infections" would leak back into Puritania. At the same time, Williams and his associates were rushing ahead with plans for their new colony. Williams had already arranged with Canonicus for a tract of land large enough to support it. A summons was issued for Williams's arrest, but he stalled the authorities by contending that he was too ill to withstand an ocean voyage.

In fact, aware of his impending arrest, Williams had set out three days earlier during a blinding blizzard, walking south by west to the lodge of Massasoit at Mount Hope. Walking eighty to ninety miles during the worst of a New England winter, Williams suffered immensely and likely would have died without Indian aid. Near the end of his trek, Williams lodged with Canonicus and his family.

Week by week, month by month, Williams's family and friends filtered south from Plymouth and Salem to his new community. By spring, houses were being erected, and fields were being turned. The growing group also began to erect an experimental government very novel by European (or Puritan) standards of the time. For the first time among English-speaking people in America, they were trying to establish a social order based on liberty of conscience and other natural rights.

Very quickly Williams's house became a transcultural meeting place. He lodged as many as fifty Indians at a time—travelers, traders, sachems on their way to or from treaty conferences. If a Puritan needed to contact an Indian, or vice versa, he more than likely did so with Williams's aid. Among Indian nations at odds with each other, Williams became, according to the Massachusetts colony's governor William Bradford, "a quencher of our fires." When citizens of Portsmouth needed an Indian agent, they approached Williams. The Dutch did the same thing after 1636. Williams often traveled with Canonicus, Massasoit, and their warriors, lodging with them in the forest. The Narraganset Council sometimes used Williams's house for its meetings.

Williams had collected material for an Indian grammar book much of his adult life, but the press of events left him little time to write. It was not until 1643, on a solitary sea voyage to England, that Williams composed his *Key into the Languages of America*, the first Indian grammar in English, as well as a small encyclopedia of his own observations of the Native Americans. In the *Key*, Williams also began to formulate a critique of European religion and politics that would be a subject of intense debate on both sides of the Atlantic for decades to come.

Some of Williams's American lessons were offered in verse:

I've known them to leave their house and
    mat
        To lodge a friend or stranger
When Jews and Christians oft have sent
        Jesus Christ to the Manger

Oft have I heard these Indians say
    These English will deliver us

Of all that's ours, our lands and lives
    In the end, they'll bereave us.
            [Grinde and Johansen]

In some ways, Williams found what Europeans called "Christian values" better embodied in Native American societies: "There are no beggars amongst them, nor fatherless children unprovided for." The *Key* was not only a grammar. It was also a lesson in humility directed at the most pompous and ethnocentric of the English:

When Indians heare the horrid filths,
    Of Irish, English men
The horrid Oaths and Murthurs late
    Thus say these Indians then:

We weare no Cloathes, have many Gods,
    And yet our sinnes are lesse:
You are Barbarians, Pagans wild,
    Your land's the wildernesse.
            [Grinde and Johansen]

When some Puritans asked whether a society based on individual choice instead of coerced consent would degenerate into anarchy, Williams found the Indians' example instructive: "Although they have not so much to restraine them (both in respect of knowledge of God and lawes of Men) as the English have, yet a man shall never heare of such crimes amongst them [as] robberies, murthurs, adultries &c., as among the English." [Grinde and Johansen]

Among the colonists of Providence Plantations, as among the Indians he knew, Williams envisioned a society where "all men may walk as their consciences perswade them." Williams's ideal society also shared with the Native American societies he knew a relatively egalitarian distribution of property, with political rights based on natural law: "All civil liberty is founded in the consent of the People"; "Natural and civil Right and Privilege due . . . as a Man, a Subject, a Citizen."

Establishing such a utopian society was easier said than done. As Williams watched, some of his fellow settlers set up land companies similar to those in other colonies in an attempt to hoard land reserved for future arrivals. The land had been set aside to prevent the growth of a landless underclass in the colony. In 1654, in a letter to the town of Providence, Williams showed how isolated he sometimes felt in his quest for a new way of life: "I have been charged with folly for that freedom and liberty which I have always stood for—I say, liberty and equality in both land and government."

Entering his sixties, Williams's body grew old quickly. In 1663, he complained often of "old pains, lameness, so th't sometimes I have not been able to rise, nor goe, or stand." The mantle of leadership among the Wampanoag had fallen to METACOM, who was called King Philip by the English. Aged about twenty-five in 1662, Metacom distrusted nearly all whites, Williams being one of few exceptions. Metacom grew more bitter by the day. He could see his nation being destroyed before his eyes. The devastation of alcohol and disease and the loss of land destroyed families and tradition. These were Metacom's thoughts as he prepared to go to war against the English.

When Indians painted for war appeared on the heights above Providence, Williams picked up his staff, climbed the bluffs, and told the war parties that if they attacked the town, England would send thousands of armed men to crush them. "Well," one of the sachems leading the attack told Williams, "let them come. We are ready for them, but as for you, brother Williams, you are a good man. You have been kind to us for many years. Not a hair on your head shall be touched."

Williams died in early 1683 in Providence.

FOR MORE INFORMATION:

Brockunier, Samuel H. *The Irrepressible Democrat: Roger Williams.* New York: Ronald Press, 1940.

Chupack, Henry. *Roger Williams.* New York: G. K. Hall & Co., 1969.

Covey, Cyclone. *The Gentle Radical: A Biography of Roger Williams.* New York: Macmillan, 1966.

Davis, Jack L. "Roger Williams Among the Narragansett Indians." *New England Quarterly* 43 (1970).

Ernst, James. *Roger Williams: New England Firebrand.* New York: Macmillan, 1932.

Grinde, Donald A., Jr., and Bruce E. Johansen. *Exemplar of Liberty: Native America and the Evolution of Democracy.* Berkeley and Los Angeles: University of California Press, 1991.

Miller, Perry. *Roger Williams: His Contribution to the American Tradition.* Indianapolis: Bobbs-Merrill, 1953.

Parrington, Vernon Louis. *Main Currents in American Thought.* New York: Harcourt, Brace, and Co., 1927.

Rider, Sidney S. *The Lands of Rhode Island as They Were Known to Caunonicus and Miantunnomu When Roger Williams Came.* Providence, R.I.: Sidney S. Rider, 1904.

Savelle, Max. "Roger Williams: Minority of One." In *The American Story,* edited by Earl S. Miers. Great Neck, N.Y.: Channel Press, 1956.

Slotkin, Richard, and James K. Folsom, eds. *So Dreadful a Judgement: Puritan Responses to King Philip's War, 1676–1677.* Middleton, Conn.: Wesleyan University Press, 1978.

Vaughan, Alden T. *New England Frontier: Puritans and Indians, 1620–1675.* Boston: Little, Brown, 1965.

Williams, Roger. *The Complete Writings of Roger Williams.* New York: Russell & Russell, 1963.

———. *A Key into the Languages of America.* 1643. Reprint, Providence, R.I.: Tercentenary Committee, 1936.

Winslow, Elizabeth Ola. *Master Roger Williams.* New York: Macmillan, 1957.

WILSON, RICHARD
Oglala Lakota
1936–1990

Richard Wilson was chairman of the Pine Ridge Indian Reservation Tribal Council during the 1973 Wounded Knee occupation as well as its violent aftermath. From the early 1970s until his 1976 defeat for the chairman's office, Wilson outfitted a tribal police force that was often called the "goon squad." This police force—for which "GOON" meant Guardians of the Oglala Nation—was financed with tribal money from the federal government.

One result of the escalating conflict between Oglala Lakota traditionalists allied with the American Indian Movement (AIM) and Wilson was the seventy-one-day occupation of Wounded Knee in 1973. The local context of the occupation included an effort to publically confront Wilson's policies, which often favored non-Indian ranchers, farmers, and corporations.

The struggle between AIM and Wilson was also taking place within the realm of tribal politics. When Wilson sought reelection in 1974, Russell MEANS, an Oglala who had helped found AIM, challenged him. In the primary, Wilson trailed Means, 667 votes to 511. Wilson won the final election over Means by fewer than 200 votes in balloting which the U.S. Commission on Civil Rights later found to be permeated with fraud. The Civil Rights Commission recommended a new election, which was not held; Wilson answered his detractors by stepping up his terror tactics against them, examples of which were described in a chronology kept by the Wounded Knee Legal Defense-Offense Committee. One of the goons' favorite weapons was the automobile. Officially, such deaths could be reported as traffic accidents.

Wilson had a formidable array of supporters on the reservation, many of whom criticized AIM for being urban-based and insensitive to reservation residents' needs. Mona Wilson, one of Wilson's daughters, who was seventeen years of age when Wounded Knee was occupied, recalled him crying in his mother's arms at the time. Recalling the events two decades later, Wilson's wife, Yvonne, and two daughters remembered him as a kind and compassionate father who had the interests of his people at heart. They said that Wilson supported AIM when it protested the 1972 murder of Raymond YELLOW THUNDER in the reservation border town of Gordon, Nebraska. Only later, as events culminated in the siege of Wounded Knee, did Wilson and AIM leaders become deadly enemies.

Wilson was the first Oglala Lakota tribal chairman to serve two consecutive terms. He worked as a self-employed plumber, owner of a gas station, and on other short-term projects after his defeat by Al Trimble for the tribal chairmanship in 1976. Wilson's family recalled that he also had a traditional side. He was a pipe carrier (roadman) in the Native American Church and also a practicing Episcopalian. Wilson was known for feeding anyone who came to his door; he had a major role in beginning a Lakota community college on the reservation as well as a number of other tribal enterprises.

Wilson died of a heart attack in 1990 as he was preparing to run for a third term as tribal chairman.

FOR MORE INFORMATION:

LeMay, Konnie. "20 Years of Anguish." *Indian Country Today*, February 25, 1993.

U.S. Commission on Civil Rights. "Report of Investigation: Oglala Sioux Tribe, General Election, 1974." Civil Rights Commission,

Washington, D.C., October 1974. Mimeographed.

WINEMA (KAITCHKONA WINEMA; TOBY or TOBEY RIDDLE)
Modoc
1836–1920

Born along the Link River in northern California, she was originally called Nonooktowa, meaning "Strange Child," because of her reddish brown hair. Winema's father was called Secot (there is no record of her mother's name). She was a cousin of the Modoc leader CAPTAIN JACK. Winema gained her adult name, which means "Strong-hearted Woman," as a young girl when she safely guided her canoe through rapids and rocks. As a young woman, she shot a grizzly bear and fought alongside men in battle. She gained the further respect of her people when, as a girl of fourteen, she rallied Modoc braves to victory after a surprise attack by another tribe.

At fifteen, Winema refused to marry the Modoc husband chosen for her and then married Frank Riddle, a Kentucky miner. After her marriage, she was known as Toby Riddle among the whites. Although her tribe rejected her at first for marrying Riddle, the Modocs later called on her and her husband to function as interpreters in negotiations with whites. On several occasions, she aided in the calming of tense and potentially violent situations.

After the Modocs departed to Klamath, Oregon, under Captain Jack (Kintpuash), to lobby for a Lost River Reservation, he allegedly stated that Winema was dead in the eyes of the Modocs and she had become a white woman. But in the tense negotiations that ensued, Frank Riddle and Winema served as interpreters and intermediaries between white officials and Modoc traditionalists, shuttling between the army camp and the Modoc chiefs in their natural stronghold, the Lava Beds along Tule Lake.

In February 1873, after extensive fighting, a peace commission was created, including General Edward Canby, Alfred B. Meacham, and Eleazar Thomas, and a tent was pitched on neutral ground. At the first meeting, Captain Jack asked for the Lava Beds as a reservation and refused to turn over HOOKER JIM for the killing of white ranchers. Before the second talks, Winema told Meacham that some Modoc leaders wanted Captain Jack to kill Canby because they thought he could not be trusted. Although Meacham became concerned, Canby ignored the warning and proceeded with the talks as planned on April 11, 1873. As Winema feared, Captain Jack shot and killed Canby; another warrior, Boston Charley, killed Thomas. SCHONCHIN JOHN fired on Meacham, hitting him, but Winema used her body as a shield to protect Meacham. After the Modocs left the camp, she put Meacham in her saddle blanket and went for help. During the next weeks, Winema nursed the wounded Meacham back to health.

Winema traveled to Washington, D.C., where a parade was held in her honor in recognition of her bravery, and where she met President Ulysses S. Grant. From 1874 to 1881, she toured eastern cities with Meacham, her husband, their son Jeff, SCARFACED CHARLEY, and other Modocs, portraying herself in a dramatic play entitled *Winema*, which detailed the reasons for the Modoc War.

In 1881, Winema returned to Oregon, where she lived for the remainder of her life. In 1890, she was given a pension for her service to the federal government. She donated most of the pension to her people. Her son, Jeff Riddle, used her as the basis for his book, *The Indian History of the Modoc War*, published in 1914. Winema died on the reservation on May 30, 1932, and was buried in the Modoc cemetery. The Winema National Forest is named for her.

WOODEN LEG (KUMMONK'QUIVIOKTA)
Northern Cheyenne
1858–1940

Wooden Leg was a veteran of the 1876 Battle of the Little Bighorn and later a tribal judge. As judge, he was told at one point that the Bureau of Indian Affairs had issued an edict that Indian men could not have more than one wife. This was part of a general governmental offensive against polygamy, which also affected the Mormon settlers of Utah.

Wooden Leg.
[National Anthropological Archives]

As tribal judge, Wooden Leg was charged with enforcing the new rule. He sent a tribal police officer to gather all Northern Cheyenne men who had more than one wife and gave them the news. Initially, most of them resisted, but then they came up with strategies to circumvent the law: telling Indian agents that the extra wives were really in-laws, for example, or maintaining two households with one wife in each of them.

Wooden Leg related a story of how he pondered telling his own two wives of the order. He was stricken with remorse as his younger wife, who had no children, was moved out of his house. "A few years later, I heard that she was married to a good husband. Oh, how glad it made my heart to hear that!"

Wooden Leg related his memoirs to Thomas B. Marquis, who published them in *A Warrior Who Fought Custer* (1931). The chief related the story to Marquis in sign language, aided by a few words of English, as other Cheyennes stood by confirming or correcting what he said.

FOR MORE INFORMATION:
Nabokov, Peter. *Native American Testimony.*
New York: Viking Penguin, 1991.

WOVOKA (JACK WILSON; WANEKIA)
Northern Paiute
c. 1856–1932

Born along the Walker River in Mason Valley, Nevada, Wovoka ("The Cutter") is usually said to be the son of TAVIBO, a Paiute spiritual leader. As a youth, Wovoka learned the spiritual ways of Tavibo and also knew of the prophetic messages of John SLOCUM and SMOHALLA. As a teenager, Wovoka also lived for a while with a white family of devout Christians, the Wilsons, on a ranch in western Nevada. As a result, he became known to them as Jack Wilson.

Wovoka caught a severe fever in late 1888. Delirious during a solar eclipse on January 1, 1889, Wovoka later stated that he had been transported to the spirit world and had communed with the Great Spirit. After this visit with the Creator, he believed he was to carry a message that the earth would come to an end but then regenerate itself into a place only for American Indians and the new messiah. This reborn world would be for all Native peoples, dead and alive. Thus, Wovoka talked of a new existence free from suffering. To gain this new existence, Indians must live in honesty and harmony, purify themselves often, and avoid Euro-American habits, particularly alcohol. Similarly, he deemphasized the importance of mourning, since he prophesied that the deceased would be reborn soon. He sought to replace these mourning practices with meditation, prayers, singing, and most importantly, dancing the Ghost Dance, in which men and women held hands in large circles and danced slowly while singing prescribed songs.

He contended that through the Ghost Dance a follower might die for a few moments and gain a brief vision of the new paradise for Indians—a world of verdant prairie grasses, large buffalo herds, and all of one's relatives. This powerful spiritual message spread rapidly through the Indian boarding schools and thence to reservation communities, particularly the Arapaho, Cheyenne, Shoshoni, and Lakota. As a result of his prophesies, his devotees considered him to be the "Red" messiah and called him the "Red Man's Christ."

Many of the Lakota people, seeking solace for their defeats, developed a new militance after a group of eleven of their leaders, including SHORT BULL and KICKING BEAR, traveled to see Wovoka in Nevada during the winter of 1889–1890. Interpreting Wovoka's words to suit their agenda, these leaders chose to heighten his message about the eventual elimination of whites from the Americas. Special Ghost Dance shirts could stop bullets, according to some interpretations.

The Ghost Dance and Wovoka's message caused white authorities to become nervous. The military decided to intervene and forcibly stop the dances. This resulted in the death of SITTING BULL and the slaughter of BIG FOOT's band at Wounded Knee in December 1890. Wovoka, appalled by the violence, counseled peace with the white population. Subsequently, the Ghost Dance religion subsided, but some groups, including the Cheyenne and Arapaho, have kept some aspects of the rituals in other tribal ceremonies.

Wovoka and his wife, Mary, had three daughters and a son. He died in 1932 near Schurz, Nevada, on the Walker River Reservation.

WRIGHT, ALLEN (KILIHOTE)
Choctaw
1825–1885

Allen Wright, who would become a principal chief, translator, and preacher, was born along the Yaknukni River in Attala County, Mississippi. (His Choctaw name, Kilihote, means "Let's Kindle a Fire.") Wright's father was Ishtemahilubi and his mother was of the Hayupatuklo clan. They were both Choctaws. During preparations for Choctaw removal, Wright's mother died. A few years later, after removing to Oklahoma, his father died, leaving Wright with only a sister. As a result, Cyrus Kingsbury, a Presbyterian missionary, became interested in the young lad and sent him to local missionary schools. Wright continued his education in New York, graduating from Union College in 1852 and from Union Theological Seminary in 1855. By that time he had mastered English, Greek, Latin, and Hebrew. After marrying a white missionary from Ohio, Harriet Newell Dayton, he fathered eight children.

Wright was ordained into the Presbyterian Church in 1856, after which he began work among Native people. After becoming involved in tribal issues, he was elected to the Choctaw house of representatives and the senate. He later became his tribe's treasurer. In 1862, during the Civil War, he served briefly in the Confederate army. After the war, Wright served as principal chief for two terms, from 1866 to 1870. In 1866, during negotiations for Choctaw and Chickasaw treaties, he proposed the name Okla-homma for the region encompassing Indian Territory. It meant "Red People," and the suggestion became the official name of the state of Oklahoma in 1907. In the 1870s and 1880s, Wright translated many works, including the Chickasaw constitution and codes of law, into English, as well as the Psalms from Hebrew to English. In 1880, his *Chahta Leksikon*, a Choctaw dictionary, was published. He died at Foggy Depot, Oklahoma, on December 2, 1885, and is buried there near his home.

WYANDANCH (WYANDAUGH)
Moutauk
c. 1600–1659

Wyandanch, "the Wise Speaker," assumed leadership of the Moutauks after the death of his brother Pogattacut in 1653 at his home village on the eastern end of Long Island, New York. He was the last grand sachem of the Moutauk Confederacy. In that same year, Niantics led by NINIGRET raided a wedding ceremony for Wyandanch's daughter Quashawan and kidnapped her. Lion Gardiner, an Englishman to whom Wyandanch had earlier sold land, met the ransom for Quashawan and was rewarded by Wyandanch with grazing rights on Moutauk land. Wyandanch died in 1659, probably from a smallpox epidemic that is known to have killed many of his kin. A Long Island town is named for him.

γ

YELLOW HAIR (NAPE-ZI)
Northern Cheyenne
c. 1850–1876
Yellow Hair, also known as "Yellowhand," was killed July 17, 1876, during the battle for the Black Hills probably by William ("Buffalo Bill") CODY, who was working as a scout for the U.S. Army at the time. Yellow Hair was reportedly scalped by Cody just three weeks after George Armstrong CUSTER and his force of 225 men had been killed by Sioux and Cheyennes at the Little Bighorn. The confrontation between the scout Cody and Yellow Hair became the seed of many dime novels of the time.

YELLOW THUNDER (WAKUN-CHAKOOKAH)
Winnebago
1774–1874
Yellow Thunder was a principal chief of the Winnebagos and an opponent of removal at a time when the U.S. government was trying to move them from the vicinity of present-day Green Bay, Wisconsin.

Yellow Thunder and other chiefs were persuaded to sign away their lands without knowing it and then were told they had only eight months to move out. Yellow Thunder and several other chiefs traveled to Washington, D.C., in 1837 to assert their right to their ancestral homes, but President Andrew Jackson refused to meet with them.

The Winnebagos under Yellow Thunder refused to move. In 1840, troops arrived to force them to a reservation in northeastern Iowa. Yellow Thunder was briefly held in chains, then released, as the chiefs agreed that resistance would cause their people to be exterminated.

Late in his life, Yellow Thunder and his wife departed the Iowa Reservation and returned to Wisconsin, where they homesteaded a forty-acre farm. He died there.

YELLOW THUNDER
Sioux
fl. 1850s
Yellow Thunder was chief of a Sioux band camped near Ash Hollow, in western Nebraska,

and became the target of a punitive raid by troops under the command of Colonel William HARNEY. Harney freely admitted that Yellow Thunder's band had had nothing to do with the Indians he had been sent to punish, another band that had devastated a small army force under the command of Lieutenant J. L. GRATTAN.

The brash, young Lieutenant Grattan, fresh out of West Point, had said he thought that all Indians were cowards and dogs. In an action that presaged the similar "FETTERMAN Fight" a few years later, Grattan and thirty men entered a sizable Sioux camp near Laramie, Wyoming, to arrest a young Native man who was accused of stealing an immigrant's wayward cow. Grattan proposed to "whip all the Sioux on the Plains and make them run like rabbits." Instead, the Indians in the camp killed Grattan and all his men. Colonel Harney was dispatched shortly thereafter with orders to punish this Sioux camp, but he couldn't find them; so he descended on Yellow Thunder's band instead and killed eighty-six people. The village was laid waste and many horses killed. In his report on the incident, Harney admitted that he had attacked the wrong band of Indians and that he was looking solely for scapegoats.

The evening after the battle, a young Oglala warrior whom his compatriots called "Curly" surveyed a battlefield filled with the bodies of dead and mutilated men, women, and children. He rescued one Cheyenne woman who had escaped death by huddling under a blanket with her infant son. The experience made him swear to fight the army. After that, he came to be known as CRAZY HORSE, who would become a master strategist in the Plains wars.

FOR MORE INFORMATION:

Wiltsey, Norman B. *Brave Warriors.* Caldwell, Idaho: Caxton, 1963.

YELLOW THUNDER, RAYMOND
Oglala Lakota
1921–1972

Raymond Yellow Thunder was kidnapped, probably by a gang of white toughs, during a drinking episode on February 12, 1972, in Gordon, Nebraska, a town straddling the border of the Pine Ridge Indian Reservation. Yellow Thunder was stuffed into an automobile trunk and transported to a dance at an American Legion Hall. He was stripped from the waist down and shoved onto the dance floor. Later, Yellow Thunder was similarly humiliated in a laundromat. He spent the night in jail and was released the next day.

Sometime during the next week, Yellow Thunder was murdered. His body was found on February 20 stuffed into the cab of a pickup truck on a Gordon used car lot. He had died of cerebral hemorrhage from a blow to the head. Four Gordon-area whites were charged with manslaughter and released on bond. Two men, Melvin and Leslie Hare, were later convicted of manslaughter.

The fact that perpetrators of an unusually brutal murder would be convicted of manslaughter and not murder outraged many Lakota and became a symbol to them of all the injustices that had been forced upon them by white society. A year later, the American Indian Movement (AIM) hosted a march of one thousand to fifteen hundred people in Gordon to protest the treatment of American Indians in the town. (Gordon is actually named after a bootlegger of liquor to Indians. John Gordon may have been the last bootlegger to be punished for illegally running liquor into the Oglalas' Paha Sapa, or Black Hills. An army officer burned his wagon as gallons of contraband liquor fed the flames.)

The AIM protest brought considerable media coverage to the group and was one of a number of incidents that led up to the seventy-one-day siege of Wounded Knee, a hamlet on the Pine Ridge Reservation, in 1973 (see Dennis BANKS, Russell MEANS, and Leonard PELTIER).

FOR MORE INFORMATION:

Matthiessen, Peter. *In the Spirit of Crazy Horse.* New York: Viking, 1983.

YELLOW WOLF (HERMENE MOXMOX)
Nez Perce
1855–1935

Yellow Wolf left to history one of the few narratives of the final days of the Long March of Chief Joseph (see JOSEPH, YOUNGER), describing the harsh days before the Nez Perces' surrender to General Nelson A. Miles.

Born Hermene Moxmox, a nephew of Chief Joseph, Yellow Wolf was a warrior during the Nez Perces' Long March; he was only twenty-one years of age at the time. He had already earned a reputation among the Nez Perce as a hunter and sharpshooter. He was also an expert at training horses.

Yellow Wolf said, in part:

I felt the coming end. All for which we had suffered[,] lost.

Thoughts come of the Wallowa[,] where I grew up, of my own country when only Indians were there, of tipis along the bending river, of the blue, clear lake, wide meadows with horse and cattle herds. From the mountain forests, voices seemed calling. I felt as dreaming, not my living self.

The war deepened, grew louder with gun reports. I raised up and looked around. Everything was against us. No hope! Only bondage or death! Something screamed in my ear. A blaze flashed before me. I felt as burning. Then[,] with rifle I stood forth,

saying to my heart: "Here I will die fighting for my people and their homes." [Hamilton]

During the last battle of the Long March, between September 30 and October 5, 1877, Joseph and most of the survivors decided to surrender. A small band, including Yellow Wolf, escaped and took refuge with SITTING BULL's Hunkpapas in Canada.

Yellow Wolf's recollections are contained in Lucullus McWhorter's book, *Yellow Wolf* (1940). Yellow Wolf died at Colville, Washington, in 1935, shortly after completing the narrative for the book.

FOR MORE INFORMATION:

Hamilton, Charles. *Cry of the Thunderbird.* Norman: University of Oklahoma Press, 1972.

McWhorter, Lucullus V. *Yellow Wolf.* Caldwell, Idaho: Caxton, 1940.

YONAGUSTA (DROWNING BEAR)
Cherokee
c. 1760–1839

As a peace chief of the Mountain Cherokees of North Carolina, Yonagusta was known for his oratory and diplomacy. Originally, the Mountain Cherokees resided along the Tuckaseigee River; but after 1819, they relocated to the Oconaluftee River area. At about sixty, Yonagusta became desperately sick and subsequently became comatose. Believing that he had died, his people began to mourn him. Later, he was revived and stated that he had seen the world of the spirits. As a result of this vision, he became a prophet. His teachings forbade the use of alcohol.

In 1829, fifty-eight Mountain Cherokees and Yonagusta left the Cherokee nation and became citizens of Haywood County, North Carolina. Acquiring a tract of land through the aid of Will Thomas, a lawyer and Yonagusta's adopted son, Yonagusta and members of his group managed to avert removal to Indian Territory.

YOUKIOMA (YUKEOMA, YOUKEOMA)
Hopi
c. 1880–1929

Born about 1880 at Old Oraibi, Youkioma ("Nearly Complete" or "Almost Perfect") was a member of the Kokop clan. He grew up in the village of Old Oraibi on Third Mesa in Arizona. When the U.S. government forced assimilation and acculturation upon the Hopi, the village of Oraibi became factionalized into the Progressives or Friendlies (those who wanted to accommodate to white authority) and the Conservatives or Hostiles (those who rejected white ways). Youkioma would become a leader of the Conservative faction.

During the summer of 1891, Lonahongyoma split from the Friendlies and claimed to be the "real chief" at Oraibi. Most of the people in Oraibi believed that Lomahongyoma's leadership served them better. As a result, the ceremonial life of the village began to split and

A traditional Hopi village.
[Nebraska State Historical Society]

children were taken from school. Troops were brought in to compel the rebellious Hopi to return to the settlement at Keams Canyon with their children. Although friendly to the whites, the Progressive leader Loloma was arrested at this time and taken to Fort Wingate.

In 1902, Loloma died and his nephew, Tewaquaptewa, succeeded him as the leader of the Progressive faction. Loloma's rival, Lonahongyoma, too old to pursue his role as chief of the Conservatives, handed over the reigns of leadership to Youkioma. As a result, the division between the two factions deepened. Rather than have one ceremonial ritual for all Hopis, each side took an unprecedented step and began to sponsor its own ceremonies—splitting the spiritual life of the Hopi in two.

Late in summer 1906, as the important Snake Dance Ceremony approached, the factions become more hostile toward each other. The arguments and fights were so intense that many feared it would turn into a civil war. The U.S. government warned that military force might be used if things got out of hand.

On September 5, 1906, Conservatives decided to hold the Snake Dance. With tensions mounting over the conducting of separate rituals, Progressives and Conservatives faced one another outside the village on the night of September 6. On the morning of September 7, some minor skirmishes occurred and Youkioma was pushed out of the house of a prominent Progressive. However, Youkioma proposed a way to avert violence. Late in the afternoon of September 7, he drew a line in the sand outside the village and placed himself in the center of the line. He then asserted, "If your people force us away from the village and are strong enough to pass me over this line, it will be done. But if we pass you over the line, it will not be done." After a "push war," the Progressives overwhelmed the Conservatives and as promised they departed

Oraibi to form another village of about four hundred people, Hotevilla, on Third Mesa.

After the bloodless scuffle, white authorities jailed Youkioma on several occasions and also sent him to the Carlisle Indian School in Pennsylvania for rehabilitation. This behavior by white authorities deprived the Conservative Hopi faction of a much needed leader during distressing times. In 1911, Youkioma and the Hopi Indian agent, Lawshe, traveled to Washington, D.C., to lobby for Hopi self-determination. There he met and had his picture taken with President William Taft. Embittered by white interference and the factionalism in his community, Youkioma lived the remainder of his life at Hotevilla until his death in 1929.

Z

ZOTOM (PODALADALTE)
Kiowa
c. 1853–1913

Zotom, who would become a renowned Kiowa artist, missionary, and warrior, was born probably in 1853. His father was Keintikead ("White Shield") and his mother was Sahpooly ("Owl"). His name means "Hole Biter" or "The Biter."

As a youth, Zotom participated in the customary Kiowa raids on Texas and Mexico. Captured in 1875 and sent to Fort Marion, Florida, for imprisonment and rehabilitation, Zotom became a skilled artist during his incarceration. He was known especially for his decorated ladies' fans. Zotom was also an accomplished dancer, the camp bugler, and one of the hardest workers at the fort. In 1878, he became a student at Hampton Institute in Virginia. After a few months there, he moved to Paris Hill near Utica, New York, to train for the Episcopal ministry. He was christened Paul Caryl Zotom at this time. After being ordained a deacon in 1881, Zotom went to Indian Territory as a missionary to his people.

After his conversion, Zotom tried to strike a balance between his two cultures. He participated in the Sun Dance, but the Episcopal Church reprimanded him for that practice and for dressing as an Indian. Zotom appealed repeatedly to the Episcopal Church for more missionaries in the field, but to no avail. In 1894, Zotom was stripped of his deaconship. He turned briefly to the Baptist religion before becoming a member of the Native American Church, which finally seemed to answer his spiritual needs.

In his later years, he turned more and more to art for his economic support, painting model tepees for the 1898 Omaha Exposition and later a series of painted buckskin shield covers that contained significant ethnological and artistic data.

Zotom was married three times. His first wife was a Kiowa woman named Keahpaum, or "Prepared Meat," and they had one son. His second wife was a Crow-Comanche called Mary Yeagtaupt, or "Thrusting the Lance to Both Sides"; they were childless. His last wife was Mary Aungattay (sometimes known as Mary Buffalo), or "Standing in the Track," who bore him several children. Zotom died in Oklahoma on April 27, 1913.

FINES 5¢ PER DAY FOR OVERDUE BOOKS

‹ ‹ ‹ *Index* › › ›

About the Authors

BRUCE E. JOHANSEN, Ph.D., is Professor of Communication and of Native American Studies at the University of Nebraska at Omaha. He is the author of several books, including *The Forgotten Fathers: How the American Indians Helped Shape Democracy*.

DONALD A. GRINDE, JR., Ph.D., a Yamasee by birth, is Director of the ALANA (African American, Latino, Asian American, Native American) Studies Program and Professor of History at the University of Vermont. Among his several books are *Ecocide of Native America: Environmental Destruction of Indian Lands and People* and *Exemplar of Liberty: Native America and the Evolution of Democracy*, both written with Bruce E. Johansen.